Persian Nativities IV:

ON THE REVOLUTIONS
OF THE
YEARS OF NATIVITIES

by Abū Ma'shar

The Complete Edition from Arabic

TRANSLATED & EDITED BY
BENJAMIN N. DYKES, PHD

The Cazimi Press
Minneapolis, Minnesota
2019

Published and printed in the United States of America
by The Cazimi Press
515 5th Street SE #11, Minneapolis, MN 55414

© 2019 by Benjamin N. Dykes, Ph.D.

All rights reserved. No part of this publication may be reproduced, stored in or introduced into a retrieval system, or transmitted, in any form or by any means (electronic, mechanical, photocopying, recording or otherwise), without the prior written permission of both the copyright owner and the above publisher of this book.

The scanning, uploading, and distribution of this book via the Internet or via any other means without the permission of the publisher is illegal and punishable by law. Please purchase only authorized editions and do not participate in or encourage electronic piracy of copyrighted materials. Your support of the author's rights is appreciated.

ISBN-13: 978-1-934586-49-5

Acknowledgements

I would like to thank the following friends and colleagues, in alphabetical order: Steven Birchfield, Charles Obert, Tania Daniels, Sharon Knight, Monadhl al-Mukhtār, Hitomi Oshita, Allison Simon, and Mohammed Vaez.

Also available at www.bendykes.com:

Designed for curious modern astrology students, *Traditional Astrology for Today* explains basic ideas in history, philosophy and counseling, dignities, chart interpretation, and predictive techniques. Non-technical and friendly for modern beginners.

This new translation of six works by Sahl b. Bishr is a required text for Benjamin Dykes's traditional natal astrology course, and is the first translation of Sahl's huge *Book of Nativities* from Arabic.

Dorotheus's *Carmen Astrologicum* is a foundational text for traditional astrology. Originally written in a lost Greek version, this is a translation of the later Arabic edition. It contains nativities, predictive techniques, aspect and house combinations, and a complete approach to elections or inceptions.

This excellent and popular introduction to predictive techniques by contemporary Turkish astrologer Öner Döşer blends traditional and modern methods, with numerous chart examples.

The first two volumes of this medieval mundane series, *Astrology of the World*, describe numerous techniques in weather prediction, prices and commodities, eclipses and comets, chorography, ingresses, Saturn-Jupiter conjunctions, and more, translated from Arabic and Latin sources.

Two classic introductions to astrology, by Abū Ma'shar and al-Qabīsī, are translated with commentary in this volume. *Introductions to Traditional Astrology* is an essential reference work for traditional students.

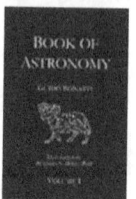

The classic medieval text by Guido Bonatti, the *Book of Astronomy* is now available in paperback reprints. This famous work is a complete guide to basic principles, horary, elections, mundane, and natal astrology.

This first English translation of Hephaistion of Thebes's *Apotelesmatics* Book III contains much fascinating material from the original Dorotheus poem and numerous other electional texts, including rules on thought-interpretation.

The largest compilation of traditional electional material, *Choices & Inceptions: Traditional Electional Astrology* contains works by Sahl, al-Rijāl, al-'Imrānī, and others, beginning with an extensive discussion of elections and questions by Benjamin Dykes.

The famous medieval horary compilation *The Book of the Nine Judges* is now available in translation for the first time! It is the largest traditional horary work available, and the third in the horary series.

The Search of the Heart is the first in the horary series, and focuses on the use of victors (special significators or *almutens*) and the practice of thought-interpretation: divining thoughts and predicting outcomes before the client speaks.

The Forty Chapters is a famous and influential horary work by al-Kindī, and is the second volume of the horary series. Beginning with a general introduction to astrology, al-Kindī covers topics such as war, wealth, travel, pregnancy, marriage, and more.

The first volume of the *Persian Nativities* series on natal astrology contains *The Book of Aristotle*, an advanced work on nativities and prediction, and a beginner-level work by his student Abū 'Alī al-Khayyāt, *On the Judgments of Nativities*.

The second volume of *Persian Nativities* features a The second volume of *Persian Nativities* features a shorter, beginner-level work on nativities and prediction by 'Umar al-Tabarī, and a much longer book on nativities by his younger follower, Abū Bakr.

This compilation of sixteen works by Sahl b. Bishr and Māshā'allāh covers all areas of traditional astrology, from basic concepts to horary, elections, natal interpretation, and mundane astrology. It is also available in paperback.

Expand your knowledge of traditional astrology, philosophy, and esoteric thought with the *Logos & Light* audio series: downloadable, college-level lectures on MP3 at a fraction of the university cost!

Enjoy these new additions in our magic/esoteric series:

Astrological Magic: Basic Rituals & Meditations is a basic introduction to ritual magic for astrologers. It introduces a magical cosmology and electional rules, and shows how to perform ritual correctly, integrating Tarot and visualizations with rituals for all Elements, Planets, and Signs.

Available as an MP3 download, *Music of the Elements* was composed especially for *Astrological Magic* by MjDawn, an experienced electronic artist and ritualists. Hear free clips at bendykes.com/music.php!

Nights is a special, 2-disc remastering by MjDawn of the album GAMMA, and is a deep and powerful set of 2 full-disc MP3 soundtracks suitable for meditation or ritual work, especially those in *Astrological Magic*. Hear free clips at bendykes.com/music.php!

Aeonian Glow is a new version of the original ambient work mixed by Steve Roach, redesigned by MjDawn and Vir Unis from the original, pre-mixed files. This MP3 album is entrancing and enchanting: hear free clips at bendykes.com/music.php!

Table of Contents

Table of Abbreviations viii
Table of Figures ix
INTRODUCTION 1
  §1: Abū Ma'shar, and how to read this book 1
  §2: A few definitions 7
  §3: Theory of prediction, defense of revolutions 14
  §4: Interpreting planets: 25
  §5: Profections 37
  §6: Whole signs, quadrant cusps, intercepted signs 49
  §7: Distributions 61
  §8: Solar revolutions 75
  §9: Monthly revolutions and monthly profections: 88
  §10: The Moon 106
  §11: Transits 108
  §12: *Fardārs* 115
  §13: The lord of the orb 121
  §14: Ninth-parts 129
  §15: Summary statements about timing 132
  §16: Longevity 135
  §17: Lots 140
  §18: Fixed stars, eclipses, comets 142
  §19: Manuscripts and editorial remarks 143
BOOK I: ON THE REVOLUTIONS OF YEARS 145
  Chapter I.1: Introduction 145
  Chapter I.2: On the knowledge of the revolution of the years of nativities… 148
  Chapter I.3: On responding to those rejecting the year of the Sun, & our proving of it, & its months & days 150
  Chapter I.4: On what is invoked by people in invalidating the years of nativities, & what our response to them is 152
  Chapter I.5: On the excellence of knowing the conditions from the revolution of the years of nativities 158
  Chapter I.6: On making the image of the revolution of the year: what is drawn in it 159

Chapter I.7: On the Ascendant of the year, & knowing the conditions of the planets at the revolution 162
Chapter I.8: On the knowledge of the indicators of the Ages of Man ... 165
Chapter I.9: On the knowledge of what is necessary for the astrologer, concerning the condition of the owner of the revolution 172

BOOK II: ON THE LORD OF THE YEAR **179**
Chapter II.1: On the number of indicators of the year.......................... 179
Chapter II.2: On the knowledge of the indicators of the soul, the body, & the rest of the conditions, in the revolutions of years......................... 183
Chapter II.3: On the knowledge of the sign of the terminal point, & the lord of the year, & their indications for matters.................................. 185
Chapter II.4: On the indication of Saturn if he was the lord of the year & is in a suitable condition 190
Chapter II.5: On the indication of Saturn when he is the lord of the year & is in a bad condition 196
Chapter II.6: On the indication of Saturn in the houses of the circle, when he is the lord of the year 210
Chapter II.7: On the indication of Jupiter when he is the lord of the year & is in a suitable condition... 213
Chapter II.8: On the indication of Jupiter when he is the lord of the year & is in a bad condition 219
Chapter II.9: On the indication of Jupiter in the houses of the circle, when he is the lord of the year.. 225
Chapter II.10: On the indication of Mars when he is the lord of the year & is in a suitable condition 227
Chapter II.11: On the indication of Mars when he is the lord of the year & is in a bad condition... 231
Chapter II.12: On the indication of Mars in the houses of the circle, if he was the lord of the year... 238
Chapter II.13: On the indication when the Sun is the lord of the year & is in a suitable condition 241
Chapter II.14: On the indication of the Sun when he is the lord of the year & is in a bad condition.. 245
Chapter II.15: On the indication of the Sun in the houses of the circle, if he was the lord of the year 248
Chapter II.16: On the indication of Venus when she is the lord of the year & is in a suitable condition... 250

CONTENTS iii

Chapter II.17: On the indication of Venus when she is the lord of the year & is in a bad condition 253

Chapter II.18: On the indication of Venus in the houses of the circle, if she was the lord of the year 256

Chapter II.19: On the indication of Mercury when he is the lord of the year & is in a suitable condition 259

Chapter II.20: On the indication of Mercury when he is the lord of the year & is in a bad condition 260

Chapter II.21: On the indication of Mercury when he is the lord of the year, in the houses of the circle 262

Chapter II.22: On the indication of the Moon when she is the lord of the year & is in a suitable condition 264

Chapter II.23: On the indication of the Ascendant of the revolution & its lord, & their partnership with the terminal point & the lord of the year, & with others, in the indication 268

BOOK III: ON DIRECTIONS..**286**

Chapter III.1: On directing, the distribution, the distributor, & its partner in the management 286

Chapter III.2: On the indication of the fortunes & infortunes, & the distributors & their partners in the indication, & in the management of the distribution by body or rays, & the shifting from one to another 293

Chapter III.3: On the management of Saturn if he was the distributor, & the partnership of the planets with him in the management 316

Chapter III.4: On the management of Jupiter when he is the distributor, & the partnership of the planets with him in the management 319

Chapter III.5: On the management of Mars when he is the distributor, & the partnership of the planets with him in the management 322

Chapter III.6: On the management of Venus when she is the distributor, & the partnership of the planets with her in the management 325

Chapter III.7: On the management of Mercury when he is the distributor, & the partnership of the planets with him in the management 327

Chapter III.8: On the partnership of the lord of the year, the distributor, & the Ascendant, in the indication 337

Chapter III.9: On the knowledge of the ninth-parts & their lords, & their direction & distribution, & the division of each one of them into thirds, & the knowledge of the lord of each division by its indication, &

the one partnering with it by body or ray, according to what the people of India said.. 347

Chapter III.10: On knowing the lord of the year from the method of the lords of the ninth-parts, according to the belief of the people of India.. 361

BOOK IV: ON THE *FARDĀRS* OF THE PLANETS..................................364

Chapter IV.1: On the indication of the *fardār* of the Sun....................... 364

Chapter IV.2: On the indication of the *fardār* of Venus 373

Chapter IV.3: On the indication of the *fardār* of Mercury..................... 375

Chapter IV.4: On the indication of the *fardār* of the Moon 378

Chapter IV.5: On the indication of the *fardār* of Saturn 384

Chapter IV.6: On the indication of the *fardār* of Jupiter....................... 387

Chapter IV.7: On the indication of the *fardār* of Mars 390

BOOK V: ON THE TRANSIT OF THE PLANETS, EACH TO THE OTHER 395

Chapter V.1: On the indication of the transit of the planets 395

Chapter V.2: On the indication of Saturn when he transits in the revolution over his own rooted position & the position of the rest of the planets 407

Chapter V.3: On stating the indication of Jupiter if in the revolution he transited his own rooted position & the position of the rest of the planets 410

Chapter V.4: On the indication of Mars if in the revolution he transited his own rooted position & the position of the rest of the planets 412

Chapter V.5: On the indication of the Sun if in the revolution of the year he was in one of the twelve houses 415

Chapter V.6: On the indication of Venus if in the revolution she transited her own rooted position & the position of the rest of the planets..... 417

Chapter V.7: On the indication of Mercury if in the revolution he transited his own rooted position & the position of the rest of the planets 419

Chapter V.8: On the indication of the Moon if in the revolution of the year she transited her own rooted position & the position of the rest of the planets 421

BOOK VI: ON THE CONDITION OF THE PLANETS IN THE SIGNS 426

Chapter VI.1: On the lord of the orb... 426

Chapter VI.2: On the turning of the houses of the root, & the direction of degrees 430

Chapter VI.3: On the indication of the sign of the terminal point & the Ascendant of the revolution of the year, when one of them coincides with one of the houses of the root, & in the revolution one of the seven planets was in it 435

Chapter VI.4: On the indication of the year's terminating at a sign in which there is a planet in the root, or its rooted position is the Ascendant of the year 458

Chapter VI.5: On the indication of the planets when they are in one of the houses in the root of the nativity, but at the revolution of the year they pass into another house 465

Chapter VI.6: On the indication of the connection of the lords of the houses with one other, & their separation from one another 468

BOOK VII: ON THE SHIFTING OF THE PLANETS IN THE SIGNS THROUGHOUT THE WHOLE YEAR 476

Chapter VII.1: On the conditions of the planets in the signs & houses of the circle, in the revolution 476

Chapter VII.2: On the indication of Saturn in his transit in the twelve houses 480

Chapter VII.3: On the indication of Jupiter in his transit in the twelve houses 489

Chapter VII.4: On the indication of Mars in his transit in the twelve houses 494

Chapter VII.5: On the indication of the Sun by his transit in the twelve houses 500

Chapter VII.6: On the indication of Venus by her transit in the twelve houses 503

Chapter VII.7: On the indication of Mercury by his transit in the twelve houses 508

Chapter VII.8: On the indication of the Moon by her transit in the twelve houses 514

Chapter VII.9: On the indication of the Head & Tail during their transit in the twelve houses 517

BOOK VIII: ON THE PRESENCE OF THE PLANETS IN THEIR OWN SHARES AND THOSE OF OTHERS 523

Chapter VIII.1: On the indication of Saturn by his presence in the shares of the planets 523

Chapter VIII.2: On the indication of Jupiter by his presence in the houses of the planets 524
Chapter VIII.3: On the indication of Mars by his presence in the houses of the planets 526
Chapter VIII.4: On the indication of the Sun by his presence in the houses of the planets 527
Chapter VIII.5: On the indication of Venus by her presence in the houses of the planets 529
Chapter VIII.6: On the indication of Mercury by his presence in the houses of the planets 530
Chapter VIII.7: On the indication of the Moon by her presence in the houses of the planets 531
Chapter VIII.8: On the indication of Saturn by this presence in the bounds of the planets 532
Chapter VIII.9: On the indication of Jupiter by his presence in the bounds of the planets 534
Chapter VIII.10: On the indication of Mars by his presence in the bounds of the planets 535
Chapter VIII.11: On the indication of the Sun by his presence in the bounds of the planets 537
Chapter VIII.12: On the indication of Venus by her presence in the bounds of the planets 538
Chapter VIII.13: On the indication of Mercury by his presence in the bounds of the planets 540
Chapter VIII.14: On the indication of the Moon by her presence in the bounds of the planets 542
Chapter VIII.15: On the indication of the planets by their presence in the wells of the signs 545
BOOK IX: ON THE KNOWLEDGE OF THE CONDITIONS OF A MAN IN THE MONTHS, DAYS, AND HOURS, AND THE KNOWLEDGE OF THE CUTTERS AND INDICATORS OF THE YEAR 552
Chapter IX.1: On the knowledge of the indicators of the months 552
Chapter IX.2: On the knowledge of the condition of the first month... 564
Chapter IX.3: On the image of the revolution of the month 575
Chapter IX.4: On the combinations of the seven planets...................... 577
Chapter IX.5: On looking into the conditions of the eleven months 601

Chapter IX.6: On the indication of the planets for lasting things [&] change..625
Chapter IX.7: On the indicators of the days & hours, & their indications... 630
Chapter IX.8: On the cutters, which of them is true, friendly, superior, loved for wisdom..645
Chapter IX.9: On the special indicators in the indication of the conditions of the year..667

APPENDIX A: CALCULATING DISTRIBUTIONS..................671
APPENDIX B: TABLE OF ASCENSIONAL TIMES................675
GLOSSARY..678
BIBLIOGRAPHY 705
INDEX..708

Table of Abbreviations

ASB1	Sahl, *The Astrology of Sahl b. Bishr Volume I*
AW2	Dykes, *Astrology of the World, Volume II*
BA	The Book of Aristotle (in *PN1*)
Carmen	Dorotheus, *Carmen Astrologicum*
Da.	al-Dāmaghānī excerpts, in Burnett and al-Hamdī 1991/1992
Gr. Intr.	Abū Ma'shar, *The Great Introduction to the Science of the Stars*
Introduction	Sahl, *The Introduction*, in *ASB1*
ITA	Dykes, *Introductions to Traditional Astrology*
JN	Al-Khayyāt, *On the Judgments of Nativities* (in *PN1*)
Nativities	Sahl b. Bishr, *On Nativities* (in *ASB1*)
PN1 – PN3	Dykes, *Persian Nativities* Vols. I - III
WSM	Dykes, *Works of Sahl & Māshā'allāh*

CONTENTS

Table of Figures

Figure 1: Natal chart, whole sign houses and bounds 8
Figure 2: Distribution of natal Ascendant 9
Figure 3: Profection to age 34 10
Figure 4: SR for age 34 11
Figure 5: Bi-wheel for age 34 11
Figure 6: Three predictive frameworks and relations to time 14
Figure 7: SR planet looking at activated natal position 17
Figure 8: Comparing natal and SR conditions 18
Figure 9: Jupiter in and ruling three places in both charts 19
Figure 10: Saturn lord of the year, trining Jupiter in both charts 22
Figure 11: Jupiter in good place 26
Figure 12: Mars in good place, Jupiter in bad place 28
Figure 13: Jupiter in good condition, Mars in bad condition 30
Figure 14: Houses for profected ASC, to Age 59 38
Figure 15: "Phil," Ascendant and Lot profected to Ages 2, 14, 26, etc. 39
Figure 16: Abū Ma'shar's proxies when luminary is lord of year ... 44
Figure 17: Profection example: "Phil," Age 27 48
Figure 18: When cusp falls on different sign 52
Figure 19: When two cusps are on same sign 53
Figure 20: Transits in intercepted signs 56
Figure 21: Abū Ma'shar's explicit and likely rules for cusps and houses 59
Figure 22: Nativity with bounds and list of distributions 63
Figure 23: Table of Egyptian bounds 65
Figure 24: 24 transitions between distributors and partners 70
Figure 25: Abū Ma'shar's distribution example 74
Figure 26: SR example: "Phil," Age 27 82
Figure 27: SR bi-wheel: "Phil," Age 27 83
Figure 28: Total significations for Venus 86
Figure 29: Monthly profection of natal Ascendant 91
Figure 30: Monthly profection of natal Lot of Fortune 92
Figure 31: Monthly profection of natal third 92
Figure 32: Monthly profection of SR Lot 93
Figure 33: Profected Month 5 for natal and SR Ascendants 94
Figure 34: Seven monthly indicators 96
Figure 35: Activation of assets in first month 98

Figure 36: Quick summary of how to look at year 99
Figure 37: Abū Ma'shar's monthly profections, sign of year fixed 103
Figure 38: Abū Ma'shar's monthly profections, sign of year convertible 104
Figure 39: "Phil," MR for Age 27, Month 10 105
Figure 40: Transits, modern view 108
Figure 41: Transits, ancient view 108
Figure 42: Venus return to same bound 111
Figure 43: *Fardār* sequences and years 116
Figure 44: Planetary *fardār* lords by sect and number of years 117
Figure 45: Planetary hours 123
Figure 46: Lords of the orb, continuous looping 125
Figure 47: Table of lords of the orb (continuous loop version) 126
Figure 48: Table of lords of the orb (single cycle version) 128
Figure 49: Longevity: releasing and cutting 137
Figure 50: Comparing terms in longevity and distributions 138
Figure 51: Simplified Abū Ma'shar revolution 160
Figure 52: Abū Ma'shar's 154 preferred points 162
Figure 53: The Ages of Man 169
Figure 54: How a native's revolutions continue to indicate living relatives 178
Figure 55: Comparing natal and SR conditions 188
Figure 56: Activating natal infortune, reinforced in the revolution 271
Figure 57: Activating natal fortune, reinforced in the revolution 272
Figure 58: Activating natal infortune, angular in the revolution 273
Figure 59: Combination of leadership, unhappiness, and danger 274
Figure 60: Activating natal infortune, angular to self in revolution 277
Figure 61: Activating natal fortune, good condition and configured, lord of year angular 278
Figure 62: Lord of year in tenth at both times, good condition and place . 282
Figure 63: Jupiter safe, angular, looking at lord of year 283
Figure 64: A complex scenario with an infortune 284
Figure 65: Chart example 290
Figure 66: Seven "static" distributor-partner combinations 296
Figure 67: Example: "the brink of death" 299
Figure 68: Transitions 1-8, between distributors or partners 305
Figure 69: Four shifts between distributors 306
Figure 70: Four shifts between partners 307
Figure 71: Eight shifts from bound to bound, same partner 309

Contents

Figure 72: Eight shifts from partner to partner, same bound 311
Figure 73: Transitions 9-24, both bounds and partners 312
Figure 74: When time lords' effects change, based on quadruplicity 333
Figure 75: Mercury activated by planetary years and ascensions 336
Figure 76: Order of ninth-part lords 348
Figure 77: Ninth-parts and first-level subdivisions, fiery and earthy signs 349
Figure 78: Ninth-parts and first-level subdivisions, airy and watery signs . 350
Figure 79: Lords of convertible signs 352
Figure 80: First three ninth-parts of Aries, with subdivisions 354
Figure 81: Order of subdivisions in any ninth-part 355
Figure 82: Venus return to same bound 396
Figure 83: Persian planetary orbs (on each side), and intensity of transits 397
Figure 84: Venus transiting Jupiter, houses derived from Sagittarius and Pisces 399
Figure 85: Duration of effect, planetary return 401
Figure 86: Saturn return to 6th, in 12th from sign of year, 7th from SR ASC 402
Figure 87: Duration of effect, transit to a different planet 404
Figure 88: SR Venus transiting natal Jupiter in 6th, looked at by SR Jupiter... 406
Figure 89: Table of lords of the orb (continuous loop version) 428
Figure 90: Abū Ma'shar's theory when cusp falls on different sign 434
Figure 91: Abū Ma'shar's theory when two cusps are on same sign 435
Figure 92: SR planet looking at activated natal position 459
Figure 93: Profection distance between planet and domicile, as a process 464
Figure 94: A revolutionary planet in three derived houses 467
Figure 95: Lord of each Ascendant, with its own lord of the second 474
Figure 96: Lord of each Ascendant, with each others' lords of the second 475
Figure 97: Transits in intercepted signs and with two cusps 476
Figure 98: The wells in the signs (*Gr. Intr.* V.21) 547
Figure 99: Monthly indicator #1: Basic profection 554
Figure 100: Seven annual and monthly indicators 555
Figure 101: Monthly indicator #3: Basic profection 556
Figure 102: Monthly indicator #5: Basic profection 557
Figure 103: Abu Ma'shar's special rules for quadruplicities in monthly profections 560
Figure 104: General template for the indications 565
Figure 105: Cancer-Moon as governor of 1st house 566

Figure 106: Activation of assets in first month 568
Figure 107: Indicators for relationship of topic to native 570
Figure 108: Basic interpretations for configurations 571
Figure 109: Monthly revolution in a tri-wheel 576
Figure 110: Combinations for planets with two signs 578
Figure 111: Planets with two houses, 1st division 580
Figure 112: Planets with two houses, 2nd division 581
Figure 113: Planets with two houses, 3rd division 582
Figure 114: Planets with two houses, 4th division 584
Figure 115: Combinations for planets with one sign 585
Figure 116: Planets with one house (Moon), 1st division 586
Figure 117: Planets with one house (Sun), 1st division 586
Figure 118: Planets with one house (Moon), 2nd division 588
Figure 119: Planets with one house (Sun), 2nd division 588
Figure 120: Planets with one house (Moon), 3rd division 589
Figure 121: Planets with one house (Sun), 3rd division 589
Figure 122: Planets with one house (Sun or Moon), 4th division 590
Figure 123: Table comparing planetary combinations 591
Figure 124: Planet with two houses, 1st division, first way 597
Figure 125: Venus combinations for 1st division, first way 598
Figure 126: Seven monthly indicators 602
Figure 127: Seven monthly indicators, general appraisal of any month 605
Figure 128: Six indicators, general appraisal of any month 607
Figure 129: Four other methods of monthly timing 612
Figure 130: Fortunes looking at profected sign of month 614
Figure 131: Infortunes looking at profected sign of month 616
Figure 132: Quick monthly method 1 622
Figure 133: Quick monthly method 2 623
Figure 134: Quick monthly method 3 624
Figure 135: Events indicated by houses 628
Figure 136: Lord of weeks and days, Method 1 631
Figure 137: Nineteen cutters, planets, and fixed stars 652
Figure 138: Combining house meanings 669
Figure 139: Combining house meanings 670
Figure 140: Distribution of Mars-Mercury, Age 17.97 672
Figure 141: Distribution of Saturn-Jupiter, Age 42 673

INTRODUCTION

§1: Abū Ma'shar, and how to read this book

Nine years ago I published *Persian Nativities III* (*PN3*), my translation of the Latin version of *On the Revolutions of the Years of Nativities*, Abū Ma'shar's book on predictive techniques. It was an important book to make available, because at the time very little had been published about some of the central techniques of traditional astrology. However, I was always conscious of the fact that the Latin edition was incomplete: of the original nine Books, the Latin had only Books I-V and a tiny portion of IX. I always wondered what could be in the full Arabic version, and the known chapter titles weren't necessarily helpful.

But after some years of using the techniques and now regularly translating Arabic, I present *Persian Nativities IV* (*PN4*), the complete English edition of Abū Ma'shar's book. In *PN4* the student will find not only neater and clearer explanations than in *PN3*, but the restored portions contain numerous delineations of planets in the places, how to interpret the activation of a natal planet versus a revolutionary planet, how to handle intercepted signs and signs with multiple cusps, the "lord of the orb," better timing of events, copious comments and advice on longevity techniques, and extremely detailed instructions about monthly revolutions and smaller units of time. There is probably no other book on the central techniques which is as all-encompassing, and it's much more sophisticated and subtle in places than I had previously realized.

Abū Ma'shar recognized that his ordering of topics isn't always presented in the easiest way for the student,[1] and this Introduction is meant to help with that. Here are the highlights:

- Each section presents some aspect of Abū Ma'shar's primary techniques, but students at different levels will benefit in dif-

---

[1] See II.1, **25-26**.

ferent ways. The first parts tend to be more suitable for beginners.
- I've inserted "reading tables" so you may read specific sentences and passages by Abū Ma'shar which illustrate my summaries. Beginners might get more out of them over time and with more experience.
- The extensive Glossary at the back of the book explains just about every technical term you might find, so please use it!

Abū Ma'shar was one of the most famous astrologers of the 9th Century, a contemporary of the astrologer Sahl b. Bishr, and perhaps 30 years old when the astrologer Māshā'allāh died in about 815 AD. He is said to have learned astrology only after age 47, following an engagement with al-Kindī;[2] this would have been in about the year 834.

He was allegedly born in or around Balkh (in modern Afghanistan), in about 786 AD: this is generally accepted because according to the biographer and historian al-Nadīm, he died in 886 AD in Wāsit (in modern Iraq) at the age of 100.[3] And since the nativity in *PN4* III.1 is from August 10, 787 AD, David Pingree had argued as early as 1962 that this was the nativity of Abū Ma'shar himself.[4] However, even if we overlook the difference in years (786 vs. 787), there are two good reasons to doubt Pingree, and one more circumstantial one. The first good reason is that Abū Ma'shar's student Shādhān b. Bahr reports that "epilepsy used to afflict Abū Ma'shar at the fullness of the Moon every month, *and he did not know his own nativity*—but he had done a question [chart] about his lifespan and its conditions...."[5] That is, Shādhān isn't only claiming that Abū Ma'shar did not know his nativity, but ex-

---

[2] Al-Nadīm, p. 656.
[3] Al-Nadīm, p. 657.
[4] Pingree 1962, p. 487.
[5] Translated by me from the Arabic (Oxford Bodleian Hunt. 546/2, f. 65a, and Tehran, Milli 1634-10, slide 39a, full translation forthcoming). This student is the "Sadan" known from the Latin *Albumasar in Sadan*.

plains that *because* he did not know it, he had to resort to a question chart to look into his own health.

The second good reason is an inconsistency involving when Abū Ma'shar learned astrology. According to al-Nadīm, it was *after* age 47:[6] if he was born in 787, this would put his first year in astrology after 834 AD. But the Latin edition of Shādhān provides a question chart posed to Abū Ma'shar in October 832.[7] If authentic, then either Abū Ma'shar was born earlier, or learned astrology earlier: either way, al-Nadīm must be wrong about the length of his life or when he began astrology.

The more circumstantial reason is that Abū Ma'shar was allegedly sentenced to be lashed by Caliph al-Musta'īn:[8] but al-Musta'īn reigned from 862-866, which means that Abū Ma'shar would have been between age 75-80: is that really plausible? Maybe, but in any event I side with Abū Ma'shar's student for now and do not accept the chart in III.1 as his nativity. In fact, I suspect is it meant to be the nativity of Caliph al-'Amīn or al-Ma'mūn (both born 786-787), or perhaps the Persian vizier al-Fadl b. Sahl. I describe it and its many problems in §7 below, which include what may be a two-stage process of calculation and alteration.

Abū Ma'shar had a mixed reputation even in his own day. Some accused him of outright plagiarism,[9] which may be explained in some cases because authors didn't always attribute sources properly at every turn. In other cases he was accused of sloppiness or doctoring data, such as the claim that he used an observational device (a gnomon) of a certain length for measurements in his tables, but made calculations as though it was of another length.[10] Be that as it may, to my mind *On the Revolutions of the Year of Nativities* is of a special character and shows quite a bit of thoughtfulness, if not outright originality. Abū Ma'shar

---

[6] Al-Nadīm, p. 656.
[7] See Vescovini pp. 327-28.
[8] Al-Nadīm, p. 656.
[9] Reported by al-Nadīm, p. 654.
[10] Kennedy 1956, pp. 133-34.

himself recognized it as a stand-out book, remarking that there had never been anything like its intricacy and philosophical rigor before.[11] Currently I have no reason to doubt him, even if I don't agree with all of his approaches or emphases. Moreover, he notes that it's a product of his old age, after much effort and persistent thought,[12] composed after writing the famous *Great Introduction*;[13] and in one late chapter he produces some philosophical reflections on life and astrology, including a classification of the houses insofar as they relate to prediction and the course of life.[14] Finally, in one of the last chapters, he seems to produce a lecture in response to student demands, addressing students directly and chiding them a bit for being too interested in longevity techniques—before providing pages of valuable advice on them.[15]

Before introducing the approach I'll take in this Introduction, let me make a few more remarks on what *PN4* reveals about Abū Ma'shar's sources and his astronomy. As for his sources, he definitely uses the following:

- Rhetorius on planets in the places (*PN4* VI.3), although from precisely what source is hard to say.
- Dorotheus, from *Carmen* (*PN4* II, V, VI.4, VIII, maybe IX.7), on aspects, planets in each other's signs, transits, and profections. He also refers to Dorotheus or Valens in IX.1, **40-41**.
- Al-Andarzaghar (throughout *PN4* II-IV), adapting and elaborating his material for profections, distributions, and *fardārs*.[16]

---

[11] Ch. I.1, **1-3**; IX.5, **104-06**.
[12] III.9, **13**.
[13] III.9, **11**; VIII.15, **20**.
[14] Ch. IX.6.
[15] Ch. IX.8.
[16] These attributions to both al-Andarzaghar and Abū Ma'shar are found in al-Dāmaghānī (see Burnett and al-Hamdi, 1991/1992). In the footnotes I have added "Da." numbers to indicate the al-Dāmaghānī passage numbers. In this way, between Sahl's *ASB1*, *PN4*, and Burnett and al-Hamdi's translation of al-Dāmaghānī, we have virtually all of the natal and predictive portions from al-Andarzaghar's book on na-

He is also probably using al-Andarzaghar in IX.7, on planetary weeks and days.
- Perhaps Māshā'allāh in *PN4* II. There, Abū Ma'shar groups his discussion of planets in the houses in the same way that Māshā'allāh does in his *Treatise on Lots* (as one can see throughout Sahl's *Nativities*).
- Ptolemy, both the *Almagest* and *Tetrabiblos* (see for instance IX.1, **42, 44** and IX.8, **33-50**).

As for his astronomy, his fixed stars are calculated for a date of about 820 AD, as he refers to them using the calendar of Alexander for that period,[17] but I don't know which book of tables or *zīj* he was using for them.[18] In Ch. I.4, **29** he shows familiarity with three famous *zījes*: the *Sindhind*, Ptolemy's *Almagest*, and the Sasanian Persian *Shahriyār* (also known as the *Zīj al-Shāh*), suggesting that even in the mid- to late 800s there were still astrologers using sidereal zodiacs on a regular basis.

Chapter I.4, **23-31** offers other insights into astrological practices of his day, and the fact that even Abū Ma'shar mixed and matched sidereal and tropical values for different purposes. First, he used a sidereal year of 365.259 days for his Saturn-Jupiter conjunctions, as I described in *AW2*.[19] But in two places here[20] he endorses the Hipparchan tropical year of 365.24667 days (from *Almagest* III.1) when calculating solar revolutions. (He also uses a year of 365.25 days when calculating periods for the Indian ninth-parts.)[21] These discrepancies help to

---

tivities which later appeared as the Latin *Book of Aristotle* (translated by Hugo of Santalla) in its Arabic translation.

[17] IX.8, **51**.

[18] He is credited with devising two of his own: see Kennedy 1956, p. 133 (#63). But why didn't he use those values instead of 820 AD (before he came to astrology), especially since he wrote this book in the late 800s?

[19] See the Introduction, the table at the end of §5.

[20] Chs. I.4, **31**; IX.7, **10**.

[21] Ch. IX.7, **55**.

show how easy it was for other astrologers to find fault in Abū Ma'shar's technical work.

The passage in Ch. I.4 is especially puzzling because Abū Ma'shar is responding to precisely this criticism: that mixing different astronomical systems will result in charts being cast for the wrong time. His response is that we should use the mean Sun for the nativity (in whatever tables one uses for that), and then apply the Hipparchan tropical year to calculate the revolutions. To me this response doesn't make sense. In layman's terms, in traditional astronomy the "mean Sun" is the uncorrected Solar position: it's the position the Sun would be in if he moved at a uniform rate every day, which he does not—that's why astronomers and astrologers then used a special table to apply a correction or "equation" to it, so as to get the "true" position we find in the ephemeris and in a normal chart. But Abū Ma'shar seems to be suggesting we embrace it as a "fudge" factor; and even if he does want the corrected position, what is the point of applying the Hipparchan tropical year if the *zīj* being used for the mean Sun doesn't use a tropical zodiac to begin with or even has a different rate of precession? Luckily for us, we're interested in Abū Ma'shar's theory of prediction and interpretive methods, rather than his calculations.

Like many traditional astrology books, *PN4* is heavy on technique rather than chart examples (indeed, it only contains one problematic example, the nativity in III.1); Abū Ma'shar claims that he wrote a book of example charts illustrating the techniques in detail,[22] but it seems to have perished. Because the book is so thorough in its techniques, and especially in combining them, the reader really needs a helpful guide: this was recognized by Abū Ma'shar himself,[23] and in the rest of this Introduction I'll review the techniques in a way that will be more friendly to the practitioner. I will also supply my own reading lists and tables of information (with sentence numbers in boldface), so the student may quickly read the essential passages and then return to

---

[22] Ch. I.1, **14**.
[23] Ch. I.1, **13**; II.1, **25-26**.

my descriptions and examples. Specialized vocabulary will be presented in the relevant sections, and also as part of the Glossary.

Reading: Overview of book	
Overview of book and topics	I.1 (all)

§2: A few definitions

This book is about "revolutions," which has both a general and a particular meaning. In a general sense, it refers to a whole suite of predictive techniques which are recalculated every year at the solar revolution,[24] when the Sun returns to his natal position in the zodiac. Not every technique involves events for precisely one year, but enough of them do or can, that they're viewed together annually at the "revolution of the year of the nativity."

In a particular and narrow sense, a revolution is one specific technique: casting a chart for the moment of the solar revolution. This is almost always what Abū Ma'shar means when he speaks of a revolution. I will often abbreviate this as SR ("solar revolution"). In addition, one may cast monthly revolution (MR) charts for the moment when the Sun enters the degree of any sign corresponding to his natal position. For example, if the natal Sun is at 12° 22' Gemini, the SR is cast every year when he returns to 12° 22' Gemini. But during that year, each MR will be cast when he enters 12° 23' Cancer, 12° 23' Leo, and so on.[25]

---

[24] In modern astrology, this is called a solar "return."
[25] As we will see in §9, the annual SR also acts as the first month of the year, which requires special rules for determining which features refer to the year, and which to the first month alone.

Although many concepts and techniques are described in *PN4*, several of them are central and form a hierarchy in relation to the natal chart. Let's look at each of them briefly, and learn some vocabulary:[26]

1. Root, rooted. This refers to the natal chart, which is called a "root" because it's the foundation for the other techniques and charts. All charts must ultimately be understood in relation to the root. In Latin the word is *radix*, so some English-speaking astrologers have adopted this as "radix" or speak of a "radical" chart.[27] The root is fixed in time at the moment of birth. Figure 1 is a nativity with the natal or rooted Ascendant at Taurus, 18° 26'.

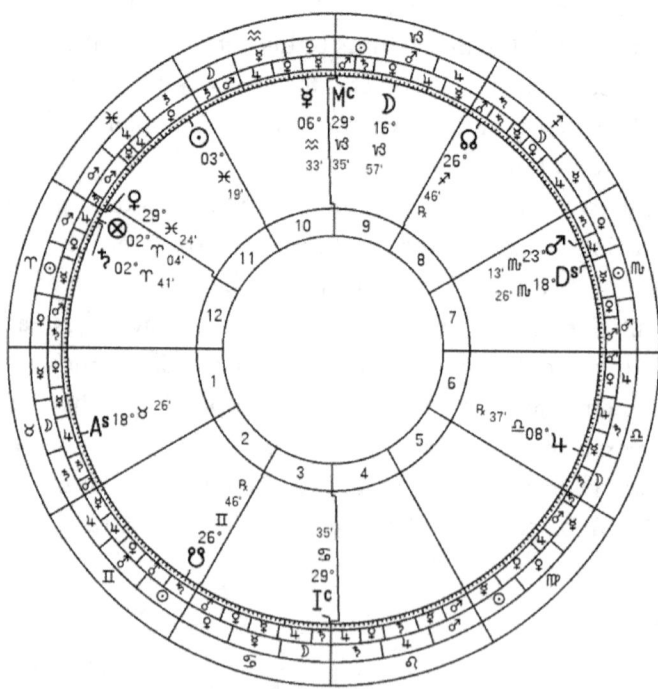

Figure 1: Natal chart, whole sign houses and bounds

---

[26] See also the Glossary for other technical terms, which I sometimes put in boldface in the lists here.

[27] See the Glossary. Actually, many charts can be roots, if they are foundations for other charts. In some ways the annual SR chart is a root chart in relation to monthly or MR charts.

2. Distribution. This is a technique applied directly to the natal chart, in which we direct the natal Ascendant (or any other point) forward in the zodiac through the bounds or terms, and as it moves along it also encounters the bodies and aspect rays of the planets. The lords of the bounds (called **distributors**), and the planets or rays encountered (called **partners**), describe what the time period will be like, measuring 1 year for each 1° of ascensions (not zodiacal degrees). This type of motion and measurement is known as "primary directions." In Figure 2, the Ascendant of the root is treated as moving from the end of Taurus through Gemini.

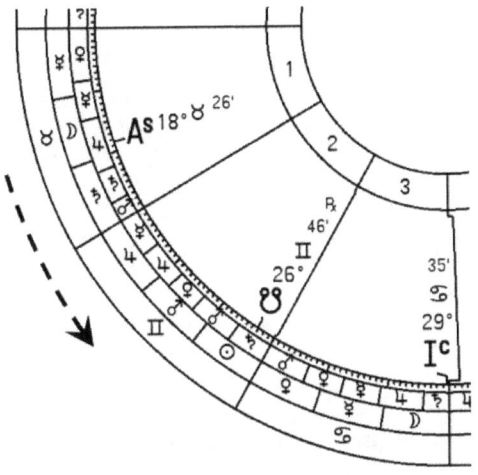

Figure 2: Distribution of natal Ascendant

3. Profections. Also called "turning" in Arabic, profection is also applied to the root but as a sign-based technique. The sign of the Ascendant (or other things) is advanced or turned one sign per year, until it reaches its **terminal point**: the **sign of the year** for the age we want. The Ascendant is in its natural place at birth or Age 0, then jumps to the second sign at Age 1, and so on around and around. In Figure 3 the natal Ascendant has profected or turned so as to terminate at Pisces, the eleventh sign, Age 34. (Everyone's Ascendant will profect to the eleventh at Age 34.) This particular profection activates the natal planets in it (Venus and the Sun), as well as its lord Jupiter, who is called the **lord of the year**. Below I provide a table with profections of the Ascendant to all houses through Age 59.

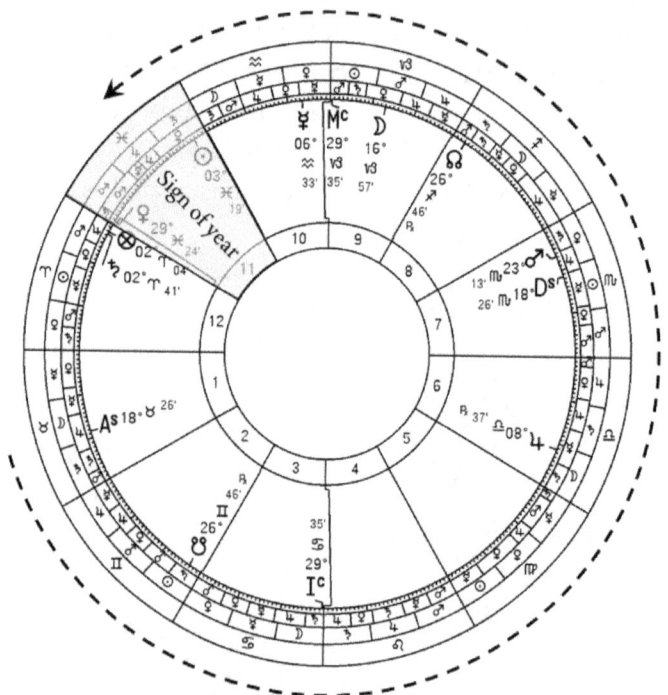

Figure 3: Profection to age 34

4. Revolution, revolutionary. This refers mainly to the annual SR chart, cast every year for the moment of the Sun's return to its natal position, and for the birth location. It's interpreted partly on its own, but also in comparison with the root. In Figure 4 I've cast the SR for Age 34 as a separate chart and then shown it in Figure 5 as a bi-wheel, with the nativity at the center:[28] this allows us to judge easily how the planets in the SR relate to the rooted positions.

---

[28] In the Janus program, cast the charts separately and click Wheels > Bi-Wheel. This will allow you to choose which wheels are inner and outer, and even which points you want to show in each (Select > Planets Inner Chart, Planets Outer Chart).

Introduction

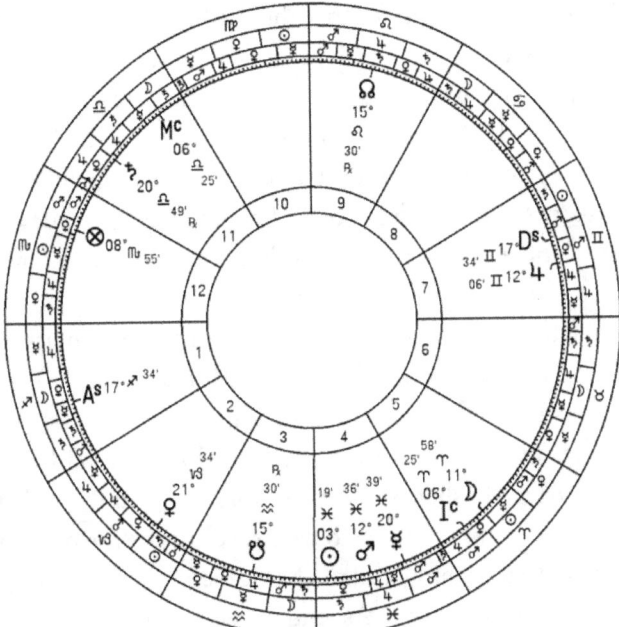

Figure 4: SR for age 34

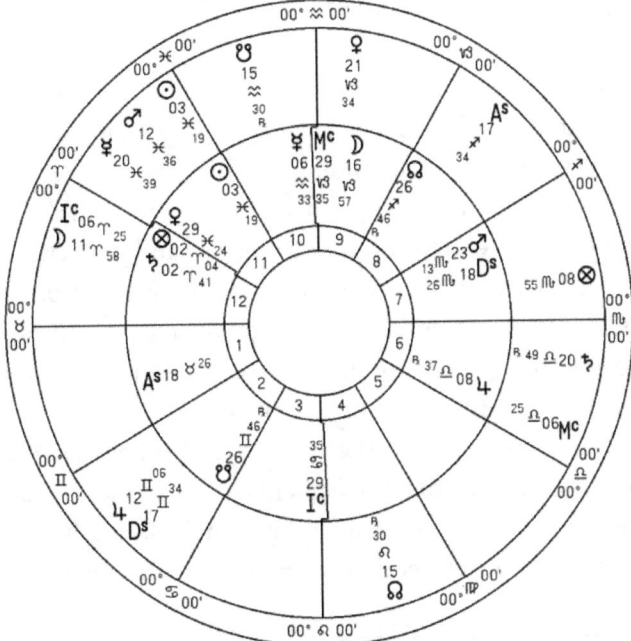

Figure 5: Bi-wheel for age 34

Abū Ma'shar seems to prefer that the SR be the inner wheel, but to me this seem unnatural and I only do it to illustrate his instructions in Ch. I.6. In Figure 5 you can see that the two Suns are in the same position, and also that the revolutionary Midheaven at 6° 25' Libra (outer circle) is virtually on the natal Jupiter at 8° 37'. I only include the seven traditional planets, the Nodes, Lot of Fortune, and axial degrees. You may calculate and add other Lots and things as you like—Abū Ma'shar certainly does!

Since the late Renaissance there have been three primary views on the location to use for the SR: (1) the location at birth, (2) where the native happens to be at the moment of the SR, and (3) the city where the native lives at that time. I use the birth location, and I don't see evidence that Abū Ma'shar or other authors of his time used anything else. Astrologers routinely used to cast revolutions for many years in the future using something called the "excess of revolution," which calculates how far forward the Ascendant will jump from year to year: since this is sensitive to geographical latitude, it can only work if we assume a fixed location: the birth location.

5. Time lords. A "time lord" is a natal planet or place which rules life or some area of life, for a particular span of time: it's "activated" for that time because a symbolic timing mechanism has been applied to it.[29] Note that while the nativity is fixed for all time, and the SR is cast in "real time" at a later date, both distributions and profections apply a kind of symbolic motion and symbolic time: in distributions we move or pretend to move something degree-by-degree, and in profections we go sign-by-sign. When we do this, we treat these various planets and places as time lords with administrative power over life.

In the charts above, when the profection symbolically reaches Pisces at Age 34, it means that the natal planets in it and the lord of that sign (Jupiter) are activated for one year, namely during Age 34: at that age, the themes of the eleventh, Jupiter, the planets in it and the places

---

[29] For "activating" or "setting into motion" (حرّك, تحرّك), see Ch. V.8, **26**; VII.1, **2**, and Sahl's *On Times* Ch. 3, **36** (in *ASB1*).

they rule, and so on, will take center stage in the native's life. Or when the distribution of the Ascendant moves through the bound of Mercury at the beginning of Gemini, and those degrees are converted into a span of years, it means that Mercury becomes an active time lord in those years of life.

It's hard to underestimate the importance of time lords: indeed, many if not most traditional predictive techniques involve them. For our purposes here, we can say that they do several things: they (1) show the orderly activation of the configurations in the nativity itself; and they (2) allow the course of life to have intelligible themes over periods of time, like a story. This second point stands in sharp contrast to the usual treatment of transits, progressions, or simple primary directions, in which you might have nothing at all happening in any of these techniques for many years. In traditional astrology *some time lord is always active*.

6. Indicators. Finally, whenever we try to understand any life topic in traditional astrology, we must identify the significators or indicators. These are planets or places which act as guides to that topic: such as the seventh, the lord of the seventh, Venus, and the Lot of marriage for the topic of relationships. In *PN4*, Abū Ma'shar frequently provides lists of indicators to guide us through the maze of planets, places, and charts. The most common indicators are the Ascendants in each technique and their lords, but time lords are also important indicators.

Reading: Introduction to revolutions and practice	
Definitions of SR and profection	I.2 (all)
Benefit of revolutions	I.5 (all)
Life context, Ages of Man	I.8-I.9 (all)
The SR chart	I.6 (all)
Ranking and overview of techniques	IX.9 (all), II.1 (all)[30]

---

[30] For Ch. II.1, note the footnotes guiding you to the Chapters and Books which discuss each item on the list.

§3: Theory of prediction, defense of revolutions

For most people it's not obvious why we need a theory of prediction: we normally just use the techniques we like. But are all techniques alike? Does a profection or primary direction predict in the same way, or predict the same kinds of things, and with comparable causes, as a solar revolution or transit does? Today we have a polite, live-and-let-live approach to prediction just as we do with house systems, but it may come as a surprise to learn that some Persian and Arab astrologers debated the meaning and value of different predictive techniques. For instance, in Ch. I.4 we see some unnamed astrologers deny that revolutions have value. In defending solar revolutions, Abū Ma'shar develops his own theory of prediction, and how techniques and events are related. Here I'll present the main points, but in my course and perhaps in a later article I'll show how the theory has important implications for how we view astrology and metaphysical levels of reality.

In order to make it easy to follow, let me lay out Abū Ma'shar's three predictive frameworks, each with its own form of time (the terminology is my own):

Nativity	Profections	Revolutions
Timeless	Symbolic time	Real time
Promise	Activation	Real conditions

Figure 6: Three predictive frameworks and relations to time

The nativity is *timeless* in the sense that it's static: it's only an image of the moment of birth, it does not change over the life, and by itself it does not say when its significations (such as for marriage) will occur. Profections and other time lord systems applied to the nativity have *symbolic time*: by counting signs, letting the sphere rotate, and so on, they assign sequences to the natal indications, allow for their development, and show the activation of the planets managing them. The SR has *real time* or represents *real conditions* through which the natal promise and activated time lords are expressed. Note also that the table contains a thick line dividing the nativity and time lords from revolutions: this is because the theory of prediction here puts them into different categories of knowledge and being. I will address this in my course and article.

Let's focus first on the contrast between the nativity and the SR. The nativity says that something will happen later. But since it's only an image of the moment of birth, it can only indirectly refer to actual events at a later time. So when do events actually manifest? When the proper, real-time conditions for them exist: and we have techniques for assessing just that, through transits, question charts, event charts, elections—and solar revolutions. The basis of Abū Ma'shar's theory of prediction is precisely this point: since any future event indicated by the nativity inherently pertains to the conditions which will actually exist at that time, prediction *requires* a real-time technique (revolutions), by which we can *compare* what's prefigured in the nativity, with their real conditions in the revolution.[31]

This comparison is also necessary because the nativity does not show each event in every detail. First, the nativity only refers generally and indirectly to the future (as I just stated), so it can't describe everything. But second, many things in the nativity can happen multiple times, or are complicated affairs which last and change over many years.[32] Third, those later conditions will have stronger or weaker indications for the event's manifestation, as compared with the nativity.[33] For example, if a natal planet in a middling condition promises something, and in a revolution it's dynamically angular (such as being on the Midheaven), its manifestation can exceed expectations, because the conditions for fulfilling it are better than they were in the nativity; but this requires a later chart and a process of comparison. For greater accuracy we might even need multiple charts, such as an SR which

---

[31] Remember that "revolution" here stands for any real-time technique, and could include monthly revolutions, ongoing transits, and so on.
[32] Abū Ma'shar addresses precisely this point in IX.6, **9-20**.
[33] Indeed, the nativity even indicates things about past things and people who existed before birth under other real-time conditions, like parents and other relatives.

indicates the conditions over a year generally, and then MRs for shorter units of time, as well as transits. So a real-time technique, which we're assuming to be an SR, retards or enhances something good, improves or worsens something difficult, changes something's quality, and so on. Prediction not only states the "when," but tries to understand the "what" and "how," the more and the less, the better and the worse.

Reading: Theory of prediction, defense, reflections	
Why revolutions are needed	I.4, **1-12, 16, 22** II.1, **1-4** II.23, **3** IX.6, **5-6**
Statements about comparing charts	I.4, **6, 10-11** I.7, **25-26** II.3, **5-8** VI.4, **3-8** IX.9, **16-23**
Reinforcement, repetition, continuity	II.23, **14** and **17** III.2, **18-19** VI.3, **3, 150-52** VI.4, **27-28** VI.6, **38-40** VI.4, **29-30**
Defense of revolutions, real-time conditions	I.3 - I.4 (all)
Reflection on life and astrology	IX.6, **1-8**
Houses, prediction, existence	IX.6, **9-20**

Abū Ma'shar gives many examples of this type of comparison, but let's take two from the reading table. First, a simple one from Ch. IX.9, **16-20**. If a natal planet in the second place indicates gaining assets, but in real time at the SR it's transiting in the SR ninth and the natal fifth, then the assets will manifest in relation to things such as travel and children—something which the natal position by itself could not have shown. Thus a planet which is determined to one topic in the nativity, will direct it towards or have its source in, some other house topic due to its SR position.

Next let's consider a more advanced example in Figure 7. In Ch. VI.4, **3-8**, he imagines that the natal Saturn is activated by having the profected or SR Ascendant on it: this indicates Saturnian themes for that year. Now if the SR Saturn looks at his natal sign, then his themes and issues will be fully present because there will

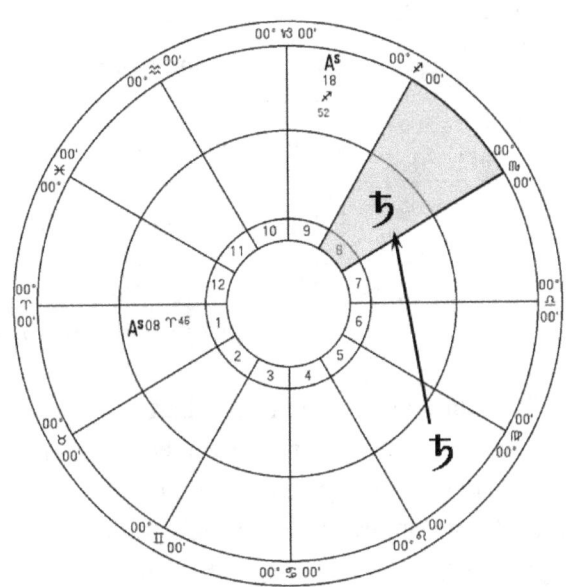

Figure 7: SR planet looking at activated natal position (VI.4, 3-8)

be a kind of similarity between his natal meaning and his producing it by aspect in the SR: he is able to elicit it and draw it forth. But if he isn't looking at his natal position while the SR fortunes do, then although the natal Saturnian influence will still be active, its full nature will not carry through and the fortunes will retard the problems, making them lighter and offering protection. Thus, the essence of the natal indication is altered by the real conditions that exist at the time of its activation. When we remember that Saturn will be activated again by profection in 12 years, it shows the importance of knowing the SR conditions because it's not possible for the same natal Saturn to manifest in exactly the same way twice.

Comparing natal and SR conditions of lord of the year	
Comparison	Basic meaning
Good in root, good in SR	Safety, good, and delight in what it indicates
Good in root, bad in SR	Weakness and decrease in what it indicates
Bad in root, good in SR	Condition will improve, introduce delight
Bad in root, bad in SR	Excess of adversity in what it indicates

Figure 8: Comparing natal and SR conditions of lord of the year (II.3, 5-8)

In addition to comparison, Abū Ma'shar points out that predictions become more firm by reinforcement and repetition. For every planet (especially a time lord) is doing *something* at the SR in relation to the nativity, and indeed does multiple things: it's potentially in and ruling three places in the nativity, and in and ruling three others at the SR.

An example of this would be Jupiter being natally in the fifth while ruling the ninth and sixth, and then at the SR being in the SR Ascendant (which is the natal seventh), and ruling the SR twelfth and third. This involves lots of possibilities, and life rarely exhibits all of them equally. Certainly as astrologers we don't want to bet on *everything* happening: we want to focus on what's most important and likely.

So instead of predicting just everything, we need to focus on indications which are multiplied in the same chart, and especially *across* charts, so that there is reinforcement, repetition, and continuity—leading to more certain predictions. Again, I've listed many examples in the reading list, but I can mention a simple one here, when the same signs or rulerships are activated by profection and in the SR. Suppose that the profection comes to the natal Mars in the tenth, and the SR Mars is in the SR tenth: thus we have a repetition of the house position across two charts. This kind of repetition doesn't just confirm the existence of an event, but what its *causes* and *manner* will be—namely, through tenth-house affairs. The same planets, in or ruling the same houses in multiple charts, will be more reliable and suggest a more prominent event.

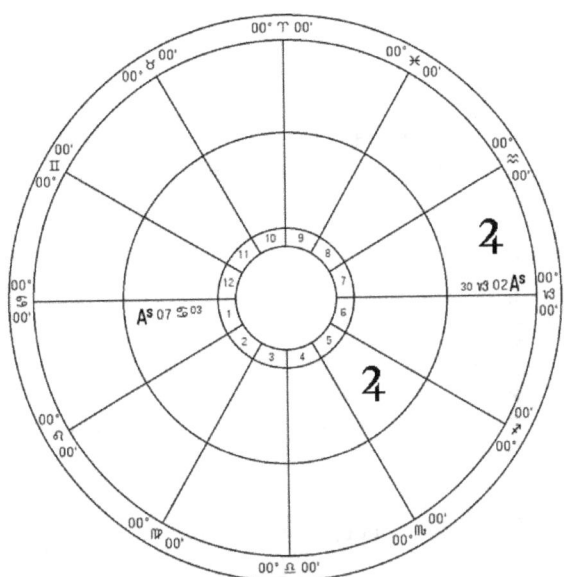

Figure 9: Jupiter in and ruling three places in both charts

So far we have focused on the opposition between the nativity and the SR.[34] Now let's address time lords, because in Abū Ma'shar's theory they play an essential role, mediating between the nativity and the SR. People commonly pick and choose freely among the techniques, and fair enough: life is too short to use all of them. However, I believe we can make a strong case for needing at least one time lord technique: an SR or transits isn't enough.

Imagine that a nativity is expressed solely and directly through real-time techniques, whether an SR or transits. If so, then every indication in the nativity would simultaneously be in a constant state of change and expression. Like a plant blooming in every direction, a child would be constantly be developing a profession or having it hindered, marrying or divorcing, becoming ill and improving, as every planet became angular, withdrew, entered its fall, and so on. This would lead to ridiculous interpretations, but without a way of putting natal indica-

---

[34] Remember that for the sake of discussion the SR is our model for all real-time techniques.

tions in a certain order, there would be no *astrological* reason not to predict all of these things for a baby.

Reading: Time lords, meanings of different charts	
Central role of time lords	I.2, **6** I.8, **27-29** III.1, **2** III.2, **24** IV.7, **27-28** VI.2, **1, 4-5**
Natal, profected, SR meanings	II.4, **7-11** III.1, **1** III.2, **1-2** VI.3, **1-2** VI.5, **23**

Time lords establish an order or sequence to the natal indications, using symbolic time. They do this in many ways: the Ages of Man apply astronomical periods of the planets to stages in human development; profections convert distances between signs into time, activating planets, their rulerships, house topics, and their lords through these relationships; distributions assign units of time and life topics to distances on the celestial equator, as the heavens rotate between one point and another; the lord of the orb uses the lords of the planetary hours in conjunction with the houses of the nativity, in order; the *fardārs* assign time lords to periods of human life based on the sect of the nativity; and so on. Converting these relationships into units of time shows when planets take on the *management* (Ar. تدبير) for life in general or for a particular topic.

So by contributing an intelligible *order* to the nativity (and life), time lords are more closely aligned with the nativity than with an SR, which again is why I put a thick black line between them in the table above. Time lords show changing *priorities* over time and periodic *development* in the natal topics. It's not simply that they have psychological value in making things understandable, but they play a metaphysical role in providing meaningful order.

For Abū Ma'shar, natal and time lord indications have different characteristics:

1. Natal indications are always "strongest," because they generally dominate life's possibilities. Time lords are the next most powerful, and revolutions the least powerful.

2. Time lords are conceptually closer to the nativity than to the SR, because they're really a conversion of natal configurations *as they natally exist*, into time.

3. Even among time lord systems, distributions tend to be more powerful than profections, because they almost always last longer and have fewer factors which could point in divergent directions, while profections are generally considered along with SRs and have other things like the Moon to consider.

4. Although an SR does modify the expression of natal indications and time lords, its indications are also for more recent and incidental things, with more incidental causes, which may not even be directly connected to the nativity. The SR therefore has more independence from the nativity than a profection does.

An example by Abū Ma'shar may help explain this idea of the SR as being more incidental and independent.[35] If Saturn trines Jupiter in the nativity, then when Saturn is the lord of the year it will indicate good things in that year, because the native's life is *generally predisposed* to that due to the nativity. Indeed, his life will normally manifest that theme in repeatable ways. But if Saturn trines Jupiter in that year's SR as well, then it won't only manifest but be occasioned by special Jupi-

---

[35] See II.4, **7-10**.

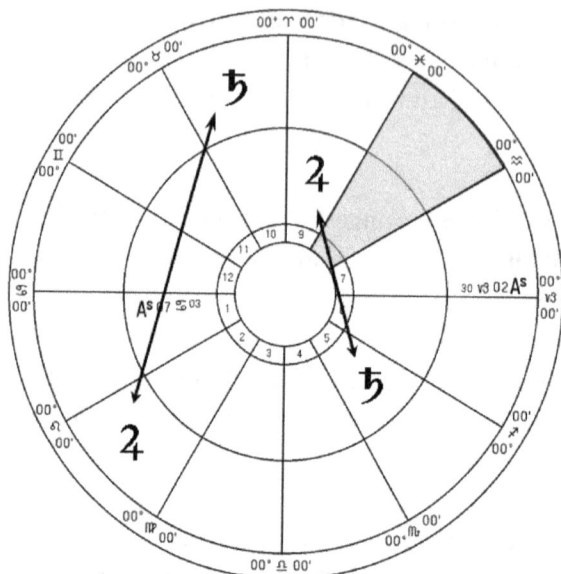

Figure 10: Saturn lord of the year, trining Jupiter in both charts (II.4, 7-10)

terian circumstances at that time, and due to recent influences—which are probably *not* repeatable, but only specific to that year.

One important consequence of these points is this: *you ought to use at least one time-lord technique*. I think you should focus on profections, but even something like the Ages of Man (Ch. I.8) is better than nothing. For it's a physical and social fact that people go through phases of life which we can at least roughly represent using the planetary years in the Ages of Man. So at a minimum, the Ages of Man are a well-motivated astrological tool, in which we treat each planet as managing any human life in a general way for many years. But everyone will also experience their Venus period in a *particular* way, and that particular way is shown in the nativity. So while the activation of Venus as a time lord at the appropriate age is necessary, it's not enough: it must be a *particular* Venus, in *this* person's nativity. That Venus will then be modified by the real conditions described in the SR.

Finally, I want to mention one other factor: the Lot of Fortune. Traditional astrology draws on the ancient concept of Fortune as a web of causes which occasionally produces "surprise" or apparently random events. These events aren't actually random, but because we have a limited ability to understand how all things are connected, predictive techniques involving the Lot of Fortune allow us to discuss sudden events which contribute to one's story by inserting surprises and the opportunity to make important decisions in response to them. Profections of the Lot of Fortune are mentioned a lot by Abū Ma'shar, and we should start paying more attention to them.[36]

༃   ༄   ༄

The only thing we have not discussed is why the revolution must be *solar*. After all, many people calculate lunar returns, or Venus returns, and many other things. But Abū Ma'shar calculates revolutions solely based on the Sun's position. Why?

The key to his thinking is that, in order to reflect and express the nativity, the revolution must have a "likeness" to the "original condition."[37] This word for "likeness" (مثل) refers to anything that is an example or comparable. In other words, it must be a moment which approximates the natal conditions in a suitable way. Of course we cannot replicate the nativity exactly, so we must find some time unit or planetary motion which does so sufficiently. Abū Ma'shar believes that the example of nature recommends the Sun, since a full cycle of seasons and natural development elapses between solar revolutions: the natural condition of the world will be in a "likeness" to the nativity. We could also point out that a solar revolution combines both a planetary position (his natal degree) and a consistent time-unit (the year). So in both time and position, the Sun is an obvious choice. Abū Ma'shar suggests that only the Sun allows for a consistent standard of measurement.[38]

Reading: Why revolutions are solar	
Why the revolution is solar	I.3

Another option would be the Moon, but this presents some complications. For one thing, the most obvious thing about the Moon and

---

[36] For more on the Lot of Fortune, see §17 below.
[37] I.3, **3-4**.
[38] I.3, **8-13**.

her motion is that it's highly coordinated with the Sun, and her phases are based on her relation to him. So if we wanted to create a likeness to the nativity, it might make more sense to calculate a lunar *phase* chart, so that she is in the same phase as she was at the nativity. But since the Sun also moves in the meantime and she is also somewhat variable, these lunar phases will seem to happen at irregular times and drift across the seasons. This irregularity doesn't seem to bear a consistent "likeness" to the natal conditions (and even less so if we believe that cycles of natural processes like the seasons are important).

Note also that it's hard to put lunar returns or phases into any larger time frame such as a year: there's simply no way to add up lunar months to equal a solar year, so "years" made up of lunar months would vary in relation to each other. Lunar months are not parts of a solar year. (Likewise, Abū Ma'shar explicitly rejects Ptolemy's method of monthly profections based on the Moon: see IX.1, **42** and **44**.)

There is also a matter of consistency, as so many predictive methods use the solar year: *fardārs*, annual profections, ascensions and distributions, the lord of the orb. Only the Sun's cycle provides that consistently, not an integer number of lunar months or phases.

Another option I've heard from Robert Schmidt, is his interpretation of a passage in Valens (*Anth.* V.3): calculate the SR position of the planets for the date of the solar revolution as normal, but calculate the *Ascendant* for the time when the Moon returns to *her* natal position (so long as the Sun is still in his proper sign). So, let the natal Sun be in 15° Gemini, and the Moon in 15° Scorpio: we calculate all planets for the moment the Sun returns to 15° Gemini, but then calculate the SR Ascendant for the time when the Moon returns to 15° Scorpio *while the Sun is still in Gemini*. If this is what Valens means, then his revolution mixes two real-time charts (the solar return and the lunar return) to create a third one which doesn't actually exist: namely, a chart with an Ascendant that did not exist at the time the planets were in that position.[39] Note that this also doesn't actually replicate the lunar phase: instead, it finds the Ascendant for a date that might be up to

---

[39] Actually, it could have existed, but might have been on the other side of the world.

about 29 days off, when she is actually in a different phase.[40] But astrology can be strange: some techniques seem like they have no right to work, but they do! If this is Valens's method and it's the true one, it would *not* invalidate anything we've said so far about time lords and real-time conditions. But it would mean that the chart which has the proper "likeness" to the nativity would be rather unusual.

§4: Interpreting planets:

This section provides a general overview of how to interpret a planet, whether natally, or in a revolution, or when comparing them across charts. Much of the arrangement and commentary is mine, but it's based on readings and advice from Abū Ma'shar.

Planetary nature, infortunes vs. fortunes, sect. Of course the first thing we have to remember is what the natural signification of the planet is, and its basic categories: is it a fortune or infortune, and of the sect or not? This gives use a *prima facie* expectation of what range of activities and effects to expect: Mars is more likely to indicate fighting, and Venus affection and friendliness, although this can change based on other considerations. Planets of the sect of the chart are more likely to have constructive expressions with less disruption or distortion, but planets contrary to it are the contrary. So although both Saturn and Mars are infortunes, Saturn is likely to be more suitable in a diurnal chart and Mars in a nocturnal one, because they are of those sects. However, this isn't absolute: there are indications in *PN4* that if an infortune had "testimony" in the nativity or SR by ruling a key area of

---

[40] For example, let the natal Sun be at 1° Gemini, and the Moon at 10° Sagittarius, so she is a recent Full Moon but waning. Then let there be some SR in which the Moon is in Aries: this means she has about 20 days to go before she makes her lunar return and we can calculate the Ascendant of the SR chart. But by that time, the Sun will also have moved about 20°, and when she reaches her natal position at 10° Sagittarius, she will be a *waxing* Moon, not replicating the natal phase.

the native (such as the Ascendant), then its indications are likely to be more beneficial.

Location: more immediate than rulership. Whether you're interpreting a place (house) or planet, location always comes before rulership. In Figure 11 natal Jupiter is in Leo, the fifth. If we interpret the fifth, the fact that Jupiter is in it comes before the fact that the Sun is its lord and is somewhere else. Likewise if we interpret Jupiter, his being in the fifth comes before the fact that he rules the ninth and twelfth. Some astrologers say that location is "stronger" than rulership, but I think this is not quite precise: it's better to say that it's more "immediate," because a planet acts immediately where it is, and only indirectly by places it sees or rules. Abū Ma'shar says that it has greater "relevance" or "applies" more to, its location than to other things.[41] For similar reasons, a conjunction is considered more powerful than aspects because a planet's immediate power surrounds it like a glow—commonly called its "orb." In practical terms, we can say that a planet focuses its quality directly on that place's topic (such as children), so that it helps manage that topic and becomes a primary indicator of it. Thus in this example, Jupiter directs his benefic energy to children, and becomes a significator for children by being there.

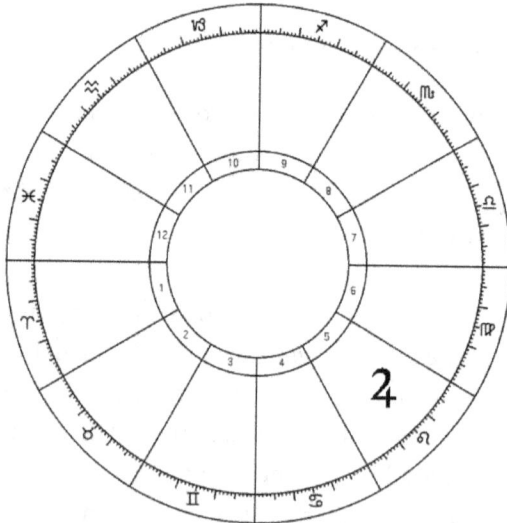

Figure 11: Jupiter in good place

---

[41] IX.5, **92**.

Abū Ma'shar has three lists of planets in the places, but I only recommend two of them. The first is found throughout Book II, describing the lord of the year in the places: use Saturn in Ch. II.6 as a model. The second is Ch. VI.3, **4-149**, when the SR Ascendant or profection comes to a sign, and an SR planet is in it. Both are largely based on solid ancient delineations, so as long as you remember that natal planets have deeper and longer-lasting effects than SR planets do, you can use these for any house delineation.

The third list—which I don't recommend—is in Chs. VII.2 – VII.9, the planets transiting through the twelve houses. These are shot through with odd and unlikely interpretations, with too much repetition to be of value. One of his principles seems to be that a planet won't just affect the place it transits, but will also have indications based on every other place it sees. So for example, Saturn in the third not only affects the siblings, but also has indications for illness because it squares the sixth; and means good things for authorities, because it trines the tenth.[42] In other cases he seems to be using derived houses, so that a planet in the twelfth from some place, will mean enmity for that topic. But Abū Ma'shar doesn't spell any of this out, so any chance to prioritize the indications and organize the mess is lost.

Good and bad places. The houses or places are divided into "good" and "bad" places (Abū Ma'shar's usual terms are "suitable" and "bad"), primarily on the basis of whether they see or are configured to the Ascendant. Places which are configured by aspect to the rising sign are generally "good," and those in aversion are "bad." This has two important consequences. First, it can mean that (1) the planet will be benefited or harmed, or diverted in a good or bad direction, by the place: so because the fifth and eleventh are considered very good places, even infortunes in them can indicate good or somewhat good things—of their planetary type. Mars in the fifth can show good fortune in Martial things, such as vigorous Martial entertainments, or success in war. But because planets never lose their fundamental na-

---

[42] See VII.2, **13**.

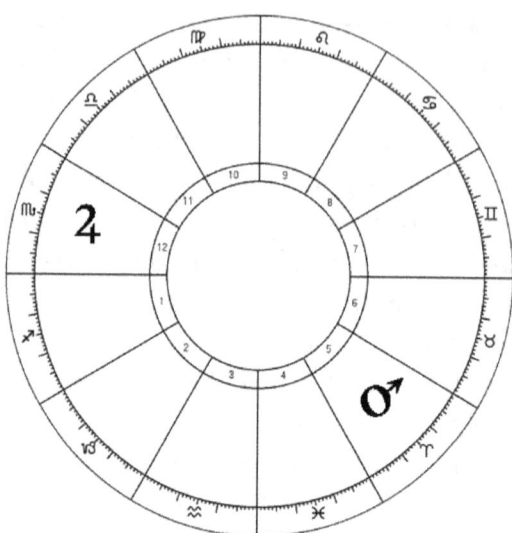

Figure 12: Mars in good place, Jupiter in bad place

tures, (2) they will actively modify the good or bad things indicated by the houses. Thus Mars in the fifth, depending on his condition and aspects, could also indicate that success in Martial things is accompanied by risk-taking and accidents. Or, Jupiter in the twelfth can indicate Jupiterian enemies (so that the direction of Jupiter's energy becomes bad), but because he is Jupiter he can often rescue the native from the worst things. You will see this throughout Book II and Ch. VI.3. One example from Ch. II.9, **15-16** captures this nicely. If Jupiter is in a bad place (such as the twelfth), and not in his own dignity nor received (i.e., so that he has no special strength there), the native will *not* have normal Jupiterian benefits like respect and rank; this is an example of (1), but could also be an example of (2) because he is too weak as an alien planet to counteract the nature of the twelfth. On the other hand, if he were there and is actually made unfortunate (such as by a square from Saturn), then something actually bad would be indicated, of a Jupiterian nature or because of Jupiterian things.

Rulership. After analyzing a planet's place, consider the place or places it rules: it will connect the topics of the houses it rules, to the place where it is, and try to manifest them through its place. So, the lord of the ninth in the second can show income (the second) coming from travel or relations with foreigners (the ninth). We can look at this from two perspectives: as the lord of the ninth, it will lead the native's travels to manifest somewhere else—namely as money. But we can also look at it through its position: as a planet in the second, it will produce a particular kind of money: travel-related money. A similar thing is done below, when we compare the planet's significations in the nativity, with its new house and rulerships in the SR. Thus a planet in the natal ninth (signifying travel), and in the SR second (money), might show applying one's travels to making money *in that year*.

Strength, dignity, angularity. Understanding a planet's strength or weakness by dignity and angularity, is essential. In much contemporary astrology, planets are treated as though they always operate at full capacity, namely in a strong way. But traditional astrology had many ways to evaluate a planet's operations. One form of strength is being in a dignity, especially one's own sign or exaltation (such as the Sun in Leo or Aries): this allows a planet to act in a more consistent, authoritative, and unwavering way. Lesser dignities like triplicity and bound are better than nothing but less effective. If a planet has no dignity so that is it more neutral (called "alien" or "peregrine"), this is somewhat precarious because it's as though it doesn't "belong" where it is, and has no authority. Finally, a planet in its detriment or fall is in an unstable or even destructive condition. A second form of strength is being angular or succeedent by quadrant division (in Arabic, "advancing"), as opposed to being cadent or falling (in Arabic, "withdrawing"). Advancing planets have more vigor and intensity, and are more likely to rise to the threshold of effective action and public notice, while withdrawing planets are weaker, unstable, or private and unnoticed.

In Figure 13 Jupiter is in an excellent condition: he is in a good place (the Ascendant or rising sign), his own sign (Sagittarius), and advancing very close to the degree of the Ascendant. Mars is in a bad place (the sixth sign), in his detriment (Taurus), and middling in strength (in a succeedent quadrant division). Mercury is in a good place but in his fall and retrograde, and withdrawing.

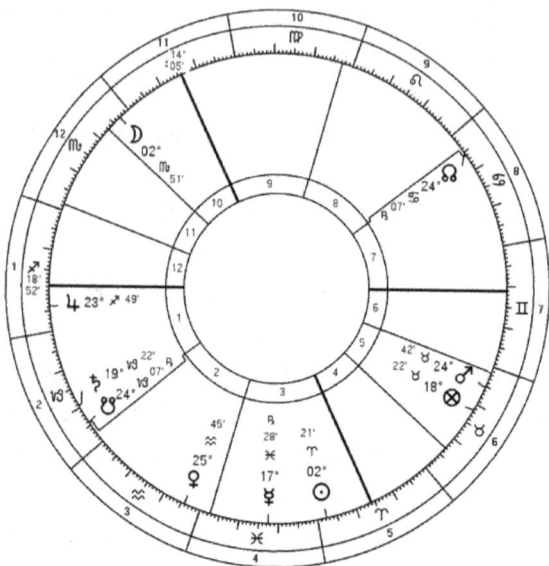

Figure 13: Jupiter in good condition, Mars in bad condition

It's pretty easy to understand how a powerful planet will manifest: just you expect it to, in full vividness and clarity, with fortunes granting obvious goods and rescuing from evils, and infortunes creating obvious problems and thwarting goods. The difficulty comes with the middling and weaker conditions. Abū Ma'shar makes a number of valuable statements about this. Here are some which illustrate his thinking:

- *Strong vs. weak planets.* When a planet is very strong, its indication won't only manifest more fully in terms of quality, but will actually appear objectively in the world; but the weaker a planet is, the more it will only appear in the mind, in one's plans and wishes—or will be fleeting even if it does appear.[43]
- *Weakness corrupts.* A planet in a weak and bad condition might not prevent or wholly cancel whatever it would normally indicate, but it will often corrupt or alter it, and those things will be accompanied by fear, unhappiness, or only a portion of the expected results.[44]
- *Weak fortunes.* Fortunes which are weak or in a bad condition, and in sextile or trine with another weak or bad condition,

---

[43] VIII.15, **29-30**.
[44] VIII.15, **27-28**.

won't have excessive problems, because their aspect allows some harmonization. But the weakness inhibits their potential, and will even add something bad to the situation along with distress and labor, and decrease the good.[45] To me this sounds like someone with a weak business plan who opens a shop with a friend lacking the requisite skills: the business will probably limp along for a while, with worry, and perhaps even lead to debts. Or, it's how a weak or unskilled person can not only fall short, but under pressure can be led to failure and unhappiness, even if he has good intentions.

Configuration (aspects). Configurations or aspects (whether just by sign or by degrees and orbs) are partnerships and relationships between planets. Since the planets already mean things by themselves, it's important to get a sense of each planet by itself first. I'd like to reference two nice templates which Abū Ma'shar uses in *PN4*, as well as a more general statement.

In the first template or treatment (II.4, **1-4**), Abū Ma'shar considers how fortunes and infortunes can harm or bring benefit, depending on their condition and aspect. Normally, an infortune indicates something bad or difficult by its nature, although this can differ based on the type of aspect (trines being better than squares). But an infortune in a good condition won't harm another planet and can even indicate something good, *if* it's configured by trine or sextile (**3**). On the other hand, an infortune in a bad condition will corrupt another planet, no matter the aspect (**2**). As for fortunes, although they typically indicate something good, a fortune in a bad and weak condition will have its good indication weakened, so that it will be easily corrupted and influenced if it's configured to a corrupting infortune or planet in a bad condition (**4**). This is like an insecure but well-meaning person who can be adversely influenced or manipulated by bad friends. But a lot can also depend on whether the aspecting planet is advancing (angular or succeedent by quadrant division) or withdrawing (cadent or fall-

---

[45] II.8, **4-6**.

ing): advancing planets have a greater ability to affect others, as well as maintain their own integrity.[46]

The second treatment (II.5, **58-66**) has too many permutations to list here, but here are some of the basics:

- Two planets in aspect will each act on the other, but in their own ways: so a lot depends on which planet you're interested in. If a planet in a good condition is looked at by one in a bad condition, the bad planet will decrease the suitability of the first one, in accordance with the bad planet's condition and place. But the planet in the good condition will improve the bad planet.
- We expect trines and sextiles to be better than squares and oppositions, but a lot depends upon the planetary condition. When a planet in a bad condition trines or sextiles, it will still do bad things, but more at the level of confusion, distress, and toil (**60**)—but when a planet in a good condition does it, it will improve things a lot (due to the condition and type of aspect). As for squares and oppositions, a planet in a bad condition will actually harm (**60**), while a planet in a good condition will improve things only a little (**62**). Conjunctions are more neutral and so depend more on the planetary type and condition (**66**).

The more general statement (II.11, **13**) is that if two planets are in a bad condition (especially if one of them is an infortune), then a trine or sextile won't really help them: they will more likely show misfortune in the category of things that they *would* have indicated, if they had been in a suitable condition.

Eliciting the natal indication in an SR. Throughout *PN4*, Abū Ma'shar repeats two major ways in which we can be more sure of the natal meaning being elicited and brought forth in a given SR. The first way

---

[46] III.7, **15-18**.

is by a similarity of condition and aspect, such as if the natal planet, aspects, and house, are very similar between the nativity and the SR. This means that it's allowed to manifest more straightforwardly, with fewer filters and conditions which would modify it.

But the other way, which Dorotheus also emphasizes, is that the activated planet ought to see its natal position, in the SR: such as if the profection comes to the natal Jupiter, and in the SR Jupiter is configured to his natal position (VI.4, **29-30**). This allows him to more reliably manage and elicit the effect in that year. Note that this doesn't mean the effect is *good*: it just means that it's more guaranteed.

Comparing natal and SR situations for the same planet. Again, comparing a planet's condition between the SR and the nativity can be done in many ways: its condition by dignity can enhance or degrade its quality; the SR house will direct its energy in a different way or through a different area of life; a cadent planet may only show an impulse for something that isn't carried through. Also, the greater the dissimilarity between the houses in the charts, the more diverted the effect is: a natal planet in the sixth and in the SR twelfth (which are similar places), will operate more straightforwardly and fully than if it were in the SR fifth.

The advice above can be followed in any chart. Abū Ma'shar also adds lists of delineations for planets in other situations which are less commonly studied or used:

Planets in each other's signs (list). One important way of interpreting a planet in a sign, is by means of whose sign or domicile it is. Just as staying in Dracula's castle is different from staying with a friend, it makes some difference whether a planet is in a sign of Saturn's or a sign of Venus—or perhaps, whether a planet is in a sign owned by a planet of the same sect or the contrary one, such as Jupiter in a sign of Saturn (both being diurnal planets and so somewhat friendlier to each other). A basic list is in Chs. VIII.1 – VIII.7, which is ultimately based on Dorotheus (*Carmen* II.32 – II.37), but it's so similar to al-Khayyāt (*JN* Chs. 40-45) and the Latin Māshā'allāh,[47] that it's probably based either on one of them or some common source. However, Abū Ma'shar sometimes omits important details found in the other sources, such as if the planet in a particular sign is also angular: he was probably only interested in the most generic interpretation.

Planets in each other's bounds (list). A list of these is in Chs. VIII.8 – VIII.14, and could be used both natally and in the SR. In general, traditional authors are vague about the precise meaning of a planet in a bound, and especially how a bound differs from a sign. Dorotheus often follows this pattern, and admits that his delineations assume that the sign and bound are ruled by the same planet (such as if the Moon is in both the sign and bound of Mercury).[48] By contrast, Abū Ma'shar's lists for the bounds do differ from those of the signs, so that Saturn in a sign of Mercury (VIII.1, **7**) is very different from Saturn in a bound of Mercury (VIII.8, **5**). However, the interpretations for the bounds are so much more elaborate, and sometimes perplexing, that it's hard to know how they were constructed. They're similar in complexity and detail to those of the Latin Māshā'allāh,[49] but not so close I can identify Māshā'allāh as his immediate source. Some sect descriptions may also have been omitted. For another list of the Ascendant and each planet in each other's bounds, see Firmicus Maternus in *Mathesis* V.2.

Abū Ma'shar also agrees with other authors that a planet's bounds will mean different things depending on their sign:[50] thus the bound of Venus in Gemini, means something different from the bound of Venus in Capricorn. Lists giving separate interpretations for every single

---

[47] *On the Significations of the Planets in a Nativity* Chs. 1-7 (in *WSM*).
[48] *Carmen* II.37, **15**.
[49] See Māshā'allāh, *On the Significations of the Planets in a Nativity* Chs. 20-26 (in *WSM*).
[50] VIII.14, **8-9**.

bound are attributed to Critodemus[51] and found in Valens,[52] but they don't include planets in them. One suspects that the principle of interpretation is some combination of the planetary natures, so that the bound of Jupiter in Aries, will be a function of how Jupiter and Mars combine—but what if it's Saturn *in* the bound of Jupiter, in Aries? Rhetorius Ch. 12 claims that generally, the lord of the sign sets the baseline assumption of benefit or harm (based on it being a fortune or infortune), and the bound either improves it (bound of fortune), or makes it worse (bound of fortune).

Planets in the "wells" (list). Readers of English-language traditional astrology (especially Lilly) may have heard of the "pitted" degrees, although in both Latin and Arabic these are really "wells." I find it surprising that Abū Ma'shar spends so much time on them here, as they're usually obscure and marginal in practice. But in Ch. VIII.15 he does a service by saying more about them than I've seen before, and I've added a table of them from *Gr. Intr.* V.21. Like his planets in the bounds, I'm not sure exactly how these delineations were developed, but they're similar to planets in their falls. As for the Moon, her position in the wells sounds a lot more like Venus in the licentious signs and decans, in Rhetorius Chs. 68 and 76. Following is a provisional translation of his description of the wells from *Gr. Intr.* V.21:

> **1** In the signs there are degrees called "wells," such that if one of the planets occurred in those very degrees of the signs, without being powerful,[53] then the disappearance of its brilliance will not be delayed, and its indication being very weak.[54] **2** So if the fortunes occurred in them, their condition will be like what we stated about weakness, but as for the infortunes, if they occurred in them their indication will be weakened (and sometimes they

---

[51] See the *CCAG* VIII.1, pp. 257-61 (in Schmidt 1995 [*Sages*], pp. 53-57).
[52] *Anth.* I.3.
[53] غير متقدّر
[54] ضعف عن, which usually means "is too weak to."

will indicate incidental good fortune due to their inability to [create] misfortune), and sometimes the nature of their misfortune will be strengthened.

3 And the ancients have already stated the places in which they indicate suitability or corruption, but we will state that in its own place. 4 Now as for the exactness of the degrees of the wells in their signs, they certainly do disagree about them; but we will leave aside any mention of their disagreement about them, but will state their degrees in the signs in accordance with what the generality of the old scholars of the people of Persia and Egypt agree on.

Reading: Interpreting a planet	
Nature, fortunes and infortunes	V.2, **4-5**, **6-7**, **9-10**
House location	IX.5, **92** II.6 (Saturn example) VI.3, **4-149**
Good and bad places	II.9, **15-16**
Strength, dignity, angularity	II.8, **4-6** VIII.15, **27-30**
Configuration	II.4, **1-4** II.5, **58-66** II.6, **16-18** II.11, **13** III.7, **15-18**
Eliciting the effect by SR aspect	VI.4, **29-30**
Comparing conditions between charts	II.5, **63-64** II.5, **67-74** II.23, **65-71** VI.5 (all) IX.9, **16-20**

Other lists	
Planets in each other's signs (list)	VIII.1 – VIII.7
Planets in each other's bounds (list)	VIII.8 – VIII.14
Planets in the wells (list)	VIII.15

§5: Profections

Now let us turn to the techniques themselves. The easiest but most important time lord technique is "profections," which comes from a Latin word meaning "to set out on a journey," and in the older Greek[55] and Arabic texts refers to "turning" or moving around in a circle. Since there are already so many other terms which refer to turning, rotating, and circles, I'll use the Latinate "profection" here.

Abū Ma'shar focuses mainly on the profection of the Ascendant. At birth, when the native is Age 0, the Ascendant is the rising sign itself, and that first year of life is indicated by that sign, planets in it and looking at it, and its lord (the "lord of the year"). But at Age 1, the Ascendant profects so as to terminate at the second sign, and *that* becomes the indicator for that year (along with planets in it, its lord, etc.). The profection continues around for as long as the native is alive, returning to itself in multiples of 12: Ages 12, 24, 36, and so on. In Figure 14 you can see that everyone's Ascendant will likewise come to the seventh sign or place at Ages 6, 18, 30, and so on. I recommend that you memorize some of the ages for the angular signs, so you can quickly count forwards and backwards to find the sign you need for any age.[56]

---

[55] See Heph. III.20, **3**.

[56] In older texts, particularly in Vettius Valens, people's years are given in ordinal form ("the thirteenth year," "the fortieth year"), rather than the cardinal form ("Age 13," "Age 40"). This can cause confusion, because the "thirteenth" year is Age 12, not Age 13. Stick to identifying people's ages, because that is how people actually speak.

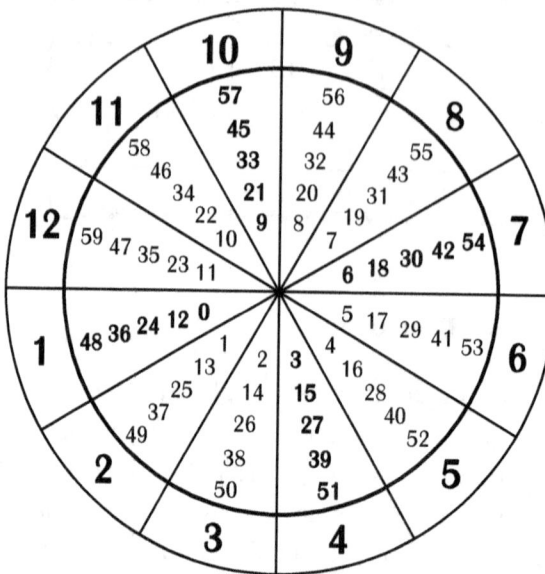

Figure 14: Houses for profected ASC, to Age 59

Because the Ascendant signifies life generally, the profection of the Ascendant shows how the theme of life is affected and expressed every year. A year which is in Scorpio (and its lord of the year Mars), will have different characteristics than one which is in Cancer (and its lord of the year the Moon); a profection which terminates at a planet in fall, is different from one which terminates at a planet in exaltation. Note that this is explicitly a *sign-based* technique; but Abū Ma'shar will give some extra advice if you're using a house system with cusps and they don't fall on the expected sign.[57] Also, when the profection terminates at any given sign, it will often take on the meaning of that house topic: so profections of the Ascendant to Age 22 will often have eleventh-house meanings. But this isn't always the case: it seems that the house meaning is emphasized mainly when there is actually a planet in it (natally or in the SR).[58] But the house position of the lord of the year always matters.

The student should also note that with profections comes a new house scheme: profected houses. Just as natal houses follow from the natal Ascendant, and SR houses from the SR Ascendant, Abū Ma'shar has profected houses which follow from the sign of the year. So if the natal Ascendant profects to Scorpio, Scorpio is indeed the profected

---

[57] See §6 below.
[58] See below.

Ascendant and the sign of the year; but Sagittarius becomes the profected second and its lord Jupiter the lord of the year *for the second house*; Capricorn becomes the profected third and its lord Saturn the lord of the year *for the third house*; and so on. On the one hand, this gets complicated quickly because in Abū Ma'shar's full natal-profection-SR method we will have three Ascendants for *everything*, and I don't like that. And just wait until we add MRs and monthly profections. But, since we can profect everything it does follow logically that we would have to look at, say, the natal third, the profected third, and the SR third to see how the topic of the third house manifests. Nevertheless I'll mainly ignore it here.

Below I offer reading lists and examples for how a profection is interpreted, step-by-step. But it's worth noting that Abū Ma'shar occasionally emphasizes the profection of the Lot of Fortune, and indeed we could profect anything: each thing signifies its own topic and nature, and profects at the same rate, simultaneously. So in Figure 15, the profected Ascendant terminates at the third sign (Cancer), with certain natal planets in it and its lord of the year the Moon. But at the same time, the Lot of Fortune (with its meaning of Fortune) profects to the third sign *relative to itself*. So while the meaning of the na-

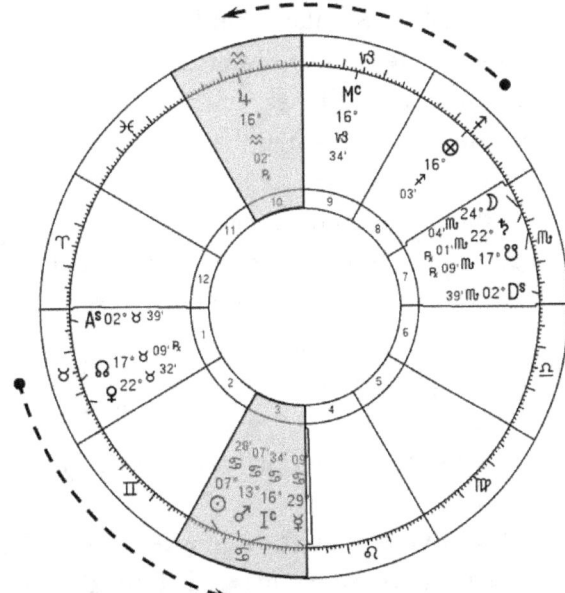

Figure 15: "Phil," Ascendant and Lot profected to Ages 2, 14, 26, etc.

tive's body, mind, and life is characterized by Cancer and everything in it (and the Moon), the topic of Fortune takes on the qualities of Aquarius, the tenth, Jupiter in it, and its lord Saturn. Thus everything profects so as to activate some new planet, topic, and lord each year: there is a sign of the year for the Ascendant, a sign of the year for the Lot—for everything. If you're a beginner, definitely stick to the Ascendant only.

Figure 15 is also an example of something which I discovered years ago and now can say was known to Abū Ma'shar: what I call a profection "process." Time lords convert relationships in the nativity into time, and this also goes for planets and the signs they rule. When a sign is activated by profection, it not only indicates matters for that year, but also begins a process which continues on past that year until the profection reaches its lord: then the process culminates with some event in that year. So, the Lot of Fortune will profect back to itself at Age 24, making Sagittarius and its lord Jupiter the indicators of that year. But Jupiter is also several signs away, and this meaning of Fortune-Sagittarius will set other things into motion, which will culminate at Age 26 when the profection terminates at Jupiter. Some of these processes can last for years, and for that reason it's harder to notice them: shorter distances are easier.

Following is some vocabulary you should familiarize yourself with, followed by the first readings. The last set of readings (in Chs. II.3 – II.6) gives basic instructions for all profections, and interpretations for Saturn as a model lord of the year.

- **Turning** (Ar. إدارة, Gr. *kuklōmenon*). Equivalent to **profection**.
- **Sign of the year**. The sign where the **profection** or **turning terminates**. Sometimes called "the sign of the terminal point."
- **Terminal point, termination** (Ar. انتهاء), **sign of the terminal point**. Equivalent to the **sign of the year**.
- **Terminate at** (Ar. ينتهي). To reach a certain sign in a given **profection**.

- **Lord of the year** (Ar. صاحب السّنة, Pers. سال خدای). The planet ruling the **sign of the year**.

Reading: Profections or "turning"	
Definition of profections	I.2, **5** II.3, **1**
What to profect	VI.2, **1-20**
Profection "process"	VI.4, **32-33**
Method of interpretation, using Saturn as a model	II.3 (all) II.4, **1-17** II.5, **1-24** II.6 (all)

ೞ ಞ ಞ

Interpreting a profection in its *natal* meaning is virtually identical to interpreting any house: one looks at the sign and any planets in it (and what houses they rule), planets looking at the sign, then its lord and its condition and configurations. What we then add are the SR conditions: planets in and looking at the sign in the SR, what house it occupies in the SR, what its lord is doing at the SR, and so on. If you would like a brief model for this whole process, simply read the sections of Chs. II.3 – II.6 in the last entry of the table above. But since Abū Ma'shar discusses profections throughout the book, it's best to survey all of the most important passages, which I provide in separate tables below.

Interpreting the sign of the year. The first step is to interpret the whole-sign house itself, both natally and at the SR: remember profections are a sign-based method, and for the sake of convenience Abū Ma'shar assumes that if you use a quadrant house method, all cusps will fall on their associated signs. (In the next section I'll say more about this.)

The sign's natal condition is pretty straightforward: we evaluate the natal planets in it and looking at it, by their natures, house locations, rulerships, and types of aspects. The most notable aspects are squares and oppositions by infortunes or trines and sextiles by fortunes, because the planets and aspects reinforce each other's natures. Harm or benefit can be assumed to come from the topic of the houses they are in or rule: if the eighth, fear or debt or matters pertaining to death; if the ninth, foreigners and travel. Natal planets in the sign will be active in that year as topics which are more constant or fundamental to the native's life; SR planets in it will be more incidental and connected more with that year's story. But if the sign of the year is empty, the story of the year is more likely to manifest through the lord of the year and whatever it's doing: so if the profection came to Aquarius and the third place (it being an empty sign), siblings might be not that important but its lord Saturn and his place will be.

Let's now turn to the lord of the year.

Reading: Interpreting the sign of the year	
Its natal condition (and natal planets in it)	II.3, **2** II.23, **20-71** III.8, **15-16** VI.2, **1** VI.4, **1-31**
Its SR condition (and SR planets in it)	II.3, **3-4** II.23, **5, 20-71** VI.3, **4-148** (skim)

Alternative lords of the year. By default, the lord of the year is the lord of the sign of the year. However, both Abū Ma'shar and older texts identify alternatives or similarly important planets, and have special rules for the Sun and the Moon.

If the profection comes to Aquarius, we assume that Saturn is the lord of the year—and indeed, by the rules of astrology, Saturn will play an important role. However, if another natal planet such as Venus is in Aquarius, there's a good argument to be made that her influence will be more obvious than Saturn's, and she could perhaps be treated as the lord of the year. Abū Ma'shar endorses this approach, saying that such a planet will be "like" the lord of the year or the lord of the SR Ascendant, because it will be more "powerful" than both.[59] This is akin to the view of Valens in *Anth.* IV.11 (Schmidt pp. 25-26), who says that if the profection comes to an empty sign, then take its lord as the usual lord of the year; however, he says if the sign is empty but there is a *transiting* planet in it (obviously, at the SR), then one may use it instead. The operative principle here is that location is more immediate or "powerful" than rulership, so a planet actually present in the sign should attract more of our attention. This was also the reason for my suggestion above that if the sign of the year is empty, don't emphasize its house topic (unless it's an angle): instead, focus more on the lord of the year and its place. So in the nativity above, if the profection came to Virgo and the fifth (an empty sign), with no SR planet in it, then focus on Mercury and his location in both charts, but avoid overemphasizing the fifth. If the profection came to Aquarius and the tenth, emphasize both the tenth and Jupiter (with his rulerships) because he is there. But if the profection came to Capricorn and the ninth, I would definitely emphasize the fact that the MC is there, in addition to Saturn being the lord of the year.

Another thing to note is SR planets which are highly angular or advancing, especially if they were in the sign of the year. So, let the sign of the year be Virgo, and the natal Venus in it, and in the SR Venus is advancing close to the Midheaven: this would be a powerful argument for focusing on her, because she is both activated (by profection) and prominent (by angularity. But suppose she was natally in one of Virgo's whole sign angles (which are active places relative to a sign), and *transiting* in it at the SR, *also* close to the SR Midheaven: that would probably be even more important. Even if Venus was simply near one of the axial degrees in the SR, it would be wrong to ignore her.

---

[59] III.8, **15-16**.

A third consideration happens when Cancer or Leo is the sign of the year. Many traditional texts are reluctant to give the luminaries roles as time lords, perhaps because they're thought to be so universal in scope: therefore when they become lords of the year, we're supposed to use another planet I call the "proxy" planet. Although Abū Ma'shar gives delineations for the luminaries as lords of the year, he does report some version of the alternatives as found in al-Andarzaghar. The report by al-Dāmaghānī vaguely states that one ought to look at their signs, the lords of their signs, and their mixtures with the other planets.[60] That's not very helpful. The table here shows Abū Ma'shar's suggestions.

Sun PN4 II.13, **1**; II.14, **1**	Moon PN4 II.22, **1-5**
Distributor[61]	Distributor
Lord of directed releaser	Lord of directed releaser
Planet in Leo (in root or SR)	Planet in Cancer (in root or SR)
Planet to which Sun hands over, while still in same sign	Planet to which Moon hands over, while in same sign[62] (but if empty in course, the lord of her sign)
Place of Sun	
	Condition of Moon

Figure 16: Abū Ma'shar's proxies when luminary is lord of year

While I understand the logic behind these choices, I suggest the following. Use the luminary as lord of the year for purposes of evaluating its condition, location, and rulership. But use a different planet for the

---

[60] See Burnett and al-Hamdi (2011/2012), p. 318. This is repeated in the Latin *BA*, Ch. IV.7.
[61] This may be the distributor for the directed longevity releaser.
[62] See the special rules for multiple planets in II.22, **2-3**.

ongoing *transits*, especially transits through the whole-sign angles of the sign of the year: that planet will likely be one closely conjoined with the luminary in the SR. So if the profection comes to Leo, make the Sun a normal lord of the year: see what houses Leo occupies, what houses the Sun is in, his condition, and so on. But if he is closely conjoined with Mars in the SR, track *Mars's* transits through the whole-sign angles of Leo. You can still monitor the direction of the SR Ascendant around the SR chart to the position of the Sun for further timing.

What the lord of the year does, how it's affected. When interpreting the lord of the year it's useful to begin with a list of significations: Venus in Virgo in the eleventh suggests Venusian things, friendships and hopes; being in fall means something disappearing, abject, tragic, and so on. But the lord of the year isn't simply "turned on" like a light switch, or a list of significations. It is an *agent*: it actively manages things and affects their operation. Like the main character in a drama, the events and actions revolve largely around it. If we're profecting the Ascendant, then the lord of the year indicates what the native is interested in and is doing, because it represents both the year as a whole and the native. (Profections of other places won't show the native so directly.) The house location of the lord of the year may show things the native is doing or is interested in.[63]

As an agent, the lord of the year has several ways of carrying its activity through into the SR, and affecting other topics. Expressing its own natal significations is more direct and effective if it sees its natal place and is in the same or similar SR house. The worse its condition and place (or if it's in aversion to its natal place), the less effective it is: this might mean actual idleness (for the native and the planet's management), or that the native is busy doing things that don't bring

---

[63] But I would more likely associate this with the lord of the SR Ascendant, or what the lord of the natal Ascendant is doing in the SR. Abū Ma'shar wants us to look at the house of the lord of the year, *relative to the sign of the year*, so that the three systems of Ascendants are kept distinct. But I'm less convinced of the value of derived profected houses.

benefit or even harm. And just as in any other chart, the next aspect which the lord of the year will complete (while still in its sign) will also shed light on what it's doing or "what comes next"; but if it's empty in course one should look at the lord of its sign instead.

Reading: Interpreting the lord of the year	
Alternative candidates	III.8, **15-16**
Proxies for Sun and Moon	II.13, **1**; II.14, **1** II.22, **1-5**
What the lord of the year does	II.4, **6, 12-13, 23** II.5, **58-84** II.6, **25-26** II.22, **23-25** II.23, **61** III.8, **22** VI.4, **29-30** VI.6, **1-2**
How the lord of the year is affected	II.4, **1-5, 7-12** II.5, **58-66, 75** II.6, **16-18** II.8, **4-6** II.11, **30-34** II.22, **26-28** III.8, **7, 20-21, 27-28, 39-40**
The lord of the year by dignity and place	II.3, **9-20** II.6 (all)
Lord of the year: comparing conditions between charts	II.3, **5-8** II.5, **67-74** II.12, **20**
Saturn as a model for lord of the year	II.4 II.5, **1-57** II.6

Comparison between charts. The table of readings provides several checklists for how to analyze the lord of the year based on its condition in the two charts: this is essential for Abū Ma'shar's theory of prediction.

Other placements, connections, principles. Lastly, some other considerations. It's good to see which SR house a planet is in, because it will express the natal placement through the SR house (this is especially useful for the lords of major houses). For instance, if the lord of your natal Ascendant is in the SR fifth, then you (lord of the Ascendant) will be interested in the topic of children, entertainments, pleasures, and so on.

Reading: Other placements and connections	
Planets changing houses between charts	VI.5 VII.9, **25-27**
Connections between lords of houses	VI.6
Reinforcement, repetition	II.6, **25-26** II.12, **20** II.23, **14-17, 37, 40, 70**

You can also look at the connections between the lords of houses, so that if in the SR the lord of your natal second squares the lord of your natal ninth, it shows a connection between finances and ninth-house matters. But don't mix the house meanings of two different charts, like if the lord of the *natal* second squares the lord of the *SR* ninth. Stick within one system and keep it simple.

Finally, remember the principle of reinforcement and repetition: the more that natal and SR planets are in the same or similar conditions, places, rulerships, and configurations, the more certain we can be that natal indications will follow through directly and clearly.

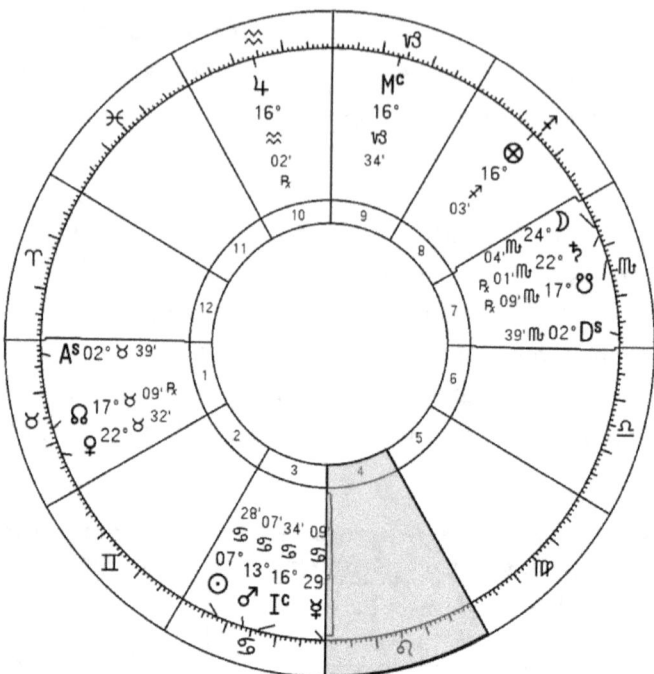

Figure 17: Profection example: "Phil," Age 27

Let me say a few words about this nativity, to illustrate some of these principles. When the Ascendant was profected to the fourth, Leo, at Age 27. There is no planet natally in the sign, and its lord the Sun is in aversion to it, in the third place, not in his own dignity, and conjoined with (and burning) a Mars in fall. Normally I wouldn't emphasize the topic of the fourth place because there is no planet in it, but it's an angular house so it will usually show its indication. Here are some major things I see: the topic of family, parents, and his living situation (fourth house), and some kind of dislocation or disruption there because the Sun is in aversion to it; siblings or brothers, and people he deals with every day since the Sun is in the third, and probably some conflict and instability with them because the Sun is in no dignity and is conjoined to a Mars in fall; this Mars in fall is the lord of the seventh, so expect some problems in relationships. All of this was true: his parents were threatened with losing their home, he was living with some fraternity brothers as roommates and the situation was deteriorating rapidly, with anger and conflict; and in his romantic relationship there was also repressed anger and resentment. I'll wait until §8 to look at the SR for this year.

§6: Whole signs, quadrant cusps, intercepted signs

This section is a bit more advanced, and will make more sense if you're aware of recent controversies about how house systems were treated by traditional astrologers, especially the shift from whole signs to quadrant divisions. For the purposes of this section, "signs" and "places" will always refer to whole-sign houses, and "divisions" will always refer to quadrant-based house systems, like Porphyry, Placidus, or Alchabitius Semi-Arcs. Refer to the Glossary if you need help with the terminology.

Through my own and others' translations, we have seen various ways in which astrologers recognized, described, and used signs and divisions. Most delineation texts assume whole signs, which begin with the sign on the horizon and count the rest of the signs in order from there. But because of the obliquity of the ecliptic, the meridian (which defines the MC) and divisions of the quadrants (or their cusps) won't always fall on the signs of the corresponding number: the eleventh sign and eleventh division will almost never coincide exactly. This is an inevitable result of astronomy, and there's no way to avoid it: it must be recognized, understood, and solved somehow. However, astrologers rarely showed much reflection on this fact in their terminology or practice. Then we see that people like Ptolemy and Valens layered divisions on top of signs in order to judge the suitability of longevity releasers, and then fostered confusion because they applied the same house-names to both signs and divisions in the same chart:[64] for example, normally the eleventh sign is called "Good Spirit" by the Greek-speaking astrologers, but Valens also applies this name to the division which partially overlaps the sign. Of course by the time of

---

[64] See *Tet.* III.10 (Robbins pp. 273-75), and *Anth.* III.2.

Morin and Lilly in the 16th - 17th Centuries scarcely anyone would even have recognized whole signs, but the full-blown shift was pretty much complete even by the time of Bonatti in the 13th Century.

Our new translations of the 8th and 9th Century astrologers in Baghdad reveal that they were *fully* aware of the controversy, and applied some solutions. We know this in part because astrologers like Sahl, Māshā'allāh, and Abū Ma'shar used special terminology. For instance, whole-sign houses are called houses by "counting" or "number" (عدد),[65] while divisions are called houses by "equation" (سواء) or (تسوية)[66] or "calculation" (حساب)[67] or "division" (قسمة).[68] They make other distinctions which I explain elsewhere, but the point is that they recognized there was an issue, and wanted to add clarity by applying different terms to signs and divisions. Following is a translation of a couple of sentences from Abū Ma'shar's *Great Introduction* VIII.3, where he discusses this matter in relation to certain Lots. These Lots are calculated from the lord of a house to that house, or to the "degree" of the house—but is this the first degree of a sign, or some cusp? It depends on your house system. In this example, Abū Ma'shar uses the Lot of assets or money, which is measured from the lord of the second to the second (and projected from the Ascendant):

> (*Gr. Intr.* VIII.3) **14** And know that sometimes in the work of Lots one needs to take from the lord of one of the houses up to that house, but that house by *counting* is one of the signs which is withdrawing by *equation*[69] towards another house: so that it ought to be taken from the lord of the sign by equation, to that degree in which the calculation occurs. **15** And an example of that is that the Ascendant was Cancer by degree, in the fourth clime, and the house of assets by counting was Leo, but by calculation it was Cancer, [in] a known degree: so it ought to be taken

---

[65] See *PN4*, VI.2, **21-24**.
[66] See *Gr. Intr.* VIII.3, **14-15**.
[67] See *Gr. Intr.* VIII.3, **15**.
[68] See *PN4*, VI.2, **25**.
[69] That is, by calculation of a cusp.

INTRODUCTION   51

from the *Moon*, who is the lord of Cancer, up to that known degree of it, and one would not focus on the Sun and Leo.

In this case, because the cusp of the second division falls on the rising sign, he totally ignores the second sign itself, favoring divisions over signs. This is a case of two cusps on the same sign, but we also have the issue of "intercepted" signs, in which a sign has no cusp on it at all.

In *PN4* Abū Ma'shar raises the issue again in predictive techniques, which turns out to be necessary because, even though he uses divisions, he knows that profections are a sign-based technique. Dorotheus profects one year for each sign,[70] and in his own account of annual and monthly profections Ptolemy refers to them as signs,[71] as does Sahl (who is probably quoting Māshā'allāh).[72] Likewise, Abū Ma'shar makes it absolutely clear that the default approach for annual profections is by sign.[73]

But as with the Lots, where should we profect from if the cusp of the division doesn't fall on the corresponding sign? Abū Ma'shar treats profections and directions together in his answer:

- **Cusp on different sign:** profect from both, but direct from the cusp.

In Figure 18, Scorpio is the rising sign, and Pisces the fifth. But the cusp of the fifth *division* falls in the sixth sign, Aries. So if we wanted to profect "the fifth" for the topic of children, where should we profect from? Abū Ma'shar says from *both* signs: the expected fifth sign Pisces, and the sixth sign Aries (with the fifth cusp on it). To perform directions or distributions of the fifth, use the degree of the cusp itself (in Aries). It's hard to know if this is another example of Abū Ma'shar's

---

[70] *Carmen* IV.1, **1-2**.
[71] *Tet.* IV.10 (Robbins pp. 453-55).
[72] Sahl, *Nativities* 1.24, **1**.
[73] *PN4* I.2, **5**.

"try everything" approach, or whether Abū Ma'shar's intention here is considered and sincere: for he certainly knows that planetary configurations to Pisces aren't the same as those to Aries; Jupiter isn't the same as Mars; monthly profections from one aren't the same as the other. Indeed, if we actually followed his advice on monthly profections, in some years the months would go in opposite directions at the same time (see §9 below).

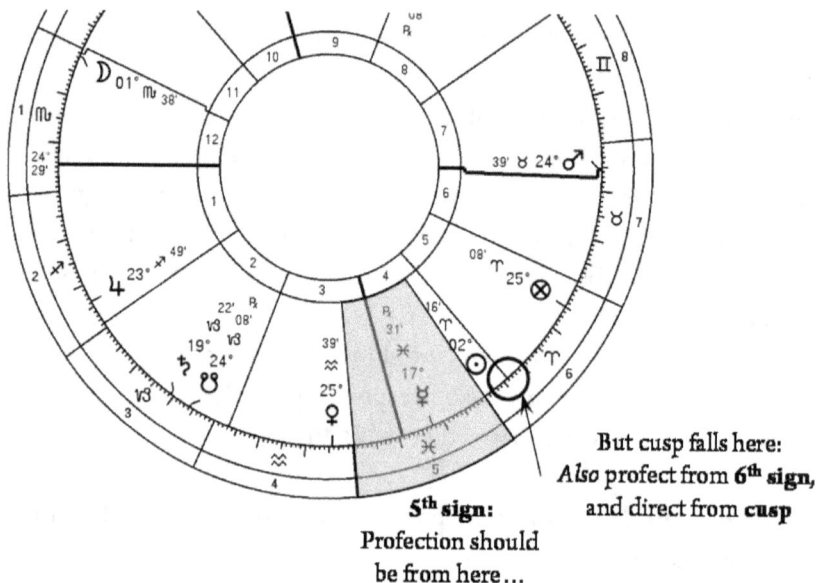

Figure 18: When cusp falls on different sign (VI.2, 21-24)

If two cusps fall on a single sign, Abū Ma'shar seems to treat it as though the power has shifted over to that sign, so *only* that sign should be used for profection, but directions can be made from each cusp individually. In Figure 19, Libra is the eleventh sign but the cusp of the eleventh division is in Scorpio, the twelfth sign; the cusp of the twelfth division is also in Scorpio, its expected sign. In this case, for the topic of friends we shouldn't profect from the eleventh *at all*, but *only* the twelfth (Scorpio), and direct from the cusp in early Scorpio. For profections and distributions of the twelfth, we also use Scorpio and the cusp of the twelfth division in late Scorpio.

- **Two cusps on one sign:** profect from the sign with cusps, and direct from each cusp.

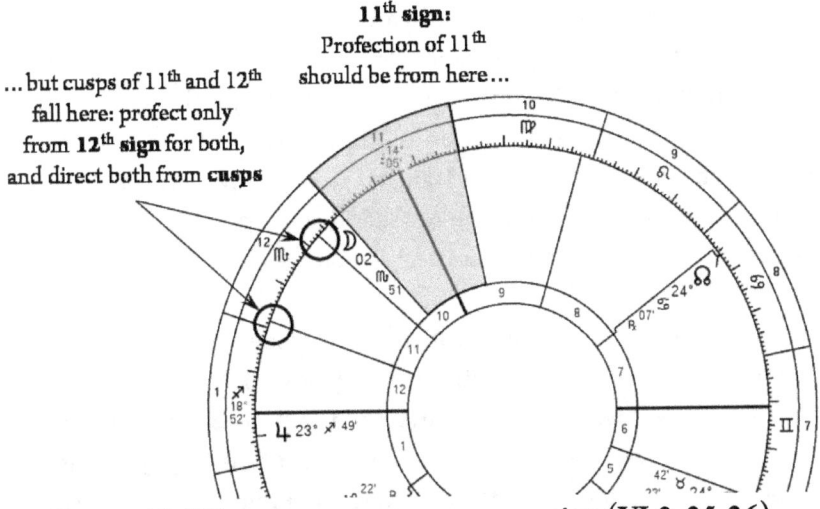

Figure 19: When two cusps are on same sign (VI.2, 25-26)

To extend this thought, I suppose that when profecting and directing the tenth in this chart, we would likewise profect from Virgo (the tenth sign) and Libra (where the cusp of the MC is), and direct from the MC in Libra. That would be an instance of the first rule above because in the case of Virgo, we simply have a single shifted cusp. But if both the MC and the cusp of the eleventh division had been in Libra, then we wouldn't use Virgo at all, as with the second rule given here.

This second rule about two cusps implies that the eleventh sign wouldn't even be used in natal interpretation for the topic of friends. For remember that in profections, each sign is on itself at birth, and is profected forward after that. But if Libra cannot be used for profections of the eleventh house, that is equivalent to saying that it's not even the eleventh house at birth: only Scorpio is.

Both here and in the first rule above, we can see the problems which result from using both whole signs and divisions for techniques and interpretations: either you have to use both and entertain contradictory indications (first rule), or give up on one of them, most likely the signs (second rule). Since the apparent shifting of the cusps is what creates these scenarios, it's probably inevitable that someone using divisions would eventually just start ignoring the signs. This is what happened in the Latin and early modern West: signs dropped away, and only houses by division were used for profections. All of this results from using both whole signs and divisions for the topics of life.

Abū Ma'shar doesn't mention intercepted signs in relation to profections, but he does with transits, so let's now turn to that. In a short passage (VII.1, **1-4**), Abū Ma'shar discusses how transiting planets will activate the "signs or houses" which they pass through:

> (PN4 VII.1) **1** Everything which has preceded whose planetary indications we have mentioned, belongs to their positions[74] which they have at the revolution of the year. **2** And for every one of them, when they come to be in one of the <u>signs or houses</u> of the circle after that,[75] they activate the indication of that <u>sign or house</u>. **3** And if a <u>single sign</u> is apportioned out to <u>two houses</u>,[76] and then a planet comes to be in it, then its indication <u>in that sign</u> will be in accordance with what is apportioned from it <u>to each house</u>. **4** And if two or three <u>signs</u> were apportioned <u>to a single house</u>,[77] then the indication of the planet when it comes to be in it, will be in accordance with the indication of <u>the house</u> which they are apportioned to.[78]

Here Abū Ma'shar opens by saying that while previous delineations have described planets' indications at the SR, he will now discuss how they indicate things by ongoing transit "after that," since we need to know how they will activate the meanings of the remaining signs and houses over time (**1-2**). So far, so good. But in a sense he has skipped

---

[74] This word (موضع) is normally a synonym for "place" (مكان), and does not inherently mean a specific degree.
[75] That is, by ongoing transits throughout the year.
[76] That is, two cusps on one sign.
[77] That is, intercepted signs.
[78] That is, by the division or quadrant house it is actually in.

over something important: why do transits need to be explained at all? For if we already know what a planet means by its position at the SR, why would any later transit be any different? If an SR planet means something by being in a certain sign, then later transits should work the same way; if they mean something by division, then later transits should work by division. Remember too that SR planets are themselves essentially transits to the nativity, cast for a specific moment (the SR): so why is this even an issue?

I think a clue may be found in his vocabulary, which I've underlined. Remember that in *PN4* VI.2, **21-25** he called *both* signs and divisions "houses": signs are houses by counting, and divisions are houses by division. But in the passage above, he *only* identifies divisions as houses (**2-4**), and even identifies the house with the cusp itself. In the first case we have two cusps or "houses" on the same sign (**3**), and in the second case we have an intercepted sign (**4**), which had been omitted in the profection material above. I don't think this is just carelessness, and it might reflect something specific to profections. Normally a transit over a planet occurs at a specific degree, but transits are also *ingresses* into signs, so that in whole-sign houses a transit into a sign automatically stimulates that house topic. Since he recognizes both signs and divisions, he needs to solve a problem: what if a planet enters a sign but isn't in the quadrant division associated with it and defined by a cusp? If a planet transits into an intercepted sign, it is a new sign—but it's still in the same quadrant division as before. So what do we do? His two rules in **3-4** are:

- **Two cusps on a sign:** interpret the transit using only cusps and divisions.
- **Intercepted sign:** interpret the transit using only the division.

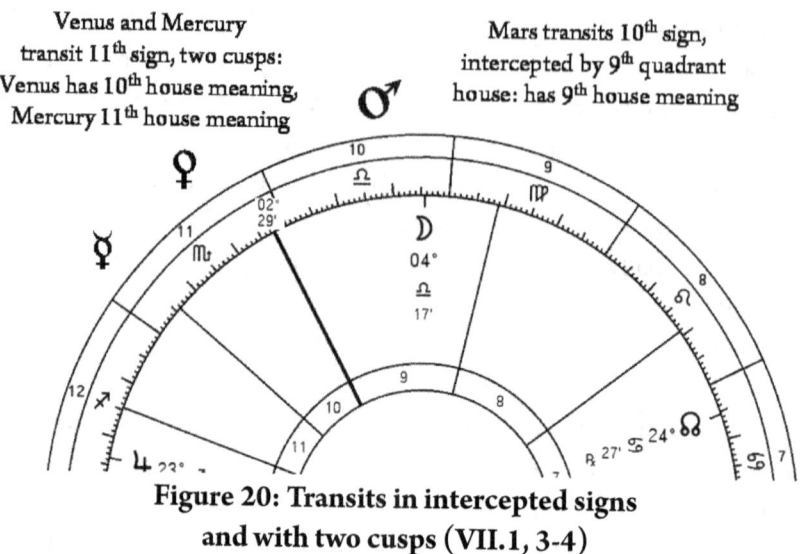

Figure 20: Transits in intercepted signs and with two cusps (VII.1, 3-4)

In Figure 20 Scorpio is the eleventh sign, with two cusps on it: the Midheaven and the eleventh. We want to know what a planet will mean when it transits through Scorpio. According to **3**, each portion of Scorpio is allotted to whatever division overlaps it: a planet entering Scorpio would have ninth-house meanings because it's still in the ninth division; but between the Midheaven and the eleventh cusp (where Venus is) it will have tenth-house-meanings; and between the eleventh cusp and the end of Scorpio (where Mercury is) it will have eleventh-house meanings. And according to **4**, Mars will have ninth-house meanings all the way from about 21° Virgo to 2° Scorpio.

So according to these rules, Abū Ma'shar seems to have made a complete shift to quadrant divisions for house topics—which is reflected by the fact that in VII.1, **1-4** he no longer refers to signs as houses. And this would be perfectly legitimate and *assumed* in modern astrology. But there are three indications that it's not so simple.

First, remember that Abū Ma'shar feels the need to explain this to his audience. If the shift to divisions had already been completed, or if transits were thought to activate *only* a zodiacal sign's qualities but not any particular house topic,[79] there would be nothing to explain. For it would be obvious that Mars entering Gemini would only pertain to the qualities of Gemini, and by house would only pertain to his quadrant division. Note also that Abū Ma'shar didn't feel the need to explain this about SR positions themselves, as though SR positions were obvious: that is, perhaps astrologers already assumed quadrant divisions for the SR chart. And yet he feels the need to explain it for ongoing transits. This suggests that, *like profections,* people knew transits were a whole-sign technique involving ingresses, but were unsure how to handle them *given that* the transition to divisions was still taking place. So this must have been something of an obvious problem for people of his time, with a not-obvious solution he felt compelled to provide.

Second, unless Abū Ma'shar really is simply shifting over to divisions, he has omitted two other obvious scenarios, one of which he defined above for profections: what if (1) the correct cusp is on the corresponding sign, all by itself? And what if (2) the correct cusp is on the next sign, but without a doubling of cusps or intercepted signs? (That is the fifth-house profection scenario from above). In Figure 20, let (1) a planet be in late Cancer, the seventh sign and division. Now let it ingress into Leo, the eighth sign, with the eighth cusp on it at 11°: what does it mean? Since the correct cusp is in the sign, all alone, does all of Leo have an eighth-house meaning? Is the same true for the ingress into Virgo, which has the ninth cusp in it, all alone? Or, let (2) a planet in Figure 18 ingress into Pisces, the fifth sign. The fifth cusp is in the sixth sign, but without doubled cusps or an intercepted sign. Does the transit in Pisces activate the topic of children *in addition to* its transit in Aries where the cusp is—just as we're supposed to profect from both? I don't know Abū Ma'shar's answers, but the unevenness in

---

[79] In some modern mundane astrology, ingresses into signs is thought to activate the meaning of the sign, but not a house topic. So, if Pluto enters Capricorn people say it activates the meaning of *Capricorn* itself, but not a house topic defined by cusps in a particular chart.

treating these cases is further evidence that there was no consensus in his day.

Third, although he distinguishes between "sign" and "house" (division) in VII.1, **1-4**, just after this passage in sentence **6** there is more ambiguity. There, Abū Ma'shar describes how Jupiter can travel up to 38° or more over the course of a year; if so, then his management or stimulating activity will appear in three signs; the end of the first sign, the entire next sign, and the beginning of the third sign. But the phrasing is somewhat unusual: "sometimes he shifts from house to house, and his management will appear in three signs." What does that mean? If by "house" he means "shifting across a cusp, between two divisions," then surely that will happen in most years—and in some years he will shift across two cusps (when there are two cusps on one sign) or none at all (in an intercepted sign). And what is the relationship between this and the part about three signs? If he travels 38°, then *obviously* he will be in three signs. And Abū Ma'shar doesn't say he will shift from house to house *because* his management will be in three signs. Or is this just a clumsy way of saying the same thing in two ways—but that would identify houses with signs, contrary to what he had just done. If Abū Ma'shar had an absolutely clear theory and solution, we wouldn't expect this ambiguity.

I suspect that these passages are revealing the following things: (1) Abū Ma'shar had shifted mainly or solely over to quadrant divisions for topics when interpreting charts. (2) But as I mentioned before, he knew that when constructing revolutionary charts one needs to match the signs together because the cusps shift around, so the signs are still somehow important bases for chart-reading. (3) He also knew that some techniques were clearly and traditionally based on signs: profections and transits. This created a problem for someone using only or mainly divisions. Therefore (4) he offered some of his own opinions, but did *not* supply a complete explanation of all scenarios, because even in his own mind he had not fully worked it out. Rejecting or ignoring whole signs was probably just around the corner, but had not been accomplished yet.

Cusp:	On same sign	On next sign, no other cusps	On next sign, two cusps	Intercepted sign
Profection	*Same sign*	Both signs	Next sign only	*Same and previous?*
Direction	*Cusp?*	Cusp	Cusp	*Cusp?*
Transit	*Same sign?*	*By division?*	By division	By division

Figure 21: Abū Ma'shar's explicit and likely rules for cusps and houses

One final matter to discuss is a third option for profections which is sometimes mentioned: profecting by 30° increments. There are some indications of using increments in *PN4*, but I think some of these are by report only, and aren't standardized. In other cases they're used for specific purposes.

Profecting by 30° increments essentially means profecting by "equal houses." Let the natal Ascendant be at 20° Gemini: the interval used for the profection isn't Gemini as a whole (older method), nor by divisions and counting cusps (later method), but strictly the thirty degrees from 20° Gemini to 20° Cancer. The next profection would be from 20° Cancer to 20° Leo, and so on. Thus, this method ignores cusps and sign boundaries. From there, one has important choices to make. Since the interval begins in one sign but ends in another, who is the lord of the year? It could be the lord of the initial sign, for the whole year. But maybe that planet rules only the proportion of the year indicated by the amount of the sign in the interval: in this example, only 10° or 1/3 of the interval is in Gemini, so maybe Mercury only rules 1/3 of the year, and the Moon rules the rest. These are some of the questions one must answer.

Be that as it may, I think it's clear that Abū Ma'shar doesn't use, or perhaps doesn't fully appreciate, the notion of increments. The main reason is that if we used increments, there would be no question of what sign to profect from: we would simply profect from one 30° increment to the next. No matter what we were profecting, we could divide the chart into equal houses starting from that degree, and all of the annual increments would be spaced out equally. But he does not do that.

Abū Ma'shar does mention increments in other places, but they don't form a profection technique. In one passage he *seems* to cast out 30° because he speaks of "the *degree* of the terminal point,"[80] which could only be done by using cusps or an increment. However, he does this only to find a point which he can match to a fixed star, and he doesn't use it interpretively (indeed, he also does this with the Ascendant and the degree of the distribution). In another he seems to do the same thing, but only to see what part of a common or double-bodied sign it falls into, because he wants to know whether to profect backwards or forwards.[81] In a third passage he makes it seem like the Indians use 30° increments, in a confusing sentence.[82] But he explicitly does *not* do this in his examples.[83] Finally, in a fourth example he uses it as a sensitive point for transits, instead of the entire sign of the year.[84]

In two other places he uses continuous profections, which occur when one treats the profection not as a fixed block of degrees, but a continuous flow of degrees which progress over the course of a year or month. For example, if a sign or 30° increment were considered as a continuous profection, then each degree would represent a little over 12 days (365.2422 / 30° = 12.17 days). In both of these passages Abū Ma'shar is copying from a long list by al-Andarzaghar, so it's hard to know if he ever used them. The first passage is a kind of hybrid of distributions of profections, which moves continuously but also uses distributors and partners (and isn't used for monthly profections).[85] In another, he does daily profections of a degree per day, in increments from the degree of the profection;[86] but this doesn't even treat annual

---

[80] See III.8, **9**.
[81] See IX.1, **28-30**. I discuss these monthly profections below.
[82] See III.10, **1**.
[83] See III.10, **5**; IX.1, **11**; and IX.7, **44-45**.
[84] See V.8, **26**.
[85] See IX.7, **23-28**.
[86] See IX.7, **34-36**.

profections as a block, anyway. It's more like the symbolic timing of degrees we would expect in a horary chart.

§7: Distributions

Our second technique is "distributions through the bounds," which we could say is the full version of what's normally called "primary directions." They're really interesting and important: you should start experimenting with them immediately. Don't get intimidated by calculations: in Appendix A I will show you good software, and also how you can use either ascensional times or the animation function on your computer to calculate many of them without special software modules.

Like the equivalents in Latin (*partitio*) and Greek (*diairesis*), the Arabic term for this technique (*qismah*, قسمة) can mean simply "division." But it really means to divide something *out into* categories, or distribute pieces of something out to others. So, I stick with "distributions." Abū Ma'shar says they were used by the Babylonians, Persians, and Egyptians, and they seem to have had a close relationship with longevity techniques (which I discuss in a later section below). But more importantly, they use time lords: two of them simultaneously.

The zodiacal signs are each divided into five unequal portions call the "bounds" or "terms," each ruled by one of the planets. In Figure 22 below these are in the innermost ring, and I use the oldest, "Egyptian" series of bounds.[87] In Aries, the series runs: Jupiter, Venus, Mercury, Mars, Saturn. The series is slightly different in each sign, with different numbers of degrees. Note that the Sun and Moon do not rule any bounds.

In distributions we move or "direct" some planet or point forward in the zodiac through the bounds, and to the bodies or rays of other planets. The planet or point is called a "releaser," as though we're re-

---

[87] See the table below. If you use a computer program with bounds, be sure to change the setting to "Egyptian."

leasing it to run forward in the zodiac. (Actually the releaser doesn't move at all: in astronomical terms we're pretending it stands still, and letting the whole heavens rotate. But since astrologers work with paper diagrams it's easier to imagine that the releaser moves forward.) Practically anything can be directed or distributed this way, and Abū Ma'shar acknowledges that a special planet signifying the native's longevity is the most important one; but the next most common one is the Ascendant, so we will only use that. Just like in profections, the Ascendant means "life": so whatever happens to the Ascendant and whoever acts as its time lords, will help tell a general story about life. If we had distributed the Midheaven, we would be looking at action, projects, and career.

In Figure 22 below you can see that the Ascendant is at 9° 45' Aries, in the bound of Venus. Soon it will enter the bound of Mercury from 12° - 20°, and then the bound of Mars from 20° - 25°. The primary time lord for the Ascendant are these bound lords, called "distributors," and they're in effect for exactly as long as the Ascendant moves through those bounds. So we can see in the table above (from the Janus astrology program) that the Ascendant is in the bound of Venus at birth (Age 0), and by calculation will enter the bound of Mercury about a year later on July 2, 2020. At that point the distributorship of Venus ends, and Mercury becomes the distributor. In the distributor column you can see that Mercury remains the distributor until October 19, 2024, when Mars takes over.

However, notice that the Ascendant has recently left the body of Venus, and it will soon encounter the left or sinister sextile of the Moon, at 12° 17'; then it will hit the body of Mercury at 14° 09'. Each of these planets becomes the second time lord, the "partner." Like the distributors, a partner remains a partner until the next one takes over. Since at birth an Ascendant won't be exactly on some body or ray, Abū Ma'shar says to use whatever the previous partner would have been, by its body and ray in the same sign. In this case, Venus is the most recent partner and so is the partner at birth in addition to being the first distributor.

Introduction

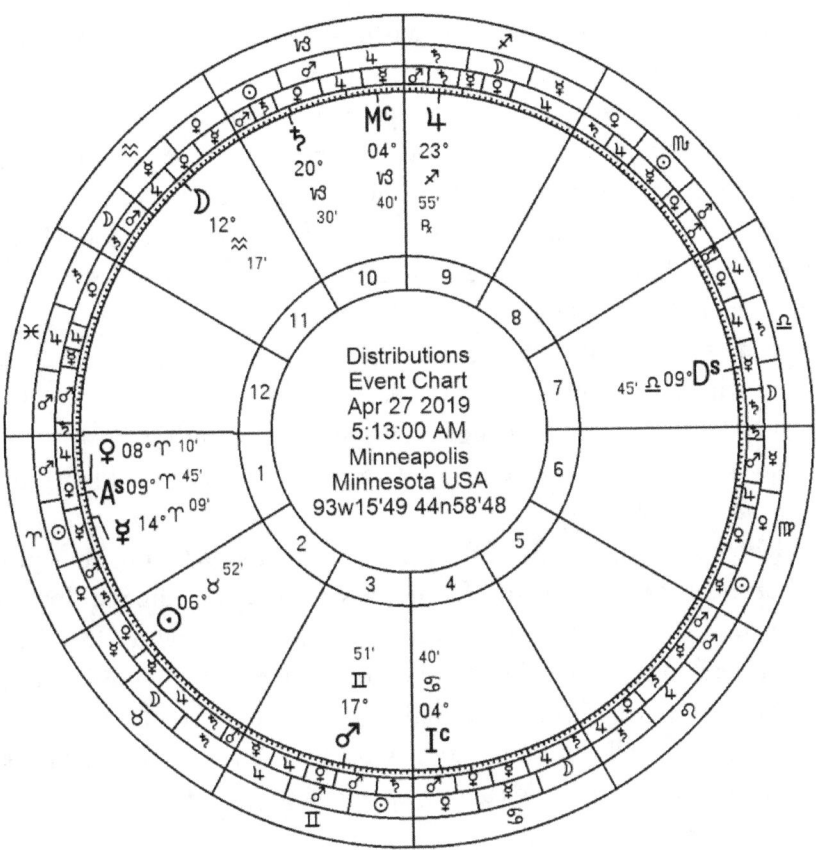

Arc	Date	Distributor	Partner
000d 00m 00s	Apr 27 2019	♀	
001d 10m 54s	Jul 02 2020	☿	
001d 19m 57s	Aug 26 2020	☿	sin ✶ ☽
002d 19m 36s	Aug 24 2021	☿	☌ ☿
004d 18m 54s	Aug 20 2023	☿	dex ✶ ♂
005d 28m 58s	Oct 19 2024	♂	
005d 45m 50s	Jan 30 2025	♂	sin □ ♄
007d 38m 54s	Dec 19 2026	♂	sin △ ♃

Figure 22: Nativity with bounds and list of distributions

In this way, the Ascendant has a pair of time lords which run in parallel, but change at different times: so to be complete, one must refer to both of them when identifying a particular distribution. In this case, the distribution at birth is Venus-Venus; then the Ascendant moves to the bound of Mercury but still retains Venus (Mercury-Venus); then while still in the bound of Mercury it hits the sextile of the Moon (Mercury-Moon); then the conjunction of Mercury (Mercury-Mercury); then the sextile of Mars (Mercury-Mars), then it enters the bound of Mars while retaining Mars (Mars-Mars), and so on. Only in cases where a planet or its ray is *exactly* at the beginning of a bound, would both time lords change at the same time; otherwise one of them is always carried over from the previous period, creating some overlap and continuity.

Below I'll review some of the principles of interpretation, but since all of this is astrology it still follows basic rules: each time lord indicates something for the native based on its planetary nature, location, and rulerships, modified by its condition. So if the distributor is Mars, that means Martial effects and events; if he is the lord of the Midheaven, the period will pertain to action, reputation, and profession; if he is natally in the fourth, it adds family, parents, and real estate.

Vocabulary:

- **Distribution** (Ar. قسمة). Several meanings: (1) the technique of **directing** a **releaser** (a planet or point) through the **bounds**; (2) the pairing of its two **time lords**, called the **distributor** and **partner**, such as being in "the distribution of Venus-Mars"; (3) the location of the bound of the distribution itself.
- **Distributor** (Ar. قاسم). A **time lord** in **distributions**: the lord of the **bound** which a **directed** point or **releaser** is moving through.
- **Direct, direction** (Ar. تسيير, سيّر). To move something in the chart by **primary motion**, using some form of **ascensions**.

- **Partner** (Ar. شريك, مشارك). A **time lord** in **distributions**: the most recent planet which the **releaser** has encountered by body or ray.
- **Manager** (Ar. المدبّر). Sometimes, the planetary **partner** in **distributions**; sometimes a term for the longevity **releaser**. But also a generic name for planets which have any kind of **management**.
- **Management** (Ar. تدبير). A generic term referring to how a planet "manages" a topic by signifying it. Typically, planets **hand over** and "accept" management to and from each other, simply by **applying** to one another.
- **Jār bakhtār** (Ar. جار بختار, from Pahlavi or middle Persian). An Arabic transliteration of a Pahlavi phrase said to mean "distributor of time."

♈	♃ 0°-5°59'	♀ 6°-11°59'	☿ 12°-19°59'	♂ 20°-24°59'	♄ 25°-29°59'
♉	♀ 0°-7°59'	☿ 8°-13°59'	♃ 14°-21°59'	♄ 22°-26°59'	♂ 27°-29°59'
♊	☿ 0°-5°59'	♃ 6°-11°59'	♀ 12°-16°59'	♂ 17°-23°59'	♄ 24°-29°59'
♋	♂ 0°-6°59'	♀ 7°-12°59'	☿ 13°-18°59'	♃ 19°-25°59'	♄ 26°-29°59'
♌	♃ 0°-5°59'	♀ 6°-10°59'	♄ 11°-17°59'	☿ 18°-23°59'	♂ 24°-29°59'
♍	☿ 0°-6°59'	♀ 7°-16°59'	♃ 17°-20°59'	♂ 21°-27°59'	♄ 28°-29°59'
♎	♄ 0°-5°59'	♀ 6°-13°59'	♃ 14°-20°59'	♀ 21°-27°59'	♂ 28°-29°59'
♏	♂ 0°-6°59'	♀ 7°-10°59'	☿ 11°-18°59'	♃ 19°-23°59'	♄ 24°-29°59'
♐	♃ 0°-11°59'	♀ 12°-16°59'	☿ 17°-20°59'	♄ 21°-25°59'	♂ 26°-29°59'
♑	☿ 0°-6°59'	♃ 7°-13°59'	♀ 14°-21°59'	♄ 22°-25°59'	♂ 26°-29°59'
♒	☿ 0°-6°59'	♀ 7°-12°59'	♃ 13°-19°59'	♂ 20°-24°59'	♄ 25°-29°59'
♓	♀ 0°-11°59'	♃ 12°-15°59'	☿ 16°-18°59'	♂ 19°-27°59'	♄ 28°-29°59'

Figure 23: Table of Egyptian bounds

The distributor vs. the partner. The two time lords are not of equal meaning or significance. The primary lord is the distributor, and even then Abū Ma'shar says that the partners can be ranked according to their aspect: partners by body or conjunction are most significant in life, then by opposition, square, trine, and lastly sextile. Thus in the example above, Mars-Saturn (2025-2026) would be more significant than Mercury-Mars (2023-2024), because Saturn is a partner by a square, while Mars is a partner only by sextile. But this rule cannot be absolute because other conditions apply, such as if the same planet is the distributor and the partner. The example above has several instances, because Mercury not only rules one of the bounds but is actually in it: so when the Ascendant reaches his body, the distribution will be Mercury-Mercury. Likewise when the Ascendant is in the bound of Mars it will also encounter his sextile, so it will be Mars-Mars. If the same planet is performing both roles, it stands to reason that it will manifest more clearly and directly, no matter the ranking of aspects.

But more generally, the distributor sets the tone and parameters, it says what that period is fundamentally *like*; it has more to do with the native himself; it shows how things are fundamentally resolved, even if the partner alters it somewhat or grants some other kinds of actions. So in a period of Saturn-Jupiter, Jupiter will modify Saturn and describe all sorts of other Jupiterian things, including whatever house topics he rules or the house he is in—but it will occur against a Saturnian background, with a Saturnian feeling of sorrow, labor, responsibility, and so on. In some cases, it seems that the distributor is more like the overall "objective reality," while the partner describes one's reaction to them. In Ch. III.2, **37**, Abū Ma'shar describes a scenario in which the distributor is a fortune, and the partner an infortune: even though they might both be in a good condition, and there will be objectively good things happening (especially because of the distributor), the partnering infortune will indicate some unhappiness with those things.

The partner modifies the distributor. Because the distributor is primary, the partner adds to the situation and modifies it. If you read through the combinations of planets in Chs. III.3 – III.7, we can see some general and unsurprising trends. (1) When an infortune is a partner it can spoil or minimize the good indicated by a good distributor (or make a bad distributor worse), while fortunes as partners usually improve things. But (2) the planets' qualities seem to play a role as well: for example, Mars-Sun seems to be a problem because of the excessive heat and dryness, whereas Venus-Sun is more balanced. (3) The intrinsic compatibility of the planets makes a more harmonious or discordant partnership. Finally, the partner makes its own contribution by helping to explain *why* there are sorrow or problems (or benefits and joy): it does this through its own significations. So if Mars is a partner, his nature, place, and rulerships should add information about *why* unhappiness might accompany the general themes of the period.

The partner shows people and actions. But the partner also has its own special significations: it especially indicates people and actions which go on during the period, and especially those which help explain the themes of the distributor. So in Ch. III.6, **13-14**, Mercury as the partner indicates gossip, while the Moon indicates female relatives or family relatives.

Distributions can activate natal configurations. Since a distribution has two time lords, it not only activates them individually, and combines them for the purpose of the distribution, but if they were also configured closely in the nativity it will activate *that specific aspect*. For instance, a Venus-Saturn distribution will activate Venus and Saturn separately in their own roles; because Saturn is the partner he will also combine with Venus and contribute to her meaning as a distributor (for better or worse). But if in the nativity they're *also* in a close trine by degree in particular houses, such a distribution will activate *that specific trine*.

Planets connecting with the distributor (or partner). In the Latin *PN3*, I detected a trend describing planets natally aspecting the distributor, which I called "mood" planets. An example in the chart above would be Mercury: because he is connecting closely with Mars from a sextile, when Mercury acts as the distributor he will also bear the influence of Mars—no matter which bound of Mercury the Ascendant happens to be moving through. I would have called Mars a "mood" planet because it seemed as though Mars would contribute feelings, attitudes, and interests to the native (who is represented by Mercury). Thus during distributions of Mercury, the native would be thinking about Martial things, fighting, might be argumentative, and so on—no matter who the partner happened to be. Now that we have the Arabic, I feel less strongly about the notion of a mood, but several passages do suggest that such a planet will indicate some of his behavior and what the native will pay attention to or be occupied with. But whether or not there is such a mood planet, configurations to the distributor and partner will certainly modify the expression of each independently.

Special rules for SRs. In his *Nativities* Ch. 1.23, **27**, Sahl credits Māshā'allāh with the view that we must examine the real-time conditions of the planets on the day when the distribution changes. This is probably too much to ask, and would demand exceedingly precise birth data. Abū Ma'shar would probably want something like that too, but his method is based on solar revolutions, so he focuses on that.

One rule in Ch. III.8, **7** is rather straightforward: fortunes with the distributor or partner in the SR can help alleviate problems indicated by them. This is an extension of the principle of applying real-time conditions. But another set of passages is more intriguing: since at the SR there might be planets transiting in or looking at the bound of the distribution itself, they can also play a role in modifying the effect.[88] For example, let the Ascendant in the chart above be in the distribution of Mercury in Aries (from 12°-19°59'). If some planet is transiting in that bound or looking at it by ray in one of the SRs during that period (between July 2020 and October 2024), it will affect the meaning of the distribution *in that year*, but in only an incidental way, in the mind, or with a social effect. (This is because things which appear only in the SR are more incidental.) For example, if a very good planet does this during a difficult distribution, the native will still have a bad situa-

---

[88] III.2, **38, 43, 46-47, 54**.

INTRODUCTION 69

tion but people will admire how he handles it. Or, if a bad planet affects the distribution, people will be burdened by his situation.

Interpretation: combinations and transitions. At this point I'd like to turn to the central interpretive chapter on distributions, III.2. It's long but worth putting in outline form so you can track what Abū Ma'shar is doing. The first part provides the basics of interpretation:

- III.2, **1-3**: How to integrate with other techniques, including their relative weight.
- III.2, **4-9, 102-04**: Factors in interpreting a distribution.

With respect to **4-9**, I disagree with some of the list. Sentence **6** refers to the meaning of the sign relative to the three Ascendants (natal, profected, SR), but any releaser will spend many years or even decades in only a few signs, and it doesn't make sense that that would play an important role (besides, in terms of directing the natal Ascendant, hardly anyone will get past the third or fourth sign anyway). I think this is a case of Abū Ma'shar simply trying to do too much. Likewise **7** (all the other dignities) is just too much unfiltered information and creates background noise. I would recommend **5**, **8** (SR only), and **9**.

Next we move to what I call the seven "static" models of interpretation. Models #1-#2 give interpretations for the distributor by itself, and #3-#7 give their combinations with partners:

- III.2, **10-29** (Models #1-#2): Static interpretation of distributors.
- III.2, **30-54** (Models #3-#7): Static fortune-infortune combinations of distributor-partner, including how to compare the natal condition to the SR condition, and SR planets affecting the bound.

If you're new to distributions, the rest of Chapter III.2 might be confusing at first, but it's pretty simple. Because we experience life as a transition from one thing to another, and previous experiences and events affect later ones, Abū Ma'shar exhaustively reviews all of the ways in which a distribution may pass from one state to another. Transitions #1-#8 are simply from bound to bound, or partner to partner, such as a transition from the bound of a fortune to the bound of an infortune. But because the two time lords run in parallel, over time the transitions are actually more complicated. For example, in the list of distributions for the chart above, the last ones are Mars-Saturn and Mars-Jupiter. This means that the native will change from an infortune as the partner (Saturn) to a fortune (Jupiter), while remaining in the bound of an infortune (Mars). This is transition #22 in Abū Ma'shar's list. Following is a breakdown of the rest of the chapter, with a table that will help you organize the transitions in your mind and find them:

- III.2, **55-101**: 24 transitions and their interpretation:
    - III.2, **55-57**: The factors involved.
    - III.2, **58-62** (#1-#4): 4 transitions between distributors.
    - III.2, **63-67** (#5-#8): 4 transitions between partners.
    - III.2, **68-76**: (#9-#16): 8 transitions between distributors, same partner.
    - III.2, **77-86**: (#17-#24): 8 transitions between partners, same bound.
    - III.2, **88-91**: Interpretations of simple transitions #1-#8.
    - III.2, **92-101**: Interpretations of complicated transitions #9-#24.

24 Transitions between distributors and partners		
#1-8	Between distributors or partners only	III.2, **55-67** (See table after **62**)
#9-16	Between distributors, same partner	III.2, **68-76** (See table after **76**)
#17-24	Between partners, same distributor	III.2, **77-85** (See table after **85**)

Figure 24: 24 transitions between distributors and partners (III.2, 55-86)

INTRODUCTION

Another short summary. For another short summary of how to interpret distributions, see also Ch. III.7, **20-31** (which includes more advanced timing information):

- III.7, **20-21**: What to consider about the time lord: nature, location, rulerships.
- III.7, **22-23**: Look for a distribution activating a natal configuration.
- III.7, **25-31**: Interpreting shifts over time.

Timing of events in distributions. Unlike profections which last only for a year, distributions can last up to twelve years or more (depending on the bound and birth latitude). This makes it important to know what to expect about the timing, because a distribution isn't going to be fully active at all times. Abū Ma'shar gives three basic rules for identifying which years will be more active, and one difficult passage with many more considerations:

- When the situation of the distributor (or the partner?) is "multiplied" by being in a similarly good or bad real-time situation (compared with the nativity), or perhaps by being in the same house, etc.
- When the distributor also happens to be another time lord in some year, such as also being the lord of the year, or if the profection comes to its natal position (or even to a Lot similar to its nature).
- When the distributor or partner looks at the bound itself in the SR and other key places.

A more difficult passage discusses whether a distributor will be active more than once over the lifetime, and when, along with techniques using ascensional times, planetary years, and other things (III.7, **32-42**).

Reading: Distributions	
Basic theory, definitions	III.1, **1-18, 24-25** III.2, **102** III.3, **1-2** III.8, **51** III.9, **1** VI.2, **1-20**
Distributor vs. partner	III.2, **37, 103-04** III.3, **8** III.7, **6**
Partner modifies distributor	III.3, **5-6** III.1, **49** III.4, **4**
Partner indicates people and actions	III.3, **5-6** III.5, **10, 12, 14** III.6, **13-14**
Activating natal configurations between distributor and partner	III.5, **5, 7** III.6, **5** III.7, **7, 22-23**
Planets connecting with distributor	III.3, **12** III.6, **5, 9** III.7, **4, 14-18**
Special rules for SRs	III.2, **38, 43, 46-47, 54** III.8, **7, 23**
Lists of combinations	III.2 – III.7
Interpretation template (see below)	III.2, **1-9, 102-04** (basics) III.2, **10-54** (static models) III.2, **55-101** (transitions)
Shorter interpretation summary	III.7, **20-31**
Timing events	III.2, **18-21** III.6, **1** III.7, **32-42**

*Abū Ma'shar's chart example (III.1, **19-45**).* At the beginning of Ch. III.1, Abū Ma'shar illustrates distributions with a chart example, but there are three problems with it and I recommend the reader ignore it. First, recall from §1 that according to his student Shādhān, Abū Ma'shar didn't know his own nativity (and there are doubts about when he learned astrology versus when he was born): so right away this should make us doubt it.

But the second and more important point is that the example contradicts Abū Ma'shar's own method, and in the strangest ways. Remember that when a point is directed through the bounds, (1) *that point* is the topic of interest: such as the Ascendant for life generally, the Sun for honors, and so on. Then, (2) it gains and loses time lords as it encounters them in succession: so when the Ascendant moves from the bound of Mars to the bound of Venus, Mars's distributorship is over. And (3) every point is directed from its own natal position, from the time of birth: thus the Ascendant is distributed from its natal position, starting at birth; the Sun from his position, starting at birth—and this would also pertain to any other point, including Lots. So for instance if we want to distribute a Lot (which Abū Ma'shar explicitly endorses in VI.2), we must distribute it for its own topic, from its natal position, starting at birth. In this way it will have its own series of time lords, at its own rate of speed based on the type of sign and the birth latitude. In Abū Ma'shar's example, the Lot of courage is said to be at 7° 14' Taurus. This means that while we can distribute the Ascendant from the date of birth from *its* natal position (2° 54'), the Lot of courage must be distributed from the date of birth from *its own* natal position. Each distributed point has its own story and timeline.

However, this nativity violates principles (1) and (3) and makes a mess in the meantime. For as the Ascendant encounters the Lots which appear in the Ascendant, Abū Ma'shar's text *accumulates* them so that (1) they become the topic of interest as though each of them is a releaser, and (3) they're not activated from birth, but from the age the Ascendant meets them. Thus in **26-27** the Ascendant encounters the Lot of courage: and fair enough, we could say that the native encounters something related to the topic of courage at that age. That could be considered a primary direction, and if he meant it that way he ought to consider it a partner which is left behind when the next one is encountered. But instead the text picks up each Lot *cumulatively*, and actually distributes all of them as topics, from the age when each encounters the next. This example is so contrary to his own method, and unusual, that it seems more likely to have been lifted from some other source.

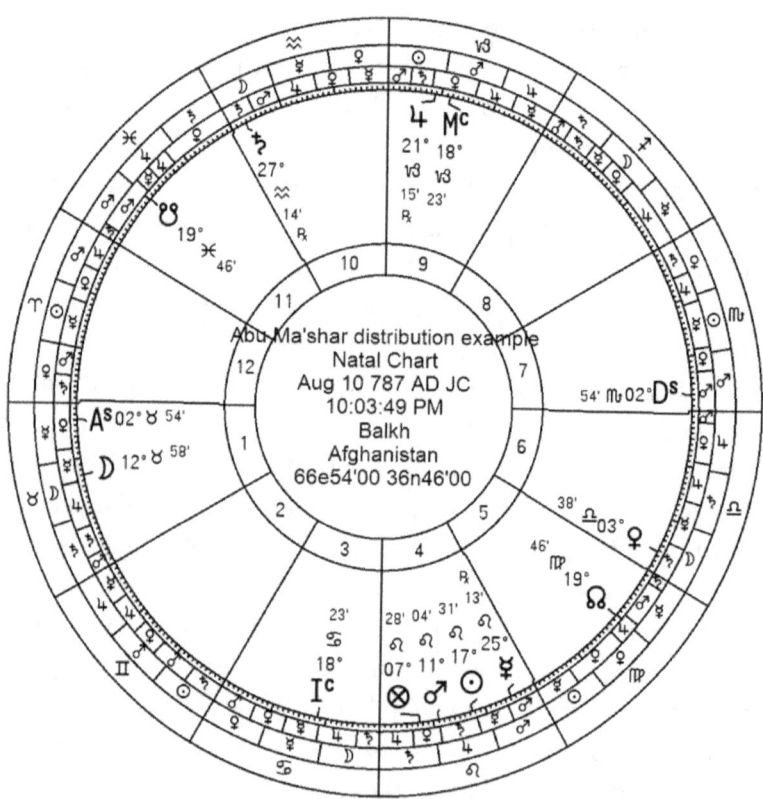

**Figure 25: Abū Ma'shar's distribution example
(III.1, 19-45), Sasanian zodiac**

A final oddity in the chart has to do with the calculations, because there seem to have been two stages in the chart data. (This is apart from any question of scribal error.) The initial planetary positions in

19 are very close to the values in the "Sasanian" sidereal zodiac (as calculated by the Janus program), so those seem to be calculated from birth data. However, **22** presents a different set of data used to work out the example, which clashes with **19** and cannot be internally explained. For example, **19** gives the position of Saturn as 28° 26' Aquarius, which would make him square Taurus; but **22** says he actually sextiles Taurus from 9° 24', which would put him in Pisces, and the worked example uses the values from **22**. Similarly, the Lot calculations in **22** and elsewhere cannot be reproduced from the given data and the known calculations. As I mentioned before, I suspect is it meant to be the nativity of Caliph al-'Amīn or al-Ma'mūn (both born 786-787), or perhaps the Persian vizier al-Fadl b. Sahl., but has undergone changes.

For these reasons I believe the entire presentation of the chart example has been corrupted and ought to be ignored.

§8: Solar revolutions

Revolutions are our primary real-time technique, followed by ongoing transits. In this section I'll focus more on the SR chart and evaluating it alone, even though we cannot ignore how it expresses natal and time lord significations. But because things will begin to get complicated, remember this rule: *Prioritize and keep things simple before jumping to the complex and unusual.*

In an earlier section I mentioned some of the differences between revolutions and other charts, but it's worth saying a few more words here. In one important passage, Abū Ma'shar says that an SR "resembles" a profection, but that a profection is "more powerful."[89] This is because the sign of the year and lord of the year are determined to matters indicated in the nativity—that is how they're activated, by profections in the nativity—and their causes can be found in the root. What this really means is that their indications are more inherent to

---

[89] VI.3, **1-5**; see also II.5, **70-74**.

the meaning of the native's life. They're also likely to be repeated through further profections and in more time-lord techniques.

Now of course, since the SR Ascendant activates natal planets by being on them, it will draw out those natal indications already (but not in the way a time lord does). And if the SR Ascendant happens to fall on the sign of the profection or the lord of the year, then there will be a more direct expression of the natal sign and planet because the two will coincide: this would happen if both the sign of the year and the SR Ascendant fell on Aquarius, or if the sign of the year was Aquarius and the SR Ascendant fell on Saturn (the lord of the year), or something similar. But taken by themselves, the SR's indications are more incidental, occasional, and limited in their meanings, and their causes are more recent; and it's hard for something merely occasional to override something in the nativity which says the contrary. So if your natal Venus has a lot of problems, a single SR with a good Venus might only be a temporary (but memorable) episode which must still be understood against the background of the difficult natal Venus.

A similar situation exists between SR and MR charts: just as the SR shows an annual activation of a natal indication, an MR shows the monthly activation of what was in that SR. So, if there is some significant planet in the SR (or even another planet closely aspecting it by degree), those planets will become more manifest when they manage one of the monthly ingresses—and especially if they have management power in the SR as well.

Reading: Revolutions vs. other charts	
How revolutions differ from the nativity and profections	II.5, **70-75** VI.3, **1-3, 150-52**
Special combinations of distributions, profections, and SRs	III.8, **1-8, 15-54**

One difficulty faced at the level of revolutions, is that there are now three Ascendants, with their own sequences of houses: the natal Ascendant, the profected Ascendant, and the SR Ascendant. Ideally each system could be kept separate, but we know that's not possible. Since natal planets and time lords are evaluated in real time at the revolution, there will be a mixture. Thus the lord of the year may be in the natal fifth, but at the SR it could be transiting in a sign which is the natal third, the SR seventh, and the profected ninth. What can we do? I don't have a complete answer, and as I mentioned above I'm reluctant to add a full-scale set of profected houses. But if the lord of the year was in the SR seventh, and that happened to be in the natal third, I would say it was immediately and most directly involved in the topic of relationships (the SR), which would draw in or pertain to siblings or other third-house people (natal).

Vocabulary:
- **Owner of the revolution** (Ar. صاحب التّحويل). The native, the person whose revolution it is.
- **Revolutionary** (Ar. تحيولي). A placement or object in a revolution chart.
- **Ascendant of the year** (Ar. طالع السّنة). The Ascendant of a solar revolution.
- **Governor** (Ar. مستولي). In revolutions, a special **victor**: a sign (and its lord) which is the same activated place for all or most of the various indicators: such as if the profected Ascendant, profected Lot, SR Ascendant, and SR Lot are all on Taurus. This would make Taurus and Venus the predominating influences and triggers for the events of the year and their timing.

The SR Ascendant and its lord. Let's begin our review with the SR Ascendant and its lord. Abū Ma'shar says that the SR Ascendant represents the native's body, while its lord is the soul (that is, the native's inner outlook, interests, and emotions). I'm not sure I would draw the distinction that cleanly, but either way the SR Ascendant pertains more to the native himself and personally, as opposed to the year in a general sense. The same would go for the MR Ascendant and its lord in a particular month. By its position in the SR houses, the lord of the

SR Ascendant will show something of what the native is interested in, motivated by, or is involved with.

Reading: Interpreting the SR Ascendant	
Meaning of SR ASC and its lord (basic)	II.2, **4**, **9** and **10**, **18** II.23, **6** VI.6, **1-2**
SR ASC operating with time lords	II.23, **1-2**, **41** III.8, **17-19**, **31**
Importance of SR ASC and its lord	III.8, **29-30**, **32** II.23, **6-13**, **25**, **41**, **65-67**, **70**
Complex scenarios with SR ASC	II.23, **14-17**, **25**
Lists and checklists	
Checklist for analyzing the SR ASC	I.7, **1-6** VI.3, **4-5**
SR ASC on natal sign, SR planet in it	VI.3, **6-149**[90]
SR ASC on natal sign, natal planet in it	VI.4, **3-25**, **31**

Thus the SR Ascendant (and its lord) is a "partner" with the distributor and the lord of the year, because it's a major representative of the native in the SR chart, just as those planets are his time lords during that period. So despite having a lot to do with how the native personally feels and experiences the year, it does have a general significance. The good or bad quality of the SR Ascendant should be balanced against the lord of the year and the distributor: in a good condition it can help confirm and enhance other indications, or be diminished by (or unable to override) bad ones.

The SR Ascendant is a primary position for the whole chart, so whatever affects it will affect the year. It will activate a natal planet by being on its sign, and if some planet is in the SR Ascendant by transit,

---

[90] Focus on the first paragraph for each house; note that Abū Ma'shar often relies on derived houses here.

it will have a powerful effect on the year. Just like the natal Ascendant, SR planets which are configured to the SR Ascendant will be brought into direct relation to the native, so we especially want fortunes and planets in a good condition to do that. (The same goes for the lord of the SR Ascendant, just like the lord of the natal Ascendant in a nativity.) But an infortune in the SR Ascendant, especially if it *also* had harmed the natal Ascendant, or the SR Ascendant was on that same planet, will indicate great trouble and disruption.

In II.23, **25** Abū Ma'shar presents an interesting scenario: what if Jupiter is in the SR Ascendant, but there are other significant indications of misfortune? He says the native may be personally elevated and have leadership, but he won't be made happy by any of it because so many other things go wrong. To me this suggests that while the good things are real and vivid (Jupiter in the SR Ascendant), they're fleeting or maybe even superficial because they're outweighed by the rest of the problems—like someone who is voted employee of the year and receives a bonus, but nevertheless his house burns down and his mother dies. Another interesting and complex scenario can be found in Ch. II.23, **14-17**.

SR planets in a stake, advancing, angular. Part of evaluating a revolutionary chart is identifying which planets stand out and are more intense: this is shown by their being dynamically angular or advancing (i.e., moving by diurnal motion towards the axial degrees). Such planets will command more attention, and Abū Ma'shar says planets are made *powerful* by their SR positions.[91] Not all natal planets which are activated as time lords will be equally strong in the SR; some will be weak and their impulses less active.

The converse is also true: any dynamically angular planet in the SR is important, but especially if it also happened to be natally in the sign of the year (or even in its whole-sign angles): in that way it would be both activated in relation to the profection, and highly stimulated and noticeable by the SR. For example, let Venus be natally in a whole-sign

---

[91] II.23, **3.**

square with the sign of the year; then let her actually be transiting in the sign of the year at the SR, and also on the SR Midheaven: we would be forced to regard Venus and her topics as being central to the year. And in general we should ask: what planets are on the angles of the SR, and what were they doing in the nativity? Those matters will be more prominent. This doesn't mean they will be successful, though: in II.23, **18** Abū Ma'shar says that infortunes in the SR Midheaven will show either sluggishness and slackening (i.e., they will strongly inhibit action), or the native will be working hard at something which doesn't actually bring benefit.

Abū Ma'shar sometimes emphasizes that advancing towards the axial degrees doesn't just mean something is "strong," but that is *public*; planets which are dynamically cadent and still configured to the SR Ascendant are more personal in their meaning and confined to one's inner circle; if they were actually in aversion to the SR Ascendant, they would be secret.

The sign or planetary "governor." Although I generally shy away from using planetary victors, it's hard to ignore a sign or its lord which keeps appearing in the same year. So it's worth noting if there's a sign (and its lord) which acts as a "governor" for any particular month, and that is if all or most of the monthly indicators happen to be on the same sign (IX.2, **4**). This is normally something Abū Ma'shar refers to in reference to MRs, but it's worth mentioning here because the SR also acts as the first month of the year.

The SR Lot of Fortune. Abū Ma'shar does recommend that we recalculate Lots for the SR chart (so that there's a natal Lot of marriage but also one in every SR). It would be a good idea to pay attention to the SR Lot of Fortune, just as we ought to remember to profect the natal Lot of Fortune. The SR Lot would refer to how the native is confronted by webs of causes, events, and opportunities which are unexpected and he probably has to make choices about; the good and bad condition of its sign and lord ought to tell us how favorable that is. Following our astrological logic, the SR Lot should give us real-time information on how fully and well the profected natal Lot is expressed, just like we do with the lord of the year for the profected natal Ascendant.

Planets changing houses between charts. One principle nicely emphasized by Jean-Baptiste Morin but only mentioned in a few places by Abū Ma'shar, is watching how planets change signs between charts.[92] (I mentioned this above.) Since the nativity determines or focuses planets generally on certain topics for the whole life, they will undergo modifications to this in subsequent SRs. So, suppose there is a natal planet in the second, permanently but generally describing something of the native's assets and lifestyle: if that planet is in the SR fifth, then the native's finances will be connected to children or spending on pleasures in that year; if in the SR third, in relation to travel or learning; and so on. Obviously the lords of the natal angular houses and planets in them are usually the ones we want to track most carefully, especially the lord of the natal Ascendant.

Reading: Identifying and interpreting SR planets	
SR planets in a stake / advancing / angular	II.3, **15-18** II.18, **18** II.23, **4-18, 37, 39-40**
Planets changing houses between charts	VI.5 (all) VII.9, **25-27**
The annual or monthly "governor"	IX.2, **4** IX.4, **90, 92, 106** IX.9, **10-11**
Connections between lords of houses	VI.6, esp. **1-7, 38-45**

---

[92] See for example Morin's *Astrologia Gallica* XXIII Ch. 18 (p. 131).

Let's look in Figure 26 at the SR for "Phil," whose profection for Age 27 we examined briefly above. First, the SR chart by itself. Right away we can see that an exalted Saturn is in the SR Ascendant and the Sun in the tenth, indicating something of a good status and recognition. Both fortunes are in the ninth, suggesting good influences from a trip, foreign things, or education. This was true: at his new job he was well liked and was groomed for promotion very quickly; he also took a long-needed vacation.

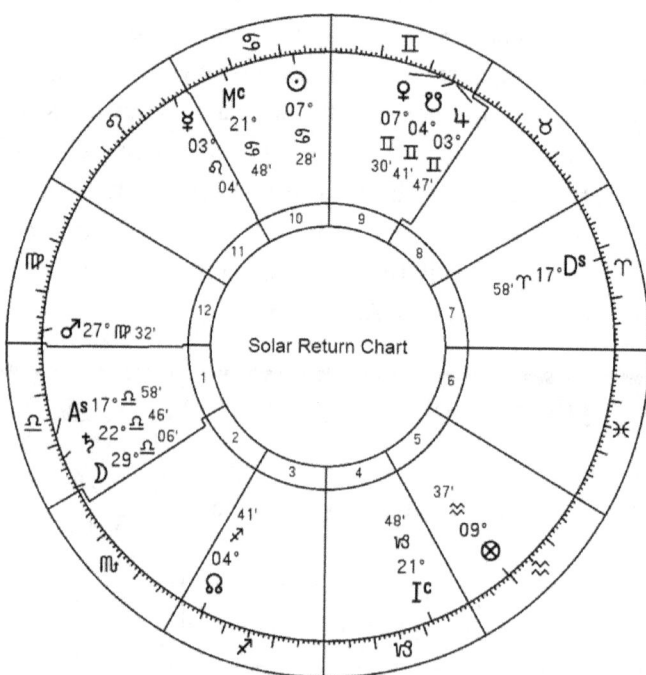

Figure 26: SR example: "Phil," Age 27

But let's now combine the nativity of Phil (from Figures 15 and 17) with this SR in a bi-wheel in Figure 27, so we can see other things more clearly. The nativity is the inner circle, the SR the outer circle. I said that the exalted Saturn in the SR Ascendant showed recognition: now we can see that Saturn was the natal lord of the tenth sign and the MC: so this supports the indications for recognition.

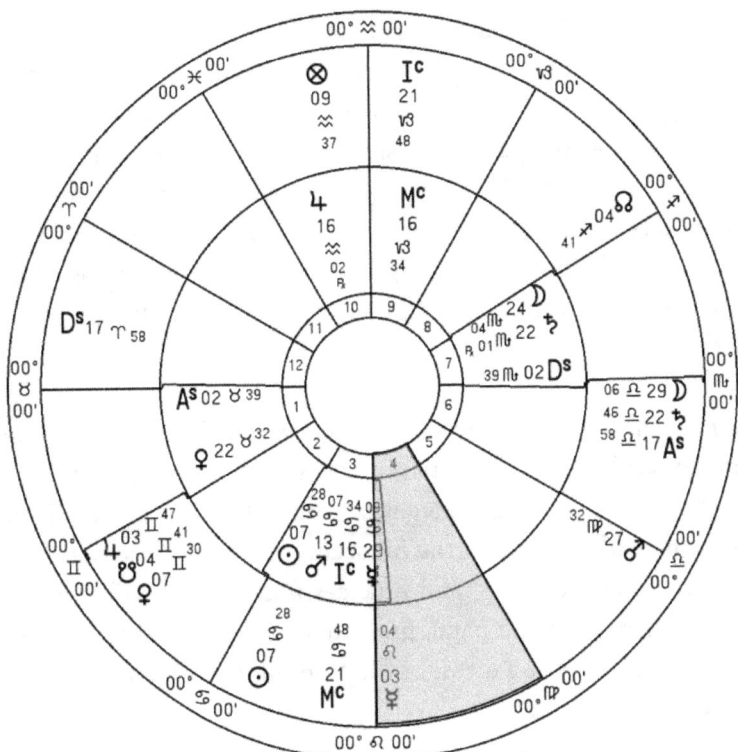

Figure 27: SR bi-wheel: "Phil," Age 27

Next, note the following placements: (1) the natal Ascendant Taurus is the SR eighth; (2) the SR Ascendant Libra is the natal sixth; and (3) the SR Saturn—who is still an infortune—is in the SR Ascendant. These suggest suffering and illness, and indeed he not only had much stress and anxiety, but also a major surgery and food poisoning which could have seriously hurt him without good treatment.

Then, note the following: (1) the fortunes are in the SR ninth as I said, but that happens to be the natal second house of assets and livelihood; (2) the lord of the natal Ascendant, Venus, is one of those planets; (3) Jupiter was natally in the tenth and so indicates recognition and action; and (4) Mercury, the natal lord of the second, is transiting in the sign of the year, in a nice trine with that same SR Jupiter and Venus. In this year the native was indeed promoted and made a lot more money, supporting the other indications for recognition.

Finally look at Mars, who was with the lord of the year (the Sun) in the nativity. The SR Mars is transiting in the natal fifth (Virgo), which is also the SR twelfth. In this year he did have a lot of fun and excitement (Mars in fifth) with his fraternity brothers and roommates (natally in third), but this quickly turned sour and he experienced isolation and disappointment (harmed natal Mars in fall, now in SR twelfth).

Lords of houses connecting with each other. Because the SR can be interpreted partly by itself, we can treat connections between planets in its houses and their lords straightforwardly: the lord of the SR ninth connecting with the lord of the SR second, indicates a connection between travel and learning, and finances. But as I stated before, since planets play roles in the natal, profected, and SR schemes of houses, this can easily become a mess. In Ch. VI.6, Abū Ma'shar provides some guidelines:

- Favor the natal meanings of two planets, over their SR places and rulerships.
- Favor the meanings *within* a house scheme, before assuming any connection *across* schemes.
- Favor applying connections, over separating ones. Separations suggests that any benefits will be less, or some plan will be abandoned or not be completed.

Abū Ma'shar gives specific chart examples at the end of VI.6, but the idea is this. Let the lord of the natal Ascendant be Mars, so the lord of the natal seventh is Venus. But suppose that at some SR, they rule the SR tenth and SR fourth respectively, and they're connecting with each other. Abū Ma'shar's principles say that their natal first-seventh meanings should be considered before their SR tenth-fourth meanings, and that these relationships *within* each scheme should be considered before we cross them and say that Mars, the lord of the *na-*

tal Ascendant, is connecting with Venus, the lord of the *SR fourth*. Keep it simple, and remember which charts and planets have priority.

Timing in a revolution. Since an SR represents the whole year (as the nativity represents the life), not every indication will manifest at the same time. Of course Abū Ma'shar offers many different ways to know when an SR indication will manifest, but here we can name six: (1) when an SR planet comes by later transit to the same planet's sign or bound, as it was in the SR; (2) when a planet becomes a monthly lord; (3) for as long as a planet is actually transiting in a place, in real time; (4) when a monthly profection reaches a planet, or perhaps when an MR Ascendant is on it; (5) the direction or distribution of the SR Ascendant around the entire SR chart, for exactly one year; (6) the direction or distribution of other points around the SR, such as Lots or the lord of the year.

Reading: Some timing ideas	
When an SR planet transits the same planet's sign or bound	VIII.14, **6-7**
When a planet is a monthly lord	VIII.15, **21-22**
As long as a planet is transiting somewhere	VIII.15, **21-22**
When a monthly profection (or perhaps MR ASC) reaches a planet	VIII.15, **21-22**
Direction of SR Ascendant around chart	IX.7, **27**
Direction of other SR points around SR	IX.7, **29-33**

Total house significations: the complex method (IX.4). This is an advanced topic, more of an exercise by Abū Ma'shar, and of little practical value. In Chapter IX.4, Abū Ma'shar presents an obsessively detailed account of all of the ways in which a planet may be interpreted by its house meanings in all three of the annual Ascendant schemes: natal or rooted, profected, and SR. As the reader will see, some of this is based on his (to my mind) forgettable theory of derived houses for transits: according to this theory, a planet will have a fourth-house meaning if it's in the fourth place from its own sign—and vice versa, its sign would be in the tenth place from it, conferring a tenth-house meaning.

The idea is that, for each of the three Ascendants, a planet can be either in its own sign (or not) in the root, and likewise be transiting in it (or not) in the SR, and be in some relation (or not) to the signs it rules. This gives us a total number of possible interpretations for each planet in any particular year, from a maximum of 32 down to 6. In his usual desire to be thorough, he even multiplies the possible combinations by the number of months, to yield a total of 3,300 combinations per year.

The reader will see that there is no way Abū Ma'shar's scheme could be of practical use, despite his attempt to give a chart example in IX.4, **91-106**. But in order to make things absolutely clear, I have painstakingly designed images for all of his schemas, and will illustrate them using his Venus example:[93]

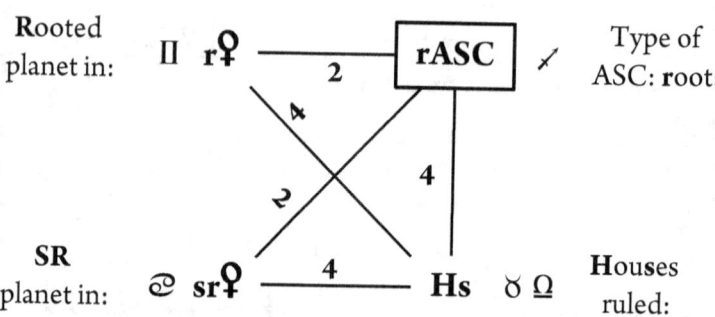

Figure 28: Total significations for Venus (IX.4, 91-104)

In this example, we want to know the number of possible interpretations for Venus in some year, in relation to the natal or rooted Ascendant, when she is *not* in any of her signs in either chart (the na-

---

[93] This is an instance of his "first division, first way" of calculating combinations, in IX.4, **8-9**.

tivity or the SR). In the top right we see that the type of Ascendant is the root or natal Ascendant ("rASC," in the box), and it was Sagittarius. In the top left we see that Venus was natally in Gemini. In the bottom left, she was in Cancer at the SR. In the bottom right, we see that she rules two signs or houses (Taurus, Libra). This means that this Venus has 16 possible ways to generate house significations in relation to the natal Ascendant, indicated by the small numbers:

- The natal Venus has 2 derived-house possibilities between her and the natal Ascendant. In this case Gemini and Sagittarius are in the seventh place from each other (1-2).
- The signs ruled by Venus have 4 possibilities with the natal Ascendant. (3) Taurus is the sixth from Sagittarius, and (4) Sagittarius the eighth from it; (5) Libra is the eleventh from Sagittarius, and (6) Sagittarius the third from it.
- The natal Venus has 4 possibilities with her two signs, since she is in neither one: (7) Gemini is the second from Taurus, and (8) Taurus the twelfth from it; (9) Gemini is the ninth from Libra, and (10) Libra the fifth from it.
- The SR Venus has 2 possibilities with the natal Ascendant. (11) Cancer is the eighth from Sagittarius, and (12) Sagittarius the sixth from it.
- The SR Venus has 4 possibilities with the her two signs, since she is in neither one: (13) Cancer is the third from Taurus, and (14) Taurus the eleventh from it; (15) Cancer is the tenth from Libra, and (16) Libra the fourth from it.

After this, the angry student of Abū Ma'shar must look at Venus's relationships to the profected Ascendant and SR Ascendant, for a total of 32 interpretations. Abū Ma'shar could only force himself do these first 16.

§9: Monthly revolutions and monthly profections:

Abū Ma'shar's treatment of monthly revolutions was missing in the Latin version, and it's by far the most fascinating and complicated of the methods—perhaps a bit too complicated, because the reader needs a lot of help in understanding the details. I've provided many tables and diagrams, but we must also go slowly so as not to get confused. By way of overview, here is the list of chapters on monthly revolutions, and their subjects:

- IX.1: Summary of the monthly indicators, and method.
- IX.2: The first month.
- IX.3: How to draw a chart.
- IX.4: Total method of house indicators.
- IX.5: Months 2-12 (with some "quick" methods).
- IX.7: Weekly, daily, and hourly indicators.

The most important chapters are IX.1, IX.2, and IX.5. Chapter IX.3 is straightforward, and I've already discussed IX.4 above. Chapter IX.7 is on smaller units of time and I won't really address it much here.

To my mind there are three reasons why the theory of monthly revolutions (including monthly profections) is so complicated. The first is that not all months are treated the same. The SR chart and the sign of the year stand for both the entire year and the first month, so the same chart shows two things; but months 2-12 have separate charts and profections. You can see above that Chs. IX.2 and IX.5 deal with different months. This means that for the first month (IX.2) we need a special way of knowing which indications are for the year as a whole, and which are for the first month alone. Then we have to deal separately with the later MRs (IX.5).

The second reason is that it becomes even more complicated to compare the planets in real time (in the MR) with causally prior charts. For MRs are a real-time technique which express both the annual SR (as a smaller unit of time), and also the nativity—since anything deriving from the nativity, also expresses it. Therefore an MR has two charts acting as its root: the SR and the nativity. Abū Ma'shar's solution is to draw up a list of seven monthly indicators to be examined in each MR: five of them are "rooted" because they depend directly on the nativity and the natal position of the Sun (which is when we cast the SR), while two depend on the MR and its recalculation of the Sun's position every month. (We will look at this below). This needs to be read very carefully and I've only recently experimented with it.

The third reason is that Abū Ma'shar begins a new type of comparison in the monthly charts. That is, he not only evaluates the houses and their lords for what they predict about life topics themselves (such as money or marriage), but then compares them to special indicators for the native, to see how these topics directly *impact* the native.

Abū Ma'shar's theory thus becomes so complicated, that by the end of Ch. IX.5 (**95-126**), he has condensed these down to three simpler and quick methods. These are probably the best place to start, once you understand the basics of the theory.

He also recommends that we identify a monthly "governor" or victor, which is a sign or planet in which all or most of the monthly roles coincide: such as if the sign of the year, the profected natal Lot, the SR Ascendant, and the SR Lot were all the same sign.[94] This is the monthly version of the annual governor I mentioned in the previous section, and would act as a chief significator for the month instead of dividing the interpretation among many different signs and planets.

---

[94] He also adds that it should be a convertible sign, because he insists on occasionally including the Indian ninth-parts. I will ignore them as much as possible.

Reading: Overview of monthly revolutions	
Justification of method	II.1, **29-33**
Levels of time, with indicators	IX.1, **1-8**
	IX.5, **95-98**
Monthly governor	IX.2, **4-7**
	IX.5, **2**
Three quick methods	IX.5, **107-26**

Monthly profections and revolutions. First let's understand the mechanics of monthly profections and revolutions, beginning with following rules:[95]

1. Everything may be profected.
2. All profections are sign-by-sign.
3. Months are measured from the date of the SR and the MRs, not by calendar months.
4. The sign of the profection in an annual chart (the nativity or the SR) is also the first month.

In a natal chart, we profect the place whose significations we want, to the year we want. That sign represents the year and the first month *for that significator*. After that, each successive sign represents the rest of the months of the year, again measured by the date of the revolutions. (But for easy reference it's simplest to refer to the same date in each month: such as if the SR and birthday are on August 27, then the first month is from August 27 to September 27, the second month from September 27 to October 27, and so on.)

---

[95] Remember that I will *not* follow Abū Ma'shar's special rules for quadruplicities, because they will cause confusion and they seem highly unlikely to me. I will describe them at the end of this section.

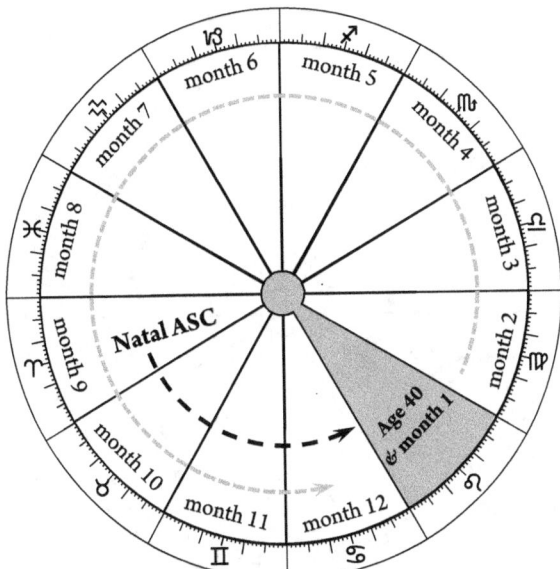

Figure 29: Monthly profection of natal Ascendant (IX.1, 9-10)

So in Figure 29, let Aries be the natal Ascendant, and suppose we're interested in Age 40. The natal Ascendant profects to the fifth place or sign (Leo), so Leo is both Age 40 as a whole, and its first month. The second month is Virgo, the third month Libra, and so on—these are the months *for the topic of the Ascendant*. So just as there is a lord of the year and the first month (the Sun, ruling Leo), there are also lords of the other months (Mercury for Virgo, Venus for Libra, etc.). This profection of the natal Ascendant and its months, is Abū Maʾshar's "rooted" indicator #1.

Let's do the same with the natal Lot in Figure 30. This natal Lot is in the fifth, Leo, and we profect to Age 39: we come to *its* Age 39, which will be the eighth, Scorpio, ruled by Mars. This is both the year as a whole *for the Lot*, and also the first month. The second month for the Lot's Age 39 is Sagittarius, the third is Capricorn, and so on. Therefore the Lot itself will have a lord of the year and of the first month (Mars) and also the other monthly lords (Jupiter, Saturn, etc.). This profection of the natal Lot and its months, is Abū Maʾshar's "rooted" indicator #3.

92 ON THE REVOLUTIONS OF THE YEARS OF NATIVITIES

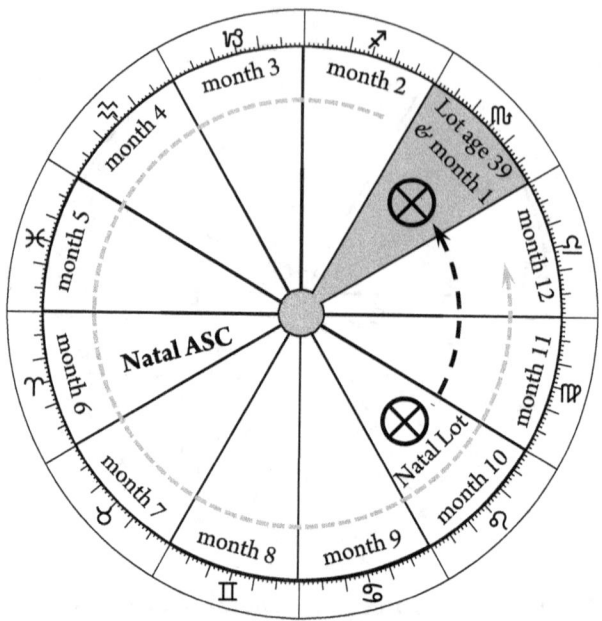

Figure 30: Monthly profection of natal Lot of Fortune (IX.1, 17-19)

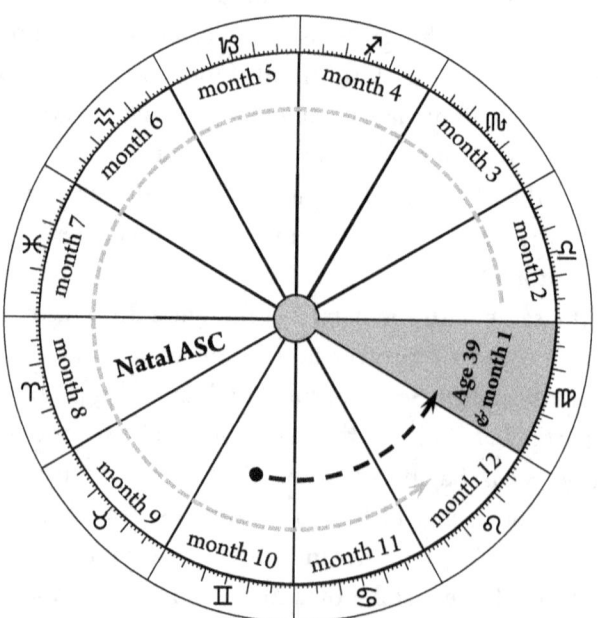

Figure 31: Monthly profection of natal third

We could do the same with the natal third in Figure 31. Let the natal third be Gemini, and we profect to Age 39: we come to *its* Age 39 at the sixth, Virgo, ruled by Mercury. This is both the year as a whole *for the third*, and the first month. The second month for the third's Age 39 is Libra, the third month is Scorpio, and so on. Therefore the third itself will have a lord of the year and of the first month (Mercury), and also the other monthly lords (Venus, Mars, etc.).

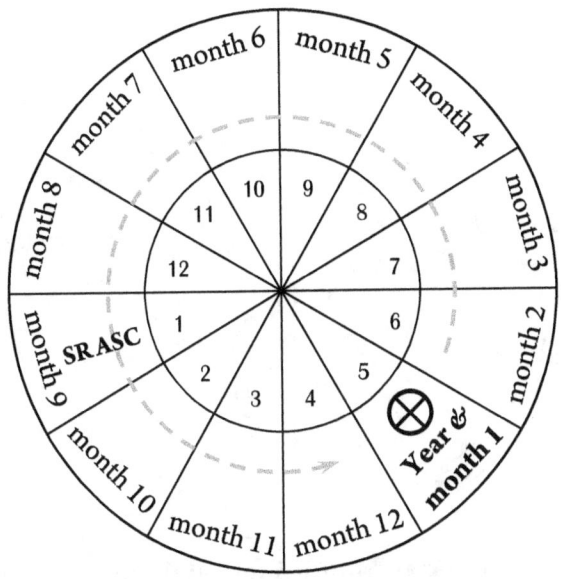

Figure 32: Monthly profection of SR Lot (IX.1, 21)

So far we have profected natal positions. We can also profect SR positions to particular months, and the most important places would be the SR Ascendant and SR Lot. In Figure 32 let's profect the SR Lot, which is Abū Ma'shar's "rooted" indicator #5. Let it be in the SR fifth. It represents the Lot in the SR chart for the whole year, but also its first month. The second month for the SR Lot is the sixth place, the third month is the seventh, and so on.

Note well that the profected *natal* Lot (or anything else we profect) won't necessarily match its profected counterpart in the SR. This is why monthly profections become so complicated, and why Abū Ma'shar would like to find cases where the indicators coincide on the same sign. Figure 33 illustrates what I mean. Let the natal Ascendant be Aries (inner circle), and let's profect it to Age 39, the fourth, Cancer. Let's also cast the SR for Age 39, and suppose that the SR Ascendant is in Leo (outer circle).

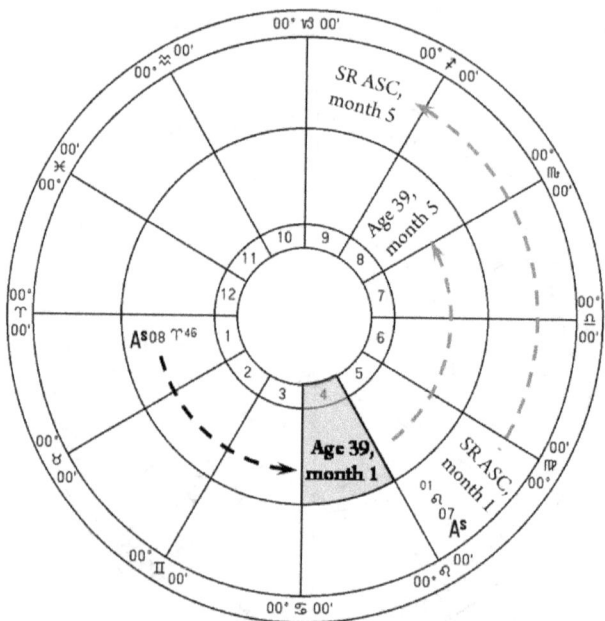

Figure 33: Profected Month 5 for natal and SR Ascendants

Because the sign of the year and the SR Ascendant are in different signs, you can see right away that the months won't coincide: the fifth month for the profected natal Ascendant is Scorpio, while the fifth month for the profected SR Ascendant is Sagittarius. Mars and Jupiter (the monthly lords) are rather different planets, so we don't have a clear meaning being projected from the nativity through the SR. If we now add an MR chart whose Ascendant happens to be in Capricorn, the waters are more muddied. So while we can understand Abū Ma'shar's criticism of his predecessors' not doing much with monthly profections and MRs (since years aren't as specific as months), complications like these can make us more sympathetic to them. We can also understand why Abū Ma'shar would like to find a governor so that the same sign and planet repeats across charts. But such governors will be rare.

The monthly revolution chart is easy to cast: it's the time when the Sun is in the degree of any sign, which corresponds to the natal degree. (And we will use the birthplace for the location). If the natal Sun was at 15° 29' Scorpio, then the SR (and first month) is calculated for his return to 15° 29' Scorpio; the MR for the second month is at 15° 29' Sagittarius; the MR for the third month at 15° 29' Capricorn.

The general principles for interpreting monthly signs and charts by themselves are pretty much the same as those for annual profections, although I've provided a list of passages in your reading table. For example, if most or all of the indicators and their lords are in a good condition, that topic will be easier and successful; if not, not. Transits at the MR can be made to the SR positions, just like transits at the SR can be made to natal positions.

Reading: Monthly profections and revolutions	
Definition and timing of monthly revolution	I.3, **9** IX.1, **9-10, 17-25** IX.3, **1-3**
Basic interpretive principles	III.1, **5-6** V.1, **9** IX.2, **18ff** IX.5, **60-83, 93-94**

The seven monthly indicators (IX.1). The purpose of Ch. IX.1 is to list and explain Abū Ma'shar's seven monthly indicators, and reject three alternatives (in **40-45**). Three passages list and explain them, which you can find in the reading table below. Following is a table which also appears twice in the text:[96]

Rooted	#1	**Profected natal Ascendant** (1st month) and monthly profections from it	Old, rooted causes Slow to disappear
	#2	**Ninth-part of sign of year** (1st month) and monthly profections from it	
	#3	**Profected natal Lot of Fortune** (1st month) and monthly profections from it	
	#4	**SR Ascendant** (1st month) and monthly profections from it	Recent causes Limited to year Not constant
	#5	**SR Lot of Fortune** (1st month) and monthly profections from it	
Not	#6	**Ascendants** of: monthly revolution charts	Recent causes Months, days Short duration
	#7	**Lots of Fortune** in: monthly revolution charts	

Figure 34: Seven monthly indicators
(IX.1, 9-25, 35-39; IX.5, 95-98)[97]

The first five are "rooted," because their position depends on a chart which uses the natal Sun: namely, the nativity and the SR. Of these, those which are actually in the nativity [#1-#3] are more essential to the native, their causes are older and last longer. Those which are calculated in the SR [#4-#5] are more recent, limited to that year, and less persistent. The last two indicators are not rooted because they're calculated when the Sun is in a *different* sign, at an MR chart. These have more recent causes (sometimes in the SR), and are more confined in duration. So if we start at the top and work our way down, the indica-

---

[96] See around IX.1, **17**, and IX.5, **2**. The table in IX.5 has slightly different wording, because there Abū Ma'shar is speaking about a *particular* month, not just in a general way.

[97] For comparing the subject-matter of each significator, see IX.5, **99-102**.

tors decrease in universality, power, and length of time (both in their origin and how long they last).

Notice that all of these—apart from the ninth-part, which I ignore—are Ascendants and Lots. This should alert us that they give general characteristics for the year and month. One short passage describes just this (IX.5, **99-103**): the main idea is that they refer to life in general, the native's experience, *not* particular life topics such as assets or marriage. Abū Ma'shar claims that the signs are more objective about the quality of the time, and the lords describe the native's thoughts (and probably, actions). This follows astrological logic, but in practice it probably isn't so simple.

Reading: The seven monthly indicators	
List, and summary of time	IX.1, **5, 9-25**
	IX.1, **35-39**
	IX.5, **95-98**
What each means	IX.5, **99-103**
Three rejected methods	IX.1, **40-45**

The first month (IX.2). Since the signs of the annual profections and places in the SR chart act as both the year and the first month, we need to identify which indicators stand for the year, and which for the first month (or perhaps, both). Here is Abū Ma'shar's rule:

> To indicate the first month, the *lord* of a place should be in a *sign* which indicates the first month, especially in the SR Ascendant (and perhaps in the other angles) and if they are fast in motion.[98]

Since all five of the "rooted" indicators can be profected by month, all of them can be one of these signs. (I ignore [#2] the ninth part, but will keep saying there are five because Abū Ma'shar does.)

---

[98] IX.1, **3** and **35**.

So, let the lord of the natal second be Venus, and let's do our annual profections and cast the SR for some year, identifying indicators #1-#5. In the SR she would have to be in one or more of: the [#1] profected natal Ascendant, [#3] profected natal Lot, [#4] SR Ascendant, or [#5] SR Lot—especially in the SR Ascendant or perhaps one of its angles: then the topic of assets will be activated in the first month of the year. This gives us up to five places for Venus to be in, increasing her chances of being in a place indicating the first month. But she isn't the only planet to indicate assets: there is also the lord of the profected second and the lord of the SR second. In that case we could have a motley mixture of some lords in those signs, and some not. Again: complicated.

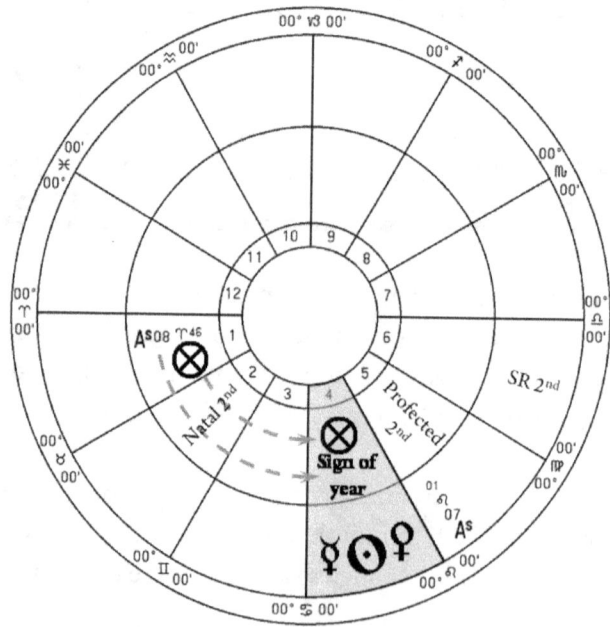

Figure 35: Activation of assets in first month (IX.2, 9-11)

Obviously it would be easier if all of the rooted indicators were the same sign or only a couple of signs, so that there are fewer places for the planets to be in. Figure 35 is an example. The natal Ascendant and Lot are both in Aries (inner circle), and we're profecting to Age 39 which is Cancer, the fourth. Let's say that the SR Ascendant happens to be in Leo (outer circle). The lords of the natal, profected, and SR second houses are Venus, the Sun, and Mercury. By some miracle, all three of them happen to be in the sign of Cancer, which is [#1] the profected natal Ascendant and [#3] the profected natal Lot. That's a good argument in favor of their significations for assets being active in the first month, especially since all three are there. (If we counted [#2] ninth-parts, it would be even better.)

Abū Ma'shar's topic for the first house (the body) is treated somewhat oddly, either because it's so over-determined by significators which happen to also indicate the first month, or because he gets lost in his discussion of the monthly governor.[99] But in the rest of Ch. IX.2 he explains that we also need to interpret the condition of the house topics (for the topics themselves), and how their lords are configured with the native's indicators (for how they affect the native). I've included two tables in the text to explain this but his general approach can be summarized here:

House indicators…	should…	in order to:
Natal house (& lord) Profected house (& lord) SR house (& lord)	Be in a good/bad condition	Be good/bad for the topic
	Mix with the five rooted indicators *and* the lord of the natal ASC	Affect the native for good or ill
	Be in the sign of the five rooted indicators	Indicate the first month

Figure 36: Quick summary of how to look at year and first month (IX.2)

---

[99] IX.2, 4-8. It seems that he wants the lords of the five rooted indicators to all be *in* those signs (whether their own or each other's).

Reading: The first month	
Why the first month is different	IX.2, **1-2**
The rule for indicating the first month	IX.2, **3** and **35**
Model for house topics in first month	IX.2, **9-17**
How house topics affect the native	IX.2, **18-29, 32-34**

Months 2-12 (IX.5). For the rest of the year we have separate MRs, so we can now use all seven of the monthly indicators: the five "rooted" ones, along with the MR Ascendant and MR Lot. Again we will have a somewhat different treatment of the first house versus the other house topics, but let's begin with Abū Ma'shar's nice appraisal of the month as a whole.

For the month as a whole (independent of specific topics like assets or marriage),[100] first identify each of the seven indicators. Then, organize them into two groups. The first group [#3, #5, #7] includes all of the Lots of Fortune, which indicate the flow of events.[101] The second group [#1, #4, #6] includes all of the Ascendants, which indicate the native and what he wants and does. By interpreting each group separately and how they interact with each other, we can talk about the month and how the native is affected by it, just as we did with the house topics and how they affect the native above.

For the body and soul (a first-house topic),[102] look at the seven monthly indicators: their condition in themselves, the type of place they're in, and how they interact with each other. The signs indicate the body, their lords the soul. This section has some nice delineations about personality and general temperament based on planetary condition.

---

[100] See IX.5, **19-29, 99-102**.
[101] Again I omit [#2] the ninth-part. Note that in IX.5, **21** he classifies the ninth-part with the Lots, while in **100** he puts it with the Ascendants. The latter is more faithful to Abū Ma'shar's theory, but it doesn't matter to me because I'm ignoring it.
[102] IX.5, **1-18**.

For all other house topics,[103] Abū Ma'shar again picks *six* indicators for the native (all Ascendants and their lords), just as he did with the other house topics in the first month. These are to be compared to the houses and lords relative to each of them, in order to appraise the topic and how it affects the native. So for assets, we compare the MR Ascendant and its lord with the MR second and its lord; or the SR Ascendant and its lord with the SR second and its lord. Some of these derive from rooted indicators (the nativity and the SR), some from only that month. Of these combinations, relationships *within* the same house scheme are more powerful than across schemes (**46-47**). Thus the relationship between the lord of the MR Ascendant and lord of the MR second (same scheme) will be more significant than its relationship with the lord of the profected second (across schemes).

Reading: Months 2-12	
The month as a whole (with table)	IX.5, **19-29, 99-102**
Body and soul	IX.5, **1-18**
Other house topics (with table)	IX.5, **30-53**
Basic interpretation of monthly sign (again)	IX.5, **60-83**
Three quick methods (again)	IX.5, **107-26**

Days and hours. Chapter IX.7 is devoted to methods which assign time lords to planetary "weeks," days, and hours. I won't say anything about this section here except to note that both IX.7, **29-33** and III.1, **3-6** endorses the method of directing (or rather, distributing) the SR Ascendant around the SR chart for the period of one year. In IX.7, **32** Abū Ma'shar acknowledges that one could use a variation based only on zodiacal degrees (instead of equatorial degrees or ascensions), but admits it's only an approximation: that's an understatement, because as the birth latitude increases it introduces huge distortions.

---

[103] IX.5, **30-53**.

In my course I describe how I use this directive method.

Timing methods in the months. Rules for timing in months and smaller units of time, follow general rules I've already discussed and will return to below. Here is a reading table with a few of them:

Reading: Timing in months, weeks, days	
Transits	IX.5, **71**
Moon	IX.5, **91, 93-94**
	IX.7, **73-75**
Monthly profections	IX.5, **54-58, 86-90**
MR Ascendant, MR management	IX.5, **59**
	II.5, **75**
Timing for days	IX.5, **71, 93-94**
	IX.7, **29-33**

*Abū Ma'shar's rule for quadruplicities and profections (IX.1, **26-34**).* This is an advanced topic and I have deferred it until now because it's complicated, probably wrong, and an over-zealous application of quadruplicities. Actually this is probably not Abū Ma'shar's own idea, as it's alluded to in the context of converse directions by Māshā'allāh in Sahl's *Nativities* Ch. 1.23, **36**).

The rule concerns the practice of changing the direction of monthly profections based on the quadruplicity of the annual sign. For any annual profection, whatever sign it lands on will represent the year as well as the first month (as normal). However, the quadruplicity of the sign and degree of the profection will determine in which direction we count for *all subsequent months*. Fixed signs like Taurus have no change at all. Convertible or movable signs like Cancer go backwards. Double-bodied signs like Gemini will go forward or backwards depending on where the degree of the profection or terminal point falls in that sign. This means that for convertible signs and some double-bodied signs, the months will form a backwards-rotating circle.

INTRODUCTION

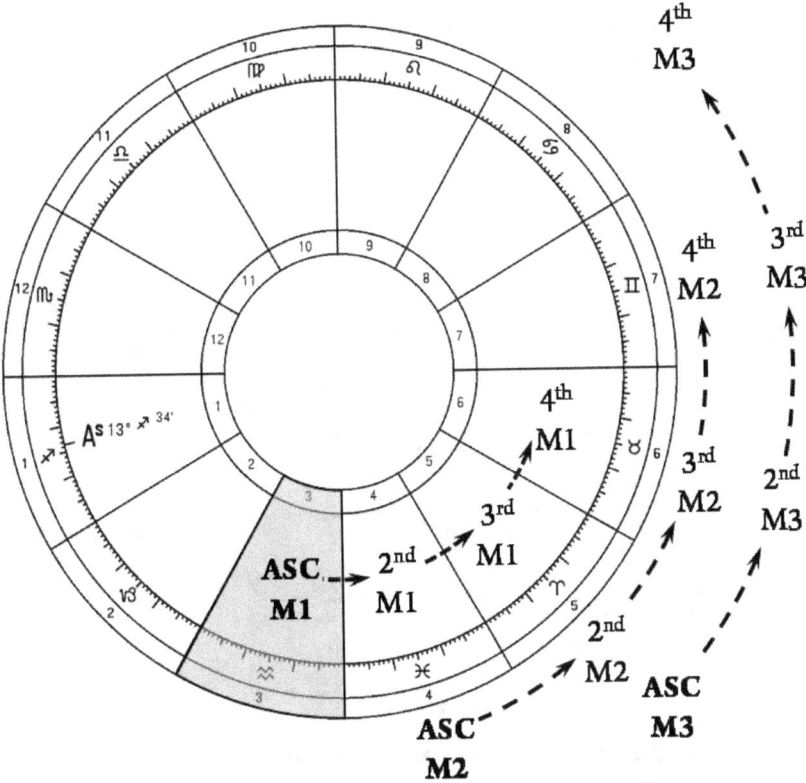

Figure 37: Abū Ma'shar's monthly profections, sign of year fixed

In the text of IX.1 I provide four diagrams for the profected Lot, but let's use the profected Ascendant here because we can also profect houses, and we need to know how these houses fit in. The rule is that no matter in which direction we count the months for the Ascendant, all of the other profected houses will still follow in the usual order.

In Figure 37, the natal Ascendant is profected to Age 26, the third place: in this case, the fixed sign Aquarius. Aquarius is the sign of the year as well as the first month, *for the Ascendant*. The rest of the signs represent Month 1 (M1) for the other topical houses at Age 26: Pisces is the profected second for the year and M1, Aries the profected third for the year and M1, and so on.

For the second month, we proceed in the order of signs and assign M2 for the Ascendant to Pisces (middle ring of arrows), and every sign thereafter represents M2 for the rest of the houses. For the third month we again advance the Ascendant by one sign and derive all of the rest in the same way (outer ring). So in the third month of Age 26, the lord of the month for assets is Venus, the lord of Taurus.

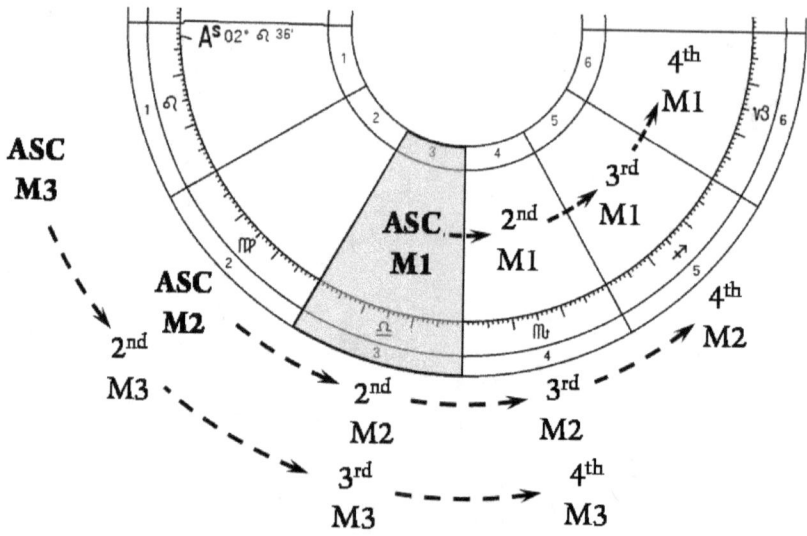

Figure 38: Abū Ma'shar's monthly profections, sign of year convertible

If the sign of the year is convertible, although in the first month all of the signs are as we expect, every month thereafter we go *backwards* in the order of signs for the Ascendant, again deriving the rest of the houses from it. In Figure 38, Age 26 is Libra, a convertible sign. The sign of the year and M1 for the Ascendant is Libra, M1 for the second house is Scorpio, and so on—just as above.

But for the second month, we set M2 for the Ascendant back one sign to Virgo, and derive the rest of the houses from it: M2 for the second house is Libra, M2 for the third house is Scorpio, M2 for the fourth house is Sagittarius. In the third month we again go back one sign: M3 for the Ascendant is Leo, M3 for the second is Virgo, M3 for the third Libra, M3 for the fourth Scorpio. This is like a backwards-rotating circle.

You can see that the difference between the two methods gives very different results. In Figure 38, M3 for the second house is Virgo and its lord Mercury; but if we didn't use any quadruplicity method and just profected forward as usual, M3 for the second house would be Capricorn and Saturn.

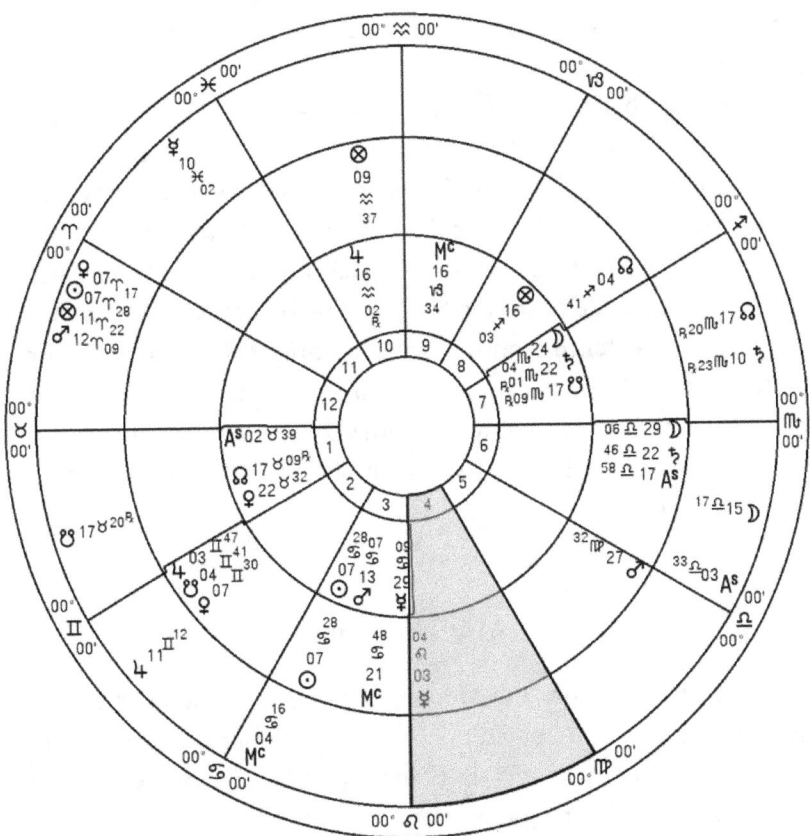

Figure 39: "Phil," MR for Age 27, Month 10

Let's take a final look at Phil's SR for Age 27, Month 10 (outer circle). Above I said that he took a long-needed vacation: that happened during this month when Jupiter, who had indicated it in the SR, exactly trined his natal position.

I also said he had food poisoning: that happened in this month, and you can see that the MR Ascendant has replicated the SR sign, in the natal sixth (illness). The MR Moon is also in these Ascendants in both charts, now opposed to the MR Mars. She also happens to be the lord of the month for the profected SR Ascendant (if you profect from Libra for ten months, it reaches Cancer). So, she is the lord of the month in the SR, in the MR Ascendant, replicating an SR configuration that indicated illness.

I also said that there was conflict with his fraternity brothers and roommates. You can see that Mars is in the MR seventh (conflict), and he had a big fight with one of them when Mars reached 22° Aries, opposing the SR Saturn in the SR Ascendant (which indicates the native); this also squares the SR MC. Mars also happens to be the lord of the month for the profected SR Lot (the SR Lot is in Aquarius, and by profection its tenth month is Scorpio). So Mars was an indicator of conflict due to the natal profection (being joined to the lord of the year, the Sun), and in the SR 12th showed more enmity, and when he was the monthly lord of the SR Lot and in the MR seventh (conflict), there was a fight.

§10: The Moon

As mentioned before, the Moon is an important general indicator in any revolution, and we ought to consider her a "partner" with the other indicators, because in all branches of astrology her motions, separations, and connections show the flow of events. Abū Ma'shar recommends that we focus on the planet she connects with to see what topics and themes will be highlighted—where the management is going. If however she is empty in course, we ought to look at the lord of her sign. This last part seems odd to me, because normally we would either say that her emptiness indicates problems, or we would see whom she connects with after entering the next sign, which would also imply an important shift of focus and attention, and a change of circumstances. But in his *Introduction*, Sahl makes a point with respect to question charts that Abū Ma'shar may have in mind.[104] There, Sahl says that if the Moon is empty in course but the first planet she connects with in the next sign is the domicile or exalted lord of the previous one (in which she had been empty), then it's like being received: so perhaps we could consider this—otherwise, being empty in course would have no special meaning to begin with.

Abū Ma'shar also offers lists of interpretations for the SR Moon transiting over natal planets, as well as in the houses (see table below). As usual, the houses are tricky because Abū Ma'shar wants us to consider all three types: natal, profected, and revolutionary. He emphasizes that the indication will be much stronger if all three happen to share the same Ascendant, so there is no division across several areas of life. And I suppose this is right: but I would normally just look at the revolutionary house.

Finally, Abū Ma'shar has many interesting special scenarios and combinations involving both the natal and SR Moon, which illustrate her importance for life in general.

Reading: The Moon	
Statements of her importance	IX.5, **91-92** and **125**
Her connections and lord of her sign	• II.1, **12** • II.22, **14-22**
Lists of her transits over natal planets, if she has testimony in the year	V.8, **1-20**
Lists of her transits in the houses[105]	VII.8
Special rules and configurations, illustrating her importance	• II.23, **30, 46, 48-55, 65** • III.8, **19, 26, 29, 31, 35, 39-40, 41** • V.8, **21-26**

---

[104] Sahl, *Introduction* Ch. 3, **57**.

[105] These are especially if the three main Ascendants (natal, profected, and revolutionary) are the same sign.

§11: Transits

Transits are a common technique in contemporary astrology, and they were also used by the traditional astrologers. But the strict meaning of "transit" meant something different, and they were used in different ways. In this section we'll look at how the older astrologers treated transits, and especially some of the particular ways Abū Ma'shar handles them.

The word "transit" in our three primary languages means to physically move across something:[106] that is, it has to do with the *body* of a planet passing over a sign or the *body* of something else. In a similar way modern astronomers refer to a "transit of Mercury" as the passing of Mercury's body across the body of the Sun. So when we look at older texts for transit delineations, we rarely see delineations like "transiting Mars square natal Venus": really what's happening is that Mars is transiting a sign or degree which *Venus* squares. Strictly speaking, transits only happen where the transiting planet actually is. This was the older view.

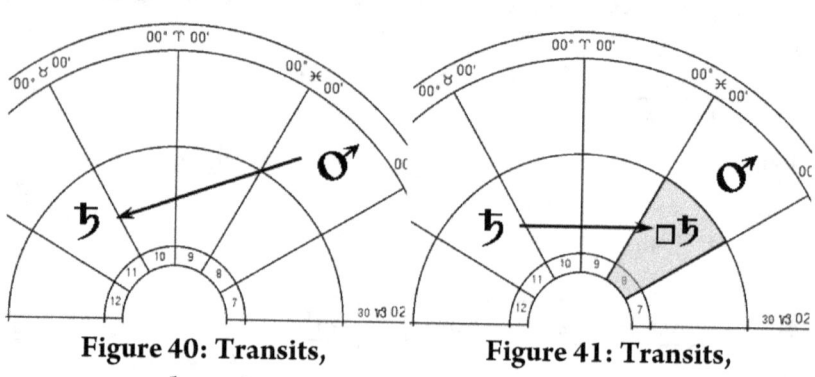

Figure 40: Transits, modern view

Figure 41: Transits, ancient view

The figures here illustrate what I mean, as explained by several examples in *Carmen* IV.1, **1-8**. Figure 40 on the left shows the modern view: in it, the natal Saturn is in Taurus (inner circle), and by transit

---

[106] Greek: *epembasis* ("to tread upon"). Latin: *transire* ("to go across"). Arabic: مر (*marra*, "traverse, pass over").

the SR Mars squares natal Saturn. In this case, transiting Mars is doing the squaring. But Figure 41 on the right shows the ancient view: in it, the natal Saturn in Taurus is *squaring Aquarius,* and by transit the SR Mars affects the harmed Aquarius by his body crossing through ("transiting") it. This isn't simply a trivial difference, because it reveals what the ancient significance of a transit is: *a transit activates something from a root chart.* The natal Saturn *was* doing something, namely squaring Aquarius: that is a natal signification. By Mars's transit to Aquarius at some later time, that natal Saturn square is activated. This is the kind of scenario we would especially look for if Aquarius had actually been the sign of the year, because the interpretive emphasis would already be on it.

Now, it's not quite as simple as this. You might object that because planets are always casting rays, Mars *should* be squaring the natal Saturn—or maybe, since Saturn is no longer there, he is squaring the sign *affected by the body of Saturn* (Taurus), just as above he is transiting the sign *affected by the square of Saturn* (Aquarius). And this is a valid point. But Dorotheus would put it like this: "Mars is indeed making a superior square to the natal Saturn, but that's because he's transiting the *sign* which does so." Aquarius still has a superior square relationship to the natal Saturn, so any plant transiting in it will partake of that relationship *because it is in that sign.*

Like many things in traditional astrology, this is partly a matter of emphasis. If Aquarius was the sign of the year, Mars's transit through it would be more significant than his square to the Saturn, because Aquarius is the main concern in that year.[107] Furthermore, among a planet's transits, being in a place is more powerful than looking at or aspecting it. And even then, not every configuration is equal: conjunctions are the most powerful, then oppositions and squares, then trines, and lastly sextiles.

But the fact remains that according to this older view, transits alone aren't necessarily important—they are triggers and timers for *other*

---

[107] In such a case it would also matter that Saturn is the lord of the year.

things, they are secondary and relational. I would say that this happens in two primary ways (which can overlap):

- Transits trigger or affect a configuration or situation in a previous chart. Recall that in the section on profections, transiting planets activate profections to natal planets.
- Transits to and by time lords are more significant. For example, the lord of the year's transiting position in the SR, but even throughout the rest of the year, can show when its events will be active. The ongoing transits of other significant SR planets like the lord of the SR Ascendant should also be noted, because they're akin to time lords when compared to the rest of the year.

Thus if SR Venus happens to be transiting through the sign of the year, or she is the lord of the SR Ascendant, her ongoing transits should have greater significance.

In Ch. V.8, **32-35**, Abū Ma'shar builds on these ideas to track the source or cause of the event—and by extension, its meaning in the native's life. Suppose that, some weeks after the SR in some year, transiting Venus comes to the body of Mars (I believe he means the natal Mars). This will indicate some event, especially if one of them is a time lord, in an angle, etc., so that it's more notable and important. But what role does it play in the native's life? Since transits primarily activate previous configurations, then if Venus and Mars were already configured in the nativity, the source of the event will be an "old" matter, or one more typical and inherent in the native's life. But if she had only been configured to him at the SR and not the nativity, it will be something new, and probably incidental or unconnected to much else (but maybe meaningful in *that* year's course of events). If she was configured to him in both charts, then it's both old and new, or both inherent and incidental. But if she had not been configured to him in either chart (and so it's happening for the first time later in the year), it will be "from a matter not known," probably an apparently random thing.

Planetary returns. Many people have heard of a "Saturn return," when Saturn returns to the sign or even degree he was in at birth, approximately every 29 years. Abū Ma'shar does mention Saturn returns,[108] but any planet can make one, and Abū Ma'shar opens his treatise on transits with a discussion of them (see the table of readings below). Typically we look for planetary returns in the SR. Following our astrological logic, the more notable planetary returns are those of time lords: such as if Saturn was the lord of the year by profection, and was also making a return to his natal sign. Abū Ma'shar affirms exactly this point in Ch. IX.9, **14**.

The fundamental meaning of any planetary return is "renewal": that is, it will activate anew, whatever it had indicated in the nativity—subject to how closely it connects with the natal position, and its condition relative to the nativity: so for instance it matters whether the planetary return is happening in a good or bad SR house. The more the revolutionary conditions are good, angular, and configured to the Ascendant (probably of both the root and the revolution) as well as the sign of the profection, the more they will bring success and prestige, especially if the planet was in a good condition in the nativity,[109] and especially if it has "testimony" in the year by indicating the native in some way (such as ruling the natal or SR Ascendant).[110]

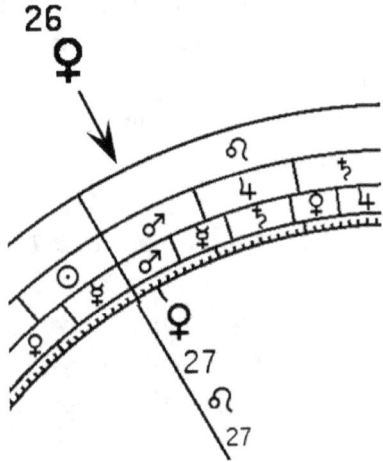

Figure 42: Venus return to same bound (V.1, 3)

---

[108] See II.23, **51**; V.1, **28** and **30**; V.2, **1-3**.
[109] See V.4, **5-8**.
[110] See V.2, **4**.

The "completeness" of the return refers to how closely the planet returns to its natal degree, and whether this is applying or separating. If at the revolution it's on the degree or in the same bound, it's complete, as in Figure 42 where Venus has returned to the bound she was in at the nativity. If it's outside the bound but the natal position is still within one half of its "orb," it's less complete; if not within the orb at all or only in the same sign, it will be even less—if applying. If it's only in the same sign but separating, then it will be even less or something only in the imagination.

Sometimes a fast-moving planet like the Moon or Venus will return to its SR position again, later in the year. In that case, Abū Ma'shar says that it will mean something similar to what it did in the SR, but not the same thing because in the meantime the conditions of the other planets will have changed.[111] But it would seem that it's a "mini" planetary return nonetheless.

Abū Ma'shar's approach to interpretation. In Ch. V.1, **7**, Abū Ma'shar affirms that the same "completeness" principles for planetary returns (in the same bound, applying, separating, and so on) also apply to other transits, such as transiting Venus to the natal Saturn. Then he helpfully suggests three approaches to transit interpretation:[112]

1. **"Cookbook combinations."** We can go by the generic natures of the planets in their aspect combinations.[113] I suggest you review the models of aspects to the lord of the year in Book II, and the pairing of planets in distributions and *fardārs* in Books III-IV. This is a good way to think about general combinations. Abū Ma'shar also mentions cases where the planets' natures and places or rulerships are similar.
2. *Transiting planet affecting natal planet.* This is the more traditional approach, in which the transiting planet does

---

[111] See VII.1, **16**.
[112] See V.1, **11-23**.
[113] V.1, **12**.

something to the rooted planet, in accordance with their natures, conditions, and so on,[114] rather than just being a generic mixture or combination. For instance, Venus transiting Saturn might loosen him up and make him more friendly, but Saturn transiting Venus could cool her down or sour her pleasantness.

3. *Derived domiciles.* This approach may be unique to Abū Ma'shar.[115]

According to Abū Ma'shar's method of derived domiciles, we take the signs ruled by each of the planets and interpret their derived positions from each other. For example,[116] if Venus transited the natal Jupiter, then because Taurus (a sign of Venus) is the sixth relative to Sagittarius (a sign of Jupiter), this transit indicates an illness; but because they're both fortunes, the native will recover. Of course normally we wouldn't expect a Venus-Jupiter transit to indicate an illness *unless* they ruled or were in the sixth house of a chart, or we were specifically talking about illnesses brought on by too much eating, drinking, sex, and so on. So this type of interpretation departs greatly from the usual approaches. One refinement he makes is treating the planet with the most testimony for the year as the primary planet, and derives the other signs from it. So even if Venus was transiting the natal Jupiter, if she had more testimony (such as ruling the SR Ascendant or being the lord of the year), we would see where *his* signs fall relative to *hers*, rather than the other way around.

Frankly, I think this derived-domicile approach is a shame and should be ignored, for three reasons. First, it doesn't even seem to be based on correct delineation principles, and actually contravenes them. For normally, house-based topics must be derived from planets'

---

[114] Compare V.2, **6** and V.4, **2**. Some of these delineations are outlined in *Carmen* IV.4.
[115] V.1, **15-23**.
[116] V.1, **17**.

house locations and rulerships—but Abū Ma'shar is trying to derive house topics from sign relationships alone.

Reading: Transits	
"Completeness" of transit	V.1, **1-7** VII.1, **16**
Planetary returns	V.1, **1-6, 8-10** V.2, **1-3** (model) II.23, **51** IX.9, **14**
How transiting planets improve or worsen natal configurations	V.1, **13-14**
How testimony in the year changes the interpretation	V.2, **4-5, 6-7, 9-10** (model)
Managing the three Ascendants	VII.1, **17, 19-21** VII.1, **26-27** VII.9, **25-27**
Special scenarios and rules about timing	V.8, **21-35**
When the effect will happen	V.1, **24-25** V.8, **21, 24-29** VII.2, **7-8**
Delineation lists (model combinations of planets to study)	Book II Book III Book IV
Duration of the effect: transits to planets	
Planetary return (transit to self)	V.1, **27-35**
Transit to a different planet	V.1, **36-45**
Transit with multiple planets	V.1, **46-52**

Second, it leads to the kind of confused mess we often see in the "astrological alphabet" in modern astrology, when people conflate Taurus, Venus, and the second house. If Abū Ma'shar is right, then Venus and Jupiter transits will *always* mean illness, friends, authorities,

INTRODUCTION

land, siblings, and inheritance—all of them—just because of how Sagittarius, Pisces, Taurus, and Libra are related. If we then add the meanings of the houses where Venus and Jupiter actually are, then these or any planets will mean practically anything.

Third, his delineations in Book V are misleading because he blends his derived meanings with everything else. For example, no normal combination of Mercury and Jupiter would lead us to believe that they indicate marriage; but that is what Ch. V.7, **3** says. This can only be because the signs of Mercury are in the seventh from those of Jupiter (Gemini-Sagittarius, Virgo-Pisces): therefore because they rule the seventh from one another, conjunctions of Mercury and Jupiter indicate marriage. Frankly this seems bogus to me, and so I've underlined all phrases and key words in those chapters, where it seems clear to me that he could *only* have gotten his interpretation this way. I invite you to ignore these underlined parts.

The table of readings and explanations in the text should give you pretty much everything else you need, including various instructions for timing.

§12: Fardārs

One time-lord method which isn't well known today is the *fardār* (Ar. فردار) called in some books the *firdariyyah* (Ar. فرداريّة). The word is probably a Persian transliteration for the Greek *periodos* ("cycle, period"). Almost all of the material about *fardārs* is in the short Book IV, which to me is something of a giveaway that, like the lord of the orb, they are an alien system not well integrated with the other techniques. The fact that they employ the Nodes also suggests that they were invented in India, or among Persians familiar with Indian thought. Indeed, Abū Ma'shar gets almost all of his material from the Persian al-Andarzaghar, or else they share a common source. In the footnotes to Book IV I refer to the al-Andarzaghar passages in al-Dāmaghānī (Da.), from Burnett and al-Hamdi (1991/1992).

Like the Ages of Man, the *fardārs* assign a standardized set of time lords for all humans over the course of life, with one difference: diurnal births get one series, nocturnal births get another. Thus, whereas the Ages of Man associate the periods and order of planets to the *natural* development of the human being, *fardārs* imply that sect differences lead to different life experiences, in different orders.

Diurnal		Nocturnal	
☉	10	☽	9
♀	8	♄	11
☿	13	♃	12
☽	9	♂	7
♄	11	☉	10
♃	12	♀	8
♂	7	☿	13
☊	3	☊	3
☋	2	☋	2

Figure 43: *Fardār* sequences and years

If the nativity is diurnal, then the time lord for the native's life as a whole is the Sun, for 10 years; then Venus for 8, and so on, in descending Chaldean order. After the Moon the order loops back to the top, running through Saturn, Jupiter, and Mars. When the series is ended after 70 years, there are 5 years for the Head (3) and Tail (2) of the Dragon. If the nativity is nocturnal, one starts with the nocturnal sect light, the Moon, then loops back up to Saturn and so on. Again, the Head and Tail of the Dragon come at the end. If the native lives longer than 75 years, the sequence returns to the sect light, as at birth.

In the Middle Ages, a variation developed so that the Head and Tail were thought to always follow Mars: according to this view, in a nocturnal birth they would come between Mars and the Sun, at Ages 39-43. Most likely this view developed because al-Qabīsī, in his popular *Introduction*, doesn't make it clear that they always come at the end. Instead, he runs through the diurnal sequence and then says that the nocturnal one works just the same, except that it begins from the

Moon.[117] Abū Ma'shar's *Great Introduction* likewise just lists the years for the diurnal sequence. Since the list of planets is already known to involve looping around in order, it would have been easy for someone to assume that the Nodes work the same way, and always come after Mars. But Abū Ma'shar is clear in the Arabic and Latin versions of this book that they always come last (IV.7, **24**).

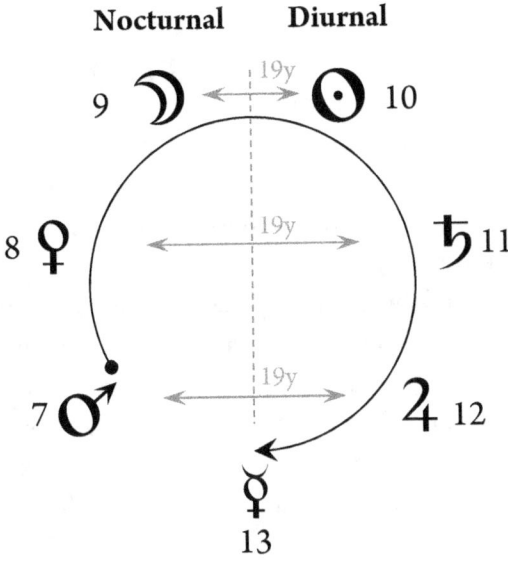

Figure 44: Planetary *fardār* lords by sect and number of years

The reason for the number of years assigned to the *fardārs* isn't obvious. There is more than one coincidence between the number of years assigned to the planets, and other cycles (such as Venus and Jupiter each getting their lesser years), but other planets are puzzles. What is certain is that years can be paired up between the diurnal and nocturnal planets, and the fortunes and infortunes, to suggest the 19-year Metonic cycle (which is a function of solar years and lunar months). If we take the planets out of Chaldean order and organize them by their number of years, we find something interesting. All of the nocturnal

---

[117] See al-Qabīsī IV.21 (in *ITA* VII.1).

planets come first, then the diurnal, with Mercury (who is variable) coming last. If we put them in a circle, we see that they come in neat pairs of luminaries, fortunes-infortunes, diurnal-nocturnal, and that the years for each pair adds up to 19, the length of the Metonic cycle.

The Metonic cycle refers to the fact that 19 tropical years (6,939.602 days) is almost exactly equivalent to 235 synodic or lunar months (6939.688 days): the difference is about 2h 4m. Because of this, the positions and phase of the Sun and Moon repeat at almost exactly the same time on the same day, every 19 years; this is useful for predicting eclipses. (It's not wholly precise because the difference between the periods accumulates after several cycles.)

Other patterns include the fact that the Moon's number (9), multiplied by 12 months, yields 108, a well-known number associated with the Moon (her greater years) and in Hindu thought. The Sun's number (10) multiplied by 12 yields 120, a solar number (his greater years). The years of Venus and Jupiter are their lesser years. But I don't understand the years of Mars, Saturn, and Mercury (although I have some ideas). Nor do the years of the Nodes make sense to me, and if they were supposed to be added to Mercury's 13 to make 19, then they should have 6 years, not 5. It may be that some of the years were assigned in order to yield an idealized longevity of 75 years. Thus it seems that the planets, divided by sect and other pairings, and arranged so as to replicate the Metonic cycle, are then put in Chaldean order to yield the *fardārs*.

Reading: *Fardārs*	
Instruction, meaning, use	IV.1, **1-10** IV.4, **4-11** II.2, **15** IX.8, **113**
With profections and transits	IV.2, **24-25** IV.7, **27-28**
Interpretations	IV.1 – IV.7 (all)

INTRODUCTION

The other technical point is that each period (but not the Nodes') is subdivided into seven equal parts: the lord of the *fardār* rules the first one-seventh of its own period, then the next planet in order co-rules the next one-seventh, and so on.[118] Therefore the 10 years of the Sun are ruled in this order: Sun-Sun, Sun-Venus, Sun-Mercury, *etc.* In this way the *fardārs* act like distributions, with a primary lord and its partner. Now to my mind, if the planets get unequal years for their *fardārs*, it would make sense that the partners or sub-lords should also rule for unequal times: so each partnering planet would co-rule with the Sun in proportion to its allotment of time in the scheme as a whole. But according to Abū Ma'shar they don't. (To me this seems like something worth investigating.) Abū Ma'shar carefully calculates the exact length of each sub-period, but the reader should be careful with this because his months are standardized at 30 days. For example, each sub-period of the Sun is 1.42857 years (the result of dividing 10 years by 7 planets). If we remove the 1 and multiply the remaining .42857 by 12 we get 5.14284 "months" of 30 days. If we remove the 5 and multiply the remaining .14284 by 30, we get 4 days and some hours. For most people this kind of exactness is unimportant, but Abū Ma'shar does recommend looking at the real-time transits of the planets when they take over management of the sub-periods, so you must be careful about how many days are really involved. To be really exact, you want to get the actual number of days and not idealized months of 30 days.

As for other time measurements in Book IV, they are either from, or distortions of, the values found in the al-Andarzaghar sections of al-Dāmaghānī. An example of this is IV.4, **29**, which speaks on an illness for 17 days. I'm not sure how these are calculated.

The interpretation of the *fardārs* is similar to distributions. First, the natural compatibility of the planets affects the general character of the period: so, the Venus-Saturn combinations are predictably difficult. Their combination should also affect the types of people and activities normally indicated by their natures, such as marriage and family for

---

[118] For a complete table, see the end of Ch. IV.1.

Venus, or assets and honor for Jupiter. The Moon's *fardār* is based in part on the symbolism of waxing and waning in the lunar cycle: the native will have joy and wealth (akin to waxing), then be in distress, poverty, and low rank (akin to waning).[119]

More importantly, the natal meanings of the time lords are activated according to their condition, place, and rulerships. These natal indications are then compared with their real-time conditions at the time when they take over the management. For all of the major *fardār* lords, this will obviously be at an SR. For all of the sub-lords except those of Mars, they will be at unusual times which must be calculated (as I stated above). Just like with distributions, when a *fardār* lord also happens to be the lord of the year by profection, the indication will be more evident and intensify during that time.

This new Arabic edition now allows us to understand something which puzzled me in the Latin. Sometimes Abū Ma'shar simply adopts al-Andarzaghar's delineation for a particular period, and sometimes he applies it only to the diurnal version and then invents his own (usually similar) nocturnal version. Now we see that the Latin version omitted Abū Masher's explanation, which appears in Ch. IV.4, **4-11**. There, Abū Ma'shar politely refrains from naming al-Andarzaghar specifically but says that previous scholars hadn't made diurnal and nocturnal distinctions: instead, they gave only a single interpretation for, say, Moon-Saturn, and designed it to apply to an adult client. Abū Ma'shar rightly points out that this isn't sufficient: it's not just that diurnal and nocturnal people might experience a combination differently, but these combinations will happen at different times of life. It may be fine to write a delineation for the Moon *fardār* which speaks about a male native's wife, but that is only appropriate for a diurnal native (Ages 31-40): nocturnal natives have their Moon *fardār* from Ages 0-9, which is far too young for that. Therefore Abū Ma'shar assigns some of al-Andarzaghar's interpretations to only one sect, then invents his own for the other sect at a suitable age. Since all natives will be adults dur-

---

[119] See IV.4, **2**.

ing the *fardārs* of Mercury, Jupiter, and Mars, he simply adopts the essentials of al-Andarzaghar as they stand.

Abū Ma'shar's point can be taken further than just speaking about what's suitable for a particular age. It also speaks to the fact that in a diurnal nativity, Mars is the contrary-to-sect infortune: therefore, the Mars periods should generally be more troublesome for diurnal natives; the same goes for Saturn in nocturnal nativities. We can also go further: the order of *fardārs* asserts that diurnal and nocturnal people will also experience such highs and lows and different times of life. Since the Saturn *fardār* comes right after the Moon's, a nocturnal birth will experience things like hardship and loneliness in childhood and adolescence—powerful things which must be coped with early, but then could be managed more easily later on. A diurnal native won't experience Saturn till much later, but even then he is the diurnal infortune and so not as bad; but the Mars *fardār* will hit later in life (and so perhaps harder). If all of this is true, it allows us to explain the contours of people's lives in ways that are more subtle than the Ages of Man, which are indeed developmental but are the same for everyone.

§13: The lord of the orb

The lord of the orb (Ar. صاحب الدّور) is a time lord used in connection with profections from the Ascendant. It is the lord of a planetary hour, which cooperates with the profected Ascendant and the lord of the year: according to Abū Ma'shar, Hermes attributes it to the Babylonians. The main readings are found in Ch. VI.1, and IX.7, **7-9**. I've never seen an astrologer use this in practice, and it quickly becomes complicated—probably too complicated to be useful. If you're a beginner, skim the next few paragraphs to learn about planetary hours, but ignore this technique.

Planetary hours are divisions of actual periods of daylight and nighttime, as determined by actual sunrise and sunset: since the length of day and night differs according to season and latitude (except on the equinoxes), planetary hours are almost never our "civil" hours of 60 minutes apiece. Most astrology computer programs calculate this, but here is how it works (and it might be useful to know this, because not everyone agrees on when "day" begins).[120] If the nativity is by day, divide the total number of civil hours and minutes between sunrise and sunset, by twelve: this is the length of each of the twelve planetary hours of that day. Assign the lord of the planetary day to the first planetary hour, then the next one down in Chaldean order to the next hour, the next planet to the next hour, and so on, rotating through the seven planets until you assign them to all of the hours. If the nativity is by night, do the same thing for the period between sunset and sunrise.

Thus if your nativity was on a Tuesday, during the day but just before sunset, then add up the total hours and minutes between sunrise that morning and sunset. (You can often find these times in your newspaper or on a weather website.) In this case, let it be 13h 14m. Divide by 12 to get 1h 6m 10s, which will be the length of each planetary hour for that day in that location. Since Tuesday is ruled by Mars, Mars has the first planetary "hour" of 1h 6m 10s, the Sun gets the second "hour," and so on, until finally the Moon gets the last and twelfth hour. In this example, because the native is born just before sunset, he is born during the planetary hour of the Moon. If the nativity was by night, we would do the same for the hours between that sunset and the next sunrise.

As you can see in the tables here, the hours for the entire week occur in one continuous loop, starting with the Sun at sunrise on Sunday, through Saturn at sunset, but continuing with the next planet Jupiter in that evening, and so on throughout the week. Finally, at the end of the night on Saturday (just before sunrise on what we would consider Sunday morning), Mars is the lord of the hour, before the week begins again at sunrise on Sunday.

The lord of the orb is pretty straightforward, but Abū Ma'shar adds some details that make me wonder exactly where he is adding his own ideas: one could derive two different versions of the lord of the orb. I'll

---

[120] In the Janus astrology program, open a chart in the Traditional module, and click the General tab. The planetary hour is listed near the top.

follow his first description, since it also uses this idea of a continuous "loop" of planets.

	Sunday	Monday	Tuesday	Wed.	Thursday	Friday	Saturday
	Diurnal hours: from sunrise						
1	☉	☽	♂	☿	♃	♀	♄
2	♀	♄	☉	☽	♂	☿	♃
3	☿	♃	♀	♄	☉	☽	♂
4	☽	♂	☿	♃	♀	♄	☉
5	♄	☉	☽	♂	☿	♃	♀
6	♃	♀	♄	☉	☽	♂	☿
7	♂	☿	♃	♀	♄	☉	☽
8	☉	☽	♂	☿	♃	♀	♄
9	♀	♄	☉	☽	♂	☿	♃
10	☿	♃	♀	♄	☉	☽	♂
11	☽	♂	☿	♃	♀	♄	☉
12	♄	☉	☽	♂	☿	♃	♀
	Nocturnal hours: from sunset						
1	♃	♀	♄	☉	☽	♂	☿
2	♂	☿	♃	♀	♄	☉	☽
3	☉	☽	♂	☿	♃	♀	♄
4	♀	♄	☉	☽	♂	☿	♃
5	☿	♃	♀	♄	☉	☽	♂
6	☽	♂	☿	♃	♀	♄	☉
7	♄	☉	☽	♂	☿	♃	♀
8	♃	♀	♄	☉	☽	♂	☿
9	♂	☿	♃	♀	♄	☉	☽
10	☉	☽	♂	☿	♃	♀	♄
11	♀	♄	☉	☽	♂	☿	♃
12	☿	♃	♀	♄	☉	☽	♂

Figure 45: Planetary hours

At birth, the lord of the planetary hour is assigned to the Ascendant and the first year (Age 0). In a general sense it's called simply "the lord of the orb," but as we will see it has a special role indicating that house, so it's also "the lord of the hour *of the Ascendant.*" So, just as we interpret the Ascendant and its lord for Age 0 in a profection, we also interpret this lord of the orb and use it to describe the native's health, life, etc. Then in each year thereafter, the lord of the next planetary hour becomes the new lord of the orb, along with the new profected lord of the year—and just like the profected lord of the year, we're supposed to look at the real-time condition of the lord of the orb at the SR. But in the way Abū Ma'shar speaks about it, the lord of the orb also seems to have a *special* meaning for that house. When we profect the Ascendant, we're always concerned mainly with the native's life—because the Ascendant means *his* life, which undergoes various things as we turn it by profection. The lord of the orb does also seem to have this general quality, but then specifically means the people and topics of the sign of the year: thus when the profection comes to the third, the lord of the orb for that year specifically denotes the condition *of the siblings*—when the profection might not always have a lot to do with them. I don't think I'm reading too much into Abū Ma'shar's description about this special quality: otherwise the lord of the orb would be just another time lord thrown onto the general heap of things to do.

Actually, one thing which does save this from being just another technique, is that the order of lords of the orb seems to change every twelve years—and this is where we have to make a decision about Abū Ma'shar's description. If we assign the first twelve hour lords to the twelve places and then stop, each lord of the hour would be permanently assigned to a particular house. That would be like profections, where we go around again with the same natal planets and configurations every twelve years. But in Ch. VI.1, **8**, Abū Ma'shar makes it absolutely clear that the order of planetary hour lords *continues on*, even though by profection we return to the same lord of the year. If so, then the lords of the orb offer some variety every twelve years. Let's look at an example.

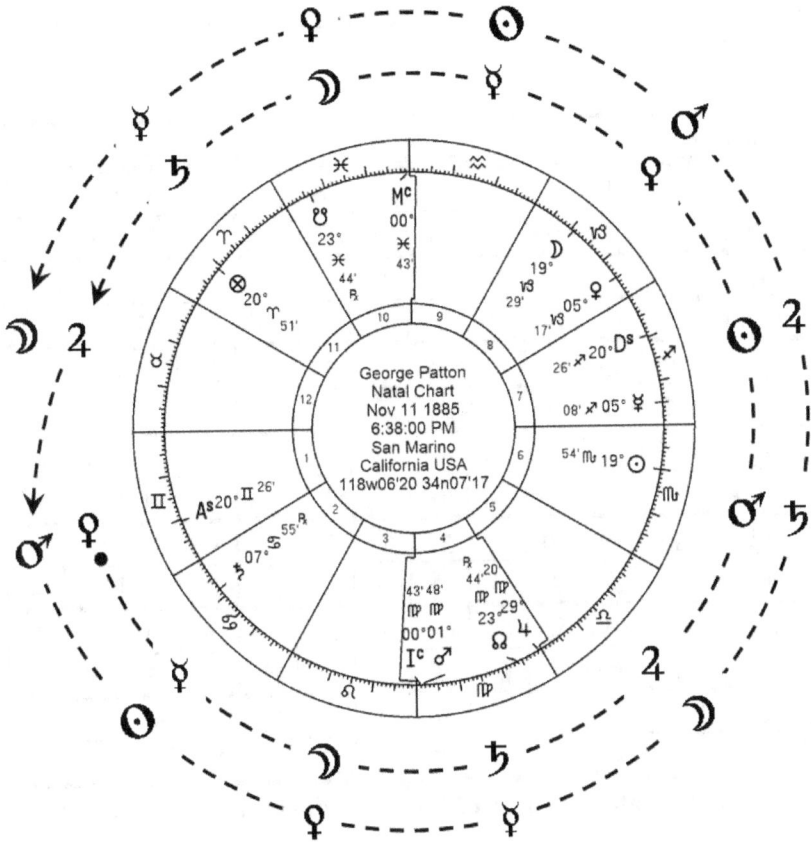

Figure 46: Lords of the orb, continuous looping (VI.1, 8)

The nativity is nocturnal, at 6:38PM on a Wednesday, which happens to be the second planetary hour of the night (i.e., after sunset). According to the table, the lord of the second nocturnal planetary hour on Wednesday is Venus. Therefore at Age 0, the lord of the year by profection will be Mercury (the lord of the Ascendant, Gemini), and the lord of the orb Venus. At Age 1 the lord of the year is the Moon, with its lord of the orb Mercury—and so on. However, once we complete a full cycle and the profection returns to Gemini, the lord of the year will be Mercury again, but the looping of planetary hour lords continues independently, so the new lord of the orb for Age 12 is

Mars, not Venus. At Age 13 the lord of the year is the Moon again, but the lord of the orb the Sun. The table below shows this:

House	1	2	3	4	5	6	7	8	9	10	11	12
Age	0	1	2	3	4	5	6	7	8	9	10	11
Hour	N	2	3	4	5	6	7	N	2	3	4	5
Age	12	13	14	15	16	17	18	19	20	21	22	23
Hour	6	7	N	2	3	4	5	6	7	N	2	3
Age	24	25	26	27	28	29	30	31	32	33	34	35
Hour	4	5	6	7	N	2	3	4	5	6	7	N
Age	36	37	38	39	40	41	42	43	44	45	46	47
Hour	2	3	4	5	6	7	N	2	3	4	5	6
Age	48	49	50	51	52	53	54	55	56	57	58	59
Hour	7	N	2	3	4	5	6	7	N	2	3	4
Age	60	61	62	63	64	65	66	67	68	69	70	71
Hour	5	6	7	N	2	3	4	5	6	7	N	2
Age	72	73	74	75	76	77	78	79	80	81	82	83
Hour	3	4	5	6	7	N	2	3	4	5	6	7

Figure 47: Table of lords of the orb (continuous loop version)

At Age 0, the profection is at the first house (the Ascendant), and the lord of the orb is the natal (N) lord of the hour. Then at Age 1 the profection moves to the second house, and the next or second lord of the hour, and so on. At Age 12 the profection returns to the first house, but the lord of the orb is the sixth hour lord. You can confirm this above in the table of planetary hours: on Wednesday evening, if you count Venus as the natal lord of the hour, the sixth lord is Mars as we stated before. Again, at Age 82 the profection will return to the eleventh house, and Mars will likewise be the lord of the orb, as Mars is always the sixth lord from Venus.

At this point we come to a special refinement which Abū Ma'shar offers in Ch. VI.1, **18-19**. In any year, just as we could track the real-time or SR condition of the lords of the natal first, tenth, and eleventh (sometimes called the "excellent" places in Arabic), so too we can track their associated lords of the orb. For instance, in the nativity above it would be normal for us to examine Mercury in every SR, because he rules the natal Ascendant and so always indicates the native. The same goes for Jupiter and Mars, which rule his natal tenth and eleventh. But Abū Ma'shar says we can track their associated lords of the orb as well. I believe he means the lords of the orb in the *first* cycle of assigned lords, corresponding to ages 9 and 10: in the nativity above, the Moon and Saturn. If so, those lords of the orb are permanently associated with those natal houses.

However, in line with his usual penchant for derived houses from the sign of the year, Abū Ma'shar says we should *also* do this with the sign of the year and the tenth and eleventh from *it*. Again, I think this means we should take the nativity as a cycle of twelve profections, and stick to whatever lords of the orb pertain to that cycle only. So, let the native be Age 14: the profected Ascendant comes to Leo, the sign of the year. By now we're in the second cycle of profections, so the lord of the orb for Age 14 and the third place is the natal hour lord (Venus). But the tenth from Leo is Taurus: its lord of the orb in the first cycle *was* Jupiter (at Age 11), but in the present, second cycle *will be* the Moon (at Age 23): which do we use? Likewise the eleventh from Leo is Gemini: its lord of the orb recently in the second cycle *was* Mars (at Age 12), but in the third cycle *will be* Saturn (at Age 24). I think we should "reset" the lords at each cycle, so once we reach Age 12, every sign gets a new lord of the orb simultaneously, and retains that lord until Age 24. Thus in our example at Age 14, the lords of the orb for these three places are Venus, Moon, Mars. When the native is Age 24, they will all reset again as shown in the next rows of the table.

Of course, all of this continuous looping and my idea of resetting cycles is based on Ch. VI.1, **8**, where Abū Ma'shar says that we should keep counting in the same order of planetary hours. Another solution to this whole issue is that we only assign a *single* set of lords of the orb, and when we reach the twelfth house we simply stop, letting those lords remain the same for the whole life. It's possible that Abū Ma'shar added this continuous looping on his own and has gotten it wrong: in that case, the planetary hour lord at birth (Venus) is *always* the lord of the orb for this native's Ascendant, and so Mercury and Venus will be the lord of the year and lord of the orb *whenever* the profection returns to it (Ages 12, 24, 36, and so on). This would also mean that whenever the profection comes to the third (Leo), the lords of the orb for its tenth and eleventh will *always* be the first set, Jupiter and Venus. In that case, our table ought to look like this:

House	Hour	Age						
1	Natal	0	12	24	36	48	60	72
2	2nd	1	13	25	37	49	61	73
3	3rd	2	14	26	38	50	62	74
4	4th	3	15	27	39	51	63	75
5	5th	4	16	28	40	52	64	76
6	6th	5	17	29	41	53	65	77
7	7th	6	18	30	42	54	66	78
8	Natal	7	19	31	43	55	67	79
9	2nd	8	20	32	44	56	68	80
10	3rd	9	21	33	45	57	69	81
11	4th	10	22	34	46	58	70	82
12	5th	11	23	35	47	59	71	83

Figure 48: Table of lords of the orb (single cycle version)

In this version, the lords of the hour are assigned to the twelve houses only once, so every time the Ascendant profects to some place, its lord of the orb will be the same one as 12 years before: this isn't possible if the lords of the hour are assigned continuously. This also allows a consistent set of lords of the orb for the sign of the year and its derived tenth and eleventh. However, it does contradict Abū Ma'shar's statement that the lords of the hour are assigned in a continuous loop (Ch. VI.1, **8**).

§14: Ninth-parts

For the most part Abū Ma'shar sticks to the classical Hellenistic system of prediction: distributions, profections, revolutions. But we have also seen him use a Persian or Indian technique, *fardārs*, and one he attributes to the Babylonians, the lord of the orb. In Books III and IX he describes another technique attributed to the Indians, "ninth-parts" (Ar. تساعير). This is not for beginners.

As Abū Ma'shar explains (III.9, **1-3**), the ninth-parts are an Indian version of both profections and distributions. While the Babylonians, Persians, and Egyptians used the bounds for distributions, this was allegedly found to be too crude: dividing a sign into ninths (and smaller subdivisions) was more precise and true.[121] Each sign is divided into nine equal portions of 3° 20', but their principle of rulership is based on triplicities, quadruplicities, and the order of signs. The first ninth-part of all signs in a particular triplicity is ruled by the lord of the convertible sign in it, and each ninth-part thereafter is ruled by the lords of each of the signs following that convertible one, in order. Let's use the airy signs as an example, because they illustrate what I see as a potential flaw. The convertible airy sign is Libra, ruled by Venus. This means that the first ninth-part of every airy sign will be ruled by Venus. Since the sign after Libra is Scorpio (ruled by Mars), Mars will rule the second ninth-part of all airy signs—and so on. You can see this visually in my diagrams and tables for Ch. III.9.

If you work out whole sequence of ninth-parts, you can see that they're nothing more than the lords of each sign, in order, beginning with Aries. This is because if we start counting out nine from any convertible sign, we will come to an end just before another convertible sign, which will start the next triplicity sequence. For example, the first ninth-part of Aries is ruled by Mars, the lord of the convertible fiery sign (Aries itself). If we assign the rest of the ninth-parts to Aries in the order of signs, the last one will be Jupiter, who rules Sagittarius.

---

[121] But as my friend and colleague Charlie Obert likes to point out, precision in calculation is not the same as accuracy in interpretation.

Now, the next sign is Taurus, an earthy sign: but the lord of *its* first ninth-part is Saturn, who rules Capricorn—which was the next sign after Sagittarius anyway.

We might think that this is simply a nice coincidence, and that there was no need to refer to the triplicities. But the ninth-parts really are tied to the triplicities, because as we subdivide them we will use the lords of the signs in each triplicity to rule them. So when we subdivide the first ninth-part of Aries (ruled by Mars) into three, each of the three subdivisions will be ruled by the lords of the fiery signs: Mars, Sun, Jupiter.

Restricting the rulership of the ninth-parts to only the lords of nine signs in order, has the unusual consequence that three planets are left out of certain triplicities. Saturn cannot rule a ninth-part in any fiery sign, because the sequence from Aries to Sagittarius ends before Capricorn. Likewise, neither the Moon nor Sun can rule a ninth-part in any of the airy signs, because the sequence from Libra to Gemini ends before Cancer and Leo. To me this seems like a flaw, as though schematizing by nine was more important to the inventors than representing all of the planets.

A more unusual feature are the profections. When the Ascendant profects to some sign, the lord of the year is the lord of the first ninth-part. But by definition that must be the lord of the convertible signs, which means that there can only be *four possible lords of the year*: Mars, Moon, Venus, Saturn. Abū Ma'shar may be misunderstanding the Indian method, but he definitely believes that's what it is.[122]

A third and even stranger feature has to do with the distributions. According to Abū Ma'shar, when the Ascendant is distributed through the ninth-parts, it cannot simply start where it is and proceed directly onwards: first it must complete *all* of the subdivisions, even if they're already past. So, let the natal Ascendant be in the middle of the first ninth-part of Aries. This ninth-part has three subdivisions, ruled by Mars, the Sun, and Jupiter. Now if the Ascendant is in the middle, somewhere in the subdivision of the Sun, we would expect that it

---

[122] See III.10, **1, 4-5**.

INTRODUCTION

could then proceed directly to Jupiter's, then leave that ninth-part and enter the next one. But no: according to Abū Ma'shar, it must then circle back and complete the Mars subdivision, as though each ninth-part is an integral whole which must be fully experienced before moving on. It seems hard to believe. On the other hand, when directing the SR Ascendant around the chart of the SR in the Indian fashion, it sounds as though Abū Ma'shar believes the Ascendant cannot begin where it is, but must start at the beginning of the sign (IX.7, **70, 72**). The normal way of doing this is in IX.7, **29-33**.

I'm not really sure how devoted Abū Ma'shar was to the ninth-parts. He suggests that he is adding them to the book to make it complete, and accepts them as excellent knowledge,[123] but they don't really fit in with anything else. He recommends that we use them in addition to normal distributions,[124] but that just seems like trying to do everything possible in case we missed something, and without any inherent way of distinguishing the two systems. Likewise he regularly adds them to the normal indicators of the native in the monthly revolutions (Book IX), but to me this seems forced and artificial.

Reading: Ninth-parts	
Definitions	III.9, **1-11**
Annual profections	III.10 (all)
Monthly profections	IX.1, **11-16, 32**
Days and hours	IX.7, **43-72**
Distributions / directions	III.9, **12-49**
In longevity calculations	IX.8, **127-28**

---

[123] See III.9, **13**.
[124] See III.9, **3**.

§15: Summary statements about timing

So far we have discussed many different predictive techniques. Here I would like to summarize some of the key ideas about timing and time-lord activation, so when we identify some topic or object in the chart we can quickly answer the question, "when will this thing happen?" I cannot vouch for every method Abū Ma'shar uses, but this is what he says.

When will a natal planet be activated?
- Generally, when that planet is a time lord (including when it manages one of the sub-periods of the year, such as a month), or some profection reaches it. *Example: natal Venus will be active when she is the lord of the year or the profection reaches her.*
- When a planet is in the same SR house, as it was in the nativity. *Example: natal Venus in the natal tenth will be active in a year when she is in the SR tenth.*
- Planets configured to the lord of the year will be active when they manage one of the sub-periods of the year, *especially if they look at the lord of the year or other key points in real time.*[125] (This might also apply to a planet looking at the distributor, such as if it was the lord of the year during the period of that distribution.) *Example: if Venus is the lord of the year and natally trines Saturn, then Saturn's trine to her will be more active if he is lord of one of the MRs or perhaps the SR, especially if he looks at her in real time.*
- When the planet plays two or more time-lord roles at the same time. *Example: if Venus is the distributor for six years, and is also the lord of the year during one of those years, the effect will be more notable at that time.*

---

[125] II.5, **75**. This is just another way of saying that natal planets are activated when they are time lords, and that they activate natal configurations. If there was a natal Venus-Saturn trine, then it stands to reason that that trine will be activated when she is the lord of the year *and* he is some other time lord.

- When that planet reaches the fortunes or infortunes (probably by transit, but perhaps by direction).[126]
- A planet's manifestation will more certain and notable when its condition in a later chart or in real time is strong (such as being angular, in a dignity, etc.).

When will an SR position or transit be active?

Just as a natal planet holds good for the whole life, an SR planet's position is supposed to hold good for the whole year. But just as the natal planet isn't always active, the SR planet isn't, either. So when will an SR position or transit be active, later in the year?

- A planetary return: right away or very soon, or else when that planet becomes a monthly time lord.
- An SR transit to a rooted planet: when they both combine by transit later on in real time. *Example: SR Venus transits natal Jupiter. The effect should be when they connect in real time later in the year.*
- An SR/MR planet or place which is harmed or benefited: when it's the time lord for a smaller sub-period, or the Moon reaches it. *Example: the lord of the SR Ascendant harmed. The harm will be more obvious when that planet rules one of the months or its sign is activated by a monthly profection.*
- An SR planet or place which is harmed (or benefited): when the monthly profection comes to its whole-sign angles.
- A planet harming (or benefiting) a place: when it rules one of the smaller sub-periods. *Example: Mars squaring the sign of the year. He will be more active when he rules an MR Ascendant or rules a monthly profection.*
- As long as a planet is in its sign, until it leaves it. *Example: SR Mars opposes and harms the sign of the year. He will harm that sign and topic until he leaves the sign and is in aversion to it.*

---

[126] III.1, **2**.

Reading: Summaries concerning timing	
Activating a natal planet	II.5, 75 III.1, 2 III.5, 4 III.6, 1 VIII.15, 21-25
An SR position or transit	V.1, 24-26 VII.2, 7-8 VIII.15, 21-22 IX.5, 84, 86, 93-94
Moon's condition	V.8, 21, 24-25
Sensitive positions to transit	V.8, 26
Ongoing transits	VIII.14, 6-7

When will the Moon indicate something?

Because the Moon is such a key planet and moves so quickly, she has lots of opportunities to manifest what she indicates in the SR or MR. This will be:

- When she reaches the square or opposition of her SR or MR position.
- When she reaches the body or rays of a planet affecting her in the SR.
- When she reaches the body (or rays?) of a planet indicating something in the root.
- We can also treat the degrees between her and some planet (or its rays) as days or months.

What sensitive positions can show timing by a transit to them?

- The degree of the distribution or distributor.
- The SR Ascendant.
- The degree of the profection (considered as a 30° increment).
- The degree of the natal or SR Moon.

Special rules about ongoing transits in the year:
- When an SR planet is in some bound or sign, and later transits through a sign or bound ruled by the same planet, it will repeat a similar theme. *Example: SR Venus in the bound of Saturn. She should trigger similar things when transiting the bound of Saturn in the other signs.*
- The lord of the year is the most important planet for tracking its transits in the bounds. (But I can attest that that is also true for other planets transiting through the whole-sign angles of the sign of the year.)

§16: Longevity

Chapter IX.8 presents some of Abū Ma'shar's rules about predicting the length of life, and has several interesting features. All of them show his own thoughtful reflection on this difficult and controversial topic. This is more suitable for intermediate and advanced students.

First there is the conversational and personal way it begins, as a response to student inquiries (**1-3**): one can see how Abū Ma'shar cautions against having too much curiosity about longevity as well as making too much out of difficult revolutions. One of his purposes is to help students tell the difference between an actually disastrous or lethal ("cutting") year, and one which is only difficult (**3**).

Second, Abū Ma'shar gives an exhaustive and creative list of all sorts of time lord combinations and primary directions which can indicate disasters and death. These include directions to fixed stars (not usually mentioned in other texts), special degrees and planets, distributions, and complicated scenarios in revolutions.

Finally, Abū Ma'shar makes his own comments on the standard methods of longevity prediction, so let me explain what they are, and his vocabulary. All of this is in **4-13** and **119-26**.

The dominant theory of longevity prediction in traditional astrology was the releaser–house-master theory: it can be found virtually everywhere from Dorotheus (1st Century AD) to Lilly (17th Century).¹²⁷ Ptolemy's version in *Tet.* III.10 is virtually the same but he notably omits the house-master. In its essence, it's simply a special application of distributions through the bounds. According to this approach, the native's life or life force is represented by a special planet or point called a longevity "releaser," which is identified by a special method. It's usually one of the luminaries, the Ascendant, Lot of Fortune, sometimes the conjunction or prevention before birth, and sometimes something else. This longevity releaser is then directed (or rather distributed) through the bounds, to determine when periods of crisis will occur.¹²⁸ A point which threatens severe problems or even death, is called a "cutter" (and sometimes, "destroyer" or "killer"), as though it cuts off the life force. A cutter is therefore a dangerous promittor in directions or partner in distributions.

But not every difficult distribution threatens death, so how can we distinguish between hardship and death? This brings us to the second major planet, the "house-master." This planet is normally one of the lords of the longevity releaser, and preferably its bound lord: note that this would make the house-master the distributor of the releaser's natal position! Abū Ma'shar calls the house-master the "indicator of the lifespan," because the house-master determines the standardly-expected length of the lifespan, called the "foundation of the lifespan" (**4-6**). It does this in several ways, including through its planetary years, its angularity, and by other planets connecting with it: these other planets either increase its years or decrease them, hence Abū Ma'shar calls them the "increasers" and "decreasers" (**5, 7**).

After identifying these planets and determining the expected lifespan, the longevity releaser is then distributed through the bounds.¹²⁹ If it encounters a difficult distribution (and especially a partnering planet) long before the house-master's lifespan, then it probably is just a difficult year. But if it encounters one right around that lifespan, and especially if there are other indications of problems

---

¹²⁷ See the table below for citations from Sahl's *Nativities* on this topic.
¹²⁸ See Ch. III.1, **3-4**, where Abū Ma'shar refers to precisely this.
¹²⁹ Some texts say that one can also distribute the house-master itself, but to me that seems like a misunderstanding.

in the SRs around that year, then it might be a "cutting" year, and the partner planet is probably a cutter indicating death (**8-9**). To this general theory, Abū Ma'shar adds the observation that the natal indications for a healthy life also matter: if the indications for the life force are already weak in the nativity, then even a normal-looking distribution might be disastrous (**10-13**). This isn't unique to Abū Ma'shar, as Māshā'allāh mentions the same thing;[130] but it's good advice and shows that traditional astrologers sought to have a nuanced approach.

In order to make this clearer, let's imagine the nativity in Figure 49. As we know, the Ascendant is always a releaser which we should distribute through the bounds: Abū Ma'shar does this throughout Book III and elsewhere. But let's assume that according to the longevity methods we have also identified it as the longevity releaser: this means that when we distribute it we're also looking for threats to life.

Now notice that our longevity releaser is in the bound of Mercury. In any normal distribu-

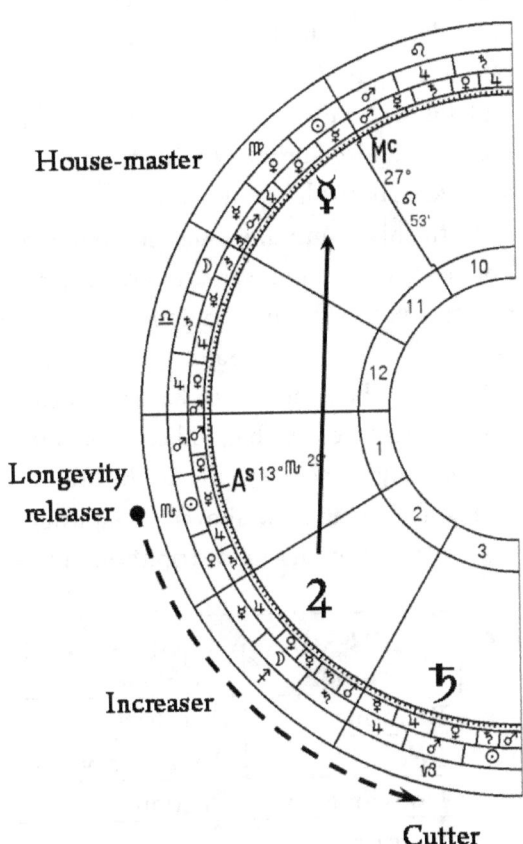

Figure 49: Longevity: releasing and cutting

---

[130] See Sahl, *Nativities* Ch. 1.23, **61-63**.

tion this makes Mercury the distributor of the Ascendant's natal position. Note also that Mercury looks closely at it by a sextile (and let us assume his ray is actually in the bound): this makes Mercury the natal distributor *and* partner of the Ascendant. In the longevity methods, this combination makes Mercury the house-master for the native's whole life.

Mercury is in a good place, advancing towards the Midheaven, in a good condition, etc.; this means that he will grant many of his possible years (don't worry about how many, this is just for illustration), so the "foundation of the lifespan" or expected longevity will be long. And because Jupiter (a fortune) is closely connecting with him, Jupiter will add some more years. In distributions this would simply benefit the meaning and quality of the distributor, but in longevity methods it adds years to the lifespan.

With this in mind, we distribute our releaser forward through the bounds. At some point the Ascendant will encounter Jupiter as a partner, as it passes through Sagittarius. But then in Capricorn, after many years, it will encounter Saturn as a partner. If we assume that Saturn is sufficiently bad, and this happens near the end of the expected lifespan, and we have bad indications in the SR and so on, then Saturn will actually be a cutter and end the life.

The following table shows the equivalencies between this standard longevity technique and distributions, followed by the key vocabulary:

Longevity technique	Distributions through bounds
Releasing	Distributing
Releaser	Point distributed
House-master	Distributor of natal position (usually)
Increaser, decreaser	Planets connecting with distributor
Cutter, killer	Partner (in directions, "promittor")

Figure 50: Comparing terms in longevity and distributions

Introduction

Vocabulary:

- **Releaser, longevity releaser** (Ar. هيلاج, from Persian). The planet or point which indicates the native's life force, and is directed or distributed to find years of crisis or death.
  - *Hyleg, hīlāj.* Latin and English transliterations of the Arabic for **releaser**.
- **House-master** (Ar. كدخداه, from Persian). Usually the bound lord of the **releaser**, indicating the expected length of life or **foundation of the lifespan**.
  - **Indicator of the lifespan** (Ar. دليل العمر). The **house-master**.
  - *Kadukhudāh, alcochoden.* Latin and English transliterations of the Arabic for **house-master**.
- **Foundation of the lifespan** (Ar. أصل العمر). The expected longevity shown by the **house-master**.
- **Increaser, decreaser** (Ar. زائد, ناقص). A planet which natally connects by body or ray to the **house-master**, and increases or decreases the **foundation of the lifespan**.
- **Cutter, killer, destroyer** (Ar. قاطع, قاتل). A planet or point which ends the life when the **releaser** meets it by distribution.

Reading: Longevity	
General comments	IX.8, **1-3**
Longevity releaser	III.3, **1-2** III.1, **3-4** *Nativities*, 1.15 – 1.16
House-master, its years	*Nativities*, 1.20
Increasers, decreasers	IX.8, **4-5** *Nativities*, 1.21
Upbringing, short lives	*Nativities*, 1.19, 1.29
Cutters, cutting	IX.8, **6-18, 120-23**

§17: Lots

In a previous section I described how the Lot of Fortune plays an important role in Abū Ma'shar's techniques, primarily by profection. Ultimately this may have been because the Lot is also one of the five natal releasers and indicators of life from which the longevity releaser is selected.[131] But I've also suggested that the Lot plays an important role in allowing the native to experience surprise or apparently random events, fresh trends, and opportunities for making decisions. The reason for this is because, since antiquity, the principle of Fortune has referred to how we find ourselves in relation to changing webs of events which confer meaningful benefit or harm: sometimes events shape up to open doors, close them, produce benefits or harm—and sometimes we find ourselves left outside of these webs of causes. Houses and planets on the Lot and its whole-sign angles, and the planet ruling it, describe life topics and themes which are subject to changing events and opportunities: they allow the unexpected, something new taking place which isn't strictly determined in the nativity.

In Ch. IX.5, **101-02**, Abū Ma'shar sums up this generic sense of benefit and harm for the Lot of Fortune, when he says that the Lot by (1) natal profection, (2) calculated in the SR, and (3) as calculated in the MR, generally shows assets, relationships with people or everyday livelihood, trade, good fortune, social prominence, praise, and so on. But throughout *PN4* he also mentions other roles that Lots play, both natally and as calculated for the revolutionary charts.

First, the lord of the year will activate the Lot which it's on or looks at (natally and in the SR). This makes normal astrological sense, since a time lord will also activate whatever else it's affecting. This also goes for any Lot which a time lord rules (natally and in the SR). For example,[132] if the lord of the year is the lord of the Lot of brothers or siblings, and the Lot is natally in a bad place, with infortunes, then something bad will happen to the brothers in that year. Now if that

---

[131] Recall that the other four are the Ascendant, the luminaries, and the pre-natal lunation.
[132] Ch. III.8, **52-54**.

time lord also affects the lord of the Ascendant, then those things won't only affect the brothers, but their affairs will spill over to affect the native.

Also, SR planets which are looking at or on natal Lots (or perhaps even SR Lots?) will affect the matters of that Lot. This is another way of saying that transits affect Lots, since the SR is in part a set of transits to the nativity. The SR transit of Jupiter to the Lot of marriage for example, is a classic indicator of marriage.[133]

To this we could add that profections to a Lot also activate it, just like they do anything else in that sign. Again, a classic example pairing this with a transit is Dorotheus, who says if the profected Ascendant comes to the Lot of marriage but transiting Saturn is *not* squaring or opposing it, then the native will marry.[134] For, the profection activates the natal Lot, but the real-time transit of Saturn lays conditions upon its success in that year.

Finally, Abū Ma'shar uses Lots as confirming devices for other time lords. Let's look at two examples. (1) Suppose the distributor of the Ascendant is Venus for some years: we already know that if she happens to be the lord of the year during that period, then her topics (like marriage) will be more manifest in that year; but it would also be so if the profection in one of those years came to a sympathetic Lot, the Lot of marriage. The first profection would activate her as a general significator of love, the second one the Lot as a web of events allowing one to meet or marry someone. (2) Similarly, because a Lot is one of the factors supporting the quality of a topic, its harm or benefit at that time will support or detract from it. So, if the lord of the year is Saturn and he is configured with Venus, this isn't normally a great indicator for love and passion. But several things could make this worse: one would be if they're in a poor condition (Saturn indicating a lack of passion, Venus ruined passion), but another would be if the Lot of marriage and its lord are in a bad condition at the time. In that case, the poor Lot and its lord would add bad luck or few opportunities to

---

[133] See for example Sahl, *Nativities* Ch. 7.4, **1**; *Carmen* II.5, **7**.
[134] See for example Sahl, *Nativities* Ch. 7.4, **1** and **4**; *Carmen* II.5, **7** and **9**.

an emotionally more sterile situation. But, if the planets and Lot were all in a good condition, it would add opportunity and events to stronger emotions.

Reading: Lots	
Fortune	IX.5, **101-02**
General rules and examples	II.4, **12-14** II.4, **21** II.5, **34** III.6, **1** III.8, **43, 52-54**

§18: Fixed stars, eclipses, comets

Abū Ma'shar occasionally refers to fixed stars, and in distinctive ways; he rarely refers to eclipses and comets.

The first way in which he discusses fixed stars is by applying the method for eminence and prosperity from natal astrology. In that method (which Sahl's *Nativities* describes in detail), we are to see if one of the thirty or so brightest fixed stars is on the natal Ascendant or Midheaven, or perhaps with the lord of the Ascendant or a luminary: if so, it's an indication of the native's prosperity and eminence (whether for good or bad reasons). In *PN4*, Abū Ma'shar applies this to the positions in SR and MR charts.

The second use of fixed stars is in the matter of longevity, in which he identifies nineteen stars, clusters, and nebulae, which can kill when the longevity releaser encounters them by distribution. (For an explanation of this, see above.) One thing I find interesting about this, is that Abū Ma'shar uses some unexpected stars: they're all from Ptolemy's *Almagest*, but I have not otherwise seen them used, or they're normally employed in delineating things like blindness and illness.

Reading: Fixed stars, eclipses, comets	
Fixed stars (prosperity, eminence)	I.6, 7 III.2, **107-08** III.8, **9-10** IX.3, 7 IX.5, **59** IX.7, 75 *Nativities* Chs. 2 – 2.2
Fixed stars (longevity)	III.2, **109** IX.8, **33-55**
Eclipses	II.23, **33** III.8, **13-14**
Comets	III.8, **11-12**

§19: Manuscripts and editorial remarks

This edition was translated from four Arabic manuscripts:[135]

- **B**: Oxford, Bodleian, Digby Or. 5. This was my primary manuscript, and had marginal notes and passages which are not found in the other MSS, suggesting that later scribes omitted this necessary material.
- **P**: Paris, BNF Ar. 2588. This is very close to **B**.
- **E**: Escurial Ar. 917. This often differed in numerous details (which did not always affect the meaning of sentences), and sometimes offered better readings.
- **T**: Tehran, Majlis 6433. This incomplete manuscript contains Chs. III.2, **31** to Ch. IX.7, **61**. I used this mainly to clarify questions in the other MSS; it is closer to **B** and **P** than to **E**;

---

[135] Another manuscript which I was not aware of until early 2019, is Leningrad (St. Petersburg), Or. Inst. B 807, as described in Sezgin p. 372. I will include it in a future second edition.

some of the same errors and alternative words are shared between **T** and **P**.

The Arabic edition now allows me to bring Abū Ma'shar's meaning more fully to light than the Latin edition did, and so I will sometimes italicize words or add quotation marks for emphasis because the text really invites it. These are my own additions because Arabic manuscripts, like Latin ones, almost never have punctuation or any way of indicating these kinds of emphases.

In this volume I make use of both square and pointed brackets:

- Square brackets [ ] either add my own section divisions to help the reader, add a clarifying word, or indicate that something is illegible or uncertain. For example, if two planets are both referred to as "him," I may write [Mars] to identify which one is meant in a particular situation. If something is illegible or unclear, I put that in italics to indicate that the problem lies in the manuscript: [*uncertain*]. So, square brackets are always *my* way of alerting or helping the reader.
- Pointed brackets < > *only* indicate words or passages which are actually omitted in the manuscripts but must be there. For example, if a sentence needs a "not," I will write <not>. If part of a sentence is missing or omitted, I write <*missing*> or <*omitted*>, again using italics to indicate that the problem is with the manuscript.

I also use boldface sentence numbers, to make it easy to find references. When I give references I will typically give the Book and Chapter number, and then the sentence: III.2, **3** refers to Book III, Chapter 2, sentence 3. When I refer to a sentence which appears in a section I'm footnoting or am already discussing I will often simply put it in boldface and parentheses: (**3**).

ON THE REVOLUTIONS OF THE YEARS OF NATIVITIES

In the name of God the Merciful, the Compassionate,
and prayer and peace be upon Muhammad and his family,
the good and the pure:

This is the book of Abū Ma'shar Ja'far b. Muhammad the astrologer,
On the Revolutions of the Years of Nativities
And it is in nine Books

BOOK I: <ON THE REVOLUTIONS OF YEARS>
In nine chapters

<Chapter I.1: Introduction>

1 Ja'far b. Muhammad, known as Abū Ma'shar, said: In general, each of those who have gone before (of the masters of the profession of the stars) has written a book on the revolution of the years of nativities (and their months and days), but some of them mentioned things others did not, and we have not found a book by any of them which elaborates on everything which [pertains to] this subject; indeed, I see their deficiency in it as being due to two sources. **2** One of them is that some are incapable of knowing what is needed for the science of it,[1] and the second is that in their writing they do not apply the philosophical distinctions which are necessary in a book [like] this.[2]

3 But we have composed this book of ours based on a deep inquiry into what is needed in it, in terms of reporting the indications of the higher bodies, as to what affects people in the revolution of the years of their nativities (of the good and the bad, benefit and harm, illness

---

[1] Or more simply, "incapable of understanding what knowledge of it is necessary."
[2] See also IX.5, **104-06**.

and health, and afflictions both easy [and] surmountable as well as difficult, decisive, and ruinous), from the years of their lifespans and the rest of their conditions (the apparent and powerful as well as the internal and hidden): and we have assigned the indication for each of the topics to an individual Book, and there are nine Books and ninety-six chapters.

4 The First Book is in nine chapters:[3] [I.2] on the knowledge of the revolution of the years of nativities, and [I.3] our proving of them, and [I.4] responding to one who disagrees with that, and [I.5] what benefit there is in the knowledge of the revolutions of years and [I.7] the knowledge of the planets' conditions in them, and [I.6] the work of the image of revolutions, and [I.8] the knowledge of the Ages of Man, and [I.9] what knowledge is needed first by the astrologer before passing judgment on revolutions.

5 The Second Book is in twenty-three chapters: [II.1] on the number of indicators of the year, and [II.2] the indicators of the soul and indicators of the body, and [II.3] the knowledge of the sign of the terminal point, and [II.4-II.22] the knowledge of the lord of the year and its indication, and the indication of the rest of the planets over things when they look at [the lords of the year] and they're in a suitable condition or in a bad condition, and the indication of the place of the lord of the year in the houses of the circle in the revolution of the year, and [II.23] the indication of the Ascendant of the revolution as well as its lord, and their partnering in the indication with the terminal point and the lord of the year, and with other things besides them.

6 The Third Book is in ten chapters: [III.1] on the knowledge of directing, distribution, the distributor, and the one partnering with it in the management, and [III.2] the indication of the fortunes and infortunes as distributors, and those partnering with them in the indication, in the management of the distribution by body or by rays, and the shifting over of one of them to another, and [III.3-III.7] the indication of the seven planets if one of them was the distributor or

---

[3] The first chapter is the present one; I have added numbers in brackets throughout for the rest.

one of them partnered with it in the management, and [III.8] the partnership of the lord of the year, the distributor, and the Ascendant in the indication, and [III.9] what the people of India say about the direction of the ninth-parts and their distribution, and the lord of each of their divisions, and its indication for good or bad, and [III.10] the knowledge of the lord of the year [according to the Indians].

7 The Fourth Book is in seven chapters, on the indication of the *fardārs* of the seven planets, the Head, and the Tail.

8 The Fifth Book is in eight chapters, on the indication of the transit of the planets in the revolutions of years over their own rooted position, or the transit of one of them over the [rooted] position of another.

9 The Sixth Book is in six chapters: on [VI.1] the indication of the lord of the orb, and [VI.2] on the turning[4] of the houses of the root and the direction of the degrees, and [VI.3] on the indication of the sign of the terminal point or the Ascendant of the revolution, if one of them coincided with one of the houses of the root, and [VI.5] on the indication of the seven planets and the Head and Tail if they were in a house in <the root, but in another one in>[5] the revolution of the year, and [VI.4] on the indication of the year terminating at a sign in which there was a planet in the root, or its rooted position was the Ascendant of the year, and [VI.6] the indication of the connection of the lords of the houses with each other, or their separation from each other.

10 The Seventh Book is in nine chapters, on the indication of the shifting of the planets, Head, and Tail, in the houses of the circle, house-by-house, throughout the whole year.

11 The Eighth Book is in fifteen chapters: on [VIII.1-VIII.7] the indication of the planets upon their alighting in their own houses or in the houses of another, or [VIII.8-VIII.14] in their own bounds or the bounds of another, and [VIII.15] their indication if they were in the wells or in the rest of the positions of the circle.

---

[4] That is, profection.
[5] Adding based on the topic and title of that chapter.

12 The Ninth Book is in nine chapters: on [IX.1-2, IX.5] the indicators of the months, and [IX.3] the work of the images of their revolutions, and [IX.4] the conditions of the planets and their houses relative to the four indicators, and the conditions of the four indicators relative to them, <and [IX.6] the indication of the planets for lasting things and change>,[6] and [IX.7] the knowledge of the indicators of the days and hours, and the indication of each of these indicators individually, and [IX.8] the knowledge of the "cutting" year, and [IX.9] the special indicators in the indication of the conditions of the year.

13 And even though we have mentioned these things in it according to this division, and all of the knowledge in it is easy to express from an external point of view, we know that when using [it] and judging the conditions of people in the revolutions of years, much of it is far from the understanding of many people of this profession, and the application of it is obscure to them, as well as distinguishing one thing from another. **14** So, afterwards we will write a book in which there are examples of revolutions of the years of nativities, with images, and in it we will establish, with explanations, everything which is doubtful to them or which is believed to be far from their understanding.[7]

Chapter I.2: On the knowledge of the revolution of the years of nativities

1 If the Sun was in some place of the circle in the root of the nativity, and then moved along in all of the signs until he came back to his position in which he was at the root, then he will have traversed 360° in 365 days (and a fraction), and a solar year will have been concluded for the nativity. **2** And at the beginning of his traveling in his rooted

---

[6] Adding the missing chapter from IX.6.
[7] Abū Ma'shar did indeed write a *Book of Examples* on the revolutions of years (Sezgin p. 149, #27), and according to Sezgin it is excerpted in al-Nāsirī, who wrote an astrological compilation in 1358 AD. I do not currently have a copy of al- al-Nāsirī, but see Sezgin p. 25. It is also (allegedly) partly excerpted or summarized in Majlis 6452 (ff. 69b-71b) and 6485 (ff. 84b-87b), but there are no chart examples.

position [after that], it is the revolution of the second year: so when he has traversed the twelve signs in his travel and has returned to his position another time, then his second year will have been completed. **3** And when he has begun the motion from his rooted place [again], then the third year for the native will be revolved, so when through his travel he has reached his rooted position again, then the third year will have been completed; and likewise [for] each of the native's solar years.

4 And at the revolution of every year, one ought to derive its Ascendant and calculate[8] the twelve houses of the circle according to it, and understand the positions of the planets for that time: because even if the Ascendant of the root of the nativity was some sign and degree, and its planets at that time in some position, in the second year the Ascendant will be another sign, and its planets in another position than what they were in at the root of the nativity—and in the third year it will be likewise, in terms of the difference of the degree of the Ascendant and the positions of the planets.

5 And the beginning of the year in which the native is born, has[9] the indication of each of the indicators according to the condition of the sign in which it is; then from that, the indication of every year terminates at the sign which follows it, a sign for every year, until the end of his lifespan:[10] so the indicator of the year of birth is the sign of the Ascendant, and the indicator of the second year is the second sign from it, and the indicator of the third year is the third sign from it, and the fourth year is the fourth sign from it—and the termination of the year of each of the indicators at one of the signs will be in this manner. **6** And since the terminal sign of the indicators, the Ascendant of the revolution, and the positions of the planets, will be different in every year from the next year, for that [reason] the conditions of people's years will differ.

---

[8] يسوّي.
[9] Reading more naturally for "is."
[10] Abū Ma'shar is hinting at the annual profection of multiple significators, not just the Ascendant.

Chapter I.3: On responding to those rejecting the year of the Sun, & our proving of it, & its months & days

1 Now, people have disputed what the ancients have stated about the year of the Sun, and they said, "Why did they make the year be from the motion of the Sun relative to one of the positions of the circle and his return to it, but they didn't make it be from his reaching the opposition of his place, or other positions in the circle?" **2** And they have also said, "If the year is twelve months, then why did they make the year of the nativity be from the *Sun's* traversing the twelve *signs*, and they didn't make it be from the Moon's reaching the position which *she* was in at the root of the nativity, twelve times—since every time the Moon reaches it, it is a month?"[11]

3 So our response to them in what they dispute concerning the year of the Sun, is that there are four seasons in a single year (and they are the spring, summer, fall, and winter): so when these seasons are completed, the year is completed, and the time[12] returns to the condition it was in at the beginning; but if one subtracted anything from any of the seasons, the year would not be completed and the time would not return to a likeness of the original condition. **4** And indeed, the completion of these seasons comes to be through the course of the Sun in the twelve signs: because if he was in some position in the circle and then traveled in it until he came back to it, then the four seasons of the year would have cycled around us. **5** (But if he fell short of reaching the position which he was in by any [amount], the seasons of the year would *not* cycle around us entirely, and it would be less than that in accordance with his falling short of that position.) **6** And if he began traveling from that [original] place for a second time, the condition of the time would return to a likeness of what it was the first time. **7** But for the Moon we do not find this activity in the completion of the sea-

---

[11] In other words, in a calendar that uses lunar months, or cultures that observe lunar months, why isn't the year equivalent to twelve lunar returns rather than twelve solar months?

[12] الزَّمان. Interestingly, this word can also mean "destiny" or "fortune." Abū Ma'shar may have intended this ambiguity, because he could have used another word.

sons of the year (nor for the other planets): so for this reason they made the year of the native be from the start of the Sun's motion from his place in which he was at the root of the nativity, to his return to it, and [so] the four seasons (which are spring, summer, fall, and winter) become the portions of the year, and the months of nativities come to be from the transit of the Sun in the signs, a month for every sign.

8 And our response to them in what they dispute concerning the months is also that [1] since the parts of a single solar year are the four seasons, and [2] the year has a beginning and an end, and [3] each one of these seasons which are its parts [also] has a beginning and end, and [4] everything which has a beginning and end has a middle, therefore every one of these four seasons has three conditions (a beginning, middle, and end), so that a single year has twelve parts, each part being called a month.[13] **9** And in each of the years the Sun traverses 360°: so when he traverses these degrees according to the parts of the year—and there are twelve parts—each part gets 30°, and that is the amount of a "month of the Sun"; and each of their degrees makes up a single one of the parts of the month of the Sun. **10** So now we will say that when the Sun begins [his] course from any of the positions of the circle, so that he travels 2' 30", that is one of the "hours" of a day of the Sun.[14] **11** And when he travels a complete degree of the equal degrees,[15] that is one of the "days" of the Sun. **12** And when he travels 30 equal degrees, that is one of the "months" of the year of the Sun. **13** And when he traverses 360°, that is a complete year of the Sun—except that some of the hours, days, and months of the Sun are at variance with other hours, days, and months,[16] due to the variation of his course in the degrees and signs.

---

[13] By this criterion, the year itself ought to be divided into thirds, but never mind.

[14] Here Abū Ma'shar continues to apply our words for time analogously to the Sun's motion in the signs. He is aware that the Sun does not always move 2' 30" in one of *our* clock hours, as he points out in **13**. But just as 1 clock day has 24 hours, so 1° in the zodiac has 24 units of 2' 30" apiece: an "hour" of a day *of the Sun*.

[15] That is, zodiacal degrees.

[16] That is, in the way that *we* measure them by calendars and clocks.

Chapter I.4: On what is invoked by people in invalidating the years of nativities, & what our response to them is

1 Now,[17] those people who disagree with the masters of the science of the stars claim that one does not need a revolution of the years of nativities, and they advance two arguments regarding that.

[Objections #1 and #2: Whether revolutions have no significance, or a weaker one]

2 One of them is that they say *nativities* are what indicate the conditions of the people, and not the meaning of the revolutions of years.[18]

3 The second argument is that they say, "Astrologers claim that the indication of the root of the nativity is 'stronger' than the indication of the revolution of the year—but if one of the planets of the root of the nativity had indicated by its condition that something detestable would affect some man in some year, and then that year was revolved for him, and that planet did *not* indicate the occurrence of that detestable thing by its condition [in the revolution], then would [the detestable thing] be made null? **4** Now if [the astrologers] said yes,

---

[17] This is a very interesting chapter. Up to the part about the *zījes* (**23-31**) it can be seen as responses not to skeptics, but to other astrologers who *do not use real time*. The first two objections (**2-4**) are from people who only use symbolic timing and time lords, so they see no need to add real time in the form of a solar revolution (or maybe even transits). The third objection (**18-19**) has to do with primary directions, which are indeed based on real diurnal motion, but are only calculated for a few hours after birth: after that, the timing system is symbolic (a year per equatorial degree). In that case we would have an astrologer who only applies time at the nativity, so again sees no need to use revolutions. In his response to this third objection (**20-22**), Abū Ma'shar is in agreement with Morin (or rather, Morin agrees with Abū Ma'shar) that even with a primary direction, we need a revolutionary chart to see how well the direction is able to manifest the natal indication *at that time* (*Astrologia Gallica* XXIII Ch. 12).

[18] That is, that revolutions are totally irrelevant. The next argument (**3-4**) tries to show that even if revolutions were *weaker* than nativities, they would still be irrelevant. The main problem with the objections is that they are expressed in extreme, all-or-nothing language, while at the same time they admit that the astrologers are only claiming one chart is "stronger," a comparative concept.

BOOK I: ON THE REVOLUTIONS OF YEARS　　　　　153

then they have already destroyed their own statement that the indication of the root of the nativity is stronger than the indication of the revolution of the year; but if they said no, then [the indication of a revolution] is useless."

[Responses to Objections #1-2]

5 We will tell them what the need for the revolution of the years of nativities is, and in responding to their statement we will object with three arguments.

6 The first of them is that we say one does not draw conclusions about the essence of the matter from a single condition of the planets, but the indication for it is made sound through the knowledge of two or more of its conditions: so whenever a planet indicates through its condition in the root of the nativity that something would come to be in one of the years, we do need knowledge of its condition in that year [itself], so that we know the essence of its indication of that matter from [all of] its conditions.

7 And the second argument is that if a planet in the root of the nativity indicates that something good or bad will come to be for [one] year or more, one does not [necessarily] know the *magnitude* of that thing from the root of the nativity, nor its particular *manner* [of coming about] in detail, since of course it may be a great good, a middling good, or a small good (and the bad is [also] like this). **8** But we *will* know the abundance (or scarcity) of what the planet indicates for every one of them, as well as its increase and decrease, if we do measure its condition in the revolution of the year in which it had indicated it would come to be through its condition in the root. **9** So, if the planet had an indication for good in that year like it did in the root, that good will be great; and if its condition in the revolution of the year was contrary to what we stated, the good will be below that. **10** For it does not happen that [1] a planet in the root indicates (by one of its conditions) that the native will obtain good in one of the years, but [2] if it was that year and it does not indicate the benefit of [that] good, that [3] he will not obtain that kind of good *at all*: rather, it indicates that a *lesser* good will affect him. **11** Because the indication of the revolution does not nullify the indication of the root, but manifests it and brings it to light: so that from the difference between its condition in the root and in the revolution, one knows the essence of its indication of that thing, in terms of strength and weakness, and abundance and scarcity. **12** And if it were not for the difference between the planets' conditions in each time, we would not need to have knowledge of their conditions in the revolutions of years: because through the difference of their conditions in the revolutions of years relative to their condition in the root, is known their indication in strength or weakness, or abundance and scarcity.

13 And[19] the third argument is that the planets have an indication for what has passed away (of the condition of a man), as well as what [currently] exists of it, and what is coming to be. **14** Now as for [a planet's] indication of what [currently] exists in that time, that is known from the condition of the planet at the time of that very same indication. **15** But as for its indication of what was or will be, one understands what is possible to understand about the condition of that thing by mixing its condition at the time of the indication,[20] with each of the two [other] indications individually: then the judgment will be according to that. **16** So because of that, they said if one of the planets in the root of the nativity indicated the coming-to-be of something in a past or future time, we should look at its condition in these two times, then compare its condition in each of those two times with its rooted condition, and then by its condition we should draw conclusions about that thing which it had indicated in the past or future time—except that its indication over things which will come to be in future years inherently [pertains] to the time in which it is rendered into action. **17** Therefore, one certainly does need the revolutions of years for the knowledge of people's conditions.

---

[19] For this response, as well as the footnote to **22** below, see my Introduction.
[20] That is, the nativity. But this could also apply to an election chart, where the conditions of the planets *at* the election also promise something for the future.

BOOK I: ON THE REVOLUTIONS OF YEARS

[Objection #3: Primary directions make revolutions unnecessary]

18 Now [some other] people from among the masters of the stars also rejected the revolutions of years, and in that they have advanced two arguments. **19** One of them is that they say one ought to direct [only] the rooted indicators, so that the year in which they reach the fortunes or infortunes will indicate good or evil in accordance with their condition in the root, but not the meaning in the revolution of the year.

20 But in this way they have already erred in their rejection of the revolution of years, and they have not rejected it except due to their inability to mix the indication of the condition of the planets of the root, with the indication of the condition of the planets of the revolution, and [because of] its difficulty for them. **21** Because if the rooted indicators were directed so that they reached one of the indicators having an indication over something in one of the years, then one ought to know their condition in the root along with their condition in the year in which their direction has reached that indicator: then one mixes those conditions so one may know the essence of its indication in that year. **22** And if you didn't know their condition in the root and you do not know their condition in that year, knowledge of their indication with precision would not be possible: so there is no escaping the knowledge of the condition of the planets in the revolution of the year along with their condition in the root, and the mixture of the indication of one of the conditions with the other, just as we have stated in what preceded.[21]

---

[21] This is not an excellent argument, because the objector has simply refused to admit that future planetary conditions are relevant. Abū Ma'shar might have said the following: (1) The condition of the planets at birth is precisely their condition *at that time*, and only refers indirectly, and in a general way, to what will happen in the future time they point to. (2) But at that future time, the real conditions in the world will be different in many details that are relevant to the event's manifestation. (3) And those details are exactly what we would expect to find in the chart of a solar revolution (for the year as a whole) and through things like transits during time of

[Objection #4: That different tables make revolutions inaccurate]

23 And the second argument is that they say the work in the revolutions of years should be according to the sign of the terminal point and the direction of the indicators: but [that] as for the Ascendants of the revolution,[22] it isn't possible to make a judgment about them, because they will not be correct. **24** For if the nativity was calculated for the man with one of the *zījes*, but then you worked out the revolution of the year with another *zīj* of a different type, there would be a discrepancy between them in the degree of the Ascendant, and perhaps they would [even] differ in the sign, and also in the day. **25** And if the sign of the Ascendant of the revolution, and its degree, and [even] its day, did not match the *zījes* of a different type, one could not rely on its truth for a [particular known] thing, and one would have measured these things with a corrupted measurement [so that] they would be far from the path of truth in it.[23]

26 But[24] everyone who rejects the Ascendant of the revolution and claims that it does not comport with the truth, has already rejected his own recognition of the beginning of the coming year, and is already ignorant of the end of the outgoing year (in any of the years), because the last season of the outgoing year connects with the first season of the coming year. **27** And if a man was ignorant of the beginning of the year as well as its end, then he would be ignorant of its entirety due to his ignorance of when the year begins, and how many years have come upon the native, and at which sign the year terminates,[25] and the rest of what goes along with that, of that sort of thing; and this is the height of ignorance and being blind to any understanding. **28** For the beginning

---

the manifestation. (4) Therefore we do need to mix the natal promise with the conditions shown in a future chart.

[22] Abū Ma'shar is probably thinking of all of the monthly revolutions as well.

[23] This is an indication that astrologers sometimes used different (and incompatible) *zījes* for different purposes, as we know Abū Ma'shar did with mundane and natal revolutions (see **31** below). Obviously, if you cast a nativity with one set of tables, and revolutions with another, you will not get the beginning of the year right.

[24] Reading more naturally for "because."

[25] That is, by profection.

BOOK I: ON THE REVOLUTIONS OF YEARS 157

of the year *is* known, and it is the returning of the Sun to his rooted place: and if the beginning of the year is known in this way, then its day, hour, and portion of the hour *are* known; and if that is known, then the sign of the Ascendant is known to its very degree.[26]

29 Now there is indeed a discrepancy between the *zījes*, in the degree of the Ascendant of the revolution, and in its sign or its day, because the circuit of the Sun in each of the *zījes* is different from his circuit in the others (such as the *Sindhind* [being different] from Ptolemy, and the *Shahriyār* with both of them,[27] and likewise the rest of them), so that due to the discrepancy among them in his circuit there occurs a discrepancy in his mean [position] and his equation,[28] and in the Ascendants of the revolutions of [the Sun's] years, and their degrees—and perhaps they will differ in the day as well. **30** But the way of good sense in the discovery of the day of the revolution, and the sign of the Ascendant and its true degree, is that one calculates the Ascendant of the revolution of years using the mean Sun and his circuit as set down in the *zīj* which one used for the root of the nativity, so that its sign, degree, day, and the Ascendant of the revolution of years will be sound, the knowledge of which is needed for judging it. **31** And the most correct of the circuits of the Sun for the work of nativities, and the Ascendants of the revolutions of their years, is the circuit

---

[26] The argument here is really in favor of using some *zīj* for everything, and being consistent. Of course if one *intentionally* uses incompatible tables, it makes no sense to complain about the differences between them!

[27] The *Sindhind* was a *zīj* made from one of the Sanskrit Siddhāntas (perhaps by Brahmagupta), translated in Baghdad in the last third of the 700s: it exerted great influence on later *zījes*. The reference to Ptolemy is to the *Almagest*. The *Shahriyār*, also known as the *Zīj al-Shāh*, was a Sasanian Persian *zīj* that was translated into Arabic in the late 700s. See Kennedy 1956 for a nice survey.

[28] In traditional geocentric astronomy, an equation (Ar. تعديل) is a correction found in a special table, which one applies to the approximate or "mean" position of a planet, in order to get the "true" position.

which is taken with the instruments that Ptolemy mentioned in the book *The Almagest*, and it is 365 ¼ days, minus 1/300 of a day.[29]

Chapter I.5: On the excellence of knowing the conditions from the revolution of the years of nativities

1 As for the excellence of knowing the conditions of people from the revolution of their years, it is evident: because all of the nations of the Babylonians, the people of Persia, India, and the Egyptians, both their kings and the common people, did not make a start in anything in any year, unless they first looked at the revolution of the years of their nativities. **2** For if its condition in that matter was indicative of a suitable condition in it, they did it—and if not, they avoided it.

3 Now as for the kings, they used to look for the revolution of a year benefiting those wanting to head out to war: so if they saw strength over their enemies in it, they did it; and if not, they left off it. **4** And if they saw, in the revolution of the years of those managing their wars and affairs[30] (and their messengers), effectiveness in the works which they directed them towards, they would direct them [to do it] and put them in charge over those things, so long as the planets were indicative of their advancement in it. **5** But if in any of their years they saw weakness and inability for them in the indications of the planets, they would substitute for them people whose revolutions of years did indicate carrying out what they directed them to do.

6 And if the kings wanted to get involved in any affairs, and in the revolutions of their years they saw that that type of thing would not be suitable for them in that year, they would not get involved in it. **7** And they as well as the common people used to look for things which [their] revolution of the year indicated would be suitable for them—of medical treatments, eating, drinking, entertainment, sexual inter-

---

[29] That makes 365.24667 days (or 365d 5h 55m 12s), the tropical year as measured by Hipparchus and continued by Ptolemy in the *Almagest* III.1, p. 139. The tropical year is currently measured at 365.24219 (365d 5h 48m 45s).

[30] **P** reads, "assets."

course, buying and selling, and the rest of their whims—so that they would do them and put them into operation, and they would avoid what the revolutions indicated harm for them in, in those years.

8 And certainly they used to draw conclusions about some matters by means of the revolution of their own years and the years of others, like a man seeking a child from a woman in some year: for if he saw in the revolution of his own year as well as her year, that she would become pregnant and bear a child from him, he would seek that from her. **9** But if not, he would approach someone else, whose revolution of *her* year indicated that she would give birth.

10 So, the knowledge of these matters and what is like them in revolutions, indicates their excellence and benefit.

Chapter I.6: On making the image of the revolution of the year: what is drawn in it

1 If you wanted to fully work out an image of the revolution of the year, along with what is in it, then make the image be circular or square, and divide it into twelve divisions in the widespread manner which is done in the hands of [current] people.

2 Then, know the Ascendant of the year by its degree and minute, and write it down in one of those houses, then after that write down the twelve signs in succession, a sign in every house, calculating the houses by their degrees and minutes, in the way that you calculate the houses by the portions of hours and the ascensions of the right circle.[31]

3 And in [those houses] write down the planets of the revolution of the year, with their conditions in rising and falling,[32] and retrogradation, and the rest of what goes along with that, and their rays and twelfth-parts, and the twelfth-parts of the degrees of the houses: and

---

[31] Or, "right ascensions." In other words, the twelve quadrant-based cusps.

[32] الصّعود والهبوط. This probably means either their motion in zodiacal latitude, or their positions in their astronomical circles (which can show speed in addition to judging which planet is stronger in transits).

write down the Lots in [the houses], and the Head of the Dragon and its Tail, so that all of them are in the signs in which they are at the revolution of the year.

4 Then after that, write down in them the planets of the root of the nativity, with their conditions and rays and twelfth-parts, and the twelfth-parts of the signs, and the Lots and Head and Tail, in their positions in the signs which they were in at the root of the nativity.

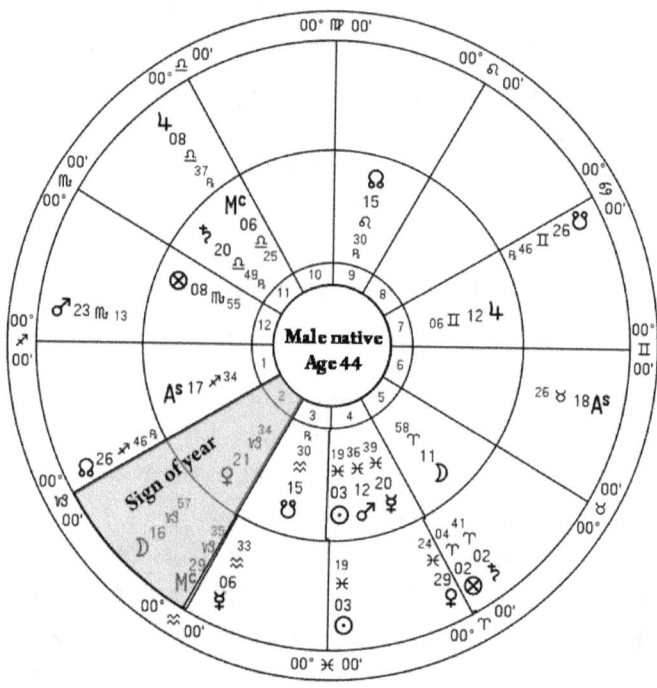

Figure 51: Simplified Abū Ma'shar revolution (Ch. I.6), with natal positions in outer circle[33]

5 Then, write down in them the position of the Ascendant of the root, and the position of the terminal point of the year [which was

---

[33] In this image I have followed Abū Ma'shar in putting the revolution in the inner wheel, and the natal positions in the outer wheel—in the rest of the book I will put the nativity in the center. The native is 44 years old, so the profected natal Ascendant comes from Taurus to the natal ninth, Capricorn, which I have shaded in grey. I have also used whole-sign houses to make the image easier to understand.

profected] from it as well as from the Lot of Fortune of the root, and from the rest of the indicators, all of them in their signs in which that year terminates.

6 Then, write down in them the positions of the endpoint[34] of the distribution, the distributor and the one partnering with it in the management, and the lord of the *fardār*, and the one dividing [its *fardār*] with it, and the lord of the orb, each of them in their signs and bounds which they are in.

7 And if,[35] in the root of the nativity, one of the fixed stars was in the very degree of the Ascendant, or in the very degree of the stake of the Midheaven, or with one of the luminaries, or with one of the seven planets which are in the stakes, then write it down in them.

8 And once you have done that, then there will be gathered together for you in the image of the revolution of the year, 14 planets, and the Head and the Tail (each of them in two places), and the rays of the planets of the root of the nativity and the revolution of the year in 98 places, and the twelfth-parts of the degrees of the houses, the planets of the revolution of the year, and the root of the nativity, in 38 places, and the Lots according to how you do it ([using] many or few). **9** But if in one of the houses you wanted to write down something of the planets, and there are several of them in it, then you ought to start with the one that is first in degrees, then after that you write down the one which follows it in degrees, until you have the planet in the most degrees as the last of them. **10** Then you look at the rays, Lots, and twelfth-parts, and you do it with them like that, until you finish with everything in the twelve houses, in this manner.

---

[34] That is, the very degree which the distribution had reached. Reading for "terminal point" (انتهاءه), which is the usual term for profections.

[35] This fixed star method is one of the "eminence" methods in nativities (see Sahl, *Nativities* Ch. 2.2). It deals with about 30 of the brightest fixed stars. Later (III.8, **9-10**) he will include such stars doing this in the revolutionary chart.

11 And if you did that, then you have properly made the image of the revolution of the year, along with what is in it, completely and fully.[36]

Significators	Root	SR	Total
Planets	7	7	14
Planets' rays	49	49	98
Head	1	1	2
Tail	1	1	2
			116
Twelfth-parts of houses	12	12	24
Twelfth-parts of planets	7	7	14
			38
Lots	(*varies*)	(*varies*)	(*varies*)
			154

Figure 52: Abū Ma'shar's 154 preferred points in a revolutionary chart (Ch. I.6)

Chapter I.7: On the Ascendant of the year, & knowing the conditions of the planets at the revolution

1 If you made the image of the revolution of the year, then understand:

2 Its Ascendant, which house it is in the root (of the houses of the circle, which are the stakes and what follows them).[37]

---

[36] **P** now continues this sentence with comments that seem to be by Abū Ma'shar, but they are written a bit oddly and repetitively (so they may be by another astrologer). The gist of it is that some of the ancient opinions are correct, and some are in error. One of the errors seems to be using the lords of the pre-revolutionary lunation or its bounds; another has to do with looking at planets that have much testimony and are in a good position in addition to the Ascendants of the quarters and months, but I do not understand it. The passage concludes by telling the reader to simply do everything in the way we are taught here.

Book I: On the Revolutions of Years

3 And who was in it in the root and the revolution (of the planets and the rays, and the Lots and the twelfth parts).

4 And who of them is looking at it, in both of the times.

5 And who is making a claim on it,[38] and where they are relative to it, and in which position each one of them is: either in a position in which it has a share, or in the contrary of that (being in exile).

6 And does it have one house or two—for if it has two houses, does it look at one of them or at both, and where is it relative to its house and where are its two houses relative to it; and if it has one house, then does it look at it or not, and where is it relative to its house, and where is its house relative to it.

7 And[39] the ones direct [in motion], and retrograde.

8 And the strong ones, and the weak.

9 And those rising and falling in their direction, and in which condition it is (of strength or weakness, and rising and falling).

10 And the falling away of some from looking at others.[40]

11 Or the assembling of some with others, or one of them looking at another.[41]

---

[37] This probably means not only its house (second, third, fourth, etc.), but its dynamic angularity.

[38] That it, who has a dignity there: this would especially be a victor among the various lords, but the rest of the sentence suggests that one should look at all of them.

[39] At this point Abū Ma'shar transitions from just looking at the revolutionary Ascendant and its lord, to all of the planets. But of course it is still very relevant which of the planets in, looking at, or ruling the revolutionary Ascendant are in these conditions.

[40] That is, being in aversion to each other.

[41] This is by whole-sign.

12 And the hurling of their rays from the seven directions.[42]

13 And their connection and separation.

14 And the reception of one by another.

15 And those of them supporting their associate or corrupting them.

16 And those hostile to them and friendly towards them, and those harmonizing with others or being contrary to them, and those of them combining with their associate apart from that.[43]

17 And those of them in their own domain or not in their domain (of the diurnal [planets] and the nocturnal ones).

18 And likewise their twelfth-parts.

19 And the arrival of each one of them in the revolution, at their own rooted position[44] or at the positions of other planets.

20 And their course in the twelve signs.

21 And their transiting the planets of the root of the nativity, as well as the planets of the revolution of the year, and the revolution of the months (and their rays and twelfth-parts).

22 And all of the Lots[45] of the year.

23 And their condition relative to the stakes of the circle.

---

[42] This is by degree-based aspects or connections.

[43] This last part might refer to how their qualities combine in conjunctions, such as a hot planet with a hot planet.

[44] Otherwise known as a planetary "return."

[45] The text actually says "*their* Lots." This could actually refer to the seven Hermetic Lots, each of which is correlated with one of the seven planets. See the worked example in Ch. III.1. But since Abū Ma'shar and others also want us to calculate things like the Lot of marriage in the revolution, we should not limit it to those seven.

24 And their position relative to the Sun (such as being eastern, western, in the heart, and burned or under the rays, and one which has already gone out from his rays and is in its own glow), and the rest of the conditions which are added to the planets based on their nearness to him or distance from him.

25 So, you ought to look into these conditions (both the excellent ones and the bad ones) for each planet, in both the root and the revolution. **26** For sometimes a planet in the root is in some position, in some condition, and inspecting a position or one of the planets (whether friendly or hostile to it), while its place, condition, and aspect in the revolution of the year is contrary to that: then its indication will be according to its place and condition in the two times together—the root and the revolution.[46]

Chapter I.8: On the knowledge of the indicators of the Ages of Man

1 In the revolutions of the years of nativities you ought to begin by knowing the age level which the native is at (of childhood, youth, maturity, old age, and senility): because each one of the seven planets has an indication whose nature is rooted in one of the periods of his lifespan, and his condition in the revolutions of years does not proceed by any other [means].[47] **2** And that is like a boy who, due to the delicacy of his character, and his weakness and ignorance, if the management of one of the planets offered sexual intercourse, and children, and a desire to collect assets and real estate, and travels, and pursuing difficult works, or one of the affairs which one like him would not be able to do—his condition at that age would not be like the condition of a youth having strength, toughness, reason, and proper management

---

[46] See some brief statements about this in Ch. I.4, **7-11**. Abū Ma'shar will elaborate on this throughout the book.
[47] Cf. the classic account in *Tet.* IV.10 (Robbins pp. 441-47).

[ability] for the things he pursues. **3** Or, it is like a decrepit, weak old man if the management of one of [the planets] offered children or something which someone like him would need the condition of youth for: a child will not be born to him, nor would it promote that situation, nor many things according to this condition. **4** So because of that, you ought to know the age of the native so that the judgment will be in accord with it.[48]

5 And [some] people have rejected that, saying "surely we do see children and small youths marrying, and they have rank, authority, slaves, riding animals, and they travel in their youth, and sometimes they inherit assets having value, and own real estate, and many things which are like that!"

6 Well, we say: "These things (and what is like them) are done *for* him by one of those who take care of him, like the parents or others besides them; and that is prepared for him when the management of one of the planets indicating what we mentioned offers it, without that being according to his own will, choice, and acquisition."[49] **7** And the meaning of our statement is that he does not obtain any of that through his own management, choice, action, and motivation, nor will he have sex, nor will a child be born to him, nor will he pursue difficult works with his own hands, and nothing will be prepared for him which resembles this, because at that age he is too weak for that situation [and] is ignorant of it. **8** But when he is in one of the [appropriate] periods of his lifespan, in the nature of one of the planets' ages, it enables the activity of that thing which is in the indication of its nature.

9 And indeed their indication for the ages of a man is according to the ordering of their circles (from the lower to the higher), and the ancients made the number of years of each planet in this subject be of two types: one of them according to the amount of its lesser years, and the other according to the number of one-half or one-tenth of its lesser

---

[48] See Ch. I.9 for more on this.
[49] See a similar comment in Ch. IV.4, **4-11** (esp. **10-11**).

or middle years, along with the correspondence of any of them with the number of the four elements.[50]

10 Now as for the first four years of his lifespan, which are called the years of upbringing,[51] they are managed by the Moon, who is the closest of the planets to us: because what is found to belong to the body of a child is of a moist nature, weakness, tenderness, and little food, and a poor character, and ignorance of things, and the soul's refraining from work, stratagems, thinking, and opinion, and the quickness of the upbringing, and much susceptibility to[52] natural changes—indicating that the Moon is the one in charge of the native's management for four years, from the beginning of birth. **11** And indeed they made this be the number of the years of upbringing in accordance with the four elements, which are the foundations of bodies, for each element a year; and it is made clear to us that these years are the completion of the years of upbringing, because if the native reaches this age, he shifts from the conditions which we stated above, into another one.[53]

12 And some of the ancients said the reason why the Moon is the indicator of the upbringing, when her middle years are 39 ½,[54] [is that] we take one-tenth of it, and that is approximately 4—so it becomes the years of upbringing. **13** And they took one-tenth due to its relationship with 4,[55] and because it is the middle of the numbers for those years: for if one had taken one-tenth of her *lesser* years,[56] that would have been 2 ½ years, and the native does not find a shift at that time from the condition of childhood and weakness; and if they had

---

[50] Lit., the four "natures."
[51] Or, "nourishment" (التَّرْبِيّة).
[52] Lit., "acceptance of."
[53] According to this logic, children should be ready to begin basic education after age 4.
[54] This is the amount which Abū Ma'shar reports, while others sometimes say 66 ½.
[55] I.e., the four years which Abū Ma'shar says were independently gotten by other means, in **10-11**.
[56] The Moon's lesser years are 25.

taken one-tenth of her *greater* years,[57] that would have been close to 11 years, and before that time he would already have shifted from its condition: therefore the years of upbringing are 4.

14 Then after that he will be in the second age, in the indication of the nature of Mercury, for 10 years (and it is one-half of his lesser years);[58] and it makes clear to us that this management is the number of these years, due to what is found at the end of[59] this time (of the years of a man's lifespan), of his transfer from condition to condition.[60] **15** And the knowledge that it is in the nature of Mercury is because his circle follows the circle of the Moon in height, as well as due to what is found in the nature of a man at that age, of cleverness, thinking, discrimination, and beginning in the study of knowledge and natural social graces, and an acceptance of those; and the end of this age is the conclusion of childhood.

16 Then after that he will be in the third age, in the indication of the nature of Venus, for 8 years, in accordance with her own lesser years. **17** The beginning of this age is the beginning of youth, and indeed the knowledge that it is in her nature is because her circle follows the circle of Mercury in height, and due to what is found in the nature of a man at that time, of the beginning of the stirrings of passion, puberty, seeking sexual intercourse and the occasions for it, and impulses in that, and little abstention from it.

---

[57] The Moon's greater years are 108.

[58] Omitting here a puzzling statement (which reads differently between **P** on the one hand, and **B** and **E** on the other). It speaks of an "average" or "half" (النصف) of two numbers he assigns or which are assigned to him, with **B** and **E** describing them as "the first" of the amounts and "the greatest" of them, while **P** speaks of the "first half/average of the numbers" and "the least of them." Now, it is true that Mercury's middle years (48) are the average between his lesser years (20) and his greater years (76), and this statement may represent a comment to that effect which has been garbled by scribes; but it has nothing to do with 10 years being one-half of 20. Ptolemy does not make anything like this comment in *Tet.* IV.10.

[59] **E** omits "at the end of."

[60] This period ends at age 14, which is the end of a basic formal and social education: see the next sentence.

18 Then after that he will be in the fourth age, in the indication of the nature of the Sun, for 19 years, in accordance with his own lesser years. **19** And indeed the knowledge that it is in [the Sun's] nature is because his circle follows the circle of Venus in height, and due to what is found in the nature of a man at that time, of the love of reputation and nobility, seeking elevation, and shifting from the child's condition of amusement, and leaving games behind, and a restriction in pleasures and behaving like a child. **20** And just as the Sun is in the middle of the superior and inferior planets, this period of the years of the native becomes a turning point[61] between being younger and maturity; and the end of this age is the completion of youth.

Planet	Years	Ages	Period of life
☽	4	0-3	Upbringing
☿	10	4-13	End of childhood
♀	8	14-21	Beginning of youth
☉	19	22-40	End of youth
♂	15	41-55	Beginning of maturity
♃	12	56-67	Maturity, transition to old age
♄	30	68-97	Old age

Figure 53: The Ages of Man (I.8, 10-26)

21 Then after that he will be in the fifth age, in the indication of the nature of Mars, for 15 years, and it is the amount of his lesser years. **22** And the beginning of this age is the beginning of maturity, and the knowledge that it is in [Mars's] nature is because his circle follows the circle of the Sun in height, and due to what is found in the nature of a man at that time, of the forcefulness of his eagerness for earthly things, and thinking about them, and an abundance of labor and trouble, and the planting of worry,[62] the mastering of fears, and the abatement of much of the amusements and forcefulness of youth.

---

[61] الفصل.

[62] Reading with Ptolemy's phrasing for, "and planting, and worry."

23 Then after that he will be in the sixth age, in the indication of the nature of Jupiter, for 12 years. **24** And the knowledge of that is because his circle follows the circle of Mars in height, and because it enters the age which is the time of old age, and abstaining from much labor, seeking, eagerness, and leaving behind the mastering of fears in the search for worldly things, and his worry and thoughts will be about the merits of moral qualities, and powers (and rejecting a desire[63] for them), and he will meditate on the life to come,[64] and good works.

25 Then after that he will be in the seventh age, in the indication of the nature of Saturn, until the end of his lifespan. **26** And the knowledge of that is because his circle follows the circle of Jupiter in height, and due to what is found in a man at that time, of the nature of old age, turning away[65] from life, the disappearance of strength, the coldness of the body, being deprived of energy, the idleness[66] of thought, weakness of the soul, the abatement of the strength of [his] nature, the expiration of his hope, a scarcity of desires (and their corruption), and an abundance of ailments.

27 And in each one of these seven ages which we have mentioned, the indication of that planet's nature will be according to what its condition <had indicated> in the root, as well as at the time when it took over management of that age. **28** So if it was in a suitable condition in both of the times, it indicates the utmost of suitability in the subject of its indication in that age, while if it was corrupted in them it indicates an excess of corruption in it. **29** And if they differed, so that its condition in the root was contrary to its condition in the year[67] it takes over the management of that age, the condition of suitability or corruption will be below what we stated. **30** And if a man did not reach the time of old age (so as to complete all of the ages of the planets), his death will be in the age of the planet which he did reach.

---

[63] Reading with the sense of Ptolemy, as a version of the verb شىأ, for an uncertain Arabic word that might be related to "evening."
[64] Or perhaps, "retirement" (المعاد).
[65] تولّى.
[66] Lit., "idle chatter" (غلبة).
[67] E: "at the age."

31 Now as for [some] people, they said that a man will be in the seventh age (in the management of Saturn) for 30 years: so if he did go beyond that he will return to the management of the Moon, to the condition of weakness, moisture, and little eating, and refraining from many excitements, then after that to Mercury, then to the rest of the planets, each planet according to the number of its years in the manner we stated before. **32** But [they said] if he did return to the indication of the nature of the Moon and the rest of the planets, his condition at that time would not be like his original condition (in terms of drinking milk, and breastfeeding, and the rest of the conditions), because in the original condition he would take on (from the strengths of the planets) the nature which partook of the age of childhood and youth, and advancing and increasing strength. **33** But when [the planet] gets the management the second time, he will be decreasing in strength, too weak in body to take on that strength, so that one who is strong in each one of them will take on the contrary of the original thing.[68]

34 And there were also people who used to look at the native so that when he reached one of the ages of any of the planets, they divided the years of that planet among the seven planets, and judged his conditions in that age according to [those planets'] conditions, in the way they do it with the years of the *fardārs*.[69] **35** But it is not like that, because the years of the *fardār* of each planet are derived with regard to [how] all of the planets cooperate together with it in that topic, and their order is in accordance with the succession of their exaltations in the signs.[70] **36** But as for these years, they are in accordance with the harmonizing of each planet's nature with the nature of the Ages of man, in the succession of their circles; and the years of their ages are

---

[68] I believe Abū Ma'shar is saying that such an old person could be overwhelmed and distressed by the experience, if the time lords at the relevant periods were stronger than his old age would allow him to enjoy.

[69] For example, let the years of the Sun be 19. If we divide these into seven, then the first period will be Sun-Sun, then Sun-Venus, Sun-Mercury, and so on. See Book IV.

[70] That may be true in Abū Ma'shar's mundane *fardārs*, but it is not true for the natal ones. The series is still in accordance with the "Chaldean" order of the planets.

derived from the condition of each one of them in itself.[71] **37** So because of that, if a native was in the indication of the nature of any of the planets, at some age of his lifespan, his years are not divided among the seven planets, but he will be in the nature of the planet itself, for the amount of those years.

Chapter I.9: On the knowledge of what is necessary for the astrologer, concerning the condition of the owner of the revolution

1 When[72] judging a revolution of the years of nativities, it is necessary that the knowledge of four things be presented to us beforehand: the first is [1] that we know in which age the owner of the revolution is, of the ages of the planets; second is [2] of what class he is, of the classes of people; the third is [3] the conditions which are possible to judge for one like him; and the fourth is [4] that we first have knowledge of many matters of his affairs.

2 Now as for the knowledge of [1] the first thing, it is that we know what year [of life] the native has come to at the revolution of his year: because if we know that, then it will be evident to us which age of the planets he is in.[73] **3** And that is necessary because many of those who are deprived of success in one of the sciences do not want people to think they are incapable of excellence in that knowledge, so they leave it out intentionally due to [their] incorrectness in it, and[74] ridicule it among the people so as to move ahead to their own incorrect fancies and gain the upper hand, and involve the sciences in errors with many

---

[71] Abū Ma'shar might mean that each planet's age here is closely tied to the natural development of the human (as he has emphasized above), and those developmental states do not have natural subdivisions, like the age of the Sun having a natural experience corresponding to Sun-Sun, Sun-Venus, and so on. Most time lord systems are gotten via schematic permutations, running through lists of combinations of planets and/or signs, like monthly profections that subdivide the zodiac.

[72] Much of this chapter is an expansion of ideas in *Tet.* IV.10 (Robbins pp. 439-43).

[73] This was discussed in Ch. I.8 above.

[74] Reading this clause a little more smoothly and naturally than the original.

things from them: so they will revolve the year of a small child and a decrepit man too weak to act, and then offer it to the astrologers to judge his conditions, without informing them what age he has reached. **4** So if [the astrologers] used one of the conditions (of the planetary indications) to judge something in that year which its owner is incapable of doing, they would make a mistake in it:[75] and [the skeptics] make that the reason for slandering the science of judgments. **5** So because of that, it is good that we know what year the native has reached at the time of the revolution, and in which of the ages of the planets he is, so that the judgment for him may be in accordance with that.

6 And as for [2] the second thing, it is that we ought to know beforehand that people have four classes: kings lasting in good fortune, those who are [directly] below them,[76] the middle [class], and the lower [class]. **7** And that is needed because many of those who are hostile to the sciences, and the people [among] them who are ignorant by nature, want [to create] confusion in the sciences: so they offer a revolution of the year of a king to the astrologers, so that it may be judged, but without informing them of the condition of its owner. **8** So when the astrologer does not know which of the classes of people he is in, and he sees good fortune and victory over enemies in the revolution of his year, he cannot[77] inform them of the essence of what that indication is, and that will invite them to slander this science. **9** Because if a king had an indicator in his year which was in a suitable condition, strong, it indicates his victory over one of the kings who are his enemies, and his capturing of fortifications, cities, and climes, and his hoarding of treasures—but if it belonged to another one of the people, it indicates his victory over one of *his* enemies and his connecting with kings, and his elevation over [the other] people of *his*

---

[75] See I.8, **2-8**.
[76] That is, the nobility.
[77] Reading for "will not."

own class.⁷⁸ **10** So because of that, the astrologer needs to have knowledge of the classes of people in the revolution of years.

11 And as for [3] the third thing, it is that you know the conditions which are able to come to be for that man, because the indications of the planets through their own natures are according to what is in this world: and if they are lasting, then individuals of their nature which are *able* to take on that indication, are acted upon by them.⁷⁹ **12** So if an astrologer saw, in the revolution of the year of a eunuch, one of the indicators of children, in a condition indicating the production of children, it would not be possible for him to judge the production of children for him, for at the time of the eunuch's birth the planets would already have indicated the uselessness of procreation for him: for how would it be possible for him to have children in any of the years, if the planets of the root had already indicated that he would not have the ability in him to take on that indication?⁸⁰

13 And likewise a child: if one of the indicators in the revolution of the year reached a position indicating something like the production of children, one would not judge that for him, for two reasons. **14** One of them is if the root of his nativity makes it pointless because he is in a planetary age which does not indicate the production of children in its time.⁸¹ **15** And the second is that his *nature* in his condition does not take that on from the indications of the planets—and thus everything of the conditions of people which is like this.⁸²

---

⁷⁸ In other words, in both cases it would show success for the native, but in a way appropriate to his class: the normal native will not do what kings can, but he might be able to associate with them. See III.4, **1-3** and III.5, **1-3** for examples of this in practice. For another general statement, see III.8, **11-12**.

⁷⁹ This category concerns the physical inability to embody the planets' significations, rather than age level or social rules.

⁸⁰ In other words, it's not the eunuch's age or class that prevents children (as above), but his physical condition, which ideally should be seen in the nativity (but even if not, it is necessary to know it). See **32** below, where he implies that "even if" these details can be gotten from the chart, it's best just to ask.

⁸¹ This refers to the first type of knowledge (**2-5**).

⁸² Again, like the eunuch it is not just his status or age (which might involve only social hindrances), but his physical inability to embody the indications.

16 And likewise if an astrologer had seen, in the revolution of the year of a dead man, the positions of the planets in a condition indicating various things of the good or bad, it would not be possible to judge a single thing of that for him, because [a corpse] will not take that on from their indications.[83]

17 And so of course in all of this, one ought to state that "the planets indicate such-and-such for so-and-so, *if* it is in the nature of that man at that time to be able to take on that indication from that planet." **18** But if in his nature he is not able to take it on from [the planet], then one should not say that it indicates that thing for *him*, but that "the planet has a general indication for the nature of such-and-such." **19** And indeed if the nature of this man was able to be in a condition like this and [at] this time, being receptive of this indication from it, then it *would* be such-and-such.

20 And as for [4] the fourth thing, it is that we should know beforehand many things of the situation of the owner of the revolution, so that our judgment for him will be in accord with what happens to him: because for one who does not have assets, if the indicators in the revolution of one of his years indicate the benefit of assets, then let it be said that he will *earn* assets; but if he [already] had assets, let it be said that he will *increase* in his assets. **21** And for one whose parents are both alive and he does not have brothers, but the indicators indicate their production, then let it be judged that he will *have* brothers; but if he had brothers [already], then let an *increase* in them be judged for him; and likewise the judgment of real estate, authority, and the rest of what is like that. **22** But as for one whose parents have already died, and some of the indicators were in a condition indicating something like their death in the revolution of the year, or that he would have a [new] brother, then one should not judge a single one of [those things]. **23** And for one who does not have brothers, one should not judge the death of his brothers, and for one who does not have villages or crops or assets, one should not judge the destruction of his villages

---

[83] But see **33** below, where a dead man's solar revolution might continue to give information about living relatives.

nor the corruption of his crops, nor the ruin of his assets—nor the suitability of anything of those; and likewise what resembles this type [of thing].[84]

24 Now[85] as for people of the ancients who used to judge similarly in these matters, they said if the indicators judged the death of the parents for the owner of the revolution, or the destruction of their assets, or the birth of a brother, and his parents are not alive, nor do they have assets, then that death will be among the "elderly people of his house"; or it will be [a birth] of someone "like his brothers," and it will destroy the wealth of someone with him who is "like [the parents], in a condition like theirs," and he will benefit from one who is of [a similar] status. **25** And for one whose root of the nativity indicated he would not have children at all, but the planets in the revolution of his year were in a condition indicating children, then he will *adopt*[86] a child and make him be *like* a son. **26** And for one who did not have villages nor crops, and the revolution of his years did not indicate that he would acquire them [personally], and yet it indicates a suitability of condition (or corruption) in them, then that will come to pass with the aid of someone else. **27** And for one whose revolution of the year indicated that he would marry, perhaps in that year it will prepare for him sexual intercourse with a woman [but] without marriage. **28** And for someone whose year indicated the companionship of kings and the benefit of wealth from them, perhaps that will be from the leaders of the people and their nobles[87]—and they used to do likewise with what

---

[84] This is a nice reminder that astrology is not psychism, and does not answer all possible questions from a single chart. Sometimes we have to ask the client questions, just as a good lawyer should talk to clients instead of just reading documents, and a doctor ought to speak to patients instead of just reading medical charts.

[85] In the previous paragraph (**22-23**), Abū Ma'shar wanted to *avoid* making predictions for people who are not in the right situation. But in this paragraph we see that ancient people wanted to preserve the predictions by saying they will involve *similar* people and situations. So they might say, "you may not have a natural child, but you might adopt one" (**25**).

[86] **P**: "rear, bring up."

[87] That is, from socially elevated people relative to the native's status, but not an actual king.

resembles these matters. **29** And perhaps the judgment about these things they have said, and what resembles it, will be correct.

30 And of the things which ought to come first in the astrologer's knowledge, it is also that he know whether the revolution belongs to a woman or a man: for if that belongs to a man, the path in the judgment will be according to what we have stated in this book of ours; but if the revolution belonged to a woman, the judgment for her will be according to what resembles the nature of women, of the management of a household, and the servants of the men, and the conditions which resemble [women]. **31** But if the woman was of those managing cities and pursuing various works and professions, the judgment for her will be according to that.[88]

32 And these things, and what is like them, are what ought to come first in the knowledge of the astrologer concerning the condition of the owner of the revolution, before judging the revolution of the year: because even if nativities had indicated these conditions, deriving the knowledge of [the conditions] in them at the revolution of every year takes a long time and is very difficult.[89]

33 And of course one knows from the revolution of the year of a man, even if he has already died, [that] the condition belongs to his child alone, because his relationship to him is established in life; and after death it is just like [how], from the revolution of the year of a native who has come out from the belly of his mother alive, one knows the condition of his parents so long as they are alive, as well as the time of their death, even if the native is already dead.[90]

---

[88] For a similar statement by Sahl, see his *Nativities* Ch. 1.4, **2-3**.

[89] This is especially since Abū Ma'shar has suggested it was the practice to simply show up at the astrologer with a chart already cast, wanting a quick answer.

[90] In other words, because the native has a natural and permanent relationship with parents and children, his solar revolutions will continue to indicate things for those relatives, even after his death: and this includes years in which we see that his charts indicate *their* deaths (I suppose Abū Ma'shar also includes things like profections and directions here). But once those relatives die—whether during the native's life or after—they cease to be relevant to the chart. We can also imagine that (1) the information about those surviving people will become less relevant over time be-

Native's SRs while still alive	Native's SRs after his death
The native's living parents and children, including SRs which indicate their death in a particular year.	
All other things pertaining to the living native	No other things pertaining to the dead native

Figure 54: How a native's revolutions continue to indicate living relatives (I.9, 33)

cause they do still have their own independent charts and lives, and (2) spouses are not included here, because their relationship to the native begins during life, and ends by divorce or death. Remember too that some authors claim the nativity gives information about the native's burial and reputation after death, but that is not what Abū Ma'shar is referring to here.

BOOK II: ON THE LORD OF THE YEAR

And it is in twenty-three chapters

Chapter II.1: On the number of indicators of the year

1 A single year is divided into months, days, and hours, and each one of what we have stated has a number of indicators.[1] **2** And through the difference of their own conditions the planets indicate different conditions for a man in each year, and among them are what they indicate through their condition at the revolution about the suitability or badness of the *whole year's* condition: and it is a "complete" indication. **3** But among them is [also] what their indication is for [the year] in a way more specifically than that: and it is what they indicate in any of the [other] times of the year through the rest of their conditions and positions at the time of their transits in the twelve signs, in terms of increasing in that good and bad, and decreasing from it. **4** And among them [also] is what they indicate at the revolution of the months and days, and they are [only] "particular:" and that is because they are *parts* of the year.[2] **5** So, let us now state the indicators of the year, and there are 19:[3]

6 The first is the sign of the terminal point, and its lord.[4]

7 The second is the distribution and the distributor.[5]

8 The third is the one partnering with [the distributor].[6]

---

[1] For a list of these and chapter references, see IX.1, **5-7**.
[2] See IX.3, **1-3** for a similar statement. Abū Ma'shar seems to mean that the revolution stands as a complete but *general* statement about the whole year, since it also stands specifically for the first month: after that, we look at the ongoing transits and monthly revolutions.
[3] Note the absence of the Indian ninth-parts in this list.
[4] See all of Book II; III.8; VI.2, **21-26**; VI.3-VI.4.
[5] See Book III; VI.2.
[6] See Book III; VI.2.

9 The fourth is the planet which has the *fardār*, and the one partnering with it in the division [of its periods].[7]

10 The fifth is the lord of the orb.[8]

11 The sixth is the Ascendant of the revolution of the year, and its lord.[9]

12 The seventh is the Moon and the planets she connects with so long as she is in her own sign; and if she were empty in course, then [use] the lord of her house.[10]

13 The eighth is the transit of the planets over their rooted positions, and the transit of one of them over another.[11]

14 The ninth is the indication of the lord of the year, insofar as[12] in the revolution it was in one of the twelve houses.[13]

15 The tenth is the positions of the planets relative to their own houses, and the positions of their houses relative to them.[14]

16 The eleventh is the turning of the planets and the twelve houses.[15]

17 The twelfth is the coinciding of the sign of the terminal point or the Ascendant of the revolution, with one of the houses of the rooted circle, [and a planet is in it in the revolution].[16]

---

[7] See Book IV.
[8] See VI.1.
[9] See II.23, III.8, VI.3-VI.4.
[10] See II.22.
[11] See Book V.
[12] Reading more in the sense as إذ أنّ, for إذا ("if, when"), since every planet is always in one of the houses.
[13] See II.6, II.9, II.12, II.15, II.18, II.21.
[14] This may refer to IX.4, but see also VI.6, **1-2**.
[15] See VI.2.
[16] Adding the bracketed material because Abū Ma'shar is clearly referring to VI.3.

18 The thirteenth is the coinciding of the sign of the terminal point or the Ascendant of the revolution, with the positions of the planets of the root.[17]

19 The fourteenth is a planet which was in one of the houses in the root of the nativity, and in the revolution it comes to be in another house.[18]

20 The fifteenth is the indication of the connection of the lords of the houses with each other.[19]

21 The sixteenth is the indication of each planet at the time of its shifting in the houses of the circle throughout the whole year, or its transits of them (so long as it is in one of the signs), in the bounds of the planets, and their rooted and revolutionary bodies, rays, twelfth-parts, and Lots.[20]

22 The seventeenth is the indication of the connection of the planets with each other, when they come to be in one of the signs throughout the whole year.[21]

23 The eighteenth is the indication of each planet when it comes to be in its own house or the house of another, or in its own bound or the bound of another.[22]

24 The nineteenth is the indication of the Head and Tail.[23]

25 So these are the indicators of the revolution of the years of nativities, and each one in turn is stronger in indication than the one which is after it: so one ought to compose their indications in this order, trea-

---

[17] See VI.4. That is, if those Ascendants are "on" a natal planet.
[18] See VI.5.
[19] See VI.6.
[20] See generally Books V, VI, and VIII.
[21] This probably refers to Ch. VI.6, and Book VII generally.
[22] See VIII.1-VIII.14 (Abū Ma'shar probably intends to include VIII.15 as well).
[23] This may refer to VII.9.

tise after treatise. **26** But in some places we have given priority to some of them over others in accordance with what seems better for their ordering, and the arrangement of the discussion, and the connection of the meanings of one of them with another.

27 And each one of these indicators has a special indication over something which differs from that of others, though sometimes a number of these indications come together in a single one of the planets, so one ought to investigate that. **28** (And we have certainly discovered that when we examine some of these indicators in detail up to the end of the year, their indication combines with that of the indicators of the months days, and hours.)

29 But when most of the masters of the stars wanted to examine the revolution of the years of nativities by its months, days, and hours, they used to apply[24] only these indicators which indicate the conditions of the *whole* year, to the months, days, and hours, without consulting any others along with them. **30** So, oversights and error used to occur in their judgments about the revolutions of months (and what follows upon that), because the conditions of these indicators differ in the [various] times of the year, and there was no detailed examination of their indication for it. **31** The manner of the investigation in it *should* be that you look at [1] the Ascendant of a month, and its planets and rays, and its twelfth-parts and Lots according to their conditions, and combine these indicators with those you have applied to[25] [2] the beginning of the year and [3] the root of the nativity: because the positions of [1] the planets of the revolution of the months[26] (and their conditions), will differ from [3] the positions of the planets of the root of the nativity, as well as [2] the positions of the planets of the revolution of the year (and their conditions).[27] **32** So in this way each month will come to have individual indicators from its own Ascendant and planets which are consulted for information, and by means of those other indicators [it will be informative] for the con-

---

[24] سيّروا...إلى.
[25] See footnote above.
[26] **P**: "year."
[27] For three summary ways of doing this, see Ch. IX.5, **107-26**.

ditions of the months, days, and hours. **33** For if a single man had [only] a single indicator, then his motivations and conditions would be [only] according to that indicator; but every man at every time has several indicators, in different conditions: so because of that, his conditions at each time period will be different.[28]

Chapter II.2: On the knowledge of the indicators of the soul, the body, & the rest of the conditions, in the revolutions of years

1 Among the indicators which we made clear in the chapter which was before this, are those which indicate [1] the condition of the soul, and those which indicate [2] the condition of the body, and those which indicate [3] the rest of a man's conditions, of his impulses and exploits, in every one of the times.[29] **2** So the first thing we ought to look at for him in the revolution of the year, is the indicators which show the condition of the soul, the body, and their harmony.[30] **3** For when they indicate a blending, harmony, and survival, look after that at the rest of the man's conditions for that whole year; and if they do not, then the examination in it should be [only] for the time which indicates his survival.

4 Now as for those indicators which indicate [2] the condition of the body, there are five:

5 The first is the sign of the terminal point.

6 The second is the bound which the distribution has reached, from the Ascendant.

7 The third is the bound which the distribution has reached, from the [longevity] releaser.

---

[28] An extensive treatment of monthly revolutions is in Book IX.
[29] In Ch. IX.5, **99-100** Abū Ma'shar will give an alternative list based solely on his detailed method for annual and monthly revolution charts and profections.
[30] Or more literally, "congruity," but that is not natural English.

8 The fourth is the Moon.

9 The fifth is the Ascendant of the revolution of the year.

10 And there are eight things which indicate [1] the soul:[31]

11 The first is the lord of the year.

12 The second is the distributor of the Ascendant.

13 The third is the distributor of the [longevity] releaser.

14 The fourth is the one partnering with them both, by body and ray.

15 The fifth is the lord of the *fardār*.

16 The sixth is the lord of the orb.

17 The seventh is the one accepting the connection of the Moon, or the lord of her house <if she were empty in course>.[32]

18 The eighth is the lord of the Ascendant of the revolution of the year.

19 And what indicates their harmony and duration, is the existence of the indicators of the soul and the body (all or most of them) in the suitable places of the houses of the circle, and their safety from the infortunes.

20 Now as for [3] the rest of the indicators, they indicate the impulses and exploits: but if in one of the times one of them [happens

---

[31] Abū Ma'shar does not mean anything particularly deep about "soul" here, but rather the mind and emotions generally (as distinct from the body). In Ch. IX.9, **1-9**, these are the indicators for his basic annual template, without any distinction as to body or soul.

[32] Adding with the parallel statement in II.1, **12.**

to] indicate something of the topic of the soul and body, then that indication is not rooted.[33]

21 And the indicators which we have stated as indicating the harmony of the soul and body, do certainly have indications for the rest of the conditions as well, except that they have a special indication for the soul and body which other indicators do not.[34]

Chapter II.3: On the knowledge of the sign of the terminal point, & the lord of the year, & their indications for matters

1 In the revolution of years you ought to look at the Ascendant of the root, and for every year the native has completed, cast out one sign from it: the sign which the intended year reaches is the "sign of the terminal point," and its lord is the "lord of the year" (and in Persian it is called the *sālkhudhāh*).

[Analyzing the sign of the year: in the nativity]

2 So you ought to examine this sign in the root of the nativity, [and see]: [1] in which of the houses of the circle it is (which are the stakes or what follows them, or those falling from them),[35] and [2] whose house, exaltation, and triplicity it is in (of the fortunes or infortunes), and [3] which of the planets is in it in the root,[36] as well as the Lots and twelfth-parts, and [4] who had been inspecting it or casting its rays at it from the seven directions, and [5] from which sign and degree they were looking at it or casting their rays at it (of the signs

---

[33] That is, it only pertains to that year, because it does not *intrinsically* denote the soul or body.

[34] For example, the Moon always indicates the topic of whatever house Cancer occupies, but in herself she specifically indicates the body.

[35] Specifically discussed by house topic in VI.3.

[36] Specifically discussed in VI.4.

helpful to it, or undermining it, or befriending it or hostile to it,[37] or from the signs great in the length of day or shorter [in it], or matching in ascensions or matching in the belt),[38] and [are they] in the glowing degrees or the contrary of that),[39] and [6] are they[40] fortunes or infortunes, and [7] to what bound, face, ninth-part, and degree (of the bright or dark degrees)[41] they cast their rays, and [8] [if] perhaps the sign of the terminal point in the root was falling away from[42] the view of the planets and the casting of their rays to it.

[Analyzing the sign of the year: in the revolution]

3 Then you should look in the revolution of the year, [to see]: [1] if one of the planets of the revolution (or its rays or twelfth-parts) is in the sign of the terminal point,[43] or [2] whether any of them is looking at it, or [3] whether it is devoid of their alighting in or looking at it in the revolution, and [4] whether one or all of them is looking at it, and [5] from what direction their aspect is, and [6] where those planets were in the root, and where they are in the revolution,[44] and [7] how their condition is in the root and how their condition is in the revolution. 4 (And the condition of each one of them, and especially the condition of the lord of the year, is known in the way we stated it in Chapter I.7 of this book of ours.)

---

[37] See *Gr. Intr.* VI.4. These are the signs configured to it by sextile, trine, square, and opposition.
[38] See IX.2, **32-34**.
[39] These are probably the degrees called "smoky," "bright," etc., from *Gr. Intr.* V.20 (see *ITA* VII.7).
[40] That is, the ones looking at the sign of the terminal point.
[41] Again, probably from *Gr. Intr.* V.20 (see *ITA* VII.7).
[42] That is, "in aversion to."
[43] This is specifically discussed in VI.3.
[44] This is specifically discussed in VI.5.

[Analyzing the lord of the year by condition]

5 Now if the sign of the terminal point[45] was [1] safe from the harmful infortunes (both those rooted and revolutionary), and its lord is direct in course (in both the root and the revolution), in its own domain[46] (of the condition of day or night), in its own glow, in a sign in which it has a claim, and it is strong, in a suitable condition in itself and in relation to the aspect of the planets and their rays, and with respect to their twelfth-parts, in an excellent place from the Ascendant of the root (as well as [from] the sign of the terminal point and the Ascendant of the revolution), then that is an indicator of the safety of the body for the owner of the revolution of the year, and the goodness of his soul, and his delighting in the things which the lord of the year indicates (as well as the planets supporting it in the root of the nativity and the revolution): such as assets, class and rank, the acquisition of property, the production of children, the ownership of slaves or an increase in them, or delighting in women—in accordance with their natures and houses.

6 But if the lord of the year was [2] of a suitable condition in the root just as we stated, and in the revolution it was contrary to that (in terms of retrogradation, burning, being under the rays, or exile, and westernization from[47] the Sun, or the assembly of the infortunes or their inspection, or its being in the contrary of its domain,[48] or the rest of what is like that), then it indicates weakness in that year, and a decrease in everything we stated, in accordance with what the combination of planets [would indicate][49] (of an abundance of beneficial conditions or their scarcity).

---

[45] And its lord, as we will see: Abū Ma'shar now runs through his customary permutations of being good or bad in the root and the revolution.

[46] حيّز. This should probably be understood as "sect," so that it is simply of the sect of the chart.

[47] B reads, "or nearness to," which would be redundant. For the superiors, this would mean going under the rays, which is probably what Abū Ma'shar intends.

[48] Again, this should probably be understood as "sect."

[49] Reading more naturally for, "in accordance with what the planets *combine*."

7 Now if the lord of the year was in [3] a bad condition in the root, and in the revolution it was in an excellent condition, it indicates that his condition will improve somewhat in that year, and it will revive things for him in it, which he will delight in: because the indication of the lord of the year is very powerful for the conditions of the year.

8 And if the lord of the year was in [4] a bad condition in both the root and the revolution, it indicates an excess of adversity in the category of what it indicates.

Comparing natal and SR conditions of lord of the year	
Comparison	Basic meaning
Good in root, good in SR	Safety, good, and delight in what it indicates
Good in root, bad in SR	Weakness and decrease in what it indicates
Bad in root, good in SR	Condition will improve, introduce delight
Bad in root, bad in SR	Excess of adversity in what it indicates

Figure 55: Comparing natal and SR conditions of the lord of the year (II.3, 5-8)

[Analyzing the lord of the year by place and reception]

9 And along with this, you should look at [the lord of the year]: where it is, in the houses of the circle (in the root as well as the revolution), and whether it is received but not made unfortunate, or made unfortunate [as well as] not being received:

10 For if it was in a suitable condition in both of the times, excellent in its position in the circle, received, then it indicates obtaining good, benefit, and power. **11** But if it was in an excellent condition and position in the root, and in the revolution it was like that as well except that it is *not* received, then it indicates that he will come to the brink of gain, benefit, and much good, but then it will decrease after that and be corrupted.

12 And if in the root and the revolution it was in a bad condition and position in the houses of the circle, but it *is* received, then it indicates that he will have a little good and benefit from the underclass, and from every bad work and loss. **13** And if in addition to the badness of its condition in the two times the lord of the year was in a stake of the Ascendant of the year in the revolution, and a planet not receiving it was making it unfortunate from the square or opposition, then it indicates a detestable thing and illnesses appearing in that year. **14** Now if that infortune was retrograde or going towards burning, then it indicates that the harshness will reach him from no [particular] direction.⁵⁰

15 And if [the lord of the year] was made unfortunate in both of the times, in a stake, it is harsher and more powerful for the tribulation. **16** But if the lord of the year was *not* in the stakes in the two times and is made unfortunate [while still] looking at the Ascendant, it is below what we stated, and no one apart from his family and close friends will know what afflicts him. **17** And if it was in the four positions which do *not* look at the Ascendant (and they are the second, sixth, eighth, and twelfth), then that detestable thing will be hidden, with no one knowing about it. **18** And if, along with its falling away from an aspect to the Ascendant, a planet does look at it⁵¹ from a stake, then that will appear after being concealed; but if [the lord of the year] was [the one] connecting with a planet in the stake, he himself will be the one who divulges that, by himself.

19 And be sure to examine the assembling of the lord of the year with the planets and [their] rays, and the Lots and the twelfth-parts: because the indication of each one of them will appear in accordance with its condition in itself (in terms of suitability or corruption).

20 And now we will state the indication of each planet when it is the lord of the year, and we will begin with Saturn.

---

⁵⁰ Or perhaps, for no particular "reason" (من غير وجه).
⁵¹ Or rather, "connects with": see later in the sentence. The applying planet makes the matter public.

Chapter II.4: On the indication of Saturn if he was the lord of the year & is in a suitable condition

[General comments on planetary condition]

1 As for Saturn, he is an infortune by his nature, indicative of corruption, while Jupiter is a fortune by his nature, indicative of good fortune and suitability; but sometimes an infortune indicates good fortune and a fortune [indicates] misfortune, through the difference of [their] conditions. **2** For if an infortune was in a bad condition, then through its nature as well as the badness of its condition it indicates a detestable thing and corruption—and if it assembled with or looked at another [planet] in that condition it is in, from whatever direction the aspect was, then it makes it unfortunate. **3** But as for if the infortune was in a suitable condition, then it will not do harm from the trine and sextile, but does indicate suitability and the good. **4** And if a fortune was in a bad condition, weak, the indication of its good fortune is weakened; so if a corrupting infortune or a planet in a bad condition looks at it [while it is] in that condition, [the fortune] will take on its detestable thing and the badness of its condition, and will indicate misfortune and corruption, in the category [of things] which its nature indicates, and the reason for it will be due to the nature of the infortune.

5 [So] when Saturn is in a bad condition, and Jupiter or (one of the fortunes in a suitable condition) looks at him, it blunts his evil, and the more that the corruption of his condition is reduced, his indication for evil will be weaker; and the more that he[52] increases in the suitability of his condition and looks at one of the planets, his corruption due to that planet, and his indication for something detestable, will be reduced and less.

---

[52] I believe this is Jupiter. But the point is clear: a good condition can either indicate something suitable, or protects against corruption.

[Saturn as lord of the year, considered alone]

6 So[53] if Saturn was the lord of the year and in both the root and the revolution he is[54] eastern, in his own glow, direct in course and increasing in it, in his own house or exaltation, or in the rest of the places in which he has a claim, or in the position of one of his friends and those supporting him, and he is in an excellent position in the houses of the circle, and in his own domain, then [the native] will be a manager for beneficial works, being effective in them, strong, enduring in them, and especially in what there is of the management of lands and villages, and construction in real estate, and acquiring it, and building houses and dwellings, and the discovery of water for wells, and the planting of trees, and sowing [crops].

[Saturn-Jupiter]

7 Now[55] if the nativity was of the births of nobles and kings, and Saturn was just as we have stated concerning a suitable condition, and he is in the trine of Jupiter *in the root*, then it indicates for the owner of the revolution in that year, the building of cities and castles, and enclosures[56] encircling them, and the raising of walls which are like that, and making use of gardens, and drawing [water from] channels, and the excavation of streambeds and rivers, and putting in order what had already been corrupted of [those things] before that. **8** And if Jupiter looked at him from a sextile in the root, his condition will be close to that as well. **9** Now if Jupiter was looking at him in the revolution from the trine or sextile, from an excellent position, *in addition to* his looking at him in the root, then (along with those things which we stated) it indicates that he will have dignity and delight, and he will acquire assets from the powerful and the nobles, along with their praise to-

---

[53] For this sentence, cf. Da. 130.
[54] **P** adds, "safe from the infortunes."
[55] For this sentence, cf. *Carmen* II.14, **1**.
[56] **E**: "rivers."

wards him, and he will be a master of favor,[57] judgment,[58] dignity, and prudence, and he will be benefited in every work he does, and will delight in children. **10** And[59] if Saturn (in that year, or in the root, or in both times) was in the signs of kings[60] when Jupiter looked at him, then in that year he will manage the works of kings.

11 And[61] Saturn indicates things like these suitable conditions when Jupiter assembles with him in both of the times, and they are both in a suitable condition.

12 And you should also look at the rays, the Lots, and the twelfth-parts which are in the root of the nativity and in the revolution, [to see] which of them is with Saturn or which one[62] he looks at in the two times with an aspect of power and friendship, for it will indicate suitability in the category [of things] which they indicate. **13** Now if Saturn had a share in his own place, or the lord of the house of the Lot was looking at the Lot from a sign in which [Saturn][63] has a claim, or from the sign of his friend, and[64] the place of the aspects to it are like that, the good which the Lot indicates will be from a known direction, or from a male or female friend. **14** But if he[65] was in an alien sign or in a sign of his enemy, that will be from a foreign man or woman, and enemies.

---

[57] Reading with **P** as تودّد. That is, someone who is powerful enough to grant favors and to ingratiate oneself with.

[58] **P** reads, "intelligence" or "gentleness."

[59] For this sentence, cf. Da. 131.

[60] That is, the fiery signs.

[61] Cf. *Carmen* II.18, 1.

[62] Lit. "where."

[63] Reading for "it," since the purpose of the paragraph is to link Saturn as the lord of the year with the meaning of the Lots.

[64] Reading with **E** for "or."

[65] **P** reads, "they." But this should probably be understood to mean any of the planets just mentioned.

[Saturn-Mars]

15 Now[66] if Saturn was the lord of the year, and he and Mars are in a suitable condition in the root and the revolution, and Mars looked at him from the trine or sextile in the two times, and one of them receives his associate (or they were both received by a single planet), then in that year [the native] will embark upon what will benefit him, and he will increase in his assets and rank, and will associate with kings, and will delight in brothers, and their condition will be suitable.

16 And[67] if Mars assembled with him in the two times and they are in a suitable condition in both, then in that year he will be of a good character, correct in his opinion, and the satisfying of his needs will become easy, and he will be eminent[68] in his expenditures, and he will squander assets.

17 But if the assembling of Mars with him or his looking at him was in [only] one of the two times, it decreases everything we stated.

[Saturn-Sun]

18 And[69] if Saturn was the lord of the year, and he and the Sun are in a suitable condition in the two times, and [the Sun] looked at him in both from the sextile,[70] and they are in a place of the day[71] or[72] Saturn is eastern from him, and the Sun is made fortunate in the two times,

---

[66] For this sentence, cf. *Carmen* II.14, **4**.

[67] For this sentence, cf. *Carmen* II.18, **2**.

[68] Or, "a noble," or "like a noble" (يشرف, reading with **P**). But **B** and **E** read that his expenditures will be "nine-fold" (يتسع \ يتسّع): this suggests they are excessive, but that would make the next clause redundant.

[69] For this sentence, cf. *Carmen* II.14, **5-6**.

[70] Abū Ma'shar should probably have added, "or from the trine, provided that Saturn is not retrograde," because in **19** he specifically warns against that. Saturn always turns retrograde around his eastern trine with the Sun, but then turns direct in his western trine, so there is no reason not to allow a trine provided that he is not retrograde. See also II.7, **9**.

[71] This probably means a diurnal chart, with Saturn above the horizon.

[72] **E** reads, "and."

then in that year it indicates an increase in his rank and power,[73] and in the suitability of his father's condition, and their both benefiting from the nobles and those having importance. **19** And if [the Sun's] aspect to [Saturn] in both was from the trine and [Saturn] is retrograde, it is below that. **20** And if the aspect of the Sun to him was [only] in one of the times, it decreases everything we stated.

[Saturn-Venus]

21 And[74] if Saturn was the lord of the year, and he and Venus were in a suitable condition in the root and the revolution, and she looked at him from the trine or sextile in the two times, and he receives her, and Venus is in a place of the night[75] (and especially if she was receiving him as well), and the Lot of marriage is made fortunate, then in that year he will delight in women, and will increase in his cleanliness, and the fertility of his home,[76] and he will be devoted to decorations and paintings in [his] dwellings, homes, and buildings.

22 And if the aspect of Venus to him was in [only] one of the two times, his indication in that year will be similar, except that [the native] will have no delight in it, and people among the underclass will envy him, and treat him badly, and he will be distressed because of women, eunuchs, and effeminate men, and generally it will be made difficult for him in whatever he seeks, of the things which are of the category of the indication of Venus; and distress will find some of his women, and something of his property and his goodness[77] will be spoiled, and he will show hatred for his own entertainments,[78] and he will be distressed in times of delight.

---

[73] **E**: "nobility."
[74] For **21-22**, cf. Carmen II.14, **8** and II.18, **7**.
[75] Ideally, this is probably with her below the horizon but him above it.
[76] خصب منزله. Or perhaps, "productivity," "plenty."
[77] Reading as طيبه. But perhaps this is طيبة, his "good nature, geniality."
[78] But **P** reads, "he will show hatred in his thinking."

[Saturn-Mercury]

23 And[79] if Saturn was the lord of the year, and he and Mercury are in a suitable condition in the root and the revolution, and he looked at him in the two times from the trine or sextile, and one of them receives his associate, and Mercury is strong, and the Lot of slaves, the Lot of children, and the Lot of work (and their lords) are in a suitable condition, then in that year he will increase in his dignity, and intelligence,[80] and knowledge, and the excellence of his thinking, and he will be of a firm opinion in those things he is concerned with,[81] and he will be devoted to [types of] management, writing, calculation, accounting, and various sciences, and he will delight in children, slaves, and attendants, and[82] will increase in them.

24 Now[83] if Mercury assembles with him in the two times and both of their conditions were like that, then in that year he will have a good understanding, be excellent in memory and thought, clever in matters.

25 But if his assembling with him or looking at him was in [only] one of the times, even if they are both like that in suitability, it decreases everything we stated.

[Saturn-Moon]

26 And[84] if Saturn was the lord of the year, and he and the Moon are in a suitable condition in the root and the revolution, and he looks at her in both times from the trine and sextile, and he receives the Moon, or[85] the Moon is received and made fortunate, increasing in

---

[79] For this sentence, cf. *Carmen* II.14, **9**.

[80] Or, "gentleness" (حلمه).

[81] This verb implies both actual concern, and in general whatever he happens to be thinking about or planning (يهمّ).

[82] **E** and **P**: "or."

[83] For this sentence, cf. *Carmen* II.18, **8**.

[84] For this sentence, cf. *Carmen* II.14, **7**.

[85] Reading for "and," or else the next instance of "received" would be redundant. But it is possible that this should simply read, "and he receives the Moon, *and the Moon is made fortunate...*".

glow and calculation, then in that year [the native] will increase in his assets and rank, real estate, and places of sowing, and he will benefit in what he is devoted to (of the conditions of planting, rivers, channels, and whatever of them he digs), and he will increase in his status among the nobles and kings, and he will be blessed by a good reputation among the people, and he will delight in mothers and women.

27 And if her aspect to him was in [only] one of the two times, even if they are both in a suitable condition, it decreases everything which we stated.

☙ ❦ ❧

28 Now as for the assembling of the planets with Saturn generally, or their looking at him from the square and opposition, we have omitted [any] mention of that and their indications in this place, because if they were like that in relation to him, and he is taken only in virtue of [that],[86] then perhaps he would make them unfortunate so that they indicate corruption. 29 But in this place we are sticking to the conditions which indicate *suitability* when they have an aspectual relation[87] to him.

Chapter II.5: On the indication of Saturn when he is the lord of the year & is in a bad condition

1 If[88] Saturn was the lord of the year and in [both] the root and the revolution he is falling, in a bad position, and in an alien sign, and is burned or under the rays, or retrograde (and especially if he was in a sign of his enemy), and Jupiter does not aid him by looking at him and combining [with him] from one of the signs in harmony with him, and the revolution is nocturnal and he is above the earth (and the stake of

---

[86] Abū Ma'shar is reminding us that planetary condition makes a big difference in configurations, so he is distinguishing configurations in a good condition from those in a bad condition. He will repeat this many times in the chapters which follow.

[87] Reading as مناظرة.

[88] For this sentence, cf. Da. 132.

the west and the Midheaven are worse), or the revolution is by day and he is under the earth (and the stake of the fourth is worse), then in that year it indicates detestable things in old men of the people of his house, and fathers, and grandfathers. **2** And if he was in a male sign, most of that will be in males, while if he was in a female sign most of it will be in females; and if he was in a sign having two bodies, that will be in [both] males and females.

3 And[89] in all of this he indicates that the owner of the revolution will have powerful catastrophes, as well as a long illness from moisture, and a shivering fever, trembling of the body, coldness, stinking, the retention of urine, the stirring-up of black bile, and throbbing and pains which resemble what we have stated, along with damages in assets and building, sowing, waters, and in everything which resembles that of ancient things, of works, lands, real estate, and slowness in things which are needed, and trouble for him in them, and poor management in the things he devotes himself to, and error in them as well as in his opinion, and he will associate with people of blame, malice, and deception: and that will be worse if he is slow or stationary.

4 Now[90] if Saturn was just as we have explained and he is in an alien sign, then these things will find him in foreign travel; and if he was in a house of his friend, then that will find him from friends and because of them; and if he was in a sign of his enemy, then that will find him from enemies, and it will be more conclusive and harsh.

5 But if the lord of Saturn's house is looking at him in the root, that will be because of an enemy with an old enmity; but if the lord of his house looked at him in the revolution, then because of a new enemy; while if it looked at him in both times, it will be from both types together. **6** And in these three ways the owner of the revolution will be aware of [who it is]—but if it does not look at him in the two times [at all],[91] it will be from both an old and new enemy, neither of whom he will be aware of.

---

[89] For this sentence, cf. Da. 132.
[90] For this sentence, cf. Da. 133.
[91] That is, being in aversion to him.

7 And if Saturn was the lord of the year and he was under the rays in the root and in the revolution, then in that year it indicates contention, alarm, and fear of the Sultan, and he will become ill in a hidden place, and harm in relation to fathers, grandfathers, and old men (in accordance with what that sign indicates). **8** Now if the Sun was stronger, that will be greater and worse; and if [the Sun] was weaker, it will be less.[92]

9 And if Saturn had this bad condition but then assembled with a planet or its rays, or with one of the Lots or twelfth-parts, or he looked at any of what we stated, in both of the times, with strength [and] an aspect of contrariety and hostility, then it indicates corruption in the category of what that thing indicates.

10 And if Saturn indicated something detestable in a diurnal revolution, and he is in his domain, then it will be quick to disappear.

[Saturn-Jupiter]

11 Now if Saturn was the lord of the year and he and Jupiter are in a bad condition in the root and in the revolution, and he looked at him in both of them from the trine or sextile (and especially if Jupiter was in one of the bad houses of the circle), then in that year it indicates the destruction of something of dwellings, real estate, and the disappearance of part of [his] assets, and the corruption of [his] rank, and idleness, and indifference[93] to what would benefit him.

12 And[94] if Jupiter looked at him in the two times from the square, and they are in a bad condition in both of them, then in that year it indicates a decrease in assets, and indifference, and difficulty in every work he begins, and he will not be correct in his works, and misfortune will afflict his parents, and it will take away from their rank.

---

[92] Abū Ma'shar discusses his theory of planetary strength and elemental mixtures in conjunctions in *Gr. Intr.* VII.4, but I do not understand how it applies here. He may have in mind that Saturn is in a better dignity than the Sun.

[93] This word (التَّواني) also connotes slowness and negligence.

[94] For this sentence, cf. *Carmen* II.15, **2-3**.

13 And[95] if Jupiter looked at him in the two times from the opposition, and they are in a bad condition in both of them, then he will have bad management and work in that year, and he will be distressed because of children.

14 And if they assembled in the two times and they are in a bad condition, it indicates the corruption of assets, and fines, and quarreling in that.

15 And if his assembling with him or looking at him in these ways was in [only] one of the two times, or they were in a suitable condition, it will be below that.

[Saturn-Mars]

16 If[96] Saturn was the lord of the year and he and Mars are in a bad condition in the root and in the revolution, and he looks at him (from whatever direction the aspect was), and they are both in a sign of the image of people, and especially if they were in the house of enemies, then it indicates that in that year the owner of the revolution will have misfortune, injustice, and incarceration by enemies or some of the leadership, or because of them, and he will be distressed because of brothers.

17 Now if Mars looked at him in the two times from a trine or sextile, and they are in a bad condition in both, then in that year it indicates indifference, and idleness, and the corruption of [his] condition,[97] and the death of the brothers, or a powerful catastrophe will afflict the owner of the revolution and his brothers.

18 And[98] if Mars looked at him in the two times from the square, and they are in a bad condition in both, and Saturn is looking down upon [Mars], then an illness from heat will afflict him, and a fever, and it will corrupt the assets of his parents, and some of his brothers will

---

[95] For this sentence, cf. *Carmen* II.16, **1**.
[96] For this sentence, cf. Da. 135.
[97] الحال. Or, "[his] situation." But perhaps this should be المال, "assets."
[98] For this paragraph, cf. *Carmen* II.15, **5-6**.

die. **19** But if Mars was the one looking down upon Saturn, then he will envy[99] his relatives, and a bad ailment will afflict the father, and it will corrupt many of the conditions of the owner of the revolution, as well as the condition of his father.

20 And[100] if Mars looked at him in the two times from the opposition, and they are in a bad condition in both, then in that year he will be afflicted by a decrease in his assets and livelihood, and be made extremely unhappy, and he will become ill, and a detestable thing will afflict him because of envy, slander, and defamation, and he will quarrel with his family and relatives. **21** And if they were looking at each other like that from signs of water, then something detestable will afflict him from water and moisture; and if they were both in a sign having four feet, the misfortune will afflict him from a blow,[101] or bite, or venom, or a corrupting treatment.

22 And[102] if Mars assembled with him in the two times, and they are both in a bad condition, then it indicates that in that year he will have many distresses, have a bad character, bad management, and what he needs will be made difficult for him, and a detestable thing will afflict his older brothers. **23** And if at their assembling they combined in a single nature, it will be easier; while if they combined in two natures, it will be a small thing.[103]

24 And if Mars's assembling with him or his looking at him from these directions was in [only] one of the two times, or they were in a suitable condition, [the indication] will be below that.

[Saturn-Sun]

25 If Saturn was the lord of the year, and he and the Sun were in a bad condition in the root and the revolution, and [the Sun] looked at

---

[99] Or, "bear a grudge against" (يحسد).
[100] For this paragraph, cf. *Carmen* II.16, **1-5**.
[101] Or perhaps this should be understood as a "kick," such as from a horse.
[102] For this sentence, cf. *Carmen* II.18, **2**.
[103] As with **7-8** above, this refers to Abū Ma'shar's theory of how planets mix their qualities together (such as the hot and the dry).

him in both (from whatever direction the aspect was), in that year it indicates distresses, malicious gossip, the defamation of him and his father, and a decrease in their assets and rank. **26** And if Saturn was like that and he was with the Lot of the father or its lord, or they were both corrupted by another, then it indicates a detestable thing for the fathers and the paternal uncles, or that will affect the native from them or because of them.

27 And if the Sun looked at him in the two times from the trine or sextile, and they were both in a bad condition in both (and especially if the revolution was by night), then it introduces various distresses upon him and his parents in that year, as well as damage in assets and a decrease in rank and power, and confusion in affairs.

28 And[104] if the Sun looked at him in the two times from the square, and they were in a bad condition in both, and the Sun is looking down upon [Saturn], then in that year it will destroy what assets he inherits from his parents, and his relatives will be hostile to him, and he will become ill from cold and leprosy, and toil and fatigue will be prepared for him. **29** And if Saturn was the one looking down upon [the Sun], then distresses will afflict him which he will be perplexed by, and he will be imprisoned or put in fetters, and he will be unemployed from [any] beneficial works.

30 And[105] if the Sun looked at him in the two times from the opposition, and they are in a bad condition in both, then poverty and need will affect him and his father in that year, and an ailment resembling a chronic one will afflict them both.

31 And[106] if Saturn was under the rays in the two times, then in that year he will scatter his father's assets, and the outcome of his matter generally in what he does will be corruption and something detestable, and it indicates wounds[107] and illnesses [such as][108] a long-lasting case

---

[104] For this paragraph, cf. *Carmen* II.15, **7-8**.
[105] For this sentence, cf. *Carmen* II.16, **10**.
[106] For this paragraph, cf. *Carmen* II.18, **4-5**.
[107] Or, "ulcers" (قروح).
[108] Reading loosely as تأتيه for بأنه (appears only in **B**).

of measles. **32** And if the revolution was by night then it is worse, and detestable things will affect his children and brothers—and if the Sun was in fewer degrees than [Saturn] it is [even] worse in all of that, and it will undermine his rank, and his status will decline, and he will be enthusiastic in quarreling, litigating, and fighting.

33 And if the assembling of the Sun with him or his looking at him from these directions was in [only] one of the times, or they were both in a suitable condition, it will be below that.

[Saturn-Venus]

34 If[109] Saturn was the lord of the year, and he and Venus are in a bad condition in the root and the revolution, and she looked at him in both (from whichever direction the aspect was), and the Lot of wedding or its lord is corrupted by an assembly of the infortunes or their aspect, then a detestable thing will affect his women, or that will affect him because of them, and he will have what is unpleasant[110] because of his good [qualities], household effects, clothing, and dishes.[111]

35 And if Venus looked at him in the two times from the trine or sextile, and they were in a bad condition in both, then in that year he will be devoted to dirty places, and it will corrupt his possessions, and he will be disturbed in[112] his way of life, [his pleasure] in it being spoiled, and he will befriend adulterers both male and female, and suffer damage from men and women of the underclass.

36 And[113] if Venus looked at him in the two times from the square, and they are in a bad condition in both, and Saturn is looking down on her, then the owner of the revolution will not delight in women in that

---

[109] For this sentence, cf. Da. 136.

[110] آفة. Normally I translate this generically as "misfortune," but it also has special connotations of dirtiness and disgust (see also the next sentence, which uses a different word).

[111] Note that three different factors here point to a decrease in love: that the nature of the lord of the year (Saturn) is not very amorous, that the natural significator of love (Venus) is in a bad condition, and that the Lot of marriage is in a bad condition.

[112] Or even, "filthy in" (كدر العيش).

[113] For this paragraph, cf. *Carmen* II.15, **9-10**.

year, and some of them will be ruined, or estrangement will occur between him and them, and separation, and different distresses will afflict him because of them and in everything which Venus indicates.

37 And if Venus was the one looking down upon him, then he will be blessed with the obedience of women, and their affection towards him, and the goodness of their character, and likewise they will be blessed by [similar things from] him.

38 And[114] if Venus looked at him in the two times from the opposition, and they are in a bad condition in both, then in that year he will have little delight, and he will see poverty and meanness in his women and relatives, and chronic illness and sickness, and something detestable will afflict him from women and from different things of the category of the indication of Venus, or some of his women will be ruined.

39 And[115] if Venus assembled with him in the two times, and they are in a bad condition in both, then in that year he will have sex with harlots and vile women, or a sterile woman, or he will shift from one to another, and will not love them, nor will they love him.

40 And if her assembling with him or looking at him from these directions was in [only] one of the times, or they were in a suitable condition, it will be below that.

[Saturn-Mercury]

41 If[116] Saturn was the lord of the year, and he and Mercury are in a bad condition in the root and the revolution, and he looked at him in both (from whatever direction the aspect was), and the Lot of children, the Lot of slaves, or the Lot of work, or[117] their lords, were made unfortunate, then in that year it indicates harm, and a detestable thing,

---

[114] For this sentence, cf. *Carmen* II.16, **11**.
[115] For this sentence, cf. *Carmen* II.18, 7.
[116] For this sentence, cf. Da. 137.
[117] **P**: "and."

corruption, distresses, sorrow, and regret, in owned people[118] and slaves, and children, and partners, and works which he does, or that will afflict him for these reasons and because of corrupt management, bad thought, and disasters.

42 And if Mercury looked at him in the two times from the trine or sextile, and they are in a bad condition in both, then distresses will afflict him because of calculation, writing, the sciences, assets, and he will be slack, with bad management, desisting from what would benefit him.

43 And[119] if Mercury looked at him in the two times from the square, and they are in a bad condition in both, and Saturn is looking down upon [Mercury], then distresses and disasters will afflict him in his way of life and assets, and the beneficial works which he busies himself with will pass out of his hands, and he will serve [other] people because he will need them, and something detestable will afflict him because of speech, and an ailment in his mouth or ear. **44** But if Mercury was the one looking down upon [Saturn], it indicates little of what we stated.

45 And[120] if Mercury looked at him in the two times from the opposition, and they are in a bad condition in both, then an ailment will afflict him in his mouth and tongue, and a detestable thing will affect him because of speech, and he will be ill-tempered in his works, cold in disposition, corrupt in reason and thought, and he will become ill from windiness, and he will be distressed because of betrayal and theft, and he will encounter a detestable thing from everyone who contends with him, and his hope will be cut off, and he will love solitude and being isolated, and he will be afflicted by loss in his assets because of something ancient. **46** (And his looking at him from the square is indicative in this manner, too.)

---

[118] المماليك. In normal discourse this simply means a slave, but I'm not sure how Abū Ma'shar means this to differ from the next word "slaves" (العبيد).
[119] For this paragraph, cf. *Carmen* II.15, **11-12**.
[120] For this sentence, cf. *Carmen* II.16, **12**.

47 And[121] if Mercury assembled with him in the two times and they are in a bad condition in both, then different distresses will affect him, and he will be lazy, shrinking from speaking and works, and bad thoughts will overtake him, and his reason and opinions will be mixed up, and the people will not accept much of his talk, and a detestable thing will affect him in [his] children and slaves, and he will become ill, and types of tribulation will afflict him in that year.

48 And in all of this, if his assembling with him or looking at him from these directions was in [only] one of the times, or they were in a suitable condition, it will be below that.

[Saturn-Moon]

49 If Saturn was the lord of the year, and he and the Moon are in a bad condition in the root and the revolution, and she looked at him in both (from whatever direction the aspect was), and especially if the Moon was decreasing in glow and calculation in the two times, then in that year it indicates an illness of the body, and distress because of mothers and reports, and what resembles those things.

50 And if the aspect of the Moon in the two times was from the trine or sextile, and they are in a bad condition in both, then distresses will affect him in that year because of the nobles and kings, and reports, and he will be criticized.

51 And[122] if the Moon looked at him in the two times from the square, and they are in a bad condition in both, and Saturn is looking down upon her, then he will be lazy, bad in management, not correct in what he does, and he will scatter the assets of his parents. **52** And if the Moon was the one looking down upon him, then he will be put to the test by quarrels, and the hostility of people, and by illness, and he will scatter the assets of his parents, and be distressed by children. **53** And if in the revolution of the year the Moon was in a feminine sign,

---

[121] For this sentence, cf. *Carmen* II.18, **8**.
[122] For this paragraph, cf. *Carmen* II.15, **13-14**.

then his woman will be hostile to him, and she will seek his misfortune.

54 And[123] if the Moon looked at him in the two times from the opposition, and they are in a bad condition in both, then pains will afflict his parents in a hidden place, and the owner of the revolution will devastate their assets, and he will have a bad character, have many worries, and it introduces damage upon him in assets and his way of life. **55** And if they were both in signs having four feet, then misfortunes will afflict him from riding animals—and one should look in this manner if they were both in signs of wild animals or the signs of humans.

56 Now[124] if the Moon assembled with him in the two times and they are in a bad condition in both, then it indicates the ailment of his mother and the weakness of her body.

57 And if her assembling with him or looking at him from these directions was in [only] one of the two times, or they were in a suitable condition, it will be below that.

[A general comment on aspects and conditions]

58 So these are the indications of Saturn when he is the lord of the year and [1] he is in a suitable condition in the two times, and planets in a suitable condition looked at him in both, or [2] he was in a bad condition in both and planets in a bad condition assembled with him or looked at him.

59 But as for if Saturn was the lord of the year and [3] he is in a suitable condition in the two times, and a planet in a bad condition (or made unfortunate) looked at him, then the planet looking will decrease the indication of Saturn's suitable condition, in accordance with *its* own condition and the situation of the place from which it looks. **60** So if that aspect was from a trine or sextile, it introduces confusion and distresses and toil into it; and if it was from a square or opposition, there will be diminishment and harm in it.

---

[123] For this paragraph, cf. *Carmen* II.16, **14-17**.
[124] For this sentence, cf. *Carmen* II.18, **9**.

61 And if Saturn was the lord of the year and [4] he is in a bad condition in the two times, and a planet in a suitable condition (or made fortunate or received) looked at him, then it improves his condition. **62** So if that aspect to him was from a trine or sextile, that improvement will be great, but there will [still] be toil and distresses in it; and if the aspect was from a square or opposition, the improvement will be below that.

63 And if the planet looking [at him] was in an excellent condition in one of the times, and in a bad condition in the other time, then it will take away from *its own* indication, whether that thing was good or bad.

64 And if one of the planets in the root looked at the lord of the year from [some] direction (such as the square or opposition), and that planet looked at it in the revolution from another direction (such as the sextile or trine), then blend its two conditions: because the aspect of the trine is more powerful than the aspect of the sextile in the indication of good fortune and the good, and likewise its power in repelling evil and injury; and the aspect of the opposition is more powerful than the aspect of the square in the occurrence of something detestable, and is weaker [than the square] in the acquisition of good fortune.

65 And if several planets looked at [the lord of the year], then one should judge each one of them individually, in accordance with its condition and its indication in its place,[125] in the manner which we stated.

66 But as for the assembling of the lord of the year with the planets, or the assembly of one of them with another, in all conditions, then look: for if one of them assembled with another in fitness and adaptation,[126] or reception, or a suitable condition, it indicates good and good fortune; and if that was [with] contrariety or misfortune or a bad condition, it indicates corruption.

---

[125] **B** and **E**: "its condition and its place."

[126] ممازجة, which usually just means "combination."

67 And you should know the quantity or quality of the suitability or corruption in all of this (concerning the condition of the lord of the year in itself and the condition of each one of [the planets] in relation to it) upon [their] looking at it or assembling with it, and their condition relative to the houses of the circle: because when Saturn is in a bad condition in the root and the revolution just as we have said, then the evil he indicates in that year will be greater, harsher, and more fixed. **68** But if Saturn was in a bad condition in the revolution but a suitable condition in the root, then all of the evil we have explained will be little; and if the fortunes looked at him and they are in a suitable condition, he will escape from [the evil], and especially if the revolution was by day and Saturn above the earth. **69** And if he was in a bad condition in the root, and in the contrary of that in the revolution, the evil will be middling.

70 And when a planet in the root indicates something good or evil, and it also indicates it in the revolution, then that thing will be complete, abundant, powerful in its category [of events]. **71** But if it indicates [it] in the root and not in the revolution, or it indicates it in the revolution and not in the root, then see which of the two indications is more powerful. **72** For if they were equal, that thing will be middling, but if the indication of the root was more powerful, it will be above average, while if the indication of the revolution was more powerful, it will be below average. **73** And if it indicated that thing in the revolution alone, it will indicate that thing [only] weakly: that thing will be slight, or in that year there will be an impulse [for it] which is not completed. **74** And in all of this, its duration will be [only] for that year, or so long as that indicator has power over that indication, but then it will be corrupted.[127]

75 And when a planet indicates something good or evil through its looking at the lord of the year, then its indication will be manifest when it manages one of the times of the year: and that is more firm if it

---

[127] This suggests both that the indication might be very short, but also that it might last longer than the year: such as with a slow planet transiting in a key sign, but not leaving the sign until after the following revolution begins.

BOOK II: PROFECTIONS

[also] looked at the lord of the year at that [later] time, or at the sign in which the lord of the year was at the root or the revolution, or it looked at the sign of the terminal point, or at the Ascendant and its lord, or at the indicator of the month or day.

76 So, these are the conditions of Saturn by himself and at the planets' looking at him or their assembling with him, and their being in the houses of the circle, and there are eight ways [to examine it]:

77 One of them is the suitability of his condition in himself.[128]

78 The second is the badness of his condition in himself.[129]

79 The third and fourth is the aspect of the planets to him, in every one of their conditions.[130]

80 The fifth is the suitability of his condition in himself and the aspect to him by planets in a bad condition.[131]

81 The sixth is the badness of his condition in himself and the aspect to him by planets in a suitable condition.[132]

82 The seventh is the assembling of the planets with him.[133]

83 The eighth is his condition in the houses of circle (and we will state that now).[134]

84 And the remaining conditions of the planets quick in course in the revolutions of years, are [also] in this manner.

---

[128] See especially **67-74**.
[129] See especially **67-74**.
[130] The third is their suitable condition when *he is also* suitable (**58**), and the fourth is their bad condition when *he is also* bad (**58**).
[131] See **59-60**.
[132] See **61-65**, and **68**.
[133] See **66**.
[134] Or rather, in the next chapter.

Chapter II.6: On the indication of Saturn in the houses of the circle, when he is the lord of the year

1 If Saturn was the lord of the year and he is in a suitable condition in the two times, in his own house or in a position where he has a claim, and he is in one of the stakes of the Ascendant of the root, or of the terminal point, or of the Ascendant of the revolution (and the strongest of that is the Midheaven), then in that year he will take possession of villages for himself, and be devoted to building and the improvement of lands, and the digging of rivers. **2** And if he was in an alien sign and he is received, then he will assume responsibility for that on behalf of someone else, in the manner of [holding it in] trust and [as a] household manager, and he will be praised, and good will come to him because of it. **3** But if he was in an alien sign, *not* received, then he will [still] assume responsibility for that on behalf of someone else like we said, but he will be blamed and accused in it—and if along with that he was in the aspect of one of the corrupting planets, he will encounter harm and something detestable because of it.

4 And if Saturn was the lord of the year and he was in the eleventh or fifth in the two times, in a suitable condition, and he is in his own house or received, then in that year he will delight in friends, and be devoted to guarantees,[135] building, and expenditures on lands and things whose benefit he is hoping for, in what he faces [in the future],[136] and he will be praised in that. **5** But if he was alien, not received, he will be distressed because of children and brothers, and he will be blamed along with a shortage which will affect him in his possessions; and if in addition to that he was retrograde, then it will destroy some of his dwellings or real estate, and it will introduce a loss[137] in his assets, and it will corrupt some of his crops and revenues. **6** Now if Mars looked at him with a harmful aspect, then in addition to

---

[135] That is, sureties, bail, contracts, and other relationships of trust that benefit people (قبالات).
[136] **P**: "in what he earns."
[137] وضيعة. This particularly refers to things that are sold or resold at a loss.

what we mentioned it indicates damage in assets, the corruption of friends, and distress over children.

7 And if Saturn was the lord of the year and he is in the third or ninth in the two times, in his own house or received, in a suitable condition, then in that year he will do works in which he hopes for recompense and reward by God, and benefit from some of the people in what he faces [in the future], and the management of a building for himself or for one of the people of his concern, and he will travel to a place he knows or his toil will multiply because of benefit he hopes for, and he will be devoted to the conditions of his relatives, brothers, and foreigners.[138] **8** And if he was in these two places and he is alien [but still] received, then it indicates what is like that, except that he will go on a distant journey in which he will find the benefit. **9** And if he was in them and he is alien [but] not received, evil gossip will be said about him because of religion and worship, and evil ideas will get the better of him in his motives, and something detestable will find him while abroad, and he will contend with his family and relatives. **10** And if Saturn was retrograde, his opinions will be mixed up, and he will have doubts in his religion, and will do a work which will be attributed to corruption in religion because of him.[139] **11** And if he was in this bad situation and Mars looked at him with a harmful aspect, then in addition to what we stated something detestable will afflict him because of theft and fire.

12 And if Saturn was the lord of the year and he is in the second in the two times, in a suitable condition, in his house <or received>, then it indicates that his situation in his assets will be set aright, and he will increase in them. **13** And if he was in it and his condition was like that, and he is in an alien sign [but still] received, then he will increase in his assets from a direction he had not hoped for and was not aware of, and he will be blessed by sowing. **14** And if he was in it and he is in a corrupt condition, *not* received, it indicates the corruption of assets, vegetation, and fields, from sinking or water.

---

[138] Or, "strangers" (والغرباء).
[139] Or perhaps, "due to *it*" (i.e., due to his doubt and confusion).

15 And if Saturn was the lord of the year and he is in the eighth in the two times, in his own house or received, he will have good from the dead in that year; and if he was not received or he was retrograde, it indicates the decrease of his assets and their squandering, and distresses because of ancestors and destruction.

16 And if Saturn was the lord of the year and he is in the sixth in the two times, in a suitable condition, he indicates few pains in that year, from cold and moisture, and benefiting from being treated for those ailments; but if he was in a bad condition, it indicates pleurisy[140] and chronic illnesses. **17** And if he was received [and] made fortunate, he will recover from them, and the days of his illnesses will be few, and he will benefit from remedies. **18** Now if in addition to that the lord of the sixth was made unfortunate, then it indicates the ruin of his slaves and riding animals; but if it was received, in a suitable condition, an ailment will afflict them but they will escape it.

19 And if Saturn was the lord of the year and he is in the twelfth in the two times, in his own house or received, he will be victorious over his enemies, and they will befriend him, and they will praise him well—but he will be little occupied in works which would benefit him. **20** And if he was alien [and] not received, or retrograde, then he will encounter hardship from prison, confinement, and enemies. **21** And if along with his being alien he was in a bad condition or Mars looked at him with an aspect of corruption, then torment and beating will find him.

22 And if Saturn was the lord of the year and in the revolution he was in the four places falling away from view of the Ascendant (and they are the second, the sixth, the eighth, and the twelfth), in a bad condition, then it indicates leisure, laziness, and despairing of being blessed and [having] beneficial things. **23** And if in addition to that he was not received, then it is harsher for that, and he will be dispossessed,[141] and will encounter hardship, and evil will be said about him, and illness will afflict him from cold and moisture or cold and dryness;

---

[140] That is, inflammation of the lung.
[141] **P**: "saddened."

and if he was retrograde, it is [even] harsher for what we stated. **24** Now if he was in these positions and was eastern, received, or in his own house, he will be in a suitable condition except that he will be at leisure, being little occupied in what will benefit him.

25 Now if Saturn was in any of the houses of the circle in the root (such has the second, or third, or others) in one of the conditions, and in the revolution he was also in the same [house] relative to the sign of the terminal point or the Ascendant of the revolution of the year, in a similar condition, then it is firmer and more powerful for the indication of what he indicates from his own nature and the nature of the house, and especially if he looked at [his] position [in] the root.[142] **26** But if it was the contrary of that, blend the indication of the two places in the manner we have made clear to you, and make its indication act in partnership with everything which is attributed to that house, so that the judgment about him is correct.

27 And you should look in this manner at the conditions of the rest of the planets in the houses of the circle, just as we have discussed the condition of Saturn and his indication in isolation as well as with the aspect of the planets to him (or their assembly with him), and his condition in the houses of the circle in the revolutions of years. **28** And [so] we likewise ought to state the indication of the rest of the planets in the manner which conforms with this book.

Chapter II.7: On the indication of Jupiter when he is the lord of the year & is in a suitable condition

1 If[143] Jupiter was the lord of the year and he is in a suitable condition in the root and the revolution, then in that year he will befriend kings, the mighty, and celebrated nobles, and he will have good man-

---

[142] For example, let the natal Saturn be in the eleventh (say, Gemini), but in the fifth of the revolution (say, Virgo): in that case he would be able to see his natal position from his revolutionary one, and thereby link and reinforce his natal promise.

[143] For **1-4**, cf. Da. 139.

agement, being successful because of what [he does] correctly, being praised [in] the results of matters, having patience and good relationships,[144] and he will increase in his rank and power, be well praised, and will have responsibility for works in his own country. **2** And if it had already indicated the generating of children for [the native] in the root of his nativity, then [the native] will be blessed with children in that year,[145] and he will have benefit and delight from various directions, and assets will pass to him from supplications or other things, and perhaps he will inherit the assets of his father in an unplanned way. **3** Now if the owner of the revolution was in the upper class, of the nobles, then in that year he will gain power and rule over the people, and over the people of metropolises, and assets will pass to him. **4** And if the native was of the middle [class], then in that year he will have leadership over his peers, and will delight in various things (of beneficial and fortunate occupations), and especially if Jupiter was in his own house, bound, and triplicity.

5 And you ought to look at the rays, the Lots, and the twelfth parts which Jupiter assembles with or looks at in the two times with an aspect of affection and power, [to see] what things they and their lords indicate: for it indicates suitability in them, in accordance with the suitability of Jupiter.

[Jupiter-Mars]

6 If[146] Jupiter was the lord of the year and he and Mars are in a suitable condition in the root and the revolution, and he looked at him in both of them from the trine or sextile, then it indicates that in that year he will be a leader, informed about works, acquiring [wealth][147] in them, and he will have respect, a high status, and benefit from rulers, and in general he will be well commended.

---

[144] Or perhaps, "favor" (تودّد).
[145] Perhaps in old age this could take the form of grandchildren, along with the ideas in I.9, **25**; thanks to Steven Birchfield for this observation.
[146] For this sentence, cf. *Carmen* II.14, **10**.
[147] Reading with **E**, for "being preoccupied."

7 Now[148] if Mars assembled with him in the two times and they were in a suitable condition in both, then in that year he will gain power and status in his land and his homeland, and he will have a good way of life; and if they were both like that and they were both in the house of one of them, then he will be powerful, and will have leadership.

8 And if Mars assembled with him or looked at him in [only] one of the times, it will be below that.

[Jupiter-Sun]

9 If[149] Jupiter was the lord of the year and he and the Sun were in a suitable condition in the root and the revolution, and [the Sun] looked at him in both from the sextile, and the Sun is made fortunate, then in that year he will increase in his good fortune, and the goodness of his way of life, and he will be blessed by an appropriate marriage, and good children. **10** And if [the Sun] looked at him from the trine and [Jupiter] is retrograde, or [the Sun's] looking at him was in [only] one of the two times, and their condition was like that, it will be below what we said.

11 And[150] if the Sun assembled with him in the two times and [Jupiter] is easternizing from [the Sun], then he will have rank and various elevated benefits, and his parents will delight in him, and they will benefit by him. **12** And if he assembled with him in [only] one of the two times, and his condition was like that in terms of easternization, it will subtract from everything we stated.

13 And[151] if the Sun assembled with him in the two times and he is under the rays, it indicates something detestable in the whole category

---

[148] For this sentence, cf. *Carmen* II.19, **1-2**.
[149] For this sentence, cf. *Carmen* II.14, **15**.
[150] For this sentence, cf. *Carmen* II.19, **4**.
[151] For this paragraph, cf. IX.8, **92**, and *Carmen* II.19, **3**.

[of things] indicated by Jupiter. **14** If the Sun was more powerful[152] and [also] made unfortunate, there will be much corruption, and death will be feared for him (although if he was made fortunate, that will be less); but if Jupiter was more powerful than [the Sun], the corruption will be little.

[Jupiter-Venus]

15 If[153] Jupiter was the lord of the year and he and Venus are in a suitable condition in the root and the revolution, and she looked at him in both (from whatever direction the aspect was), then in that year it indicates an increase in his assets in relation to women, and that will happen with the help of some of the nobles, and the powerful, and friends, and he will delight in women and in feminine men, and will benefit by them.

16 Now if Venus looked at him in the two times from the trine or sextile, and they were in a suitable condition in both, then in that year he will increase in his power, rank, and assets, and his clothing, and his fornication, delight, entertainment, and music, and that will be due to women; and perhaps a child will be born to him or he will delight in children or in the children of kings. **17** And if Venus had testimony in her sign, or she was in the sign of her friends, then that will be from a known direction, and in relation to a female friend; and if she was in an alien sign or that of an enemy, it will be from strangers and enemies, [both] men and women.

18 Now[154] if Venus assembled with him in the two times and they were both in a suitable condition, then in that year he will increase in his power among the leaders and administrators, and he will be exalted above the people, and his friends will multiply, and he will be well

---

[152] Abū Ma'shar discusses his theory of planetary strength in conjunctions in *Gr. Intr.* VII.4, but I do not understand how it applies here. Perhaps he means that the Sun is in a better dignity, angular or advancing, and so on.
[153] For **15-16**, cf. *Carmen* II.14, **11**.
[154] For this sentence, cf. *Carmen* II.19, **5**.

commended, and he will benefit because of fathers, places of worship, and mosques, and he will delight in women, marriage, and children.

19 And if Venus assembled with him or looked at him in [only] one of the times, it will diminish everything we said.

[Jupiter-Mercury]

20 And[155] if Jupiter was the lord of the year and he and Mercury are in a suitable condition in the root and the revolution, and he looked at him in both from the trine or sextile, then in that year he will acquire assets having value, and he will benefit from business, buying and selling, writing, and management, and he will maintain watch over things and assets in a judicious way, being knowledgeable about things, and he will precede his peers in rank and power, writing, effectiveness, and discernment, and due to the nobles he will assume responsibility for works and [types of] management,[156] and he will be praised among the people, and be pleasing among them, persevering in conditions of righteousness and what resembles that (of the matter of religion). **21** And if the owner of the revolution was of the lower [people], then he will benefit from courtesy and skill in working with his hands, and the professions.

22 And[157] if Mercury assembled with him in the two times and they are in a suitable condition in both, then in that year he will increase in his righteousness, religion, reason, the excellence of his thought, and eloquence, and he will benefit by that and benefit from different things,[158] and he will be devoted to writers who have importance, and will manage their affairs.

---

[155] For this sentence, cf. *Carmen* II.14, **12**.
[156] This could also be read, albeit less grammatically, as "and he will assume responsibility for the works and [types of] management which belongs to the nobles."
[157] For this sentence, cf. *Carmen* II.19, **8**.
[158] Reading for "and others besides him will benefit from different things."

23 And if Mercury's assembling with him or his looking at him was in [only] one of the times, it will subtract from everything we have stated.

[Jupiter-Moon]

24 If[159] Jupiter was the lord of the year and he and the Moon are in a suitable condition in the root and the revolution, and she looked at him in both from the trine or sextile, then it indicates that in that year he will increase in his rank, and be blessed by the people, having praise and beautiful speech, and whatever works he begins will be completed by his own hands; and if he sought children one will be born in that year (or his woman will become pregnant), and he will inherit the assets of his fathers. **25** And if the owner of the revolution was of [the status of] kings, and the Moon was increasing in glow, then he will take hold of a status having power; and if he was of the middle [class], he will be in charge of a group of the people, and will act with fairness among them, and his conduct will be good; and if he was of the lower [class], he will have leadership over his peers. **26** And in everything we stated, it indicates benefit from buying, selling, and business.

27 And[160] if the Moon assembled with him in the two times and they are in a suitable condition in both, then he will increase in his power, rank, and assets, and especially if the revolution was by day.

28 But if Moon's assembling with him or her looking at him was in [only] one of the times, it will subtract from everything we stated.

29 Now as for the aspect of the planets to Jupiter from the square or opposition while they are in a suitable condition, we have left off [any] mention of that here, because when they are in these two places relative to him, sometimes they indicate something detestable; and we have already discussed that before.[161]

---

[159] For **24-25**, cf. *Carmen* II.14, **13-14**.
[160] For this sentence, cf. *Carmen* II.19, **9-11**.
[161] See II.5, **58-66**.

Chapter II.8: On the indication of Jupiter when he is the lord of the year & is in a bad condition

1 If[162] Jupiter was the lord of the year, and in the root and the revolution he was retrograde, under the rays, alien, in the west, or he was in exile, in[163] the houses of the infortunes, or falling from the stakes in bad positions, then it will destroy the native's assets and subtract from his good fortune, and undermine his rank, and multiply his distresses, and it indicates an abundance of expenses, and the unjust extraction of [his] assets, and that will be due to the kindness of his soul and his seeking praise and appreciation, and he will be distressed because of fathers, children, and the nobles, and different things, and by the badness of his condition in his way of life; and that will be worse if Jupiter was in the sixth.

2 Now[164] if the corrupting infortunes[165] assembled with him or looked at him from the square or opposition and they are looking down upon him, and Jupiter is in a bad condition, and he is in the house of fathers or the house of children (or he had testimony in them), and the Lot of the father, the Lot of the mother, and the Lot of children (and their lords) were made unfortunate, then it indicates that distresses will come upon the owner of the revolution because of the death of children, fathers, or mothers, in accordance with the indication of the sign in which Jupiter is, as well as the nature of the Lot and its lord.

3 And if he assembled with the rest of the Lots, or one of the rays or twelfth-parts in the two times, or he looked at them with strength [and] a contrary aspect, and he is in a bad condition, it indicates distress and something detestable from the category of the indication of that thing.

---

[162] For this sentence, cf. Da. 140.
[163] **E**: "and in," so that he would be both in exile (peregrine) and in the house of an infortune.
[164] For this sentence, cf. Da. 141.
[165] **P** reads simply, "if the planets."

4 And when Jupiter is in a bad condition you ought to understand the conditions of the planets, and their assembling with him (and the direction[166] of their aspect to him), because even if his condition was like that but then planets[167] in a bad condition also assembled with him or looked at him from the trine or sextile, it does *not* indicate excessive, destructive corruption from these three directions,[168] due to the harmonization of the nature and their blending [with him] via affection—but due to his weakness and the badness of his condition, it will keep his indication from reaching complete good fortune. **5** And the planets in a bad condition will also *add* badness to him, so that it will introduce harm and decrease in the thing which he *would* have indicated at a time of [having] a suitable condition and they would be with him or be related to him in these two places;[169] and the owner of the revolution will have distress and labor because of those things. **6** But as for their looking at him from the square or opposition, it is contrary to that, and we will discuss that now.

[Jupiter-Mars]

7 If[170] Jupiter was the lord of the year and he and Mars are in a good condition in the root and the revolution, and he looked at him in both from the square, and [Jupiter] is looking down upon Mars, then it will establish his forcefulness,[171] and perhaps he will have rulership over his own rank, and he will gain power and rank and benefits from kings, generals, and their sons,[172] except that he will be distressed because of children and assets, and corruption will enter upon a portion of his parents' assets. **8** And if they looked at each other from this direction in the two times and they are both in a bad condition, it will subtract

---

[166] Not the technique of primary directions, but the type of aspect from which they look at him.

[167] **P** reads, "Venus."

[168] That is, the assembly, sextile, and trine.

[169] Again, from the sextile or trine.

[170] For this paragraph, cf. *Carmen* II.15, **15-16**.

[171] وطأته. This has connotations of a ruler's vehemence and even violence.

[172] **B** reads, "and those resembling them."

from everything good we stated before, and the owner of the revolution will find something detestable and the spending of money because of those things. **9** But if Mars was looking down upon [Jupiter] (in whatever condition they were), then the owner of the revolution will have something detestable from older people, workers,[173] and the masters of allies, and he will be distressed because of benefits, assets, [his] way of life, and children, as well as cheating, envy, slander, and quarreling, and his labor will multiply—except that if they were in a suitable condition in the two times (during their mutual aspect from this direction), it will be below what we stated.

10 And if Mars looked at him in the two times from the opposition, and they are in a bad condition in both, then distresses will afflict him in that year because of rank, and women, and children, and he will see the death of some of those relatives who are meant [by that], and perhaps he will marry and a child will [be born] to him, and his quarreling will multiply, and matters will become confused for him, he will waste assets but then acquire assets again, and the worst conditions of that year from this indication will be until one-half of it has passed. **11** But if they were both in a suitable condition in the two times, then there will be a little of what we stated, or there will be [some] movement indicating something detestable in the category of these things, but then it will not come to fruition.

[Jupiter-Sun]

12 Now[174] if Jupiter was the lord of the year and he and the Sun are in a suitable condition in the root and the revolution, and [the Sun] looked at him from the square in both, and the Sun is looking down upon him, then in that year he will increase in his rank and the rank of his father, and they will benefit from different things. **13** And if they were both in a bad condition, then restriction will afflict him and his father in assets, and they will go to a foreign country and travel on a

---

[173] Or perhaps, "administrators" (العمّال).
[174] For this paragraph, cf. *Carmen* II.15, **17-18**.

journey in which they will not be pleased, and enmity and envy will occur between them and those having importance, among their acquaintances, neighbors, and their families. **14** And if Jupiter was the one looking down upon [the Sun] and they are in a suitable condition in the two times, then benefit and good, rank, power, and an elevated status will come to the owner of the revolution and his father in that year. **15** But if they were both in a bad condition, distress will afflict them because of these things.

16 And if the Sun looked at him in the two times from the opposition and they are in a suitable condition or made fortunate in both, then in that year there will be delight in his whole situation, and he will increase in his power and rank, and on behalf of the Sultan and the nobles he will be responsible for works involving many people, and kings will seek his advice in their affairs, and they will come to his point of view. **17** Now if they looked at each other from this direction and they are in a bad condition in both, or made unfortunate, it will subtract from everything we said, and distresses will find him because of these things.

[Jupiter-Venus]

18 If[175] Jupiter was the lord of the year, and he and Venus were in a suitable condition in the root and the revolution, and she looked at him from the square in both, and Jupiter is looking down upon her, then in that year he will increase in his rank, and will benefit by women, and he will have a good way of life, a friend of purity[176] and cleanliness, and he will adhere to [his] religion and its causes, and he will do works of piety. **19** But if they were both in a bad condition, something detestable will afflict him because of what we stated. **20** And if Venus was the one looking down upon him, and they were in a bad condition in the two times, then he will be eager for amusement and women, and distress will afflict him because of them, and he will acquire assets from some of them due to something detestable which

---

[175] For this paragraph, cf. *Carmen* II.15, **19-20**.

[176] Reading tentatively for undotted and different spellings in the MSS.

will afflict them from someone other than the owner of the revolution, and he will treat people badly, and he will be dissatisfied with some of his siblings, and it will corrupt some of his possessions and food. **21** And if they were both in a suitable condition, he will benefit from and delight in everything we said.

22 And if Venus looked at him from the opposition in the two times and they were both in a suitable condition, then he will increase in his rank and in the praise of the people for him, and their love towards him, and he will be in charge over the people of his house, will acquire assets, and be protective of his assets. **23** And if they were in a bad condition or made unfortunate, it will subtract from everything we said, and distresses will find him because of it.

[Jupiter-Mercury]

24 If[177] Jupiter was the lord of the year and he and Mercury were in a suitable condition in the root and the revolution, and he looked at him in both from the square, and Jupiter is looking down upon [Mercury], then he will be devoted to writers, and be an ally of the people, and because of his aid to them he will have good and benefit. **25** And if they were both in a bad condition, it will subtract from that, and distress will find him for that reason. **26** And if Mercury was the one looking down upon [Jupiter] in the two times, and they are in a bad condition in both, restriction will afflict him because of assets, and he will rejoice in little profit and benefit, and he will have little thankfulness towards the people, having bad dealings with them, and will treat people badly and be unjust towards them. **27** And if they were both in a good condition, he will benefit by and rejoice in everything we said.

28 And if Mercury looked at Jupiter from the opposition in the two times and they are in a suitable condition in both, then in that year he will increase in his culture and knowledge, and he will know hidden secrets, be devoted to buying and selling, be well commended, and be dear to the people of his house. **29** And if they were in a bad condition

---

[177] For this paragraph, cf. *Carmen* II.15, **21-22**.

in both, or made unfortunate, it will subtract from everything we have stated, and he will be distressed because of it.

[Jupiter-Moon]

30 If[178] Jupiter was the lord of the year and he and the Moon are in a suitable condition in the root and the revolution, and she looked at him from the square in both, and Jupiter is looking down upon her (whether the revolution is by day or night), then the owner of the revolution and his parents will be in a suitable condition in their way of life in that year, being praised, well commended, and they will benefit from their relatives, and increase in their power and rank. **31** And if they were in a bad condition it will subtract from that, and something detestable will afflict him because of them. **32** And if the Moon was looking down upon him and they were both in a suitable condition, beautiful things will be said about them, and the leaders and the masses will respect them. **33** And if they were in a bad condition in both it will subtract from that, and quarrels will afflict them, and decrease in their rank and assets, and they will be frustrated in their management.

34 And[179] if the Moon looked at Jupiter from the opposition in the two times, and they are in a suitable condition in both, and the Moon is in fewer degrees than him, then in that year he will increase in his rank, and will acquire assets, and will delight in [his] family, assets,[180] and children, and he will be devoted to kings and leaders, and will be in a suitable condition, proud of himself, autocratic in his opinion, and if he travels in it he will return from his journey. **35** And if they were in a bad condition in the two times, and the Moon is in more degrees than him, then it indicates a decrease in his assets, and distresses will afflict him from different directions, and especially at the beginning of the year.

36 And in all of this, if the assembling of the two (or their aspect) in the two times indicated suitability and the good, but then she assem-

---

[178] For this paragraph, cf. *Carmen* II.15, **23-24**.
[179] For this paragraph, cf. *Carmen* II.16, **24-25**.
[180] **P** and **E** omit.

bled with him or looked at him in [only] one time, it subtracts from everything we said. 37 And if the indication was for corruption, it will be below that.

܀ ܀ ܀

38 Now as for his condition with Saturn, we have already discussed that in what preceded, whereas these are the indications of Jupiter when he is in [1] a suitable condition, and planets in a suitable condition assembled with or looked at him, or he is in [2] a bad condition and planets in a bad condition assemble with or look at him. 39 But as for if Jupiter was in [3] a suitable condition and planets in a *bad* condition looked at him, or he was [4] in a bad condition and a planet in a *good* condition looked at him, the work in that (and other things, of the things which we are discussing in this category) will be in the manner we discussed for the indication of Saturn.[181]

Chapter II.9: On the indication of Jupiter in the houses of the circle, when he is the lord of the year

1 If Jupiter was the lord of the year and he is in a suitable condition in the root and the revolution, in his own house or in a sign in which he has a claim, or is received, not made unfortunate, in the four stakes from the Ascendant of the root (or relative to the terminal point or Ascendant of the revolution), then in that year he will be celebrated by the people of his class, praised, respected, and he will increase in his status, rank, and assets. 2 Now if he was in the Midheaven, that will be because of those having importance; and if he was in the Ascendant it will be in relation to his own motives and work he does; and if he was in the opposite[182] it is because of women and antagonists; and if he was in the stake of the earth that is because of fathers, the family, lands, and real estate. 3 And if he was in these four positions and is in a bad con-

---

[181] See II.5, **58-66**.
[182] That is, the seventh or Descendant.

dition, retrograde, not received, then it indicates the decrease of his assets, and their corruption, and a scarcity of his eagerness to gather them, and worries and distresses, because of the indication of the stake in which he is.

4 And if Jupiter was the lord of the year, and he is in a suitable condition in the two times, in the eleventh, received, not made unfortunate, then in that year he will have a good way of life, be delighted, being well commended, and his friends will have good from him. **5** And if he was in it and is in a bad condition, not received, or made unfortunate, he will have many worries, have bad thoughts, with no work being prepared for him in which there is benefit, and he will be distressed because of friends, hopes, and wishes.

6 Now if Jupiter was the lord of the year and in the two times he is in the fifth, in a suitable condition, received, then he will be blessed with children (if the root of his nativity had indicated children), or he will delight in children (if he had them). **7** And if he was in it and is not received, or is made unfortunate, he will be distressed because of children, messengers, and gifts.

8 And if Jupiter was the lord of the year and in the two times he is in the ninth or third, in a suitable condition, received, then good things in his religion will be reported about him in that year, and he will go on a journey for the sake of piety, religion, and good deeds, and he will be praised, and will delight in brothers and reports. **9** And if he was in them and is in a bad condition, or made unfortunate, not received, then reports will reach him in that year which he will be distressed by, and harms and distresses will enter upon him in relation to brothers, and he will be negligent in his religion, and he will have doubts about it, and if he traveled in [that year] he will encounter something detestable.

10 And if Jupiter was the lord of the year and in the two times he was in the second or eighth, in a suitable condition, received, it indicates leisure,[183] and a scarcity of work, except that benefits will be

---

[183] Reading as العطلة with **E**. But **P** reads الغبطة, "happiness," which goes well with the "cheerfulness" in the next sentence.

produced for him without seeking [them], or because of the dead. **11** And if he was in them [but] made unfortunate, not received, then it indicates an abundance of spending without cheerfulness, and distresses, and contention because of assets.

12 And if Jupiter was the lord of the year and he is in the sixth or twelfth in the two times, in a suitable condition, received, then it indicates that the lowest [people] will praise him, and he will benefit from those who are confined, and enemies will make peace with him. **13** And if he was in them [but] not received, or made unfortunate, illnesses will befall him from windiness and other things, and distresses from enemies or confinement.

14 And if Jupiter was in one of the houses in the root, in one of the conditions, and in the revolution he was in another house in that [same] condition (or [even] its contrary), then combine the indication of his two conditions in the manner we stated in the chapter on Saturn.

15 And if Jupiter was the lord of the year, and in the revolution of the year especially he was in the four positions which do not look at the Ascendant, and he is <not> received,[184] then the owner of the revolution will not have eminence, nor will he increase in his rank, and many of his brothers and acquaintances will shun him, and he will be little occupied in what would benefit him. **16** And if he was in them and he is made unfortunate, something detestable will find him because of these things.

Chapter II.10: On the indication of Mars when he is the lord of the year & is in a suitable condition

1 If[185] Mars was the lord of the year and in the root and the revolution he is in his own glow, direct in course, increasing in it, in suitable

---

[184] Without the "not," this could also be read as *even if* he is received.
[185] For this sentence, cf. Da. 143.

places of the circle, in his own domain or[186] in a sign in which he has a claim, or received, then [any] depression of the soul, distresses, and laziness, will disappear from the owner of the revolution, and his mind will be strong, and he will increase in his reason and his concentration, and his acuteness in things, and the quickness of his getting things done[187] in works, and his eagerness for profits, and he will be victorious in what he seeks (of the work of the Sultan),[188] and he will be awe-inspiring among the people of his class, and he will acquire benefits and assets generally from those things he is devoted to, and the outcomes of his affairs will be suitable.

2 And if Mars was just as we explained (in terms of the suitability of his condition), and he is in an alien sign, that good will come to him from foreigners;[189] and if he was in a sign of his friends or he was received, that will be from friends and acquaintances; and if he was in a sign of people, then he will see love and delight from people, and will benefit from them, and he will be well commended; and if he was in one of the signs of water, that will be because of waters and moisture. **3** And seek information in the rest of the signs in this manner.

4 And you ought to look at the rays, the Lots, and the twelfth-parts which Mars assembles with or looks at in the two times with strength, in an aspect of harmony and affection, whatever indication they and their lords have: because it indicates suitability in them, in accordance with the suitability of Mars's condition.

[Mars-Jupiter]

5 If[190] Mars was the lord of the year, and he and Jupiter are in a suitable condition in the root and the revolution, and he looked at him in both from the trine or sextile, and the owner of the revolution is of [the status of] kings who are lasting in good fortune, then he will in-

---

[186] **E** and **P**: "and."
[187] إبرامه. This has connotations of concluding a treaty, confirming things, and so on.
[188] Or perhaps, "of the work of authority."
[189] Or, "strangers" (الغرباء).
[190] For **5, 7,** and **8,** cf. Da. 145.

crease in his good fortune and good, and his servants, and his entourage and followers, and his army, and he will lead troops, and be a leader over many people, and his enemies will come to be in his power. **6** And[191] if Mars was in Aries or Capricorn, then he will be victorious over his enemies and will increase in his courage and his undauntedness,[192] and his riding animals and weapons, in everything which Mars indicates. **7** And if the native was of the middle [class] whose root of their nativities do not indicate victory in that rank, he will connect with the nobles and powerful people of the generals and masters of wars, and he will get from them what delights him, with respect to benefit and advantages. **8** But if the native was of the lowest [class], then he will have good or benefit from the army, and people who deal in Martial trade professions. **9** And[193] you also ought to examine the signs in which Mars is, in the root and the revolution—are they of the signs of kings, or the signs of those in the middle, or the lower [class][194]—then blend his condition in himself with the nature of his sign.

[Mars-Sun]

10 And[195] if the Sun looked at him in the two times from the trine or sextile, and they are in a suitable condition in both, then he will increase in his good fortune and his assets, and he will be blessed with marriage and children, and an increase in power with the Sultan and those having importance, and generals, and those waging wars, and he will be mentioned well among the people.

---

[191] For this sentence, cf. Da. 143.
[192] Or perhaps, the "assistance" (نجدة) that others give him.
[193] For this sentence, cf. Da. 144.
[194] The fiery signs are the royal signs or signs of kings. Gemini, Virgo, Libra, and the first half of Sagittarius belong to the administrative and middle classes, while Aquarius belongs to the lower class (Sahl, *Nativities* Ch. 1.38, **11-12** and **46-47**). But the earthy signs are also attributed to the lower and slave classes (Sahl, *Nativities* Ch. 6.10, **1**). See also Sahl's Ch. 2.8, **4-9** and 4.5, **26-27**.
[195] For this sentence, cf. *Carmen* II.14, **16**.

[Mars-Venus]

11 And[196] if Venus looked at him in the two times from the trine or sextile, and they are in a suitable condition in both, and the lord of the Lot of wedding is in the seventh, in view of the fortunes [which are] in a suitable condition, then he will increase in his assets and advantages, and will be blessed with marriage, and remaining close to women as well as having sex with them, and delight, and benefit from them, and he will have sex with some of them in secret, and he will increase in his children, garments, and possessions, and his women will befriend people who have power and authority. **12** And if Mars and Venus were in a sign in which they both had a claim,[197] then that will be in relation to his own woman or from a known direction; but if they were in an alien sign, that will be abroad or with foreigners.[198]

[Mars-Mercury]

13 And[199] if Mercury looked at him in the two times from the trine or sextile, and their condition in both was like that (in terms of suitability), then it indicates that there will be an increase in the mind of the owner of the revolution, and in his cleverness, and he will be diligent in works, quick to move in things, praised, lucky, and he will increase in his logic, culture, knowledge, and understanding.

[Mars-Moon]

14 If[200] the Moon looked at him in both times from the trine or sextile, and their condition in both was like that (in terms of suitability),

---

[196] For this sentence, cf. *Carmen* II.14, **18**.
[197] Abū Ma'shar means, "they are *each* in a sign in which *each independently*" has a dignity or claim, not that they are in the same sign and both have a claim in it.
[198] Or, "strangers" (الغرباء).
[199] For this sentence, cf. *Carmen* II.14, **19**.
[200] For this sentence, cf. *Carmen* II.14, **20**.

BOOK II: PROFECTIONS

and they are in a place of the night,[201] and the Moon is decreasing in glow, then it indicates the advantage of goodness and benefit, and success in the needed things he seeks out, and an abundance of delight in those things he is devoted to.

15 Now as for the assembling of the planets with him, and their looking at him from the rest of the directions,[202] that generally indicates corruption in matters; and because of that we are not mentioning it here.[203]

Chapter II.11: On the indication of Mars when he is the lord of the year & is in a bad condition

1 If[204] Mars was the lord of the year and in the root and the revolution he is retrograde, or under the rays, or burned, western, or alien, in the shares of the infortunes, not received, falling from the stakes in the bad places, then in that year it indicates his fury,[205] and absence,[206] and the independence[207] of his opinion, and his reason being mixed up (and its weakness), and the corruption of his mind, and the badness of his thought, and his astonishment and confusion, and misfortune will

---

[201] Ideally, this would probably be in a nocturnal chart above the horizon, or in a diurnal chart below it.

[202] That is, the square and opposition.

[203] See the next chapter.

[204] For this sentence, cf. Da. 149.

[205] حدّة. Normally this would mean "sharpness," "keenness," and even "passion" and "excitability," which are also Martial and useful; but in the negative range of emotions it means violence, rage, and fury.

[206] Adding with **E**. Remember that Mars is a travel planet, so this suggests independence, "doing his own thing," and perhaps deliberately showing stubbornness and non-cooperation.

[207] تصرّف. This has connotations of arbitrariness and freedom; it is evidently considered negatively here because it is not tied to the usual goals, standards, and customs.

afflict him from wild animals and riding animals, and fires, heat, blood, illnesses, and bad journeys,[208] and being away from the country without benefit, and with the badness of his brothers' and sisters' condition—and everything which will affect him from that will be according to the category of the indication of Mars and the sign in which he is. **2** Now[209] if the corruption was as we stated and he is under the rays, then it indicates misfortune from fire, conflagration, theft, and hidden, secret matters, and deception and stratagems, and illnesses, and internal sicknesses.

3 And[210] if Mars was just as we stated in terms of the badness of [his] condition and he is made unfortunate, not received, then the owner of the revolution will have complaints[211] and detestable things from the category of the indication of Mars, and from the nature of the infortune corrupting him, and from the nature of their two signs. **4** So if they were both in signs of the image of people, then the complaint will afflict him from works he does, and from speech, contention, injustice, enemies, theft, and highway robbers. **5** (And[212] if in addition to the corruption of his condition Mars was slow or stationary, that will be harsher and uglier, because sometimes along with what we mentioned it will indicate beating, chains, confinement, and anger, and especially if he was in the sign of his enemy.) **6** And if he was in a sign in the image of predatory animals and beasts, and rough [animals][213] of the earth, then that complaint will be from predatory animals, and riding animals, and rough [animals]. **7** And if he was not in those signs, then it will be from the spilling of blood, ulcers, bile, and illness, burning by fire and from hot things, and travel in which there is no benefit.

---

[208] Reading الأسفار with **E** and **P**, for B's الأسقام ("illnesses, sicknesses").

[209] Reading for "because," which does not really make sense here. For this sentence, cf. Da. 147.

[210] Between **3-13**, cf. the first half of Da. 146.

[211] الآفات. But this could also be understood as "misfortunes."

[212] For **5-7**, cf. Da. 146.

[213] حرشة. This also has connotations of being prodded and excited, such as when animals are goaded to attack each other. I would have expected "reptiles" as the Latin has it, and maybe Abū Ma'shar or his source is thinking about scorpions and snakes in a state of excitement.

8 But if in all of this he was in his own house or in the house of his friend, the complaint will be easier, and it will be from a direction already known. **9** But if he was in exile or in the house of enemies,[214] then it will be harsher and more powerful, and longer-lasting. **10** And if Mars was in his own domain it will be less for the harm—and if he was in the contrary of that and he is in a stake, it will be greater in corruption and harm.

11 And you ought to examine the rays, the Lots, and the twelfth-parts which Mars assembles with or looks at in the two times, with power [and] an aspect of hostility, for it will indicate disaster from the category of their indication.

12 And if Mars indicated something detestable in nocturnal revolutions, then it indicates the quickness of its disappearance.

13 And if Mars was the lord of the year, and some planet looked at him in the root and the revolution from the trine or sextile, and they are in a bad condition in both, then it indicates that harm and something detestable will enter upon the owner of the revolution, in the category of what that planet *would* have indicated if they looked at each other from these two directions, and they had been in a suitable condition.

[Mars-Sun]

14 If[215] Mars was the lord of the year and he and the Sun are in a bad condition in the root and the revolution, and [the Sun] looked at him in both from the square, and Mars is looking down upon [the Sun], then the owner of the revolution will leave common sense[216] behind, be hasty, with little vision and thought in things, and his contentions will multiply, and his distresses in different matters, and because of assets and a decrease in it, and [his] children will find a

---

[214] Or more likely, "a" house of enemies (that is, his planetary enemies).
[215] For this paragraph, cf. *Carmen* II.15, **25-26**.
[216] التَّمييز. But this really has to do with the ability to distinguish between things, or have a sense of discrimination between things.

harsh disaster, or some of them will be destroyed. **15** And it is harsher in all of this if the revolution was by day and they were both above the earth. **16** And if the Sun was the one looking down upon [Mars], then different illnesses and disasters will afflict him, and if one of the authorities needed to be cast out, he will see something detestable from him,[217] and it indicates travel.

17 And[218] if the Sun looked at him in the two times by day from the opposition, and their conditions in both were like that in terms of badness, or they were both made unfortunate, then different distresses and disasters will afflict him in that year, and perhaps he will fall from an elevated thing, and a bad disaster will affect the father, or he will die a bad death. **18** But if the condition of both of them was like that and the revolution was by night, then he will be lazy in motivation, and the works he begins will not be completed at his hands, and assets will leave him, and poverty will afflict him in his possessions.

19 And[219] if the Sun assembled with him in the two times and they are in a bad condition or made unfortunate in both, then in that year he will have many whims, not remaining firm in one condition, and the people will speak of him badly, and will slander him, and different distresses will afflict him, and a disaster from iron or fire, and distress from the Sultan, and he will squander the assets of his father, and his eye will become diseased or an ailment will afflict it, and his father will have a powerful disaster or be destroyed; and it is more confirmed in all of this if he was in a stake or what follows it.

20 And if the Sun's assembling with him or looking at him from these directions was in [only] one of the two times, or they were in a suitable condition, it will be below that.

---

[217] I believe this means that the *native* will see something detestable from the authority, and will fail at casting him out.
[218] For this paragraph, cf. *Carmen* II.16, **26**.
[219] For this sentence, cf. *Carmen* II.20, **1**.

[Mars-Venus]

21 And[220] if Mars was the lord of the year and he and Venus are in a bad condition in the root and the revolution, and she looked at him in both from the square, and Mars is looking down upon her, then he will be distressed because of women and enemies, and the hostility of people towards him will be renewed, and because of them something detestable will afflict him, and perhaps he will have sex with servant-girls, or due to marriage and sex he will be devoted to bad, disgusting things. **22** And if Venus was the one looking down upon him, and their condition was like that in terms of badness, then those things will [still] be like that, except that [his] condition in that will be better and finer.

23 And[221] if Venus looked at him in the two times from the opposition, and they are in a bad condition in both, then in that year he have much free movement from condition to condition, and he will be distressed because of children, enemies, and women, and he will become ill or some of the [women] will be ruined.

24 Now if Venus assembled with him in the two times and they are in a bad condition in both, then it indicates what is similar to what it indicates when they look at each other from the square.

25 And if Venus's assembling with him or her looking at him from these directions was in [only] one of the two times, or they were in a suitable condition in both, it will be below that.

[Mars-Mercury]

26 If[222] Mars was the lord of the year and he and Mercury are in a bad condition or made unfortunate in the root and the revolution, and he looked at him in both from the square, and Mars is looking down upon [Mercury], then in that year he will treat people badly with open

---

[220] For this paragraph, cf. *Carmen* II.15, **27-28**.
[221] For this sentence, cf. *Carmen* II.16, **27**.
[222] For this paragraph, cf. *Carmen* II.15, **29-30**.

insult for no reason, and he will slander people, and spread rumors about them, and he will quarrel many times because of [types of] management and things he does, and powerful adversity will find him because of that and because of speech, and [deeds and words] will be claimed by him which he did not do and did not say, and perhaps good or assets will be presented to him²²³ which he will not accept.²²⁴ **27** And that is harsher if the revolution was by day and Mars is not in his own domain; but if it was by night, it will subtract from everything we mentioned. **28** And if Mercury was the one looking down upon [Mars], then in that year he will treat people unjustly, and he will have ugly thoughts and opinions, be bored, spiteful, an embezzler of things, eager to gather wealth.

29 And²²⁵ if he looked at him in the two times from the opposition and they are in a bad condition in both, then in that year he will have little shame, be impudent,²²⁶ loving what is worthless and detesting the truth, and practicing deception and stratagems, and manipulation, and treatments²²⁷ because of [his] insult towards people, and poverty will afflict him in his possessions, and he will be devoted to putting down collateral and quarreling, and writers and the authorities and judges will resist him, and he will be afflicted by fear of them, and something detestable will find him because of what we stated, and he will flee from his land (and especially if Saturn had a claim in the position of Mercury).

30 And²²⁸ if Mercury assembled with him in the two times, then in that year he will increase in his forms of knowledge, and he will be devoted to cheating, deception, lying, and quarreling. **31** And if they

---

²²³ عرض عليه. Meaning unclear.

²²⁴ Meaning unclear: it does not make psychological sense to me that he would also reject being known for something good he *had* done. Carmen does not contain this statement so is of little help here.

²²⁵ For this sentence, cf. *Carmen* II.16, **29**.

²²⁶ Or, "brazen" (صفيق الوجه).

²²⁷ الأدوية. Normally this refers simply to medical treatments (just as "manipulation" often does), but perhaps this is some older sense of using one's authority to control and mistreat people.

²²⁸ For this paragraph, cf. *Carmen* II.20, **4-8**.

were both in a bad condition, something detestable will find him because of it; and if they were in a suitable condition, he will see what he loves because of it. **32** And if they were both made fortunate or received, he will have good and benefit because of these things, and be well praised; and if they were made unfortunate he will encounter something detestable because of it. **33** And if they were both in a bad condition and they were under the rays, he will be devoted to robbers, and he will fabricate forged, false books. **34** But[229] if they were made fortunate or received, he will have good and benefit because of it, while if they were made unfortunate, he will have detestable things and complaints for that reason.

35 But if Mercury's assembling with Mars or his looking at him from these directions was in [only] one of the two times, it will be below that.

[Mars-Moon]

36 If[230] Mars was the lord of the year and he and the Moon are in a bad condition in the root and the revolution, and she looks at him in both from the square, and Mars is looking down upon her, then in that year diminishment and corruption will afflict the mother in her assets and way of life, and one of those whom she is concerned about will die, or the owner of the revolution will die, or one of his relatives, and an ailment will afflict him in his brain, corrupting his reason, and especially if Mars was in a bound of Saturn, and the Moon in a bound of Mercury or a bound of Mars. **37** And if the Moon was the one looking down upon him, then in that year humiliation and something detestable will afflict his mother, and harm and diminishment in assets and [their] way of life will afflict both her and the owner of the revolution.

38 Now[231] if the Moon looked at him in the two times from the opposition, and they are in a bad condition in both, then he will become

---

[229] This sentence repeats the essentials of **32**.
[230] Cf. also IX.8, **93**, and *Carmen* II.15, **31-32**.
[231] For this sentence, cf. *Carmen* II.16, **30**.

ill with a powerful illness, or one of his limbs will be cut by iron, and distresses will afflict him because of women, and from different directions.

39 But[232] if the Moon assembled with him in the two times and they are in a bad condition in both, then he will be exhausted, and a bad illness will afflict him, and some of his body will be cut by iron.

40 And if the Moon's assembling with Mars or her looking at him from these directions was in [only] one of the two times, or they were in a suitable condition, it will be below that.

41 Now as for [Mars's] indication with Saturn and Jupiter, we have already discussed that when we mentioned their indications [earlier]; but these are the indications of Mars when he is the lord of the year and is in [1] a suitable condition, and planets in a suitable condition look at him, or he is in [2] a bad condition and planets [also] in a bad condition assemble with or look at him. **42** But as for if Mars was in [3] a suitable condition and a planet in a bad condition looked at him, or he was in [4] a bad condition and a planet in a suitable condition looked at him, the work in those [cases] and others (of the things we are discussing in this category) will be like what we said about the indication of Saturn.[233]

Chapter II.12: On the indication of Mars in the houses of the circle, if he was the lord of the year

1 If Mars was the lord of the year, and in the root and the revolution he is in a suitable condition, in the four stakes, received, not made unfortunate, then in that year the owner of the revolution will be successful in what he seeks (in relation to the Sultan's authority and the masters of wars), and he will inspire awe in the people of his class,

---

[232] For this sentence, cf. *Carmen* II.20, **9**.
[233] See II.5, **58-66**.

defeating one who contends with him, being praised in his whole situation, and he will gain status and power. **2** Now if he was in the Midheaven, he will see what he loves from the Sultan; and if he was in the rest of the stakes his condition will be in accordance with the indication of that stake, in terms of religion, good, and suitability. **3** But if in the root and the revolution he was in the stakes [and] made unfortunate, not received, misfortune will be feared for him from conflagration, robbers, blood, and from every hot, bad, [and] moist illness. **4** And if he was retrograde he will flee from his country, and his condition will become harsher, and it will be feared for him due to iron, and he will spend money because of traveling and children. **5** And that will be harsher if it was by day and he is in the Ascendant or in the Midheaven, while if he was in the west ailments will afflict him, and illnesses, and cutting by iron, and different distresses, and he will be victorious over his enemies; and if he was in the fourth his real estate, home, and dwelling will be corrupted, and he will spend money, and encounter something detestable from different affairs, but then be rescued.

6 And if Mars was the lord of the year and in the two times he was in the eleventh or fifth, in a suitable condition, received, not made unfortunate, then it indicates delighting in the people, and an increase in children, and rank and status from friends and brothers, and generally that will be from the masters of allies,[234] and wars, and authorities, and benefits will be prepared for him for these reasons and from the working of fire and blood, and time after time[235] he will plan to travel, but perhaps that will not be prepared for him. **7** (And sometimes Mars will be in the stakes or in these two places, in a suitable condition just as we stated, and the owner of the revolution will [already] be away from his country, so that he will return to it.) **8** And if he was in [these] two in the two times and he was made unfortunate, not received, then it indicates distress and accidents in the family and children, and feuding with friends and brothers.

---

[234] Or, "assistants," or even military adjutants (المعاون).
[235] Or perhaps, "on occasion" or "occasionally."

9 And if Mars was the lord of the year and in the two times he is in the ninth or third, in a suitable condition, received, not made unfortunate, then he will travel and gain good in it, and he will be strong [and] praised in his travel. **10** And if he was in them in the two times and he is in a bad condition, made unfortunate, not received, then evil things will be reported about him because of [various] matters, some of which are true, and some false; and he will travel, and loss and hardship will affect him, as well as an illness from heat, and fear, and misfortune from wild animals, and especially if Mars was in Leo or Scorpio.

11 And if Mars was the lord of the year and in the two times he is in the second, and he is in a suitable condition, received, not made unfortunate, then he will have good and benefit from a direction he is not aware of. **12** And if he was in it and he is in a bad condition, made unfortunate, not received, he will spend his money and squander it.

13 And if Mars was the lord of the year and in the two times he is in the eighth, received, not made unfortunate, then he will benefit because of the conditions of the dead, ancestors, and inheritances. **14** And if he was in it and is made unfortunate, not received, then for that reason he will have something detestable, and quarrels, and his assets will be squandered.

15 And if Mars was the lord of the year and in the two times he is in the twelfth, in a suitable condition, received, not made unfortunate, he will be little occupied in what would benefit him, and he will see what he loves with respect to runaways and those who are confined, and he will be safe from his enemies. **16** And if he was in it and he is made unfortunate, not received, then something detestable will affect him from these directions which we mentioned.

17 But if Mars was the lord of the year and in the two times he is in the sixth, and he is in a suitable condition, received, not made unfortunate, then his body will be healthy, and he will be victorious over his enemies. **18** And if he was in it and is made unfortunate, not received, then pains will afflict him from heat and moisture, and a disturbance[236] of the blood. **19** And if Saturn looked at him or was with him, he will have an illness from bile and pus, and an illness from black bile.

20 And if Mars in the root was in any of the houses of the circle, in one of the conditions, and in the revolution he was in the corresponding house relative to the sign of the terminal point or the Ascendant of the revolution, and he is [also] looking at the position of the root or was in it, then it is firmer in indication for what he had indicated; and if he was contrary to that, then blend the indication of his two conditions and two places, in the manner which we stated before.

Chapter II.13: On the indication when the Sun is the lord of the year & is in a suitable condition

1 If[237] the Sun was the lord of the year, then the majority of that judgment in that year should be in accordance with the condition of [1] the lord of the sign in which the distribution of the lifespan from the [longevity] releaser was (whether the releaser-ship belonged to [the Sun] or to another),[238] and partnering with it in the indication is [2] the planet which is in Leo in the root of the nativity or in the revolution, and [3] the planet to which the Sun hands over the management (so long as it is in its sign),[239] and then along with that[240]

---

[236] This refers especially to agitation and excitement (خیجان), but probably could refer to any blood condition.

[237] Although Abū Ma'shar lists many different significators besides the Sun here, he *can* be interpreted as the lord of the year by himself: i.e., what revolutionary house he is in, his condition in that year, and so on. But for transits, I would use [3], if he was closely configured to a planet within a few degrees, either in the nativity or the revolution. See also II.14, **1** and II.22, **1-2**, which allows the distributor (probably of the longevity releaser) to be the proxy planet. (For a possible source in al-Andarzaghar, cf. Da. 129.)

[238] For example, if the longevity releaser is currently being directed through Virgo, then Mercury is a candidate for being the primary planet.

[239] This should refer to the Sun (i.e., the planets he can connect with so long as he is in *his* sign), just as with the Moon in II.22, **1-2**. (But grammatically it refers to the

you see [4] where the Sun is, calling upon [that] as a witness with them.²⁴¹

2 Now if in the root and the revolution [the Sun] is in a suitable condition, in his own house or exaltation, or he is in some other sign suitable for him, and he is above the earth, in the suitable places, then in that year it indicates being close to kings, victory over the enemy, a celebrated status, an increase in rank, assets, and benefits, and the goodness of [his] condition in them, and beautiful things will be said about him in gatherings and crowds, and he will increase in his knowledge,²⁴² speech, logic, and his understanding of things, and he will treat [some] people badly and treat others well, and will be devoted to authorities and the just, and religious people, and the conditions of religion, and his condition as well as the condition of [his] fathers and middle brothers will be improved, with benefit.

3 And you ought to look at the rays, the Lots, and the twelfth parts which the Sun assembles with or looks at in the two times, in strength, with an aspect of affection, and he is in a suitable condition: for it will indicate suitability in the category of their indication.

[Sun-Venus]

4 If the Sun was the lord of the year and Venus looked at him in the root and the revolution from the sextile, and they are in a suitable condition in both, then the praise of the people for him²⁴³ will multiply in that year, and he will have good management, and will increase in his forms of knowledge, and he will be in conformity with the truth in his speech, and his vision of true things [with] suitable interpretations will multiply.

---

other planet.) Note that Abū Ma'shar does not specify whether this planet to which the Sun applies is in the root or the revolution.
²⁴⁰ E: "then *after* that"
²⁴¹ Or perhaps "with him," referring to the Sun. This suggests simply the lord of the natal sign of the Sun.
²⁴² Or perhaps, "perception" (علم).
²⁴³ P reads, "the *need* of the people for him," which is a plausible alternative.

5 Now[244] if Venus assembled with him in the two times and they are in a suitable condition in both, and the revolution was by night and Venus western (or the revolution was by day and she is eastern), far from his rays, appearing in both situations, then in that year he will see what he loves from kings and their children, and he will be well commended and thanked, and will be praised in his management and works, and will delight in things which Venus indicates. **6** And if what we stated about the condition of day and night was the contrary (except that her assembling with the Sun is [still] far from his rays, in the east or in the west), then that will subtract from some of the suitability.[245]

[Sun-Mercury]

7 If[246] the Sun was the lord of the year and he and Mercury are in a suitable condition in the root and in the revolution, and he is assembling with [the Sun] in both of them, being far from [the Sun's] rays in the east or west, then in that year he will be in charge of work for a group of people, and he will increase in his culture and knowledge, and will be devoted to writing and writers who have power, and he will be praised among the people, contented in his situation, and he will benefit by everything Mercury indicates, and he will earn assets having value, and will benefit by slaves and servants.

[Sun-Moon]

8 If the Sun was the lord of the year and the Moon looked at him in the root and the revolution from the trine or sextile, and they are in a suitable condition in both, made fortunate, then he will acquire assets having value, and he will increase in his rank and children, and will be

---

[244] For this sentence, cf. *Carmen* II.21, **1**.
[245] Reading for "subtraction."
[246] For this sentence, cf. *Carmen* II.21, **3**.

in a suitable condition in those things (which the Moon indicates) to which he devotes himself.

9 And if the Moon looked at him from the square in the two times, and they are in a good condition in both, made fortunate, then it indicates that he will have respect, assets, and different benefits, and he will be well praised and have good management.

10 And if the Moon looked at him from the opposition in the two times, and they are in a suitable condition in both, then his contention and quarreling with others will multiply, and his speech will multiply, and he will increase in his reason, and be victorious over his enemies.

11 And if the Moon assembled with him in the two times, and they are in a suitable condition in both, and she is far from his rays, then in terms of suitability it indicates something like what she indicates in his sextile, except that distresses will pass over him, and the outcome of it will pass over to good and safety, and he will be devoted to stratagems and hidden things. **12** And if the Moon was under the rays in the two times, and they are in a suitable condition in both,[247] then he will be devoted to stratagems, betrayal, and cheating, but he will be safe from adversity.[248]

13 And in all of this, if her assembling with him or looking at him was in [only] one of the times, it subtracts from everything we said.

14 And if the planets were in the heart of the Sun, in a suitable condition, made fortunate, then it indicates suitability and goodness in the category of their indication; but if they were in a bad condition, made unfortunate, it indicates the contrary of that.

---

[247] Abū Ma'shar is apparently distinguishing being merely under the rays (implying hiddenness), from being actually harmed by burning.

[248] This actually reads as though "she" will be safe from "his" adversity (i.e., the Moon and the Sun), but could also be read as though the native is safe from the adversity that could come from the deception, etc.

Chapter II.14: On the indication of the Sun when he is the lord of the year & is in a bad condition

1 If the Sun was the lord of the year, the majority of the work in it is in accordance with the condition of the distributor,[249] and the lord of the sign in which the distribution from the releaser is, and partnering with it is the rest of what we stated before.[250]

2 Then after that, look: for if he was in a bad condition, made unfortunate, then it indicates that something detestable will affect the owner of the revolution from everything the Sun indicates (of what we stated before), and the condition of fathers will be bad, as well as his condition in authority and rank.

3 And you ought to examine closely his assembling with the rays, Lots, and twelfth-parts, for he would indicate corruption in accordance with their categories.

[Sun-Venus]

4 If the Sun was the lord of the year and Venus looked at him in the root and the revolution from the sextile, and they are in a bad condition <or> made unfortunate in both, then it indicates that he will be distressed because of the Sultan, women, household furnishings,[251] and possessions, and he will be dissatisfied, with many distresses, have bad management, and malicious gossip about him will multiply.

5 And if Venus assembled with him in the two times, and they are in a bad condition in both, made unfortunate,[252] and she is under his rays, burned, then distresses will affect him from women (and because of them), and from enemies, and because of assets and children, and his

---

[249] This was not mentioned in II.13, **1**, but is included for the Moon in II.22, **1**. It is probably the distributor for the directed longevity releaser.

[250] See II.13, **1**, and compare with II.22, **1**.

[251] **E** reads, "personal servants."

[252] Adding منحوسان with **B** and in accordance with sentences below; this portion of the sentence seems to have been garbled a bit, and **E** and **P** omit this word, while **B** seems to have at first abbreviated it greatly before adding the rest in a marginal note.

body will be in an uproar from an ailment and illness, and he will be spoken of badly, and he will be devoted to stratagems and hidden matters, and something detestable will affect him from the category of the indication of Venus.

[Sun-Mercury]

6 If the Sun was the lord of the year and Mercury assembled with him in the root and the revolution, and they are in a bad condition in both, or[253] made unfortunate, and [Mercury] is under [the Sun's] rays, then distresses and different detestable things will affect him from the Sultan and from people having power, and some of the authorities will be angry with him, and he will be devoted to stratagems and [types of] management, and writers, and authorities, and those who are confined, and those who are doomed, and he will be in someone else's power, and he will quarrel because of different matters, and will be distressed because of children, slaves, and servants.

[Sun-Moon]

7 If the Sun was the lord of the year and the Moon looked at him in the root and the revolution from the trine or sextile, and they were in a bad condition in both, or made unfortunate, then it will subtract from everything we mentioned about her looking at him from these two directions when they are both in a suitable condition; and he will have much confusion in the works he devotes himself to.

8 Now[254] if the Moon looked at him in the two times from the square, and they are in a bad condition or made unfortunate in both, then quarrels, ailments, and illnesses will affect him, and it will undermine his way of life, and he will be distressed because of assets and people who treat him unjustly and envy him, and it enables him to mistreat whom[ever] he wants.

---

[253] Reading for "and."
[254] For this sentence, cf. *Carmen* II.15, **33-34**.

9 Now if the Moon looked at him from the opposition in the two times, and they are in a bad condition in both, <or made unfortunate>,²⁵⁵ then contentions and quarrels will afflict him, and something detestable from the Sultan, time after time, and some of the authorities will be angry with him, and he will be distressed because of women, children, the family, and assets.

10 And if the Moon assembled with him in the two times and she is under his rays, and they are in a bad condition in both, or made unfortunate, alarm and fear will affect him, and types of detestable things, and he will be distressed for various reasons pertaining to the Sultan²⁵⁶ and fathers.

        ✦ ✦ ✦

11 And in all of this, if these planets assembled with him or looked at him in [only] one of the two times, it will be below that. **12** But as for his indication with the planets which are above him,²⁵⁷ we have already discussed that in what preceded; this is the indication of the Sun if he was in [1] a suitable condition and planets [also] in a suitable condition assembled with him or looked at him, or he was in [2] a bad condition and planets in a bad condition assembled with him or looked at him. **13** But as for if the Sun was in [3] a suitable condition and a planet in a bad condition looked at him, or he was in [4] a bad condition and a planet in a suitable condition looked at him, the work in those two [cases] and others (of the things which follow that in this category) is like what we discussed in the indication of Saturn.²⁵⁸

---

²⁵⁵ Adding in accordance with the previous paragraphs.
²⁵⁶ **E**: "the authorities."
²⁵⁷ That is, the superior planets.
²⁵⁸ See II.5, **58-66**.

Chapter II.15: On the indication of the Sun in the houses of the circle, if he was the lord of the year

1 If the Sun was the lord of the year and he is in a suitable condition in the root and the revolution, in the stakes, received, free of the infortunes, then the owner of the revolution will increase in his rank, he will gain good, and he will be commended and praised. **2** And if he was in the Ascendant or the Midheaven, then he will increase in his rank and will be renowned, having a voice among the people of his class, and he will have good from the Sultan; and if he was in the seventh he will be devoted to different managements, and will be victorious over enemies, and will be healthy in his body, and see what he loves from women; and if he was in the fourth he will gain good because of real estate, fathers, and old men. **3** And if the Sun was in these positions in the two times but he is made unfortunate, not received, then something detestable will affect him from the category of the indication of the stake in which he is, and he will have little benefit, and fear of the Sultan will afflict him.

4 And if the Sun was the lord of the year, and he was in the eleventh or fifth in the two times, received, not made unfortunate, then he will be in a suitable condition in his food and clothing, and he will see what he loves from his brothers, and will delight in children, and will increase in them and in his crops and revenue, and he will be devoted to gifts and messengers. **5** And if he was in them in the two times and is made unfortunate, not received, then he will be distressed because of friends who have authority, and they will undermine him, and he will contend with them, and he will be distressed because of children.

6 And if the Sun was the lord of the year and he is in the ninth or third in the two times, received, not made unfortunate, then he will travel because of the Sultan, and beautiful things will be said about him because of religion, and he will have good from brothers and relatives, and they will have [it] likewise from him as well. **7** But if he was in them [while] made unfortunate, not received, then ugly things will be reported about him because of religion, and he will go on a journey he will not benefit from, and something detestable will afflict him in it, and he will be distressed because of travelers, brothers, and relatives.

8 And if the Sun was the lord of the year and he is in the second and eighth in the two times, received, not made unfortunate, then it indicates mild-temperedness and leisure time, and benefits and revenue will be prepared for him in accordance with [his] spending, without labor. **9** And if he was in them and he is made unfortunate, not received, then it indicates leisure time but a scarcity of benefit, and a bad condition in his way of life, and negligence and laziness in what would benefit him.

10 And if <the Sun> was the lord of the year and he is in the sixth in the two times, received, not made unfortunate, then it indicates mild-temperedness and safety. **11** But if he was made unfortunate, not received, then it indicates illness, heat and dryness, and a pain in his eyes and the upper part of the body, and in the head.

12 And if the Sun was the lord of the year and he is in the twelfth in the two times, received, not made unfortunate, then it indicates that beautiful things will be spoken about him, and he will be safe from enemies. **13** But if he was made unfortunate, not received, then it indicates confinement, and distresses because of confined people and enemies, or he will be banished from his country.

14 And if in the root the Sun was in one of the houses of the circle, in one of the conditions, and in the revolution he is in what corresponds to that house (relative to the sign of the terminal point or the Ascendant of the revolution), and he is looking at the position of the root or is in it, then it is more firm for the indication of what he indicates. **15** And if it was the contrary of that, blend the indication of his two conditions and places, according to what we discussed about Saturn.

Chapter II.16: On the indication of Venus when she is the lord of the year & is in a suitable condition

1 If[259] Venus was the lord of the year and she is in a suitable condition in the root and the revolution, in her own house or in a position in which she has a claim (or she is received), not made unfortunate, then the owner of the revolution will have much amusement, delight, listening to songs, and he will increase in his clothing, sexual intercourse, perfume,[260] and possessions, and he will associate with friends and brothers, befriend men and women, get married, and be devoted to colors[261] and fornication. **2** And if she was in her own house or exaltation, or she was received, that will be from a direction he is aware of; and if she was in exile [but still] received, that will be while abroad and from foreigners.[262]

3 And you ought to examine the rays, Lots, and twelfth-parts which Venus assembles with or looks at in the two times with power [and] an aspect of affection and harmony: for it will indicate a suitability of condition in them, in accordance with their indication.

[Venus-Mercury]

4 If Venus was the lord of the year and she and Mercury are in a suitable condition in the root and the revolution, and Mercury looked at her from the sextile in both, then in that year he will crave delights and amusement, and will increase in his children and women, and will associate with women who have good culture, elegance, charm, and knowledge, and frequently he will be occupied with delighting in them and in fornication, and in beautification, and colors, and he will be devoted to men having culture and elegance, having writing and

---

[259] For this sentence, cf. perhaps Da. 154.
[260] طيبه. Or more broadly, "goodness."
[261] Or perhaps, "make-up" (الأصباغ).
[262] Or, "strangers" (الغرباء).

knowledge,²⁶³ and he will be made aware of many hidden secrets, and he will be distressed in some of the times because of what we stated.

5 And²⁶⁴ if Mercury looked at her in the two times from the square, and they are in a suitable condition in both, and Mercury is looking down upon her (or Venus is looking down upon him), then in that year he will be loved, very much devoted to culture, writing books, the sciences, adultery, and colors, and friendliness, and he will increase in his power, and will delight in women who have beauty—except that he will be distressed in some of the times of his delight and be disturbed in what is prepared for him.

6 Now²⁶⁵ if Mercury assembled with her in the two times and they are in a suitable condition in both, then the love of amusement and joy²⁶⁶ will conquer him in that year, and an increase in women who have culture and elegance, and he will delight in them and in children, and he will be devoted to composing speech and writing poetry, and friendliness, colors, adultery, adornment, paintings,²⁶⁷ perfume, and scents, and he will increase in his cleverness, and will treat people well, and will know many hidden secrets, and will labor much, and²⁶⁸ will travel.

[Venus-Moon]

7 If²⁶⁹ Venus was the lord of the year and the Moon looked at her in the root and the revolution from the trine or sextile, and they are in a suitable condition in both, then in that year he will be pleased, cheerful, with a joking disposition, enjoying his own women and the women of others, and perhaps he will have sex with male youths, and amuse himself in [a number of] ways.

---

²⁶³ Reading with **B**. **E** and **P** read confusingly, and then add "frivolity and flirtation."
²⁶⁴ For this sentence, cf. *Carmen* II.15, **35**.
²⁶⁵ For this sentence, cf. *Carmen* II.22, **1**.
²⁶⁶ **E**: "exuberance."
²⁶⁷ Or, "sculptures."
²⁶⁸ This should probably be "or."
²⁶⁹ For this sentence, cf. *Carmen* II.14, **23**.

8 And[270] if the Moon looked at her from the square in the two times, and they are in a suitable condition in both, and the Moon is looking down upon Venus, then in that year he will increase in his assets, furnishings, and possessions—except that he will be distressed because of something of the affairs of women, pleasures, and decorations. **9** And if Venus was the one looking down upon [the Moon], then in that year he will be loved, putting on affectations,[271] having cleanliness and decorations, having good management, desire, clothing,[272] and way of life, and he will be distressed because of marriage and women, and he will be devoted to corrupt women, of a bad type, and there will be an increase in the suitability of his mother's condition.

10 And[273] if the Moon assembled with her in the two times and they are in a suitable condition in both, he will increase in his culture, elegance, cheerfulness, and delight, and he will concern himself with eagerness and desire for some foreign women whom he does not know while abstaining from those he has authority over, and his irritation with them (and because of them) will multiply.

11 And[274] if the Moon looked at her in the two times from the opposition and they are in a suitable condition in both, then distress and toil will affect him often because of hidden secrets, and fleeting confusions and distresses will affect him because of women, children, managements, and different works.

12 And in all of this, if their assembling with her or looking at her was in [only] one of the times, it will subtract from everything we stated.

---

[270] For this paragraph, cf. *Carmen* II.15, **36-37**.
[271] Reading متخلّقًا with **B** and **E**. **P** reads, "a fabricator / making things up" (مختلقًا).
[272] **E** reads, "religion." **B** seems to read "profit" (الرّبى).
[273] For this sentence, cf. *Carmen* II.22, **3**.
[274] For this sentence, cf. *Carmen* II.16, **32**.

Chapter II.17: On the indication of Venus when she is the lord of the year & is in a bad condition

1 If[275] Venus was the lord of the year and she is in a bad condition in the root and the revolution, in an alien sign, then distresses and harsh disasters will afflict him in that year, [which] appear in all of the things of Venus, and his distress with women, children, and friends will multiply, as well as decoration, entertainment, delight, clothing, and food.

2 And if she was in a place of exile and hostility, in a sign of the image of people, the distresses will affect him in women and because of them: but if she was in exile, that will affect him from foreigners,[276] while if she was in a sign of her enemies that will affect her from enemies and because of them. **3** And if she were in a sign of her friends, that will be from friends.

4 Now if the sign in which she is, was not of the image of people, then it indicates the weakness of the body, illness, sorrow, and confusion, and distress with spouses, mothers, and their situations.

5 And if Venus was retrograde or under the rays, then what we mentioned will be [more] firm and corrupt, and his delight and pleasures will vex him, and he will loathe them, and misfortunes will happen to him because of food. **6** But if her condition was like that and she was with the Lot of marriage, then it indicates distresses in relation to women.

7 And you ought to examine the rays, Lots, and twelfth-parts which Venus assembles with or looks at, with strength [and] an aspect of conflict while she is in a bad condition, because they will indicate corruption in the category of their indication.

[Venus-Mercury]

8 If Venus was the lord of the year and she and Mercury were in a bad condition in the root and the revolution, and he looked at her in

---

[275] For **1-6**, cf. Da. 156.
[276] Or, "strangers" (الغرباء).

both from the sextile, then it indicates distresses and confusion in everything they would have indicated if they looked at each other from this direction and were both in a suitable condition.[277]

9 And[278] if Mercury looked at her from the square[279] in the two times and they were in a bad condition in both, then he will be distressed, and something detestable and a bad reputation will affect him because of women and management, and in every matter they would have indicated if they looked at each other from this direction and they were both in a suitable condition.[280]

10 And if Mercury assembled with her in the two times and they were in a bad condition in both, then in that year he will be eager for women, amusement, and delight, and something detestable and distresses will afflict him from them and from writers and writing, and works he does, and from every matter they would have indicated if they had been assembled and in a suitable condition.[281]

[Venus-Moon]

11 If Venus was the lord of the year and she and the Moon were in a bad condition in the root and the revolution, and she looked at her in both from the trine or sextile, then in that year there will be much change in the condition of women and sexual intercourse, and distresses will affect him because of them and because of mothers, and he will be devoted to conflicting[282] reports (and they will generally cause him grief), and much of his delight and entertainment will undermine him.

12 And[283] if the Moon looked at her in the two times from the square and they are in a bad condition in both, and the Moon looked

---

[277] See II.16, **4**.
[278] For this sentence, cf. *Carmen* II.15, **35**.
[279] This could only happen by whole signs.
[280] See II.16, **5**.
[281] See II.16, **6**.
[282] Or simply, "different" (مختلفة).
[283] For this paragraph, cf. *Carmen* II.15, **36-37**.

down upon [Venus], then he will be defamed because of women, and be distressed because of assets. **13** And if Venus was the one looking down upon [the Moon], and their conditions were like that, then in that year he will have bad management, and will be distressed because of advantages and his way of life, and women, and marriage, and he will be devoted to corrupt, low-class women, and it will corrupt much of his possessions and dishes.

14 And if the Moon looked at her in the two times from the opposition, and they were in a bad condition in both, then he will be distressed because of marriage and women, and some of his children will become ill or will be ruined.

15 And if the Moon assembled with her in the two times and they are in a bad condition in both, then he will be annoyed and distressed because of people who have culture, sciences, and the knowledge of writing, and he will separate from his family, and a disagreement will occur between him and them, and he will withdraw from them, and he will be eager for close relations with foreign women who are not known, and his family will prefer other men besides him.

16 And in all of this, if the assembling of [Mercury and the Moon] with her or their looking at her was in [only] one time, it will be below that.

⁂

17 And as for the indication of Venus with the planets which are above her, we have already discussed that in what preceded; these are the indications of Venus when she is in [1] a suitable condition and these two planets assemble with her or look at her when they are in a suitable condition, or she is in [2] a bad condition and a planet in a bad condition looks at or assembles with her. **18** But as for if Venus was in [3] a suitable condition and a planet in a bad condition assembled with or looked at her, or she is in [4] a bad condition and a planet in a good condition assembled with or looked at her, the work in those [cases] and others[284] (of everything which is of this category) is like what we stated about Saturn.[285]

Chapter II.18: On the indication of Venus in the houses of the circle, if she was the lord of the year

1 If Venus was the lord of the year and she is in the four stakes in the root and the revolution, received, not made unfortunate, then it indicates that the owner of the revolution will delight and rejoice in various ways due to the Sultan, and those having importance, and an increase in assets, rank, and animals, and he will reach the gates of the kings, and will gain clothing and possessions, and will delight in women, and his sexual intercourse will multiply, and he will be successful in [gaining] what he needs, and he will increase in his real estate. **2** And if she was in them and she is retrograde, he will gain what we mentioned, except that it will be from a direction which is not good and some of it will be spoiled. **3** And if she was in these four positions and she is made unfortunate, not received, then he will be disturbed in his way of life, and loss will afflict him, and evil things will be reported about him, and quarrels will happen to him, and confusion and distress in accordance with the category of the indication of the stake she is in. **4** Now if the one making her unfortunate was Saturn, various cold, bad pains will happen to him, like paralysis on one side of the body, cold, and pleurisy;[286] and if the one making her unfortunate was Mars, something detestable will afflict him because of women and sex, and his possessions will be burned and stolen, and his blood will be agitated. **5** And if she was in this condition in the fourth, then perhaps his woman will die.

---

[284] Reading the rest of the sentence with **B**. **E** and **P** read: "and in everything else of the things which are discussed of this category, [it] is like what we stated for the indication of Saturn."
[285] See II.5, **58-66**.
[286] An inflammation of the lung.

6 If Venus was the lord of the year and in she is in the fifth or eleventh in the two times, received, not made unfortunate, then he will increase in his friends, women, and possessions, and he will delight in children, and increase in them—if the root of his nativity had indicated that. **7** And if she was in them and she is made unfortunate, not received, then distresses will afflict him for no purpose, and in general that will be because of women and children (if he had them), and he will be hostile to his friends.

8 And if Venus was the lord of the year and she is in the ninth or third in the two times, received, not made unfortunate, then the native will travel in that year, and on his journey he will have status and rank,[287] and good, and his social relationships with friends will be good, and he will be well commended, and benefit by brothers, the family, and relatives, and some of his women will travel, and he will be [well] dressed, and pray, and be kind to the people. **9** Now if she was in them and she is made unfortunate, not received, then reports will reach him which will distress him, and he will go on a distant[288] journey on which something detestable will happen to him, and he will be defamed in his religion, and he will contend with his brothers, and his assets will be ruined, and he will encounter something detestable because of buying and selling.

10 If Venus was the lord of the year and she is in the eighth or the second in the two times, received, not made unfortunate, then he will have benefit from the underclass or from base work; and her being in the eighth especially indicates an abundance of spending. **11** Now if Venus was in the second [but] made unfortunate, not received, then it indicates the corruption of his assets, and his negligence and idleness, and the stagnation of his work, if he was of those who are devoted to one of the trades. **12** And if she was in the eighth, it indicates leisure time and a scarcity of benefit, and contention regarding assets, and corruption in them.

---

[287] Adding with **E**.
[288] Adding "distant" with **P**.

13 And if Venus was the lord of the year and she is in the sixth or twelfth in the two times, received, not made unfortunate, then he will benefit because of the underclass, remedies, drugs, food, and provisions. **14** And if she was made unfortunate, not received, and she is in the sixth, then it indicates leisure time, and illness from the essence of the infortune: if that was Saturn, then from black bile; if it was Mars, from blood; and if it was the Sun, then from heat. **15** And if Venus was in the twelfth, made unfortunate, not received, something detestable and distresses will affect him in relation to enemies, and the confined, confinement, and punishment.

16 And if Venus was the lord of the year and she is in one of the houses in the root, in one of the conditions, and in the revolution she is in the corresponding house relative to the sign of the terminal point or the Ascendant of the revolution, and she is looking at her own position in the root or is in it, then it is firmer for the indication of what she indicates. **17** And if it was the contrary of that, then blend the indication of her two conditions and two places, in the manner we described for the indication of Saturn.

18 And if Venus in the revolution was falling from the stakes or what follows them, it indicates that the owner of the revolution will loathe amusements and delight, and eating and drinking, or he will be harmed by that; and it is firmer for that if the year had terminated at the position of Saturn in the root, and Saturn[289] was in one of the stakes of the sign of the terminal point or the Ascendant of the revolution.[290]

---

[289] This is probably the transiting Saturn, at the time of the revolution.
[290] In that case, the natal and revolutionary presence of Saturn would spoil the pleasure which Venus would be trying to produce.

Chapter II.19: On the indication of Mercury when he is the lord of the year & is in a suitable condition

1 If[291] Mercury was the lord of the year and he is in a suitable condition in the root and the revolution, then it indicates the earning of money in that year, and his collecting [of it], and praise, and a livelihood and benefit because of business, reason, the sciences, culture, speech, logic, quarrels, debating, and suitable works, and praised management, and he will have good praise, and [there will be] beautiful talk about him, and the satisfaction of the people in what he says, and their being together with him in that.

2 And you ought to examine the Lots, the rays, and the twelfth-parts which Mercury assembles with or looks at in the two times, in strength, for it will indicate suitability in the category of what they indicate.

[Mercury-Moon]

3 And[292] if Mercury was the lord of the year, and he and the Moon are in a suitable condition in the root and the revolution, and she looked at him in both from the trine or sextile, then the owner of the revolution will be devoted to various sciences, and he will preserve them.

4 Now if the Moon looked at him in the two times from the square, and they are in a suitable condition in both, and Mercury is looking down upon her, then he will increase in his logic and reason—but he will be distressed by a group of the people. **5** And if the Moon was the one looking down upon him, then malice will get the best of him, and recklessness, and a scarcity of stability in one thing.

6 And if the Moon looked at him in the two times from the opposition, and they are in a suitable condition in both, then people who are

---

[291] For this sentence, cf. Da. 160-61.
[292] For this sentence, cf. *Carmen* II.14, **24**.

enemies will appear to him, and he will be victorious over everyone who contends with him and quarrels with him, and is hostile to him.

7 And[293] if the Moon assembled with him in the two times, and they are in a suitable condition in both, then he will increase in his culture and knowledge in that year, and things will be preserved by him, and he will be praised in his opinion, and associate with men or people who are low in importance, and there will be an increase in the suitability of his mother's condition, and her culture and knowledge, and the goodness of her management.

8 And in all of this, if she assembled with or looked at him in [only] one of the times, it will subtract from everything we mentioned.

Chapter II.20: On the indication of Mercury when he is the lord of the year & is in a bad condition

1 If Mercury was the lord of the year and he is in a bad condition in the root and the revolution, then types of harm will afflict him in that year from children, enemies, slaves, and low-class people, and from business and teaching, associates, calculation and accounting, partners, books, management, speech, controversy, contentions, and lawsuits, and his hope will be cut off, and he will despair of [any] types of benefit. **2** And[294] if Mercury was in the west (in addition to the badness of his condition), and he is made unfortunate, and the Lot of children is with him, something detestable will affect children and slaves;[295] and if he was with the Lot of friends, the adversity will be from friends; and if he was with the Lot of work and authority, then the adversity will affect him in relation to his works and the authorities, and he will pass over to chains of iron, and harm, and different distresses. **3** And if his condition was like that and he is *not* in the west, that will be less.

---

[293] For this sentence, cf. *Carmen* II.23, **2**.
[294] For this sentence, cf. Da. 164.
[295] But perhaps this should read, "will affect *him from*" children and slaves, as with the other Lots below.

4 And you should look in this way when he assembles with the rest of the Lots, rays, and twelfth-parts, or looks at them with strength.

[Mercury-Moon]

5 If Mercury was the lord of the year and he and the Moon are in a bad condition in the root and the revolution, and she looked at him in the two times from the trine or sextile, then distresses will afflict him because of travel, siblings, and the sciences, and he will be deprived of[296] things.

6 And[297] if the Moon looked at him from the square in the two times, and they are in a bad condition in both, and Mercury is looking down upon her, then detestable things and different distresses will afflict him from groups of people, and from writing, writers, and betrayal, and he will be confined or shackled. **7** And if the Moon was the one looking down upon him, then in that year he will be restless,[298] with little patience, fickle, with little stability in one opinion.

8 And[299] if the Moon looked at him in the two times from the opposition, and they are in a bad condition in both, then in that year he will shrink from logic and speech, and he will be tested by quarrels and enmity, and a group of the people.

9 And[300] if the Moon assembled with him in the two times and they are in a bad condition in both, then in that year he will have little stability in one opinion,[301] and will be devoted to concocting falsehoods, and will be distressed by people whose importance and social esteem is low.

10 And in all of this, if she assembled with or looked at him in [only] one of the times, it will be below that.

---

[296] E: he will "pretend" or "fake" things.
[297] For this paragraph, cf. *Carmen* II.15, **38-39**.
[298] Or, "anxious" (جزوع).
[299] For this sentence, cf. *Carmen* II.16, **33**.
[300] For this sentence, cf. *Carmen* II.23, **1**.
[301] P: "condition."

11 Now as for the indication of Mercury with the planets which are above him, we have already mentioned that in what has preceded; but these are the indications of Mercury when he is in [1] a suitable condition and planets in a suitable condition look at him, or he is in [2] a bad condition and planets [also] in a bad condition look at him. **12** But as for when Mercury is in [3] a suitable condition and a planet in a bad condition looks at him, or he is in [4] a bad condition and a planet in a suitable condition looks at him, then the work in those two [cases] and others (of the things which pertain to them in this category) will be just like what we stated about the indication of Saturn.[302]

Chapter II.21: On the indication of Mercury when he is the lord of the year, in the houses of the circle

1 If Mercury was the lord of the year and he is in the four stakes in the root and the revolution, in a suitable condition, received, not made unfortunate, then the owner of the revolution will gain status, rank, and benefits from writing and business, and serving the Sultan, and he will increase in the quickness of his instruction and his accepting of the sciences, and his preservation of them, and he will be praised because of these things, and good will be said about him: and that will be stronger if he was in the Ascendant or the Midheaven. **2** But if Mercury was in these four positions in the two times, in a bad condition, made unfortunate, not received, in that year he will encounter something detestable because of writing, writers, and calculation, and illnesses will befall him, and he will be accused in those works he pursues; and if he was devoted to business, selling, and buying, then he will suffer loss in it. **3** And in the seventh and fourth especially, it indicates quarreling and contention with his family. **4** And if he was retrograde, something detestable will be reported about him because of sexual intercourse, and an illness will befall him, of the nature of the star making him unfortunate.

---

[302] See II.5, **58-66**.

5 And if he was in the fifth or eleventh in the two times, in a suitable condition, received, not made unfortunate, he will have much good in that year, and he will befriend the nobles and authorities, and will profit in business, and in selling and buying, and if he had children he will delight in them, or he will have children (if the root of his nativity indicated that). **6** And if he was in them and he is in a bad condition, made unfortunate, not received, his friends will be hostile to him in that year, and <it indicates> the slowness of his understanding of things; and if he had a child, an ailment and illness will afflict it, and death will be feared for him.[303] **7** And if Mercury was retrograde, the owner of the revolution will be confused.

8 And if Mercury was in the ninth or third <in the two times>, then in that year the owner of the revolution will travel, and will see what he loves on his journey, and he will have good visions[304] with a true interpretation, and good will be spoken of him because of his commitment to religion, and an increase in reason as well as good, praised management, and good will affect his brothers and acquaintances, and he will be praised in his situations, and he will increase in knowledge and his insight into things. **9** And if Mercury was in them in the two times and he is in a bad condition, made unfortunate, not received, then in that year he will travel, and something detestable and damage will afflict him on his journey, and he will have doubts in religion, and ugly things will be reported about him because of it, and he will have bad visions, and suffer loss in buying, selling, and business, and it will corrupt what is between him and his brothers, and the people of his house.

10 And if Mercury was in the eighth or the second in the two times, and he is in a suitable condition, received, not made unfortunate, he will benefit from selling and buying, and will profit in them both, and his associations with the people will be praised, and he will have a good condition. **11** But if Mercury was in them and he is in a bad condition, made unfortunate, not received, he will suffer loss and a

---

[303] I'm not sure if this is the native or the child.
[304] Or, "dreams," here and below.

downturn[305] in business, and he will be incriminated, blamed in his management, and will quarrel because of assets.

12 And if Mercury was in the twelfth or sixth in the two times, and he is in a suitable condition, received, not made unfortunate, then in that year he will not be eager for collecting assets, and he will withdraw from business and [finding] advantage, and he will acquire benefits from the underclass and every low work. **13** And if he was in them and he is <in a bad condition>, made unfortunate, not received, illnesses will befall him of the nature of the planet making him unfortunate (if it was Saturn, then from windiness, cold, pains of the joints, nerves, and veins; and if it was Mars, then from blood and what is like that), and he will be seized for [a crime] he did not commit, and evil will reported about him for what he did not do, and confinement and distresses will afflict him.

14 And if Mercury was in one of the houses of the circle in the root, in one of the conditions, and in the revolution he is in what corresponds to that house relative to the Ascendant of the root, or the sign of the terminal point, or the Ascendant of the revolution, and[306] he is in what is like that condition, then it is more confirmed for what he indicates. **15** And if it was the contrary of that, blend the indication of his two conditions and his two places, in the manner which preceded in our discussion.

Chapter II.22: On the indication of the Moon when she is the lord of the year & is in a suitable condition

1 If[307] the Moon was the lord of the year, then the majority of the judgment about the conditions of the owner of the revolution will be in accordance with the condition of [1] the distributor[308] and [2] the

---

[305] وضع.
[306] Reading with **E** and **P**. **B** reads, "or."
[307] For a possible source of this sentence in al-Andarzaghar, cf. Da. 129.
[308] As with the Sun in II.14, **1**, this is probably the distributor for the longevity releaser.

lord of the sign in which the distribution from the [longevity] releaser[309] is (whichever releaser the directing was from), and acting as partner with the lord of the sign of the distribution in the indication, is [3] the planet which was in Cancer in the root or the revolution, and [4] the planet which the Moon connects with, so long as she is in her [current] sign. **2** Now if in that sign she connected with not just one, then see how many there are: for if it was two planets, the year is divided into two halves; and if her connection in that sign of hers was with three planets, then that year is divided into equal thirds; and if it increased beyond that, then the year is divided according to their number. **3** So, his condition in each one of the portions of the year (in terms of good fortune and misfortune, and good and evil), will be in accordance with the condition of the planet which owns the portion. **4** But if the Moon was empty in course, his situation will be in accordance with [5] the condition of the lord of her house, whether it looked at her[310] or not. **5** And along with what we mentioned, you ought to call upon [6] the conditions of the Moon as a witness: for if she was in a suitable condition, it generally indicates the suitability of the category of what she indicates; and if she was corrupted, it indicates corruption in it, and indicates an illness of the body, and the badness of the mother's condition.

6 And if the Moon was northern, increasing in calculation, then it indicates a suitability of condition; and that is more excellent if she was rising in it,[311] increasing in glow. **7** But if she was northern [and] decreasing in calculation, then his condition will be middling.

8 And if the Moon was southern, decreasing in calculation, then his condition will be bad, and that is worse if she was decreasing in glow. **9** And if she was southern [but] increasing in glow and calculation, then

---

[309] I clarify that this is the longevity releaser in accordance with the similar phrasing in II.13, **1**.

[310] Or, "it." That is, it does not matter whether the lord of her sign is in aversion to it or to her. But perhaps it would make a difference in the interpretation: see **17-22** below.

[311] This probably means "in latitude."

his condition will be middling. **10** And if she was descending in the south, decreasing in glow and calculation, then his condition will be very bad.

11 And you ought to examine her assembling with the rays, Lots, and the twelfth-parts, and her looking at them, so that the judgment about each one of them will be in accordance with their condition relative to it.

12 But as for her indication upon the planets' looking at her, we have already discussed that in what preceded.

13 And as for her condition in the houses of the circle, the judgment about that is according to [the house's] nature and her condition, in the manner of judging the rest of the planets.[312]

[Other rules for the Moon]

14 And you ought to look at the sign of the Moon of the revolution: for indeed its power is close to the power of the Ascendant of the year. **15** So if the Moon in her sign was connecting with a planet [which was] received,[313] made fortunate, in a suitable condition, then everything which he begins in that year in terms of works will be completed quickly, and he will increase in works beneficial for him, and in the goodness of his condition. **16** And if it was in a bad condition or made unfortunate, then it indicates something detestable in the category of its indication and the indication of the planet making it unfortunate.

17 But if she was empty in course, you should see which planet's house she is in. **18** For if she was in a house of Saturn, and Saturn is in a suitable condition, then he will benefit by sowing and lands, and everything which relates to that (of rivers and digging them, and the digging of canals, and planting); and if Saturn was in a corrupt condition and he is in a sign of the image of people, then it indicates that something detestable and troubles will afflict him from people, time

---

[312] See also VII.8 for a list of the Moon in the houses.
[313] **B** adds "by her." This would indeed be even better.

after time.³¹⁴ **19** And if the Moon was in a sign of water, made unfortunate by Saturn or another, then it indicates wounds and ulcers.

20 And if she was in a house of Jupiter and he is in a suitable condition,³¹⁵ then he will be well commended among kings and the nobles, and every work he begins will be completed, and if he sought children a child will be born to him, and he will inherit the assets of his fathers, and will do work having power. **21** But if Jupiter was falling, in a bad condition, then it indicates distresses because of different things, and malicious gossip about him, and the people will slander him.

22 And if she was in a house of Mars,³¹⁶ and Mars was in a stake in <the root> and the revolution, and especially in the Midheaven by day, then it indicates damages from riding animals, and something detestable because of work and the Sultan,³¹⁷ and malicious gossip regarding him, and the cutting of his body with iron, and the flowing of blood from him.

[Other rules for the lord of the year]

23 And of course in all of the times³¹⁸ you should look at the lord of the year, whether it was the Moon or not, connecting or empty in course, in whichever planet's house it is, in the revolution.³¹⁹ **24** For if

---

³¹⁴ Or perhaps, "on occasion" or "occasionally."

³¹⁵ **B** and **E** add, "from it" or "from her." Certainly we would want him to be well configured to that sign and to the Moon, but the sentence for Saturn does not add this.

³¹⁶ Reading the next clause with **P**, but adding "in the root" to explain its use of "*and the revolution.*" The next closest reading is **B**, "and Mars was in a stake of the revolution," which is not quite as strong as making him angular in both charts. **E** simply has "in the revolution, in a stake," which would mean that *the Moon* is there rather than Mars.

³¹⁷ Or, "authority."

³¹⁸ That is, the nativity and the revolution; but Abū Ma'shar might also be referring to the monthly returns.

³¹⁹ This is stated badly. What Abū Ma'shar means is that the lord of the year *is* in fact empty in course: in that case, see whose sign it's in. That is why he reminds us of the rule for the Moon in **27**.

it was in a house of Saturn and both it and Saturn are in a suitable condition, they indicate suitability in the category of what Saturn (who is the lord of its house) indicates—just like what we stated about the indication of the Moon when she is in one of the signs. **25** And the indication of the lord of the year will be like that when[ever] it is in a house of one of the planets.

26 And when a planet is elevated above[320] the lord of the year, its indication will appear: and that is like if Jupiter was the lord of the year and the Sun was elevated above him, then [the Sun] will grant him authority. **27** Or, like if Mars was the lord of the year and the Sun was elevated above him: for he will travel—and if the Sun was excellent in condition, the travel will be praised [and] beneficial, while if he was in a bad condition it will be spoiled [and] bad. **28** Or, like if Saturn looked down upon the Sun and undermined him, and [the Sun] is in the house of enemies: it indicates tribulation and detestable things entering upon the native's father because of spending, and travel, and being banished from his country, and fleeing from the Sultan, along with chains and confinement.

Chapter II.23: On the indication of the Ascendant of the revolution & its lord, & their partnership with the terminal point &the lord of the year, & with others, in the indication

1 After the sign of the terminal point, the power of the indication belongs to the distributor.[321] **2** But we discuss the Ascendant [of the revolution] after [the sign of the terminal point] because the Ascendant and its lord act as partners with the sign of the terminal point and its lord, in the indication of many things: so we discuss it after [the sign of the terminal point] so that the sequence and composition of both may be even better.

---

[320] استعلى على: this most likely means "overcoming," as in **28** ("looked down upon").
[321] This may be true for a *particular* year, but as III.2, **2** points out, the distribution is stronger for activating rooted matters because of its broader scope and development over years.

3 So you ought to know the Ascendant of the year, and the position of its lord as well as the rest of the planets relative to it, because the power of the planets of the root and revolution is known from their positions in the revolution relative to the Ascendant of the year and its stakes, and the rest of its houses.[322]

4 And each house has an indication over a known thing: for the stakes indicate the condition of the body, rank, women, and fathers; and what follows them indicates the condition of assets, children, the dead, and good fortune (and friends, and good praise or criticism);[323] and the falling ones indicate the condition of brothers, illness, travel, and enemies (and bad speech, contention, chains, and confinement)—but each one also has an indication over other things, which are apparent to scholars of the science of the stars. **5** (And indeed the indication of each house will be manifest when one of the planets comes to be in it.)

6 So if the lord of the Ascendant of the year was in a suitable condition in the revolution, free of the infortunes, in its own glow, received, then he will gain good and authority in that year. **7** So if it was in the Ascendant or Midheaven, he will be healthy in his body, and will gain power and status; while if it was in the seventh or fourth, he will increase in his family, women, and attendants. **8** But if it was in one of them and he was corrupted, something detestable will affect him from the category of its indication.

9 Then after that you look at its condition in the rest of the houses of the circle,[324] as well as its connection with the planets (and their connection with it, and their indication) individually[325] and[326] in its combination with the lord of the year, and with the Ascendant of the

---

[322] This is an important point: it is the angularity of the *revolution* that allows even the *natal* significance and power to be greater or less.
[323] Instead of criticism, **P** reads "and good works."
[324] This seems to mean, "if it is *not* in one of the stakes."
[325] Or perhaps, "in isolation" (على الانفراد). The MSS differ in their reading of "their" and "its" here, and in how this parenthetical comment ought to read. The point is that each planet matters.
[326] Reading for "or."

root and its lord, and the Moon, and the rest of the planets, and the positions of the fortunes and infortunes in the houses of the root and the terminal point, and the Ascendant of the revolution.

[Infortunes harming the Ascendant of the revolution]

10 Now[327] if there was an infortune in the Ascendant of the year, that is very bad, and especially if that infortune was doing violence to the Moon and the lord of the year. **11** If that infortune was Mars it indicates the injustice of enemies towards him, and if it was Saturn it indicates illness, distress,[328] and confinement, and what resembles his indication; and the nature of the sign should also be called upon as a witness.

12 Now if one of the two infortunes was in the square of the Ascendant of the year, but the lord of the Ascendant was in a suitable place and with the fortunes, in witness to the Ascendant, then it will repel from him much of the adversity of that infortune.

13 And if one of the two infortunes was in the Ascendant of the year, and the other in the Ascendant of the root, then it indicates the badness of the year, and its harshness; but if a fortune was with one of them, it will subtract from the adversity.

[A complex Ascendant scenario involving a natal infortune or fortune]

14 And[329] if there was an infortune in the root and the year reached it,[330] or that sign [with the rooted infortune] was the Ascendant of the year, and that infortune was looking at it in the revolution with an aspect of hostility, while the rest of the planets are in a suitable condition, then due to the nature of the infortune it indicates that something detestable as well as illnesses will afflict him in that year, in

---

[327] For this paragraph, cf. Da. 171-73.
[328] Reading with **E. B** and **P** read "wrong, injustice," using a different word than for Mars. It may be accurate, but certain distress and anxiety are more Saturnian.
[329] This resembles a scenario by Māshā'allāh in Sahl, *Nativities* Ch. 1.23, **6-7**.
[330] That is, by profection.

accordance with its indication; and the suitability of the rest of the planets' condition indicates that he will gain good.[331]

15 And if the condition of the infortune was like that, but it was not what we stated about the suitability of the [other] planets, and in addition to that the lord of the Ascendant of the revolution or the lord of the sign of the terminal point[332] was made unfortunate by one of the infortunes, death will be feared for him. **16** And if that infortune was in the four stakes and their misfortune[333] was from it, the fear will be more corroborated.

17 But if it was a fortune instead of the infortune, it indicates health, safety, delight, and the benefit of good, according to the essence of the fortune.

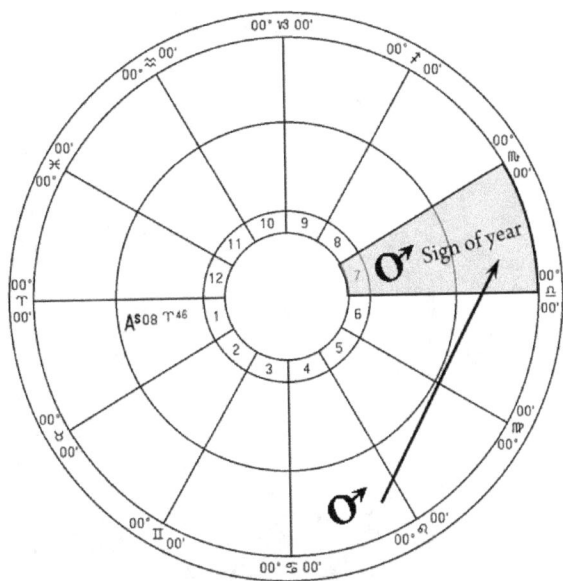

Figure 56: Activating natal infortune, reinforced in the revolution (II.23, 14)

---

[331] This probably means, "he will gain good in other areas of life," otherwise we would just be left with a mushy mixture. The point ought to be that the infortune's relation to the Ascendant has a more personal and direct bad effect on the native himself.

[332] This probably means, "whichever one the infortune was in," because in **14** this natal infortune is either in the sign of the terminal point or the Ascendant of the revolution.

[333] Probably one of the lords just mentioned, but being in the stakes would also affect life generally.

Figure 57: **Activating natal fortune, reinforced in the revolution (II.23, 17)**

[*Combinations in the Midheaven and the fourth*]

18 If Mars and Saturn were in the Midheaven of the Ascendant of the revolution, it will bequeath sluggishness and an economic slump in work, and a slackening in all of the benefits of the year, and he will spend assets without benefit; and if any of the planets indicated something good in that year, he will be quick to pursue it, but with little perseverance beyond what is necessary.[334]

19 And if the Sun and Moon in the revolution were with Saturn in the fourth stake, it indicates the death of the fathers and mothers.

---

[334] Reading this last clause as a combination of **B** and **E** (دوام, "perseverance"), and **P** (انتقال, "beyond the necessary/minimum"). The word in **P** also has connotations of booty, so we might add that there will be some reward but not much.

[Profections to houses]

20 If the year terminated at an excellent position and its lord was in a bad place,[335] or the year terminated at a bad position and its lord was in an excellent place, then it indicates a middling condition, in good and evil.

21 If the year terminated at the house of an infortune, and the infortune was in it in the revolution, it indicates harm.[336]

22 And if the year terminated at the Midheaven of the root, in the place of the rooted infortunes, then it indicates harm in work.

23 And if the year terminated at the house of assets, and the infortunes were in it in the root, then it indicates corruption and loss in assets; and that is harsher if those infortunes were in the stakes or what follows them, in the revolution. **24** But as for if they were in the withdrawing places, it will be easier.

Figure 58: Activating natal infortune, angular in the revolution (II.23, 23-24)

---

[335] I'm not sure if this is in the nativity alone, or in the revolution.

[336] This is ambiguous and should be taken in a general way: infortunes in their own signs can be very effective, and good for their own particular task, even if it is not pleasant.

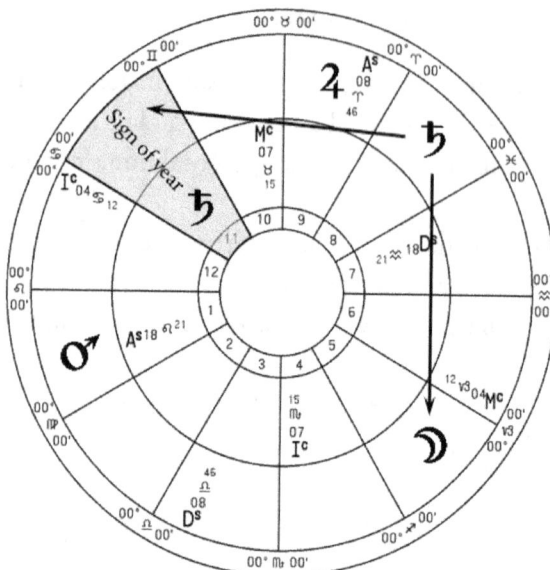

Figure 59: Combination of leadership, unhappiness, and danger (II.23, 25)

25 And[337] if the year terminated at the house of hope of the root, and Saturn is in it in the root, and Saturn also looks at it in the revolution, from a bad place, and he looked at the Moon from the square,[338] and in that year Mars was in the Ascendant of the root,[339] stationing, and Jupiter was in the Ascendant of the year, then [1] Jupiter's being in the Ascendant of the revolution indicates elevation and leadership and power, even though it will be hateful to him, not being cheerful in it; and [2] the condition of Saturn and Mars indicates harm, chains, confinement, punishment, fear of robbers, cutting, fleeing, hostility, wrong, weeping, and screaming.

26 And[340] if the sign of the terminal point was the house of illness in the revolution, and the infortunes looked at it, and nothing of the fortunes looked at it, it indicates a powerful illness.

27 And if the year terminated at the sixth, twelfth, fourth, seventh, and eighth, there is no good in it, and especially if in the revolution their lords were alien,[341] retrograde, with the Sun, or with the infortunes.

---

[337] For this sentence, cf. Da. 177 and 175.
[338] This is probably the revolutionary Moon.
[339] P reads, "the terminal point."
[340] For this sentence, cf. Da. 176.
[341] P reads "western," but that does not fit well in this standard list of bad conditions.

Book II: Profections

28 And if the year terminated at the house of disease[342] of the root, and Venus is the lord of the year, and she is with Saturn in the stake of the earth,[343] connecting with him, and the Ascendant of the revolution is the house of death of the root, it indicates chains and powerful adversities.

29 And if the year terminated at the twelfth sign of the root, and its lord was Jupiter, and he is with Saturn in the stake of the west,[344] and Saturn is retrograde, and Mars is in the stake of the earth, it indicates powerful harm, and the soul's coming to the brink of destruction.

30 And if the year terminated at the house of wedding [of the root], and in the revolution its lord and the Moon are opposing their own houses or exaltations, then the owner of the revolution will hate his own country, and will travel to another.[345]

31 And if the lord of the year was in the stake of the west from the Ascendant of the revolution, or it was withdrawing from the stakes and what follows them,[346] and is made unfortunate, then it indicates fleeing from his country, and powerful disasters.

32 And[347] if the year terminated at the house of the father, and one of his indicators had reached a sign whose lord was with the lord of the

---

[342] وبال. This is probably the twelfth, especially since that would complete here the triangle of places that show confinement and sorrow: twelfth, eighth, fourth.
[343] This is probably in the revolution.
[344] This and the position of Mars are probably in the revolution.
[345] **E** and **P**: "into exile."
[346] I.e., being dynamically cadent, or withdrawing.
[347] From here through "the Ascendant of the root," reading with **P**. In **P**'s reading, the Ascendant is profected to the natal fourth or the Lower Midheaven, and there is also a profection (or less likely, a transit) of some significator of the father (perhaps the Lot of the father) to a place whose lord is with the lord of the natal third. But **B** and **E** read, "And if the year belonging to the father reached, from one of its indicators, a sign whose lord was with the lord of the third of the Ascendant of the root...". In this latter reading it is hard to know what we are talking about. Is the year "belonging to the father" the same as the profection of the Ascendant to the fourth, as with **P**? At any rate, despite the double profection, **P**'s reading fits better with the other paragraphs, in which the Ascendant is profected to some natal house.

third of the Ascendant of the root, then it indicates that the father will be blessed with a child and the native blessed with a brother.

33 And if the terminal point or the Ascendant of the revolution was [also] the Ascendant of the root, and one of the luminaries was the lord of the year, and it is eclipsed or is with the Tail, and Saturn looked at it, then it indicates that something detestable and damage will afflict him from the masses.

34 And if the house of children in the root was Sagittarius, and Sagittarius became the Ascendant of the revolution, and in it was the Saturn of the year,[348] and Jupiter, Mars, Venus, and Mercury were in Leo (in the Ascendant of the root), and Mars was looking at Moon with an exact opposition but the rest of them in a wide aspect from her, the position of Saturn and the condition of the Moon relative to Mars indicates fear, and confinement, and chains for the owner of the revolution, and detestable things in children; and the nature of the fortunes indicates release from those detestable things [later].

35 And if the house of children in the root was a house of Saturn, and in the revolution that house came to be in the stake of the earth, being made unfortunate in the revolution, then it indicates the death of children, and a powerful disaster afflicting him.[349] 36 And if it was just as we stated and the year terminated at the house of children, and Saturn was the lord of the year, and he is in a suitable condition, it indicates that [only] a little adversity will affect the children.

37 And if the year terminated at the place in which Saturn or Mars was in the root, and that planet returned to its place or to its square in the revolution (and especially if that one of the two from whom one gets the indication is in a stake or what follows them), then it indicates that he will have injustice, harm, and a bad condition in his way of life.

---

[348] **P** omits "of the year." So, **B** and **E** are talking about the revolutionary positions of Saturn and other planets.

[349] This might mean that a child (singular) will die *or* a powerful disaster will afflict it (without it having an indication for the native). Sometimes Arabic uses the singular "child" to mean "children."

38 And if the lord of the year was Saturn or Mars, and in the revolution of the year he was in the Ascendant of the revolution, not in his own domain, and especially if in the root he was in the Ascendant of the nativity or in its opposition or square—if that was Saturn it indicates illnesses and emaciation, and if it was Mars it indicates fear, confinement, and damage in assets.

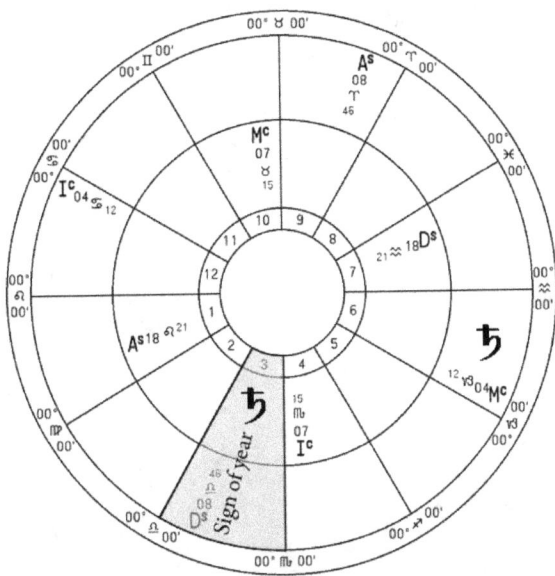

Figure 60: Activating natal infortune, angular to self in revolution (II.23, 37)

39 And if Saturn was the lord of the year and he is under the earth, and Mars reached[350] his own rooted place, and he assembled with Saturn there, and the lord of the Ascendant of the revolution was in the seventh or under the rays, and the fortunes were withdrawing from the stakes, then it indicates adversity and evil in the whole year.

40 And if the year terminated at the place of Jupiter, and in the revolution he is in a suitable condition, looking at his own rooted place, and the lord of the year was <not>[351] falling, then it indicates

---

[350] Abū Ma'shar uses the word for profection here ("terminates at") but he means a return by transit.

[351] Adding with the sense of the Latin. Without the "not" it would read, "*even if* the lord of the year was falling," as though Jupiter himself is able to convey this goodness despite the lord of the year withdrawing. But I would distinguish the angularity of the planet with its condition (such as being in a dignity, etc.), so I follow the Latin.

powerful good fortune and great good,[352] and that is stronger if the lord of the year was in a suitable condition.

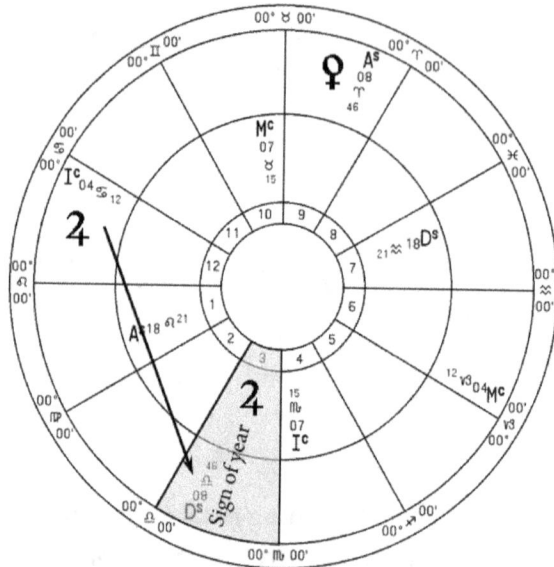

Figure 61: Activating natal fortune, good condition and configured, lord of year angular (II.23, 40)

41 And if the Ascendant of the year corresponded to one of the signs in which the infortunes were in the root, and[353] the year terminated at that sign, then let that infortune be made to be like the lord of the year, especially if the lord of the terminal point or[354] the lord of the Ascendant was falling away from an aspect to its own house.[355]

42 And if Mars was the lord of the year, and in the revolution Saturn reached the place of the rooted Mars, and Mars in the revolution of the year was in the stakes or what follows them, looking down upon Venus, and the fortunes are falling from the stakes, it indicates the roughness[356] of the year, as well as fear, chains, confinement, and something detestable from generals and leaders.

---

[352] **B** and **E** add that he will have a position of status, but the rest of the sentence is somewhat garbled in them.

[353] **B** reads "or," but to my mind that is not good enough because otherwise this would simply be saying that any rooted infortune would automatically be like the lord of the year. But if *both* the profection *and* the Ascendant of the year fell on it, it would be more emphasized.

[354] In this case I retain the "or," because the scenario allowing the infortune to act as the lord of the year is already complete, and this condition is simply extra.

[355] That is, in aversion to its own house.

[356] فظاظة. This can also mean "rudeness," "crudeness," etc.

BOOK II: PROFECTIONS

43 If the Ascendant of the year as well as the sign in which the Sun and Moon were in the revolution, were corrupted, then the indication for them will be from the lord of the house of the luminary which is greater in testimony in the year.

44 And[357] if the Sun and Moon were both corrupted, made unfortunate in the revolution of the year, in the seventh or fourth place from the Ascendant of the revolution, [and] especially if they were with the Head or Tail, it indicates the death of the parents; and that is more corroborated if in the root they had both indicated [the parents'] condition.[358]

45 And if Jupiter was in Capricorn in the revolution, and he was corrupted by Saturn, Mars, and the Sun,[359] then it indicates detestable things and corruption.

46 And if an infortune was with the lord of the year in the Ascendant of the root,[360] and it corrupted the Moon as well, then it indicates the badness of the year.

47 And if the lord of one of the houses of the root or the revolution[361] was retrograde, or burned, or the infortunes made it unfortunate, or it came to be in one of the bad positions, then it indicates harm via the category of the indication of that house (whether assets, or real estate, or something else).

---

[357] For this sentence, cf. perhaps Da. 188.
[358] Or rather, if the Sun and Moon had also been harmed in the nativity (al-Andarzaghar). But perhaps Abū Ma'shar is thinking of the possibility that other planets could indicate the parents: namely Saturn (in a nocturnal chart) or Venus (in a diurnal one).
[359] This should probably be understood as "or" for all of them, not that they all must corrupt him together.
[360] I believe this means that *at the revolution* they are transiting in the natal Ascendant.
[361] Perhaps this should be understood as one of the houses of the root being retrograde, etc., "*in* the revolution." But it would not help if the lord of a revolutionary house was retrograde, either.

48 And[362] if the lord of the year was an infortune, and in the root of the nativity it was in the house of illness, and in the revolution of the year[363] that infortune did violence to the Moon, and the fortunes are also looking at the Moon in the revolution from a suitable place, and the infortune was in the Ascendant of the year, then it indicates powerful adversities, and a long-lasting illness.

49 And[364] if the lord of the year was a fortune, and an infortune was in the Ascendant of the revolution, and the other infortune in its setting, and the Moon in the year was corrupted by one of the two (or by others), it indicates powerful harm from enemies in [his] assets, or one of his limbs will be cut, and he will fear for himself, and especially if a fortune is not looking at the Ascendant of the revolution.

50 And if the lord of the year was a fortune but it is retrograde, and Mars looked at it in the revolution from the opposition, and at the Moon from the square, and it[365] is in the fourth of the Ascendant of the revolution, and the Ascendant of the year is made unfortunate by the Sun or the Dragon, and its lord is not looking at it, then it indicates [many] types of detestable things in the body, and harm from enemies and robbers, and the disappearance of assets, and loss in them.

51 And if Saturn is the lord of the year, and he returned to his rooted place,[366] and in the revolution Mars came to be in his opposition, it indicates something detestable, and harm in accordance with the indication of the house in which Saturn is: so if he was in the Ascendant of the year or with the Moon, it indicates harm in the body—and one should speak this way about the rest of the houses.

52 And if the lord of the year, and the Ascendant of the revolution and its lord, and the Moon, are corrupted by the infortunes from an assembly or square or opposition, then it indicates corruption, and the enemy's having power over him, and loss in assets. **53** And if Jupiter or

---

[362] For this sentence, cf. Da. 186, except that al-Andarzaghar says the fortunes are *not* looking at the Moon.
[363] **B** and **P** read, "in the *Ascendant* of the year."
[364] Cf. also IX.8, **94**, and Da. 9.
[365] Grammatically, this could be either Mars or the lord of the year.
[366] This would be a Saturn return.

Venus were with the Moon or with the lord of the year, it indicates a release from that adversity.

54 And if the Moon[367] in the revolution was in Cancer, and the Sun in Aries, and they were both corrupted by Mars from Capricorn, it indicates detestable things, harm, and corruption.

55 And if the Moon in the revolution was in a sign of the image of people, and she was corrupted by Saturn and Mars together, and the lord of her house was an infortune, it indicates adversities and bad things.

56 And if the lord of the year was harmed by the infortunes, it will be a year of fear and worry, and loss and injustice in assets; but if Jupiter looked at it, it indicates a repelling of that.

57 And if the lord of the year was Mercury, and he was made unfortunate by Mars in the fourth of the Ascendant of the revolution, or in the fourth of the sign of the terminal point, or in the fourth of the Ascendant of the root, then it indicates the death of brothers. **58** And likewise if Mercury was the lord of the year and he is made unfortunate by Mars in the stake of the west from one of the three positions,[368] it also indicates the death of brothers.

59 And if the lord of the year was in the tenth in the root, and in the year it is in the tenth of the revolution (or in its eleventh), in a suitable condition and place, it indicates the gaining of assets and authority. **60** And if the lord of the year was in the tenth of the root and the revolution, it indicates victory over the Sultan.[369]

---

[367] E reads, "the lord of the Moon."
[368] That is, the seventh of the root, terminal point, or revolution.
[369] Some condition must be missing, because this is the same scenario as is included in the previous sentence.

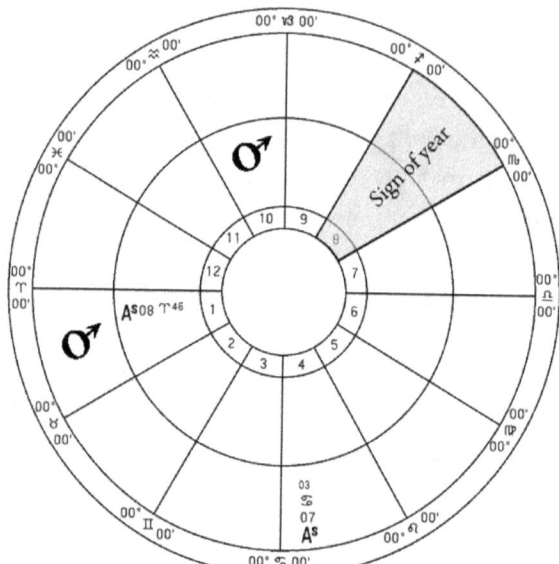

Figure 62: Lord of year in tenth at both times, good condition and place (II.23, 59)[370]

61 And if the lord of the year in the root was in a falling place, or under the rays, and in the revolution it is in the sixth or eighth, or burned, and Saturn is looking at it in the revolution, it indicates his being dismissed from works, and his leisure time and idleness, and disasters resembling death will afflict him.

62 And if Jupiter in the root was free of the infortunes, in a suitable condition, and in the revolution he is in a stake and looks at the lord of the year, it indicates the gaining of assets and status, and respect from the Sultan and kings, and he will be devoted to works he will benefit by, and he will be correct in his management and works.[371]

63 And if the lord of the year was alien,[372] in the sign of his enemy, and in the sixth or twelfth, in the inspection of Mars or Saturn, and Jupiter is falling away from an aspect to the Moon and the lord of the

---

[370] In Figure 62 the Ascendant is profected to Scorpio, so the lord of the year is Mars. The natal Mars is exalted in the natal tenth (inner circle), and the revolutionary Mars is in the tenth of the revolution, in his own domicile (outer circle).

[371] In Figure 63 the natal Jupiter is exalted and in a good place (inner circle), and presumed to be in aversion to the infortunes. The year is profected to the third, Gemini. In the revolution, the transiting Jupiter looks at the lord of the year Mercury, from an angle of the revolution, by a sextile (outer circle.

[372] With slightly different pointing this could also be read as "western," but in this scenario being alien or peregrine makes more sense.

year, then it indicates that he will encounter disgrace and damage from enemies.

64 And[373] if the year reached the stake of the earth or the stake of the west of the root, and Saturn is in it or looks at it with an aspect of hostility,[374] death will be feared for him.

65 And of the roots which are used in the revolutions of years, one should know that the most harmful infortune in the year is one in the Ascendant of the revolution (or its division),[375] when in the root it was *already* doing violence to the Ascendant of the year and the Moon, and to the planets ruling the year, and the stakes. **66** But as for if the infortune in the revolution was in the Ascendant of the year (or any of its houses, like the house of assets, or brothers, or others), except that it was *not* doing violence to it in the root, its harm will be easier. **67** And if the infortune was looked down upon by the Sun, in the trine of the fortunes, and it had a claim in the Ascendant and

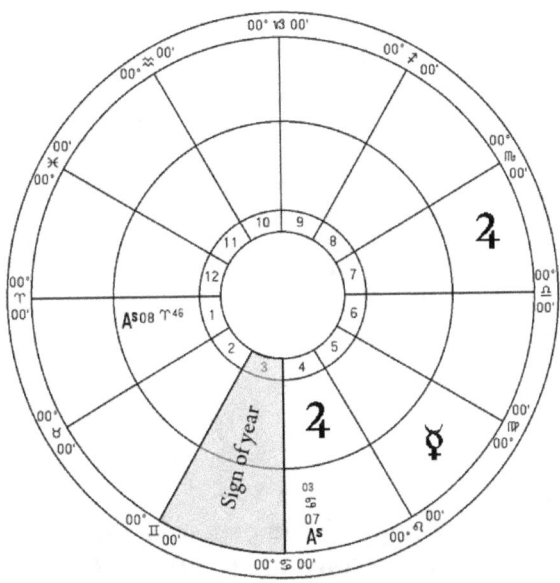

Figure 63: Jupiter safe, angular, looking at lord of year (II.23, 62)

---

[373] Cf. also IX.8, **95**.

[374] This is probably Saturn by transit in the revolution.

[375] Reading as فسمه, suggesting the Ascendant of a monthly revolution. **P** reads "distributor," which naturally suggests that it could be "the distribution," such as if the infortune is transiting in the bound of the distribution—and that *would* be like being in the Ascendant, since the distribution is primarily done by directing the natal Ascendant. But I don't think Abū Ma'shar is adding that complication, since we have not addressed distributions yet.

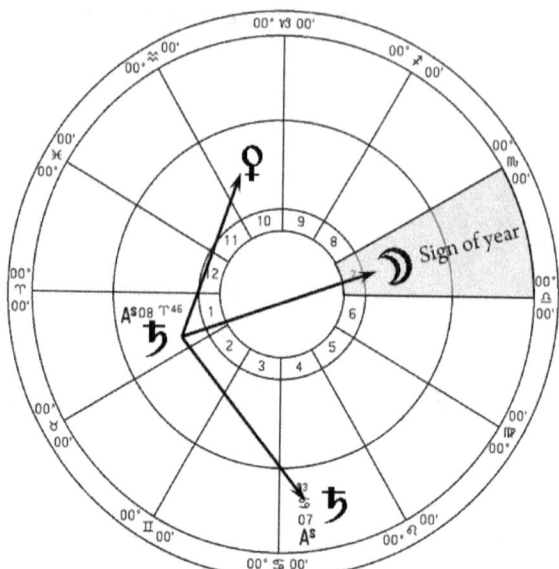

Figure 64: A complex scenario with an infortune (II.23, 65)[376]

[the place of] the Moon, it indicates good [coming from] from labor and trouble.

68 And if the fortunes were in the Ascendant of the revolution, or they came to the positions of some of the planets, or they came to be in some of the houses from the Ascendant of the revolution, it indicates little benefit *unless* [they made] a good aspect to that position in the root. 69 And if the fortune was retrograde or burned, or withdrawing, then it will be too weak to grant that good.

70 And if the Ascendant of the revolution was a sign in which there was already an infortune in the root of the nativity, or the year terminated at a sign in which there was an infortune in the root (or there was an infortune in both), and at the time of the revolution of the year an infortune was in[377] one or both of them, it indicates a change of homeland, and fleeing and ruin.

---

[376] In Figure 64 for age 66, the profected Ascendant terminates at the natal seventh house, Libra, with the Moon in it (inner wheel). The Ascendant of the year is in Cancer, and in it at the revolution is Saturn (outer wheel). But Saturn was already harming Cancer by square in the nativity, in addition to harming the natal Moon and natal Venus (the lord of this year), and the angles. So both the Ascendant of the year and the profected Ascendant are activating natally harmed signs (Cancer, Libra), and this is made more intense because the harming planet, Saturn, is actually transiting in it. This is bad for life and the body, especially because he was also harming a general significator of the body, the Moon.

[377] Lit., "corresponded to."

71 And if one of the infortunes in the root was looking at one of the fortunes, and then assembled with it in the revolution or looked at it from the square or opposition, without reception, it indicates powerful harm.

BOOK III: ON DIRECTIONS
And it is in ten chapters

Chapter III.1: On directing, the distribution, the distributor, & its partner in the management

1 In the revolutions of years one needs to direct many indicators, some of them rooted and some of them revolutionary: because each one of them has a particular characteristic in the indication which the others do not have. **2** And if the rooted indicators indicated something good or bad in the root of the nativity, their indication will appear when they govern the distribution in one of the years, or if they managed with their bodies or rays[1] (or the rest of their indications),[2] or they reached the fortunes or infortunes.[3]

3 Now, each of the five releasers[4] is directed individually. **4** As for the one which we rely on for information about the native's lifespan,[5] we direct [it] for the conditions of survival, illness, and death;[6] but as for the rest of the releasers, we direct [them] for the knowledge of health and emaciation, and disasters, and the rest of the different conditions which each of them indicates, and we will mention that in what follows. **5** And all of the planets and Lots are [also] directed, as well as the twelfth-parts and the twelve houses, in the root of the nativity, the

---

[1] That is, by being the partner in the distribution.
[2] Abū Ma'shar is probably talking about one of the other techniques like the lord of the orb or the *fardārs*.
[3] This is either a transit or profection, but probably a transit.
[4] According to III.3, **1**: the Sun, Moon, Ascendant, Lot of Fortune, and the meeting or opposition before birth. In al-Qabīsī's version (IV.12), the Ascendant is directed or distributed for things which happen to the body, the Sun for matters of esteem, nobility, loftiness, and authority, the Moon for the conditions of the soul (i.e., the emotional life) and marrying (using a word that also pertains to the family), the Lot of Fortune for matters of earning or acquisition, benefits, and restriction and abundance, and the Midheaven for the profession "and the rest of the particular conditions of management."
[5] That is, the longevity releaser, also known as the *hyleg* or *hīlāj*.
[6] So in a sense it is the most important: see III.3, **2**.

revolutions of years, and the revolutions of months: and from the direction of each of them one draws conclusions about the thing they indicate.[7] **6** And you make the degrees of direction in the root of the nativity be years, but in the revolutions of years months[8] and days, and in the revolutions of months [you make them be] days and hours.[9]

7 Now as for knowing the direction, and the knowledge of the distributor and the position of the distribution in the revolutions of years, look at the degree of the rooted Ascendant [to see] which planet's bound it is, and how many equal degrees[10] remain of that bound, and convert them into the degrees of ascensions of the country in which the native was born. **8** That is, see how many remain of the bound which belongs to the degree of the Ascendant, all laid out,[11] and you multiply that by the ascensions of the sign of the Ascendant, and divide it by 30, and take whatever comes as being a year for every degree, and a month for every 5', and whatever it is, that is what you need. **9** Then look at the bound which follows it as well, [to see] how many degrees of equality it is, and you turn that into ascensions too.[12]

10 And you work like that too with every bound you need, of the bounds of the Ascendant and the rest of the releasers, and the other planets and Lots, bound-by-bound, in succession:[13] and this is the "direction." **11** And the bound in which the position of the work is, is the "position of the distribution," and the lord of that bound is the "distributor," whether it looked at [the bound] or not.

12 (However, the Ascendant and the things in it are directed by degrees of ascensions of the country in which the native was born, while

---

[7] See VI.2, **1-20** for a listing of many of these.
[8] B adds "weeks."
[9] See Tr. IX for more on the months and hours.
[10] That is, zodiacal degrees.
[11] فتبسطه. This seems to mean, "including the minutes and seconds," rather than just rounding to the nearest degree.
[12] See my discussion of the worked example, in the Introduction.
[13] This is the older method of directing all points through any sign using the sign's ascensions; in **12** Abū Ma'shar will clarify that he prefers Ptolemy's astronomical method of proportional semi-arcs.

what is in the Midheaven or the fourth[14] is directed by the ascensions of the right sphere, and what is not in these three positions[15] is directed according to what we stated in our book [on that topic]).[16]

13 So you look at what comes out from the degrees of the direction in all of this, and you make every degree a year, and every 5' a month, and every 1' six days, and every 10" one day, and every 25'" one hour.[17]

14 And the Persians called the distributor ([of that] which is directed from the degree of the Ascendant by degrees of ascensions, in the order of the lords of the bounds) the *jār bakhtār*,[18] and did not call any of the other distributors by this name.[19]

15 And it is necessary that when directing the bounds you examine the positions of the planets and their rays: for sometimes the body of a planet or its rays will occur in [that] position. 16 So when the direction reaches one of those, the direction of the distribution will be in the "management" of what is there, from that position until it encounters another planet by its body or rays, so that the management will shift from the body or rays of the first planet, to the body or rays of the other planet; and [this] management of the planets by their body or rays acts as a "partner" in the indication, along with the distributor.

17 And you ought to understand the positions of the Lots and the twelfth-parts, for if in the distribution there were fortunes or infortunes, whether by their bodies or rays, their indications of suitability

---

[14] Or rather, the IC itself.

[15] Abū Ma'shar has omitted the Descendant, which is not usually included on these lists anyway—but why not try it?

[16] I'm not sure which book this is. But Abū Ma'shar is following Ptolemy: direct the Ascendant by oblique ascensions, the Midheaven by right ascensions, and everything else by proportional semi-arcs. For an excellent book on this topic, see Gansten 2009.

[17] This is an idealized year having 12 months of 30 days (360 days total), and is the standard way in which Abū Ma'shar multiplies out his fractions to yield specific time period.

[18] الجار بختار, an Arabization of the Persian for "distributor of time."

[19] Still, it is helpful when distributing other points to call the bound lord the distributor, too.

or corruption will be made manifest in accordance with their categories.

18 And we will work out an example in the knowledge of directing and the distribution of the distributor, in the bodies of the planets and their rays, and their management over the Lots and the twelfth-parts.

[Worked example chart][20]

19 So a native was born in the fourth clime, in a city whose latitude is 36°, and: the Ascendant was Taurus, 2° 54', and the Moon in it, 12° 48',[21] Mars in Leo 10° 29',[22] the Sun in Leo 15° 59',[23] Mercury in Leo 22° 04'[24] (retrograde), Venus in Libra 2° 54',[25] Jupiter in Capricorn 20° 26' (retrograde),[26] Saturn in Aquarius 28° 26'[27] (retrograde), the Tail[28] in Virgo, 21° 14'.[29]

20 And we have already worked out the image of it, and its rays, and the rest of what is needed for it, except that in our example we have restricted it to the positions of the seven planets and their rays, as well as the Lots which occur in the Ascendant. **21** We will direct it so that it may be more brief and easier to understand:

---

[20] For a discussion of this very troubled and misleading example, see the Introduction.
[21] By my calculation using the data in the worked example below, 12° 44'.
[22] This should be 16° 29', as found by calculation from the example: see **22** and **41**.
[23] One MS has it as 15° 49'.
[24] One MS has it as 22° 07'. According to **22** below it is at 29°.
[25] One MS has it at 7° 14'.
[26] By calculation from the example below it should be 25° 05'.
[27] One MS has it at 20° 26', and another at 23° 26'. But by calculation in the worked example it is at 9° 24' (see **22**, which also has it in a sextile to the Ascendant from Pisces).
[28] This should be the Head, not the Tail.
[29] One MS has it at 21° 24.

22 The Lot of courage, 7° 14'; the sextile[30] of Saturn, 9° 24'; the Lot of prosperity, 12° 06'; the Lot of reason, 14° 34'; the square of Mars, 16° 29';[31] the trine of Jupiter, 25° 05°; the square of the Sun, 21° 14';[32] the square of Mercury, 29° 05'.[33]

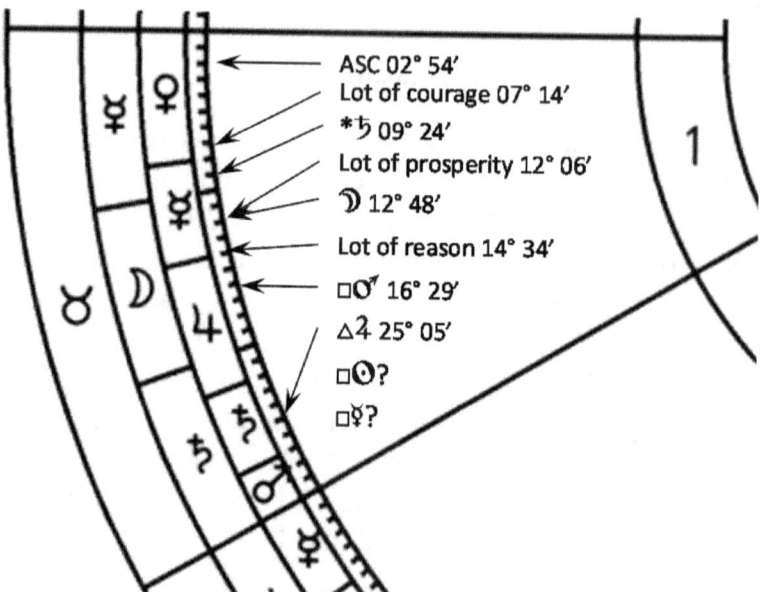

Figure 65: Chart example (III.1, 19-45)

23 When I wanted the knowledge of the distribution and the distributor (which is called the *jār bakhtār*), and the direction of the degree of the Ascendant, and its reaching the bodies of planets and their rays, and their managements, and the Lots and twelfth-parts, I looked at the degree of the Ascendant: and it was 2° 54' Taurus, the bound of Venus, and from the beginning of the sign up to the degree

---

[30] Based on **35**, this would put Saturn in Pisces. But this seems to be an error, as I can only find Saturn in Aquarius. The error is repeated below in **31, 33,** and **35**.

[31] Reading by calculation of the example. The two values in the MSS are 16° 34' and 7° 24'.

[32] By calculation based on the position of the Lots, this should be 22° 00'. But note that in the worked example below (**45**) it comes *after* the trine of Jupiter at 25°, again showing that something is seriously wrong.

[33] There is not enough information in the example to calculate this directly.

of the Ascendant there was no planet nor its rays, so the management belonged to the [distributor of] degree of the Ascendant.[34] **24** If there had been the body of a planet or its rays from the beginning of the sign up to the degree of the Ascendant, the degree of the Ascendant would have been in the management of *that* body or ray, and that planet (by its body or ray) would have been the partner of the distributor in the indication of good and bad. **25** But since I did not find a planet nor its rays from the beginning of the sign up to the degree of the Ascendant, Venus became the distributor without a planet partnering with her by its body or ray: and [therefore] she is called the *jār bakhtār*.

26 And between the degree of the Ascendant and the Lot of courage, were 4° 20' by [degrees] of equality:[35] in the ascensions of the clime of Babylon (the fourth) that is 3° 02', so Venus distributes alone for 3 years, 12 days: then in this time the degree of the Ascendant connects with the Lot of courage and risk-taking.

27 And there still remains to Venus in her bound, 46' by equality: in ascensions that is 32' 12", so we said that in her distribution of the Lot of courage and risk-taking, the management of Venus was 6 months, 13 days, and something. **28** The total of that is 3 years, 6 months, 25 days and something.

29 Then the distribution shifts over to the bound of Mercury, and in his distribution of the Lot of courage Mercury manages 1 year, 8 days, and something, and the distribution comes to the sextile[36] ray of Saturn. **30** The total of that is 4 years, 7 months, 3 days and something.

31 Then Saturn manages the Lot of courage by means of the light of his sextile in the distribution of Mercury, for 1 year, 11 months, and approximately 19 days, and his light connects with the Lot of prosperity and victory. **32** The total of that is 6 years, 6 months, and 22 days and something.

---

[34] See **25**.
[35] "Degrees of equality" are zodiacal degrees.
[36] Again, this must be the square, here and in **31**, **33**, and **35**.

33 Then Saturn manages the two Lots together (the Lot of courage and the Lot of prosperity and victory) by the light of his sextile in the distribution of Mercury, for 5 months and 29 days, and he hands it over to the body of the Moon. **34** The total of that is 7 years and 21 days and something.

35 Then with her body the Moon accepts from Saturn the management of his left sextile ray, and she manages the two Lots with her body in the distribution of Mercury for 11 months and 6 days and something, and the distribution of Mercury comes to an end. **36** The total of that is 7 years, 11 months, and 27 days and something.

37 Then the distribution shifts over to Jupiter, so the Moon manages with her body the Lot of courage and the Lot of prosperity in the distribution of Jupiter as well, for 4 months and 24 days, then they both[37] reach the Lot of reason and logic. **38** The total of that is 8 years, 4 months, and 21 days and something.

39 Then the Moon manages with her body, in the distribution of Jupiter, the Lot of reason and logic and the two original Lots which we mentioned, for 1 year, 6 months, and 9 days, and hands over the management of her body to the right square ray of Mars. **40** The total of that is 9 years and 11 months and something.

41 Then Mars manages the three Lots in the distribution of Jupiter, with the light of his square, for 4 years, 3 months, and 3 days and something, and the distribution of Jupiter comes to an end. **42** The total of that is 14 years, 2 months, and 3 days and something.

43 Then the distribution shifts over to Saturn, so that Mars manages the three Lots in the distribution of Saturn with the light of his square, for 2 years, 6 months, and 6 days and something, and hands it over to the light of the trine of Jupiter. **44** The total of that is 16 years, 8 months, <and 9 days> and something

45 Then Jupiter manages the three Lots with the light of his left trine in the distribution of Saturn, until he hands it over to the square of the Sun.

---

[37] That is, the two Lots.

46 And the directions [should be done] in this manner, and the handing-over of the one handing over among them, and the acceptance of the acceptor in the distribution, and the distributor, and the bodies of the planets and their rays.

47 Now as for the Lots and the twelfth-parts, and other indicators which resemble them, they are directed from their positions which they are in, until the end of the lifespan. **48** And sometimes several of them will coincide in the bound of [the same] planet, or in the management of its body or ray, in the manner we made clear in this example.[38] **49** So if the planet managing for them was a fortune, it indicates good in the category of what each one of them indicates; and if it was an infortune, it indicates evil in them. **50** But if one of them[39] was in the management of two planets or more, then the work in it is in accordance with their natures.[40]

Chapter III.2: On the indication of the fortunes & infortunes, & the distributors & their partners in the indication, & in the management of the distribution by body or rays, & the shifting from one to another

1 Each of the distributors individually (both fortunes and infortunes), and the one partnering with them in the indication and in the management of the distribution (by their bodies or rays), in the root of the nativity and the revolutions of years, <has> remarkable power. **2** They are stronger in the indication of rooted matters than the lord of the terminal point is, because the indication of the lord of the terminal point is only over the condition of that year: but as for the lord of the

---

[38] Again, it *does not* happen in the way portrayed in the example. See my Introduction.
[39] Reading in the plural (ﻪ), for the Arabic's dual (ﻬﻤﺎ, "one of the two").
[40] The Latin understands this to mean that one of the time lords is a fortune, and the other a fortune, so that we ought to combine them.

distribution, sometimes its indication for good or evil is for several years, and likewise the one partnering with it. **3** But in addition to that, in every year one must call upon the sign of the terminal point and the lord of the year, and the Ascendant of the revolution of the year and its lord, and the Moon, and the rest of the indicators which we have mentioned before, as witnesses to that condition (with respect to its strength or weakness, and an increase in it or decrease from it).

[How to analyze the distribution]

4 And one should begin with the position of the distribution, so look at the bound:

5 [1a] To whom does it belong, and [1b] and what is the condition of its lord in the root and the revolution, in terms of easternization or westernization, and direct motion or retrogradation, and the rest of the excellent or bad conditions that [can be] ascribed to it?

6 And [2a] in what place was that bound relative to the Ascendant of the native in the root,[41] [2b] and where it is relative to the sign of the terminal point and [2c] the Ascendant of the revolution of the year?

7 And [3] the sign in which the distribution is: whose house, exaltation, triplicity, and face is it?

8 And [4a] who was in that sign in the root and the revolution (of the fortunes or infortunes), and [4b] what sort of condition does each one of them[42] in itself have (of strength and weakness), and [4c] what is the extent of its power or weakness in the root

---

[41] This would mainly apply to points other than the directed Ascendant, as it will spend much of life in the first three signs.

[42] The natal planets in that sign, just mentioned. (The word is in the plural, not the dual.)

and the revolution, and [4d] its indication for good or evil, and [4e] is it a fortune or infortune?

9 And the bound in which the direction is, and the one casting rays to it: [5a] in which rays, [5b] who is it (of the infortunes or fortunes), and [5c] which planet was in it in the root and in the revolution?[43]

[Distributor-partner combinations: Seven types]

10 Because the condition of the distributor in isolation, and with the one partnering with it by body or ray, is of seven types. **11** The first of them is [1] if the distributor is a fortune, [acting] alone in the distribution.[44] **12** The second is [2] if it is an infortune, [acting] alone in the distribution.[45] **13** The third is [3] if the distributor is an infortune, and the one partnering with it is a fortune.[46] **14** The fourth is [4] if the distributor is a fortune, and the one partnering with it is an infortune.[47] **15** The fifth is [5] if the distribution belongs to one of the planets, be it a fortune or infortune.[48] **16** The sixth is [6] if the distributor and the one partnering with it are both infortunes.[49] **17** The seventh is [7] if they are both fortunes.[50]

---

[43] See **28**, which includes influences in both the root and the revolution.

[44] See **18-24** below. An example would be if there is no partner in the sign preceding the degree of the Ascendant (as Abū Ma'shar has already mentioned in III.1, **23-25**). But perhaps this would include cases where the same planet is both the distributor and the partner: such as if the bound was ruled by Venus, and Venus actually cast a ray into the bound.

[45] See **25-29** below.
[46] See **30-35** below.
[47] See **36-39** below.
[48] See **40-43** below. This is an ambiguous mixture of weak and strong planets.
[49] See **44-48** below.
[50] See **49-54** below.

Static Distributor-Partner Combinations			
	Distr.	Partner	Reading
#1	F	--	III.2, 11, 18-24
#2	I	--	III.2, 12, 25-29
#3	I	F	III.2, 13, 30-35
#4	F	I	III.2, 14, 36-39
#5	ambiguous mixture		III.2, 15, 40-43
#6	I	I	III.2, 16, 44-48
#7	F	F	III.2, 17, 49-54

Figure 66: Seven "static" distributor-partner combinations (III.1, 10-54)

[*Type 1: A fortune by itself*]

18 As for the first type, it is if the distributor is a fortune, [acting] alone in the indication of several years, and it is in a suitable condition in itself and in the houses of the circle (in the root as well as in the revolution of those years), and the lord of the year, the Moon, and the Ascendant of those revolutions are in a suitable condition: for if it was like that, they indicate good and good fortunes which will appear, be abundant, and be well known, and the outcomes of his affairs in them will be suitable. **19** And if their condition in suitability was like that in the root and in [only] one of the years, his condition in *that* year will be according to what we said about suitability.

20 But if the distribution belonged to one of the fortunes, and that fortune was in a bad condition in the root, or in a bad position in the houses of the circle, and it was made unfortunate, and the lord of the year, the Moon, and the Ascendant of the revolution of those years were in a bad condition, then they indicate the badness of [his] condition for the number of those years. **21** But if their condition in badness was like that in the root, and in [only] one of the years, the condition of the owner of the revolution will be bad in *that* year.

22 And if they were in a bad condition in the root, and in an excellent condition in the revolution, they will improve his condition in that year with some suitability; while if they were in a suitable condition in the root but in a bad condition in the revolution, the indication of the revolution will reduce the condition of the root by [only] a little reduction (because its condition's indication for good or evil in the root is more powerful than its condition's indication in the revolution).

23 And if some of them were fortunes and some of them infortunes,[51] then the condition of the owner of the revolution will be varied in good and evil.

24 And you look like that at the conditions of the distributors and the lords of their rays, and the other indicators, so long as they are distributing or managing, in the revolution of every year.

[Type 2: An infortune by itself]

25 As for the second type, it is if the distributor was an infortune, [acting] by itself in the indication, and in the root it is in a suitable condition, in a good position or in a sign in which it has a claim (or in the sign of one of its friends, or in a sign of the fortunes), and planets in a suitable condition are looking at it, and in the revolutions of the years the distributor is also like that in terms of a suitable condition, and the fortunes are looking at it in them, and the lord of the year, the Moon, and the Ascendant of those revolutions (and their lords) are also in a suitable condition: for if it was like that, the infortune indicates success in the fortunate things which are of its category in those years. 26 And that is more confirmed if the indicators in it were in a suitable condition relative to the houses of the circle. 27 And if it was a suitable condition relative to the infortune in [only] one of the years, his condition will be suitable in *that* year.

28 And if the distribution belonged to an infortune, and that infortune was in a bad condition in the root and in the revolutions of those

---

[51] This is a little misleading: since this type only involves a single fortune in the distribution, Abū Ma'shar should have said "fortunate and unfortunate." But since he has also thrown in the Moon and the lord of the year, he has muddied the waters a little bit.

years which you're distributing, and the fortunes are not looking at that bound in the root and revolution, and the Moon is corrupted in their revolutions, and their Ascendants and their lords are in the square of the infortunes (or their opposition), then the native will die in that distribution, and his death will be in the year in which most of these indicators are corrupted. **29** But if the distribution belonged to the infortune and its condition of badness was like that in [only] one of the years, then in that year it indicates excessive adversity, in accordance with its condition in the two times—and its condition in the root is more powerful in the indication of good or evil than the conditions of the revolution.

[Type 3: The distributor an infortune, the partner a fortune]

30 As for the third type, it is if the distributor is an infortune, and the one partnering with it by its rooted body or ray is a fortune: for if it was like that, the fortune will release him from death—except that detestable things will [still] afflict him, and in that distribution he will have a condition blended of good and evil, and he will be restricted at [some] time and free at [another], and become ill and get better, and rejoice and be distressed, and something detestable will affect him but then he will be safe from it; and the strongest of them will be the most evident in the indication.

31 And an example of that is if Saturn was the distributor, in the rooted rays of Venus, and they are both equal in condition in terms of strength: so due to the nature of Venus and her good fortune, it indicates that he will gain assets in that distribution, and will marry and have children; but due to the nature of Saturn and his misfortune, it indicates that his child and woman will die, and his distresses and anxieties will multiply, and he will weep because of them. **32** But if Venus had been stronger, it would not have indicated death, and the disaster would have been gotten past.[52]

---

[52] Abū Ma'shar discusses his theory of planetary strength a bit in *Gr. Intr.* VII.4, but I do not understand how it applies here. He may have in mind that Venus is in a better dignity, in an angle or advancing, and so on.

Book III: Distributions

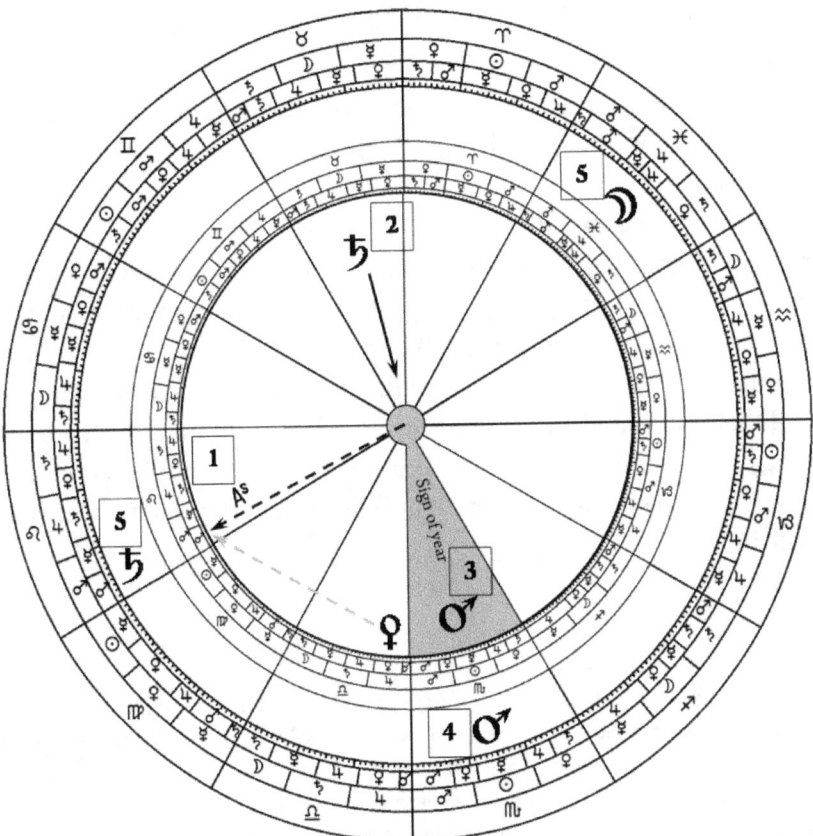

Figure 67: Example: "the brink of death" (III.2, 33)

33 And[53] if [1] the distribution belonged to one of the infortunes, and in the root there was the body of a fortune or its rays in it, and [2] in the root that distributor was made unfortunate by one of the infortunes, and [3] the position in which *that* infortune[54] was in the root, was [also] the sign of the terminal point or the Ascendant of the year (or the lords of those two [signs][55] were made unfortunate by that [same] infortune in the root), and [4] in the revolution it returned to

---

[53] This complex scenario is close to that of al-Andarzaghar (Da. 185).
[54] That is, "the infortune making the natal distributor unfortunate."
[55] The sign of the terminal point or the Ascendant of the year.

its [rooted] place,[56] and [5] the Moon and the bound in which the distribution was in those years were in bad places among the houses of the circle, or made unfortunate, with the fortunes not aiding them, then it is also very bad, and indicates that he will come to the brink to death or will die.[57]

34 And if the distribution was just as we said—belonging to corrupted infortunes—but there was *not* the body of a fortune or its rays in it in the root, but its body or ray *was* there in the revolution, it indicates a hindered[58] adversity. **35** But if along with that the sign of the terminal point for those years, and the Ascendant of their revolutions, and their lords, and the Moon, were in a bad condition, made unfortunate, then it is harsher and more powerful for the tribulation and adversity, and in that distribution he will come to the brink of death or will die.[59]

---

[56] See the example below. The natal Ascendant is Leo, and at age 39 the directed Ascendant has reached the bound of Mars in Leo, with its partner Venus sending a sextile ray to it (inner circle). So, the distribution is [1] Mars-Venus. Now also in the root, [2] the distributor Mars is being harmed by Saturn's opposition from Taurus. Since the native is 39, [3] the profection of the Ascendant terminates at the natal distributor, Mars. And at the revolution, [4] Mars returned to his natal place by transit (outer circle). Finally, [5] the revolutionary Moon is in a bad place, and the bound itself is being harmed by the presence of the revolutionary Saturn. But in a way, Abū Ma'shar is stating all of this backwards because he is focusing on distributions. We could equally put it this way: a natal infortune (Mars) is being harmed by another infortune (Saturn); at age 39 the Mars is being activated as the distributor, as the lord of the year, and through his own planetary return, with the planet natally harming him now harming the bound as well (along with the Moon being in a bad place, etc.). Put this way, we have activated a natally bad situation (Mars-Saturn) with potentially three predictive techniques: distributions, profections, and the revolution. Apparently, in such a situation the benefic contribution by Venus does not really help.

[57] But see **110-11** below.

[58] القطيع, lit. a misfortune which is "cut." Again, this is because while the revolution indicates good, it is not as powerful as the root: so it can only subtract from, or hinder, the misfortune indicated in the root.

[59] But see **110-11** below.

[Type 4: The distributor a fortune, the partner an infortune]

36 Now as for the fourth type, it is if the distributor is a fortune, and the one managing for it by its rooted body or ray is an infortune: for if it was like that, it indicates a blending of the condition and its being middling [between] what is loved and what is detested, and joy and distress, and health and sickliness.

37 So if the distribution belonged to one of the fortunes and the one managing for it was an infortune, but that infortune was made fortunate in the root, and the position in which that fortune was in the root was the [very] sign of the terminal point or the Ascendant of the year, and the lords of both [signs][60] were made fortunate by that fortune, and the Moon and the bound in which the distribution was were in suitable places in those years, then it indicates that he will have surpassing good and manifest good fortunes—except that due to the management of the infortune, he will be made unhappy by them.

38 Now if again the distribution belonged to the fortunes, but a rooted planet did not manage for it,[61] but in the revolution the body or rays of an infortune *was* in it,[62] then because of the distribution of the fortunes it indicates good fortune, and due to the rays of the revolutionary infortune it indicates *incidental* adversity and harm. **39** And the detestable thing is greater if the lord of the distribution, the lords of those years,[63] and the Moon were corrupted, in bad places in the houses of the circle.

---

[60] The sign of the terminal point and the Ascendant of the year.

[61] This would be a rare case in which no partner was in the rising sign (by body or ray) in the degrees preceding the degree of the Ascendant.

[62] That is, in the bound. In this situation, the root does not have any *intrinsic* indication for misfortune, because there is no rooted partner. This is why Abū Ma'shar says that having an infortune there in the revolution will bring only "incidental" misfortune.

[63] That is, by profection. But Abū Ma'shar consistently includes the lords of the revolutionary Ascendants too, so we should include those.

[Type 5: Mixtures of weak and strong fortunes and infortunes]

40 As for the fifth type, it is if the distribution belongs to one of the planets (be it a fortune or infortune), and its[64] position in the root is bad relative to the houses of the circle, and in that bound in the root is a powerful, corrupting infortune or its rays (from whatever direction the rays were), and nothing of the fortunes looks at that bound with a powerful aspect, or [even if] there was a fortune but if it looked at that bound in the root it was weak, and its degree was less than the degree of the infortune which was in it or looking at it with strength, and in the root there was an infortune in the sign in which the distribution was, and that infortune in the root was making the distributor unfortunate (or the sign of the terminal point or the Ascendant of the revolution, or their lords), and in the revolution it returned to its [rooted] place or undermined some of what we mentioned, then when the distribution reaches the body or ray of that rooted planet, without a doubt it will kill.

41 And[65] if the distribution belonged to one of the planets (be it a fortune or infortune), and in that bound was the rooted body of a fortune (or its ray) from a stake, and there was also the rooted body of an infortune (or its ray) in it, from positions falling from the stake, and the lords of the years of those revolutions, and their Ascendants and their lords, as well as the lord of the distribution and the Moon, were in a suitable condition, strong, then a powerful calamity will afflict him in that year, except that he will be rescued from it. **42** But if all or most of these were in a bad condition or weak, or the infortune was stronger than the fortune, he will not be freed from it, and he will die.

43 And if the condition of the distribution and these indicators was just as we said before about badness and the strength of the infortune, and in that bound in the revolution of those years there was the body

---

[64] Grammatically, this refers to the distribution (i.e., the bound), as is suggested in **6**, but this only really makes sense when directing other things besides the Ascendant. For most people, the direction of the Ascendant will be in the second sign for many years of life, but it is not a bad place in the way the sixth, eighth, or twelfth is.

[65] For this paragraph, cf. also IX.8, **80**.

of a fortune or its rays, then it will not have the power to repel death, but his death will be with reverence.

[Type 6: The distributor and partner both infortunes]

44 And as for the sixth type, it is if the distribution belongs to an infortune, in the management of the body of a rooted infortune or its rays: for if it was like that, then in that distribution it indicates harsh, powerful adversities, and the corruption of the body, and an abundance of illnesses, and a bad condition in his way of life, and in all things, and death will be feared for him in the year in which the lord of the distribution, the Moon, the Ascendant of the revolution (and its lord), and the lord of the year are in a bad condition or made unfortunate. **45** And that is more confirmed if the sign in which the distribution was, was the place of infortunes in the root or in the revolution.

46 And if the distributor was an infortune, and it was in the management of the body of a rooted infortune or its rays, but in the revolution one of the fortunes cast its ray to it, then he will not be freed from death but he will be revered in his illness and his conditions, until the time in which he dies. **47** And if in the revolution it was the ray of an infortune in it, then before death he will encounter hardship, and will be tortured, and it will be burdensome for whoever is tending to him, and he will die a bad death. **48** And if all or most of these indicators were in their own places, his death will be in a place of his own, and with his family; and if it was the contrary of that, it will be to the contrary.

[Type 7: The distributor and partner both fortunes]

49 As for the seventh type, it is if the distribution belongs to a fortune, in the management of the body of a rooted fortune or its rays, and they are both in a suitable condition: for if it was like that, then for the number of those years it indicates success in famous and great good fortune, of the category of its indication; and it is more renowned for the good fortune, and more praised, if the distributor, the sign of the terminal point of those years, and their lords, and the Ascendants of their revolutions, and the Moon, were in a suitable condition or made fortunate. **50** And it is superior to that if the lord of the distribution and the lord of the year cast their rays to that bound.

51 But if both [planets][66] were in a bad condition, they indicate badness in the category of their indication. **52** And if one of them was in a suitable condition and the other in a bad condition, each of them will indicate good or bad in accordance with its condition.

53 And if their condition was like that in [only] one of the years, then its indication in that year will be in accordance with its condition and indication [in *that* time].

54 And[67] if the distribution belonged to one of the fortunes, and the one managing for it[68] by its rooted body or rays was a fortune, and in the revolution of one of the years there was the body of an infortune or its rays in [the bound], then it indicates that he will have good fortune but he will be unhappy with it, and distresses and anxieties will affect him, in accordance with the indication of the infortune.

[24 transitions from bound to bound, and partner to partner: six factors]

55 And while of course the distribution belongs to one of the bounds, and the management belongs to the body or rays of one of the planets, for several years, sometimes within one of the years it will shift from one of them to another, so that in that year there will be a shift of the distribution from bound to bound, or a shift of the management from one planet to another planet. **56** The[69] first of them is [1] the bound in which the distribution is, and the second is [2] the lord of

---

[66] That is, the distributor and partner, which were said to be in a good condition in **49**.
[67] This sentence runs in parallel with **46**.
[68] Grammatically, this is the distribution (i.e., the bound).
[69] This paragraph introduces the six factors which account for shifting from one kind of distribution to another *while* a revolution is in effect, and in what follows Abū Ma'shar will run through 24 combinations of them. The six are: the two bounds, their two lords, and the two partners.

that bound (and it is called the first distributor), and the third is [3] the bound to which the distribution shifts, and the fourth is [4] the lord of that second bound (and it is the second distributor), and the fifth is [5] the planets <from> whose bodies or rays the direction of the distribution is, and the sixth is [6] [the planet] to which the management shifts, so that it accepts it by body or ray. **57** And these six indicators whose conditions [are examined] upon the shift in good fortune and misfortune, are in twenty-four ways.[70]

Transition	Between bounds	Between partners	Interpretation
F-F	#1 (**59**)	#5 (**64**)	**88**
F-I	#2 (**60**)	#6 (**65**)	**90**
I-F	#3 (**61**)	#7 (**66**)	**89**
I-I	#4 (**62**)	#8 (**67**)	**91**

Figure 68: Transitions 1-8, between distributors or partners[71]

[Transitions 1-4: between distributors]

58 Four of them are with respect to the *distributors*, in isolation. **59** The first is [#1] if it shifts from the bound of a fortune to the bound of a fortune. **60** The second is [#2] if it shifts from the bound of a fortune to the bound of an infortune. **61** The third is [#3] if it shifts from the bound of an infortune to the bound of a fortune. **62** The fourth is [#4] if it shifts from the bound of an infortune to the bound of an infortune.

---

[70] Transitions 1-8 are summarized in the table immediately below, with their corresponding sentence numbers; transitions 9-24 are summarized in the table following **86**.

[71] In this table, *F* means "fortune" and *I* means "infortune." Sentence numbers are given in bold.

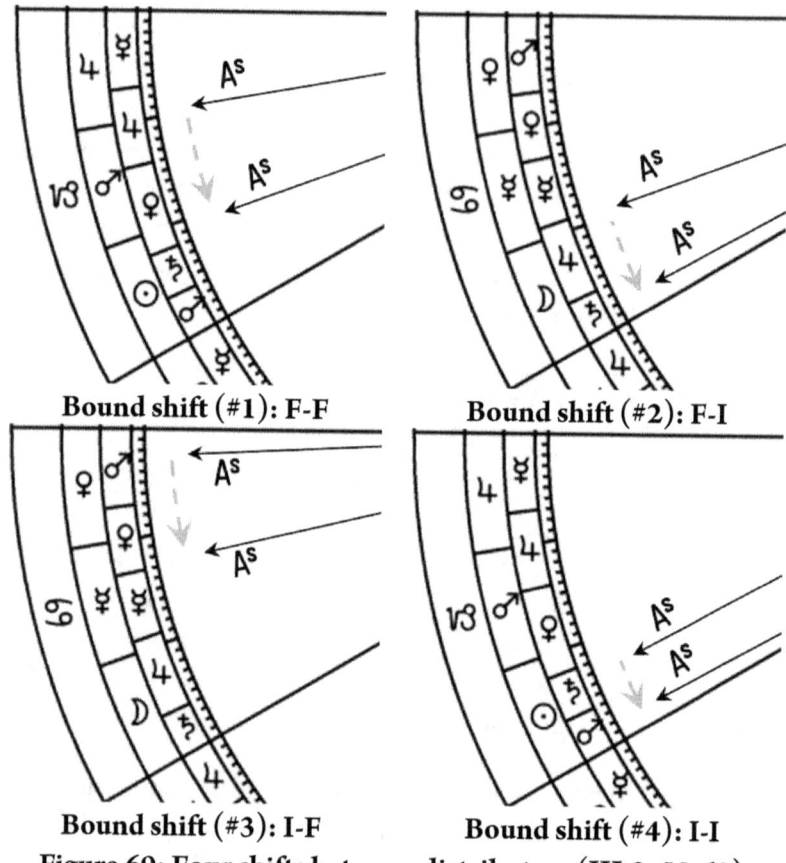

Figure 69: Four shifts between distributors (III.2, 58-62)

[*Transitions 5-8: between partners*]

63 And another four are in terms of the fortunes and infortunes *managing* for the distribution, and the shift of one of them to another by body or ray. **64** The first of them is [#5] if the management shifts from the body of a fortune or its rays, to the body of a fortune or its rays. **65** The second is [#6] if the management shifts from the body of a fortune or its rays, to the body of an infortune or its rays. **66** The third is [#7] if the management shifts from the body of an infortune or its rays, to the body of a fortune or its rays. **67** The fourth is [#8] if the management shifts from the body of an infortune or its rays, to the body of an infortune or its rays.

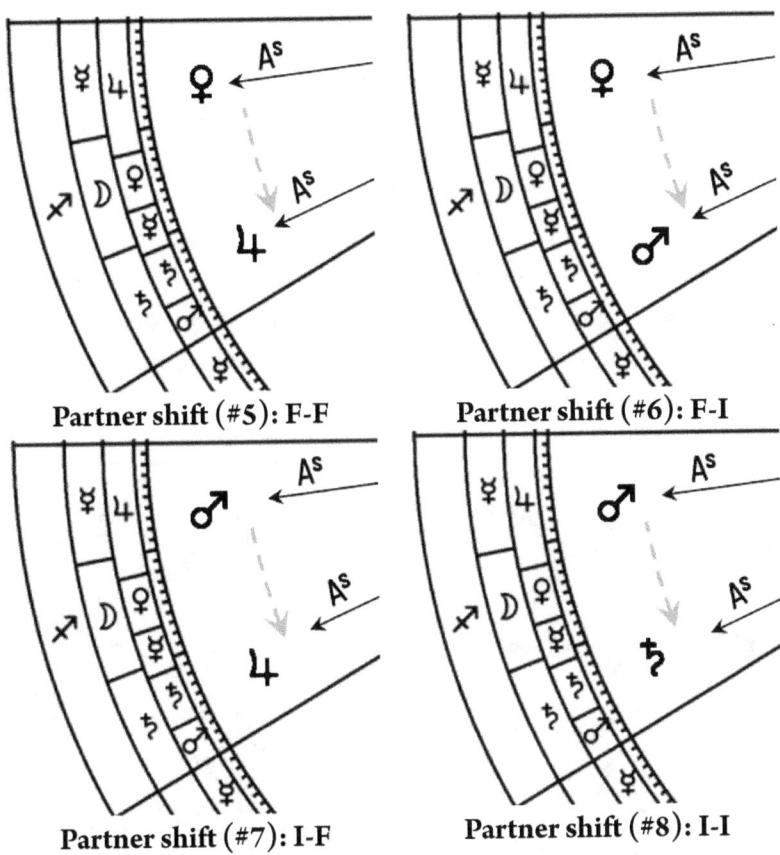

Figure 70: Four shifts between partners (III.2, 63-67)

[Transitions 9-16: between distributors, same partner]

68 And eight are in terms of the shift of the distributors *and* the partnering of the fortunes or infortunes with them, by body or ray. **69** The first of them is [#9] if the distribution shifts from the bound of a fortune to the bound of a fortune, in the management of a fortune. **70** The second is [#10] if the distribution shifts from the bound of a fortune to the bound of a fortune, in the management of an infortune. **71** The third is [#11] if the distribution shifts from the bound of a fortune to the bound of an infortune, in the management of a fortune. **72** The fourth is [#12] if the distribution shifts from the bound of a fortune to the bound of an infortune, in the management of an infortune. **73** The fifth is [#13] if the distribution shifts from the bound of an infortune to the bound of a fortune, in the management of a fortune. **74** The sixth is [#14] if the distribution shifts from the bound of an infortune to the bound of a fortune, in the management of an infortune. **75** The seventh is [#15] if the distribution shifts from the bound of an infortune to the bound of an infortune, in the management of a fortune. **76** The eighth is [#16] if the distribution shifts from the bound of an infortune to the bound of an infortune, in the management of an infortune.

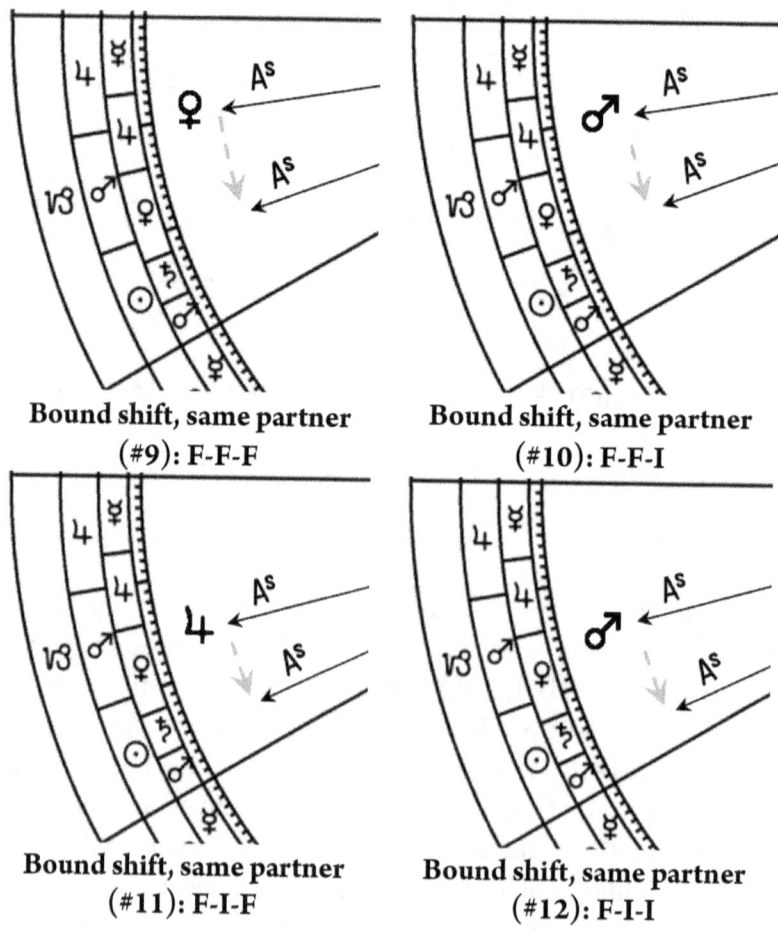

Bound shift, same partner (#9): F-F-F

Bound shift, same partner (#10): F-F-I

Bound shift, same partner (#11): F-I-F

Bound shift, same partner (#12): F-I-I

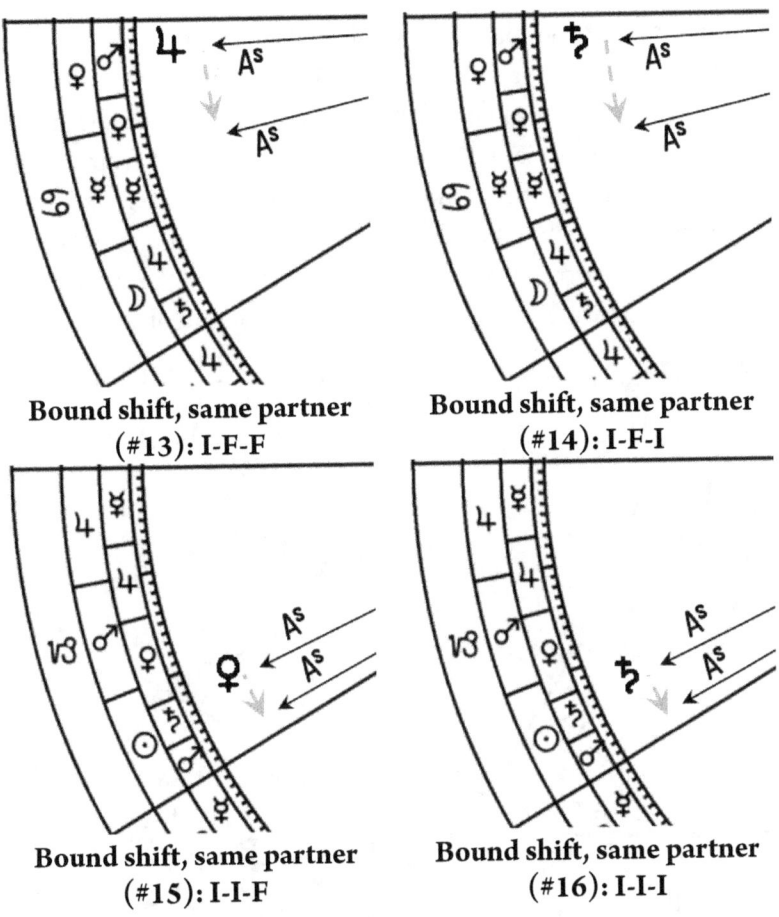

Figure 71: Eight shifts from bound to bound, same partner
(III.2, 68-76)

[Transitions 17-24: between partners, same distributor]

77 And another eight are in terms of the fortunes and infortunes managing for the distribution by body or ray, and the shift from one of them to another. **78** The first of them is [#17] if the management shifts from a fortune to a fortune, in the bound of a fortune. **79** The second is [#18] if the management shifts from a fortune to a fortune, in the bound of an infortune. **80** The third is [#19] if the management shifts from a fortune to an infortune, in the bound of a fortune. **81** The fourth is [#20] if the management shifts from a fortune to an infortune, in the bound of an infortune. 82 The fifth is [#21] if the management shifts from an infortune to a fortune, in the bound of a fortune. 83 The sixth is [#22] if the management shifts from an infortune to a fortune, in the bound of an infortune. 84 The seventh is [#23] if the management shifts from an infortune to an infortune, in the bound of a fortune. 85 The eighth is [#24] if the management shifts from an infortune to an infortune, in the bound of an infortune.

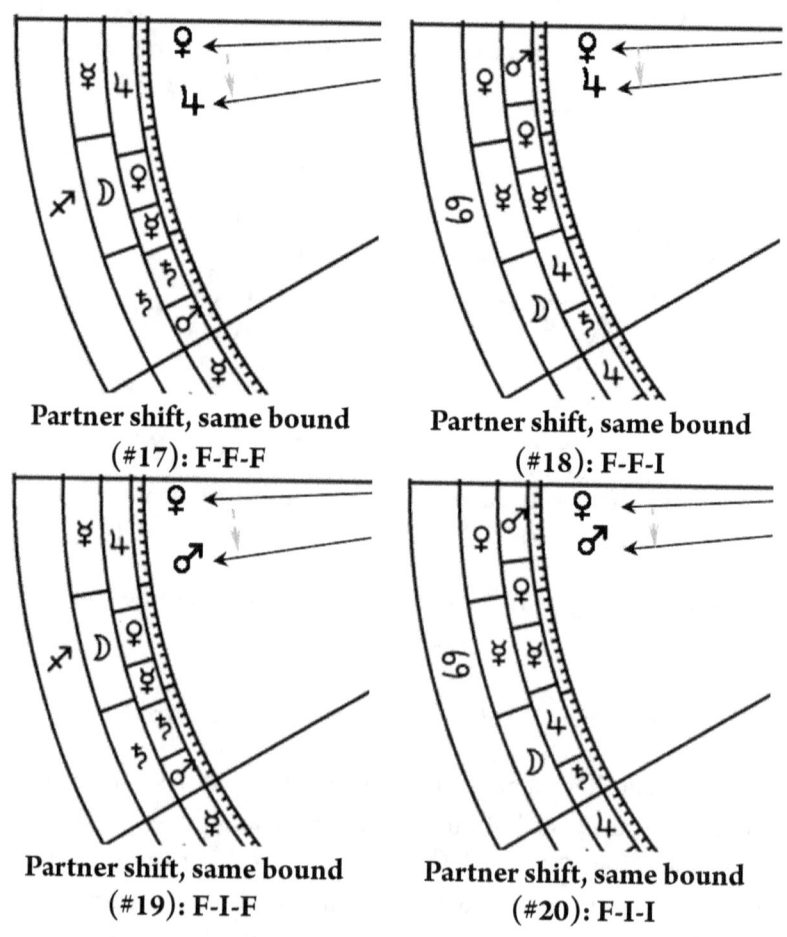

Partner shift, same bound (#17): F-F-F

Partner shift, same bound (#18): F-F-I

Partner shift, same bound (#19): F-I-F

Partner shift, same bound (#20): F-I-I

BOOK III: DISTRIBUTIONS

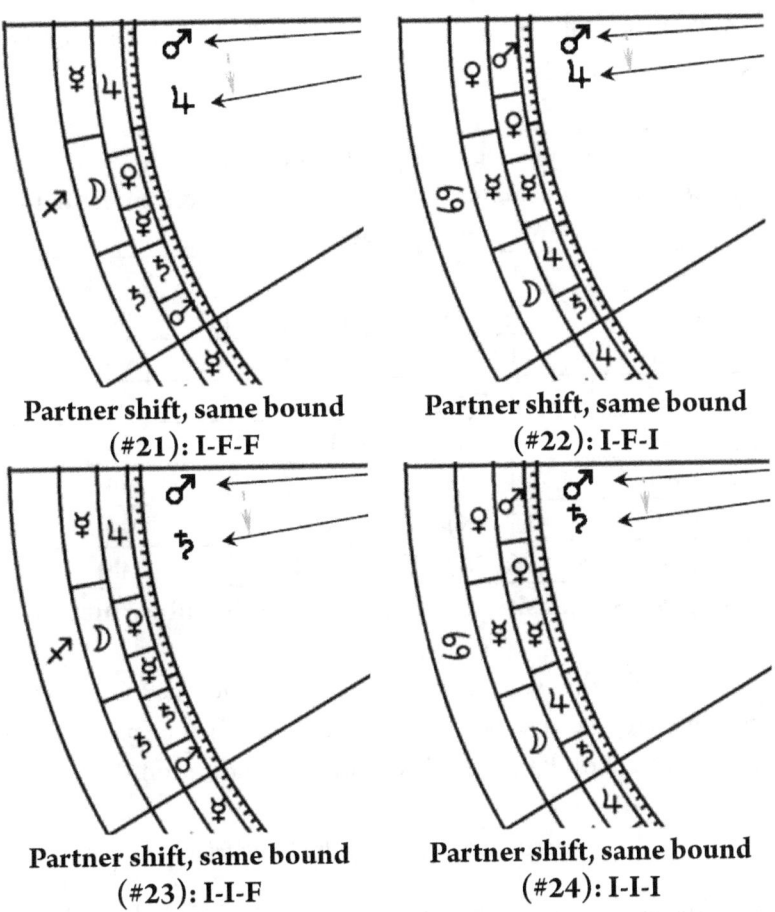

Figure 72: Eight shifts from partner to partner, same bound (III.2, 77-85)

86 And the shift of [the fortunes and infortunes] is according to these twenty-four ways.

Transition	Between bounds, same partner	Between partners, same bound	Interpretation
F-F-F	#9 (69)	#17 (78)	92-93
F-F-I	#10 (70)	#18 (79)	94
F-I-F	#11 (71)	#19 (80)	97
F-I-I	#12 (72)	#20 (81)	98
I-F-F	#13 (73)	#21 (82)	95
I-F-I	#14 (74)	#22 (83)	96
I-I-F	#15 (75)	#23 (84)	99
I-I-I	#16 (76)	#24 (85)	100

Figure 73: Transitions 9-24, both bounds and partners[72]

87 But as for the *indication* of the fortunes and infortunes in these ways, there are twelve types: four of them are called a "paired"[73] indication, and eight of them are called a "double" indication.[74]

[*Interpreting the four paired scenarios*]

88 Now as for the first of the paired ones, it is if [#1] the distribution in one of the years shifts from the bound of a fortune to the bound of a fortune, or [#5] the management shifts from the body of a fortune (or its rays) to another fortune by body (or by ray): for in that year it indicates the duration of good fortune, and the shift from good fortune to good fortune.

---

[72] In this table, *F* means "fortune" and *I* means "infortune." Sentence numbers are given in bold.
[73] Or perhaps, "parallel" (المزاوجة).
[74] These twelve categories simply present basic interpretations for the 24 combinations above.

89 The second is if [#3, #7] the distribution or its manager shifts from an infortune to a fortune: for in that year it indicates a shift from the bottom and humbleness to being raised up and greatness.

90 The third is if [#2, #6] the distribution or its manager shifts from a fortune to an infortune: for in that year it indicates a shift from good to bad, and a fear of death.

91 The fourth is if [#4, #8] the distribution or its manager shifts from an infortune to an infortune: for in that year it indicates a fluctuation in tribulations, and a shift from adversity to adversity, and from evil to evil, and that indication of the fear of death will be more confirmed.

[Interpreting the eight doubled scenarios]

92 But as for the eight doubled ones, the first of them is if [#9] the distribution shifts from the bound of a fortune to the bound of a fortune, in the management of a fortune, or [#17] the management shifts from a fortune to a fortune, in the bound of a fortune: for in that year it indicates good fortune and surpassing good. **93** Now if in addition to the shift of the distribution from a fortune to a fortune, the management of its manager also shifts from a fortune to a fortune, then that is an indicator of good fortune upon good fortune, and of good upon good; and it is the most powerful good fortune, and the most splendid in power, if the four of them were fortunes.

94 The second is if [#10] the distribution shifts from the bound of a fortune to the bound of a fortune, in the management of an infortune, or [#18] the management shifts from a fortune to a fortune, in the bound of an infortune: for in that year it indicates a suitability of condition, and the lastingness of good fortune, because the fortunes in it are greater in testimony—except that it will blend it with evil and something detestable due to the nature of the infortune.

95 The third is if [#13] the distribution shifts from the bound of an infortune to the bound of a fortune, in the management of a fortune, or [#21] the management shifts from an infortune to a fortune, in the bound of a fortune: for in that year it indicates a shift from something detestable and evil to surpassing good fortune.

96 The fourth is if [#14] the distribution shifts from the bound of an infortune to the bound of a fortune, in the management of an infortune, or [#22] the management shifts from an infortune to a fortune, in the bound of an infortune: for in that year it indicates a middling [condition] in good and evil, and excellence and badness, even though the indication of good[75] is stronger.[76]

97 The fifth is if [#11] the distribution shifts from the bound of a fortune to the bound of an infortune, in the management of a fortune, or [#19] the management shifts from a fortune to an infortune, in the bound of a fortune: for in that year it indicates a middling condition in suitability and corruption, and good and evil, even though the indication of evil is stronger.[77]

98 The sixth is if [#12] the distribution shifts from the bound of a fortune to the bound of an infortune, in the management of an infortune, or [#20] the management shifts from a fortune to an infortune, in the bound of an infortune: for in that year it indicates something detestable and much evil, and the encountering of tribulations and the fear of death, and[78] fluctuations in detestable things.[79]

99 The seventh is if [#15] the distribution shifts from the bound of an infortune to the bound of an infortune, in the management of a fortune, or [#23] the management shifts from an infortune to an infortune, in the bound of a fortune: for in that year it indicates excessive adversity and the fear of death.[80]

---

[75] **P**: "misfortune" is stronger.

[76] I believe this is in error, and that it should read that the "misfortune is stronger," since there are two instances of an infortune in it. But perhaps Abū Ma'shar means that things are improving.

[77] Again, I believe this is in error, and that it should read that the "good" is stronger," since there are two instances of a fortune in it. But perhaps Abū Ma'shar means that things are getting worse.

[78] For the rest of the sentence, **E** and **P** read, "and destruction in it."

[79] See also IX.8, **72**.

[80] See also IX.8, **73**.

100 The eighth is if [#16] the distribution shifts from the bound of an infortune to the bound of an infortune, in the management of an infortune, or [#24] the management shifts from an infortune to an infortune, in the bound of an infortune: for in that year it indicates varieties of detestable things, evil, and death.[81] **101** And it is of the greatest and harshest adversity if the four of them were infortunes.[82]

102 Now as for the good and evil which each one of them indicates, it is known from the condition of the planet one seeks the information from, and from its nature, and the nature of those houses of the circle which it owns in the root and the revolution. **103** And the strongest of the three indicators is the lord of the distribution, and the one below it in power is the one managing for it by body; but as for the lord of the ray, it is lower than both of them. **104** And the strongest of the rays is the opposition, and after that the square, than the trine, and the weakest of them is the sextile.

105 And indeed what is meant by these twelve managements is when the manager for the distribution is a planet by its *rooted* body or ray. **106** But as for when there is a planet in that bound in one of the *years*, either by its body or casting a ray to it, then its indication is *not* in the manner we have described in this chapter of the six types.[83]

[Directing to fixed stars]

107 And if the direction from the Ascendant and the rest of the releasers reached one of the thirty fixed stars indicative of good fortune,[84] and that star had indicated good fortune in the root, then

---

[81] See also IX.8, **74**.

[82] See **93** above, and IX.8, **75-76**. That is, if during the year there was a shift from an infortune to an infortune, in *both* the bounds and the partners.

[83] That is, the six indicators which Abū Ma'shar has been elaborating, starting in **55-57**. In other words, everything from **55-100** assesses the natal distribution alone, *not* what planets are doing to the bound in the revolution. Revolutionary effects are discussed in **43, 46-47, 54**.

[84] These are well-known fixed stars of the 1st and 2nd magnitudes, listed for instance in Sahl's *Nativities*, Ch. 2.2.

sometimes it will produce its indication at that time. **108** But if it does not have [such] an indication in the root, it indicates [only] part of the good fortune, of the category of the nature of the select planet in whose nature the fixed star is.[85] **109** And if the direction from one of [the releasers] reached one of the stars indicating toil[86] or killing, it will produce part of its indication.[87]

[A note about longevity and death]

110 And everything we have mentioned in this book of ours about the death of the owner of the revolution, in the distribution of any of the planets or in any of the years, is [only] if those years matched the years of the lifespan which his [longevity] indicator in the root [had already] pointed out (or if they were close to them); and likewise the death of the fathers, brothers, and others besides them.[88] **111** So if the year was in a condition indicating destruction, and that was not the time in which the years of the planets judged [it in the nativity], nor was it close to them, then he will have a disaster in it which can be gotten over.[89]

112 So this is how the topic of direction works, and we will discuss [next] what remains of this subject, if God wills.

Chapter III.3: On the management of Saturn if he was the distributor, & the partnership of the planets with him in the management

1 If you directed one of the releasers (I mean, the Sun, Moon, Ascendant, Lot of Fortune, or the degree of the meeting or degree of the

---

[85] For example, the fixed star Zosma is of the nature of Saturn-Venus: so, it would grant good fortune of a Saturnian and/or Venusian type.
[86] E reads, "blindness."
[87] Abū Ma'shar probably means things like the stars indicating blindness and other illnesses: see Sahl, *Nativities* Ch. 6.2.
[88] See also IX.8, **121-22**, and Da. 184.
[89] See also IX.8, **120**.

opposition), then understand the distributing planet, and the one partnering with it in the management of the distribution by its rooted body or ray: for each one of them individually has an indication for good or evil. **2** But the strongest of them in the indication is the distributor which you distribute from the native's releaser,[90] and the one partnering with it in the management of the distribution; but as for the rest of the releasers, they are below it in strength.

3 And[91] if Saturn was the lord of the distribution without any of the planets casting its rays to that bound, or any of them looking at Saturn, and he is in a bad condition, then in that year it indicates a long illness from cold and phlegm, and stinking, indigestion, constipation,[92] tuberculosis, swelling,[93] and a disturbance of black bile, along with depression, distress, sorrow, regret, confusion, and trouble, and a delay in every work in which there is benefit, and an abundance of quarrels, and distresses because of old things, and bad management in the works he does.

4 And if the manager for that distribution was also Saturn, by his rooted body or ray, it indicates the native's death in that year.

5 And[94] if Jupiter was the one partnering with him in the management of the distribution, then it indicates the dissolving of that evil and its minimizing, except that harm will affect the native from fathers and children.

6 And[95] if Mars was the one partnering with Saturn in the management, they indicate misfortune and harm from brothers; and if, when Mars cast his rays to that bound, he was in the inspection of Saturn without any of the fortunes looking at him, that is an indicator of death or a powerful illness, or the corruption of the brain, and some-

---

[90] That is, the longevity releaser. This is because the releaser most likely *will* be one of these five. See for example Sahl, *Nativities* Ch. 1.15, **6-15** (but especially **15**), from Nawbakht the Persian. Thanks to Steven Birchfield for pointing this out.
[91] For this sentence, cf. Da. 16.
[92] Or perhaps any kind of blockage.
[93] This especially involves tumors (ورم \ تورّم).
[94] For this sentence, cf. Da. 19.
[95] For this sentence, cf. Da. 17 and 20.

thing detestable affecting him from anger,[96] and enemies will have control over him.

7 And[97] if the Sun was the one partnering with Saturn in the management, and [the Sun] is in a suitable condition, it indicates the native's escape from death, and distresses and sorrows will afflict him, and death will be feared for his father, and different tribulations will happen to him, so long as [the Sun] is the manager in that bound.[98]

8 And[99] if Venus was the one partnering with him in the management of the distribution, they indicate that he will marry, and a child will be born to him,[100] and distresses and detestable things will afflict him, and one of his children or his women will die, so long as she is the manager in this bound.

9 And[101] if Mercury was the one partnering with him in the management of the distribution, it indicates harm from slaves or from the sciences, accounting, writers, and writing, and forged books, and from taking and giving, and buying and selling. **10** And if Mars had been looking at Mercury when Mercury cast his rays to that place, then it indicates that harm will afflict him from lies and false statements, friendliness and courtesy, and deception and cunning, and from things he does or says, so long as he is the manager of that bound.

11 And[102] if the Moon was the one partnering with him in the management of the distribution, then in that distribution they indicate an abundance of distresses and anxieties, and sorrow,[103] and adversity in his way of life, and confusion in his works and management, and his being delayed in everything he devotes himself to, and his mother and sisters will die or bad catastrophes will afflict them, so long as she is

---

[96] Reading with **E** and **P**. **B** reads "gangs" or "groups."
[97] For this sentence, cf. Da. 21.
[98] That is, if he is still the partner when the distribution shifts out of Saturn's bound, these things will go away. The same goes for similar statements below.
[99] For this sentence, cf. Da. 22.
[100] Al-Andarzaghar explains that this is due to Venus, but that the rest of the sentence is due to Saturn.
[101] For this paragraph, cf. Da. 23-24; and perhaps 25.
[102] For this sentence, cf. Da. 26.
[103] Reading with **E** and **P** for "loss."

the manager in that bound; and he will see diminishment[104] in all of his situations.

12 And[105] if the distributor was Saturn, and in the root he is in a good condition, in a suitable place, made fortunate by Jupiter, then he indicates that the native will benefit from treasures and old matters,[106] and lands, and real estate, and in everything of the indication of Saturn. **13** And the indication of the rest of the planets upon the casting of their rays to that bound in that time, will be in the manner which we spoke of in the preceding.[107]

Chapter III.4: On the management of Jupiter when he is the distributor, & the partnership of the planets with him in the management

1 If[108] Jupiter was the distributor, without any of the planets managing with him, or without any of them looking at him, and in the root he is in a suitable place, it indicates that [the native] will marry a suitable woman in that distribution, and children will be born to him, and he will associate with kings, nobles, and leaders of the people of his city, and he will increase in his rank, power, and respect. **2** Now if the native was of the middle class in good fortune, he will be a leader over his peers, and will have authority over them in his country, and will earn money. **3** And if he was of the upper class, he will gain leadership over countries and great cities, and their people, and he will increase in his power and assets, and his family, children, and his children's children.

---

[104] E: "ruin."
[105] For this sentence, cf. Da. 18.
[106] Or, old "things."
[107] I believe Abū Ma'shar simply means that they will signify the same types of things as in **6-11**, but this time they mean more positive things, since Saturn in the twelfth is now in a good condition.
[108] For **1-2**, cf. Da. 27.

4 And[109] if Saturn partnered with him in the management of the distribution, they indicate that he will corrupt the assets of his fathers, grandfathers, and the relatives on his father's side, and he will be distressed by his father and the family of his house, and a child will be born to him, but some of his children and parents will be ruined, and he will be distressed, be sad, he will weep, and be delayed in his works, and his demands will be made difficult, and he will have bad management, and become ill, and pains will afflict him (but he will recover from them).[110]

5 <And[111] if the distribution as well as the management belonged to Jupiter, he will increase greatly, and will have a cheerful face, and he will be praised in his intellect and opinion, and will do no labor on the land in that year, even though he will gain in it, and rejoice in it, and the best praise will be said about him.>

6 And[112] if Mars was the one partnering with him in the management of the distribution, they indicate that it will corrupt everything we mentioned of the good when we discussed the management of Jupiter at the beginning of this chapter, [and it indicates] diminishment in it.

7 And[113] if the Sun was the one partnering with Jupiter in the management of the distribution, they indicate that he will be in charge of work for the Sultan, and will increase in his assets, good fortune, rank, and power, and he will associate with leaders and kings, and the people attending his door will increase, and they will need him, and he will be respected,[114] safeguarded, satisfied, and he will delight in fathers, grandfathers, and relatives, and the people of his house, and different things, and the inheritances of the fathers will pass to him.

---

[109] For this sentence, cf. Da. 28.

[110] Abū Ma'shar here omits the Jupiter-Jupiter distribution, but it would likely be close to the interpretation of Jupiter alone in **1-3**.

[111] Adding the missing Jupiter-Jupiter interpretation on the basis of al-Andarzaghar (Da. 38).

[112] For this sentence, cf. Da. 29.

[113] For this sentence, cf. Da. 30-31.

[114] E: "celebrated."

8 And[115] if Venus was the one partnering with Jupiter in the management of the distribution, they indicate marrying a suitable woman from among his relatives, or from people who have nobility, and he will be blessed with suitable children, and will delight in women, and benefit by them, and will be devoted to singing and entertainment, and delights, and he will have new[116] good fortunes which have importance. **9** And if in the root Jupiter was looking at Venus, then in that distribution his condition in good fortune will increase and flourish day-by-day, and he will earn assets having value, and will increase in his clothing, perfume, furnishings, and possessions, and he will put on the clothing of kings, and dress in their fashion, and his delight and joy will multiply. **10** Now if the native was of the middle [class], he will have [what] is below everything I said.

11 And[117] if Mercury was the one partnering with Jupiter in the management, and Mercury was in a suitable condition, they indicate delight and benefit in the sciences and culture, and an increase in eloquence and judgment, and he will be devoted to those having importance (of writers, viziers, or the managers of works), and he will be correct in his management and works, and his affairs will move forward, and he will delight in children, and increase in his good fortune and the suitability of his religion. **12** And if Mercury was in a bad condition, it will be below that even though he will be successful in these matters, and something detestable will afflict him because of them.

13 And[118] if the Moon was the one partnering with Jupiter in the management of the distribution, they indicate that his body will be healthy, and he will increase in the fitness of his religion and devoutness, and in his power and rank, and he will gain prestige, and will be delighted because of mothers and sisters, and will be successful in many things which he had hoped for and has command over, and he

---

[115] For this paragraph, cf. Da. 32-33, and maybe 34.
[116] E: "great," "lofty."
[117] For this sentence, cf. Da. 35-36.
[118] For this sentence, cf. Da. 37.

will increase in his reason, knowledge, and management, and will be praised, approved among the people and kings, correct in his works and management, cheerful, joyful, delighted.

Chapter III.5: On the management of Mars when he is the distributor, & the partnership of the planets with him in the management

1 If[119] Mars was the distributor without any of the planets managing with him in that bound, or without any of them looking at him, and in the root he had indicated the granting of good things and status, then look: for if the native was of the upper class, it indicates the commanding of troops, and leadership over them, and the people's need for him, and the soldiers and common people meeting at his door, and an increase in his courage,[120] weapons, and riding animals, and his fame at horsemanship, and conquering enemies, and he will be triumphant, victorious, and earn gold, silver, and many assets, and he will manage his affairs with subjugation, superiority, boldness, contention and fighting, shouting and intimidation, injustice, and wrong. **2** And if the native was of the middle class, it indicates proximity to the Sultan and those having strength and assistance, and delight in them, and benefit will come to him from them, and he will increase in his assets, and be a leader over people, and he will inspire awe among the people of his class. **3** And if the native was of the lower class, he will connect with people having power, and will have good fortune of the category [of things] we mentioned, except that his condition in them will be below that. **4** And[121] if the distribution belonged to Mars alone and he is in a bad condition, then in that distribution it indicates an illness of the body from heat and fever, and abscesses, and the spilling of blood, and wounds, and an abundance of quarrels, distresses, and bad travels, and trouble and toil, and working hard at harmful things; and that is worse

---

[119] For **1-2**, cf. Da. 44.
[120] E: "his good fortune and courage."
[121] For this sentence, cf. Da. 39 and perhaps 41.

if in one of the years Mars was [also] the lord of the year, and his condition in them was like that in terms of badness.

5 And[122] if the distribution belonged to Mars and he is in a bad condition, and Saturn partners with him in the management (and especially if, along with his partnership in the management, he was looking at [Mars] with an aspect of hostility), then they indicate a long illness, and the corruption of the temperament,[123] and the agitation of the four humors, and his delay in beneficial works, and his negligence in assets, and the disappearance of what he has of them, and an abundance of anxieties, and his downfall in good fortune, and the decline of his condition, and his fleeing from his country or his home, and sometimes injustice will affect him, and he will pass into the hands of his enemies, and many different harms will befall him. **6** Now if Mars and Saturn were falling away from the fortunes[124] (in their condition of badness and standing alone in the distribution and the management), then after all of this a bad death will be feared for him, or an ugly killing.

7 And if the distribution belonged to Mars and Jupiter partnered with him in the management, and in the root Mars was in a suitable condition, in a house of Jupiter, and he is looking at him, then it will be like what we said in the indication of Mars about his success in good fortunes, except that he will manage his works in an unhurried way, with patience, friendliness, knowledge, fairness, impartiality, insight, and with balanced organization, and fine, good reasons, and those good things will be more numerous, and especially if the Sun in the root looked at Jupiter with an aspect of affection: for then along with what we said he will be at the hands of the greatest kings. **8** And if Jupiter was in a bad condition, something detestable will affect him from

---

[122] For this sentence, cf. Da. 42.

[123] Or more generally, the balanced "mixture" of the components of bodily health (especially the humors, mentioned next). The reason for this is especially because Mars and Saturn are excessive in their heat and cold, so this should lead to wide swings and imbalances in the body's condition.

[124] That is, in aversion to them.

administrators and the authorities, and it will impel him towards powerful people but they will be hostile towards him, and misfortune will affect him because of children.

9 And[125] if the distribution as well as the management belonged to Mars and he is in a bad condition, he will pass into the hands of his enemies, or highway robbers, and detestable things and tribulations will reach him, and death will be feared for him.

10 And[126] if the distribution belonged to Mars and the Sun partnered with him in the management, he will have something detestable from fathers, kings, and great ones of the people, as well as confinement, heat, and fires. **11** And if they[127] were in a bad condition, death will also be feared for the native.

12 And[128] if the distribution belonged to Mars and Venus partnered with him in the management, something detestable will affect him in the family and children, or because of them.

13 And[129] if the distribution belonged to Mars and Mercury partnered with him in the management, then types of detestable things will afflict him, as well as disgrace and malicious gossip, and decisive adversity from enemies, writers, books, lies and deception, and quarrels, and haughtiness and bragging, and in relation to works he does.

14 And if the distribution belonged to Mars and the Moon partnered with him in the management, illnesses and sickliness will afflict him, and contentions, and he will be distressed because of [various] managements, messengers, letters, and reports, and mothers, sisters, and women.

---

[125] For this sentence, cf. Da. 45.
[126] For this sentence, cf. Da. 46.
[127] **E** reads "he" (Mars).
[128] For this sentence, cf. Da. 50.
[129] For this sentence, cf. Da. 51.

Chapter III.6: On the management of Venus when she is the distributor, & the partnership of the planets with her in the management

1 If[130] Venus was the distributor without any of the planets managing with her, and without any of the planets looking at her, and she is in a suitable condition, it indicates a suitable, harmonious marriage, and delight in women and feminine men, and kings and their children, and success in different [types of] good fortune—and especially in the year in which the Venus is the lord of the year or[131] the year terminates at the sign in which the Lot of marriage was, in the root. **2** Now if the native was of the upper class, then in those years he will have extensive revenues, much food and furnishings, and he will increase in his women, friends, and sisters, and he will delight in them (and they will delight in him), and he will be devoted to singing, melodies, delights, and joy. **3** And if the native was of the middle class, he will marry and gain much good from women and feminine men, and he will carouse with the nobles, and gather with them in places of entertainment.

4 And[132] if the distribution belonged to Venus and Saturn partnered with her in the management, they indicate trouble[133] in the affairs he is devoted to, and abstention in the manner of women, and distresses because of them, and the illness of some of them (or their death), and something detestable and different quarrels will affect him. **5** Now if, along with his management in the bound of Venus, Saturn was looking at her and making her unfortunate, it indicates that he will find little joy in women and because of them, and then [the women] will certainly be ruined, and he will have many distresses in everything we

---

[130] For **1-2**, cf. Da. 54-55.
[131] **P** reads, "and," which of course would be even more reinforcing.
[132] For this paragraph, cf. Da. 56-57.
[133] العسر. **B** reads "coercion" (القسر), which also sounds like a Saturnian signification.

mentioned before[134] this, and he will be devoted to[135] situations of weeping and mourning.

6 And if the distribution belonged to Venus and Jupiter partnered with her in the management, and the native is of the upper class, they indicate a marriage with a free,[136] exultant woman[137] with whom he will hoard many treasures of money, garments, possessions, and dishes, and he will perfume himself with pleasurable scents,[138] and will rejoice in pretty girls and entertainment.[139] **7** And if the native was of the middle [class], he will have good fortunes in this category, except that it will be below that.

8 And[140] if the distribution belonged to Venus and Mars partnered with her in the management, they indicate a powerful, hot illness like pleurisy[141] and what is like that, and some of his women will die or become ill, and he will be harmed by them and quarrel with them and others, and he will increase in his eagerness for [women] and having sex, and he will be disgraced because of them, and something detestable will affect him from them. **9** And if Mars was looking at Venus and Mercury with an aspect of hostility in the root or at the time of the management, it indicates powerful, long-lasting quarrels and different contentions, and something detestable because of stubbornness, disputing,[142] and ugly affairs. **10** And if Jupiter looked at Mars in one of the two times, then it indicates a resolution of the quarrels.

11 And if the distribution belonged to Venus and the Sun partnered with her in the management, they indicate leadership and being devoted to kings and nobles, and benefit from them as well as fathers,

---

[134] **E**: "like."
[135] Perhaps this should read something like, "he will be involved in."
[136] حرّة. Or, "noble," i.e., someone with leisure and status.
[137] Reading the singular with **E**; but in a polygamous society the plural reading of **B** and **P** would make sense.
[138] Or perhaps more generally, "he will pamper himself with pleasurable comforts."
[139] Reading with **P**. **B**: "and he will rejoice in singers and musical instruments [or perhaps, playthings]." **P**: "and singers and musical instruments will come to him."
[140] For this paragraph, cf. Da. 58-59.
[141] An inflammation of the lung.
[142] **P** reads, "and rebels."

and victory over everyone who is hostile to him, and the governing of works which have importance.

12 And if the distribution as well as the management belonged to Venus and she is in a suitable condition, it indicates success in good fortunes of the category of what she indicates; and if she was in a bad condition, the contrary of that.

13 And[143] if the distribution belonged to Venus and Mercury partnered with her in the management, then he will have benefit from culture and abstruse knowledge, and subtle[144] management and courtesy, and he will have advantages and goods of different types, and his enjoyment and delighting in women will multiply—except that there will be malicious gossip about him because of corrupted [women].[145]

14 And[146] if the distribution belonged to Venus and the Moon partnered with her in the management, he will marry his sister or a beautiful, suitable woman of the family of his house, or he will have sex with different women having beauty, or he will have benefit and good from women or because of them, and an increase in power, rank, and elevated [status].

Chapter III.7: On the management of Mercury when he is the distributor, & the partnership of the planets with him in the management

1 If[147] Mercury was the distributor without any of the planets managing with him, or without any of them looking at him, it indicates an increase in his understanding, culture, reason, rank, and assets, and he will be devoted to writers and writing, skills, a friendly attitude, busi-

---

[143] For this sentence, cf. Da. 60.
[144] لطيفة. This also has connotations of cleverness and wit.
[145] In a marginal note, **B** adds: "And if Mercury cast his ray from the opposition, he will benefit from famous women." But since the MS does not contain a mark showing where it should be added, it probably comes from some other source.
[146] For this sentence, cf. Da. 61.
[147] For this sentence, cf. Da. 62.

ness, and associations with people, and he will delight in the types of things which Mercury indicates. **2** And if he was in a bad condition, detestable things will affect him from these things.

3 And[148] if the distribution belonged to Mercury and Saturn partnered with him in the management, he will be weak in the body, or will become ill with a bad, long-lasting illness, and his appeals will be made difficult for him, and he will be delayed in his works and managements, and he will be stupid, lazy, and moving[149] will be burdensome for him, and he will come to different distresses and contentions. **4** And[150] if in addition to Saturn's management in that bound, Mars was looking at Mercury or at that bound in one of the revolutions in which he distributes, then along with what we mentioned the native will come to powerful harm in assets, and tribulation from speech and contention, and bad management, and the malicious gossip of critics in it, and people's shaming of him. **5** And if, along with what we stated, the Moon looks at this bound as well in that distribution or those revolutions with an aspect of badness, it will be more powerful for the tribulation, evil, and something detestable, and especially if the lord of the year was an infortune or the year terminated at one of the infortunes.

6 And[151] if the distribution belonged to Mercury and Jupiter partnered with him in the management, they indicate an increase in logic, sciences, and culture, and because of them he will have fame and good, and benefits, and treasures from kings and nobles, and he will be devoted to household management, and will take over the responsibility of works for the leaders.

7 And if the distribution belonged to Mercury and Mars partnered with him in the management, it indicates a powerful illness, harm, and malicious gossip and speech, and contention, and he will act according to his own opinion and thought in [what is] wrong, detestable, and evil, and he will be blamed in his works and exploits, and an ailment

---

[148] For this sentence, cf. Da. 63 and 66.
[149] Or perhaps, "motivation" (الحركة).
[150] For **4-5**, cf. Da. 64.
[151] For this sentence, cf. Da. 65.

will afflict him in his brain—and that is more confirmed if Mars in the root was looking at Mercury with an aspect of corruption and misfortune. **8** And[152] if, in addition to the management of Mars, Saturn looks at that bound or looks at Mars or Mercury in those years in which they both are in charge of its management,[153] or the Tail was in the sign of the distribution, he will pass into the hands of his enemies, and they will take command of him, and an illness will afflict him which will diminish the benefits of [any] treatment, and the humors of his body will be corrupted, and his temperament, and his thinking and brain. **9** Now[154] if Jupiter looked at that bound or at Mars or Mercury in the time of the management, it indicates the dissolving of those detestable things and illnesses, and their being brought to light.[155]

10 And[156] if the distribution belonged to Mercury and the Sun partnered with him in the management, they indicate success in leadership and an increase in power, rank, and the excellence of his status among the authorities and leaders, and he will have leadership over a group of the people,[157] and will have authority over them, and he will gain evident high status, and will increase in his assets, and will be correct in his opinion, and concealed secrets will be laid bare for him, as well as hidden sciences, and he will be praised in his opinion.

11 And[158] if the distribution belonged to Mercury and Venus partnered with him in the management, they indicate an abundance of entertainment, and carousing with brothers, and befriending people having power and culture, and an increase in culture and children, and delighting in brothers and sisters, and he will increase in the sweetness of his speech, and the accomplishing of things, and his friendliness and

---

[152] For this sentence, cf. Da. 68.
[153] This probably means either "at the time of the solar revolution for the year in which it changes," or "by transit at the very time in which it changes."
[154] For this sentence, cf. Da. 67.
[155] وكشفها. Maybe this means that instead of festering internally without an awareness of them, they will be discovered and treated.
[156] For this sentence, cf. Da. 69.
[157] **P** reads, "his peers among the people."
[158] For this sentence, cf. Da. 70.

skill,[159] and it will prepare for him whatever he loves in terms of stratagems[160] in the matter of women and associating with them, and being with them, and delighting in them.

12 And if the distribution as well as the management belonged to Mercury and he is in a suitable condition, it indicates apparent, great good fortune of the category of what he indicates; and if he was in a bad condition, the contrary of that.

13 And[161] if the distribution belonged to Mercury and the Moon partnered with him in the management, he will increase in his culture and knowledge, and will be devoted to the knowledge of Divinity, and the heavenly sciences, and the knowledge of prophecy or the science of the stars, and he will be friendly, correct in his management and in those things he is devoted to, and he will benefit generally in what he does, and will increase in his assets and treasures.

[Planets looking at the time lords, in the nativity or revolution][162]

14 But these things which we have stated about the indication of the distributor and the one partnering with it in the management, are [only] principles: they do have other conditions besides that, which one ought to be guided by for the rest of what branches off from them.[163] **15** Because if a planetary fortune or infortune looked at one of the two in one of the two times (or [the time lord] itself was in one of the excellent or bad situations), then it will increase in good and subtract from the evil, or increase in evil and subtract from the good, or it will make it turn from its [current] condition into another one, in accordance with its own condition and the condition of the planet combining with it. **16** So if the planet had indicated good fortune but

---

[159] **P**: "and a scarcity of anger."
[160] **P**: "scenarios."
[161] For this sentence, cf. Da. 71.
[162] This may include their aspects at the very time of the shift from one distribution to another.
[163] "Branches off" seems to refer to specific planetary conditions, rulerships, and so on, which determine the planets' energy in particular ways.

then a planet made it unfortunate, and that infortune was in a stake or what follows it, it will make that good fortune turn into misfortune and corruption—and that is more confirmed if the infortune was in a fixed sign. **17** But if the infortune was withdrawing,[164] then it will not have the power to make it turn [completely], although it will change it somewhat (and especially if it[165] was in a convertible sign).[166] **18** And if the planet had indicated harm and something detestable [in the nativity], and a fortune looked at it from any of the positions [just mentioned], the work in it in terms of changing or converting it will be like what we stated.

[Corruption or support of the time lord at the nativity]

19 And you ought to look at the position of their houses relative to both of them:[167] because if [1] the planet was in a suitable position and it is made unfortunate,[168] or [2] one of the two in the root is corrupting its associate,[169] it introduces something detestable in the category of its indication and the place of its house.[170]

20 And that is like if [1] Mercury was in the Ascendant, in a suitable condition, and he is the lord of the house of enemies and the lord of the Lot of Fortune, and the lord of the distribution and of the rays as well, and he is made unfortunate: it indicates harm and quarreling in assets, and something detestable from enemies or from bad people, the masters of stratagems, lies, and deception, and he will say useless

---

[164] That is, dynamically cadent.
[165] This seems to be the aspecting infortune.
[166] The idea is that an angular infortune will have the power to force a change, and the fixed sign will make the change lasting; but a withdrawing infortune has less power, and being in a convertible sign will make the change more temporary.
[167] See the examples below.
[168] See **20-21**.
[169] See **22-23**.
[170] **P** reads: "from it." Below we will see that Abū Ma'shar means *both* its position relative to the Ascendant, *and* its position relative to its own domicile (just as he does in transits).

things.¹⁷¹ **21** But if Mercury was made fortunate, it indicates good from these types of things.

22 And [it is also] like [2] Saturn and Jupiter, if one of them was the lord of the rays and the other the lord of the distribution, and in the root of the nativity they had been hostile to each other, it indicates fighting and contention with the father or relatives.¹⁷²

23 And like [2] Venus and Mars, if one of them was the lord of the distribution and the other the lord of the rays, and one of them was doing damage to its associate [in the nativity], and they were exchanging each other's shares (and that is if each of them was in the share of the other—being in its bound, house, exaltation, face, triplicity, or joy): for they will indicate quarreling with a woman of his who is accused of fornication, and there will be malicious gossip about him.¹⁷³

24 And as for the reason for each thing we have stated, one seeks information about that from their places in the circle, and their places relative to their houses.

[How long an effect will last, in a distribution]

25 And if planets in the root of the nativity had indicated the endurance of the good or evil, the shifting from distribution to distribution and from management to management will not nullify that indication, but will change it a little bit into an increase or decrease in it, even if in the root it was in a condition at variance¹⁷⁴ with the condition in one of the two:¹⁷⁵ for each planet manifests its rooted

---

¹⁷¹ The distribution is Mercury-Mercury. Because he is made unfortunate, the Lot affects assets, the twelfth enemies and deception, and his presence in the Ascendant the native's own speech.

¹⁷² In this case, the distribution of Saturn-Jupiter or Jupiter-Saturn will activate the conflicts already shown by this *natal* aspect.

¹⁷³ Reading with **B** and **P**. But **E** reads, "her." Again, the distribution of Mars-Venus or Venus-Mars will activate the issues already shown by their *natal* aspect.

¹⁷⁴ Reading with **P**. **B** and **E** read, "it indicated a condition at variance."

¹⁷⁵ I believe "one of them" means "one of the two roles" as distributor or partner, as was just mentioned.

BOOK III: DISTRIBUTIONS 333

indication when the distribution or management passes to it, and that thing will endure so long as that planet is the distributor or manager.[176]

26 And sometimes the situation in it is at variance *within* a single distribution [or] in the management of a single planet, in terms of an increase and decrease in it;[177] and sometimes that thing will *exist* in [only] some[178] of those years: and indeed every one of [those things] is known from the sign of that planet in the nativity. **27** So if the sign in which the distributor or manager was in the root, was a fixed sign, then that thing will last for those years, and the revolutions will not change it. **28** But if in the root it was in a sign having two bodies, then its condition in it will be at variance in the revolutions of years, in terms of increase or decrease. **29** And if it was in a convertible sign, then that thing will exist in [only] some of the years of that distribution or management, and the revolutions of years will change it greatly, and sometimes it will shift from condition to condition: and you will know which one that is, from the position of the planet in the houses of the rooted circle, and the strength or weakness of that place.

Time lord in:	Changes or exists	When
Fixed	Changes	When transition happens
Double-bodied	Changes	Within same period
Convertible	Only exists	Temporarily, within period

Figure 74: When time lords' effects change, based on quadruplicity (III.7, 25-29)

---

[176] Abū Ma'shar means the following. Suppose a planet in the root indicates a wonderful, long-lasting marriage. That marriage will indeed manifest or its issues take center stage when that planet is the time lord. And even if the management or bound shifts from something good to something bad during the time-lordship of the planet, the good marriage will still exist, even though its quality might be reduced somewhat at that time.

[177] That is, without a shift of time lords taking place (as in **25**).

[178] That is, more than one.

30 And the indications of each one of them is more confirmed if, at the beginning of the distribution or management, it is in sign whose condition is like that of the sign which it was in the root (of the fixed, convertible, and those having two bodies). **31** But if the condition of the sign which it was in at the root was contrary to that of the sign which it is in at the beginning of the distribution or management, it will introduce feebleness and weakness into it.[179]

[Time lords being activated more than once over a lifetime]

32 Now[180] each one of these planets will perhaps distribute or manage twice or more in the lifespan of a man. **33** But sometimes the distributor will manifest its indication and governorship [1] only once when it distributes, and then it will definitely not take it up again;[181] and sometimes that will be [2] whenever it distributes and manages,[182] and sometimes that will be in [3] distribution after distribution, and management after management, and sometimes that will be in [4] every distribution, management, and establishing of the times, [and]

---

[179] For example, if a natal planet was in a fixed sign, but at the time of the distribution it is transiting in a convertible one, it will make the signification a little more unsteady.

[180] This paragraph is a little confusing. Abū Ma'shar is pointing out that in many cases the same planet will be a time lord more than once in the native's life, but it will not always be constant or equally manifested. Suppose the Ascendant distributes through the bound of Mercury in two different signs, many years apart: sometimes it will properly manifest in [1] only one of them, and sometimes it will do it in [2] both times. But he might also be a time lord in [3] many consecutive distributions, such as he casts a ray to the beginning of a sign, and no other planet looks at the sign: in that case, he will be the partner throughout many consecutive bounds. Or, he might be the time lord in [4] every time: this would especially be true for a short-lived native, or if the other planets were in aversion to the sign or cast their rays far away, and it was a sign of many ascensions. Finally, he may [5] never have an opportunity to manifest, especially if a short length of life and a great distance between planets do not allow it. Perhaps this would also be the case if it does not look and is in a convertible sign.

[181] See **35** below.

[182] See **36** below.

furthermore[183] it [may] have [5] a condition which is not in any distribution or management or [annual] time. **34** And indeed that is known from the sign in which the distributor is, and the number of its years, and from the ascensions of its sign. **35** For if in the root the distributor was in a fixed sign, and it is *not* looking at the position of the distribution, its indication for that thing will be weak, and will come to be in [only] [1] a single time, either when [1a] its distribution corresponds to the number of ascensional degrees of the sign which it is in at the root, or [1b] when that distribution corresponds with its greater, middle, or lesser years, in accordance with what its position in the rotation of the circle indicated in the root.[184] **36** But if it *was* looking at it[185] and it is strong in [its] indication for that thing, that will come to be [2] whenever it distributes. **37** (But as for the manager, it is contrary to that: because it is not an indicator in its own right nor [by] its rays in the root, unless [they are] in that bound: so whenever it manages it will produce its indication, in accordance with its strength or weakness.)[186] **38** And if the distributor or manager in the root was in a sign of two bodies, what it indicated in the root will come to be [3] on an occasional basis.[187] **39** And if in the root it was in a convertible sign, then it indicates that that thing (of any distribution and management) will come to be in [only] [1] one of the times, in accordance with the strength of that planet in those years.

40 And as for the *conditions of a man* in each distribution or management being different from his condition at the time of another

---

[183] Up to the colon, I have abbreviated for clarity. The original reads something like, "Furthermore its condition will be in no distribution or management, nor at any time, every condition and time being like its condition in the other time." (The MSS differ somewhat in the wording.)

[184] See **42** and its footnote, and Figure 75 below.

[185] This seems to assume it is still in a fixed sign.

[186] Abū Ma'shar means that the distributor's role is only by rulership, not by any direct connection to the bound: so its indication will not appear every time. But because the body or ray of the partner (the manager) *is* actually in the bound, it will always manifest.

[187] Lit., "time after time."

distribution or management, that is due to the *indication of the planet* in each distribution and management being different from its indication in the distribution and management of another.[188]

41 And the most manifest [situation] there can be for a planet's indication of something it had indicated in the nativity, is when [1] its testimony in any of the years is multiplied,[189] and [2] its condition in it also resembles the condition of the root, and [3] it looked at the position of the distribution, and at the lord of the sign in which the distribution is, and at the Ascendant of the root and its lord, or [4] it is the lord of the year or the year terminated at its place in the root or in the revolution; but if the contrary of that, its indication is weakened.

42 And when the indication of a planet over something is strong, and then at its distribution or management [that age of life] matches the number of ascensions of the sign in which it was in the root, or the amount of one of its own years,[190] or the rest of the times which one employs as models, that thing will be

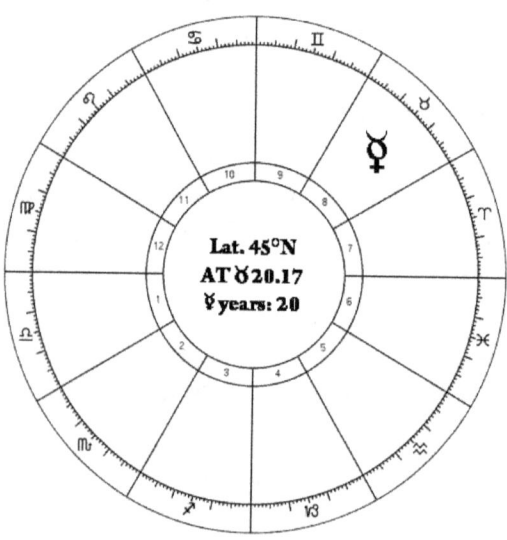

Figure 75: Mercury activated by planetary years and ascensions (III.7, 42)

---

[188] This means that if Saturn is a time lord at two different times of life, then despite the nativity not changing, what Saturn indicates specifically about the man will change because Saturn himself will be in different conditions in those two times (not to mention that the native himself will be of a different age).

[189] This may mean that it is (for example) in a revolutionary house that is the same or similar to its natal house, or plays some other important role in the year, or maybe is just well dignified.

[190] For example, its lesser years.

strong, evident, notable, [and] something which would not [normally] have been prepared for him in his whole lifespan.[191]

Chapter III.8: On the partnership of the lord of the year, the distributor, & the Ascendant, in the indication

1 If [the position of] the distribution and its lord in both the root and in the revolution were in a suitable place of the houses of the circle, and the distributor was a fortune, it indicates powerful good fortune.

2 And if [1] the year reached the fourth sign and [2] the infortunes are not looking at it, or the lord of the year is in the fourth of the root, in a suitable condition, in a sign in which it has a claim, and [3] the distributor is a fortune and in its own bound,[192] and it is not made unfortunate in the root, and [4] the Moon looked at the Lot of Fortune or assembled with Jupiter, and [5] all of them in the root are not made unfortunate, then he will have assets he desires, and he will be made fortunate with inheritances, things entrusted to his custody, and treasures. **3** And you should start to look in this at the root of the nativity: for if the root of his nativity indicated that he would have treasures or

---

[191] In Figure 75 Mercury is Taurus, the eighth. His lesser planetary years are 20, and at the birth latitude (45°N) Taurus has 20.17 ascensional times or AT. If we follow Valens, then regardless of whether or not Mercury is a time lord, he will manifest the meaning of Mercury-in-Taurus in the eighth at age 20, or at age 20.17, or their sum, or 1/3, 1/2, or 2/3 of that sum: 13.38, 20.09, or 26.75. What Abū Ma'shar adds is that we can be more confident about the effects if one of these ages occurs during a period when Mercury is *also* the distributor. When Abū Ma'shar speaks of "the rest of the times" which one uses as models, he is probably including the *fardārs* and other systems: so if Mercury were the distributor when he was also the *fardār* lord, it would also confirm the manifestation.

[192] For example, if the Ascendant is being directed through the bound of Jupiter, and the natal Jupiter is actually in his own bound as well, but somewhere else. (I read with **E** here.) But **B** reads "in the bound of its own distribution," while **P** reads "in its own bound of the distribution": that would mean that the distribution comes to a bound of Jupiter, and Jupiter is actually in that same bound, so the distribution is Jupiter-Jupiter.

inheritances, then when that planet indicative of it is the lord of the year or[193] the lord of the distribution, and in the revolution it is in the fourth, not made unfortunate, he will suddenly obtain treasures or inheritances or assets. **4** And you will know the essence of that thing from the natures of the planets. **5** For if it was Saturn it grants lands, plantations, and old, aged things from the dead, and because of grandfathers, fathers, sheikhs, and old people. **6** And if it was Jupiter, it grants gold, silver, and deluxe things because of the Sultan and nobles—and each planet will indicate like that in accordance with its nature.

7 And if the lord of the year and the distributor were both infortunes, and in the revolution they were both not in their own shares, but a fortune was with each one of them, then they will indicate a little good.

8 And if the distribution belonged to a planet, and it is in a sign of the image of people, and it is in the house of hope or is with the Lot of Fortune, it indicates the abundance of his good deeds towards the people, and charitable giving to the poor.

[Fixed stars, comets, eclipses]

9 And if in the revolution of the year one of the fixed stars indicative of good fortune was in the Ascendant of the year, or in the degree of the tenth from it,[194] or in the degree of the terminal point,[195] or in the degree of the distribution,[196] or with their lords, or with one of the luminaries, it indicates good fortune in that year.

10 And if there was one of the fixed stars having the nature of one planet, or the nature of two planets, and it had already indicated some-

---

[193] **P** reads "and," which would not only be better but would reinforce Abū Ma'shar's message about testimonies across several techniques.
[194] Or rather, the degree of the revolution's Midheaven.
[195] This sounds as though Abū Ma'shar is using 30° increments for his profections, but he does not otherwise mention this (for example, if he really did this in practice he would look at the bound lord of that degree, and so on). Instead, he seems to be mentioning this degree simply to have something a fixed star could coincide with.
[196] Omitting "from it," with **E**.

thing good or evil in the root, then when that chosen planet or two chosen planets manages one of the years or one of its times,[197] it will manifest their natures: and it is more powerful for the indication of that choice planet if, at the time it begins the management, it is in a condition indicating something like that matter.[198]

11 And if one of the stars which have a tail[199] appeared in the Ascendant of the root of the nativity, or in the sign of the terminal point, or in the Ascendant of the revolution, or in the sign of the distribution (and especially in the bound itself), or it was with the lords of some of them, then if that <nativity> belonged to kings, they will endure wars, and people will revolt against them, and enemies will be made victorious over them, and they will become ill, and their troubles and distresses will be multiplied, and they will treat the people unjustly, and perhaps something like that will indicate their destruction. **12** And if that belonged to the middle [class] of the people, and to the common people, their enemies will multiply and they will endure types of detestable things and tribulations.

13 Now if there was an eclipse[200] of one of the luminaries in one of the four positions which we mentioned,[201] or their lords were in the sign of the eclipse, then it indicates distresses, tribulations, illnesses, and types of detestable things, and the gloating of [one's] enemies. **14** And that is more evil and harsher if that sign or its lord were made unfortunate, or was in a bad condition and place.

---

[197] For example, one of the monthly revolutions.

[198] For example, let the nativity show eminence due to some fixed star of the nature of Jupiter being on the Ascendant. Then, if Jupiter was the lord of the year in some year, and in the revolution he was also exalted and in the Midheaven, it would manifest that natal promise.

[199] That is, a comet.

[200] Abū Ma'shar is using this in a general way because he mentions both luminaries; but the specific word here is normally reserved for solar eclipses.

[201] See **11**: the natal Ascendant, the profected Ascendant, the revolutionary Ascendant, and the sign of the distribution.

[Activating natal infortunes and fortunes]

15 And if the Ascendant of the year coincided with one of the signs in which the infortunes[202] were at the root of the nativity, and[203] the year terminated at that sign, or [that natal sign with the infortunes] matched [only][204] one of the two, then you should make that infortune be like the lord of the Ascendant or like the lord of the year, because it will be more powerful than them both.[205] **16** And do like that with the fortunate planets as well.

17 Then after that look at the lord of the year, the distributor, and the one partnering with it, to see if there was an infortune in one of the signs in the root, and that sign was the Ascendant of the year, and[206] that infortune in the root was making the distributor or the sign of the terminal point or[207] its lord unfortunate: for that is a bad signal. **18** And the strength of the lord of the Ascendant in that time (in [its] indication of something detestable), is like the strength of the lord of the distribution if it was made unfortunate.

19 Now if the infortunes in the revolution looked at the Ascendant of the year and at the Moon, and the fortunes do not look at them,[208] then they will be harmful, and the harm will be in accordance with the

---

[202] See also the footnote to **39**: this can also refer to planets "made unfortunate," not just the natural infortunes Saturn and Mars.

[203] **E** reads, "or."

[204] Reading for a confusing and garbled clause that seems to read, "or the revolution matched in the revolution of one of the years in one of the two."

[205] For example, let the revolutionary Ascendant be on the natal Saturn, in the year the natal Ascendant profects to that Saturn. But I think Abū Ma'shar is overstating this: activating natal planets is important, but not always more powerful than the lord of the Ascendant of the year or the lord of the year. But since location is more "immediate" than rulership, Saturn's effects here might be more up-front and obvious.

[206] **B** reads, "or." But if we followed **B**, the condition just stated would be identical to **15**.

[207] **P** reads, "and."

[208] That is, the Ascendant of the year and the Moon.

position of the Moon, and the nature of the lord of the year[209] and the distributor.[210]

20 And if the lord of the year did not have [a planet] undermining it in the root, while the lord of the year and the lord of the distribution were both infortunes, and in the revolution one of the fortunes was with the lord of the year or in its square, then even though the position of the lord of the year may be bad [or] falling, it will not harm that [native] due to its safety from the infortunes [in the root] and the testifying of the fortunes to it [in the revolution]: and his condition in that year will be in the middle. **21** And likewise, if the condition of the distributor of life[211] was like the condition of lord of the year, and the condition of the lord of the year was like the condition of the distributor.

22 If the lord of the year and the distributor were both infortunes, and in the root they were both made unfortunate, and in the revolution they were both in a bad condition, then they indicate idleness and being inactive in any and all beneficial things.

23 If the distribution and the distributor were both made unfortunate in the two times, and in the revolution they were falling away from[212] the Ascendant, then it indicates unemployment and inactivity, and harsh adversities.

24 Even if Mercury was not the lord of the year, but in the revolution he was with Mars, it indicates being dismissed from work which is in his hands, and especially if the lord of the year was in the position of the infortune which was undermining the distributor, the lord of the year, or the sign of the terminal point. **25** Now if Mercury was in an excellent position in the circle, with Jupiter and the Lot of work, then false rumors will [still] be spread about him, and he will be distressed because of it, but his dismissal will not be completed.

---

[209] Perhaps this should include, "the lord of the *Ascendant of the* year."
[210] Reading with **B**. **E** and **P** read "the position and nature of the lord of the year and the distributor," and ignore the Moon.
[211] This is probably the longevity releaser.
[212] That is, "in aversion to."

26 And if the distributor and the lord of the year are both infortunes, and an infortune or fortune which was [itself] made unfortunate is looking at them both and at the Moon in the revolution, then something detestable, and harm, will afflict him from powerful enemies.

27 And if the lord of the year was some planet, and with it in the revolution was another planet, then that [other] planet will partner with it in the indication of good or evil. **28** And look like that at the planet which is with the distributor:[213] for if the partnering planet was an enemy to the lord of the year or the distributor, and that was Mars, then harm and injustice will afflict him from enemies; and if it was Saturn, it indicates illness and hindrance in works; and if it was a fortune, it indicates good fortune of the category of its indication.

29 And if in the root there was a planet indicating harm, then when that planet comes to be in [1] the Ascendant of the root, or [2] the Ascendant of the revolution, or in [3] the position of the Moon in the root or revolution, or in [4] the position of the distribution, or in [5] the position of their lords (all of that being at the revolution of the year), it indicates powerful harm. **30** And if there was a planet in the root indicating good fortune, then when that planet comes, in the revolution, to the positions which we stated, it indicates good fortune.

31 And if the distribution belonged to the fortunes, and the lord of the Ascendant of the revolution and the lord of the house of the Moon were both fortunes, then it is excellent; but if it was like that and the sign of the terminal point and its lord were both in a bad condition, they will introduce harm and diminishment.

32 And if the lord of the year and the distributor were both fortunes, and in the revolution of the year they were in a bad place of the houses of the circle, or they were retrograde, and they are not looking at the Ascendant of the year, and one of the two infortunes in the revolution was in the Ascendant while the other is in the setting, they

---

[213] That is, by transit at the time of the revolution (or perhaps, at the time the distributor actually begins its management). Steven Birchfield suggests it could refer to the time of the monthly revolution.

indicate the hardship of the year, and its difficulty, and the victory of enemies over him, and a catastrophe from a wound caused by iron, or defamation, or falling from a raised place, and harm and loss in assets.

33 And if the infortunes were in charge of the year, and in the revolution they were in [1] the stake of the setting,[214] or in [2] the position of a [natal] infortune which had been making the distributor unfortunate, or in [3] the position of a [natal] infortune which had been making the lord of the year unfortunate, or in [4] the position of a [natal] infortune which had been undermining the sign of the terminal point, and [5] Venus and Mercury in the revolution were with that infortune, then it indicates harm in the family and children. 34 And if their condition was like that and the Sun and Moon in the revolution were with that infortune, then it indicates harm for the parents in the body or in assets, rank, and authority.

35 And if the lord of the distribution was an infortune, and in the root it was in the house of illness, and in the revolution it came to be in a bad place with the infortunes, and it undermined the Moon, then it indicates powerful harm.

36 And if the lord of the year was an infortune, and in the revolution it was in a bad place and was slow or under the rays, or[215] the distributor and the Moon in the two times were in a bad position, connecting with the infortunes, and the lord of the year or the distributor was in the sixth, it indicates illness and a chronic condition in that year. 37 And it will be likewise if the lord of the year was a fortune but in the root or revolution it was in a bad place, made unfortunate.

38 And if the year terminated at the Ascendant of the root, and if the infortunes did violence to it in a grievous way,[216] then it is very bad—and especially if nothing of the fortunes is looking at the lord of the year, and the distributor was made unfortunate.

---

[214] This either means the seventh sign, or dynamically angular, following the degree of the Descendant (or both).
[215] E reads, "and."
[216] أذى ضرر.

39 And if the lord of the year and the distributor were infortunes,[217] and in the revolution they were both in a bad position, in the opposition of the infortunes, and the fortunes are not looking at the Ascendant of the year, and the Lot of Fortune in the year[218] was made unfortunate, then it indicates the badness of the year, and fear, fleeing, chains, punishment, and harm in assets, the family, and children. **40** But if Jupiter and Venus were assembling with the Moon or looking at her, then it indicates being rescued from those detestable things.

41 And if the year terminated at the Ascendant of the root, and there was an infortune in its opposition in the revolution,[219] and the lord of the year and the lord of the distribution are both infortunes, and in that year they are doing violence to the Moon, and in the Ascendant of the revolution is the Sun, Mercury, and the Moon ([all] being made unfortunate), it indicates fear, confinement, punishment, quarreling, and contending with enemies.

42 And if the lord of the year and the distributor were both infortunes, and the Moon and Sun in the revolution were under the earth, and the fortunes are not looking at the luminaries, then it indicates the illness of the owner of the revolution, and the bad condition of his parents, and the corruption of their condition, and fear for their souls.[220] **43** But if Jupiter in the revolution looked at the Lot of the father, [the parents] will be safe and it will subtract from the detestable things. **44** And if Jupiter was the lord of the year or[221] the lord of the distribution, and in the revolution he was with Saturn under the earth, it indicates the death of children.

---

[217] Perhaps this should read, "made unfortunate," because later in the sentence they are in the opposition of the infortunes.

[218] This is probably the Lot as calculated in the chart of the revolution, not the profected Lot.

[219] That is, an infortune is transiting in the seventh *of the nativity*, so that it harms the sign of the year. But this type of rule should probably extend to any time an infortune in the revolution opposes the sign of the year.

[220] Or perhaps, for their "lives" (أنفسهم).

[221] **P** reads "and," which would be even better.

45 And[222] [whether] the distributor was a fortune or infortune, if in the revolution and root it was falling away from view[223] of the fortunes, and in the year the lord of the distribution and the Moon are both made unfortunate, and the lord of the year is corrupted, in[224] a bad position, it indicates death.

46 And[225] if Saturn was the distributor, and he and[226] Mars in the revolution were corrupting the bound which the distribution was in, without the fortunes looking at the position of the distribution, and the lord of the year or the Moon were corrupted, it indicates death.

47 And[227] if the year terminated at the Ascendant of the root, or the Ascendant of the root and the Ascendant of the revolution were a single sign, and the distributor and the lord of the year were both infortunes, and they were in bad positions in the houses of the circle, and the planets in that year were in such a condition relative to the Ascendant of the revolution that if it were like that in the root of the nativity it would not indicate an upbringing,[228] then it indicates despairing of life in that year.

48 And when the lord of the Ascendant is [located] from the Ascendant up to the degree of the Midheaven [it is] eastern, and it is the first quarter of the year (if its Ascendant was a convertible sign);[229] and up to the seventh [it is] southern, and it is the second quarter of [the year]; and up to the fourth [it is] western, and it is the third quarter of [the year], and up to the degree of the Ascendant [it is] northern, and it is the fourth quarter of the year. **49** So, you should look at the lord of

---

[222] See also IX.8, **83**.
[223] That is, "in aversion to."
[224] **P** may read, "or in." But IX.8, **83** reads simply, "in."
[225] See also IX.8, **84**.
[226] Reading with **P** for "or," since the verb indicates that both of them are involved.
[227] See also IX.8, **87**.
[228] See for example Sahl's *Nativities* Chs. 1.18 and 1.29-1.30, and *Carmen* I.12.
[229] This is an awkward phrase, awkwardly situated. But we can see below in **50** that Abū Ma'shar adds "especially" if it is convertible, so that is probably his meaning here.

the year and[230] the distributor, and at the fortunes and infortunes, to see in which quarter [of the circle] they are: for its indication will be more powerful in that quarter [of the year].

50 And if the infortunes were in the Ascendant, the eleventh, and the Midheaven from the Ascendant of the revolution, while the fortunes are under the earth, it indicates something detestable at the beginning of the year, and good at its end—and especially if the sign of the year was convertible; and sometimes the planets which are in the stakes indicate the beginning of the year, and those withdrawing and falling [indicate] the end.

51 And do not let the investigation into what there will be of good and evil, and the condition of the parents, family, and children, and the rest of the things be *only* from the distributor, the manager, and the rest of the indicators we have mentioned, but do look at the rooted Lots' reaching the fortunes and infortunes by the turning of the signs[231] or by direction (a year for every sign or degree),[232] or [the fortunes' and infortunes'] reaching the Lots in this manner.

52 And along with that, you ought to look at the lord of the year, the distributor, and the manager, to see which Lot it is lord of in the root and the revolution: and let the investigation of the Lot's indication be in accordance with that. **53** And an example of that is if the Lot of brothers and its lord were in a bad place in the root, with the infortunes: that indicates that something detestable will afflict the brothers and sisters in the time when that infortune[233] is the distributor, manager, or has taken charge of the year.[234] **54** And if the lord of the Lot was also doing violence to the lord of the Ascendant, the native will have harm from them in that year.

---

[230] **E** reads, "or."
[231] That is, by profection.
[232] Profections grant a year per sign, and directions a year per degree (of ascensions). I can't imagine that Abū Ma'shar means that some natal directions grant a year per sign.
[233] Abū Ma'shar did not say the lord of the Lot was actually an infortune, but that seems to be what he means.
[234] That is, as lord of the year.

Chapter III.9: On the knowledge of the ninth-parts & their lords, & their direction & distribution, & the division of each one of them into thirds, & the knowledge of the lord of each division by its indication, & the one partnering with it by body or ray, according to what the people of India said

1 The distribution of the bounds which we described in what preceded, are what the Babylonians, the people of Persia, and the Egyptians used. **2** But as for the people of India and those who follow them,[235] when they saw the abundant difference of people's conditions in the distribution of a single bound, they did not grant the distribution to the bounds as did those others whom we mentioned, but they granted it to the ninth-parts, so that it would be more precise[236] and closer [to the truth] in judging the conditions. **3** So when you use directions you ought to do it both ways, each by itself, so that the investigation into knowing the condition of the years will be strengthened.

4 Now as for the *nahbahar*[237] (which means "one-ninth"), it is 200': so that is 2 1/3 equal degrees,[238] and each sign has nine ninth-parts, each ninth-part having a known lord.

5 So if that sign was Aries, Leo, or Sagittarius, then the lord of the first ninth-part for each one of them is Mars (the lord of Aries); and the lord of the second ninth-part is Venus (the lord of Taurus); and the lord of the third ninth-part is Mercury (the lord of Gemini); and the lord of the fourth ninth-part is the Moon (the lord of Cancer); and the lord of the fifth ninth-part is the Sun (the lord of Leo); and the lord of the sixth ninth-part is Mercury (the lord of Virgo)—and you work like that with the lord of the signs, so that you make the lord of each sign be the lord of one of the ninth-parts, and the lord of the

---

[235] This could also be read as "those who border on them."
[236] Lit., "finer, more delicate" (ألطف).
[237] نهبهر, Abū Ma'shar's transliteration of the original word, hereafter simply "ninth-part."
[238] "Equal" degrees are zodiacal degrees.

ninth ninth-part of each one of these three signs will be Jupiter (the lord of Sagittarius).

6 And if that was Taurus, Virgo, or Capricorn, the lord of the first ninth-part for each one of them is Saturn (the lord of Capricorn), and the lord of the second ninth-part also Saturn (the lord of Aquarius), and the lord of the third ninth-part Jupiter (the lord of Pisces)—and you work like that with the lords of the signs until the lord of the ninth ninth-part for each one of these three signs is Mercury (the lord of Virgo).

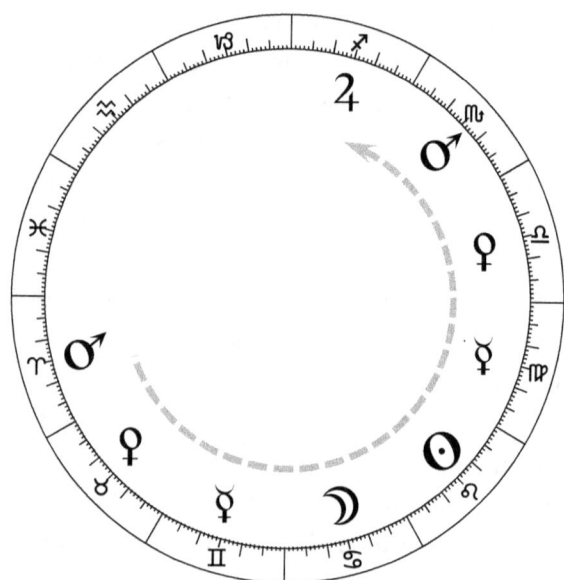

Figure 76: Order of ninth-part lords for all fiery signs (III.9, 5)

BOOK III: DISTRIBUTIONS 349

♈ ♌ ♐	Ninth-part	Sub	♉ ♍ ♑	Ninth-part	Sub
	#1: ♂ 0°00'–3°20'	♂		#1: ♄ 0°00'–3°20'	♄
		☉			♀
		♃			☿
	#2: ♀ 3°20'–6°40'	♀		#2: ♄ 3°20'–6°40'	♄
		☿			☿
		♄			♀
	#3: ☿ 6°40'–10°00'	☿		#3: ♃ 6°40'–10°00'	♃
		♀			☽
		♄			♂
	#4: ☽ 10°00'–13°20'	☽		#4: ♂ 10°00'–13°20'	♂
		♂			☉
		♃			♃
	#5: ☉ 13°20'–16°40'	☉		#5: ♀ 13°20'–16°40'	♀
		♃			☿
		♂			♄
	#6: ☿ 16°40'–20°00'	☿		#6: ☿ 16°40'–20°00'	☿
		♄			♀
		♀			♄
	#7: ♀ 20°00'–23°20'	♀		#7: ☽ 20°00'–23°20'	☽
		♄			♂
		☿			♃
	#8: ♂ 23°20'–26°40'	♂		#8: ☉ 23°20'–26°40'	☉
		♃			♃
		☽			♂
	#9: ♃ 26°40'–30°00'	♃		#9: ☿ 26°40'–30°00'	☿
		♂			♄
		☉			♀

Figure 77: Ninth-parts and first-level subdivisions, fiery and earthy signs (III.9)

	Ninth-part	Sub		Ninth-part	Sub
	#1: ♀	♀		#1: ☽	☽
	0°00'–3°20'	♄		0°00'–3°20'	♂
		☿			♃
	#2: ♂	♂		#2: ☉	☉
	3°20'–6°40'	♃		3°20'–6°40'	♃
		☽			♂
	#3: ♃	♃		#3: ☿	☿
	6°40'–	♂		6°40'–	♄
	10°00'	☉		10°00'	♀
	#4: ♄	♄		#4: ♀	♀
♊	10°00'–	♀	♋	10°00'–	♄
	13°20'	☿		13°20'	☿
♎	#5: ♄	♄	♏	#5: ♂	♂
	13°20'–	☿		13°20'–	♃
♒	16°40'	♀	♓	16°40'	☽
	#6: ♃	♃		#6: ♃	♃
	16°40'–	☽		16°40'–	♂
	20°00'	♂		20°00'	☉
	#7: ♂	♂		#7: ♄	♄
	20°00'–	☉		20°00'–	♀
	23°20'	♃		23°20'	☿
	#8: ♀	♀		#8: ♄	♄
	23°20'–	☿		23°20'–	☿
	26°40'	♄		26°40'	♀
	#9: ☿	☿		#9: ♃	♃
	26°40'–	♀		26°40'–	☽
	30°00'	♄		30°00'	♂

Figure 78: Ninth-parts and first-level subdivisions, airy and watery signs (III.9)

7 Now if that was Gemini, Libra, or Aquarius, the lord of the first ninth-part for each of the signs is Venus (the lord of Libra), and the lord of the second ninth-part is Mars (the lord of Scorpio), and the lord of the third ninth-part is Jupiter (the lord of Sagittarius)—and you work like that with the lords of the signs until the lord of the ninth ninth-part for each one of these three signs is Mercury (the lord of Gemini).

8 And if that was Cancer, Scorpio, or Pisces, the lord of the first ninth-part for each of the signs is the Moon (the lord of Cancer), and the lord of the second ninth-part is the Sun (the lord of Leo), and the lord of the third ninth-part is Mercury (the lord of Virgo)—and you work like that with the lords of the signs until the lord of the ninth ninth-part of each one of these three signs is Jupiter (the lord of Pisces).[239]

9 And there is another, abbreviated way, and it is that you look at the sign whose lords of the ninth-parts you want to know: of which triplicity is it? **10** For the lord of the convertible sign of that triplicity is the lord of the first ninth-part for each of those three signs, and the lord of the sign which follows it is the lord of the second ninth-part—and you will do like that for knowing the lords of the nine ninth-parts for every sign. **11** And we have already discussed that, along with the reason for its derivation, in the *Book of Introduction*.[240]

---

[239] In this way, Saturn will rule none of the ninth-parts in fiery signs, and the luminaries will rule none of the ninth-parts in airy signs. To me this seems like an unusual and unexplained imbalance in the theory, but because the whole theory is closely connected to triplicities and triangles, perhaps this did not bother its inventors.

[240] In *Gr. Intr.* V.17, Abū Ma'shar says that the ninth sign from any sign (which completes its triplicity) is the "completion" of its nature, apparently because it completes the third angle of a triangle. Evidently then, by dividing each sign into nine, we make reference to its complete nature. But I'm not sure whether this has to do with the triangle and triplicities, or the number nine (a significant number in Hindu thought), or alludes by analogy to the nine months of gestation.

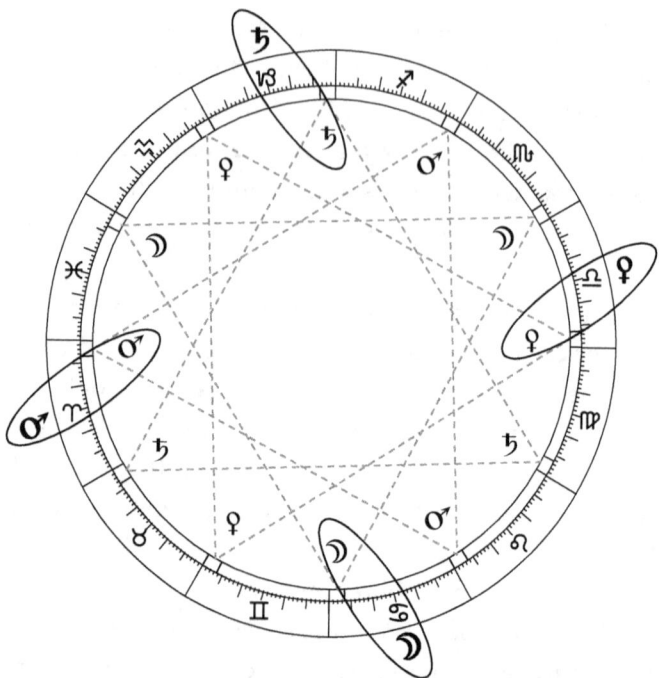

Figure 79: Lords of convertible signs
ruling the first ninth-parts (III.9, 4-10)[241]

12 Now as for the direction of the ninth-parts in nativities and other things, and their division into [smaller] thirds, and the knowledge of the lords of that division, and from which of them we should begin to draw conclusions, that pertains to what the people of India hid from the common people of the climes, and did not acquaint anyone with it unless it was scholars who waded [deeply] into it and had already gotten far in the knowledge of the stars, in the most honored ranks and the highest in ability, after they were confident that they would keep it secret, and defend it from the ignorant, and lest it be changed, and lest they would teach it except to one who knew the power of the scholars and their superiority over others of the common people (seeing that the knowledgeable person deserves to be preferred to the ignorant

---

[241] In this diagram, the points of the triangles fall on the first ninth-part of each sign: the first ninth part in each triplicity's signs, is the lord of the convertible sign of that triplicity (shown by the ovals). So, as Mars rules Aries (the convertible sign of fire), the triangle in the fiery signs shows that he rules the first ninth-part of each.

person, and compares favorably to them in his outstanding merit). **13** But we have decided to round out this noble book with every excellent [type of] knowledge reflecting the sense of what the scholars have already achieved, in virtue of [our] old age and what we have discovered through long effort and labor, and persistent thought about it for a long period of time.

14 And the knowledge and work in what we have described is that you convert each ninth-part into degrees of ascensions, and make each ascensional degree be one year: then you divide the total into three equal subdivisions, and make the lord of the first subdivision be the lord of the ninth-part itself, and the lord of the second subdivision the lord of the fifth sign from it, and the lord of the third subdivision the lord of the ninth sign from it. **15** Because [while] the lords of the ninth-parts are according to the succession of the lords of the signs, the lords of their subdivisions are in accordance with the lords of the houses of a single triplicity, in the manner of the lords of the *darījān*.[242]

16 So we begin the procedure with the lord of the first of the subdivisions—but if the work had been in the second subdivision of the ninth-part, we would begin the procedure with the lord of the fifth sign from the sign of the lord of the first subdivision,[243] then with the lord of the ninth sign from it, then with the lord of the ninth-part itself; and if the work had been in the third subdivision, we would begin with the lord of the ninth sign from the sign of the lord of the ninth-part, then after that with the lord of the ninth-part, then after that with the lord of the fifth sign from it.

---

[242] See *ITA* VII.6, and *Gr. Intr.* V.16. The *darījān* are an Indian way of assigning lords to the faces or decans. The faces of any sign are ruled by the lords of the signs of that triplicity, in zodiacal order, starting with the lord of that very sign. So the three faces of Gemini would be ruled in order by: Mercury (for Gemini), Venus (for Libra), Saturn (for Aquarius). This is the very order of subdivisions used by Abū Ma'shar: see the third ninth-part of fiery signs in the table here, the sixth one of the earthy signs, and the ninth one of the airy signs. This particular order does not appear in the watery signs, because the ninth-parts only extend for nine signs: since the watery series begins with Cancer (the convertible sign), it cannot reach all the way around the zodiac to Gemini.

[243] Reading for "ninth-part."

♈ ♌ ♐									
#1: ♂ (for ♈) 0°00' – 3°20'			#2: ♀ (for ♉) 3°20' – 6°40'			#3: ☿ (for II) 6°40' – 10°00'			
♂ (for ♈) 0°00'00" – 1°06'40"	☉ (for ♌) 1°06'40" – 2°13'20"	♃ (for ♐) 2°13'20" – 3°20'00"	♀ (for ♉) 3°20'00" – 4°26'40"	☿ (for ♍) 4°26'40" – 5°33'20"	♄ (for ♑) 5°33'20" – 6°40'00"	☿ (for II) 6°40'00" – 7°46'40"	♀ (for ♎) 7°46'40" – 8°53'20"	♄ (for ♒) 8°53'20" – 10°00'00"

Figure 80: First three ninth-parts of Aries, with subdivisions (III.9, 14-15)[244]

---

[244] The degrees of the three subdivisions here are given in zodiacal degrees; these would have to be converted into ascensions in practice.

17 And an example of that is a native born in the fourth clime, in a place whose latitude is 36° [north], and the Ascendant was the first [degree] of Aries.[245] **18** So we converted the first ninth-part to degrees of ascensions: it was 3 1/3° [in degrees of equality], so that became 2° 03' 20" [in ascensions], and that was 2 years, 20 days.[246]

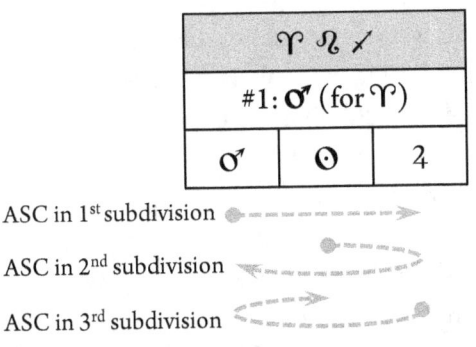

Figure 81: Order of subdivisions in any ninth-part (III.9, 16, 19-23)

19 And we divided that into thirds, [so that] each subdivision was 8 months, 6 days, and 16 hours; and the first subdivision of it fell to Mars (the lord of Aries and the lord of the ninth-part itself), and from him we draw conclusions about the conditions of one-third of the distribution. **20** Then after that we begin with the lord of the second subdivision, and it is the Sun (the lord of Leo) for 8 months, 6 days, and 16 hours: the total of that is 1 year, 4 months, 13 days, and 8 hours. **21** Then after that [we begin with] the lord of the third subdivision, and it is Jupiter (the lord of Sagittarius) for 8 months, 6 days, and 16 hours: the total of that is 2 years, 20 days. **22** And if the Ascendant or the work had been in the second subdivision of this first ninth-part, we would have begun in the subdivision with the Sun (the lord of Leo), then after him with Jupiter (the lord of Sagittarius), then after

---

[245] That is, 0° Aries: this way Abū Ma'shar can demonstrate all of the ninth-parts in order.

[246] This means that in Abū Ma'shar's table, the ascensional time of Aries at a particular latitude was 18.5.

him with Mars (the lord of Aries, and the lord of the first ninth-part). **23** And if the Ascendant or work had been in the third subdivision of this first ninth-part, we would have begun with Jupiter (the lord of Sagittarius), then after him with Mars (the lord of Aries and the lord of the first ninth-part), then after him with the Sun (the lord of Leo): so these are the lords of the subdivisions belonging to the first ninth-part of Aries, and this is how one uses each of them.[247]

24 And if the Ascendant or work had been in the second ninth-part of Aries, in the first subdivision of it, we would have divided [the ninth-part] into thirds as well, and the lord of the first subdivision of it would have fallen to Venus (the lord of Taurus and the lord of the ninth-part itself), and we would begin to make conclusions from her; and after her with the lord of the second subdivision, and it is Mercury (the lord of Virgo), then after him with the lord of the third subdivision, and it is Saturn (the lord of Capricorn). **25** And if the Ascendant or work had been in the second subdivision of this second ninth-part, we would have begun in the subdivision with Mercury (the lord of Virgo), then after him with Saturn (the lord of Capricorn), then after him with Venus (the lord of Taurus and the lord of the ninth-part itself). **26** And if the Ascendant or work had been in the third subdivision of this second ninth-part, we would have begun in the subdivision with Saturn (the lord of Capricorn), then after him with Venus (the lord of Taurus), then after her with Mercury (the lord of Virgo): so these are the lords of the subdivisions of the second ninth-part of Aries, and this is how one uses each of them.

27 And if the Ascendant or work had been in the third ninth-part of Aries, in the first subdivision of it, we would have divided it into thirds as well, and the first subdivision of it would have fallen to Mercury (the lord of Gemini and the lord of the ninth-part itself), and we

---

[247] Note well that this means *any* distribution in *any* ninth-part must run through *all* of the subperiods and complete its "triangle" or triplicity, no matter where the degree falls. So it doesn't matter if the Ascendant fell at the end of any ninth-part or its beginning: the native will still have to live through all parts of it (but in a different order based on where the natal Ascendant is). This is a significant departure from distributing through the bounds.

would begin to draw conclusions from him; then after him with the lord of the second subdivision, and it is Venus (the lord of Libra), then after her with the lord of the third subdivision, and it is Saturn (the lord of Aquarius). **28** And if the Ascendant or work had been in the second subdivision of this third ninth-part, we would have begun with Venus (the lord of Libra), then after her with Saturn (the lord of Aquarius), then after him with Mercury (the lord of Gemini). **29** And if the Ascendant or work had been in the third subdivision of this third ninth-part, we would have begun with Saturn (the lord of Aquarius), then after him with Mercury (the lord of Gemini), then after him with Venus (the lord of Libra): so these are the lords of the divisions of the third ninth-part of Aries, and this is how one uses each of them.

30 And if the Ascendant or work had been in the fourth ninth-part of Aries, we would have divided it into thirds as well, so that the first subdivision would have fallen to the Moon (the lord of Cancer and the lord of the ninth-part itself), and we would begin to draw conclusions[248] from her, then after her with the lord of the second subdivision, and it is Mars (the lord of Scorpio), then after him with the lord of the third subdivision, and it is Jupiter (the lord of Pisces). **31** And if the Ascendant or work had been in the second subdivision of this fourth ninth-part, we would have begun with Mars, then after him with Jupiter, then after him with the Moon. **32** And if the Ascendant or work had been in the third subdivision of this fourth ninth-part, we would have begun with Jupiter, then after him with the Moon, then after her with Mars: so these are the lords of the subdivisions of the fourth ninth-part of Aries, and this is how one uses each of them.

33 And if the Ascendant or work had been in the fifth ninth-part of Aries, we would have divided it into thirds as well, so that the first subdivision would have fallen to the Sun (the lord of Leo and the lord of the ninth-part itself), and we would begin to draw conclusions from him; then after him we would begin with the lord of the second subdivision, and it is Jupiter (the lord of Sagittarius), then after him with the lord of the third subdivision, and it is Mars (the lord of Aries). **34** And

---

[248] Reading in parallel with the other paragraphs, for "begin the division."

if the Ascendant or work had been in the second subdivision of this fifth ninth-part, we would have begun with Jupiter, then after him with Mars, then after him with the Sun. **35** And if the Ascendant or work had been in the third subdivision of this ninth-part, we would have begun with Mars, then after him with the Sun, then after him with Jupiter.

36 Now when the ninth-parts of Aries come to an end in this work, you will transfer the direction from it over to Taurus, and divide the first ninth-part of it into thirds as well, after which you will convert [it] into ascensions, so that the indicator of the first subdivision is Saturn (the lord of Capricorn and the lord of its first ninth-part), and we begin the subdivision from him: then after him the lord of the second subdivision, and it is Venus (the lord of Taurus), then after her the lord of the third subdivision, and it is Mercury (the lord of Virgo). **37** And if the Ascendant or work had been in the second subdivision of Taurus, we would have begun with Venus (the lord of Taurus), then after her with Mercury (the lord of Virgo), then after him with Saturn (the lord of Capricorn). **38** And if the Ascendant or work had been in the third subdivision of Taurus, we would have begun with Mercury, then after him with Saturn, then after him with Venus. **39** And in this manner you will direct the ninth-parts of the all the signs, ninth-part by ninth-part, up to what you want.

40 And you will be acquainted with the lords of the subdivision of each ninth-part individually, whether that ninth-part is ascending[249] or the direction terminates at it (in nativities and other things), in order to know the conditions of the years as well as what follows them in terms of months and days (in accordance with what results from the minutes of the division).

---

[249] That is, which ninth-part the Ascendant of the revolution is on: Abū Ma'shar confirms this in IX.7, **70**.

[Interpretation]

41 But as for knowing what each one of them signifies, one looks at the lord of each of the subdivisions of the ninth-part: [1] how is its condition in itself in the root and the revolution, and [2] how its condition is at the time of the subdivision and in the two times,[250] relative to the aspect of the Moon, the fortunes, and infortunes, and relative to the aspect of its partner to it,[251] and [3] the connection of any of the partners with others,[252] and [4] how is its strength and weakness? **42** Because from the indication of the lord of the subdivision and its partner for good fortune in nativities, the suitability of their condition, and one of them receiving its associate, or the closeness of one to the other, or the meeting of two of them in one sign or in one degree, or their coming to be in the position of the Moon, or in the places of the fortunes and their rooted and revolutionary rays, and if the lords of the subdivision of a single ninth-part are looking, one of them to its associate, from the trine or sextile, and they are fortunes—they indicate tremendous benefit and good fortune; and if in addition one of them connected with the other or connected with the lords of their houses, it will be greater and more confirmed for the good. **43** And if they were infortunes, and their condition was in accordance with what we stated about looking or connecting, it will be less harmful or it will not indicate harm at all, unless they have a bad position or are made unfortunate.

44 And if all of them (or one of them) came to be in that ninth-part (and especially in the position in which the subdivision[253] is), or they had rays in it in the root or in the revolution, or they looked at it in ac-

---

[250] The "two times" must mean the nativity and the solar revolution, but these were just mentioned.
[251] In other words, we are supposed to use partnering planets, just as with normal distributions through the bounds.
[252] This could also be understood as the *bodily* connection between them, distinguishing connections by sign from conjunctions by body.
[253] This is the same word as "distribution."

cordance with the subdivision[254] of the degrees by equality from their [own] houses, bounds,[255] or ninth-parts,[256] he will benefit by what those planets indicate, be they fortunes or infortunes.

45 And if they were made unfortunate or in the rays of the infortunes, or in a bad position, and they (or some of them) had testimony in the house of death, then they indicate death; and what indicates misfortune in the directions in nativities is the corruption of the condition of the lords of the subdivision of a single ninth-part, or if they are made unfortunate or in the position of the infortunes (or in their rooted or revolutionary rays), or one of them was in the fall of the other, or they are not looking at each other, or their condition is contrary to what we stated before about suitability.

46 And with the indication of the lord of the subdivision of the ninth-part, you should blend the lord of the ninth-part [itself], and the lord of that bound, and the lord of the *darījān*[257] in which the subdivision is, and the essence of those degrees, and their lords, and the condition of the Moon.

47 And as for the manager partnering with the lord of the subdivision of the ninth by body or by ray, if it was a fortune it indicates good fortune and suitability; and if it was an infortune, it indicates misfortune and corruption, in accordance with the category of its indication, in the manner which we stated in what preceded about the distribution of the bounds and the one partnering with them.

48 And if both the manager and the lord of the subdivision of the ninth were harmonious in nature and [their] indication for good, and one of them looks at its associate with an aspect of harmony and affection, and they both look at the position of the subdivision [while] in

---

[254] Again, this is the same word as "distribution."

[255] **T**: "shares" (i.e., dignities).

[256] Degrees of equality of zodiacal degrees, but I'm not sure how this differs from the rays he has already described, and I do not think he is combining these with distributions through the bounds.

[257] **P** and **T**: "the lord of the degrees." Again, this could be read as "the lord of the degrees in which the *distribution* is," connecting this with distributions through the bounds. See **44**.

that condition as well, then they will indicate good and suitability; and if their conditions were contrary to what we stated, it will be the contrary of that.

49 And in everything concerning the conditions of the one partnering with the lord of the subdivision of the ninth-part, act in accordance with its management with it by body or by rays, and the shifting of the management from one to another, and in the rest of the conditions, and its indication for good or evil, just as we have done for the one partnering with the lords of the bounds,[258] so that several indicators in different conditions will fall to each ninth-part, each one of them indicating something different to what another indicates: for the differences in the conditions of people in the subdivision of each ninth-part are multiplied because of that.

Chapter III.10: On knowing the lord of the year from the method of the lords of the ninth-parts, according to the belief of the people of India

1 Now when the year terminates at[259] one of the signs, the Indians make the lord of the year be the lord of the first ninth-part of the sign of the terminal point, and for them it is the lord of the year up to whatever position the year had reached from it (to the beginning of the sign or its end), in the way that other people in the rest of the climes make the lord of that *sign* be the lord of the year, until whatever place it terminates from it.[260]

2 Then, they looked at the condition of the lord of the first ninth-part, in the root and the revolution: [1] is it in its own house, exaltation, bound, ninth-part, or *darījān*, or is it in exile[261] or in an excellent place, [2] with a fortune, or with the Moon, or in the aspect of the for-

---

[258] See the combinations in III.2, and detailed interpretations in the rest of III.3-III.7.
[259] That is, by profection. Abū Ma'shar has deferred the Indian theory of profections until now.
[260] I do not really understand what Abū Ma'shar means by this.
[261] That is, "peregrine."

tunes, or [3] with the infortunes or in their aspect, and [4] where is it relative to the stakes?²⁶² **3** And along with that they looked at the rest of the conditions of the lord of the first ninth-part for that sign, and drew conclusions about the whole year from its conditions. **4** So, if the lord of the first ninth-part of the sign of the terminal point (that is, the planet which the Indians make the lord of the year) was in a suitable condition in the two times, just as we have stated about the planets' suitability of condition, it indicates suitability in that year; but if it was in a corrupt condition or made unfortunate, it indicates detestable things and corruption.

5 And an example of that is if the year terminated at 20° of Taurus (or less than that or more), then its lord would be Saturn (the lord of the first ninth-part); and if the year terminated at Gemini, at whatever position it was, then Venus is the lord of the year; and if the year terminated at Cancer, then the Moon would be the lord of the year.

6 And sometimes they saw how many ninth-parts the native had gone through²⁶³ since the day he was born, and they cast it out from the ninth-part of the Ascendant of the root [in groups of] 108, and for each time they cast it out they would reserve a single year and a single sign: and wherever it ran out, *there* was the sign of the terminal point, in the position where the ninth-parts would be reckoned.²⁶⁴ **7** (But as for knowing the conditions of the months and days from the method

---

²⁶² **P**: "the lords."

²⁶³ أتى على المولود. This may be by direction, not profection.

²⁶⁴ I think Abū Ma'shar is awkwardly trying to condense the instructions from IX.7, **43-48** into a single sentence. Every year, we profect from the Ascendant by one more sign, and the lord of the first ninth-part of the sign is the lord of the whole year represented by that sign (as he just stated: **1, 5**). But this sign not only stands for the year as a whole, but for its *first month*, with each successive sign representing the *remaining* months in the year: this is a normal monthly profection. But since each sign has nine ninth-parts, we can subdivide each month into smaller units ruled by the lords of the ninth-parts. Since each sign represents a month, and each month has nine parts, every year will have 108 subdivisions, corresponding to each ninth-part (12 * 9 = 108). The bit about "casting off" groups of 108 refers to using the native's current age to figure out which cycle of time lords one is in (see Ch. IX.7).

of ninth-parts according to what the people of India said, we will state that in the future.)[265]

---

[265] See IX.1, **11-16** and **32-33** (for the months), and IX.7, **43-72** (for the days).

BOOK IV: ON THE *FARDĀRS* OF THE PLANETS

And it is in seven chapters

Chapter IV.1: On the indication of the *fardār* of the Sun

1 Each of the seven planets, as well as the Head and the Tail, has a certain [number of] years, which are called *"fardārs"*: and every planet manages the native for the number of the years of its *fardār* at some time of his lifespan, and in that time it indicates something of good or evil.

2 The *fardār* of the Sun is 10 years, the *fardār* of Venus 8 years, the *fardār* of Mercury 13 years, the *fardār* of the Moon 9 years, the *fardār* of Saturn 11 years, the *fardār* of Jupiter 12 years, the *fardār* of Mars 7 years, the *fardār* of the Head 3 years, and the *fardār* of the Tail 2 years: the amount of all of that is 75 years, then it returns to the Sun.

3 Now as for nativities of the day, from when the native is first born one begins the distribution of the years of their *fardār* from the Sun, where[ever] he was in the celestial sphere: then after that are the years of Venus, then the years of Mercury, the Moon, and the years of Saturn, according to the succession of their spheres. **4** But as for nativities of the night, one begins the distribution of the years of the *fardār* with the Moon, then Saturn, Jupiter, [and] Mars, according to the first arrangement.

5 But when any of them manages the years of its *fardār*, it stands alone in [its] indication at first, for an amount of one-seventh of its years, then after that the rest of the planets partner in the indication of good or bad, also in the amount of one-seventh of it. **6** And so the beginning [of those sub-periods] will be from the planet which has the *fardār*, and the one which partners with it the first time is the planet which is below it in the celestial circle, and the one which partners with it the second time is the planet which is below that, in succession, until all of the planets partner with it in the years of its *fardār*, in this manner. **7** And each planet partners with the rest of the planets, because the years of each of them is derived from its shares in the twelve signs, and the twelve signs are their houses: so because of that, [each] will partner with [the other] in its management of those years.[1]

8 But as for the Head and the Tail, they stand alone in the management of their years after the years of the seven planets run out and 70 years have been completed for the native, and they do not partner with the planets (nor do [the planets] partner with them), because they do not have houses. **9** And the years of each of them is derived in a different way, however we will mention the reason for the derivation of these years in another book. **10** But for right now, we will discuss the indication of each one of [the time lords] when it manages the years of its own *fardār* by itself, and the partnership of the others [with it].

11 Now[2] as for one born by day, from the hour he was born up to 10 years he will be in the *fardār* of the Sun, except that he distributes the first one-seventh of it, and that is 1 year, 5 months, 4 days, and approximately 6 hours (and each of the rest of the planets distributes sevenths of it).

12 So if the root of the nativity had indicated good fortune for the native, then in his distribution[3] the Sun indicates that he will be brought up with the upbringing of kings, and his father will have much good, except that in the first and second months distress and something detestable will afflict his parents, [but] then that will recede from them and after that they will pass over to delight and joy. **13** And if the Sun distributed the years of his *fardār* to him and he is a young man, then he will have good from the nobles, and he will govern over the people of his house, and will increase in his assets and delight (and indeed [the Sun's] distribution to [the native] will be in his youth if

---

[1] Unless Abū Ma'shar has a different explanation, the planets' years are not actually derived from the houses.

[2] For **11-17**, cf. Da. 72.

[3] This is when a diurnal native is a small child (according to al-Andarzaghar, Da. 72, its **17.7**).

the native was nocturnal).⁴ **14** And if he distributed to him at a mature age, then he will rejoice in his family and children, and he will have types of good fortune which have [great] value (and of course his distribution to him at a mature age in diurnal nativities will be after he has passed through 75 years). **15** And if the Sun in the root of the nativity was in his own exaltation or in his own house, or in the bound of one of the two fortunes, and in the root of the nativity he indicated good fortune for [the native], then when he distributes for the native in his youth (or at a mature age), it indicates that he will be sound in his body, mild-tempered, delighted, and freed from detestable things and evil, and he will increase in his intellect and opinions, and power and rank, and the people will seek his advice in their affairs, and his word will be received, having an effective command among the people of his country, and he will do a great good thing for them, and good fortune will come to him as well as the good and types of benefits (of gold and silver, jewels, and the awards of kings), and he will be revered wherever he heads to, and kings will befriend him and carouse with him, and the nobles will patronize his door, and he will rule over lands and villages, and plant trees, and will marry, and a child will be born to him, or his father will get good fortune like this, or both [of his parents] will have that. **16** But if the Sun was in none of those places, it weakens his indication. **17** Now if the Sun in the root was in the Ascendant or with the lord of the Ascendant, making it fortunate for him, or [the lord of the Ascendant] was easternizing from [the Sun], then it indicates suitability and good fortune too.

18 Then Venus distributes in the *fardār* of the Sun 1 year, 5 months, 4 days, 6 hours, and something: the total of that is 2 years, 10 months, 8 days, and approximately 13 hours. **19** It indicates that in this distribution he will increase in his clothing, furnishings, and goods, and in the love of his parents towards him (and their fear for him), and marriage will be discussed for him or he will marry (if the root of his nativity had indicated that), and perhaps he will travel with one of

---

⁴ It is hard to believe that age 39 could be "youth," but the ancients had different ways of evaluating the ages of life.

those who care about him, and an ailment will afflict him in a hidden place. **20** Now[5] if the native was nocturnal, then he will leave the distresses he [may] be in, and his assets will multiply, and he will delight in his woman and children, and he will produce an admirable son, and will purchase many lands, and he will do a good thing for the people, and will travel for reasons of piety and to the houses of worship, and illnesses will afflict him in a hidden place of his body. **21** And if Saturn, Mars, or the Tail of the Dragon were with Venus, or they look at her with a harmful aspect, it takes away from what we mentioned (even though something detestable will afflict him because of it).

22 Then Mercury distributes in the *fardār* of the Sun 1 year, 5 months, 4 days, and 6 hours and something: the total of that is 4 years, 3 months, 12 days, and approximately 20 hours. **23** It indicates that in this distribution he will lose something of his property, and some of his relatives will slander him, and he will fall from a raised place (or will be on the verge of it), and an ailment will afflict him in the belly, which he will be safe from. **24** And[6] if the nativity was nocturnal, then in this distribution he will spend many assets, and will quarrel, and will encounter toil and trouble, and if he acted as a guarantor for a surety he will suffer a loss in it, and his profit will be little, and he will be distressed because of false testimony, and will fall from a house and will survive it, and the odors[7] of hemorrhoids will afflict him, and he will recover from it.

25 Then the Moon distributes in the *fardār* of the Sun 1 year, 5 months, 4 days, 6 hours, and something: the total of that is 5 years, 8 months, 17 days, and approximately 3 hours. **26** It indicates that in this distribution he will do harmful works, and benefit will come to him, and some of his property will be stolen, and often he will have to do with places of waters and moisture, or he will travel by water, and an ailment will afflict him in the head and eyes. **27** And[8] if the nativity

---

[5] For **20-21**, cf. Da. 73.
[6] For this sentence, cf. Da. 74.
[7] Or perhaps, "windiness" (ريح), that is, gas.
[8] For this sentence, cf. Da. 75.

was nocturnal, then it indicates that he will get involved in something which does not concern him, and assets having value will come to him, and he will increase in his crops and benefits, and a bribe no one knows about will come to him, and he will be devoted to business, and perhaps his business will be on the sea and assets having value[9] will be destroyed, and he will associate with the nobles, and will increase in his friends, and his pursuit of building and repairs will increase, and a powerful headache will afflict him, and perhaps that will be at the end of this distribution.

28 Then Saturn distributes in the *fardār* of the Sun 1 year, 5 months, 4 days, 6 hours, and something: the total of that is 7 years, 1 month, 21 days, and approximately 10 hours. **29** It[10] indicates that in this distribution he will be distressed, and something detestable will afflict him from the people of his house, and an ailment will afflict him in the belly, and a disaster from fire or hot water, and an ailment in his ears (all of which he will recover from) and he will go on a distant journey, and something detestable will afflict him from water. **30** And if the nativity was nocturnal, then he will have powerful distress, and he will quarrel with the people of his house, and he will suffer in his eyes, and water will fall in them,[11] and a bad ailment will afflict him in his belly, and he will recover from it as well as the ailment in his eye, and he will go on a distant journey, and be devoted to business, and perhaps his business will be on the sea and something detestable will afflict him from the water and his sailing, and something detestable will find him from fire and hot water because of the nature of the Sun and Saturn, and he will recover from all of it.

31 Then Jupiter distributes in the *fardār* of the Sun 1 year, 5 months, 4 days, six hours, and something: the total of that is 8 years, 6 months, 25 days, and approximately 17 hours. **32** It indicates that in this distribution he will increase in his property and furnishings, and in his parents' good opinion of him, and in their beneficence towards

---

[9] E: "assets he has with him."
[10] For **29-30**, cf. Da. 76.
[11] This probably means cataracts.

him, except that he will fall from a raised place. **33** And[12] if the nativity was nocturnal, he will increase in his power, rank, and condition, and will increase in nobility and power and good fortune, and will be a leader over his peers and village, and he will be devoted to building and repair, and will increase in his assets, and discover much, and will acquire assets having value [but] without labor, and he will be victorious over his enemies, except that at the end of this distribution he will fall from atop his house or from a riding animal.

34 Then Mars distributes in the *fardār* of the Sun 1 year, 5 months, 4 days, and 6 hours and something: the total of that is 10 years. **35** It[13] indicates that in this distribution he will shift from condition to condition, or he will travel, and perhaps he will marry, and something detestable will find him from a bite, sting, a fall, or beating, and blood will flow from him, and this management will be worse in the first four months. **36** And if the nativity was nocturnal, he will change from condition to condition, and from work to work, and he will travel or do much labor, and will be eager to have sex with women, and debauchery with them, and something detestable will afflict him because of them, and he will act unjustly towards people and quarrel with them, and something detestable will afflict him because of the quarrels, or cutting by iron will affect him, or the bite of a dog or some [other] animal, or he will become ill and perhaps his illness will disappear in[14] 15[15] days. **37** And the more that Mars and the Sun are worse in condition, the increase in the adversity will be greater; while if they were both in a suitable condition, it will be the contrary of that.

---

[12] For this sentence, cf. Da. 77.
[13] For **35-37**, cf. Da. 78.
[14] Or perhaps, "will burden him for."
[15] Reading with al-Andarzaghar (Da. 78) for "10" (see also IV.7, **5**).

Chapter IV.2: On the indication of the *fardār* of Venus

1 As for Venus, she manages her own *fardār* for 8 years after the *fardār* of the Sun, and she stands alone for the first one-seventh: and it is 1 year, 1 month, 20 days, 10 hours, and something. **2** It[16] indicates that in this distribution the native will delight and rejoice, and benefits will come to him, and perhaps he will marry and servants will come to him. **3** And if the nativity was nocturnal, then in this distribution his joy and delight in different things will multiply, and benefits will come to him, and he will rejoice in his woman, and will marry a foreign woman, and a happy child will be born to him, and he will purchase slave-girls and servants, and his sons and daughters will marry, and he will be devoted to building, and planting trees, and he will increase in his assets until he hoards them, and he will be victorious over his enemies, and friendship with people having nobility will happen to him, and he will be in charge of a work having importance, and luxurious garments will come to him from kings. **4** And according to what Hermes said, the most excellent [part] of this distribution is 5 months[17] and 25 days.

5 Then Mercury distributes in the *fardār* of Venus 1 year, 1 month, 20 days, and approximately 10 hours: the total of that is 2 years, 3 months, 12 days, and approximately 20 hours. **6** It indicates that in this distribution something will be stolen from him, or he will lose his assets, and if he travels or moves from place to place he will encounter fear from detestable things, and will become ill. **7** Now[18] if the nativity was nocturnal, it indicates that he will spend much of what he has collected, and his enemies will be victorious over him, and he will flee from them, and among the detestable things he will encounter what is prohibited to him (of eating and drinking), and his distresses will multiply, and an illness will happen to him in his whole body from drinking some remedy or eating some food.

---

[16] For **2-4**, cf. Da. 79.
[17] Al-Andarzaghar (Da. 79) reads "6 months."
[18] For this sentence, cf. Da. 80.

8 Then the Moon distributes in the *fardār* of Venus 1 year, 1 month, 20 days, and 10 hours and something: the total of that is 3 years, 5 months, 4 days, and approximately 7 hours. **9** It indicates that in this distribution his condition will be suitable, and he will associate with people who have power, and perhaps he will marry. **10** And[19] if the nativity was nocturnal, it indicates that he will leave the adversity he was in, and his condition will begin to be one of suitability, and people who are superior to him will frequent his door, and leaders will revere him, and he will be a leader of the people of his own house as well as his peers, and of assets he will gather what delights him, and if he does not have a woman, he will marry.

11 Then Saturn distributes in the *fardār* of Venus 1 year, 1 month, 20 days, and 10 hours and something: the total of that is 4 years, 6 months, 25 days, and approximately 17 hours. **12** It indicates that in this distribution he will have much labor, and will encounter powerful adversity, and due to some women adversity will pass through his hands, and he will be harmed because of them. **13** And[20] if the nativity was nocturnal, then his concerns will multiply as well as his labor, and he will be disturbed in his way of life, and his benefit will be scarce in the works which he does, and he will be in need of his companions and their charity towards him, and he will meet with them for eating and drinking, and he will be distressed by them, and his woman will die or he will become ill with a harsh illness, or quarreling and disagreement will occur between him and his woman, and perhaps he will treat her badly, and perhaps the woman will miscarry her child if she was pregnant, and he will marry an adulterous woman or a divorcée or a young girl, and he will treat his own children badly, as well as the children of others.

---

[19] For this sentence, cf. Da. 81.
[20] For this sentence, cf. Da. 82.

	Diurnal Births			Nocturnal Births	
	Period	Age		Period	Age
☉	10 years	0 – 10	☽	9 years	0 – 9
☉ ☉	1.428	0.000 – 1.428	☽ ☽	1.286	0.000 – 1.286
☉ ♀	1.428	1.428 – 2.856	☽ ♄	1.286	1.286 – 2.572
☉ ☿	1.428	2.856 – 4.284	☽ ♃	1.286	2.572 – 3.858
☉ ☽	1.428	4.284 – 5.712	☽ ♂	1.286	3.858 – 5.144
☉ ♄	1.428	5.712 – 7.140	☽ ☉	1.286	5.144 – 6.430
☉ ♃	1.428	7.140 – 8.568	☽ ♀	1.286	6.430 – 7.716
☉ ♂	1.428	8.568 – 10.00	☽ ☿	1.286	7.716 – 9.000
♀	8 years	10 – 18	♄	11 years	9 – 20
♀ ♀	1.143	10.000 – 11.143	♄ ♄	1.571	9.000 – 10.571
♀ ☿	1.143	11.143 – 12.286	♄ ♃	1.571	10.571 – 12.142
♀ ☽	1.143	12.286 – 13.429	♄ ♂	1.571	12.142 – 13.713
♀ ♄	1.143	13.429 – 14.572	♄ ☉	1.571	13.713 – 15.284
♀ ♃	1.143	14.572 – 15.715	♄ ♀	1.571	15.284 – 16.855
♀ ♂	1.143	15.715 – 16.858	♄ ☿	1.571	16.855 – 18.426
♀ ☉	1.143	16.858 – 18.000	♄ ☽	1.571	18.426 – 20.000
☿	13 years	18 – 31	♃	12 years	20 – 32
☿ ☿	1.857	18.000 – 19.857	♃ ♃	1.714	20.000 – 21.714
☿ ☽	1.857	19.857 – 21.714	♃ ♂	1.714	21.714 – 23.428
☿ ♄	1.857	21.714 – 23.571	♃ ☉	1.714	23.428 – 25.142
☿ ♃	1.857	23.571 – 25.428	♃ ♀	1.714	25.142 – 26.856
☿ ♂	1.857	25.428 – 27.285	♃ ☿	1.714	26.856 – 28.570
☿ ☉	1.857	27.285 – 29.142	♃ ☽	1.714	28.570 – 30.284
☿ ♀	1.857	29.142 – 31.000	♃ ♄	1.714	30.284 – 32.000
☽	9 years	31 – 40	♂	7 years	32 – 39
☽ ☽	1.286	31.000 – 32.286	♂ ♂	1	32.000 – 33.000
☽ ♄	1.286	32.286 – 33.572	♂ ☉	1	33.000 – 34.000
☽ ♃	1.286	33.572 – 34.858	♂ ♀	1	34.000 – 35.000
☽ ♂	1.286	34.858 – 36.144	♂ ☿	1	35.000 – 36.000
☽ ☉	1.286	36.144 – 37.430	♂ ☽	1	36.000 – 37.000
☽ ♀	1.286	37.430 – 38.716	♂ ♄	1	37.000 – 38.000
☽ ☿	1.286	38.716 – 40.000	♂ ♃	1	38.000 – 39.000

BOOK IV: FARDĀRS

	Diurnal Births			Nocturnal Births	
	Period	Age		Period	Age
♄	11 years	40 – 51	☉	10 years	39 – 49
♄ ♄	1.571	40.000 – 41.571	☉ ☉	1.428	39.000 – 40.428
♄ ♃	1.571	41.571 – 43.142	☉ ♀	1.428	40.428 – 41.856
♄ ♂	1.571	43.142 – 44.713	☉ ☿	1.428	41.856 – 43.284
♄ ☉	1.571	44.713 – 46.284	☉ ☽	1.428	43.284 – 44.712
♄ ♀	1.571	46.284 – 47.855	☉ ♄	1.428	44.712 – 46.140
♄ ☿	1.571	47.855 – 49.426	☉ ♃	1.428	46.140 – 47.568
♄ ☽	1.571	49.426 – 51.000	☉ ♂	1.428	47.568 – 49.000
♃	12 years	51 – 63	♀	8 years	49 – 57
♃ ♃	1.714	51.000 – 52.714	♀ ♀	1.143	49.000 – 50.143
♃ ♂	1.714	52.714 – 54.428	♀ ☿	1.143	50.143 – 51.286
♃ ☉	1.714	54.428 – 56.142	♀ ☽	1.143	51.286 – 52.429
♃ ♀	1.714	56.142 – 57.856	♀ ♄	1.143	52.429 – 53.572
♃ ☿	1.714	57.856 – 59.570	♀ ♃	1.143	53.572 – 54.715
♃ ☽	1.714	59.570 – 61.284	♀ ♂	1.143	54.715 – 55.858
♃ ♄	1.714	61.284 – 63.000	♀ ☉	1.143	55.858 – 57.000
♂	7 years	63 – 70	☿	13 years	57 – 70
♂ ♂	1	63.000 – 64.000	☿ ☿	1.857	57.000 – 58.857
♂ ☉	1	64.000 – 65.000	☿ ☽	1.857	58.857 – 60.714
♂ ♀	1	65.000 – 66.000	☿ ♄	1.857	60.714 – 62.571
♂ ☿	1	66.000 – 67.000	☿ ♃	1.857	62.571 – 64.428
♂ ☽	1	67.000 – 68.000	☿ ♂	1.857	64.428 – 66.285
♂ ♄	1	68.000 – 69.000	☿ ☉	1.857	66.285 – 68.142
♂ ♃	1	69.000 – 70.000	☿ ♀	1.857	68.142 – 70.000
☊	3 years	70 – 73	☊	3 years	70 – 73
☋	2 years	73 – 75	☋	2 years	73 – 75

14 Then Jupiter distributes in the *fardār* of Venus 1 year, 1 month, 20 days, and approximately 10 hours: the total of that is 5 years, 8 months, 17 days, and approximately 3 hours. **15** It[21] indicates that in this distribution his condition will be fine, and his father will have types of good fortune, and he[22] will increase in his assets. **16** And if the nativity was nocturnal, he will leave the distresses he was in, and good will be said about him, and his voice will go out far and wide for that reason, and he will increase in his real estate, assets, and dwellings, and from it he will hoard away something having value, and if the native was of those whose root of the nativity indicated good fortune, then he will reach the level of kings, and he will be put at the head of villages and lands. **17** And if Venus was with the Head of the Dragon or with Jupiter, in one of the stakes appropriate to her,[23] then he will rule over groups of people on land and sea.

18 Then Mars distributes in the *fardār* of Venus 1 year, 1 month, 20 days, and 10 hours and something: the total of that is 6 years, 10 months, 8 days, and approximately 14 hours. **19** It indicates that in this distribution he will do much labor, and will treat his siblings badly, and perhaps he will marry and connect with a man having power. **20** And[24] if the nativity was nocturnal, it indicates that he will have much labor, and will be unjust to someone else, and his siblings will have something detestable from him, and he will delight in women, and will connect with some of those having importance because of [women], or he will connect with a woman having power, or will marry, and he will be harmed by some of them, and he will have power in his own country.

21 Then the Sun distributes in the *fardār* of Venus 1 year, 1 month, 20 days, and approximately 10 hours: the total of that is 8 years. **22** It[25] indicates that in this distribution he will become have an illness in

---

[21] For **15-17**, cf. Da. 83.
[22] I take this to mean the native; it is impossible to tell in al-Andarzaghar.
[23] Or perhaps, "them." Meaning unclear: al-Andarzaghar has Venus with the Head, or Jupiter in the Ascendant (Da. 83).
[24] For this sentence, cf. Da. 84.
[25] For **22-25**, cf. Da. 85.

which there is difficulty, but he will escape it, and he will connect with the nobles, and will increase in his rank, assets, strength, and garments, and perhaps he will marry an educated woman. **23** And if the nativity was nocturnal, he will become ill with a harsh illness except that he will recover from it, and he will increase in his power and slaves and slave-girls, and he will get assets which have value, and he will dress as though in the garments of kings, and he will sit in their councils, and will be victorious over his enemies, and will marry an educated woman or one who is a writer. **24** And if Venus or the Sun was the lord of the year during this distribution, and is in a suitable condition, it is mightier for his nobility and power, and he will be victorious, and the gifts of the people to him will multiply. **25** And if at the time of the distribution Venus is in the stakes, in a suitable condition, then the benefits will multiply, and he will carouse with kings and be alone with them in their secrets.

Chapter IV.3: On the indication of the *fardār* of Mercury

1 As for Mercury, the years of his *fardār* are 13 years after the *fardār* of Venus, and he stands alone in the distribution in the first one-seventh: and it is 1 year, 10 months, 8 days, and approximately 14 hours. **2** It[26] indicates that in the first half of this distribution the native will have good, and in the last half he will have evil and something detestable, and he will travel from land to land, and he will certainly do work, except that harm will enter upon him from it,[27] and generally whatever he talks about will come to ruin, and one of his retinue or riding animals will die, and he will become will with a powerful illness, and the benefit to him by any remedy will be slight. **3** Now if Saturn

---

[26] For **2-3**, cf. Da. 86.
[27] Reading with **P**. **B** and **E** each say that it will reduce the work he does, "except that" harm will enter upon him. This would then be doubly bad, but does not make much sense of the "except," nor that Mercury has a double and ambiguous nature. Therefore, I follow **P**.

was in a bad condition and looked at him with a corrupting, unfortunate aspect, death will be feared for him; and if Mercury was of a suitable condition, it will subtract from all of the adversity we mentioned.

4 Then the Moon distributes in the *fardār* of Mercury 1 year, 10 months, 8 days, and approximately 14 hours: the total of that is 3 years, 8 months, 17 days, and 3 hours approximately. **5** It[28] indicates that in this distribution he will disturbed in his way of life, and not be prepared with food or drink, and his soul will suffer in detestable things, and if he bought a slave he will run away, and if he was devoted to business, selling, and buying, he will suffer loss in it, and if he built a building he will not complete it, and if he had a woman she will die or he will divorce her, or a powerful disagreement will occur between him and her, and if he did not have a woman he will seek marriage but will not marry, and he will become ill with a powerful illness, and he will fall from an elevated place, or a large animal will gore him, or a disaster will afflict him from which he will be on the verge of death.

6 Then Saturn distributes in the *fardār* of Mercury 1 year, 10 months, 8 days, and approximately 14 hours,: the total of that is 5 years, 6 months, 25 days, and approximately 17 hours. **7** It[29] indicates that in this distribution he will increase in his friends and assets, and he will be stingy, and assets having value will be stolen from him (and it will harm him), and his woman will become ill with a powerful illness or will die, and he will be sad about her, and he will travel and encounter distress[30] and something detestable on his journey.

8 Then Jupiter distributes in the *fardār* of Mercury 1 year, 10 months, 8 days, and approximately 14 hours: the total of that is 7 years, 5 months, 4 days, and approximately 7 hours. **9** It[31] indicates that in this distribution he will earn assets in various ways, and he will collect gold and silver, and he will spend much, and will contend with people who have power (and they will destroy him), and low people

---

[28] For this sentence, cf. Da. 5.
[29] For this sentence, cf. Da. 88.
[30] غمًّا. **P** reads, "trouble" or "labor" (عناء).
[31] For this sentence, cf. Da. 89.

will quarrel with him but then he will be free of them, then he will be put in charge of a work having importance, and he will build a magnificent building he will delight in, and he will be devoted to lying,[32] and will be close to liars and the companions of corruption.

10 Then Mars distributes in the *fardār* of Mercury 1 year, 10 months, 8 days, and approximately 14 hours: the total of that is 9 years, 3 months, 12 days, and 20 hours approximately. **11** It[33] indicates that in this distribution he will fight or quarrel with one who is lower than him in power, or one whom he does not know, and he will flee[34] to people who do have power, and he will fall into tribulation after tribulation but will be rescued from it, and he will be victorious over his enemy, and will go on a journey he will be distressed about, and if he was devoted to business he will suffer loss in it, and if he formed a partnership with a man, the man will double-cross him in it, and something detestable will afflict him from confinement, and he will be distressed because of fire and heat, and he will fall from an elevated place (or will be on the brink of that) and he will become ill with a powerful illness from which his mixture [of humors] and his brain will be corrupted (except that he will recover), and he if married, his woman will die in that year[35] (or she will be on the verge of death), and if his parents were alive his mother will die or his father will be confined, or powerful adversity will afflict them both.

12 Then the Sun distributes in the *fardār* of Mercury 1 year, 10 months, 8 days, and approximately 14 hours: the total of that is 11 years, 1 months, 21 days, and approximately 10 hours. **13** It[36] indicates that in this distribution he will increase in joy and delight, and will increase in his power day-by-day, and his retinue will increase, and a secretary and household manager will come to him, and assets will

---

[32] الكذب. P reads, "books" (الكتب).
[33] For this sentence, cf. Da. 90.
[34] P: "go."
[35] Reading and spelling with the sense of the Latin, for "will die because of it": the "it" has no proper reference in the sentence.
[36] For this sentence, cf. Da. 91.

pass to him from kings and the nobles, and he will also acquire benefits having value from others besides them, and the people of his house (and generally those he associates with) will have the good from him, and perhaps a brother older than him will die, and he will marry the woman of his brother, or he will fornicate with her, or will fornicate with his father's woman.

14 Then Venus distributes in the *fardār* of Mercury 1 year, 10 months, 8 days, and approximately 14 hours approximately: the total of that is 13 years. **15** It[37] indicates that in this distribution he will be hostile to men, and befriend women, and will desire them and delight in them, and he will be adorned with their adornments (in clothing and perfume) and will follow the harlots among them, and in their fornicating his woman will become pregnant but will miscarry her child, and if she did not get pregnant and she [already] had a child, her child will die, or one who is with her in the child's home will die.

Chapter IV.4: On the indication of the *fardār* of the Moon

1 As for the Moon, she manages the year of her *fardār* for 9 years after the years of Mercury, and she stands alone in the distribution for the first one-seventh: and it is 1 year, 3 months, 12 days, and approximately 21 hours. **2** It[38] indicates [for a diurnal nativity] that in this distribution he will be of a diverse condition in joy and distress, wealth and poverty, and he will quarrel harshly with his woman and others besides her, and he will travel and be trusted, and will profit, then he will suddenly come to rank and authority from which he will earn money having [great] value, then he will fall from that rank, but will not remain [low] except for a little while until he returns to it;[39] and at the end of this distribution fear will afflict him from iron (if not from the sword, then something else), and he will be confined. **3** Now if the

---

[37] For this sentence, cf. Da. 92.
[38] For this sentence, cf. Da. 93.
[39] This is meant to parallel the Moon's phase: increase, then decrease, then increase again.

nativity was nocturnal, and the Moon was in a bad condition, then illnesses and detestable things will afflict him, and his parents will hate him; but if the Moon was in a suitable condition, then in that distribution he will be healthy in his body, of a good character, his parents loving him, revering him, and treating him well.

[Diurnal versus nocturnal interpretations]

4 And[40] in truth, the condition of nativities of the day differs from nativities of the night in everything we have mentioned, because for those who are born by night, up to the completion of 9 years they are in the *fardār* of the Moon (just as we stated before this), and by her nature the Moon manages the first one-seventh from the beginning of this distribution, so that her indication for their condition in that distribution in that time is different from her indication for their conditions at another time: because that first condition [mentioned above][41] is suitable [only] for those people who were born by day, since the beginning of the distribution of [their] *fardār* is from the Sun, and in that time of their lifespan they will have attained the many years in which it is possible for them to have those conditions. **5** But if the nativity was nocturnal and begins the distribution of the *fardār* from the Moon, its condition will be contrary to that due to [the native's] youth and being too weak for management and pursuing works, and for this reason in the indication of the years of the *fardār* of the Sun and Venus for one born by night, we did not mention a condition *contrary* to the condition which we said belongs to those born by day. **6** And we also intend to treat the Moon and Saturn like that, stating (for each one of them) in nativities of the day an indication for something contrary to what we state about the indication for nativities of the night: because nocturnal nativities begin the distribution of the years of their *fardārs* from the Moon, and in that time the native is

---

[40] This paragraph is partly missing in **B** and **P**, and so might be missing some key transitional words.

[41] See **2** above: quarreling with a wife, having authority and wealth.

small, until he passes by all of the years of the *fardār* of Saturn. **7** So, you ought to look at the conditions which a man resembles in the period of his lifespan he is in (of youth and adulthood), so that the judgment for him will be according to that.

8 Now as for the rest of the planets (and they are Mercury, Jupiter, and Mars), for each one of them we mention the indication for a single condition, and it is done likewise for the Head and Tail: because whether the nativities are diurnal or nocturnal, one begins the distribution of the years of the *fardār* from one of the luminaries—so when one reaches the years of the *fardār* of one of these three planets, or the Head or Tail, one is in a condition to be able to have these things. **9** And we have not found this distinction (which we mentioned concerning the indication of these planets in nocturnal and diurnal nativities) in the book of any of the ancients, of the people of his art, but regarding the *fardārs* of the planets we have indeed found all of them speaking about the conditions which belong to a man when he has completed youth [and] is strong [and] discerning in the manner we have described it.[42] **10** Of course one does find special people for whom [such things] are prepared in their youth and before attaining [adulthood], of the beloved or detested conditions (such as confinement, beating, or authority or benefits from money), or shifting [their] condition from one thing to another just as it is prepared for a man who has attained it. **11** And when one does find something of that situation for some people in that time of their lifespan, then the judgment in that condition of theirs will be according to what we have revealed in the *fardārs* as well as other things of [their] situations, of the duration of that condition or shifting from it to something else.[43]

∽ ∾ ∾

12 Then Saturn distributes in the *fardār* of the Moon 1 year, 3 months, 12 days, and approximately 21 hours: the total of that is 2

---

[42] This is true of al-Andarzaghar, so this might be a polite criticism of him.

[43] Or, as he points out in I.8, **5-8**, perhaps these things will be done by authority figures who are taking care of the child.

years, 6 months, 25 days, and approximately 17 hours. **13** It[44] indicates that in this distribution he will quarrel with kings or their peers, and in his speech he will be accused of lying and falsehoods, and he will encounter something detestable from his slaves or they will flee from him, and it will ruin his cattle and riding animals, and he will squander [enough] of his money that he will be harmed and incur debts, and he will become ill with a powerful illness, and perhaps he will burned by fire or [there will be] a disaster from fire and heat, or he will be cut by iron three times (but then he will be safe), and perhaps his woman will miscarry (if she was pregnant). **14** And if the nativity was nocturnal, then an ailment will afflict him from heat but he will recover, and a disaster from fire or hot water will afflict him, and he will be treated with iron, and he will move from place to place, or he will travel,[45] and in his travels he will encounter harm, and some of those serving him will treat him badly, and some of his property will be stolen from him.

15 Then Jupiter distributes in the *fardār* of the Moon 1 year, 3 months, 12 days, 21 hours and something: the total of that is 3 years, 10 months, 8 days, and approximately 14 hours. **16** It[46] indicates that in this distribution he will be in charge of a great[47] work in which his voice will echo [far and wide], and from that work he will acquire assets having value, and he will be victorious over his enemies, and he will be well commended, and benefits will come to him from a faraway land and from villages [both] flat and mountainous, and he will plant crops and trees, and will buy slaves and servant-girls, and his delight will increase, and if he had debt he will settle it. **17** Now if the nativity was nocturnal, then he will increase in the love of his parents towards

---

[44] For this sentence, cf. Da. 94.
[45] The text includes a puzzling ﭑﭒ, which suggests that perhaps some other phrase was also included.
[46] For this sentence, cf. Da. 95.
[47] **P**: "suitable, great work."

him, and he will increase in what is saved for him (of garments and other things), and the service of a man will be renewed for him.[48]

18 Then Mars distributes in the *fardār* of the Moon 1 year, 3 months, 12 days, and approximately 21 hours: the total of that is 5 years, 1 month, 21 days, and approximately 10 hours. **19** It[49] indicates that in this distribution he will be distressed much, and will encounter harsh adversity, and some of his assets will be destroyed, and he will pay a heavy fine[50] after being tormented because of it, and if he traveled something detestable will afflict him in his assets, and fear will enter upon him from the bite of a snake or from a ship, or from hot[51] water, or from fire (then he will be safe), and he will become ill with a harsh illness, and will come to the brink of death, and he will complain about his eyesight or a powerful calamity will afflict him in the eye, and he will encounter a pain in his genitals. **20** And if Mars had testimony in the revolution of that year, it will be greater[52] for the adversity, except that his condition will improve upon [the native's] leaving this distribution. **21** And if the nativity was nocturnal, then powerful [and] varied ailments will afflict him, and some of that will be in the eye, and some of it in the belly and the lower parts, and something will sting him, or a calamity will afflict him from fire or hot water, or from hot things, and some of his property will be stolen from him, and some of those serving him will treat him badly.

22 Then the Sun distributes in the *fardār* of the Moon 1 year, 3 months, 12 days, and approximately 21 hours: the total of that is 6 years, 5 months, 4 days, and approximately 7 hours. **23** It[53] indicates that in this distribution he will treat people well, and give out money among foreign people or in a distant land, and he will delight in every

---

[48] Reading as يتجدّد. E reads يتحدّد, "will be determined." Nevertheless this is ambiguous to me. Will someone serve him, or will he serve someone else? I have a feeling it is the former.
[49] For **19-20**, cf. Da. 96.
[50] Or, "suffer a heavy loss" (يغرم غرمًا ثقيلًا).
[51] E and P omit.
[52] Lit., "more numerous."
[53] For this sentence, cf. Da. 97.

work he does, and will be a leader over people, and will be in charge of a work, and he or his woman will become ill, and perhaps that illness will be for 30 days but then he will recover, and his condition with her will be good in the first month of this distribution, except that she will miscarry her child if she was pregnant, then she will become pregnant after that. **24** And if the nativity was nocturnal he will become ill, and will shift from condition to condition, or will travel, and his parents will delight in him, and he will increase in his culture.

25 Then Venus distributes in the *fardār* of the Moon 1 year, 3 months, 12 days, 21 hours, and something; the total of that is 7 years, 8 months, 17 days, and approximately 3 hours. **26** It[54] indicates that in this distribution he will be devoted to melodies and songs, and entertainment, and his sexual intercourse with women will multiply, and the rabble will agree with him and give him praise, and at the beginning of this distribution [something] will happen to him due to the condition of his slaves which he will delight in, and he will increase in his rank, and find the good. **27** And if the nativity was nocturnal then someone serving him will loyal towards him, and he will do a work in which he will hope for glory.

28 Then Mercury distributes in the *fardār* of the Moon 1 year, 3 months, 12 days, and approximately 21 hours: the total of that is 9 years. **29** It[55] indicates that in this distribution he will be promoted and removed many times (and perhaps his appointment to be in charge of a work, and his removal from it, will be three times), and he will get involved in an intense quarrel, and he will be lied about, and he will be devoted to stratagems and hidden works, and lying and falsehood with his woman and with someone else as well, and assets having value will be squandered by him, and he will be harmed, and fear will afflict him from water and fire, and perhaps that will be at the beginning of that distribution, for 17 days but then he will be safe, and a bad ailment will afflict his child from the corruption of black bile and [his] mixture [of humors]. **30** And if the nativity was nocturnal, some-

---

[54] For this sentence, cf. Da. 98.
[55] For this sentence, cf. Da. 99.

thing detestable as well as beating will reach him, and he will be lied about, and he will be devoted to stratagems, and a calamity will afflict him from water or fire, and something of his assets will be stolen from him.

Chapter IV.5: On the indication of the *fardār* of Saturn

1 And as for Saturn, the management of his *fardār* is 11 years after the *fardār* of the Moon, and he stands alone in the distribution for the first one-seventh, and it is 1 year, 6 months, 25 days, and 17 hours and something. **2** It[56] indicates that in this distribution he will do works because of which he will be accused of stupidity and folly, and he will quarrel about useless things, and he will be publicly disgraced because of women and his female children, or he will be extremely distressed because of them, and his spending will be more than his revenue, and his assets will be corrupted, and assets will come to him from inheritance or because of a loan, and old matters, and he will have a terrible calamity in his status, and he will become ill with a powerful illness, and from it he will come to the brink of death—and if [Saturn] was made unfortunate by Mars, his illness will be harsher, and that will be from heat or fire or he will be touched by iron, and his benefit from the treatment will be little. **3** Now if the nativity was nocturnal then something detestable will find him, and his distresses will increase due to various things, and one of his relatives will die, and assets will come to him from inheritance, and some of his assets will be stolen, and he will become ill with a powerful illness, and he will do works which are unhealthy for him, and stupidity and thoughtlessness and vanity will get the best of him.

4 Then Jupiter distributes in the *fardār* of Saturn 1 year, 6 months, 25 days, and 17 hours and something: the total of that is 3 years, 1 month, 21 days,[57] and approximately 10 hours. **5** It[58] indicates that in

---

[56] For **2-3**, cf. Da. 100.
[57] Reading the more accurate 21, for 20.
[58] For this sentence, cf. Da. 101.

this distribution he will bestow honor upon kings and their peers, and will gain assets from them and others, and he will move from honor to honor, and will purchase female servants, and his joy and delight will multiply, and he will become ill, and will travel, and perhaps his illness and travel will be at the end of this distribution. **6** But if the nativity was nocturnal, then he will encounter situations he will benefit from, and he will connect with people who benefit him, and he will become ill, and will shift from condition to condition, and perhaps he will increase in his male and female servants, and will marry.

7 Then Mars distributes in the *fardār* of Saturn 1 year, 6 months, 25 days, and 17 hours and something: the total of that is 4 years, 8 months, 17 days, and approximately 3 hours. **8** It[59] indicates that in this distribution he will have a bad condition, and something detestable will find him in it, and perhaps he will fall from on top of the house or from a riding animal, or a calamity will afflict him, or he will quarrel harshly with his woman and others besides her, and the people will be hostile to him, and will lie about him, and his family will become ill with a harsh illness, or his child will die. **9** And if the nativity was nocturnal, different detestable things will afflict him, as well as lawsuits, and perhaps he will fall from a raised place and [also] become ill.

10 Then the Sun distributes in the *fardār* of Saturn 1 year, 6 months, 25 days, and 17 hours and something: the total of that is 6 years, 3 months, 12 days, and approximately 20 hours. **11** It[60] indicates that in this distribution he will increase in his power, and will be in charge of administering justice among the people and passing judgment upon them, and his joy in his family, homeland, and children will multiply, and he will travel and have a terrible headache, and complain about his eyesight, and he will quarrel with someone older than him, and be victorious over him. **12** And if the nativity was nocturnal then many of these conditions will be prepared for him in a manner which suits his age.

---

[59] For this sentence, cf. Da. 102.
[60] For this sentence, cf. Da. 103.

13 Then Venus distributes in the *fardār* of Saturn 1 year, 6 months, 25 days, and 17 hours and something: the total of that is 7 years, 10 months, 8 days, and approximately 14 hours. **14** It[61] indicates that in this distribution he will be lied about and false testimony will be made about him, and he will be involved in a powerful lawsuit,[62] but then he will be safe from it, and he will delight in the death of his enemies and in a powerful calamity which will afflict them, and an ailment will afflict him in his belly or in a hidden, secret place but he will recover from it, and his woman will die or a bad calamity will befall her, and perhaps he will not have a child born to him in this distribution, and the child [he does have] will become ill. **15** Now if the nativity was nocturnal, in this distribution he will be afflicted by whatever of these things is allowed to happen to him according to his age.

16 Then Mercury distributes in the *fardār* of Saturn 1 year, 6 months, 25 days, and 17 hours and something: the total of that is 9 years, 5 months, 4 days, and approximately 7 hours. **17** It[63] indicates that in this distribution he will labor much or travel on a journey in which something detestable will find him, and his woman will become ill, and he will be distressed because of some women or [some] man dying,[64] and he will increase in his assets as well as lose assets, and he will delight in brothers, and be devoted to the conditions of [his] children, entourage, slaves, riding animals, books, competitors, management, and associates in various things, of the good and the bad.[65]

18 Then the Moon distributes in the *fardār* of Saturn 1 year, 6 months, 25 days, and 17 hours approximately: the total of that is 11 years. **19** It[66] indicates that in this distribution he will be distressed

---

[61] For this sentence, cf. Da. 104.
[62] Or, "quarrel."
[63] This sentence should appear in Da., but Burnett and al-Hamdi do not list it.
[64] Or perhaps, "by the death of a man."
[65] Here and in the next paragraph Abū Ma'shar omits his statement about nocturnal nativities and age-appropriate events (See **6, 9, 12**), perhaps because by this time a nocturnal native will be 18, and able to do adult things.
[66] For this sentence, cf. Da. 105.

and both he and his male children will be ill, or one of his children will die, and he will be of a middling condition in it (in terms of good and evil, and benefit and spending), and he will go on a distant journey on which he will earn money, and perhaps this distribution will generally take place abroad, and at its end or upon his leaving it he will collect assets and marry another woman.

Chapter IV.6: On the indication of the *fardār* of Jupiter

1 And as for Jupiter, he manages his *fardār* for 12 years after the *fardār* of Saturn, and in the distribution he stands alone in the management of the first one-seventh, and it is 1 year, 8 months, 17 days, and 3 hours and something. **2** It[67] indicates that in this distribution he will shift from a bad condition to an excellent condition, and from every detestable thing to every desirable one, and he will increase in good fortune and assets, and he will be mentioned among kings, and he will be well commended among them, and he will be in charge of works which have importance; and if Jupiter in the root was in his own bound or the bound of Venus, or in one of the signs of his triplicity (and they are Aries, Leo, and Sagittarius), then he will be superior in the indication of good fortune and the good. **3** And if the nativity was of the highest social class in good fortune, then he will rule cities and climes, and his slaves and servant-girls will be multiplied, as well as his retinue, and he will marry a noble woman, and kings will present him with [various] types of gifts, assets,[68] and riding animals, and assets will come to him from crops and other things, or he will collect treasures, and his charity towards the people will multiply as well as his prayers for them, and he will build a magnificent building. **4** And if Jupiter was in his exaltation, then it will be greater for his good fortune.

---

[67] For **2-4**, cf. Da. 106.
[68] **P** adds, "and garments."

5 Then Mars distributes in the *fardār* of Jupiter 1 year, 8 months, 17 days, and 3 hours and something: the total of that is 3 years, 5 months, 4 days, and approximately 7 hours. **6** It[69] indicates that in this distribution he will be distressed, and will do work for the Sultan which has [something] awe-inspiring in it (except that because of that work he will encounter powerful adversity), and fear will afflict him from water,[70] and he will go on a distant journey, and his desire for women will multiply, and he will fornicate with them, and a boy will be born to him.

7 Then the Sun distributes in the *fardār* of Jupiter 1 year, 8 months, 17 days, and 3 hours and something: the total of that is 5 years, 1 month, 21 days, and approximately 10 hours. **8** It[71] indicates that in this distribution he will increase in his reason, and he will dress in the attire of kings, and will increase in assets and the good, and good fortune, and he will discover treasure or earn assets without labor, and he will be respected among the [lower] people, and rule over the people of his own social class, and kings and others will put him in charge of managing assets and their protection, and a fortunate boy will be born to him.

9 Then Venus distributes in the *fardār* of Jupiter 1 year, 8 months, 17 days, and 3 hours and something: the total of that is 6 years, 10 months, 8 days, and approximately 14 hours. **10** It[72] indicates that in this distribution he will associate with kings, and will befriend them, and will be dressed in their attire, and will have authority and good fortune, and be entrusted with assets (or will find much), or assets will pass to him without labor, and his enemies will die, and he will travel. **11** And if one of the infortunes makes one of the fortunes unfortunate, it takes away from everything we mentioned, and does the contrary of that.

12 Then Mercury distributes in the *fardār* of Jupiter 1 year, 8 months, 17 days, and 3 hours and something: the total of that is 8

---

[69] For this sentence, cf. Da. 107.
[70] Reading with **E** and **P** (and al-Andarzaghar, Da. 107), for "fire."
[71] For this sentence, cf. Da. 108.
[72] For **10-11**, cf. Da. 109.

years, 6 months, 25 days, and approximately 17 hours. **13** It[73] indicates that in this distribution he will be of good character, and will generally be without employment in beneficial works, and his enemies will multiply and his friends be hostile to him, and ugly things will be said about him, and he will marry a woman, and a dog or predatory animal or another animal will bite him, and he will destroy his home, and will corrupt some of his assets, and will fall from a raised place and from on top of his house;[74] and the worst it would be for [his] condition is in the middle of this distribution.

14 Then the Moon distributes in the *fardār* of Jupiter 1 year, 8 months, 17 days, and 3 hours and something: the total of that is 10 years, 3 months, 12 days, and approximately 21 hours. **15** It[75] indicates that in this distribution he will increase in his rank, and be a leader or be put in charge of works for the Sultan, and will have good from where he had not considered it, and his faith and hope in things will multiply, and he will rejoice at one time and be distressed at another, and a brother older than him will die, and assets will be taken from him, and he will travel, and on the road the fear of robbers will come over him; and the most that these things will be, is up to when he has passed one year from the beginning of this distribution—then after that he will pass to the good and delight.

16 Then Saturn distributes in the *fardār* of Jupiter 1 year, 8 months, 17 days, and 3 hours and something: the total of that is 12 years. **17** It[76] indicates that in this distribution his beneficence will increase, and his brothers and close companions will cut off relations with him, and his friends will be hostile to him and lie about him, and perhaps some of them will travel, and fear of kings[77] will afflict the native, and something detestable from children will afflict him, and losses in his assets

---

[73] For this sentence, cf. Da. 110.
[74] Adding the top of the house with **E** and **P**, as it is also found in al-Andarzaghar (Da. 110).
[75] For this sentence, cf. Da. 111.
[76] For **17-18**, cf. Da. 112.
[77] Reading with **E** and **P** (and with al-Andarzaghar) for "the Sultan."

will happen to him. **18** And if he loaned money[78] to a man it will not be returned to him, and if it is returned it would be with difficulty, and the people of his house will be afflicted by whatever distresses there are,[79] for an amount of 30 days.

Chapter IV.7: On the indication of the *fardār* of Mars

1 And as for Mars, he manages the years of his *fardār* for 7 years after the *fardār* of Jupiter, and he stands alone in the first one-seventh: and it is one year. **2** It[80] indicates that in this distribution he will be unjust, an oppressor, and will fall into tribulation and a long lawsuit, and his enemies will be stirred up against him, and they will undermine his status among those having power as well as the authorities, and something detestable will enter upon him from his parents but then he will be safe after that, and fear or a powerful catastrophe will afflict him from a predatory animal, fire, iron, or hot water, or from crucifixion or the crucified, and if in that year he planted something, misfortune will afflict it from fire or flooding, and he will go on a distant journey, and a headache will afflict him, or an ailment in his eyes, and he will complain about his belly for the amount of 30 days, and he will be devoted to doctors. **3** And if Mars was with Jupiter or Jupiter[81] was in a bound of Mars or in a bound of Venus, then he will encounter something detestable from enemies but then be safe from them.

4 Then the Sun distributes in the *fardār* of Mars for 1 year: the total of that is two years. **5** It[82] indicates that in this distribution his brothers will be hostile to him and something detestable will find him from his

---

[78] **P**: "something."
[79] But this could perhaps be read as them suffering distress due to the loss or trouble involved in the loaned money.
[80] For **2-3**, cf. Da. 113.
[81] Reading with **E** for "he." Hugo has Mars with Jupiter, with both of them in a bound of Mars or Venus (*BA* IV.23, **2**). The al-Andarzaghar passage has only Mars in the bound of Venus.
[82] For this sentence, cf. Da. 114.

partner,[83] or he will be confined because of his partner, and perhaps that will be for 15 days, and an illness will afflict him in a hidden, concealed place, and he will fall from atop of his house, and a king (or someone resembling a king) will kill[84] him, and his woman will die, and it will corrupt the reason[85] of one of his children, or [the child] will die.

6 Then Venus distributes in the *fardār* of Mars for 1 year: the total of that is 3 years. **7** It[86] indicates that in this distribution he will occupy himself with singing and amusement,[87] and he will befriend harlots, and will quarrel with his woman, and will associate with robbers and gain the good from them.

8 Then Mercury distributes in the *fardār* of Mars for 1 year: the total of that is 4 years. **9** It[88] indicates that in this distribution he will encounter something detestable and emigrate from his home, and will be distressed because of theft and robbing, and loss will afflict him in his assets, and he will be accused of lying, and ugly things will be said about him, and his friends will be hostile to him, and perhaps tribulation will afflict him, in which he will be ruined.

10 Then the Moon distributes in the *fardār* of Mars for 1 year: the total of that is 5 years. **11** It[89] indicates that in this distribution he will be confined in prison, and will encounter something detestable, but then he will escape from it, and loss will afflict him in every work he does,[90] and he will spend on building and repairs, and if he was wealthy he will become poor, and if he was poor he will flee from his

---

[83] شریکه. The al-Andarzaghar version (Da. 116) reads "friend" (صديق).

[84] **B** and **P** read "receive," but that does not make sense in the context of all of the rest. Hugo's reading agrees with mine (and is omitted in the al-Andarzaghar passage).

[85] عقل. **P** reads, "work" (عمل).

[86] For this sentence, cf. Da. 115.

[87] The text adds, "killing" (القتل), but al-Andarzaghar (Da. 115) reads الفتوة, "youthful" (i.e., youthful pleasures and singing).

[88] For this sentence, cf. Da. 116.

[89] For this sentence, cf. Da. 117.

[90] **P** adds, "in his assets."

country, and his condition will change to being bad, and if he bought a slave he will die or run away, and if his father was alive he will die, and he will be hostile to his friends, and fall into quarrels, and be victorious over everyone who quarrels with him.

12 Then Saturn distributes in the *fardār* of Mars for 1 year: the total of that is 6 years. **13** It[91] indicates that in this distribution types of detestable things will afflict him, and tribulation, and his son will die, and some of his assets will leave his hands, and losses will be imposed upon him, and he will become ill with a powerful illness, or a quartan fever will seize him,[92] and his reason will become confused, and [then] he will be safe from it, or his relatives and woman will hate him so that he will divorce her, or estrangement will occur between them, and a bad ailment will afflict his male children, and it will corrupt his temperament or he will die.

14 Then Jupiter distributes in the *fardār* of Mars for 1 year: the total of that is 7 years. **15** It[93] indicates that in this distribution he will be raised up from a downfall, and he will be victorious over everyone who quarrels with him, and the people will be of little importance to him, and he will have the good in killing and quarreling, and he will desire weapons and assets, and his crops will multiply, and he will rejoice in his family and children, and a boy will be born to him, and his daughter will die, and he will delight in every work he does.

◈ ❧ ◈

16 Then, after all of the planets the Head of the Dragon distributes by itself for 3 years. **17** It indicates that in this distribution he will be fortunate, and will befriend the nobility, and his speech will be received, and he will have authority over many men, and in his own land

---

[91] For this sentence, cf. Da. 118.

[92] For the rest, **E**: "and a bad ailment will afflict his male children, and his reason will become confused, and [then] he will be safe from those things, and his relatives and woman will hate him (so that he will divorce her), and a distance will fall between them and he will separate [from her], and his temperament will be corrupted or he will die."

[93] For this sentence, cf. Da. 119.

he will be put in charge of judging, and he will gain assets in lawsuits or from inheritance, and other reasons, and he will purchase slaves and servant girls, and women will desire him, and some corruption will spoil his temperament [but] then he will be well.

18 Then[94] after that, the Tail of the Dragon distributes by itself for 2 years. **19** It indicates that in this distribution he will encounter detestable things, and he will be hostile to his friends, and will quarrel with his family and children, and loss will enter upon him in his assets, and will be sad about[95] his woman or will be disgraced because of her, and he will become ill with a powerful illness which he will recover from.

<**20** And[96] if you found the Head of the Dragon in the nativity in the Ascendant of the nativity, he will live the life of kings for those three years; and if Jupiter, the Moon, Venus, or the Sun were with it, he will grow in nobility and the good.[97] **21** And if the Tail of the Dragon was in the Ascendant, he will encounter tribulation and evil. **22** And if the Head was in the house of profit, he will become rich and wealthy; and if the Tail was in the house of profit, he will become poor. **23** And if the Tail was in the house of brothers, he will be more fortunate and lucky than his brothers; and if the Tail was in the house of brothers, he will be more troubled than his brothers, and lower than them.>

24 Now,[98] the Head and Tail distribute for diurnal nativities after the years of Mars, and for nocturnal nativities after the years of Mercury:[99] and it is when the native enters year 71—and he will begin in the distribution of the *fardārs* with the Head, then the Tail, whether the native was diurnal or nocturnal. **25** And once 75 years are completed

---

[94] For **18-19**, cf. Da. 124.
[95] **P** reads, "will tyrannize."
[96] I have inserted these sentences (**20-23**) from al-Andarzaghar (Da. 121-27), since **B** has a long but only partly legible marginal note which contains phrases similar to these, corresponding exactly with these sentences in the al-Andarzaghar text.
[97] Reading more simply for "he will grow in nobility to his own nobility, and in good to his own good."
[98] For this sentence, cf. Da. 124.
[99] In other words, for Abū Ma'shar they always come at the end of full cycle of planetary *fardārs*.

for the native, the distribution of the *fardār* returns to the luminary which he began from at his birth, in the original order [of planets]: and the judgment about his condition at the time when the distribution returns to it will be like the judgment for a distinguished, mature, strong man, for whom all desirable as well as detestable conditions are appropriate, in the manner we stated in what precedes [this].[100] **26** And if his lifespan increased beyond 75 years (or fell short of it), his death will be in the *fardār* of the planet which did reach.

27 And these indications which we have stated as belonging to the planets upon their managing the years of their *fardārs* individually, or in partnership with others, we have intended to be their natural indications in this subject. **28** But the suitability of each one's condition (or its badness) in the root and at the time of the management, alters much of what we have stated about the good and the bad.

---

[100] See IV.4, **4-11**.

BOOK V: ON THE TRANSIT OF THE PLANETS, EACH TO THE OTHER

And it is in eight chapters

Chapter V.1: On the indication of the transit of the planets

1 Now, in the transit of the planets in the revolutions of years to [1] their own rooted positions, or the transit of one of them in the revolution to the position of another in the root, [there are] indications for various hidden things (of good and bad), and for [2] the duration of that thing: so you should study their positions.

[1: Transits to rooted or revolutionary places]

2 Sometimes a planet in the revolution of one of the years reaches its own rooted degree, and sometimes it reaches [only] that sign in which it was at the root of the nativity, but it does not reach that precise degree. **3** [So] as for if it goes past it or falls short of it, if in the revolution of the year it reaches its own degree which it had been in in the root of the nativity, or was in the bound which it was in at the root (preceding that rooted degree or coming after it), its indication will be complete. **4** And if the planet in the revolution was not in that bound, but between it and that rooted degree there was less than one-half its body (equally preceding it or coming after it),[1] then it will make a subtraction from its indication, whether that thing was good or bad. **5** And if between it and [the degree] was more than the amount of one-half of its body, and it is going towards it, its indication will be below that. **6** And if it was like that in distance from [the rooted degree] and it had already gone past it, then its indication will be for something small, of the category of that indication, and it indicates everything which has vanished and passed away, as well as thought, ideas, intelligence, regret, and remorse, and this type of thing.

---

[1] Also known as its "orb." See the table below.

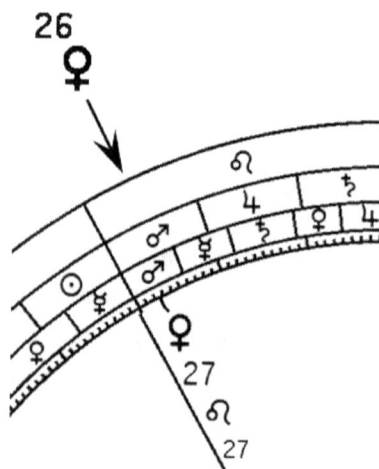

Figure 82: Venus return to same bound (V.1, 3)

7 But concerning the arrival of any of the planets in the revolution of the year at the position of another planet of the root, you ought to see if it reaches the degree of that planet exactly, or comes to be in that bound, as well as the rest of what we mentioned previously.

8 Now if a planet in the revolution of the year was in a sign, [but] then returns[2] [later] to its [natal] place, or it reaches a place other than that in that year, or another planet reaches its [natal] position in that year, then it also produces its indication; and along with that one must call upon the aspect of the planets to it in that time, or the connection of one of them with another.[3]

9 And if at the revolution of one of the months of the year, the conditions of the planets were like what we mentioned of the arrival of one of them in the revolution of that month to its position which it had been in in the root of the nativity, or its reaching the position of other planets or the root, or its reaching the position of planets of the revolution of the year, then the judgment about it in that month will be like the judgment about it in the revolution of the year.

---

[2] رجع, the usual term for being retrograde. The Greek edition understands it this way, so that the planet goes retrograde at some point and returns to its natal position. In context I think it makes more sense to simply say that it "returns," especially since in VII.1 Abū Ma'shar makes a big point of talking about how far a planet will travel over the course of the year. But either way, it means that transits later in the year will also produce its indication.

[3] That is, the planet will activate the natal meaning, but its real-time aspects at that moment will also condition it.

Planetary orbs		Transit to:	Intensity
☉	15°	Exact degree or same bound	Complete
☽	12°		
♄	9°	Within moiety	Less
♃	9°	Outside moiety, applying	Less still
♂	8°		
♀	7°	Outside moiety, separating	Small, fading, only in the mind
☿	7°		

Figure 83: Persian planetary orbs (on each side),[4] and intensity of transits

[1: Interpretation of transits]

10 Now if a planet in the revolution returned to its [own] rooted place, then at that [time] it indicates the renewal of everything it had indicated in the root of the nativity, of the good and the bad.

11 But if in the revolution it reached the position of another planet, then one should seek information from it in three ways:

12 One of them is [a] just as we mentioned before, concerning the nature of two planets if they looked at each other[5] or if they partnered together in the indication in one of the things.[6]

13 And the second is [b] from their natures, such that if a fortune in the revolution reached the position of another fortune in the root, it indicates that good and suitability; and if a fortune reached the position of a planetary infortune, it will improve the corruption and evil that that infortune had indicated [in the root]. **14** And if an infortune in the revolution reached the position of a fortune in the root, the in-

---

[4] The "orb" of the planet (sometimes called its "body") is the total number of degrees on *each* side. So, the total orb of Saturn is 18°, with 9° on each side. The amount on each side is sometimes called its "moiety" in English.

[5] That is, if they were configured in the nativity (see **8** above).

[6] This seems to mean that their significations overlapped: such as if a planet ruling the seventh transited Venus or the lord of the Lot of marriage.

fortune undermines what suitability and good that fortune had indicated [in the root]; and if an infortune in the revolution reached the position of an infortune in the root, it will be excessive in the indication of corruption, in the category which they both[7] indicate.

15 And the third is [c] that you look at the sign in which that planet had been in the root, and this other one came to its place, so that you make its house[8] be like an Ascendant: then you see where the two houses of that other planet are from it, and let the judgment be according to that.

[1: Interpretation example]

16 And[9] an example of that is if Jupiter was in one of the signs in the root (and that sign was either his own house or the house of another), and in the revolution of the year Venus came to the position of Jupiter: so we would make each of the two houses of Jupiter be like the root and the Ascendant.[10] **17** Then, we would see where the two houses of Venus are from each one of [his]: so since Taurus is the sixth from Sagittarius, we would say he will become ill; and since Libra is its eleventh, we would say he will acquire brothers;[11] and since they are both fortunes, we would say he will recover from his illness, and be fortunate in the siblings and with servants. **18** Then, we would make Pisces also be like <Ascendant of> the root, and we would say that because Taurus is the third from Pisces, he will travel; and because Libra is its eighth, assets will come to him from an inheritance, and one of those he is concerned about will die, and he will be fortunate in traveling

---

[7] **E** has only one of them, probably referring to the rooted infortune. Certainly the rooted planet is the more important one.
[8] That is, its domicile, the sign it rules.
[9] In this example, Abū Ma'shar will combine all three interpretive approaches, focusing especially on [b] and [c].
[10] Reading with **B** and **E** (**T** reads, "the Ascendant and the root," **P** "the Ascendant of the root"). This is because Jupiter is the rooted planet, and presumably more powerful in the indication: see **21-22** below, where Venus can be used if she is stronger.
[11] Or rather, "friends." But I do note that in Sahl's *Nativities* Ch. 11, the eleventh house is explicitly linked to both friends and "fraternity."

and inheritances—and you would look like that for all of the planets. **19** And so the arrival of Venus at the position of Jupiter indicates illness and death due to the position of her houses from his houses, and by their own natures they indicate assistance[12] in recovering from the illness, and good fortune with the rest of what we mentioned. **20** And if it were not for the position of her houses from his houses, then they would not have indicated illnesses, nor inheritances, nor death.

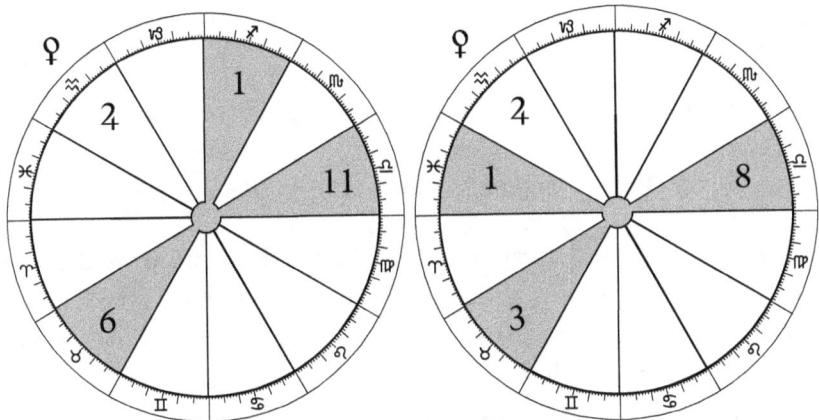

Figure 84: Venus transiting Jupiter, houses derived from Sagittarius and Pisces (V.1, 16-20)

21 And you should look in this at Venus: for if in the year *she* was greater in indication than Jupiter, then after that [you should] also make *her* houses be like the root.[13] **22** Then we would see where the two houses of Jupiter are relative to her houses, [and] then the work would be according to what we mentioned, and in this manner we would look at each of the planets—except for the Sun, because his situation in each year is not like the situation of the rest of the planets, since in every revolution [the Sun] returns to his [natal] position. **23** So we are not mentioning [the Sun's] condition in the way we have

---

[12] السَّعدة. T reads السَّعادة, "good fortune."
[13] This would probably be if she ruled the Ascendant of the revolution, or was the lord of the year.

mentioned the condition of the others, but we would [simply] make his house be like the root and the Ascendant: then we would see the place of his sign in the revolution of years, relative to his house [in the nativity]; then we would judge according to that.

24 Now as for the time in which that thing will come to be in that year, that is from its reaching its rooted place. **25** But if it managed one of the months of the year (and its days), its indication would appear [then]. **26** And if that was due to its reaching the position of one of the planets, then when one of them mixed with the other in that year by means of one of the excellent or bad combinations, its indication for good or evil will manifest in the manner that it had indicated.[14]

[2: Duration of the effect, first way (planetary return)]

27 Now as for the duration of that thing, it is in two ways. **28** The first way is that you look at the planet: for if in the root of the nativity it was in a sign, [and] then in one of the revolutions it reached its own rooted place, and it indicated something detestable due to its returning to its place and due to its position (relative to the rotation of the rooted *and* revolutionary circle),[15] the duration of that detestable thing will be in accordance with the period of that planet,[16] twice: one of them

---

[14] This seems to mean the following: if Venus transited the natal position of Jupiter, then the effect would appear later in the year when she and *transiting* Jupiter make some combination.

[15] It does not have to be in the same bad house, but can be in other, similarly bad positions (**29, 33**). Abū Ma'shar's awkward phrasing makes this unnecessarily confusing. The "rotation of the rooted circle" just means "the house which that sign occupies in the nativity," due to the local Ascendant: if Saturn is in Virgo, he is in Virgo for everyone, and that could be in any house, depending on where the native is born. But by the rotation of the circle at a particular location, Virgo will be in a particular natal house or place (such as the sixth). The "rotation of the revolutionary circle" means that at the time of the revolution, the heavens will have rotated so that Virgo occupies some place in the *revolution*: it may occupy the sixth again, or some other place. Abū Ma'shar's whole point in talking about this, is because we want to know if the revolutionary position is in a good or bad place similar to the nativity.

[16] As he suggests in **35**, the number of years in the planetary period should be converted to units of days or hours, so that they fit within a year.

due to the indication of its position in the root, and the second due to its reaching that sign in the revolution of the year.[17] **29** But if a planet in the revolution of one of the years returned to its own rooted place, and that position due to the rotation of the circle in the revolution of the year was *not* in the positions which indicate something detestable, it will take away from the indication of evil, and its duration will be in accordance with the period of the planet,[18] once.[19]

Duration of transit effect: planetary return	
Type of return:	*Duration*
Return to rooted position:	Planet's period
• In a similarly good/bad place in the SR	Adds another period
• In a dissimilar good/bad place in the SR	(Adds nothing)

Figure 85: Duration of effect, planetary return (V.1, 27-33)

30 And an example of that is if Saturn in the root of the nativity was in the seventh, and in the revolution of one of the years he reached his own rooted place, and that place was the seventh of the terminal point[20] or the seventh of the Ascendant of the revolution: his return to his rooted place indicates something detestable[21] in women and opponents, and we would say that its duration would be in accordance with the period of Saturn, doubled. **31** And if that sign had been the tenth from the terminal point or the tenth of the Ascendant of the revolution, or it was in the places suitable for Saturn, its duration would have been in accordance with his period, once.

---

[17] That is, assuming that sign is also a bad place in the revolutionary houses or relative to the profection.
[18] **T**: "in accordance with its period in the circle."
[19] So, a planet's return will always activate that natal effect, for the period of that planet in days or hours (see also **34-35**). But it must *also* be in a similar good or bad house in the revolution, to double it.
[20] المنتهى. **T** reads المشتري, "Jupiter."
[21] **P** and **T** add, "and corruption."

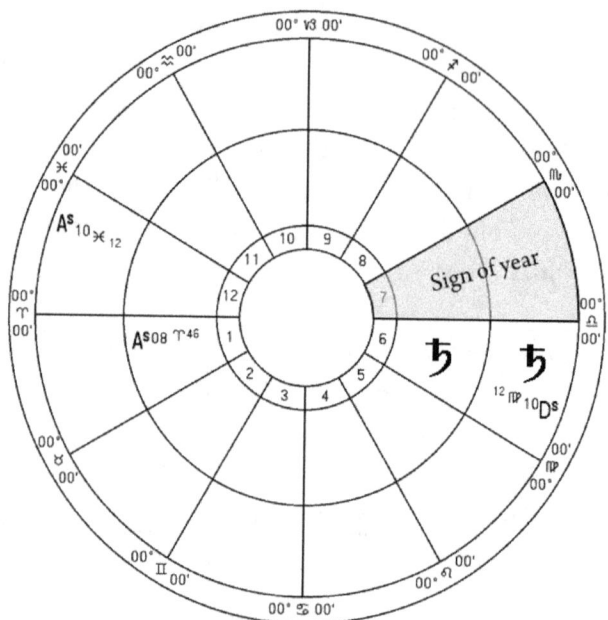

Figure 86: Saturn return to 6th, in 12th from sign of year, 7th from SR ASC (V.1, 28, 30)[22]

32 And likewise, if a planet in the revolution of one of the years reached its position which it had been in in the root, and it indicated good due to its returning to its rooted place and due to its position (relative to the rotation of the circle in the root *and* the revolution), its duration would be the amount of the period of that planet, doubled. **33** And if was different from that, and its position relative to the rotation of the rooted circle had indicated good, and relative to the rotation of the revolutionary circle it indicated evil, the duration of that good would be the amount of the period of that planet, once.

---

[22] The natal Saturn in Virgo is in a bad natal place (the sixth), and at the revolution he makes a planetary return: this activates his natal meaning for one of his periods (in days or hours). But Virgo *also* occupies a similar bad place from the sign of the year (namely, the twelfth from it)—and I have also made him be in the seventh of the revolution. Because the revolutionary Saturn-Virgo is in a similarly bad place, this adds his period a second time.

34 Now as for the knowledge of the period which one works with, look at the planet one is making the inference from: for if it was in a convertible sign, it works by its lesser period; and if it was in a sign having two bodies, it works by its middle period; and if it was in a fixed sign, it works by its greater period. **35** And if one needed to take the period twice, then double that period, and the duration of that good or evil will be in accordance with the amount of that number, in hours or days; and for help in that, turn to the stakes and what follows them, and the falling [places], as well as the number of ascensions of that sign.

[2: Duration of the effect, second way (transit to different planet)]

36 And as for the second way, it is if a planet in the root of the nativity is in a sign, and in a revolution of one of the years it comes to the position of another planet, so its reaching the position of another one indicates something, and [if] the indication of that sign in the revolution (due to the rotation of the [revolutionary] circle) harmonizes with the indication of the rotation of the rooted circle, then its duration will be [1] in accordance with the period of the *revolutionary* planet, once;[23] or[24] [2] according to what comes out of that bound,[25] or [3] its distancing itself from that degree by the amount of one-half of its body.[26] **37** Now if the rooted planet in the revolution of the year looked at the revolutionary planet,[27] then its duration will be in accordance with what we stated, and to it is added the period of the *rooted* planet.

---

[23] The reason it only gives one period despite being in good houses in both charts, is because it involves two *different* planets (instead of the same planet making a return, as with the first way above).

[24] **P** and **T** read, "and."

[25] That is, so long as it is actually transiting in the bound (see **48**): this is the real-time expression of **3** above, but using two different planets.

[26] This is the real-time expression of **4** above. For an example, see **48**.

[27] See **41**: that is, if the rooted planet which was being transit*ed*, also looked at the transit*ing* planet in real time, at the revolution.

38 But if the position of the rotation of the rooted circle was in conflict with[28] the position of the rotation of the revolutionary circle, and the two planets were looking at other, then its duration will be in accordance with the period of the *revolutionary* planet, once, or[29] by the amount that it distances itself from it, by one-half of its body—except that after that it will not cease to be in the remainders of that, for the amount of the period of the *rooted* planet.[30]

Duration of transit effect: transit to different planet	
Type of transit:	**Duration**
Place is similarly good/bad in nativity and SR	• Period of transiting planet • Or time spent in bound • Or time spent up to distance of moiety
• Natal planet also looks at transiting planet, in real time	Adds period of natal planet
Place <u>not</u> similarly good/bad in nativity and SR	• Period of transiting planet • Or time spent up to distance of moiety
• Natal planet also looks at transiting planet, in real time	Adds period of natal planet, but as diminished or after-effect

Figure 87: Duration of effect, transit to a different planet (V.1, 36-38)

39 And an example of that is if Jupiter in the root of the nativity was in a convertible sign, and that sign was the sixth of the root, and Venus

---

[28] Or, "inconsistent with." The conflict seems to be in terms of good and bad: see the example in **41**. In **39**, the natal and revolutionary places are both in the sixth, so they indicate the same difficult thing; but in **41**, Abū Ma'shar imagines that the revolutionary position is in the fifth or eleventh, so the meanings are inconsistent in terms of illness or problems.

[29] **E** and **T** read, "and."

[30] See **41** below.

in the revolution of one of the years reached[31] the position of Jupiter of the root, and that sign was [also] the sixth of the terminal point or the sixth of the Ascendant of the revolution of the year:[32] so by her reaching the position of Jupiter, Venus indicated that an ailment will afflict the owner of the revolution from windiness and a pain of the throat, and its duration will be the amount of the period of Venus, one time.[33] **40** Now if Jupiter at the revolution of the year looked at Venus, its duration would be the amount of the period of them both put together: 20 days. **41** But if that position due to the rotation of the circle in the revolution had been one of the positions indicating suitability for Jupiter and Venus (like the fifth or eleventh), it would have indicated that its duration would be the amount of the period of Venus (and that is 8 hours or 8 days),[34] [but] then it would diminish—except that after that it would not cease to be in the remainders of that, for 12 days. **42** (And if Jupiter [in the revolution] had not been looking at Venus, it would have indicated that its duration was only the period of Venus.) **43** And indeed, we made the period of Venus and Jupiter be hours or days, because they are both in convertible signs; and [because] they are both fortunes, they indicate the speed of the recovery; and you do likewise with every planet reaching its own rooted place in the revolution of the year, or the place of another planet. **44** And the work in it will be like that *if* the indication was from this way alone. **45** But as for when one infers something from this way as well as from others, the work in it will be different from that.[35]

---

[31] Reading for "terminated at," which is the term Abū Ma'shar normally reserves for profections.

[32] Or a similar house, as Abū Ma'shar has already made clear above.

[33] This is because the houses have the same or similar meaning (**36**).

[34] Just as in **28**.

[35] This may be a reference to considering multiple planets, in **46-52** below. Thanks to Steven Birchfield for suggesting this.

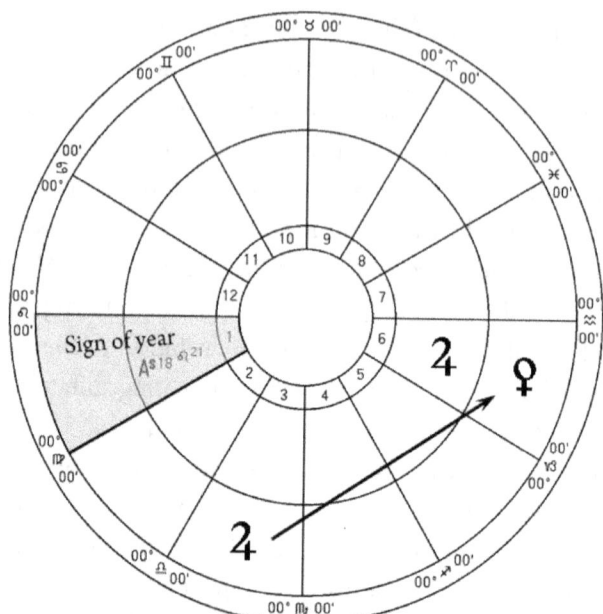

Figure 88: SR Venus transiting natal Jupiter in 6th, looked at by SR Jupiter (V.1, 39-40)[36]

[*2: Duration of the effect: second way (transit to multiple planets)*]

46 And if two or more planets in the revolution of one of the years reached the position of a single [natal] planet, or a single planet reached the position of two or more [natal] planets, the work in it is according to what is indicated by the arrival of each one of them individually to the place of the other planet. **47** And an example of that is if the Moon in the root of the nativity was in Cancer, and in the revolution of one of the years Saturn and Jupiter reached her [natal] position: so we would say that Saturn's reaching the position of the Moon indicates distress and something detestable because of women, while Jupiter's reaching the place of the Moon indicates the suitable condition of the owner of the revolution in his body and assets, and

---

[36] In this example I have made Venus be in the sixth from the terminal point, but in **39** Abū Ma'shar says she could have been in the sixth from the revolutionary Ascendant: in both cases it would be bad.

[that] pleasing reports would reach him, and he would increase in his children (if he was of those to whom children are born, and it was a time for indicating that).[37] **48** <So> since each of the two had a separate indication in one of the times of the year, the duration of that distress and adversity [in the case of Saturn] would be [1] for the amount of the period of Saturn, or [2] so long as Saturn is in that bound, or [3] until he had distanced himself from that degree by the amount of one-half of his body. **49** And their uniting [with the Moon] each also indicates something else, in the manner that we mentioned in what preceded.[38]

50 But if Saturn and Jupiter in the root of the nativity had been in Cancer, and the Moon in the revolution of the year reached their [natal] place, then the Moon reaching the position of Saturn would indicate that the owner of the revolution would marry old women and have sex with them. **51** And the Moon's reaching the position of Jupiter would indicate that he will travel to a watery place, and then he will travel from it to another.

52 And likewise working with the rest of the planets, and the timing in it, and the duration of that, will be in this way.

Chapter V.2: On the indication of Saturn when he transits in the revolution over his own rooted position & the position of the rest of the planets

Comment by Dykes. Recall from my Introduction and V.1, **15-20** above, that Abū Ma'shar delineates transits using the relationship between two planets' domiciles. In the following chapters, many of his interpretations can be derived from the planets' natures, their for-

---

[37] The Moon signifies women, the body, and reports. So Abū Ma'shar is saying that Saturn's transit to her will indicate problems due to women, while Jupiter indicates good things for the body as well as reports. Jupiter-Moon would also be a good combination for having children.

[38] Abū Ma'shar probably means his derived-domicile approach to interpretation, in **15**.

tune/infortune status, and their intrinsic compatibility (such as Venus indicating love, being a fortune, and mixing well with the Moon but not Saturn). But for the reader's interest I've underlined all phrases which can probably only be explained by Abū Ma'shar's special theory: so for example, no normal combination of the Sun and Saturn could indicate marriage; but because their signs (Leo and Aquarius) are in the seventh place *from each other*, he claims that their transit can indicates marriage (**9**). In my view, this theory is probably bogus and the underlined phrases could be ignored without loss.

1 If[39] in the revolution of the year Saturn reached his own rooted place, and in the two times he is in a suitable condition, it renews the condition of the nativity,[40] and he will move from his current status to [another] status more suitable than it. **2** Now if in the revolution of the year he was in the stakes, he will have the status and good [pertaining to them]: if he was in the Midheaven, he will have good and power from the Sultan; and if he was in the seventh, that good will be from women and quarreling;[41] and if he was in the fourth, then from fathers;[42] and if he was in the Ascendant, then from his own exertion and work. **3** And his indication will be like this in the rest of the twelve houses.

4 If Saturn in the revolution of the year reached the place of Jupiter, and in the root or the revolution Saturn was the lord of the Ascendant, or the lord of the Lot of Fortune, or he was the lord of the house of the Moon (if the revolution was by night) or the lord of the house of the Sun (if the revolution was by day), then it indicates the goodness of his condition, and an increase in his friends, education, assets, real estate,

---

[39] See the Introduction for a discussion of the underlined phrases in the following chapters, which are based on Abū Ma'shar's derived-domicile interpretations mentioned in V.1, **15-20**.

[40] Or rather, the condition he *had indicated in* the nativity (see parallel statements for other planets below).

[41] **T** reads, "partners."

[42] **B** adds الصراح ("what is obvious"), but then seems to cross it out.

and crops. **5** But if he did not have testimony in these places which we mentioned, it will do violence to his assets and real estate, and everything we mentioned, and everything which is attributed to that sign, [and] he will quarrel with his siblings,⁴³ and corrupt what is between him and them.

6 If Saturn in the revolution reached the place of Mars, and Saturn had testimony in the Ascendant of the root or in the revolution, or in the Lot of Fortune, it indicates the native's traveling, and his need for his brothers and friends,⁴⁴ and benefit [and] good from them, and often he will be passed by in his management, and will be slow in his works, malicious in his purpose, disdaining his own religion, and he will see evil because of it. **7** And if he did not have testimony in what we mentioned, he will encounter distresses and something detestable from siblings and friends because of exile and travel. **8** But if he was received, his situation will be put in order after that.

9 If Saturn assembled with the Sun in the revolution of the year, and Saturn had testimony in what we mentioned, then for the owner of the revolution it indicates hot illnesses one should be afraid of, and beating by the Sultan, and contention and quarreling with women or distress because of them, and [*illegible*]. **10** And if Saturn did not have testimony in what we mentioned, then quarreling will afflict him, and one of his women will die, and he will be confused, and will fear his father's ruin, and it will weaken his authority and corrupt it, if he had authority (and if not, something detestable will afflict him in his rank and power).

11 If Saturn in the revolution of the year reached the place of Venus, the owner of the revolution will travel, and marriage will be troublesome for him, and it will reduce his sexual intercourse, and he will hope for a child to be born to him (if the root of the nativity indicated that), and he will be tested by love, and will desire corrupted women.

---

⁴³ Pisces is the third from Capricorn (and Aquarius the third from Sagittarius), but Saturn and Jupiter are also used to construct the Lot of siblings.
⁴⁴ **E** reads, "his Sultan" or "his authority figure."

12 If Saturn in the revolution of the year reached the place of Mercury, then it will diminish his thought, and he will travel; and if he had children he will be distressed because of them, and will subject himself to fears, and will do works in which something detestable is feared for him, and he will discuss things harmful to him, and it will corrupt his business and his work.

13 If Saturn in the revolution of the year reached the place of the Moon, then a defect and state of deficiency will enter upon him because of women.[45] **14** Now if with that the Moon was in the stakes, something detestable will befall him from the category of the sign which she is in. **15** For if she was in a sign in the image of people, the detestable thing will afflict him from people; and if she was in a sign of wild animals, then from wild animals; and if she was in a sign of riding animals, then from riding animals; and if she was in Scorpio, then from burning and stinging; and if she was in Cancer or in Pisces, then from a reptile of the water and what is like that, and it will corrupt his authority and weaken it. **16** Now if with that the Moon was in the Ascendant of the root, made unfortunate, a powerful illness will afflict him and it will be feared for him.

Chapter V.3: On stating the indication of Jupiter if in the revolution he transited his own rooted position & the position of the rest of the planets

1 If in the revolution of the year Jupiter reached the place of Saturn, then his condition will advance, and it will set aright what corruption and harm Saturn had indicated in the root, and he will have good intentions, be upright in his religion, successful in his needs, and he will have good from his friends, and his enemies will make peace, and they will come into his affection.

2 If in the revolution of the year Jupiter reached his own rooted place, it will renew what good he had indicated in the root of the nativ-

---

[45] In a marginal note **B** seems to read "with a diminishment in the eyesight."

ity, and he will have assets in ways he had not hoped for, and will increase in his rank and status, and the condition of his friends and siblings will be good, and a child will be hoped for him.

3 If in the revolution of the year Jupiter reached the place of Mars, he will travel and have good in it, or benefit will be prepared for him because of traveling, or from the Sultan and the masters of wars, and he will have good from his siblings or from one who is with him in the household of the brother, and he will hope to have children born to him, if he had already reached that age.

4 If in the revolution of the year Jupiter reached the place of the Sun and assembled with him, and he is burned by [the Sun], and Jupiter had testimony in the Ascendant of the root or the revolution, or the sign of the terminal point, then destruction will be feared for the native until he goes past the burning, or the Sun goes past the degree of the terminal point or the Ascendant of the revolution. **5** But even if [Jupiter] did go past and he was safe, fear will afflict him from the Sultan (and [then] vanish from him), and illnesses will happen to him from heat, and he will have good from fathers or from one who is in their household.[46] **6** And if Jupiter was eastern, it indicates being victorious in [forms of] good fortune.

7 And if in the revolution of the year Jupiter reached the place of Venus, <u>illnesses</u> will happen to him, and the temperament of his <u>body will be corrupted</u>, and it will <u>emaciate his body</u>, and he will increase in his status and rank, and his condition will improve, and his friends will multiply, and he will be praised. **8** Now if at that time[47] Venus was made unfortunate and she had testimony in the root or in the year, it[48] will be feared for him.

---

[46] Or perhaps, "who is of their status" (بمنزلتهم).
[47] عند ذلك. I take this to mean "at the time of the revolution," but it's possible Abū Ma'shar is referring to her natal condition.
[48] E reads "death," but that seems pretty drastic for Jupiter-Venus, even if she is in a poor condition (unless Abū Ma'shar means that Sagittarius is the eighth from Taurus).

9 If in the revolution of the year Jupiter reached the place of Mercury, he will increase in his work, culture, family and servants, and his status and power, and he will gain authority. **10** Now if Jupiter was eastern, or the terminal [sign] or the Ascendant was the house of one of them, it will be greater for the good.

11 If in the revolution of the year Jupiter reached the place of the Moon, it indicates the suitability of the condition in his body and soul, and an increase in assets, children, and the arrival of pleasing reports. **12** Now if in the revolution Jupiter looked at the rooted place of Moon or assembled with her, and they were both in a suitable place, it indicates being freed from adversity (if he was in it) and the suitability of the condition in his way of life, and the delight of the soul.

13 If in the revolution Jupiter reached the rooted Ascendant, or the fifth place,[49] or their lords, or the position of Venus, or the position of the Moon, or the position of the Lot of children or its lord, whether he assembled with or looked at them, then it indicates producing a pleasing child—if the root of the nativity had already indicated the production of children.

Chapter V.4: On the indication of Mars if in the revolution he transited his own rooted position & the position of the rest of the planets

1 If in the revolution of the year Mars reached the place of Saturn, he will increase in his <u>siblings and friends</u>, and will go on a <u>nearby journey</u>. **2** Now if Mars had testimony in the year, it indicates his delay in [his] needs; but if Saturn had testimony it would be less (because Mars dissolves the slowness of Saturn as well as his coldness), except that an ailment will afflict him from wounds and injuries. **3** And if in the year in which Mars reaches the place of Saturn, Saturn also reaches the place of Mars, then they indicate fleeing from the country.

---

[49] Reading with **B**. **E** and **P** read "sign," while **T** reads "the *tenth* sign."

4 If in the revolution of the year Mars reached the place of Jupiter, it indicates <u>travel</u>, and benefits because of <u>riding animals and beasts</u>, and a child will be hoped for him, and that is more firm if the Ascendant of the root, or of the revolution, or the sign of the terminal point, were the house of one of them.

5 If in the revolution of the year Mars reached his own rooted place, and that position was one of the stakes,[50] and he had testimony in the year, and in the root he indicated benefit [and] the good, he will have power, good, and authority from the lords of wars. **6** Now if in the root of the nativity he was in a stake, he will be known, famous, and benefit from the lords of wars. **7** But if he was withdrawing, [while still] looking at the Ascendant, it indicates travel and an increase[51] in the family and [his] retinue.[52] **8** But if he was falling away from an aspect to[53] the terminal point or the Ascendant,[54] and he had testimony in them, he will gain the good from working with iron and blood.

9 If in the revolution of the year Mars assembled with the Sun and the revolution was diurnal,[55] distresses will enter upon him from the Sultan, and an ailment will afflict him from heat. **10** Now if Mars was the lord of the year and he was in a hot, dry sign, disaster will be feared from him from fire and heat. **11** And if he was in a hot, moist sign, killing[56] will be feared for him. **12** And if the revolution was by night, it will be easier.

13 If in the revolution of the year Mars reached the place of Venus, it indicates an increase in the native's sexual intercourse, and it multi-

---

[50] This probably means it is one of the stakes *in the revolution*, not the nativity. The next sentences speak of the nativity.

[51] **E**: "benefit."

[52] Ending the sentence here, with **E**, **P**, and **T**. **B** continues in a small marginal note that also lacks dotting: "And his condition in their delay will improve, and in the [*uncertain*] it will be the contrary of that."

[53] That is, "in aversion to."

[54] This is probably the Ascendant of the nativity.

[55] For this statement about sect, **E** reads "and he had testimony in it."

[56] **E** and **P** read "killing," while **B** is undotted. But killing seems extreme, and one would expect the moisture to mitigate Mars's damage.

plies his desire and his eagerness in the matter of women, and his soul will be insatiable, and he will increase in his power and rank and women, and because of [the women] hardship will afflict him, and his siblings will multiply, and he will be praised. **14** And if Mars had testimony in the year, he will become ill due to being filled with food, or from an abundance of sex. **15** And if Venus had the testimony, his ailment will be because of a medical treatment, and a disturbance of the blood, and perhaps a pain in the throat will afflict him. **16** Now if, along with her testimony in the year Venus was made unfortunate, destruction will be feared for him: and if his[57] condition was like that from his reaching the place of Venus, and Mars was corrupting for her through [his] assembly or by aspect in the root, or at the revolution or at the transit, it indicates an excess of desire and a scandal because of women.

17 If in the revolution of the year Mars reached the place of Mercury, then he will concoct lies and falsehoods, and destruction will be feared for him, or for the younger ones of his brothers, or one who has the status of a brother (of those who are younger in years than he is). **18** Now if [Mercury] had testimony in the year and was made unfortunate by Mars, it will also be feared for him. **19** And if the testimony belonged to Mars, it will be easier, except it indicates that the owner of the revolution will be in a mood of fear and ruin in that year.

20 If in the revolution of the year Mars reached the place of the Moon, and the Moon is excellent in place from the Ascendant, and she has testimony in the year, then he will have <u>authority</u> and a <u>child</u> will be born to him. **21** But if the testimony in it belonged to Mars, he will <u>travel</u>, and distress will afflict him because of the family and women; and if he had authority, it will be corrupted.

---

[57] I take this to be Mars, but Abū Ma'shar might mean the native.

Chapter V.5: On the indication of the Sun if in the revolution of the year he was in one of the twelve houses

1 If the Sun in the revolution of the year was in Leo, and he is in the stakes, in a suitable condition, not made unfortunate, and he has testimony in the root or in the year, he will be healthy in his body, and his power will be mighty, and he will have the good and benefits. **2** But if he was in one of them and he *is* made unfortunate, pains will happen to him. **3** And if he was in that condition of misfortune and he is above the earth, withdrawing from the stakes, the ailments will be easier.

4 If the Sun in the revolution of the year was in Virgo, and he is above the earth, looking at the Ascendant, and he has testimony in the year, it indicates the owner of the revolution's eagerness for seeking assets and furnishings.[58] **5** Now if the fortunes testified to him, he will get what he wanted of those assets; but if a harming planet or infortune testified to him, it indicates deprivation—and that is more confirmed if he had testimony in the year.

6 Now if the Sun in the revolution of the year was in Libra and he is above the earth, and has testimony in the year, it indicates the native's travel; and for the suitability of that and its corruption, you look from his condition in himself, and the condition of the planet mixing with him.

7 If the Sun in the revolution of the year was in Scorpio and he was in the stakes, in a suitable condition, and especially if he was in the Midheaven and had testimony in the year, then it indicates that he will have status, good, and authority, and will increase in his real estate. **8** And if he was withdrawing, free of the corrupting infortunes, yet is [still] looking at the Ascendant, the family of the owner of the revolution as well as his relatives will have good, and they will be delighted, and he will be devoted to building and repairs, and will seek hidden things.

---

[58] Reading with **B**, and treating an undotted word as an unattested Form IV noun of قسّ. **E** and **P** read, "culture" or "manners." **T** reads, "seeking children and culture."

9 If the Sun in the revolution of the year was in Sagittarius, and he had testimony in the year, and he is in the stakes, in a suitable condition, the owner of the revolution will have good, and his joy will multiply, and he will delight in his children; and if [the Sun] was connecting with Mars, a child will be born to him.[59] **10** And if he was made unfortunate, his distresses will multiply, and it will be feared for one of his children.[60]

11 If the Sun in the revolution of the year was in Capricorn and he had testimony in the year, he will be joyful and will be spoken well of, and will be in need of one who is lower than himself; and if [the Sun] did not have testimony in the year, it indicates ailments and illnesses, and an abundance of distress, and the weakness of his reputation, and his need for people who are lower than himself.

12 If the Sun in the revolution of the year was in Aquarius and he had testimony in the year, and he is free of the infortunes, it indicates marriage and an increase in the family and [his] retinue. **13** And if [the Sun] was made unfortunate, indicates the ruin of one of the family or their illness,[61] as well as contention and conflict. **14** But if he was received, it is less and easier.

15 If the Sun in the revolution of the year was in Pisces and he had testimony in the year, and is made unfortunate, it indicates the abundance of his distresses and concern, and the badness of his condition, and fear for him. **16** And if he was made fortunate, he will be distressed for no reason, and he will have little[62] good.[63]

17 If the Sun in the revolution of the year was in Aries and he had testimony in the year, and he is free of the infortunes, it indicates the

---

[59] Sagittarius is the fifth from Leo, and Leo the fifth from Aries; but Jupiter and Mars are the planets used to calculate the Lot signifying pregnancy and children (Sahl, *Nativities* Ch. 5.3, **2** and **8-9**).

[60] **P** reads, "of his family."

[61] We would expect Saturn-Sun combinations to be bad, and Saturn does indicate illness; but the common Arabic word for "detriment" (which the Sun is in, while in Aquarius) is *wabāl*, "unhealthiness."

[62] **E**: "much."

[63] **B** adds a partly unreadable and undotted phrase that seems to say "in health, [and] his joy will multiply, and the goodness of his condition."

goodness of his condition, and the suitability of his religion, and travel. **18** Now if he was in the stakes, [the native] will have authority and benefit, and his condition will improve; and if he was made unfortunate, it indicates distresses in travel and the corruption of [his] religion.

19 If the Sun in the revolution of the year was in Taurus and he had testimony in it, and he is free of the infortunes, he will associate with the Sultan and will seek what is in [the Sultan's] power,[64] and he will benefit in it. **20** And if he was made unfortunate and did not have testimony, he will have something detestable from him, and distress and malice; and that is harsher if [the Sun] was in the stakes.

21 If the Sun in the revolution of the year was in Gemini and he had testimony in the year, and he is free of the infortunes, above the earth, looking at the Ascendant or the terminal point, it indicates an increase in friends and [the native's] retinue, and a child will be hoped for him. **22** And if he was made unfortunate, he will be distressed in relation to what we stated, and his needs will be made troublesome for him.

23 Now if the Sun in the revolution of the year was in Cancer and he had testimony in the year, and he is under the earth, [his] enemies will be haughty with him, and that will be harsher if the Moon was not looking at him.

Chapter V.6: On the indication of Venus if in the revolution she transited her own rooted position & the position of the rest of the planets

1 If Venus in the revolution of the year reached the rooted place of Saturn, it indicates his eagerness for sexual intercourse. **2** Now if Venus was appearing [out of the rays], free of the infortunes, that will be from a direction suitable to her; and if she was appearing [but] made unfortunate, then from a distasteful direction; and perhaps he will be publicly exposed in that. **3** And if Venus was under the earth, that will

---

[64] **E** and **P** say he will get "assets."

be hidden. **4** Now if Venus had the testimony in the year, he will be distressed because of women and filthy things, and an abundance of ablutions and a craving for water will happen to him; and if the testimony belongs to Saturn, it indicates travel and an abundance of sex, and the production of children will be hoped for him, or one of his women will be pregnant.

5 If Venus in the revolution of the year reached the rooted place of Jupiter, it indicates uprightness in religion, and traveling to the houses of worship and the doors of piety, and assets will come to him from inheritance, and he will travel to [his] brothers and friends, and will be told about[65] siblings having importance, and will benefit by them, and will become ill and [then] recover. **6** Now if Venus had testimony in the year, an ailment will afflict him from windiness and a pain in the throat; but if the testimony belonged to Jupiter, the ailment will be from black bile.

7 If Venus in the revolution of the year reached the place of Mars, and one of them had testimony in the year, it indicates marriage, and an abundance of sex, and eagerness for it. **8** And if one of them looked at its associate, then he will not <need to> seek out any sex and pleasure, or success in it.

9 If Venus at the revolution assembled with the Sun and she had testimony in the year, and they were both in the stakes, something detestable will afflict him and he will be out of the view of the Sultan; and if they were both withdrawing, an ailment will afflict him from heat. **10** And if the testimony in it belonged to the Sun, he will increase in his rank, and will gain authority and travel and have love.

11 If Venus in the revolution reached her own rooted place, and she had testimony in the year, he will renew what she had indicated in the root of the nativity, and he will increase in his retinue, garments, and furnishings.

12 If Venus in the revolution of the year reached the place of Mercury, and he had an indication in the year, it indicates the native's

---

[65] يستفيد. This can also mean "acquire" or "utilize," but the first suggests they are infants, while the second would be redundant, given what follows.

power in reasoning, culture, and eloquence. **13** And if the testimony belonged to Venus, he will associate with male and female <u>singers</u>, and the companions of <u>amusements</u>. **14** Now if they were both (or one of them) made unfortunate, something detestable will afflict him for that reason.

15 If Venus in the revolution of the year reached the place of the Moon, and the Moon was free of the infortunes, and one of them had testimony in the year, then it indicates the suitability of his condition and the condition of his family, and his associating with the <u>Sultan</u>, and an increase in his <u>brothers</u> (if it was possible), and gaining a <u>friend resembling a brother</u>.

Chapter V.7: On the indication of Mercury if in the revolution he transited his own rooted position & the position of the rest of the planets

1 If Mercury in the revolution of years reached the rooted place of Saturn, and Mercury had testimony in the year, and he is free of the corrupting infortunes, it indicates his <u>travel</u>, and the increase of his condition[66] in that travel, and it will be hoped that a <u>child</u> is born to him. **2** Now if Saturn had testimony in the year, it indicates the ruin of the children, and the <u>illness</u> of the owner of the revolution, and the confusion[67] of his views, and the corruption of his religion, and his abstaining from many works, especially works of piety.

3 If Mercury in the revolution of the year reached the rooted place of Jupiter, and one of them had testimony in the year, he will have <u>status from one who is superior to him</u>, and he will increase in his knowledge and culture, and will <u>marry</u>. **4** Now if the one which had the testimony was corrupted or made unfortunate, corruption will enter upon him from the direction of the indication of the infortune, and it indicates conflict with enemies.

---

[66] **P**: "the badness of his condition."
[67] Or even, "insanity" (تخليط).

5 If Mercury in the revolution of the year reached the place of Mars, and they[68] had testimony in the year, it indicates that the owner of the revolution will concoct lies and falsehoods, and will spread rumors about what does not exist. **6** But if one of them was retrograde, it indicates theft. **7** Now if the testimony belonged to Mercury, it indicates the badness of his condition, and an ailment from heat and blood will afflict him; and if he was corrupted by Mars in the revolution, death will be feared for him. **8** And if along with his corruption by Mars he is entering under the rays, killing will be feared for him while in exile.[69]

9 If Mercury in the revolution of the year assembled with the Sun, and [Mercury] had testimony in it, and they were in the stakes, in a suitable condition, he will gain status from the Sultan, and that is more confirmed [if it is] the Midheaven; and if they were both withdrawing, it will be below what I mentioned. **10** And if the testimony in the year belonged to the Sun, he will have good from slaves, students, and everyone who is in his power, and they will be sincere toward him.

11 If Mercury in the revolution of the year reached the place of Venus, and he had testimony in it, it indicates the seeking of stories and poetry, and singing, and he will track down places of pleasure. **12** And if the testimony in the year belonged to Venus, it indicates an increase in knowledge, and seeking every [beautiful] thing he imagines.

13 Now if Mercury in the revolution of the year reached his own rooted place, and he had testimony in [the year], and he is in the stakes, in a suitable condition, he will increase in his power and be praised by name. **14** And if he had an indication for assets, it indicates acquiring assets; and if his indication was for brothers, he will have good from his brothers; and you look like that in the rest of the houses. **15** And if he was made unfortunate or corrupted, it introduces something detestable in the category of that thing.

16 And if Mercury in the revolution of the year reached the place of the Moon, and the Moon had testimony in the year, it indicates travel

---

[68] So read **B** and **P**. **E** reads "he," not specifying which one, but it would not be Mercury since he is singled out below. My guess is that this means "either one, but especially Mars."

[69] Or simply, "while abroad" or "while in a foreign country" (في الغربة).

as well as quarreling he will have with enemies in that traveling of his, and fear afflicting him from them. **17** And if the testimony in the year belonged to Mercury, then he will have much good, and his enemies will multiply, and he will be praised. **18** Now if the Moon was unfortunate, he will be distressed because of what we mentioned.

Chapter V.8: On the indication of the Moon if in the revolution of the year she transited her own rooted position & the position of the rest of the planets

1 If the Moon in the revolution of the year reached the place of Saturn, and the Moon had testimony in the year, it indicates marrying old women and having sex with them; now if along with that she was made unfortunate, quarrels will happen to him. **2** And if, along with her misfortune she had an indication for death in that year, it will be feared for him in it. **3** And if the testimony belongs to Saturn, bad reports will reach him, distressing him.

4 If the Moon in the revolution of the year reached the position of Jupiter, and she had testimony in it, and she was in a suitable condition, not made unfortunate, it indicates traveling to a place full of water, then he will travel from it to another one, and good will reach him in that direction of his; and if she was made unfortunate he will encounter something detestable, and illness will afflict him. **5** And if the testimony in the year belongs to Jupiter and he is looking at the Moon, then a child will be born to him.

6 Now if the Moon in the revolution of the year reached the place of Mars, and she had testimony in it, and is in a suitable condition, received, he will gain authority along with war, or he will associate with people waging war, and a child will be born to him, and pains from heat and moisture will happen to him (such as [in the] blood). **7** Now if she was in a bad condition or made unfortunate, the ailment will be powerful, and he will encounter evil and something detestable from the Sultan, and death will be feared for one of his children. **8** But if the testimony belonged to Mars, hardship will afflict him from one who is above him (such as the Sultan), and he will go on a journey that is criticized. **9** And if the condition of the Moon was like that upon her reaching, in the revolution, the position of Mars in the root, [but] then the Moon assembled with him[70] in one of the [other] days, or she looked at him, then the owner of the revolution will have his blood spilled on that day in some way, and he will quarrel and be dissatisfied; and that is more confirmed if she looked at that place in that time.

10 If the Moon in the revolution of the year assembled with the Sun, and she had testimony in [the year], it indicates something detestable which will come to him from the Sultan or from one who is more elevated than he is (like fathers and lords). **11** But if the testimony belonged to the Sun in the year, he will gain authority and good, and it will be feared for his mother and those women resembling her; and that is harsher if she is entering into burning. **12** And as for if she was going out from it, then it is easier.

13 If the Moon in the revolution of the year reached the place of Venus, and [the Moon] had testimony in [the year] and she is received, free of the infortunes, it indicates that travel will be troublesome for him (if he wanted [travel]), and perhaps he will not travel in that year; and he will be elevated in his family and be delighted in them, and will increase in his family and his retinue, and he will live in comfort, be praised, and be happy, and will acquire real estate, and be devoted to building. **14** Now if she was made unfortunate, he will be distressed because of what we mentioned. **15** And if the testimony in the year belongs to Venus, he will have rank and power and authority, and his family will benefit in this, and he will travel to the houses of worship, and to well-known people of piety.

16 If the Moon in the revolution of the year reached the place of Mercury, and she had testimony in it, it indicates that he will travel in a direction his enemy hopes for, and he will encounter conflict and hardship from the enemies or because of them. **17** And if the testimony belonged to Mercury in the year, it indicates that his condition will

---

[70] **E:** "Mars assembled with her."

be good and he will acquire <u>assets</u>, and his enemies will multiply, and good will be spoken about him.

18 If the Moon in the revolution of the year reached her own rooted place, and the revolution is by night, and she is in the stakes, in a suitable condition, free of the infortunes, then it indicates that he will be healthy in his body, and he will have reputation, power, and status from the Sultan. **19** Then you should look at what she had indicated in the root in terms of assets, brothers, and other things, for she will indicate the suitability of [his] condition in that thing. **20** Now if the Moon (or the rest of the planets) looked at her rooted position, from whatever direction that connection and looking was, some of what she had indicated in the root will appear, except that if she looked at that position from the square or opposition, it will be more powerful.

[Additional rules for transits]

21 And if the Moon was made unfortunate in one of the positions, and she reached[71] the square of her place or at its opposition, then it indicates something detestable and harm on that day.

22 And if an infortune in the revolution reached the position of the Moon in the root, and that infortune was [also] doing violence to the Moon in the revolution of the year, then it indicates detestable things and a powerful illness, especially if the lord of the year was an infortune and in the revolution it was in a bad position. **23** But if the Moon in the revolution terminated at the position of an infortune in the root it is also like that, and indicates something like what it indicates when the year terminates at an infortune.

24 And if the Moon in the revolution of the year was made fortunate or unfortunate, then when she reaches the body of that fortune or infortune (or the rays of one of them) in her course or by calculating one day or month for every degree, it indicates good or evil according to the nature of that planet.

---

[71] Reading for "terminated at," so as not to confuse it with profections (also in **22** and **24**).

25 If in her course the Moon reached a planet which indicated good in the root or in the revolution, it will produce its indication on that day; and it is like that if she reached a planet which had indicated evil in the root or in the revolution.

26 And if one of the planets in any of the times transited the degree in which the distribution or the distributor was, or the degree of the Ascendant of the root, or the degree of the Ascendant of the revolution, or the degree of the terminal point, or it reached the degree of the Moon of the root or the revolution, or any of the rays,[72] or the Lots, or the twelfth-parts, or their lords, then it will activate part of its own indication as well as the indication of that thing. **27** And if the planet looked at the position of another, from whatever direction the looking was, it will produce some of its indication.

28 And if the planet which had testimony in the year transited the twelfth-part of one of the signs or planets on one of the days, it indicates something like what the sign or planet which owned the twelfth-part, indicates. **29** And an example of that is that the twelfth-part of the fourth house fell in the second sign: so we said when the planet which had testimony in the year transited that position, he will be devoted to the conditions of real estate, assets, expenses, and crops: so this is the summary of their indication in this way.

30 And each one of the planets has indications over other things in accordance with the house of each one relative to the other, except that we have left out [any] mention of them, because one ought to seek information about that from the things which have preceded [this] mention of them.[73]

31 And the suitability of the condition of each one of them in the two times, and its badness, varies much from what we have stated about it, as well as what two planets indicate in this subject of the good and the bad. **32** So upon [any planet's] reaching the position of another in the revolution, you should look: for if that planet was [also]

---

[72] This may simply mean the Moon's rays.

[73] Abū Ma'shar must have some other sense in which the planets' houses have several meanings relative to one another, because he has certainly done enough of that already.

looking at it in the root, that thing will be because of an old matter. **33** And if its looking at it was in the revolution alone, that is because of a recent matter. **34** And if its looking at it was in both times, it is because of an old *and* new matter. **35** And if it is not looking at it in either, that is from a matter not known.

BOOK VI: ON THE CONDITION OF THE PLANETS IN THE SIGNS[1]

And it is in six chapters

Chapter VI.1: On the lord of the orb

1 In the Books which preceded, we stated the indications of the planets in isolation in accordance with the revolutions of the years, and the sum of their indications in the houses of the celestial circle.[2] **2** Now as for this Book, we will state their indications in the twelve houses according to what is needed by this Book, and we will begin in this chapter by mentioning the "lord of the orb."[3]

3 And Hermes has said concerning the hidden secrets, that the leaders of the Babylonian scholars used to study this carefully (of what there was amongst them), and they concealed it from those who were not capable in the knowledge of it [and] who [would only] imitate their knowledge—and it has a powerful indication in the root of nativities and the revolutions of years.

4 And it is that you look at the lord of the hour in which the native was born, and assign it to the Ascendant and to the first year from his birth, and by means of its conditions you judge the health of his body or its sickliness, just as you judge by means of the lord of the Ascendant of the root.

5 And you assign the lord of the second hour from it to the second house from the Ascendant of the root, and to the second year, and by means of its condition in the root and in that year, you judge the condition of assets (and other things), just as you judge by means of the lord of the second house.

---

[1] The full title runs: "The sixth statement on the revolution of the years of nativities, on the condition of the planets in the signs."

[2] This must mean the domiciles of the planets (e.g. the house of Saturn, Jupiter, etc.) in Book V.

[3] For a worked example, see the Introduction.

6 And you assign the lord of the third hour from it to the third house from the Ascendant of the root, and to the third year, and by means of its condition in the root and in that year you judge the condition of brothers and sisters (and other things besides them), just as you judge by means of the lord of the third house.

7 And you assign the lord of the fourth hour from it to the fourth house from the Ascendant of the root, and to the fourth year, and by means of its condition in the root and in that year you judge the condition of the fathers (and the rest of the occasions) just as you judge by means of the condition of the lord of the fourth house. **8** And you work like that with the lords of the hours in succession, assigning the lord of each hour to one of the rooted houses, so that the lord of the twelfth hour from the lord of the hour in which the native was born, belongs to the twelfth house from the Ascendant of the root, and to the twelfth year, and the lord of the thirteenth hour from it belongs to the Ascendant of the root and the thirteenth year, and the lord of the fourteenth hour from it belongs to the house of assets and the fourteenth year.

9 And the lord of each of the hours is called by two names. **10** The first of them is particular, like the name of the house which it resembles in the indication: so the lord belonging the first hour is referred to as "the lord of the hour of the Ascendant," and the lord of the second hour from it is referred to as "the lord of the hour of the house of assets," and the lord of the third hour from it is referred to as "the lord of the hour of the house of siblings," and the lord of the fourth hour from it is referred to as "the lord of the hour of the house of fathers"—and likewise the lord of each hour from them is called by the name of the house to which it has a likeness in its indication. **11** And the second name is general, and it is that each one of them (whichever hour it is the lord of) is referred to as the "lord of the orb."

House	1	2	3	4	5	6	7	8	9	10	11	12
Age	0	1	2	3	4	5	6	7	8	9	10	11
Hour	N	2	3	4	5	6	7	N	2	3	4	5
Age	12	13	14	15	16	17	18	19	20	21	22	23
Hour	6	7	N	2	3	4	5	6	7	N	2	3
Age	24	25	26	27	28	29	30	31	32	33	34	35
Hour	4	5	6	7	N	2	3	4	5	6	7	N
Age	36	37	38	39	40	41	42	43	44	45	46	47
Hour	2	3	4	5	6	7	N	2	3	4	5	6
Age	48	49	50	51	52	53	54	55	56	57	58	59
Hour	7	N	2	3	4	5	6	7	N	2	3	4
Age	60	61	62	63	64	65	66	67	68	69	70	71
Hour	5	6	7	N	2	3	4	5	6	7	N	2
Age	72	73	74	75	76	77	78	79	80	81	82	83
Hour	3	4	5	6	7	N	2	3	4	5	6	7

Figure 89: Table of lords of the orb (continuous loop version)[4]

12 And by means of the condition of the lord of each hour in the root and in the revolution of that year, you judge good and evil just as you judge by means of the lord of the year [by profection]. **13** So if the lord of the first hour (and it is the "lord of the hour of the Ascendant") is in a suitable condition in the root,[5] it indicates the safety of the body in the first year; and if it was in a bad condition, it indicates ailments and illnesses in it. **14** And if the lord of the second hour (and it is the "lord of the hour of the house of assets") was in a suitable condition in the root *and* in the revolution of the second year,[6] it indicates the suitability of the condition in assets; and if it was in a bad condition it indicates corruption in them. **15** And if the lord of the third hour (and

---

[4] In this table, "N" indicates the planetary hour lord for the natal hour, with the others listed in order after it in a continuous loop. For an alternative version, see the Introduction.

[5] Since this planet rules the native's first year, there cannot be a solar revolution yet.

[6] The second year of life is the first one which can have a solar revolution.

it is the "lord of the hour of the house of siblings") was in a suitable condition in the two times,[7] it indicates the goodness of their condition, and an increase in them (and if it was in a male sign, that will be in the male siblings; and if it was in a female sign, that will be in the sisters); and if it was made unfortunate, it indicates the corruption of their condition, or their ruin. **16** And if the "lord of the hour of the house of fathers" was made unfortunate in a male sign, the condition of the father will be bad; and if it was in a female sign, the condition of the mother will be bad. **17** And you look like that for the lords of the hours of the rest of the twelve houses.[8]

18 And whenever, in a revolution of one of the years, [1] the "lord of the hour of the Ascendant" of the root, and [2] the "lord of the hour of the Midheaven" of the root, and [3] the "lord of the hour of the house of hope," are in a suitable condition, made fortunate, they indicate the suitability of [1] the condition in that year, as well as [2] success in beneficial actions and authority, and [3] [other] benefits. **19** And likewise, if the lord of the hour of the sign of the terminal point[9] and the lord of the hour of these two positions from it[10] were like that, it adds in the fitness of the year; and if they were in a bad condition, they indicate the contrary of that.

---

[7] That is, the root and the second solar revolution (the revolution for the third year of life, Age 2).

[8] In this way, the lord of the orb simply becomes a kind of special or partnering lord of the year. For example, in the third year of life the Ascendant will profect to the third house, and it and its lord will not only indicate (1) the native's life generally because they rule the profected Ascendant, but they will also have (2) special indications for the brothers. But the lord of the orb, too, *because* it is specially assigned to the third planetary hour and the third house, will *also* be (2) a special significator of siblings. In the next sentence we will see that the lord of the orb assigned to that house (or perhaps only certain houses) can also have indications for any year, but again *for that topic*.

[9] That is, the lord of the orb assigned to the natal sign of the profection.

[10] That is, the lord of the orb assigned to the tenth and eleventh *relative to* the sign of the year.

Chapter VI.2: On the turning of the houses of the root, & the direction of degrees

1 Now, every one of the seven planets, the twelve houses, and the twelve Lots,[11] is turned at the revolutions of years from its own position (a year for every sign), and is directed from its degree (a year for every degree); and when any of them, by turning or by direction, reaches a sign or planetary fortune or infortune, it produces the indication of that sign or planet (whether good fortune or misfortune), according to their indication:

2 As for the planets, the Sun is turned in the houses as well as directed for rank, works, and authority, the Moon for the accidents of the body, Jupiter for assets, Venus for women, amusement, delight, and fornication—and likewise every planet is turned in the houses as well as directed from its own place, degree by degree, for making conclusions about what it indicates.

3 And as for the houses of the circle, the Ascendant of the root as well as the Moon is turned and directed for the knowledge of the condition of the body.

4 For the knowledge of the condition of assets, the Lot of Fortune of the root, and the Lot of assets,[12] and the house of assets, are turned and directed—and along with that you look at every one of the lords of the triplicities of the luminary which had the shift in the root,[13] [to see] what its condition was at that time, and what its condition is in the revolution of that year, and especially the lord of the triplicity which indicated his condition at that time of his lifespan.[14]

---

[11] Reading for, "and the Lots, and the twelfth-parts," as the twelfth-parts are not discussed below.

[12] See Sahl, *Nativities* Ch. 2.15, **1**: from the lord of the second to the second, projected from the Ascendant (and probably not reversed by night).

[13] That is, the triplicity lords of the sect light.

[14] For example, if the native was older, one would use the second triplicity lord (or for many Persian- and Arabic- language astrologers, the third one).

5 For the knowledge of the condition of the siblings, the house of siblings of the root as well as its Lot[15] are turned and directed; then along with that you look at the triplicity lords of the sign in which Mars was at the root, [to see] what its condition was at that time and what its condition was in the revolution of that year (and the first lord of its triplicity indicates the older ones of the siblings, and the second lord of its triplicity indicates the middle ones of the siblings, and the third lord of its triplicity indicates the condition of the younger ones of the siblings).

6 For the knowledge of the condition of the fathers, the Sun or Saturn is turned and directed (whichever one of the two had the shift in the root),[16] as well as the Lot of the father[17] and the fourth house of the root; then at the revolution of every year you look at the condition of the planet which was the indicator of the father, be it the Sun or Saturn. **7** And you look like that at the indicator of the brothers and sisters,[18] and the rest of what one judges by in the root.

8 For the knowledge of the condition of the mother, Venus or the Moon is <turned and> directed (whichever of them had the shift in the root),[19] as well as the Lot of the mother[20] and the tenth house of the root.[21]

---

[15] See Sahl, *Nativities* Ch. 3.11, **2**. The usual Lot (and specifically for brothers) is from Saturn to Jupiter, projected from the Ascendant, reversed at night (as confirmed by Firmicus Maternus in *Mathesis* VI.32, although many sources do not explicitly state so, or even want it to be the same by night).

[16] That is, the Sun in a diurnal chart and Saturn in a nocturnal one.

[17] See Sahl, *Nativities* Ch. 4.14, **1-2**. This is normally from the Sun to Saturn, projected from the Ascendant, reversed at night.

[18] Abū Ma'shar may mean something like using Mars for the middle brothers, Mercury for the younger brothers, Venus for sisters, and so on.

[19] That is, Venus in a diurnal chart and the Moon in a nocturnal one.

[20] This is calculated by day from Venus to the Moon, projected from the Ascendant, and reversed by night.

[21] To be consistent, Abū Ma'shar should examine the triplicity lords of Venus or the Moon.

9 For the knowledge of the condition of the children, the house of children of the root as well as its Lot²² is turned and directed.²³

10 For the knowledge of the condition of slaves, the sixth house of the root is turned and directed, as well as the Lot of slaves.²⁴ **11** And for the knowledge of the condition of illnesses, the sixth house of the root is turned and directed, as well as the Lot of illnesses.²⁵

12 For the knowledge of his condition with women, the seventh house of the root is turned and directed, as well as its Lot.²⁶

13 For the knowledge of death and catastrophes, the eighth house of the root is turned and directed, as well as its Lot.²⁷

14 For the knowledge of the condition of travel, the ninth house of the root is turned and directed, as well as its Lot.²⁸

15 For the knowledge of the condition of authority and rank, the tenth house of the root is turned and directed, as well as its Lot.²⁹

16 For the knowledge of <the condition of> hope and friends, the eleventh house of the root is turned and directed, as well as its Lot.³⁰

---

²² This is calculated by day from Jupiter to Saturn, projected from the Ascendant, and reversed by night.

²³ To be consistent, Abū Ma'shar should examine the triplicity lords of Jupiter.

²⁴ See Sahl, *Nativities* Ch. 6.10, **20**: from Mercury to the Moon, projected from the Ascendant, and reversed by night.

²⁵ See Sahl, *Nativities* Ch. 6.3.4, **2**: from Saturn to Mars, projected from the Ascendant, and reversed by night.

²⁶ For the Hermes version, see Sahl, *Nativities* Ch. 7.1, **223-24**. For men, this is calculated from Saturn to Venus, projected from the Ascendant, and reversed by night. For women, it is calculated from Venus to Saturn, projected from the Ascendant, and reversed by night. To be consistent, Abū Ma'shar should examine the triplicity lords of Venus.

²⁷ For the version used by Māshā'allāh, see Sahl, *Nativities* Ch. 8.6, **1**. It is calculated from the Moon to the eighth, and projected from Saturn (probably not reversed by night).

²⁸ See Sahl, *Nativities* Ch. 9.4, **37**: from the lord of the ninth to the ninth, and projected from the Ascendant (probably not reversed by night).

²⁹ Abū Ma'shar probably means his Lot of authority from *Gr. Intr.* VIII.4: from Saturn to the Moon, projected from the Ascendant, and reversed by night. (See Sahl, *Nativities* Ch. 10.2.5, **1-3**.) But there is also a Lot of action or work, from Mercury to Mars, projected from the Ascendant, and reversed by night (Sahl, *Nativities* Ch. 10.1.1, **14-17**), as well as others. See the table in Sahl, *Nativities* Ch. 10.2.5.

17 For the knowledge of the condition of enemies and riding animals, the twelfth house of the root is turned and directed, as well as its Lot.[31]

18 And if, for any of what we have stated (such as assets, authority, or the rest of the things of his life), there were [other] indicators from among the planets, houses, and Lots, then each of those indicators is turned and directed individually, for the knowledge of the condition of that thing. **19** And every planet and house has indications for many things: so if knowledge of something is needed in the revolutions of the year (of what[ever] any of them indicates), then that rooted planet or sign is turned and directed.[32] **20** And if anything does not have an indicator from among the houses of the circle, while one of the Lots certainly indicates it, then that Lot is turned and directed.

[A quadrant cusp in a different sign]

21 And sometimes in one of the times the houses of the circle will withdraw so that they come to be in another sign: so when it comes to be like that, *directing* it should happen from the actual degree it rests in, by the portions of the hours and the right circle.[33] **22** But as for their *turning*, that will be in two ways: the first of them is [1] from the sign which has the indication of that house by counting,[34] and the second is [2] from the sign in which that degree actually falls. **23** And an example of that is if the [natal] degree of the house of children fell in

---

[30] See Sahl, *Nativities* Ch. 11.1, **29**: by day from the Moon to Mercury, projected from the Ascendant, and reversed by night.

[31] See Sahl, *Nativities* Ch. 12.1, **48**, and my long footnote there. Three of the possibilities include from Mercury to the Lot of Fortune (reversed by night), Mercury to the Moon (reversed by night), and the lord of the twelfth to the twelfth (probably not reversed), all projected from the Ascendant.

[32] For example, real estate is an indication of the fourth, not mentioned in **6** above, and according to Abū Ma'shar (*Gr. Intr.* VIII.4), it has a Lot calculated from Saturn to the Moon, projected from the Ascendant, not reversed by night.

[33] That is, by normal proportional semi-arcs.

[34] That is, by whole-sign houses.

the sixth sign: so, the direction for the knowledge of the condition of children will be from that very same degree. **24** But the turning in the indication of the condition of children will be from two signs: one of them is [1] from the fifth house by counting, and the second is [2] from the sixth sign (in which the degree of the house of children fell).

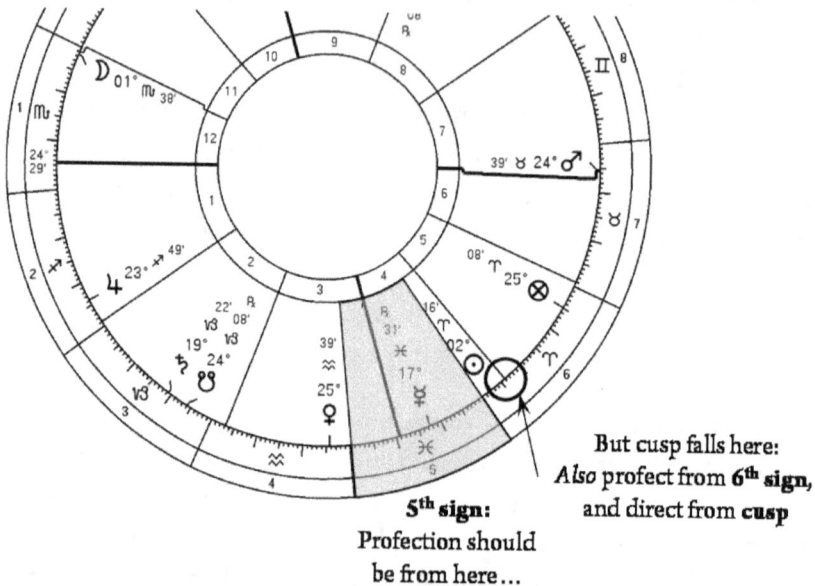

Figure 90: Abū Ma'shar's theory when cusp falls on different sign (VI.2, 21-24)

[*Two cusps on the same sign*]

25 And if the division[35] of two [different] houses fell into a single sign, then the direction for the indication of each house will be from that very degree, while as for the turning, for *both* of them it will be turned from that sign. **26** And an example of that is if the degree of the house of friends and of the house of enemies both occurred in the twelfth sign: so for each one of them you direct from its own true degree, and the sign is turned for both of them from that very same sign.

---

[35] Or, "apportioning" (قسمة).

BOOK VI: LORD OF ORB, THE ASCENDANT, CONNECTIONS

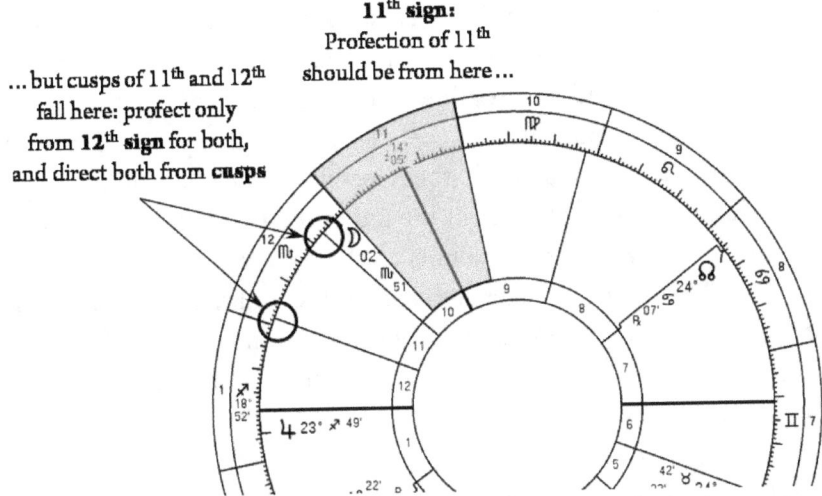

Figure 91: Abū Ma'shar's theory when two cusps are on same sign (VI.2, 25-26)

Chapter VI.3: On the indication of the sign of the terminal point & the Ascendant of the revolution of the year, when one of them coincides with one of the houses of the root, & in the revolution one of the seven planets was in it[36]

[General difference between profections and revolutions]

1 The Ascendant of the revolution and its lord, in the revolutions of years, have an indication resembling the indication of the sign of the terminal point and the lord of the year, except that the sign of the terminal point and its lord are more powerful than them in the indication; and they both[37] indicate, more so than that, the specifica-

---

[36] Simply put: this is when a planet is transiting in the sign of the year or the Ascendant of the year, at the revolution. For example, if the profection came to the natal third sign, Virgo (or the solar revolution Ascendant is on Virgo), and Venus happens to be transiting in it at the revolution.

[37] The sign of the year and the lord of the year.

tion[38] of the matters which they were an indicator of in the root, and[39] they both have an original cause in the root. **2** But as for the Ascendant of the revolution and its lord, they indicate more the things which occur incidentally,[40] and whose causes take place in that year. **3** But if the sign of the terminal point and[41] the Ascendant of the revolution were a single house of the rooted circle, the indication of the thing which that house had indicated (of good or evil) will be powerful, and in addition to that the particular characteristic of the indication of different things[42] will [also] be made available to him; and you should follow suit in what we will state of the particular characteristic of the indication of each house.

[Multiple revolutionary planets in sign of the year or Ascendant of year]

4 The statement of Hermes: And if in addition to that[43] one of the seven planets was in one of them[44] in the revolution, then it will indicate something—and the indication of a planet which has testimony in the year or in that sign, will be [even] more apparent.[45] **5** But if in the revolution of the year there were two or more planets in it, [1] each one of them by itself will indicate something different from what the other indicates, in the manner we will state; and with the occur-

---

[38] Reading as تحديد. But this might also be تجديد, "renewal." The point is that the root is more closely tied to the profection than to the revolution.

[39] Reading this last clause as a blend from the manuscripts. **B**: "or they have an original cause" or "the first of them [is] an original cause." **P** and **T**: "and it has an original cause." **E**: "and it has a cause in the root."

[40] تعرض.

[41] Reading for "or."

[42] This seems to mean, "things related to the house, but not necessarily anything clearly tied to its *natal* promise."

[43] This is a little awkward because Abū Ma'shar seems to be excerpting from material by Hermes, so we do not know what "that" refers to. But we can imagine that Abū Ma'shar is still building up his scenario in which the sign of the year and the Ascendant of the year, are the same sign.

[44] That is, the sign of the profection or the Ascendant of the revolution.

[45] That is, not just *any* planet, but one with dignity there, or ruling the Ascendant of the year, etc.

rence of two of them or more in one place, they will also have [2] a blending of their natures, especially in the indication of things apart from what we have stated—except that here we have left out [any] mention of that, as well as stating the indication of what will be produced by them upon the meeting of each one with the other, because that would resemble the statement about them in the *Book of Nativities*;[46] whereas we will [only] mention here what is appropriate and pertains to that in *this* book.

[Sign/Ascendant of year on natal Ascendant, revolutionary planet in it][47]

6 So if the sign of the terminal point or the Ascendant of the year coincided with the Ascendant of the root of the nativity, then it indicates the confirming of the rooted indications, and their strength; and if they were *both* [on] the Ascendant of the root, it is more confirmatory and powerful in the indication. **7** So if the lord of the Ascendant was in a suitable condition, in an excellent position in the houses of the circle, then he will be healthy in body and will gain the good (and if it was the contrary of that, the contrary). **8** But in particular it indicates that he will be victorious over those contending [with him], and he will associate with nobles and leaders, and he will be respected, and assets, gifts, and rewards will come to him (which have value), although he will be distressed in the sixth, eighth, tenth, and twelfth months.

9 Now if Saturn was in it in the revolution, and that was by day, then his older brothers or sisters will find detestable things, or one of them will be destroyed; and if the revolution was by night, then the harm will reach *him*, and [his] people will be hostile to him.

10 And if Jupiter was in it, then he will increase in his power,[48] and he will gain assets, and if he traveled he would have leadership and

---

[46] Abū Ma'shar may be thinking of his *Book of the Judgments of Nativities*, in Oxford, Bodleian, Hunt. 546. But in my Introduction I will refer to his theory of mixtures from *Gr. Intr.*

[47] The planetary significations here are based on Rhetorius Ch. 57 (pp. 51-56).

good on his journey, and he will return to his homeland and free himself of every adversity he gets in that year, and he will see what he loves in his enemies, but without him treating them badly.

11 And if Mars was in it, he will have much irritation and conflict, and an ailment and misfortune will afflict him from hot things, or from iron, and he will associate with commanders and the army, and he will travel and toil.

12 And if the Sun was in it, he will increase in his power and rank, and he will be in charge of works for the Sultan, and a disaster in assets will afflict his older brothers and sisters, and he will be distressed because of fathers.

13 And if Venus was in it, then he will associate with perfume vendors and dyers, and the wealthy, nobles, and kings, and ascetics and the religious, and he will see what he loves from them, and benefits and garments will come to him, and dishes and perfume, and he will do a good thing for the people, and he will devote himself to servant-girls and harlots, and he will gain assets.

14 And if Mercury was in it, he will devote himself to logic, the sciences, speech,[49] and his power will be elevated over his peers, and he will increase in his assets, cleverness, and thought, and he will collect books and seek the hidden sciences, the stars, and philosophy, as well as eloquence, and he will devote himself to the surveying of lands, buying and selling, and servants, partners, and employees.

15 And if the Moon was in it and she is empty in course, then his anxieties will multiply, and his demands will be complicated for him, and he will be disturbed in his body. 16 But if she was made fortunate, then he will associate with nobles and the religious, and will devote himself to mosques and charity for his neighbors. 17 And if she was in it and she is under the rays of the Sun, then different ailments will afflict him in the eye and in other hidden places besides that.

18 And if the Head was in it, he will increase in his power and good fortune, and will associate with leaders, and will see what he loves

---

[48] Or perhaps, "rank" (قدره).

[49] This can also refer to theological interpretation (الكلام).

from them. **19** And if the Tail was in it, then he will be injured by the rabble and will contend with them.

[Sign or Ascendant of year on natal second, revolutionary planet in it][50]

20 If the sign of the terminal point or the Ascendant of the year coincided with the house of assets of the root, then it will manifest everything which was indicated in the root concerning the matter of assets (of good or evil), and it indicates especially that he will earn assets in [that year], [and] they will remain with him; and if he quarreled with a man because of assets, he will profit from it. **21** And if he gave out money in the buying of slaves, building, the cultivation of lands, farming, planting, business, partnership, taking and giving, and because of construction, and approaching the powerful and the nobles, and managing conflicts and demands about old matters, it will be suitable, and his joy and delight will increase. **22** And if he moved to a new house or invited a man to his home, it will be suitable, though he will be distressed in the second month.[51]

23 Now if Saturn was in it at the revolution, assets will be lost for him, and he will be restricted in his possessions, and he will take on debt, and loss and damage will afflict him because of old men and slaves, or people who were slaves but were emancipated, and something detestable will afflict his parents.

24 And if Jupiter was in it, then his assets will be good, and if he spent something of them he will be compensated for it by more than what he spent, and he will be entrusted with the assets of people, and will hoard assets or bury them in the earth.

25 And if Mars was in it, then assets will be stolen from him, and what assets he acquired will not remain with him, and he will spend assets because of travel.

---

[50] The planetary significations here do not well match Rhetorius Ch. 57 (pp. 56-61).
[51] **T**: "it will be suitable in the second month."

26 And if the Sun was in it, then he will not[52] benefit from the assets of his father, though he will earn assets from suitable, prominent personalities,[53] and he will be devoted to the loaning of assets and the situations of debts.

27 And if Venus was in it his assets will be suitable, and gifts will be presented to him, and dishes and furnishings obtained.

28 And if Mercury was in it, then he will occupy himself with business, buying and selling, servants, and loaning and debts, and he will be anxious because of loss and betrayal, lying, falsehood, and cheating.

29 And if the Moon was in it, then he will devote himself to different situations in the matters of assets, and it will reduce a part of his assets.

30 And if the Head was in it, then he will be greedy for assets. **31** And if the Tail was in it, harm will afflict him and his father in assets.

[Sign or Ascendant of year on natal third, revolutionary planet in it][54]

32 And if the sign of the terminal point or the Ascendant of the year coincided with the house of siblings of the root, then there will appear what it had indicated in the root, of the good or evil of the condition of the siblings, travel, and the rest of the indications which resembles that house; and in particular it indicates distress because of relatives, and the illness of children,[55] and the hostility of some of [his] friends, and moving from place to place (or travel), and some of the brothers and sisters will have anxieties, or they will become ill, and people who have power will want him, and he will connect with nobles and kings, and he will see what he loves from them, and he will act alone in the management of things, and he will delight in women or marriage,[56] and he

---

[52] To me this seems like an error, since he does gain assets from other Solar-type people in the next part of the sentence.
[53] Or more simply, "ways" (وجوه).
[54] The planetary significations here are based on Rhetorius Ch. 57 (pp. 65-67).
[55] To me this seems wrong, and should more likely read "parents," as the third is the twelfth (illness, distress) from the fourth. **T** reads, "and some of the children."
[56] **E** and **P** read "he will marry."

will see love from [women], and he will eat of good food and it will surround him, though he will have distress in the fifth and ninth months. 33 Now if fortunes in a suitable condition are in it in the revolution, then gifts will be presented to him, and the nobles as well as those having affluence will need him, and the outcome of what deeds he does will be praised, and he will free himself of detestable things.

34 And if Saturn is in it in the revolution, then he will gain good and good fortune, and he will be sad about his friends, and some of [his] enemies will deceive him, and he will be annoyed with the people of his house, and he will stay with people whom he cares about, and he will devote himself to scholars, the religious, and the houses of worship.

35 And if Jupiter was in it, then he will benefit from women, and they will benefit from him, and he will increase in his rank because of them, and he will enter the mansions of nobles and kings, and he will see what he loves from them.

36 And if Mars was in it, then he will toil or travel, and he will associate with harlots (and in the view of the people), and he will swear false oaths, and something detestable as well as hardship will afflict him from the people of his house, and they will be hostile to him, and perhaps some of his relatives will be ruined.

37 And if the Sun was in it he will do virtuous works, and he will increase in them (as long as it is with God).[57]

38 And if Venus was in it, then he will associate with the religious, and scholars, and the masters of forces[58] and talismans.

39 And if Mercury was in it, then he will associate with poets[59] or soothsayers, and the masters of augury, and because of that he will gain what is good.

---

[57] ما عند الله.

[58] الحيل, but this word also suggests tricks and ruses, so probably includes false magicians.

[59] Literally "poetry" (الشِّعر), but this root also connotes the performance of religious ceremonies.

40 And if the Moon was in it, then he will increase in his rank and assets, and benefit from buying and selling, and he will be devoted to mosques and the masters of jurisprudence, and his travels will be praised, and he will be entrusted with the assets of some women.

41 And if the Head was in it he will delight in his brothers and sisters, and they will gain what is good. **42** And if the Tail was in it, he will be distressed by travel and relatives, and his relatives will get something detestable.

[Sign or Ascendant of year on natal fourth, revolutionary planet in it][60]

43 If the sign of the terminal point or Ascendant of the year coincided with the house of fathers of the root, then there will appear what it had indicated in the root about the condition of fathers (of good and bad), and the condition of immovable property as well; and in particular it indicates that he will become ill, and something detestable will afflict the people of his house, and some of the people will be hostile to him without [there being any] misdeed, and people will slander him and say something detestable about him, and loss will afflict him, and he will be distressed in the fourth, seventh, and twelfth months. **44** And if the fortunes were in it in the revolution, then he will get good from planting, building, and the works he will do, and he will be delighted in the people of his house as well as his friends.

45 Now if Saturn was in it at the revolution, then he will discover buried assets, or he will concern himself with the digging of wells and [with] their conditions, and it will destroy part of his home, and he will concern himself with building, and he will become ill, and conflict will occur between him and his parents.

46 And if Jupiter was in it, then he will gain benefit and good from hidden, prominent people,[61] and he will devote himself to birds and riding animals, and their care, and the houses of religion, building, and repairs.

---

[60] The planetary significations here are close to Rhetorius Ch. 57 (pp. 69-71).
[61] Or perhaps, "in hidden ways" (من الوجوه الخفية).

47 And if Mars was in it, then he will be devoted to messengers, the army, and the jockeys of riding animals, and an ailment will afflict him which he will need to treat with iron, and he will be distressed because of some women, and the people will not praise him for [his] good deeds.

48 And if the Sun was in it harm will afflict him, as well as an ailment from the corruption of the brain, and it will corrupt a portion of [his] father's assets.

49 And if Venus was in it he will befriend the nobles, and will be devoted to amusement and delight, and will often abstain from women and be separate from them, and some of his children or women will have ailments or die.

50 And if Mercury was in it he will be devoted to hidden sciences, and something detestable will come to him because of speech, and something detestable will afflict the children and siblings, and they will be in conflict with him.

51 And if the Moon was in it he will be concerned with hidden things, and an ailment will afflict him in a hidden place of his body, and he will acquire assets, and some of his assets will be diminished, and his mother will gain the good.

52 And if the Head was in it, then he will benefit from residences and lands, and he will be involved in building, and his parents will gain assets. **53** And if the Tail was in it, something detestable will afflict his home, and he will be distressed by the rabble, and his parents will get something detestable.

[Sign or Ascendant of year on natal fifth, revolutionary planet in it][62]

54 If the sign of the terminal point or the Ascendant of the year coincided with the house of children of the root, then there will appear what it had indicated in the root (of good and bad) concerning children and friends, of both men and women. **55** And in particular it indicates that he will be praised, and it will renew the friendship of

---

[62] The planetary significations here are similar to Rhetorius Ch. 57 (pp. 72-75).

people (both male and female), and he will delight in them, and he will gain the good from the powerful and kings, and he will be praised for what he does not do, and beautiful things will be spoken about him, and he will manage actions for some of those having importance, and he will be correct in his management and actions, and delighted in them, and he will increase in his assets and benefit by farms, business, crops, and building, and he will be victorious over his enemies and all whom he contends with, and if he traveled he will return from his journey, and he will quarrel with people many times, and be distressed in the eighth[63] and twelfth months.

56 Now if Saturn was in it in the revolution, then he will acquire assets and immovable property, and he will be distressed because of some of that, and he will associate with kings,[64] and his anger will be multiplied.

57 And if Jupiter was in it, then he will gain leadership, and will be fortunate in different things, and a child will be born to him, and he will see what he loves in everything he does, and if he traveled he will return to his homeland, and he will be devoted to business, and will profit in it, and he will contend with people and be victorious over those contending [with him], and he will rid himself of adversity (if he was in it), and he will do what is good for the people.

58 And if Mars was in it, then the people will revere him, and he will associate with the nobles, and he will gain the good, and one of his children will have an ailment, and provisions and expenditures will be forced upon him.

59 And if the Sun was in it, then he will befriend those who have importance, and the religious, and the pious, and he will rid himself of adversity (if he was in it), and he will have loss and injustice[65] because of things having four feet, and he will be distressed because of children, and perhaps some of them will become ill.

---

[63] **T** reads, "second."
[64] In Persian mundane astrology, Saturn is especially associated with kingship.
[65] الضّيم. **E** and **T** read "distress" (الغمّ); **P**, "knowledge" (العلم).

60 Now if Venus was in it he will be revered, victorious, and he will gain assets, authority, and power from women and the nobles, and gifts and pleasing reports will come to him.

61 And if Mercury was in it he will be victorious, with much preoccupation with diverse actions, speech, writers, and eloquence, and the management of assets, and he will be entrusted with assets, and from these things he will gain benefit and assets.

62 And if the Moon was in it, then he will gain good fortune, and will speak on religions and the situations of prophets.

63 And if the Head was in it, then assets will come to him, and pleasing reports will be returned to him, and a child will be born to him, and some of his children will be elevated, and the father[66] will benefit by them. **64** And if the Tail was in it, then his child will have something detestable, and reports which distress him will reach him.

[Sign or Ascendant of year on natal sixth, revolutionary planet in it][67]

65 If the sign of the terminal point or the Ascendant of the year coincided with the house of illness of the root, then there will appear what it had indicated in the root (of good or bad) concerning servants, slaves, illness, and a chronic condition. **66** And in particular it indicates that wounds will appear, or an ailment will afflict him in a hidden place of his body (and he will escape from it), or he will contend with people having power, and he will get close to some of the authorities, though there will be distance between him and one of [his] women, and his brothers will treat him badly, and slander will reach him (or a report of it will come to him), and he will be devoted to pleasing reports and will benefit by business, and if he moved from place to place he will delight in it, and[68] he will be distressed in the second, fourth, and seventh months.

---

[66] This could be the native, as father of these children; but perhaps Abū Ma'shar simply means the *native's* father.
[67] The planetary significations here are compiled from the lists in Rhetorius Ch. 57 (pp. 75-79).
[68] Reading for "or."

67 And if Saturn was in it in the revolution, then he will do works harming him, and it will corrupt some of his assets, and he will become ill due to moisture and dryness, or from black bile, or from wind and gout, and something detestable will afflict his slaves, and he will contend with people, and some of [his] women will be hurt,[69] and his friends will betray him and lie to him.

68 And if Jupiter was in it, then he will have something detestable from kings and authorities, or from a group of the people, and he will contend with relatives and low-class people, and he will become ill due to his liver, and perhaps that will be due to drinking wine.

69 And if Mars was in it, his toil will become great, and helpers will come to his enemies, supporting them against him, and it will corrupt the condition of his slaves, and something detestable will come to him while traveling or outside of his home, and an ailment will afflict him in the limb which belongs to that sign, or his body will be cut with iron, or a calamity will afflict him from beating, or from a man's anger at him, or from a dog biting him.

70 And if the Sun was in it, something detestable will afflict him from kings, and he will be under their power, and the father [of the native] will have a calamity.

71 And if Venus was in it, then he will become ill, and he will quarrel with his women and relatives, and he will have sex with servant-girls or corrupt women.

72 And if Mercury was in it he will devote himself to theft, and will have wicked ideas, being monstrous in logic, with ugly things being said about him, and an ailment will afflict him in his eyes or hearing, or in a place of his mouth, and he will seek the truth from people by means of documents and books.

73 And if the Moon was in it, then an ailment will afflict him in the spleen and the eye, and his mother will have something detestable from some of the leaders.

---

[69] يتأذى, which can also means to be offended or be wronged. But this can also be read as the native doing this to the women.

74 And if the Head was in it, then he will fall from an elevated place or into a well, or an ailment will afflict him in his bones, or a wound from riding animals. **75** And if the Tail was in it, then griefs and various detestable things will afflict him.

[Sign or Ascendant of year on natal seventh, revolutionary planet in it][70]

76 If the sign of the terminal point or the Ascendant of the year coincided with the house of wedding of the root, then there will appear what it had indicated in the root (of the good and bad) concerning women, conflicts, and contrariety. **77** And in particular it indicates that he will delight in women, and they will desire him, and he will be devoted to [medical] treatments and remedies, and will benefit by them, and he will do works he is praised for, and he will free himself from adversity (if he was in it), except that he will be distressed because of it,[71] and some of his relatives will have distress and something detestable, and he will associate with people having nobility, and will increase in his power, and his needs and demands will become easier for him, and he will see what he loves in his enemies, and he will marry and have a child, and he will delight in children, and be distressed in the second, fourth, fifth, tenth, and eleventh[72] months.

78 Now if Saturn was in it at the revolution, then in some of his women he will have something detestable, and he will be distressed because of some of them and the children, and an ailment will afflict him in a hidden place or in the lower area and the rear, and perhaps blood will flow from that place, and he will be idle, stingy, a miser, with much confusion in his deeds, and some of his relatives will be ruined, and he will be saddened about it, and loss will afflict him.

---

[70] The planetary significations here are based on Rhetorius Ch. 57 (pp. 80-83).
[71] Grammatically this must refer to the works or treatments just mentioned.
[72] **T:** "twelfth."

79 And if Jupiter was in it, rulership will come to him or he will be in command, and he will be restrained in[73] the assets of others, and he will have much toil or[74] he will travel, and have good fortune with women.

80 And if Mars was in it, then his conflicts will multiply as well as his confusion in his affairs, and his stubbornness and haste, and it will hasten his closeness to those who would seize him by force,[75] and perhaps he will kill a man, and misfortune will afflict him from fire, or beating, or cutting by iron, or falling from an elevated place, and assets will be stolen from him, and he will travel and toil much.

81 And if the Sun was in it he will acquire assets and become ill,[76] and he will have sex with low women or women who have an illness or defect in the front or the rear, and the father will have something detestable in his own assets, or the native will disperse the father's assets.

82 And if Venus was in it, then he will have a fine character with women, and he will come to a financial arrangement with servant-girls and harlots because of their friendship [towards him], and bad things will be said about him because of them.

83 And if Mercury was in it, he will increase in his culture and knowledge, and be devoted to foreign, astonishing books, and be entertained and play, and gain benefits, or have recourse to a well-to-do woman, and his women will seek concealed things, ruses, sorcery, and magic.

84 And if the Moon was in it, then he will travel, and his toil will multiply, and he will become ill because of the toil or travel, and loss will afflict him in his assets, and something detestable from slaves, and fighting and dogs, and he will have sex with two women who have kin-

---

[73] وينهى في. But it's possible that this could mean he "comes to a [great] result" in other's assets, even though this is not Form VIII. Steven Birchfield helpfully points out that the seventh is the twelfth from the eighth (others' assets).

[74] Reading with **B** for "and."

[75] Reading with **B** as يغصب عليه. But this could also be يغضب عليه, "who are angry with him." **T** reads an unattested Form VIII, which would mean "treat him badly" (يغتلظ عليه).

[76] **P** omits this statement about becoming ill.

ship between them.⁷⁷ **85** And if the revolution belonged to a woman, then she will desire lesbianism with women.

86 And if the Head was in it, then his women will acquire assets, and an ailment will afflict them in the eye, or he will have sex with a blind woman. **87** And if the Tail was in it, then he will have sex with a low-class woman, or a sick one, or one with a defect.

[Sign or Ascendant of year on natal eighth, revolutionary planet in it]⁷⁸

88 If the sign of the terminal point or the Ascendant of the year coincided with the house of death of the root, then there will appear what it had indicated in the root (of good and bad) concerning the causes of the dead, inheritances, and contention over assets. **89** And in particular it indicates stubbornness, conflict (and safety from that), and he will increase in his assets, and get something of the good he desires, and he will be afflicted in much of his management, depleted⁷⁹ in [his] affairs, and he will be distressed due to lies, betrayal, slander, and enemies, and some of his siblings will differ with him,⁸⁰ and he will be injured because of some foods, and will be dissatisfied, and conflicts and concerns⁸¹ will afflict him, and hidden pains (though he will be rescued from all of that), and distress will afflict him in the second, fourth, and twelfth months. **90** And if the infortunes were in it at the revolution, then he will be betrayed by his companions, friends, and those who confide in him, and people will treat him badly and be wicked to him, and trick him, and pursue him and seek to make him stumble, and he will be distressed by the death of [some] man.

91 And if Saturn was in it at the revolution, tight circumstances will afflict him in his possessions, and a catastrophe from a river or sea, or a

---

⁷⁷ Lit., "between one of them and her companion / associate."
⁷⁸ The planetary significations here are based on Rhetorius Ch. 57 (pp. 84-87).
⁷⁹ Or, "exhausted" (نافد).
⁸⁰ Reading as له يتغيّر. But **E** seems to read يعسّره, "they will make it difficult for him."
⁸¹ هموم. But **P** reads غموم, "distresses."

desert, or irritation, and he will concern himself with the conditions of the dead and the ancestors.

92 And if Jupiter was in it, then he will have good from the nobles, and because of the dead and legacies,[82] and old matters.[83]

93 And if Mars was in it, then an ailment or beating will afflict him in his face or vision, or misfortune from predatory animals, fire, or enemies.

94 And if the Sun was in it, then he will be distracted in his heart, with much reflection, and he will fall from something elevated or far away,[84] and an ailment will afflict him in his eyes, or in the stomach or legs.

95 And if Venus was in it, then he will become ill because of food or drink, or drinking wine, or poison will be given to him, and perhaps some of [his] women will do that to him.

96 And if Mercury was in it he will write a will and deal with documents and lying, and he will write counterfeit [things], and he will increase in his dependents and servants, and he will meditate on the gathering of assets and their protection.

97 And if the Moon was in it, then he will benefit from legacies and the assets of the dead.

98 And if the Head was in it, then he will fall from an elevated place, or a catastrophe will afflict him from assets. **99** And if the Tail was in it, then he will be lied about, and perhaps he will be accused falsely of [shedding] the blood of a man.

[Sign or Ascendant of year on natal ninth, revolutionary planet in it][85]

100 If the sign of the terminal point or the Ascendant of the year coincided with the house of travel of the root, then there will appear what it had indicated in the root (of good or bad) concerning travel or

---

[82] Lit., "things left behind."

[83] الأمور. **E** and **T** read "old *monies/assets*" (الأموال).

[84] Or perhaps, "unlikely" (بعيد).

[85] The planetary significations here are based on Rhetorius Ch. 57 (pp. 87-91).

the withdrawal of the Sultan,[86] and pursuing reports and the conditions of religion, and works of piety. **101** And[87] in particular it indicates that he will have the good, and benefits, and he will do deeds he had not done before that, and he will benefit by buying and selling, and lending and borrowing, and he will buy slaves and servant-girls, and his enemies will have something detestable, and some of his assets will be spent because of something he is distressed about, and he will be cautious, fearful because of things [which] will lead his condition in it to one of love, and some of his friends and relatives will have something detestable, and it will corrupt what is between him and some of them [but] then it will be made right, and he will be devoted to building, and planting trees, and his delight will be multiplied, and he will move from place to place, and be distressed in the fourth and twelfth months. **102** And if there were infortunes in a bad condition in it at the revolution, then it will ruin what he acquires (of assets and the rest of things), and he will contend with the people of his house, and be injured by them, and will be sad about his people, children, and some of his relatives and friends.

103 And if Saturn was in it at the revolution, then his pursuit of hidden things, religious people, and philosophy will be multiplied, and the interpretation of visions, and he will have astonishing dreams.

104 And if Jupiter was in it and the revolution is diurnal, then he will increase in his devotion, and he will do good deeds, and will concern himself with the houses of worship and the religious, and he will have sound dreams, with good [and] truthful interpretations; and if that was by night, then he will have dreams except that they have a misleading interpretation, and he will be shown [to] the people, and

---

[86] The idea here is probably that the ninth is declining from, or withdrawing from the tenth: so, the withdrawal of the Sultan from his position or from prominence.

[87] I confess I do not understand a lot of the significations in this sentence, even when trying to use derived houses to do so. But perhaps it is due to its whole-sign angles to the sixth (slaves), twelfth (enemies), and third (relatives), although he does not do this consistently with the other houses.

be fake to them, and will lie in his speech, and will successful in much of what he is entrusted with.

105 And if Mars was in it, then he will increase in his eloquence, and will be successful in many things, and his anger in the matter of religion will multiply (and in other things), and he will follow a false religion, and will slander the people and be punished[88] for that.

106 And if the Sun was in it, then he will increase in his faith in God and the prophets, and he will quarrel about religion.

107 And if Venus was in it, then he will be of a mixed condition with women, with little stability concerning them, and his entertainment and delight will be reduced, and he will be devoted to the houses of worship and religion, and the religious, and scholars, and the interpretation of visions.[89]

108 And if Mercury was in it, he will be devoted to writers who have power, and scholars of the various sciences, and astrologers, and medical doctors, and he will benefit from buying and selling.

109 And if the Moon was in it and the revolution is nocturnal, then he will benefit from travel and will be entrusted with the assets of some women, and he will increase in his devotion, and be devoted to the houses of worship. **110** And if the revolution was by day, then his devotion will increase and he will delight in travel, and love deserts and wastelands, and not value highly the conditions of religion and the religious.

111 And if the Head was in it, then he will have leadership and benefits because of travel or in exile,[90] and the fear of predatory animals or illness from thirst will afflict him in his travel or in some of the wastelands. **112** And if the Tail was in it, then he will see something detestable from travel and because of it, and he will spend assets because of journeys and exile.

---

[88] **P:** "criticized."

[89] Or perhaps, "dreams."

[90] Or more simply, "being away from home" or "being abroad," here and in the next sentence.

BOOK VI: LORD OF ORB, THE ASCENDANT, CONNECTIONS

[Sign or Ascendant of year on natal tenth, revolutionary planet in it][91]

113 And if the sign of the terminal point or the Ascendant of the year coincided with the house of authority of the root, then there will appear what it had indicated in the root (of good or bad) concerning rank and authority. **114** And in particular it indicates that he will rejoice at [one] time, and be distressed at another time, and he will delight in the people and the nobles of men, and he will give his attention to his own work, being praised in [his] management, and he will increase in his assets and be victorious over his enemies, and his toil will be multiplied, and if he travels he will see what he loves in it, and in it he will acquire assets, and he will be elevated above his peers, and privation will reach him (and perhaps loss if it was at the end of the year), and he will be distressed by his woman or another woman besides her, and [women] will play a trick on him and seek an enchantment and sorcery [against] him, and he will be distressed in the fifth, seventh, and eighth months.

115 Now if Saturn was in it at the revolution, and he had testimony in that sign, and the revolution is diurnal, then he will associate with kings, increase in his assets, be successful in his needs, be devoted to sowing and planting, building, and the management of lands, and he will be distressed because of women and children, and misfortune will afflict him from waters and moisture. **116** And if that was by night, then he will make people envious or be warned against them, and he will carry water,[92] and dig wells, and associate with the masters of bathhouses, peasants, and fishermen.

117 And if Jupiter was in it and the revolution is diurnal, then he will befriend the powerful, and be entrusted with assets, and will take charge of the public accounting. **118** And if the revolution was by

---

[91] The planetary significations here are based on Rhetorius Ch. 57 (pp. 91-93).

[92] Or perhaps, "channel" it, in the sense of working with canals and transport; it is possible that a preposition is missing and it means he will transport things *by* water. (The latter is the conjecture by Cumont about the uncertain Greek in Rhetorius: see Rhetorius p. 91 n. 1).

night, then his condition will be like that except that anger[93] will get the better of him, and it will decrease part of his assets.

119 And if Mars was in it and the revolution diurnal, then misfortune will afflict him from something hot or from fire, and something of his assets will be ruined, and he will be in need of the assets of someone else, and he will do works in which he will have evil consequences, and he will be distressed because of travels and being away from home,[94] and it will take away from the assets of the father, and estrangement will occur between his parents. **120** And if the revolution was nocturnal, then he will increase in his assets and power, and he will associate with soldiers, and perhaps kings will make him a leader.

121 And if the Sun was in it he will gain power due to kings, and because of fathers, and he will increase in the assets of the father, and [in] his rank and power among the powerful and nobles.

122 And if Venus was in it, then his soul will be at ease,[95] and he will be revered, and will have sex with women having importance, and they will love him, and he will have good from them.

123 And if Mercury was in it, then he will increase in his thinking and cleverness, and children and friends, and ability, and perhaps he will travel.

124 And if the Moon was in it, then he will associate with nobles and authorities, and he will devote himself to different crafts,[96] and there will be an increase[97] in the power of his mother and her assets.

125 And if the Head was in it he will associate with kings and the powerful, and he will increase in his power and benefits. **126** And if the Tail is in it, an ailment or harm will afflict him, and part of his assets will be ruined, and an illness and harm will reach his mother.

---

[93] Or perhaps, "violence" (الحِدَّة). But this seems a bit off for a contrary-to-sect Jupiter.

[94] Mars indicates travel, but being contrary to the sect means distress.

[95] Reading ينعم with **P** and **T** for "his soul will benefit" (ينفع).

[96] Or, "professions."

[97] Reading more broadly for the more straightforward "he will increase."

BOOK VI: LORD OF ORB, THE ASCENDANT, CONNECTIONS

[Sign or Ascendant of year on natal eleventh, revolutionary planet in it][98]

127 If the sign of the terminal point or the Ascendant of the year coincided with the house of hope[99] of the root, then there will appear what it had indicated in the root (of good or bad) concerning good fortune, hope, and friends. **128** And in particular it indicates that he will have much delight, be received in his speech, of good religion, exhausted in works and every action he does (even though in the outer appearance of [his] management there will be good fortune), though [his] condition in it will lead to love and what is true, and he will be victorious over his enemies [and] all who wish him ill, and he will devote himself to business, building, the cultivation of lands, and planting trees and [establishing] towers, [and] he will see what he loves in it, and will be distressed in the fifth and seventh months.

129 And if Saturn was in it at the revolution, then he will associate with kings and leaders, and will increase in his assets and earn[100] [more] assets, and especially if the revolution was by day.

130 And if Jupiter was in it he will be victorious, rejoicing, and delight in women and children, and will free himself from distress (if he was in it), and he will do a good thing for the people, and be praised for that, and will be victorious over his enemies.

131 And if Mars was in it, and especially by night, he will increase in his rank, good fortune, and assets, and will be revered.

132 And if the Sun was in it he will gain good fortune and respect, and a reputation for good[101] because of [his] fathers.

133 And if Venus was in it, he will delight in women and children, and will associate with corrupted women or have sex with young men, and he will increase in his goods, dishes, and furniture, and will befriend people having power.

---

[98] The planetary significations here are based on Rhetorius Ch. 57 (pp. 96-100).
[99] **P**: "friends."
[100] But **P** reads "corrupt." Rhetorius Ch. 57 (pp. 97-98) agrees with "earn," particularly in a diurnal chart. Rhetorius does affirm that in a nocturnal chart, assets would diminish.
[101] Or, "good will be spoken about him."

134 And if Mercury was in it he will see what he loves from women and because of them, and he will do hidden, concealed deeds, and people who have power in many things will consult him, and he will associate with surveyors of the land, astrologers, and wrestlers, and an ailment will afflict him, especially if [Mercury] was western from the Sun.

135 And if the Moon was in it, and the revolution by night, then he will have good fortune and nobility, and some of that will be because of fathers; and if the revolution was by day, then he will travel, and he will be separated from one of his parents (or both of them).

136 And if the Head was in it, then he will associate with eunuchs and the people among his friends having importance, and he will love women and increase in his good fortune. **137** And if the Tail was in it, then he will squander [his] assets and scatter them, and he will be troubled[102] in the rest of his conditions.

[Sign or Ascendant of year on natal twelfth, revolutionary planet in it][103]

138 If the sign of the terminal point or Ascendant of the year coincided with the house of enemies of the root, then there will appear what it had indicated in the root (of good or bad) concerning enemies, hardship, confinement, and something detestable. **139** And in particular it indicates that he will not have the good, and his benefits will be little from what is good, and hardship, trouble, and harm will be victorious over what good things he does or encounters, and his quarreling will multiply, as well as his irritation and distress, and evil gossip will be said about him, and his needs will be made more difficult, and he will be sad about some of his relatives, and some of them (as well as others) will double-cross him, and they will trick him and deceive him,[104] and especially in the first two-thirds of the year; but as for the last third of the year it will be more suitable, and distress will reach him in the second, sixth, and eighth months.

---

[102] Or perhaps, "toiling away" (reading as مُتعنِّيًا). But **T** reads, "unsuccessful" (مُتفشِّلًا).
[103] The planetary significations here are based on Rhetorius Ch. 57 (pp. 46-47).
[104] Reading as Form I. But as Form II, "they will consider him unreliable."

140 Now if Saturn was in it at the revolution, and the revolution was by night, then he will become ill and something detestable will afflict him from slaves, and it will decrease his assets and the assets of his parents. **141** And if the revolution was by day, then it will be below the first [interpretation], and he will be victorious over his enemies.

142 And if Jupiter was in it, then harm and conflict will afflict him, and it will arouse [his] enemies against him, and the enmity of people will be renewed against him, and that is harsher if the revolution was by night.

143 And if Mars was in it, then he will become ill, and his toil will be multiplied, and something detestable will afflict him because of slaves, and he will be subjugated or put in fetters, and that is harsher if the revolution was by day; but if it was by night, then it is less.

144 And if the Sun was in it, then he will become ill and be subjugated, and will toil because of slaves, and something detestable or harm will afflict the father.

145 And if Venus was in it, then he will be distressed because of women, and he will have sex with harlots and servant-girls.

146 And if Mercury was in it, then he will associate with kings because of buying and selling, and laborers[105] and undertakings, and for that reason he will have something detestable, and his quarreling will increase, and something detestable will afflict him because of some animals (of those having four feet).

147 And if the Moon was in it[106] and the revolution was by day, then he will be distressed because of waters and farmers, and harm will reach him due to servant-girls; and if the revolution was by night, that will be easier.

148 And if the Head was in it, then his bones will be broken, or an ailment will afflict him in the eye or ear, and his enemies will treat him

---

[105] Or, "employees."
[106] Reading the rest of the sentence with **B**. **E** and **P** read: "…then something detestable will reach him and reach his mother." **T** reads, "…then something detestable will reach his mother."

badly. **149** And if the Tail was in it, then he will acquire assets from some foreigners,[107] and his enemies will have something detestable.

150 So this indication of the sign of the terminal point and the Ascendant of the revolution is if they coincide with one of the houses of the root and one of the planets is in it at the *revolution*. **151** And if the [sign of] the terminal point and the Ascendant of the revolution are a single sign, it is stronger in the revolution; and if they differ, each one of them individually is indicative, according to its matching that sign; and the indication of the sign of the terminal point is more powerful. **152** And if one of these planets was in one of these signs, then from its condition in itself and its position relative to its house,[108] in its share (or [being] alien), it will have other indications.[109]

Chapter VI.4: On the indication of the year's terminating at a sign in which there is a planet in the root, or its rooted position is the Ascendant of the year

1 If[110] the year reached a sign in which there was a planetary fortune in the root, it being strong, received—or that sign was the Ascendant of the revolution—it indicates delight and a good condition, of the category of what the planet and sign indicates. **2** And if the year reached a sign in which there was an infortune in the root (or a planet

---

[107] الغرباء. But **P** reads, "debtors," or "rivals," or "insulters" (الغرماء).

[108] من بيته. But perhaps this simply means by its house position. Reading the rest of this sentence with **P** (which is close to **B**); **E** states it a little more elaborately and with an uncertain word. **T** reads, "and its being in signs in which it has shares and other indications."

[109] Again, all of these delineations are very general, and a lot depends on details like these, including what houses they natally rule.

[110] The interpretations in this chapter from **3-25** are elaborations of *Carmen* IV.1, **21-34**.

made unfortunate, or burned, or retrograde), it indicates something detestable.

3 Now if the year reached the sign in which Saturn was in the root of the nativity (or that was the Ascendant of the revolution), and Saturn looked at [that sign] in the revolution, then distresses will afflict him from enemies, and the appearance of disgrace, and from older people, and their nobles, and disasters from the category of the indication of Saturn, and he will become ill from black bile and coldness.[111] 4 But if Saturn does *not* look at that position in the revolution while the fortunes *do* look, that will be small, light, easy, and he will be protected from it. 5 And if a fortune looked at that place as well [as Saturn], those things and the illness will be below the first [interpretation], and he will benefit from the treatment; but if a fortune does not testify to it, it will make his liberation from it difficult, and the treatment will not benefit him. 6 And if Saturn looked at that position in the revolution by a square or opposition, it makes that harsher and will last a long time. 7 Now if a fortune [also] looked at that place in the revolution,[112] he will free himself from it after some delay, and the treatment will benefit him after hardship passes by him. 8 And if an infortune [also] looked, and that infortune

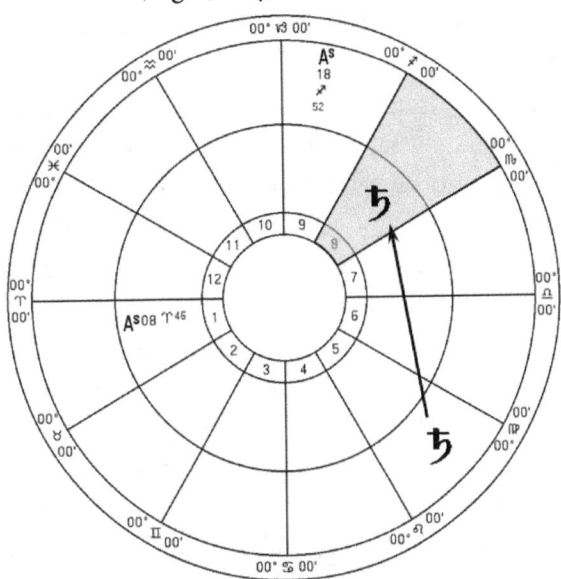

Figure 92: SR planet looking at activated natal position (VI.4, 3-8)

---

[111] **B** adds: "along with weeping and [*uncertain*]."
[112] That is, if Saturn is squaring or opposing it.

was Mars,[113] those things will be harsher and he will shift from illness to illness, and ruin will be feared for him.

9 And if the year reached the sign in which Jupiter was [in the root] (or that sign was the Ascendant of the year), and Jupiter looked at it in the revolution with an aspect of affection, then he will have status and rank with ease, and he will delight in assets, children, and friends, and he will increase in them, or marry a woman with power. **10** But if Jupiter in the revolution looked at that position which we mentioned [but] from a square or opposition, it will also be like that except that he will [only] be successful in what we mentioned through toil and contention, and some distress will stain him because of what we mentioned. **11** And if an infortune looked at that place or at Jupiter,[114] fear will afflict him from kings and from their anger, and generally it will undermine what Jupiter indicates, from the direction of the indication of that infortune. **12** Now if the infortune was in the position of Jupiter in the root,[115] it will undermine all of that, and it indicates loss, damage, and distress because of assets and children (and other things besides that, of what is of the category of the indication of Jupiter).

13 Now if the year reached the sign in which Mars was (or that sign was the Ascendant of the revolution), then the native will travel, and something detestable will afflict him from violence, anger, iron, fury, contentions, burning, and calamitous fires, and he will become ill from heat and the disturbance of the blood, and its shedding and drawing [it out], and enemies will be stirred up against him, and he will flee from his country; and that will be harsher if Mars at the revolution looked at that position with an aspect of hostility. **14** And one [should be] guided by the aspect of Mars and the fortunes to that place in the revolution, in the way one is guided in it with Saturn.

15 And if the year reached the sign in which the Sun was (or that sign was the Ascendant of the revolution) and he is in a suitable condi-

---

[113] In this scenario it could only be Mars, so perhaps Abū Ma'shar means this only parenthetically.

[114] This seems to mean that a revolutionary infortune is looking at the *natal* place of Jupiter or at the revolutionary Jupiter.

[115] This might mean that an infortune is with the natal Jupiter.

tion or made fortunate, and that position is one of the stakes of the root, then the owner of the revolution will have good from fathers and the Sultan, and from everything which [the Sun] indicates, and he will be suitable for meeting with kings and associating with them. **16** And if the Sun was in a bad condition or made unfortunate, some of the authorities will be angry with him, and something detestable will afflict him from them and from fathers, and he will become ill. **17** Now if [the Sun] was in a bad condition and the one which makes him unfortunate was Mars, the illness will be from heat and dryness, or blood, and what resembles that; and if that was Saturn, then it will be pain of the joints, and every hidden illness. **18** And if the Sun in the root was falling from the stakes, then one should look at his condition and at the house in which he was: for if he was in the second and is in a suitable condition, made fortunate, he indicates the accruing of assets and an increase in them; while if he was made unfortunate he indicates their corruption and fines in them—and his indication will be in this manner if he was in the rest of the houses.

19 And if the year reached the sign in which Venus was (or that sign was the Ascendant of the revolution), then if in the revolution she was free of the infortunes and she looked at that [natal] position he will marry, and rejoice because of[116] pleasures, women, and sex, and an increase in children, garments, goods, and he will be in good spirits. **20** But if she does not look at her [natal] place and she is in a suitable condition, it subtracts from that; and if she is in a bad condition or made unfortunate, distresses and concerns will afflict him because of women, and his sexual intercourse will be reduced, <and> his spirit foul.

21 And if the year reached the sign in which Mercury was (or that sign was the Ascendant of the revolution), and Mercury in the revolution looked at[117] his rooted place, and he is in a suitable condition, free

---

[116] Reading the rest of this sentence with **B** and **T**. **E** and **P** read: "marriage and children, and she will improve his condition, and he will be in good spirits, and increase in his goods and garments."

[117] **E** reads "returned to," which also makes sense.

of the infortunes, then in that year he will benefit by the sciences and writing, skill, cunning, reason, culture, management, and businesses, and he will profit in them, and he will be well praised; and if the root of his nativity had indicated children, a child will be born to him. **22** And if at the revolution he was in a suitable condition in the way which we stated, except that he does not look at his rooted place, his benefit in these things will be below the first [interpretation]; and if he was made unfortunate, he will be granted types of detestable things, and his reputation will be foul, and he will fabricate and falsify things, and [do] foul actions, and loss and damage will afflict him.

23 And if the year reached the sign in which the Moon was (or that sign was the Ascendant [of the revolution]), then look at her condition in the two times. **24** For if she was in a suitable condition in both, it indicates the health of his body, and the goodness of his affairs, and the praise of his relatives and the common people towards him; and if she was corrupted in them both, it indicates the badness of the condition of the owner of the revolution, as well as his mother's. **25** But if she was in a corrupted condition in the root, [and] in a suitable condition in the revolution, then[118] it indicates the corruption of [his and the mother's] conditions as well, except that it will be harsher for his mother; and if she was in a suitable condition in the root and corrupted in the revolution, the condition of the owner of the revolution will be worse.

⁂

27 So these are the indications of the sign of the terminal point or the Ascendant of the year if one of them was in the position of one of the planets of the root. **28** And if the sign of the terminal point and the Ascendant of the year were a single sign so they were both in the posi-

---

[118] Reading the rest of this sentence with **B** and **P**. **E** reads: "…the condition will be in the middle. And if she was in a corrupt condition in the root and the revolution, the condition of the owner of the revolution will be worse." **T** reads, "then it indicates the corruption of his condition as well, except that it will be harsher for the brother and mother; and if she was in a suitable condition in the root [but] corrupted in the revolution, the condition of the owner of the revolution will be worse."

tion of one of the planets, it will be more apparent for its indication, while if the sign of the terminal point was the position of one of the planets and the Ascendant of the revolution was the position of another planet, then each one of the two indicates individually according to the power of the type of its indication.

29 And the strongest that a *planet* could be in its indication, is if in the revolution it is looking at its [natal] place from the directions which resemble its rooted indication: because if in the root it indicated good, and then in the revolution it returned to its place or looked at it from a trine or sextile, then it is more abundant for its indication of good; and if it indicated bad and then returned to its place or looked at it from the square or opposition, it is stronger for that evil. **30** And the suitability of the planets' condition (or their badness) will greatly alter what we have stated, towards either the good or the bad.

31 And if the year reached where the Head was (or that sign was the Ascendant of the revolution), and the Head in the revolution was in the inspection of Jupiter or Venus, he will be made a leader in that year, and will benefit from leaders, and he will be praised; while if the year reached the sign in which the Tail was (or that sign was the Ascendant of the revolution), then he will fall into the hands of his enemies, and will disappear from their sight, and they will use force against him.[119]

---

[119] Reading ويجبرون عليه somewhat uncertainly for the undotted ويحىرون عليه. Perhaps a better to say يخبرون ("they will be notified"), but that verb does not take the preposition على. (**T** seems to read that they will let him go: ويجوزون عليه.) **B** then adds in a marginal note: "and he will have malice from enemies and the rabble."

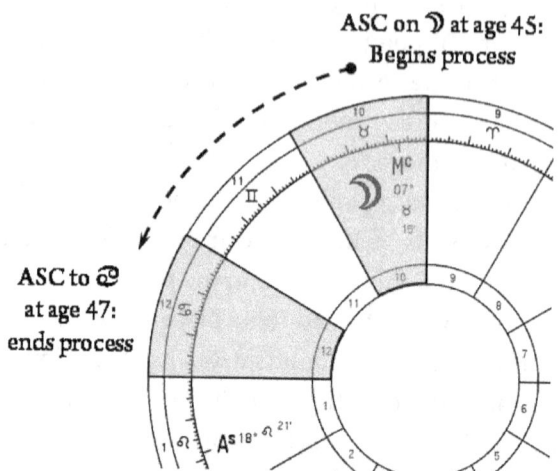

Figure 93: Profection distance between planet and domicile, as a process (VI.4, 32-33)

32 And if the year reached one of the signs, and in it was an alien planet (or [even if] it has a claim in it) be it a fortune or infortune, then it will not complete its indication in that year (whether for good or bad), but it does indicate *some* of it: and when the year reaches a sign of that planet, it will finish its indication. **33** And an example of that is if the year reached Taurus, and the Moon was in it in the root, and the Moon in this year indicates some good fortune: but when the year reaches Cancer, the Moon will complete her indication of good fortune.

34 [Now,][120] this judgment is when [planets] are excellent in the root and the revolution; but as for if one is bad in the root and bad in the revolution, then it indicates corruption in that matter in itself as well as according to the nature of the planet (whether a fortune or infortune), and according to its condition, and the connection of the fortunes and infortunes with it. **35** So judge in that like if Mars is in the house of assets in the root, and [in] <the root and> the revolution [he] is in an excellent condition: it indicates the good fortune of as-

---

[120] This paragraph (which breaks off at the end) is only in **E**. It does continue the thought about a planet in good and bad conditions, but no longer relates to the new point about the distance between a planet and its domicile indicating a years-long process.

sets. **36** But if in the root he was bad and in the revolution excellent, then it indicates suitability in his assets, and his spreading them around, in places that are necessary. **37** And if he was in a bad condition in both of them, then he will act according to his nature for corruption and spending, in what is not necessary. **38** And if Jupiter was like that, and he was excellent in the root, but bad in the revolution [*text breaks off*]...

Chapter VI.5: On the indication of the planets when they are in one of the houses in the root of the nativity, but at the revolution of the year they pass into another house

1 Now, the houses from which one is informed about the condition of the body in the revolution of the year, are three: the Ascendant of the root, the sign of the terminal point, and the Ascendant of the revolution; and those from which one is informed about his assets in the revolution are also three: the second of the root, the second from the sign of the terminal point, and the second from the Ascendant of the revolution; and those from which one is informed about the condition of brothers, sisters, and relatives, are three as well: the third house from the Ascendant of the root, the third from the sign of the terminal point, and the third from the Ascendant of the revolution. **2** And the statement is like that for the rest of the houses, so look for each one of them from the three places in this manner. **3** And certainly one should be guided in everything of what we have mentioned, by the Lots and the twelfth-parts which have the indication for that matter—except that it is not our intention to state that here, but in this place we *do* want to state the indications of the planets in the houses of the circle.

4 So if one of the planets in the root of the nativity was in the Ascendant, but then at the revolution of the year it comes to be in the second sign from the Ascendant of the root (or from the sign of the terminal point, or from the Ascendant of the revolution), then it indicates the owner of the revolution's eagerness to seek money. **5** And if the planet which was in the Ascendant in the root came to be, in the revolution, in the third or ninth from the Ascendant of the root (or from the sign of the terminal point, or from the Ascendant of the revolution), then it indicates travel. **6** But if it came to be in the fourth from one of them, he will love gentleness, the needs of the family, and the management of real estate—and you look in the rest of the houses in this manner.

7 And if a planet in the root was in the second sign, but then at the revolution it came to be in the Ascendant of the root (or the sign of the terminal point, or the Ascendant of the revolution), then it indicates that he will gain assets from a source which he had not hoped for. **8** And if it came to be in the second from one of them, it indicates earning money from a source which he had hoped for previously, and what he acquired of it will remain with him. **9** And if it came to be in the third or ninth from one of them, he will have assets from brothers and sisters, or on travels or in exile.[121] **10** And if it was in the fourth from one of them, he will have assets from fathers, lands, and immovable wealth. **11** And if it came to be in the fifth from one of them, he will have wealth from businesses, buying and selling, children, gifts, messengers, and crops.[122] **12** And if it came to be in the sixth from one of them, he will have the wealth from slaves, riding animals, the sick, and the victimized[123]—and the judgment in the rest of the signs should be in this manner.

13 And if a planet in the root was in the third sign, but then in the revolution it came to be in the sign of the terminal point or one of the [other] two Ascendants, then someone else will have precedence over him, such as a relative, or brother, or someone in such a status. **14** But if it came to be in the second from one of them, a lawsuit or conflict will occur between him and his brothers and relatives.[124] **15** And if it came to be in the third from one of them, he will increase in his brothers and sisters, and will acquire friends and brethren. **16** And if it came

---

[121] Or more simply, "being away from home."
[122] That is, from the wealth or income of the land (the fifth is the second from the fourth).
[123] Or, those who have suffered disaster (المنكوبين).
[124] The second is the twelfth (enemies) from the third.

BOOK VI: LORD OF ORB, THE ASCENDANT, CONNECTIONS   467

to be in the fourth from one of them, his brothers will gain what is good from the fathers, or from people who are in the status of fathers. **17** And if it came to be in the fifth from one of them, then a child will be born to his brothers or sisters. **18** And if it came to be in the sixth from one of them, his brothers or sisters will have an ailment. **19** And if it came to be in the seventh from one of them, the brothers and sisters will marry.

20 And this will be the manner of [every] statement about a planet which is in the house of slaves or the house of women (or the rest of the houses) in the root, but then in the revolution it comes to be in one of the houses from the Ascendant of the root (or from the sign of the terminal point, or from the Ascendant of the revolution). **21** But if it was in one of the houses from the Ascendant of the root, and was in another house from the terminal point or from the Ascendant of the year, then mix their indications together. **22** And an example of that is that a planet in the root would be in the Ascendant, but then at the

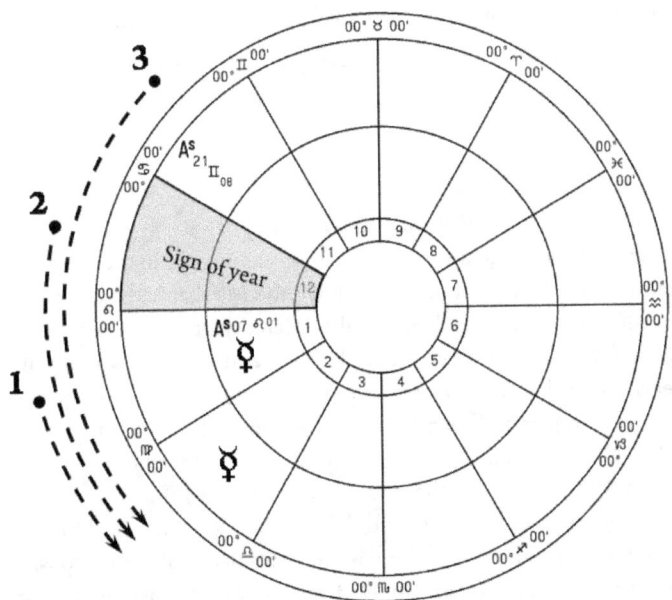

Figure 94: A revolutionary planet in three derived houses (VI.5, 20-24)

revolution it would to be in [1] the second of the root, and [2] the third of the terminal point, and [3] the fourth of the Ascendant of the revolution: so that would indicate [1] his eagerness for earning and the seeking of assets, and toil because of it, and [3] indifference to travel,[125] and [2] an increase in friends and brothers.[126] **23** And the strongest of the positions is the indication of the position of the planet from [1] the Ascendant of the root, then below that in strength is its position from [2] the sign of the terminal point, then below them both is its position from [3] the Ascendant of the revolution. **24** And the aspect of the planets towards it, and its connection with them and their connection to it, certainly increases the suitability of the condition of every one of them (or its corruption).[127]

Chapter VI.6: On the indication of the connection of the lords of the houses with one other, & their separation from one another

1 You ought to look at the lord of the Ascendant of the root, and at the lord of the sign of the terminal point, and at the lord of the Ascendant of the revolution: where each one of them is in the revolution

---

[125] Being in the fourth implies staying at home.

[126] This illustrates the difficulty in Abū Ma'shar's approach. In the diagram Mercury is in the third from the sign of the year, which Abū Ma'shar had said (in **5**) indicates travel; but he has just affirmed with **6** that Mercury being in the fourth from the Ascendant of the year means staying at home. Because these two indications contradict each other, he must change one of them: in this case, changing the third house to mean siblings and friends. In VI.6, **9** he includes both interpretations, and starts to introduce rules for telling the difference between them.

[127] In Figure 94 Mercury is in the natal Ascendant (Leo). But at age 47 (when the natal Ascendant profects to the twelfth house), he is in Virgo, and in this year the Ascendant of the revolution is in Gemini. This puts his revolutionary position in [1] the second from the natal Ascendant, [2] the third from the sign of the year, and [3] the fourth from the Ascendant of the year. But if Mars happened to square him at the revolution, each one of these significations (described in **22**) would experience disruption in accordance with the nature of Mars, and his own place and house rulership.

BOOK VI: LORD OF ORB, THE ASCENDANT, CONNECTIONS

of the year relative to its place,[128] for the owner of the revolution will be greatly preoccupied and concerned with what that house indicates. **2** And if [that Ascendant's] lord looked at it, that will be from a direction he knows about, while if its lord does not look at it, that will be from where he does not suspect nor know about.

3 Then after that you look at the connection of the lords of each one of the three indicators with the lords of the rest of the houses, as well as their connection with it.[129] **4** So, if the lord of the Ascendant of the root (or the lord of the sign of the terminal point, or the lord of the Ascendant of the year) connected in the revolution with the lord of *its own* house of assets, it indicates that the owner of the revolution will earn assets in that year, with toil and trouble, and powerful desire. **5** And if the lord of its house of assets connected with one of them,[130] he will gain assets with ease. **6** And if in the revolution each one of these indicators was separating from its associate, it indicates the scarcity of his benefit, and his ruin due to assets, and his abandoning his search [for them], with an abundance of costs. **7** And if one of them connected with an alien planet *in* the second [place] from one of these positions, it indicates his search for assets, and his eagerness for them; and if that planet [in the second] receives it he will acquire many assets, while if it does not receive it and does not mix with it, the benefit will be small.

8 And if the lord of the Ascendant of the root (or the lord of the sign of the terminal point, or the lord of the Ascendant of the revolution) connected in the revolution of the year with the lord of the third [from] its own place,[131] it indicates his travel, and that will be from his own desire and need for it. **9** And if the lord of the third from their own places connected with one of them, it will prepare travel for him

---

[128] That is, relative to its own Ascendant. So if the Ascendant of the revolution was Scorpio, see where Mars falls in the revolutionary houses, relative to Scorpio. If the profection comes to Libra, see where Venus is, relative to Libra.

[129] This is only within each respective house scheme.

[130] Again, this is only in each *respective* house scheme: the lord of the *revolution's* second connecting with the lord of the *revolution's* Ascendant, etc.

[131] That is, from the Ascendant within its own scheme.

from where he did not expect, and he will be bothered because of it, and he will increase in his brothers and sisters (and the condition of the lord of the ninth is likewise). **10** And if one of them was separating from its associate in the revolution, it does not indicate travel unless one of them is in the third or ninth signs from its own place, in the inspection of the lord of its own house, or connecting with an alien planet *in* one of these two places: for then it does indicate travel as well, except that he will be unwilling [to do] it.

11 And if the lord of one of these three positions connected in the revolution with the lord of the fourth from its own place, then he will love gentleness and leisure.[132] **12** Now if the lord of the fourth was making it unfortunate, ruin will be feared for him, while if it was received by it, he will gain benefits in relation to fathers, villages, real estate, and sowing. **13** And if the lord of their fourth connected with one of them, fathers will benefit from him[133] and he will chance upon assets in building and the improvement of homes, and sowing, and the buying of real estate. **14** And if one of them was separating from its associate in the revolution, he will abstain from everything we have mentioned, and his condition will be the contrary of that.

15 And if the lord of one of these three positions connected in the revolution with the lord of the fifth from its place, it indicates that his woman will be pregnant, and it prepares for him a preoccupation with crops and farms, and every work he hopes for benefit in, at a later date. **16** And if the lord of their fifth connected with one of them, a child will be born to him and he will get benefit from sowing, investments, and the loaning of dirhams. **17** And if one of them was separating from its associate in the revolution, the condition will be the contrary of that.

18 And if the lord of one of these three positions connected in the revolution with the lord of its sixth, it indicates his illness in that year, and acquiring it[134] will be easy. **19** And if the lord of its sixth was an

---

[132] This is probably what we would call a "homebody."
[133] But perhaps this could also mean that *he* benefits from *them*.
[134] الكاسب. The emphasis here is that the native brings it upon himself.

infortune, the illness will be harsh (and it is harsher for it if it was slow or retrograde)—and the type of illness will be known from the nature of the sixth sign and its lord. **20** And if the lord of its sixth connected with it, and its condition was as I described, an incidental illness will afflict him. **21** And if one of them was separating from its associate in the revolution, the condition will be the contrary of that.

22 And if the lord of one of these three positions connected in the revolution with the lord of its seventh, it indicates the native's marriage in that year, and his eagerness and desire in that will be from himself. **23** And if the lord of their seventh connected with one of them, women will propose marriage to him and they will be eager for him. **24** And if one of them was separating from its associate in the revolution, the condition will be the contrary of that, and he will abstain from them, and they will abstain from him.

25 And if the lord of one of these three positions connected in the revolution with the lord of its eighth, it indicates that the owner of the revolution will deceive himself, and engage in fearful things; and if it was corrupted, made unfortunate by the lord of its eighth, ruin will be feared for him. **26** And if the lord of their eighth connected with one of them, harsh things will afflict him; and if it was corrupted by it, the indication of death will be more corroborated. **27** And if one of them was received by the lord of its eighth, made fortunate by it, he will have inheritances. **28** And if one of them was separating from its associate in the revolution, it will be the contrary of that.

29 And if the lord of one of the three positions connected with the lord of its ninth, it indicates what we stated about the third.

30 And if the lord of one of these three positions connected in the revolution with the lord of its tenth, he will desire the companionship of the authorities, and seek what is in their presence,[135] and a livelihood because of them. **31** And if the lord of their tenth connected with one of them, the authorities will need him and seek him out for work.

---

[135] Or, "power" (قبل).

32 And if the lord of one of the three positions connected in the revolution with the lord of its eleventh, he will acquire brothers and friends in that year, and his condition in his way of life[136] will be improved. **33** And if the lord of their eleventh connected with one of them, the people will want him and seek out his friendship, and he will have good and status from them. **34** And if one of them was separating from its associate in the revolution, it will be contrary to that.

35 And if the lord of one of the three positions connected in the revolution with the lord of its twelfth, he will do work in that year from which he will benefit, [but] in distress and something detestable. **36** And if the lord of their twelfth connected with one of them, distresses and hardship will befall him, and confinement because of [something] he is not aware of. **37** And if one of them was separating from its associate in the revolution, it will be the contrary of that.

38 And the most corroborating thing in all of this is if the three indicators coincided in a single situation, with respect to connection and separation; and indeed that will be if the sign of the terminal point and the Ascendant of the year both coincide with the Ascendant of the root.[137] **39** And if each one of [the three] had an indication by itself, [but only] two of them coincided in [their] connecting [with other planets], it will be below the first [interpretation]; and if it happened to [only] one, it is weaker. **40** And the strongest thing in the indication of connecting [with other planets], is the connection of the lord of the Ascendant of the root with the lords of the houses of the root (or their connection with it), then below that in strength is the lords of the houses of the sign of the terminal point, then the lords of the houses of the Ascendant of the year (and the situations of their separating are like that in power).

---

[136] This especially has financial connotations, such as "salary" (معاش).

[137] But it's also possible (though even more rare) that they are in different signs, but each one is doing the same thing, *separately*, in each one of its own derived houses. So the lord of the natal Ascendant could be connecting the lord of its fourth, *and also* the lord of the revolutionary Ascendant could be connecting the lord of its fourth, and so on, with all in a similar condition.

Book VI: Lord of Orb, the Ascendant, Connections

41 And if their conditions differed, so that one of them was [1] connecting with the lord of one of the houses, and another was [2] separating from the corresponding lord of that house, and another was [3] falling away from[138] its inspection, the indication in it will be diverse. **42** And[139] an example of that is if [1] the Ascendant of the root was Libra, and at the revolution Venus was connecting with Mars (who is the lord of the house of his assets), and [2] the sign of the terminal point was Sagittarius but Jupiter was separating from Saturn (who is the lord of Capricorn), and [3] the Ascendant of the revolution was Taurus and Venus is falling away from Mercury (who is the lord of Gemini), not looking at him. **43** So due to [1] the connection of Venus with Mars, it indicates the benefit of assets, but [2] due to the separation of Jupiter from Saturn it indicates its spending, and [3] due to Mercury's falling away from the inspection of Venus, it indicates the scarcity of his eagerness for collecting and seeking [wealth]. **44** And in this manner you should mix the indications of the lords of the signs if their situations differ.

---

[138] That is, in aversion to.
[139] In this and the next paragraph I have numbered the scenarios and planets according to whether they involve [1] the root, [2] the profection, or [3] the revolution.

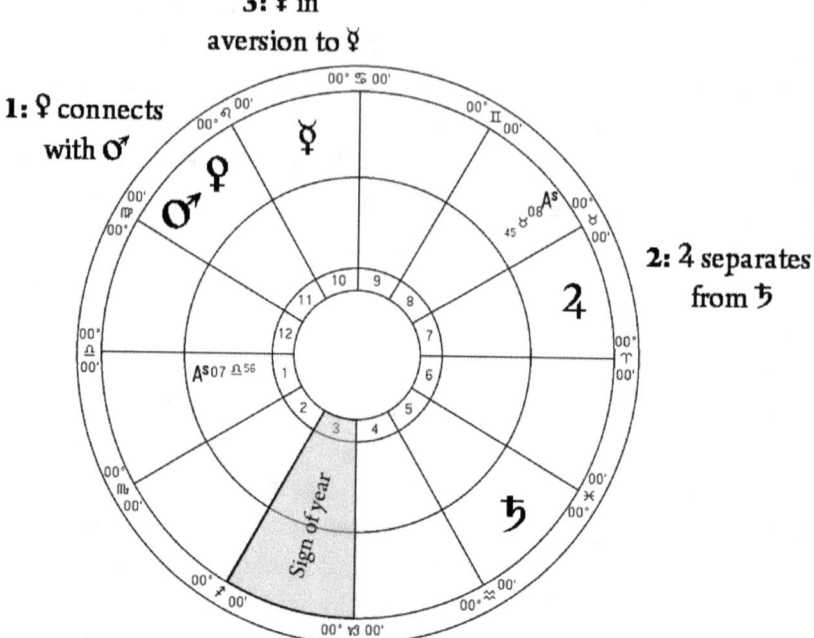

**Figure 95: Lord of each Ascendant,
with its own lord of the second (VI.6, 41-44)**

45 And if the lord of one of the houses is connecting with the counterpart of its lord [in another scheme], its indication will appear as well, except that it will be below the first [interpretation]: and an example of that is if [1] Mars (who is the lord of the house of assets of the root) is connecting with [2] Jupiter (who is the lord of the sign of the terminal point), or [3] Mercury (the lord of Gemini) is connecting with [2] Jupiter or with [1] Venus, or [1, 3] Venus is connecting with [2] Saturn: for then this also indicates benefit.

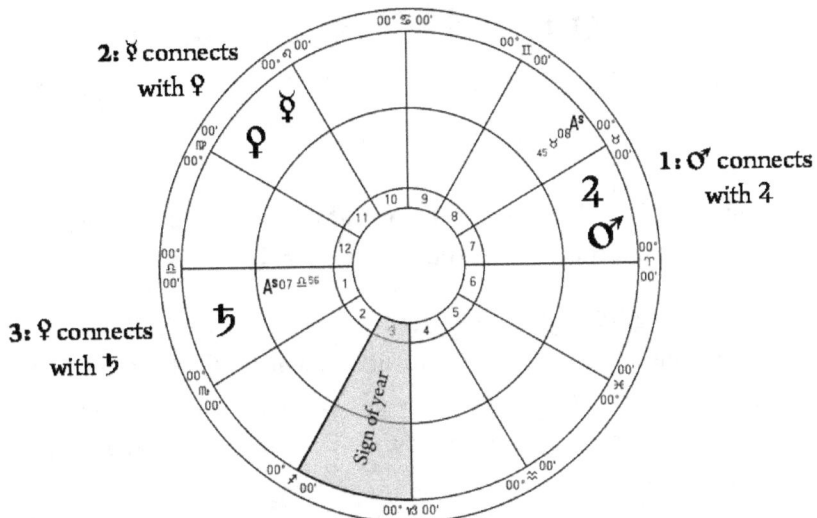

**Figure 96: Lord of each Ascendant,
with each others' lords of the second (VI.6, 41-45)**

46 The sixth part of the book is completed, and God be praised!

BOOK VII: ON THE SHIFTING OF THE PLANETS IN THE SIGNS THROUGHOUT THE WHOLE YEAR

And there are nine chapters

Chapter VII.1: On the conditions of the planets in the signs & houses of the circle, in the revolution

1 Everything which has preceded whose planetary indications we have mentioned, belongs to their positions which they have at the revolution of the year. **2** And for every one of them, when they come to be in one of the signs or houses of the circle after that,¹ they activate the indication of that sign or house.

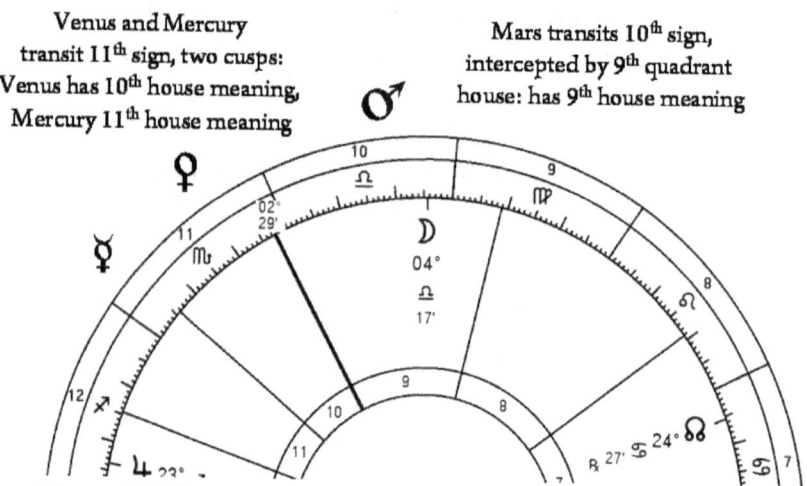

Figure 97: Transits in intercepted signs and with two cusps (VII.1, 3-4)

3 And if a single sign is apportioned out to two houses,² and then a planet comes to be in it, then its indication in that sign will be in accordance with what is apportioned from it to each house.³ **4** And if

---

¹ That is, by ongoing transits throughout the year.
² That is, two cusps on one sign (as with Venus and Mercury in Figure 97 above).
³ That is, by the division or quadrant house it is actually in.

two or three signs were apportioned to a single house,[4] then the indication of the planet when it comes to be in it, will be in accordance with the indication of the house which they are apportioned to.[5]

5 Now as for Saturn, the most he can travel in any of the years when he is quick in course in it, is 13° and some minutes; so if at the revolution of the year he was in one of the signs or one of the houses, then sometimes he will not leave that sign and house which he is in, and sometimes he will shift into the next sign or house.

6 As for Jupiter, sometimes he shifts from house to house, and his management will appear in three signs. **7** And indeed it will be like that if, at the revolution, he is at the end of the sign, and he is quick in course, [so that] in one year he will travel 38° (or an amount greater than that), so that he goes out from the sign he was in, and reaches the third sign from his revolutionary position.

8 As for Mars, if at the revolution he is in one of the signs, at its end, and he is quick in course in that year, then he will reach the tenth sign from it.

9 As for the Sun, he always returns to his own place.

10 As for Venus, if at the revolution she was in one of the signs, at its end, and she is quick in course in that year, she will return to her place and [then] go past it until she comes to the fourth sign from it, and her indication will appear in 16 signs.

11 As for Mercury, if at the revolution he was in one of the signs, then sometimes he will go past his place and come to the sign which follows it, so that his management will appear in 13 signs.

12 (And for each one of these planets, if it was slow in course, it will fail to reach these positions which we have stated, in accordance with its slowness.)

13 As for the Moon, if at the revolution she was in one of the positions, then in every one of the "months of the Sun" she will return to

---

[4] That is, intercepted signs (as with Mars in Figure 97 above).
[5] So if Mars transits the tenth sign, but it is fully intercepted between the cusp of the ninth (in the ninth sign) and the degree of the Midheaven (in the eleventh sign), then his transit in it will actually have *ninth-house* meanings. See the diagram.

her place, and go past it to the sign which follows it, or to the third sign from it, so that her management will appear[6] in 13 or 14 signs.[7]

14 As for the Head and Tail, each of them travels 20° 20' in every year, and beyond. **15** So if one of them at the revolution was in one of the houses, then sometimes it will not leave it, and sometimes it will shift from it into another.

16 And for these three inferior planets,[8] if in any of the years they reached their own revolutionary place, and went past it into another of the houses, and in the first time they indicated something, then in the second time they will not indicate something like what they had indicated at first: because upon their return to the revolutionary place (or to the rest of the positions which they were in at the first time) their condition relative to the fortunes and infortunes will be different from their condition from them which they have in the next time: and the increase or decrease in good or evil is in accordance with their condition from them.[9]

17 And upon the shifting of the planets in the twelve houses, you ought to investigate many things: seven of them are what we will mention in this Book, and the rest in the Book which follows it.[10]

18 The first of the seven, is its condition in itself.

---

[6] Reading with **E**. **B** and **P** read, "her management in every month will appear." **T**: "her management in her affairs will appear."

[7] Remember from Ch. I.3, **9**, a "month of the Sun" is exactly 30° of the Sun's motion in the zodiac, which is the basis for monthly revolution charts. So, let the natal Sun be at 17° Taurus, and the Moon in mid-Gemini. By the time he reaches 17° Gemini, she will already have made one circuit in the zodiac, past him, and entered into mid-Leo, a course of 14 signs in one "month of the Sun."

[8] Venus, Mercury, and the Moon.

[9] So, let Mercury be in some sign at the revolution, in a trine to Jupiter; by the end of the year, when he returns to that sign he might be in the square of Mars. So while he retains the same *class* of meanings due to the sign and house, the quality and outcome, and how his meanings are affected by Jupiter or Mars, will differ.

[10] Book VIII contains the planet's transits in their own and others' signs and bounds, as well as the "wells" or welled degrees.

19 The second is the position of the sign which it is in, relative to the Ascendant of the root.[11]

20 The third is its position relative to the sign of the terminal point.

21 The fourth is its position relative to the Ascendant of the revolution.

22 The fifth is its transiting the bodies of the planets or their rays, or their twelfth-parts, or the rooted and[12] revolutionary Lots, so long as it is in that sign.[13]

23 The sixth is its connection with the planets (or their connection with it), so long as it is in that sign.[14]

24 The seventh is the aspect of each of them to the other.[15]

25 And for each one of them, when it comes to be in one of the twelve houses, it indicates things in accordance with its own nature, and the nature of the sign, and in accordance with the special attributes of each.

26 And for everything we have stated about the indication of each planet upon its shifting in the houses throughout the whole year, it will be one of completeness if that planet indicated that [same] subject in both the root of the nativity and at the time of the revolution. **27** But if at any of the times of the year there was not [even] a little bit of what it had presented [in the root] (and every planet is [always] in one

---

[11] Abū Ma'shar groups this and **20-21** together in Chs. VII.2-VII.9.
[12] Reading with **B** for "or."
[13] It seems to me this was already addressed in Book V.
[14] I'm not sure if or where Abū Ma'shar address this and sentence **24**, but see Ch. VI.6.
[15] Aspects or looking is between signs, as opposed to connections (which are based on degrees: **23**).

of the signs harmonizing with it or contrary to it), it will alter some of what we will state, of the increase in it or subtraction from it.[16]

28 And these indications which belong to the planets in this Book and in Book VIII closely resemble their indications for the months and days.

Chapter VII.2: On the indication of Saturn in his transit in the twelve houses

1 If the Ascendant of the root, the revolution, and the sign of the terminal point were a single sign, and Saturn came to be in it,[17] then in that time the owner of the revolution will associate with people who have power, and he will increase in his rank, and he will have few words, be a coward, and he will be hostile to friends and brothers, and it prepares conflicts for him, and he will be devoted to the sciences, and turn his mind to detestable things because of someone else, and his anger will increase, and many of the people will fear him, and he will be distressed because of something he did not do,[18] and bad thoughts will overcome him, and he will concoct lies, and a manifest ailment will afflict him, and he will be devoted to the conditions of rivers, slaves, and servant-girls, and assets will come to him from kings or from people who have power, and it will reduce something of his assets, and he will resolve to travel, and will shift from house to house, and be distressed because of children. **2** And if Saturn was close to the degree of the Ascendant, then he will be devoted to the sciences, and know the secrets of kings and leaders, and will shift from leader to leader, and connect with people, and labor much, and increase in his

---

[16] See also VII.9, **25-27**.
[17] See VII.9, **25-27** and VII.1, **26-27** above for when the Ascendants do not coincide. We might expect that the following chapters only apply to planets transiting in the revolutionary houses, but because revolutions also activate natal indications, and we are also recognizing houses relative to the sign of the year, we have to consider all three house schemes. Therefore, for the sake of simplicity Abū Ma'shar wants to first consider the idealized case in which all three Ascendants coincide.
[18] **E** and **B** read, "because of something he does not know."

power, and leadership will come to him over people greater than him, and he will look down upon the people, and fear of the Sultan will afflict him, and he will appeal to one of the authorities, and will say things which are appropriate, and something will come to him because of things left behind and inheritances, or he will be entrusted with something of the assets[19] of the dead, and disaster will afflict his father from illness or from the anger of a man having power. 3 And if his presence in the Ascendant coincided with a male sign in which he has testimony, it indicates that he will be a master of some animals and will be distressed because of some of them, and if he devoted himself to business he would profit in it, and perhaps some of his relatives will be ruined, or distress will afflict them, and weeping will befall the owner of the revolution. 4 Now as for if he was in a female sign, alien, people will be hostile to him and he will be distressed by people. 5 But if Saturn was burned up in the Ascendant, it indicates something detestable, servitude, and service. 6 And if one of the rooted or revolutionary fortunes assembled with him in that position, it subtracts from all of the adversity we have stated, and he will increase in the good.

7 Now if Saturn came to be in the second from the three positions, then so long as he is in it [the native] will make use of sheep or other animals, and he will govern people, and do good towards the people of his house (though some of them will have adversity), and there will be estrangement between him and some of his siblings, and he will connect with the nobles so that they will drink together and support each other, and he will be well commended in places which he is absent from, and he will delight in relation to something he had not hoped for, and he will be devoted to building, repairs, buying and selling, and do business, and will be distressed because of assets of his own and those of others, and he will be extravagant in spending, and provisions will be indispensable for him, and it will take away from his assets and he will be constrained in his possessions, and his soul will be burdened by fear because of assets, and he will be distressed because of debts, collateral, and fines, [but] then that distress will retreat from him and

---

[19] **B** reads, "matters, affairs."

assets will come to him which he will delight in, and he will bury money in the earth or entrust someone else with money for safekeeping. **8** And if Saturn left the house of assets this year, he will increase in his assets and profit in business. <**9** And if Saturn was in Aries and its triplicities, then [*omitted*]>. **10** And if Saturn was in Taurus and its triplicities, he will treat the people of his house badly, and will make use of lands, and bring life to their barren [areas], and misfortune will befall part of his garments, and he will marry one of his relatives,[20] and he will have a conflict because of women, and some of them will leave,[21] and if his father was alive a debt will come upon him. **11** And if Saturn was in Gemini and its triplicities, then buying and selling will be appropriate for him, and doing business,[22] and it will produce the acquisition of money for him, and assets will come to him from some of those having importance. **12** And if he was in Cancer and its triplicities, then he will earn money from the people of his house, and his pursuit of it will be multiplied due to deserts and open country,[23] and pain will afflict him in his legs, and he will have sex with a woman having a defect or illness, and it will scatter his assets and the assets of the people of his house, and he will tear down some places and build [upon them].

13 And if Saturn was in the third from the three positions, then so long as he is in it a love of new things will overtake him, and cleanliness, and some of his siblings or relatives will treat him badly, and some of his friends will be hostile to him and quarrel with him repeatedly, and he will be victorious over those who quarrel [with him], and he will shift from place to place, and frequently he will be alone and corrupt [his] assets and goods, and come to the brink of bad adversity, and fever and pains will afflict him, as well as an ailment in the brain and head, and he will be elevated over people who are higher[24] and

---

[20] This could also be read as "one of his relatives will marry."

[21] **T** reads, "and he will live immorally with some of them."

[22] **B** and **T** add "on the water," but to me this seems more appropriate for the watery signs.

[23] Like the phrase about water in **12**, this seems more appropriate for earthy signs.

[24] This word only in **B**.

more powerful than him, and perhaps if he travels, his returning to the place which he had traveled from will be difficult, and he will be devoted to wisdom and express judgments, and especially if he was in a female sign. **14** But if he was in a male sign, then he will be devoted to scholars, philosophy, the sciences, and hidden things, and he will investigate things which are in the future, such that he will be correct in them, and will do service in piety,²⁵ and will be a leader over people.

15 And if Saturn was in the fourth from the three positions, then so long as he is in it he will be devoted to the elderly, and the nobles, and he will be respected, and will tear down a place of his residence and build [another], and be criticized, and sad because of his own assets and the assets of others, and he will squander assets, and a pain as well as a fever will afflict him, and he will enjoy many sudden delights, and marry one of his relatives,²⁶ and one of them will have something detestable, and they will have the situations which follow from them,²⁷ and some of them will be hostile to him. **16** And if Saturn had testimony in the Ascendant, then it indicates illness and worries for the owner of the revolution, and he will do works pertaining to piety for the sake of God.²⁸ **17** Now if Saturn was in his own house, then he will find a treasure or money due to [some] stratagem, and a hidden illness will afflict him, and one of his children will have an ailment or be ruined, and he will gather up much gold, and will be a custodian of assets—but if Saturn was retrograde, it subtracts from his assets. **18** Now as for if he was in exile,²⁹ then it indicates the ruin of the parents,

---

²⁵ ويخدم النّساك.
²⁶ This could also be read as "one of his relatives will marry."
²⁷ Reading with **T**: ويكون لهم حالات يتلون منها, but it does not make precise grammatical sense. Other MSS read, "the situations [which] are from them." I do not know who the "them" refers to, since it is in the feminine singular and there is no appropriate referent here.
²⁸ The word for "piety" here (بر), with slightly different voweling, is the same as the word for "land." I strongly suspect that the original source simply read "land," but someone like Abū Ma'shar took it to be "piety," and then added "for the sake of God." Saturn in the fourth sounds a lot more like farming than doing pious works.
²⁹ That is, alien or peregrine.

and the death of the father will be sudden, or a shivering fever will afflict the owner of the revolution, and degradation from some of the people. **19** And if a fortune testified to Saturn in the root or in the revolution, then he will free himself of the detestable things, and will devote himself to business, and will reach a country not his own, and will see what he loves, and will delight in male children, and a disagreement will occur between him and his friends, [but] then the matter will be settled after that.

20 And if Saturn was in the fifth from the three places, then so long as he is in it [bad] thoughts will get the best of him, and his use of high culture[30] will multiply, and he will increase in his intellect, and be distressed because of a misfortune afflicting one of his children (and it will ruin some of them), and his children will connect with people who have power, and benefit will come to them, and the owner of the revolution will increase in power without warning (and perhaps that will be because of a woman having power), and he will assume responsibility for some of the works of the Sultan, and he will be devoted to building and the management of lands, planting, trees, vineyards, and crops in several places, and he will increase in his assets, and he will become rich suddenly and be constrained suddenly, and perhaps what distresses him will afflict him in his assets, and one of his friends and his relatives will deceive him and seize[31] him, and he will shift from place to place, and will not be thanked for the good works which he does for others, and he will see something detestable in his enemies.

21 Now if Saturn was in the sixth from the three positions, then so long as he is in it he will have much grief, regret, depression, and sorrow, and he will seek treasures or old assets, and something of his assets will be destroyed time after time,[32] and he will be devoted to leaders and visit them frequently, and his value will be reduced, and he will labor much, and go on a journey he will not benefit from, and his

---

[30] الأدب, which has to do with good manners, literature, education, etc.
[31] This can also mean "murder" (يغتال).
[32] Or perhaps, "on occasion" or "occasionally."

attendance at the houses of religion will increase, and he will break his promises, and the people will find him annoying, and he will curse the people. **22** And if he was responsible for guaranteeing collateral[33] he will lose it, and some of his slaves and servants will flee, and something detestable will afflict him because of them, and the people of his house will break from him, and perhaps he will divorce his woman because of a female friend or concubine, or a disagreement will occur between them, and he will marry a woman of a bad sort, and he will not be successful in his affairs, and something detestable will afflict one of his children, and harm will afflict the father, and his enemies will gloat at his bad luck, and he will be weak in his body and become ill from a fever, or hemorrhoids will afflict him, or an ailment in a hidden place of his body, or he will be cut by iron, and [have] distresses because of fire or other things, until he weeps because of them. **23** But if Saturn was in a male sign, all of that will be less.

24 And if Saturn was in the seventh from the three positions, then so long as he is in it he will have much disorder[34] in his affairs, and his father as well as others of the people will wrong him, and they will quarrel with him because of assets, and he will be in need, poor of soul, and his friends and enemies will treat him badly, and he will be annoyed, and his children will have something detestable from him, or some of them will become ill, and his labor will multiply as well as overwhelming affliction, and his demands and needs will be difficult for him, and the people will not thank him for his charitable deeds, an ailment will afflict him which emaciates his body, and perhaps the ailment will be in a hidden place of his body, and he will fall ill due to his brain [or] head, or from moisture coming down from his brain (such as catarrh[35] or something else), or a stomachache will afflict him, or an ailment in the lower region (from which the blood is afflicted), or cold

---

[33] This can also refer to bail or any kind of deposit or guarantee (كفالة).

[34] التخليط, which covers many kinds of bad mixing or confusion: it can range from inappropriate social relations to mental disturbance.

[35] That is, an accumulation of moisture in the sinuses and upper chest, accompanied by coughing and inflammation.

will afflict him in his legs, and he will benefit from his woman, and he will serve some women and be distressed because of some of them, and will be jealous of them, and will treat them harshly,[36] and his sexual intercourse will be less—and all of this will be harsher if Saturn was in a feminine sign, western, alien. **25** But if Jupiter was with Saturn, then he will be rescued from what we stated, and his enemies will have something detestable, and he will get assets (and he will spend them).[37] **26** And if Saturn was in Aries and its triplicities, then he will hate the people and they will hate him, and cutting by iron will afflict him, or misfortune from confinement or prisoners, or from riding animals (of those having four feet). **27** And if he was in Taurus and its triplicities, then he will be devoted to agriculture, and he will benefit by it. **28** And if he was in Gemini and its triplicities, then he will be devoted to gold and silver. **29** And if he was in Cancer and its triplicities, he will be devoted to waters, rivers, planting, and waterwheels, and he will benefit from that.

30 And if Saturn was in the eighth from the three positions, then so long as he is in it he will quarrel much, and some of his enemies will die (or he will be victorious over them), and a disagreement will occur in what there is between him and his father or one of his relatives, and he will be elevated over his siblings, and some of them will have adversity, and he will mistreat some of those having importance, and he will be of diverse thoughts, many-sided, and he will do bad works, and look into hidden things, and perhaps he will be absent from his home or go on a journey in which there is [a great] distance, and he will have sex with a foreign women or a child will be born to him, and one of his children will be made unhappy by an illness or death, and he will be entrusted with money for safekeeping, and he will find something buried, or a treasure, or money with ease, and he will be devoted to the conditions of old assets, and loss will afflict him in his assets. **31** But if one of the fortunes testified to Saturn, it takes away from everything we mentioned of detestable things.

---

[36] Or, "he will shun them" (يجفوهنّ).
[37] But **E** reads, "they will benefit him."

32 And if Saturn was in the ninth from the three places, then so long as he is in it he will look into the conditions of religion and its secrets, and he will become a leader over people because of it, and he will do deeds because of which the religious and the just will disapprove of him, and he will look into philosophy and the heavenly sciences, and will report things which are in the future such that he will be accurate in them, and he will see good visions whose interpretation is true, and he will commit every deed which occurs to him, and a conflict will occur between him and the people,³⁸ and he will be devoted to the authorities and those having importance, as well as lying, deception, and stratagems, and he will command, and communicate [things] and be listened to, and he will quarrel about useless things he has no knowledge of, and [bad] words will occur between him and the people of his house, and degradation and disgrace will come to him, and assets will come to him from a disgusting source, and if he travels something detestable will afflict him on the road, and he will take a rugged, fearful path, and his return will be difficult or else he will spend his year abroad. **33** But if the fortunes testified to Saturn, it takes away from those detestable things.

34 And if Saturn was in the tenth from the three positions, then so long as he is in it he will be devoted to repairs, building, paintings and statues, agriculture, real estate, gardens, rivers, canals, ships, baths, moist places, and hunting by water, and he will associate with people who have power, and people will envy him, and he will travel or labor much, and something detestable will afflict him as well as degradation and quarrels for various reasons, and his body will be cut by a sword or iron, and he will fall from a riding animal or from a raised place, or a disaster will afflict him from some beasts, and some of his male servants, slaves, or dogs will split from him, and he will do bad deeds he will be criticized for, and have doubts in his religion, and will slander the people (and they will slander him), and he will become ill, and wounds³⁹ will afflict him or an ailment in his head, and he will shift

---

³⁸ **E** and **P** read, "and the women."
³⁹ Or, "ulcers" (قروح).

from a condition of ease to one of difficulty, and will be hostile to his relatives and parents, and something detestable will afflict [the parents] and the children of the owner of the revolution, as well as his women. **35** And if Saturn was in a sign in which he had a claim, and one of the fortunes testified to him, it takes away from the detestable things, and he will gain the good from kings, and will increase in his assets, and will be victorious over his enemies, and if he was a traveler he will return from his journey and will benefit by commerce and business dealings, and debts and loans, so that he increases in his assets, and a male child will be born to him, and he will see good, sound visions with true interpretations.

36 And if Saturn was in the eleventh from the three positions, then so long as he is in it he will increase in his good, and after [some] difficulty he will be successful in the things he seeks, and he will be distressed over nothing, and will quarrel and treat one of his parents badly, and he will be disturbed by delights and pleasures, and will be devoted to the conditions of waters and lands. **37** But if one of the fortunes testified to him, it indicates an increase in the good, assets, and accomplishment in [his] works, except that he will be distressed because of children, relatives, and slaves.

38 And if Saturn was in the twelfth from the three positions, then so long as he is in it he will be victorious over his enemies, and harm will afflict him in assets, slaves, and riding animals, and he will be cunning in his soul, and contend with someone else,[40] and he will desire evil, and a disagreement will occur between him and his women, and he will be jealous of them, and he[41] will fabricate lies, and he will act well towards some of the people of his house and his relatives, and will invite them to his meals, and [in] whatever work he begins it will diminish what is completed by his own hands, and he will have little pleasure, not being praised for whatever charitable deeds he performs for others, and harm will afflict him by reason of tricks he performs

---

[40] ينازع من غيره, reading من with **T** for عن. Still, this does not seem right in the Arabic, and seems too bland as an interpretation.

[41] **P** reads "they," referring to the wives.

against a man, and if he travels harm will afflict him in it, and he will see bad visions, and will not benefit by business, buying, and selling; and God is more knowledgeable in the truth of that.

Chapter VII.3: On the indication of Jupiter in his transit in the twelve houses

1 If the Ascendant of the root, of the revolution, and the sign of the terminal point were a single sign, and Jupiter came to be in it, then the owner of the revolution in that time will be comfortable in [his] way of life, cheerful, and he will be a leader over his peers, and the nobles will be present at his door, and he will be on intimate terms with kings, and befriend people who have power, and he will be praised, honored, and one of his brothers who is older than him will be ruined, and the power which belonged to that brother will pass to him, and he will increase in his power, assets, servants, and slaves, and will marry a woman, and be devoted to marrying and wedding, and his child will marry, and a child will be born to him (or one will be born to his child), and perhaps the one born will be male, and he will loan money to the people and benefit them, and his soul will be enlarged by the expenditure, and he will build palaces, and plant plants and vineyards, and what things he does will be completed at his hands, and will make a vow to God (and carry it out), and swear an oath over something pious.

2 And if Jupiter was in the second from the three positions, then so long as he is in it his assets will remain with him, and he will earn [more] assets and hoard them from sources both known and unknown, or because of death, and he will be entrusted with assets for safekeeping, and benefit because of a theft, and buying and selling, and slaves and servant-girls, and he will associate with nobles, and will be tight-fisted, loving to collect [wealth]. **3** Now if Jupiter was made unfortunate, something detestable will afflict him from everything which we have stated, and if he devotes himself to business he will suffer loss in it.

4 And if Jupiter was in the third from the three positions, and especially if he was in a male sign, then so long as he is in it he will be fully acquainted with the things which are, and he will do praised works of the affairs of religion and the truth, and will be mentioned with courtesy, and the people will praise him and he will treat them well, and they will treat him well. **5** And if Jupiter was in a female sign, then he will often see visions which will not come true, and he will praise himself,[42] and his devotion to scholars will increase as well as the conditions of religion, jurisprudence, and the sciences, and magic and incantations, and he will be praised, and leadership will come to him, and he will treat his siblings and the people of his house and his relatives well, and he will ingratiate himself with the people, and be [honored].[43]

6 And if Jupiter was in the fourth from the three positions, then so long as he is in it he will have good and benefit from hidden, concealed places, and he will increase in his animals, cows, and sheep, and he will store away some assets, and will be devoted to old things, and buried treasures and money, and he will benefit from business deals and profit in them, and will be a man abounding in good, and he will be devoted to the conditions of farms, lands, and rivers, and he will build buildings, and associate with the religious, and will do works of piety, and will frequently invoke God (be He exalted!) and make supplications to Him, and generally he will see what he loves in his works, and the leaders and nobility will be aware of him, and he will serve them, and he will increase in his power, and his wife will become pregnant by him.

7 And if Jupiter came to be in the fifth from the three positions, and he is not made unfortunate, then so long as he is in it he will increase in his assets, and be devoted to gifts, messengers, and reports, and taking and giving, and he will think about bad situations and poverty, and be envied for much of his actions, and tell lies about good people, and

---

[42] This could also be read as "his soul will be praised."
[43] Reading متبجّلاً somewhat speculatively, for what could also be متجمّلاً ("adorned") or مجتملاً ("anointed").

fabricate lies and falsehoods in matters of his speech, and will love idleness,[44] and a child will be born to him, and his children will be connected with people having power, and he will treat his brothers and relatives well, and will increase in his power, and see something detestable in his enemies, and frequent the houses of worship, and love fame and reputation, and report the tales of good people and the deceased, and be devoted to treasure-troves[45] and graveyards, and if he travels he will return to his homeland.

8 And if Jupiter came to be in the sixth from these three positions, then so long as he is in it he will hate the people of uprightness, and conflict and quarrels will occur between him and some of them and the people having power, due to ancient matters, and they will bring each other before the Sultan,[46] and he will also quarrel with the lower classes, and his good deeds towards the people will be burdensome for him, and he will not persist in the love of anyone, and will be sad because of his women and children, and the children of strangers, and he will squander assets in a way he does not like, and ruin the assets of his mother but gain from the assets of his father, and kings will respect him, and he will earn money from them, and fleeting distresses will pass over him, and an ailment in his liver and in his brows[47] or above his forehead, and he will become ill due to drinking wine.

9 Now if Jupiter came to be in the seventh from the three positions, then so long as he is in it he will marry a woman having power, and he will acquire jewelry for her, and have good from women and they will love him, and bad things will be said about him because of them, and his woman will become pregnant by him, and a child will be born to him, and he will increase in his friends, and his enemies will be destroyed, and he will have treasure or assets because of something old

---

[44] البطالة. **B** reads, "cleanliness" (النظافة).
[45] Only **B** contains this; if it is correct, it might pertain to trading in minerals.
[46] Reading the verb as Form VI, rather than Form VIII as it appears here ("they will be raised up to").
[47] حاجبيه. But perhaps this could be read as a variant from the same verb, "his diaphragm" (حجابه), or "his haunches" (حجبتيه).

or because of the dead, and will handle business and squander money, and fear will afflict him from waters and moisture, and his word will be accepted in many things, and generally in his works he will see what he loves in terms of advancement, and he will build buildings, and plant trees and plants, and be in charge of works having importance.[48] **10** Now if Jupiter was made unfortunate, then a disagreement will occur between him and women,[49] and they will become estranged, and something detestable and loss will afflict him in his assets, and he will quarrel with the people, and go on a distant journey. **11** And if that sign was a house of Jupiter, then it will take away from the evil and he will increase in the good, and he will gain assets having value, and delight in friends.

12 And if Jupiter came to be in the eighth from the three positions, then so long as he is in it he will shift from [one] condition to a condition more suitable than [the first], and he will be noted in the sciences and wisdom, and he will become ill, and anxieties will afflict him, and evil gossip will be said about him, and he will be lied about (except that these things will fade away from him), and his revenue will be reduced, and he will focus on the assets of the dead and what [they] leave behind, and assets will come to him for this reason, and especially if Jupiter was increasing in his course. **13** But if he was made unfortunate, it indicates a reduction in assets and much spending.

14 And if Jupiter was in the ninth from the three positions, and in a sign in which he has testimony, especially if the sign was male, then so long as he is in it he will travel from country to country, and on his journey he will have the good and benefit, and leadership, and it will involve what he loves, and he will enter into a friendship in his absence from home and because of those having importance, and he will build buildings in a foreign land, and [his] speech will be received, he being correct in it, and he will be devoted to the conditions of religion, and for that reason he will have good, and he will benefit from business and trade, and from the truth and sincerity, and be entrusted with as-

---

[48] قدر. **B** reads, "thought" (فكر).
[49] Reading النّساء with **B** and **T**. But **E** and **P** read, "the people" (النّاس).

sets for safekeeping, and collect assets, and [also] waste them, and he will come to kings and associate with them, and dress in their clothing. **15** But as for if he was in an alien sign, especially if the sign was female, he will have false visions, and it will prepare lawsuits for him, and he will swear false oaths, and lie about his enemies, and praise himself, and have a high opinion about himself, and will love sexual intercourse with women, and will have the good from them, and will look after some of them (or[50] marry [one of them]).

16 And if Jupiter was in the tenth from the three positions, then so long as he is in it he will associate with kings, and they will be on familiar terms with him, and leadership will come to him in which he will be commanding, and he will communicate and his speech will be trusted, and he will be blessed in it, and corrupt the assets of some of the people of his house, and treat others of them well, and be devoted to lands, farms, and livestock,[51] and he will be entrusted with assets for safekeeping as well as inherit money, and his children will be fortunate, and it will be suitable for him to marry, and he will benefit from partners, and he will [*uncertain*],[52] and he will be absent from his home, and carouse with strangers, and will see affection in his deeds. **17** And if he was made unfortunate, it will take away from the good and increase in the evil.

18 And if Jupiter was in the eleventh from the three positions, then so long as he is in it he will acquire assets having value, and he will marry a woman, and a male child will be born to him, and he will be devoted to taking and giving, and will associate with authorities and the powerful, and affection will come to him in his deeds, and if he was ill he will recover from his illness, and he will cling to his religion, and will quarrel because of it, and be devoted to graveyards, and build

---

[50] **P** reads, "and."

[51] **E** adds: "and cows."

[52] The MSS seem to indicate "reaching" (يأتى) his own "country" (بلده), but all read slightly differently and with odd syntax (and the next phrase says he will be absent from home). On the other hand, dotted differently it could mean that he produces pleasures (يأتى بلذة). It could also be an unusual idiom.

buildings and plant trees, and rejoice over his enemies' mishaps. **19** And if he was made unfortunate, it will take away from the good.

20 And if Jupiter came to be in the twelfth from the three positions, then so long as he is in it his father will treat him badly, and other people will treat him well, and the enmity of people will be stirred up against him, and he will be successful in lawsuits, and something detestable will afflict him in his assets, and he will have many expenses, and lend money and ask for loans, and it will prepare various disasters and quarreling for him, and evil with low, weak people, and he will go on a distant journey, and be absent from his house, and he will have much concern and anxiety, and the people will not praise him for his charitable works towards them, and he will have misfortune from some beasts, and a child will be born to him or his woman will become pregnant.

Chapter VII.4: On the indication of Mars in his transit in the twelve houses

1 If the Ascendant of the root, the revolution, and the sign of the terminal point were a single sign, and Mars came to be in it, then in that time disaster will afflict the owner of the revolution from fire or heat, or wounds will appear on him, and a pain will afflict him in a hidden place of his body due to food and indigestion, or a pain of the belly or a pain of the waist, and a blocking of the urine, and enemies will quarrel with him, and he will litigate in the matter of assets and other things (and it will be judged correctly for him in his assets), and he will move from place to place, and will have a hard heart, being quick to anger, and his father will go into confinement or some other adversity, and the owner of the revolution will treat the people of his house badly as well as his mother,[53] and it will prepare conflicts for the mother because of useless matters.

---

[53] Note that Mars in the Ascendant would be squaring the fourth and tenth, so if we assume the later assigning of the mother to the tenth, this explains the harm to both parents.

BOOK VII: ONGOING TRANSITS IN HOUSES

2 And if Mars came to be in the second from the three positions, then so long as he is in it he will apply his hand to base works, and he will litigate in the presence of leaders and the nobles, and assets will come to him from various bad directions after conflict, litigation, and labor, and some of that will be due to an old matter, and he will have many expenses he is distressed by, and some of them will be due to corrupt women, songs, and entertainment, and perhaps assets will be stolen from him, or misfortune will afflict some of his assets from fire or something else, and he will be devoted to demolition and razing, and building and repairs.

3 And if Mars came to be in the third from the three positions, then so long as he is in it he will have a high opinion of himself, and will mistreat the people of his house as well as his brothers, and he will love quarreling and lawsuits, and [bad] words will take place between him and some of his friends, and he will be devoted to deception, lying, and stratagems, as well as the army, generals, and troops, and he will carouse with the nobles, and some of those having importance will be angry with him (and he will see what he loves from some of them), and some of his relatives will go on a distant journey they will return from.

4 Now if Mars came to be in the fourth from the three positions, then so long as he is in it it indicates that an illness will afflict him in the face or in a hidden place (and perhaps that will be in the heart, spleen, or kidneys), or a pain of the joints will afflict him, or pustules and abscesses will emerge from him which one must pierce with iron, or he will fall from a raised place, and he will loan money and ask for a loan, and will tear down part of his home, and will not be praised for a good deed he does for someone else, and a lawsuit will afflict his father, and he will often become enraged, or perhaps fear of wild animals and the authorities and army will afflict him, and he will be distressed because of amusements.[54]

---

[54] This (ملهين or الملهيين) seems to be an alternate plural or phonetic variation on ملهّى ملاهٍ \. See also the end of **17** below, VIII.13, **8**, and VII.6, **1** (which reads الملهية). But even so, I do not see why it pertains to the fourth place.

5 Now if Mars came to be in the fifth from the three positions, then so long as he is in it he will be distressed because of children, messengers, and gifts, and will become ill from heat, or his body will be cut by iron, or he will fall from a raised place, and he will treat some of the people of his house badly, and evil will occur between him and some of the people, and one of his children will become ill, and he will quarrel with them or with others because of them, or something detestable will afflict some of them. **6** But if Mars had a claim in that sign or was made fortunate it will be the contrary of that, and indicates joy, delight, uprightness, and if he devoted himself to business he will profit in it.

7 And if Mars was in the sixth from the three positions, then so long as he is in it he will fall from a raised place, or an ailment will afflict him in an evident place of the body, or in the [*uncertain*],[55] feet, and legs, and his body will be cut by iron, or a disaster will afflict him from fire or hot water (and cold water), or from a predatory beast or robber, and he will treat slaves and servant-girls badly, and some of them will run away, and his children will flee or be absent from him, and misfortune will afflict his enemies and slaves, and he will discuss useless, false matters, and especially if Mars was easternizing. **8** Now as for if he was westernizing, it indicates hidden illnesses in the belly which blood will flow from, and misfortune will afflict him due to treason, and deception because of slaves.

9 And if Mars was in the seventh from the three positions, then so long as he is in it he will have much grief and regret, and misfortune will afflict him from fire or hot water, and ulcers will emerge on him, or pain will afflict him in[56] the leg, toes, and feet, or an inflammation in the eye, or there will be an ailment in a hidden place of his body, and he will be devoted to blood and its places,[57] and deception and strata-

---

[55] الحالين or الحالين, indicating a pair of something, which might mean something like "flanks" (or more likely, testicles, due to Mars). But perhaps this is just a muddled misspelling for الكليتين, "kidneys."

[56] **P**: "he will have water in," which suggest some kind of accumulation of fluid: but that is a Saturnian affliction, not Martial. **T** reads, "fire will afflict him in."

[57] دماء ومواضعها. This could also be "murders and their places."

gems, and buying and selling, and he will provoke a lawsuit against himself,[58] and will quarrel because of women and children, and will be victorious over one quarreling with him, and it will reduce part of his assets due to slaves, enemies, robbers, and labor, and he will both travel and return from his journey, and will treat slaves and the poor well, and he will create suitable wills, and associate with the leaders of the religious, and will be distressed because of relatives, and misfortune will afflict him from some of them, and his woman will become ill due to childbirth or something else.

10 And if Mars came to be in the eighth from the three positions, then so long as he is in it he will have much labor, be hard of heart, with little compassion, reducing what he surrenders to others, and he will be victorious over his enemies[59] and see what he loves in them, and his affairs will be thrown into confusion,[60] and a lawsuit will afflict him (due to which he will visit the Sultan), and he will be victorious over the one contending against him, and he will be devoted to eating and drinking, and contempt and lying, and he will discuss both what is and what is not (of useless things), and a pain will afflict him from wind or a dog bite, or a blow to the face or his eye, or something detestable because of fire and heat, robbers and enemies, and beasts, and deception and cunning, and he will be blamed for stealing, and will treat lowly people well, and be devoted to the heavenly sciences and the knowledge of religion,[61] and if he travels he will be criticized for his journey, and illness will afflict some of his relatives or brothers-in-law.[62]

11 And if Mars came to be in the ninth from the three positions, then so long as he is in it he will be isolated from his family and the people of his house, or he will shift from place to place, and will in-

---

[58] يهيّج على نفسه خصومة. But perhaps this could be read as, "he will provoke a lawsuit by himself."

[59] Reading with **B**, **E**, **P**, and **T** read, "and enemies will come to him."

[60] وتختلط عليه أموره.

[61] This interpretation does not seem right.

[62] Or more generally, relations (أصهار). Mars is a natural significator of brothers.

crease in his anger and violence, and will slander people and betray them, and invite them to his meal and will be stuffed with eating and drinking, and he will be devoted to sports and tales, and business, and types of benefits will be attributed to him, and he will delight in assets, children, and women, and he will increase in [women's] love towards him, and he will treat lowly and foreign people well, and he will increase in his power and rank, and leaders will receive his word, and he will be afraid of retaliation against him.

12 And if Mars came to be in the tenth from the three positions, then so long as he is in it a disagreement and contention will take place between him and his parents, and his women and children will have something detestable, his children will connect with a man having power, and the people of his house as well as his women will increase in their love [for him], he will desire women, and misfortune and loss will afflict him in his assets, and debt and expenses will be imposed upon him (which will hang heavy upon him), and he will offer collateral and lose something of what he is entrusted with and was watching over, and will be unjust to a man, and do works which are blameworthy,[63] and if he does something hidden it will become evident, and he will claim things he has not done, and will quarrel because of various things from which he will have something detestable, and will create evil between two people with an amulet, and will be in charge of a work or be devoted to the Sultan and generals, and he will get close to some of the authorities and be invited to some eating and drinking, and an ailment will afflict him from heat in his temples or in his bladder or knees, and he will be afflicted by fire and heat, or from hot water, or a cut by iron, or by a dog, tiger, or thief, and he will fall from a riding animal or from an elevated thing, and be swindled or deceived, and if he himself pursues deception and swindling he will be distressed by it, and its evil consequences will backfire upon him, and he will benefit by business and buying and selling, and if he travels he will encounter something detestable in it, and some of his brothers will travel. **13** Now if he was in Aries and its triplicities then he will earn

---

[63] Or perhaps, he will simply be "blamed" for them.

assets and ruin them, and estrangement will occur between him and the people of his house, and things which belong to his relatives will pass to him. **14** And if he was in Taurus and its triplicities, then he will be devoted to books and eloquence, and the opinion of some of the authorities about him will be good, and he will take on leadership over people, and will treat his enemies badly, and will move from place to place, and will make use of eunuchs, and will build in an evident, famous place. **15** And if he was in Gemini and its triplicities he will be devoted to philosophy and the sciences, and the conditions of falcons, beasts, and birds, and perfumes and amusements, and vain things, and dyes and scents, and he will spend money and move from place to place, and will be distressed because of women and children. **16** And if he was in Cancer and its triplicities a disagreement will occur between him and some of his friends, and he will be incapable of [fulfilling] many of his needs, and his works will be confused, and he will spend money on the seas, rivers, and waters, and will plant vineyards, and be in a confused condition in his soul, and he will manifest pustules and ulcers.

17 Now if Mars came to be in the eleventh from the three positions, then so long as he is in it he will delight in women and increase in his servants, weapons, and benefits, and he will get buried assets, and that will be because of an old matter or without labor, or from a direction he had no claim to, and he will benefit from some of the people of his house as well, and if he pursued business he will benefit in it, and some of his relatives will reach him from a journey, and he will tear down a place in his home, and he will be devoted to hills and mountains, and elevated places, and building and repairs, and he will associate with the powerful[64] and leaders, and will befriend people having power, and be revered, and perhaps he will be put in charge of a work for the Sultan, and he will litigate and quarrel, and be victorious over anyone contending with him, and support the people, and repel

---

64 العظماء. **B** reads, "scholars" (العلماء). **T** reads, "with leaders and scholars."

something detestable from them, and delight in women and places of amusement,[65] and he will often be away from his home.

18 And if Mars came to be in the twelfth from the three positions, then so long as he is in it he will kill a man or the corruption of a man will [occur] at his hands,[66] and his litigating and quarreling will increase, and he will be victorious over enemies and contenders, and if he travels he will encounter highway robbery or will encounter something detestable in it, and ailments and illnesses will afflict him, and he will be distressed by lowly people or slaves, and some of them will be freed or run away, and something detestable will afflict them or they will become ill, and he will increase in them or in his servants,[67] friends, and power, and he will invite the people to his meal, and be lied about, and part of his assets will disappear, and assets will come to him, and he will benefit by buying and selling.

Chapter VII.5: On the indication of the Sun by his transit in the twelve houses

1 If the Ascendant of the root and the revolution, and the sign of the terminal point were a single sign, and the Sun came to be in it, then in that time the owner of the revolution will be elevated above people, and will increase in his power, and he will do work on behalf of the Sultan, and know the secrets of kings, and be devoted to crowns and wreaths, and earn money, build a building, and do difficult labor or will travel, and he will be lied about, and for that reason he will encounter something detestable.

2 And if the Sun came to be in the second from the three positions, then so long as he is in it his eye will have an ailment, or his brain will afflict him, or a pain of the belly, or he will fall from a riding animal or from something elevated, and something detestable will afflict him from fathers or grandfathers (or because of them), and because of

---

[65] Or, musical instruments or other pleasant things (الملاهي).
[66] Or more simply, "with his help."
[67] Or, "entourage" (حشم).

debts and quarrels about them, or that adversity will be due to real estate, works, and crafts, and assets will come to him in a quarrel, and he will spend money in righteous ways and on the houses of worship, and he will build in them.

3 And if the Sun came to be in the third from the three positions, then so long as he is in it his speech will be received, and he will be in charge of his brothers and the people of his house, and he will hear something detestable from some of the crowds, and he will be accused of something ugly, and will do acts of piety, and serve the religious, increase in his devotion, be distressed because of women, quarrel with some of the leaders and chiefs, and will see what he loves from some of them.

4 And if the Sun came to be in the fourth from the three positions, then so long as he is in it he will associate with leaders and kings, and be mentioned in a good way at assemblies, and be loved, and plant seedlings and build buildings, apply himself to old things, earn money (and spend money), rejoice in women and children, pamper himself, and something detestable will afflict his parents or some of his relatives from illness or from the disappearance of assets, or something else.

5 And if the Sun came to be in the fifth from the three positions, then so long as he is in it anxieties will disappear from him (if he had them), and kings will make him mighty, and he will do their works, and increase in his power, and be devoted to the houses of religion, messengers, reports, and gifts, and a defect or something detestable will afflict some of his children.

6 And if the Sun came to be in the sixth from the three positions, then so long as he is in it he will be liable to anger,[68] subservient, humbling himself to the people, doing the work of slaves, and his reason will be confused, and an ailment in his brain or eye will afflict him, or he will be struck on one of his limbs, and harm will afflict him in his assets, and misfortune from fire or from something hot, and he will treat his slaves badly, and lawsuits will happen to him, as well as words

---

[68] Or, "choleric," which would directly relate this to a physical condition.

and contentions because of slaves and women, and an ailment will afflict his father (or he will travel).

7 And if the Sun came to be in the seventh from the three positions, then so long as he is in it he will increase in his power, assets will come to him, he will love women, illnesses and ailments will be stirred up upon him, something will be stolen from him, and he will devote himself to the conditions of robbers and thefts, as well as sheep and cows, he will be wronged by lawsuits, and will hate[69] the people.

8 And if the Sun came to be in the eighth from the three positions, then so long as he is in it he will become ill, and a pain of the heart, worry, and thirst will afflict him, and he will fall from a riding animal or from something elevated, and he will travel and return from his journey with what he loves, and his father will become ill or be ruined.

9 And if the Sun came to be in the ninth from the three positions, then so long as he is in it kings will respect him and he will be with them, and assets will come to him from travel or from being abroad, he will build a good building and plant seedlings, and gold and silver will be worked for him, and he will devote himself to paintings and the houses of worship, and increase in his own devotion, and he and his father will travel (or their labor will be multiplied), and they will benefit in that, he will be devoted to works of piety, and some of his relatives will have something detestable.

10 And if the Sun came to be in the tenth from the three positions, then so long as he is in it he will increase in his power, and some kings will befriend him and be on friendly terms with him, and he will increase in his slaves, do works with his own hands, build in an evident, famous place, good will be spoken of him in places, he will be entrusted with something for safekeeping, and he will be joyful, strong of soul, and will have good because of fathers so that he will give it to his children, and he will increase in the standing of his parents.

---

[69] Reading as ضغي. But this could also be read with alternative pointing, to yield "...lawsuits, and by the hatred of the people," or "...lawsuits, and by some of the people."

11 And if the Sun came to be in the eleventh from the three positions, then so long as he is in it he will delight in women, children, and siblings, and will treat some of the children well, and assets and property[70] will come to him, and he will spend something of his parents' money.

12 And if the Sun came to be in the twelfth from the three positions, then so long as he is in it something detestable will afflict him from fire or heat, or from hot water, and he will benefit by some of the nobles (and he will be hostile to some of them), and his parents will have a defect[71] or one of them will become ill, and they will both do the work of slaves.

Chapter VII.6: On the indication of Venus by her transit in the twelve houses

1 If the Ascendant of the revolution and the root, and the sign of the terminal point, were a single sign, and Venus came to be in it, then in that time the owner of the revolution will befriend the nobles, and will love women and befriend them, and be eager for them, and his sexual intercourse with them will multiply, and he will move from one woman to another, and will contend with them or contend because of them, and will dress them in gold, and wreaths will be placed upon his head, and he will buy garments and clothing, and be well-to-do, a gourmand, eating much, varied in his food, and he will befriend leaders, scholars, and the just, and he will know their secrets, and be devoted to stories and amusing conversations, and singing and entertainment, gardens, sowing and seeds, and he will build and paint, and money and goods will come to him, and some of that will be because of the dead, and he will do something good, grant [gifts], and pray, and he will emancipate some slaves and servant-girls and treat them well, and he will be spoken of in beautiful ways, and his enemies will

---

[70] **P** reads, "benefit." **T** seems to read "plentiful assets."
[71] Or perhaps, a state of "insufficiency" will affect them (منقصة).

make peace with him, and it will be well with one contending with him, and he will benefit by buying, selling, and travel.

2 And if Venus came to be in the second from the three positions, then so long as she is in it assets will come to him from theft and robbery,[72] and he will spend money secretly, and will be treated badly because of betrayal or a misdeed, he will travel or labor, and money belonging to him will be wasted for that reason, and some of the assets he has already inherited will be corrupted, he will spend money because of women (or others), and he will loan money, be generous of soul, devoted to markets, buying and selling, pleasant[73] places and buildings, and singing, entertainment, idleness, and playing around, and he will invite people to his meals, and support people, and will be spoken of well, and will befriend a noble woman or a eunuch, or a noble man, and he will benefit by them, and will deceive some women and lie often (though he will promise and swear oaths), and disparage some of the people.

3 And if Venus came to be in the third from the three positions, then so long as she is in it he will increase in his power, and he will be truthful of tongue, rejoicing, cheerful, and will benefit because of a woman, and have sex in secret, and will be devoted to weddings, and will invite the people to his meals, and increase in his friends, be praised among them, and they will be in need of him, and he will associate with people from whom he will exorcize jinns and spirits, and he will be devoted to composing books, the stars, engineering, and numbers, and melodies, and will treat the people of his house and his relatives well, and will benefit by them, and an ailment will afflict some of his siblings in the belly, and he will be isolated from them or some of them will be destroyed, and he will benefit from partnerships, buying and selling, and will increase in his real estate.[74]

4 And if Venus came to be in the fourth from the three positions, then so long as she is in it he will be devoted to vineyards, lands, wa-

---

[72] This seems an unlikely signification.

[73] الطَّيِّبة. But **E**, **P**, and **T** read, "moist" (الرّطبة).

[74] عقاره. But this could also be read as "medicines, drugs," (عقاره) which are sometimes Venusian indications.

ters, and building, and he will associate with plowmen and tillers, slaves, the lower class, writers, and the wise, and he will be subservient to his parents and the people of his house, and will weep because of them or will be distressed because of some of them, and will quarrel with some of the people, and be on intimate terms with people with tenderness and femininity in them, and he will treat people well and loan or advance money to them, and talk himself into poverty and a bad condition, and will move from place to place, and a pain will afflict him in one of his teeth or in his mouth, or in the urethra, and he will crave gentleness, and one of his women will become ill, and the outcomes of his matters (of those which Venus indicates), will be praised.

5 And[75] if Venus came to be in the fifth from the three positions, then so long as she is in it his labor will be multiplied, and he will associate with foreigners, and some of his needs will be burdensome for him, and he will not take debt seriously, nor anything of his purposes, nor religious people, and he will be mentioned with distaste, and will often become irritated, and will be distressed because of assets, and dissatisfied in times of entertainment and delight, and he will be harmed by women and because of them, and will have much passion for things,[76] and the people will revere him, and he will increase in his friends, and he will delight in children and increase in them (and be angry with some of them), and will be victorious, and be devoted to messengers, scholars, reports, and gifts, and will benefit in business (if he does business).

6 And if Venus came to be in the sixth from the three positions, then so long as she is in it he will quarrel with his relatives or a friend because of an allegation made against him, and he will have sex with corrupt women, and distress and a lawsuit will afflict him because of women and sex, and a pain will afflict him in his lung or head, or in a hidden place of his body, or wind will be stirred up in him, and he will

---

[75] To my mind the first half of this paragraph (up to "and because of them") does not make sense for Venus in the fifth.

[76] الأشياء. This should probably be read as "women" (النِّساء).

loathe people of uprightness, and if he travels and she is the indicator of travel, he will see what he detests in it.

7 And if Venus came to be in the seventh from the three positions, then so long as she is in it he will be graciously disposed,[77] of varying conditions in the matter of women and children, and he will increase in his love for servant girls, and perhaps he will marry a young woman whom he has a friendship with, or he will befriend some women, and much of his affairs will be faulty[78] (though his condition in all of that will result in his love), and his woman will become pregnant, and misfortune will afflict him from fire or from hot water, and he will handle weapons and medicines[79] and he will have war, and he will be devoted to stratagems, deceit, lying, and shameless[80] oaths, and assets or something else will be claimed to be in his power[81] (which he will deny).

8 And if Venus came to be in the eighth from the three positions, then so long as she is in it his drinking of wines will increase, and a detestable woman will kill him, and he will have sex with a poor woman or slave, and he will tear down a place of his home, and he will have little desire to produce benefit, and will abstain from acquiring friends, with many anxieties, being distracted in his heart, a coward, subservient to everyone, and misfortune will afflict him from water,[82] and a pain in the heart, urethra, or legs, and perhaps his body will be touched by iron.

---

[77] Reading Form IV (منعم) with **E**, but it might also be Form II ("be pampered"). **P** seem to read a longer form of a different verb (يغنى, "to be wealthy"), but the dotting does not fully make sense. **B** and **T** read that he will be abstemious or abstain from women.

[78] Or even, "denounced." Reading يعاب with **E**. **B** and **P** read different verbs but they do not quite make grammatical sense. **T** reads, "and he will be hostile towards him in many of his affairs."

[79] Reading "and medicines" only with **B**.

[80] Reading with **B**. **E**, **P**, and **T** read, "lying."

[81] Reading uncertainly for يدعى قبله. If we understood more about Abū Ma'shar's principles of interpretation in these tediously repetitive lists, it might make more sense.

[82] **B** reads, "fire."

9 And if Venus came to be in the ninth from the three positions, then so long as she is in it he will be devoted to cutting garments and tailoring them, and pictures, and in having a friendly attitude, and will handle different works with his own hands, and his labor will be multiplied as well as his trouble and distresses, and he will see what he loves from leaders, and benefits will come to him from a direction he did not know about, and he will lose something of his assets or property, he will handle different works with his own hands, and will be devoted to old tales, the interpretation of dreams, the sciences, and the religious and houses of worship, and he will travel or move from place to place, or labor (and he will benefit from that), and other things will come to be in his power, and a distasteful man will seek him, and he will quarrel in buying and selling, and fall from an elevated place,[83] and he will step down from some of his work (if he had [a position of] authority).

10 And if Venus came to be in the tenth from the three positions, then so long as she is in it he will increase in his power, and be in charge of some of the works of kings, and they will entrust him with something for safekeeping, and he will benefit from them, and be on intimate terms with their women, and will see what he loves from [the kings], and he will increase in women's love for him as well as his love for them, and he will be distressed because of something detestable which will afflict them, and he will be good to the people of his house and his dependents, and he will listen to singing and the melodies of singers, and his desire for things will be multiplied, he will handle the situations of decorating, gold, and pearls, and will spend money he had already saved up, and estrangement will occur between him and his father, and he will increase in his slaves, and be devoted to idleness and entertainment, and will increase in lands, plantings, and building.

11 And if Venus came to be in the eleventh from the three positions, then so long as she is in it he will increase in his rank, power, and assets, and his decorating and entertainment, and his listening to sing-

---

[83] **E** and **P** say "he will quarrel, and fall into a well or from an elevated place." (**T** has an elevated "thing.")

ing, and slaves will serve him, and people will come to him for hospitality or he will invite the people to his meals, and he will do something beneficial and good, and will get closer to people having power, and from them he will earn assets or something else from beneficial arts, and he will know the secrets of great people and the nobles, and will associate with the idle, and his anger will increase due to something having no foundation, and he will quarrel in useless things, and spend assets for that reason, and be hostile to people but [nevertheless] see what he loves in his enemies, and be victorious over one who contends with him, and he will delight in friends and children.

12 And if Venus came to be in the twelfth from the three positions, then so long as she is in it he will be distressed because of assets and theft, and women, servant-girls, and children, and he will contend with them as well as with others, and he will loathe the people of his house, and perform secret work, and his soul will be stingy, and if he traveled his condition in it will not be praised, and an ailment will afflict him in a hidden place of his body, or his eyes will be inflamed.

Chapter VII.7: On the indication of Mercury by his transit in the twelve houses

1 If the Ascendant of the root, and the revolution, and the sign of the terminal point were a single sign, and Mercury came to be in it, then in that time the owner of the revolution will associate with Sultans, the wise, scholars, writers, the eloquent,[84] and the powerful, and messengers will reach him as well as books from places far away from him, and the knowledge of things he did not know will be opened up for him, and evil gossip will be said about him, and enemies will make peace with him, and he will be strong of heart in the view of the people, and will attend the houses of worship, and will be victorious over one contending with him, and be truthful in his speech, and he will benefit from selling, buying, and business, and be on intimate terms

---

[84] Or, "orators" (والبلغاء).

BOOK VII: ONGOING TRANSITS IN HOUSES

with those having importance, and he will see what he loves from them, and will increase in his rank, assets, and furnishings, and be devoted to farms and gardens, and devoted to weddings and the attending of banquets, and treat slaves, orphans, and the poor well, and be entrusted with some things for safekeeping, and an ailment will afflict him in his head, and damage from[85] fire or hot water, or he will be afraid of some of the people, and will befriend a woman or delight in some women, and labor much or move from place to place, and something detestable will find his parents, or some of his siblings or his children.

2 And if Mercury came to be in the second from the three positions, then so long as he is in it he will be devoted to books of falsehood and lies, and he will compile stories and speeches and [do] business, and will loan assets and destroy part of his assets, loss will afflict him in his possessions, and he will think about the poor, and earn money from calculation and surveying, and at the doors of the nobles, and he will support his people but not be praised for that, and he will be dressed in the attire of women,[86] and will become close to the nobles, and they will esteem him, and he will know their secrets, and will be distressed because of women and children, and will travel, and his labor will multiply, and with his own hands he will handle foreign works, and be appointed as an executor for a man (or one will be appointed for him), and he will increase in his compassion for people but will quarrel, and will be distressed because of waters, and become ill in his head or ears, and if he pursued deception and stratagems a lawsuit and injury will enter upon him because of them, and his brothers will be distressed or will travel.

3 And if Mercury came to be in the third from the three positions, then so long as he is in it he will speak much of the truth, and be devoted to the sciences, proverbs, and the stars, and will know hidden

---

[85] **E, P,** and **T**: "fear of."
[86] ويتزيّى بزيّ النّساء. This seems like a strange signification, and I suspect it is a misreading for something else unless it simply means he will be somehow very fancy or foppish. See also the end of **11** below.

secrets, and will lie and slander, and seek out the defects of the people, and undermine them with the leaders, and will speak about superstitions, and he will wish something detestable upon his relatives, and treat them badly, and will hear evil gossip from them, and he will not praise anyone for [their] good deeds, and he will be on intimate terms with the poor and the miserable, and he will benefit from partnership, and the powerful will befriend him, and he will be successful in things he had hopes for, and assets will come to him, and he will fall from a place or stumble.

4 Now if Mercury was in the fourth from the three positions, then so long as he is in it lawsuits will happen to him, and it corrupts what is between him and some of his siblings or relatives, and he will treat some of them well, and people will undermine him and treat him unjustly, and he will speak detestably about people and say ugly words about them, and will be victorious over one contending with him, and be in charge of works of piety,[87] and devoted to calculation and various things of the sciences and foreign arts, and he will know hidden secrets, and think about obscure things, and something detestable will afflict him because of something concealed, and he will build buildings and increase in his real estate and going on walks, and an abscess will afflict him, or a pain in his heart or in a hidden place of his body, or an ailment from heat, or something detestable from fire,[88] and he will go to the doors of the great and connect with them, and will earn money by hidden means, and preserve it, and he will be distressed because of something stolen from him.

5 And if Mercury came to be in the fifth from the three positions, then so long as he is in it he will be devoted to messengers, reports, gifts, business, surveying, the stars, the sciences, philosophy, and writing, and he will discuss obscure matters, and will increase in his power because of speech and eloquence, and will often be delighted and joyful, and will be entrusted with assets for safekeeping, and collect assets, and spend some of it, and will settle a debt if he had one, and

---

[87] البرّ. But this can also mean "land."
[88] E: "water."

reward people, and will associate with a woman having beauty, and the people's speaking bad things about him will multiply (and he will be victorious over them), and ailments will afflict him, and he will treat his parents and the people of his house well, and will quarrel with some of them.

6 And if Mercury came to be in the sixth from the three positions, then so long as he is in it a pain will afflict him in his hearing or eyesight, or in his tongue, or an ailment in his throat from an obstruction, or in his lower parts from hemorrhoids, and he will be distressed because of speech, and will often say useless things, and be conceited, and be entrusted with [something] evil, and try to oppose the people in [legal] claims they have, and he will swear a false oath, and perhaps something will be stolen from him, and he will be wronged by the people of his house and by his women and slaves, and he will quarrel with them.

7 And if Mercury came to be in the seventh from the three positions, then so long as he is in it he will increase in his power, knowledge, and management, and he will associate with the nobles, and a man having power will be angry with him, and he will be distressed because of the people of his house, and pleasing books and reports will come in reply to him from places he reaches, and he will send out messengers and books, and he will suffer damage from some foods, and he will earn gold and silver, and merchandise from a hidden direction, and his labor will multiply, and he will quarrel with women and others besides them, and he will be devoted to whores and low people, and pimps, and will crave to have sex with young men, and folly will overwhelm his woman and she will expose her husband's secrets, and she will think about sorcery against him.

8 And if Mercury came to be in the eighth from the three positions, then so long as he is in it his pains and ailments will multiply, and he will scarcely be successful in the works he sets into motion, and he will write a false will, and he will devote himself to the matters of religion and the religious, and books and righteousness, and various [types of] management, and the condition of the assets of inheritance belonging to foreign people, and slander and speech between people will decrease, and he will ridicule them,[89] and he will call them disgusting nicknames, and he will despise them, and something will be taken [from him] which he does not know [about], and [someone will] undermine him, he will serve foreigners, and be hard of heart, foolish,[90] cowardly, shifting from work to work, and a fine will afflict him, and he will be distressed because of a theft,[91] and if he stole, [then] the thing he has will afflict him.

9 And if Mercury came to be in the ninth from the three positions, then so long as he is in it words will take place between him and his companions, and he will be undermined, and will travel, and restriction and hardship will afflict him in his property, and he will benefit from [a source] he did not consider, and assets will pass to him which he will benefit by, and he will benefit from children, and be likely [to do] something detestable and evil, and will associate with kings and their writers, and be devoted to business as well as high places or towering mountains, and leadership will pass to him because of the sciences, and he will associate with the religious, and will be with them, and be successful in works, and invent things himself from his own soul.

10 And if Mercury came to be in the tenth from the three positions, then so long as he is in it he will increase in his work and his friends, and delight in them, and they will benefit from him, and he will be spoken well of, and astonishing, expert works will pass through his hands, and he will seek the knowledge of hidden things, and obscure sciences and speech, and he will be devoted to sermonizing to the people, proverbs, and stratagems, and writers and judges, and household managers, and a man will deceive him, and he will be victorious over his enemies, and words will occur between him and his people, and the people of his house (and others besides them), and he will delight in his woman and live in luxury with women, and his playing

---

[89] Reading with **E** and **P**. But **B** and **T** read that "ridicule of *him*" will decrease. But I take Abū Ma'shar to mean that speaking will decrease, but ridicule will not.

[90] Or even "impudent" (سفيهًا); reading with **E** and **T** for سقيمًا ("ill").

[91] **P** plausibly reads, "buying."

with them and sex with them will increase, and he will invite the people to his food and drink, and he will destroy part of his assets, and be distressed because of some riding animals,[92] and will move from place to place, and benefit from business and partnerships.

11 And if Mercury came to be in the eleventh from the three positions, then so long as he is in it the nobles will respect him and praise him, and he will increase in his friends and his good fortune, and assets from a hidden source, and he will be entrusted with the assets of people for safekeeping, and he will spend money, and be successful in things he hopes for, and what he loves will originate from women[93] who have power, and they will prefer his friendship, and he will do a good deed for people but they will not praise him for that, and people he does not treat badly will envy him and speak badly about him, and he will often be exasperated and angry, and his delight will be spoiled, and he will be dressed in the attire of women, and will be devoted to wisdom, writing, and surveying, and various sciences, and images and statues, and will wrestle in front of the Sultan.

12 And if Mercury came to be in the twelfth from the three positions, then so long as he is in it he will have bad desires and exploits, and will associate with writers, soothsayers,[94] and scholars, and he will perform works he will regret and which are inappropriate,[95] and someone lower than him will come to be under his control, and he will be distressed about him because of something he did not do, and he will deceive him, and he will be forced into dealing with buying and selling, and will benefit from doing the people's accounting, and making demands and charges from them.

---

[92] الدّوابّ. E reads either "religion" or "debt" (الدّين).

[93] T: "people."

[94] Or, "priests" (الكهان).

[95] Lit., "correctness does not harmonize with them."

Chapter VII.8: On the indication of the Moon by her transit in the twelve houses

1 If the Ascendant of the root, the revolution, and the sign of the terminal point were a single sign, and the Moon came to be in it, then in that time the owner of the revolution will be preserved from detestable things and troubles, being lively, endearing himself to the people, and he will benefit from harmonizing with them and the intervention of kings and leaders, and the pursuit of lawsuits, and selling and buying, and the conditions of real estate and its purchase.

2 And if the Moon was in the second from the three positions, then so long as she is in it his revenue will be in accordance with his expenses, and he will be distressed because of old and new assets, and if something is taken from him he will not recover it (from this indication),[96] and he will quarrel in various things, and be devoted to the mountains, elevated places, and deserts, and he will have various dreams, and he will be wronged by some of his relatives, and his parents or some of his relatives will have something detestable.

3 And if the Moon was in the third from the three positions, then so long as she is in it he will be devoted to messengers and reports, and he will mock the people, and associate with leaders, and see what he loves from them as well as due to travels, foreigners, and earning money, and if something is taken from him he will recover it after trouble (from this indication), and handling sales and purchases will harm him, and he will quarrel with some of his brothers and relatives, and be elevated above them, and something detestable will afflict some of him and his parents, and he will have detestable dreams.[97]

---

[96] **E, P,** and **T** add this here and below (من هذه الدلالة), which seems to mean that the Moon's indication alone would show this, but some *other* indication would be needed to show a different result.

[97] This does not really make sense given that the Moon rejoices in the third. But perhaps Abū Ma'shar is thinking of dreams and vision practices that do *not* conform with orthodox religion (which would be the ninth house). See **9** below, which affirms that the Moon in the ninth means suitable dreams.

4 And if the Moon came to be in the fourth from the three positions, then so long as she is in it his distresses[98] will multiply, and he will be absent from his home but will often return, and he will benefit from associating with the nobles, and will have dreams with a suitable interpretation, and the handling of purchases and sales will harm him, and the acquisition of homes and lands, and if something is taken from him he will recover it, and people will be hostile to him, and a disagreement will take place between him and his parents.

5 And if the Moon came to be in the fifth from the three positions, then so long as she is in it he will often be distressed, and he will treat the people of his house well, and he will benefit from female children, and will free some slaves or treat them well, and travels will harm him as well as associating with nobles, and he will incur a loss in buying and selling, and have conflicting[99] dreams, and will be devoted to messengers and reports, and if something is taken from him he will not recover it (from this indication).

6 And if the Moon came to be in the sixth from the three positions, then so long as she is in it he will have a high opinion of himself, and mistrust[100] people, and he will think about what is evil and idle, and will labor, and do the servicing work of slaves, and an ailment will afflict him in his hands and legs, and he will quarrel and benefit because of the quarrel, as well as travel and the hunting of animals, and he will suddenly have good but will incur a loss in buying and selling, and the acquisition of lands and their cultivation will harm him, and he will not recover something which was taken from him, and frequently he will have conflicting[101] dreams.

7 And if the Moon came to be in the seventh from the three positions, then so long as she is in it a disagreement will occur between his parents, and he will be devoted to friendliness, and the authoring of maxims, and he will delight and rejoice in different things, and benefit

---

[98] P reads, "resolve, determination."
[99] Or perhaps simply, "different" (مختلفة).
[100] Reading as Form I; as Form II, "deceive."
[101] Or perhaps simply, "different" (مختلفة).

from[102] buying and selling as well as marriage, and traveling to the houses of worship, and he will benefit in that, and if something is taken from him he will recover it after a delay, and will have suitable dreams.

8 And if the Moon came to be in the eighth from the three positions, then so long as she is in it humiliation and degradation will afflict him, and he will often be distressed, and be in need of others, and provisions will be necessary for him, and expenses, and pleasing[103] reports will reach him from faraway places, and he will be devoted to the conditions of ancestors and the dead, and old affairs, and he will benefit from handling lawsuits, and the use[104] of farms and sowing.

9 And if the Moon came to be in the ninth from the three positions, then so long as she is in it he will be devoted to reports and messengers, and the authoring of maxims, and associating with foreign people, and he will have banquets,[105] and labor, and will be lively, joyful, and associate with nobles, and if he quarreled he will have something detestable because of it, and if he traveled or bought a riding animal, or acquired real estate he will benefit from it, and if something was taken from him he will not recover it (from this indication), and he will have suitable dreams.

10 And if the Moon came to be in the tenth from the three positions, then so long as she is in it he will increase in his power, and will take away the same,[106] and will have sex with some of his relatives, and will be devoted to business, waters, moist places, and will earn money and goods, and plant seedlings, and make use of gardens, and build buildings, and his children will have the good, and he will delight in children, and will benefit from travel and associating with kings,[107] and

---

[102] **B**: "be devoted to."

[103] سارّة. But if this were understood as the active participle of Form III, it would be "whispered" reports.

[104] Or perhaps something like "taking on" farms in the sense of buying them (اتّخاذ).

[105] This seems a bit better than the literal, "he will eat food."

[106] ذاهبًا بنفسه. Although the phrase is not structured like this, my guess is that it means he will also lose some authority (as the Moon signifies changeable circumstances).

[107] This phrase about kings omitted in **B**.

buying and selling, and lawsuits (as well as their management), and marriage, and he will associate with the authorities, and if something is taken from him he will recover some of it.[108]

11 And if the Moon came to be in the eleventh from the three positions, then so long as she is in it assets and goods will come to him, and he will have a position of authority over his family's assets and the assets of his parents, and he will benefit from travel[109] and going out to towns and villages, and the handling of buying and selling, and he will take on debts, and if something of [his] property is taken from him he will not find it (from this indication), and often he will have conflicting[110] dreams.

12 And if the Moon came to be in the twelfth from the three positions, then so long as he is in it he will be distressed, and he will have much labor, and be absent from his home, and degradation will afflict him, and he will be victorious over his enemies, and he will be mixed in condition (of the good and the bad), and will quarrel with his family, and if he loaned money it will not be returned to him (from this indication), and if he acted as a guarantor for collateral he will pay for it from his own money, and travels will be harmful for him as well as buying and selling, and the buying of riding animals and their introduction to his home, and his mother will have something detestable from the people.

Chapter VII.9: On the indication of the Head & Tail during their transit in the twelve houses

1 If the Ascendant of the root, the revolution, and the sign of the terminal point were a single sign, and the Head is in it, then the owner of the revolution in that time will be praised, and associate with the nobles, and marry a woman he will delight in, and do noble works, and

---

[108] See footnotes to similar phrases above.
[109] **E** adds, "and associating with kings."
[110] Or more simply, "different" (مختلفة).

some of his friends from a faraway place will be given priority over him, and he will make a journey which is distant, and his litigation and quarreling will multiply, and he will have fear of some of the people. **2** And if the Tail was in it then his distresses will multiply, and he will ruin assets, and people will envy him, and for that reason something detestable will reach him, and an ailment will afflict him in his eye.

3 And if the Head was in the second from the three positions, then so long as it is in it, it will be useful for his assets, [he will be] magnanimous, with many expenses, and he will be entrusted with assets for safekeeping by people having power, and will earn money, goods, and real estate, and will quarrel with his associates and peers, and if he put down bail he will lose it, and he will build buildings and plant seedlings and trees. **4** And if the Tail was in it then it decreases his assets, and he will have something detestable from these things generally.

5 And if the Head came to be in the third from the three positions, then so long as it is in it he will be in charge of his siblings and the people of his house, and he will be hostile to them and quarrel with them, and quarrel with others in a powerful lawsuit, and will manage his affairs with propriety, and his condition at the beginning of the year will be bad but suitable at its end. **6** And if the Tail came to be in it, then he will be worse than his siblings in condition, and perhaps he will lose one of them [in death].

7 And if the Head came to be in the fourth from the three positions, then so long as it is in it he will move from place to place or go on a distant journey, and he will increase in his power, and treat his parents well, and surpass them, and will plant seedlings and acquire real estate and livestock, and be devoted to the management of waters and rivers, and quarrel with people who are greater in power than he is, and will slander the people (and they will slander him), and he will befriend people like himself in power, and an eye inflammation and pain in the ears will afflict him, or he will be seared by fire, and decrease and loss will enter upon him in his assets, and he will be victorious over his enemies. **8** And if the Tail is in it, it indicates the illness of his parents or the ruin of the mother.

9 And if the Head came to be in the fifth from the three positions, then so long as it is in it he will increase in his friends, and will attain authority, and lawsuits will happen to him which do not have a basis, and injuries will afflict him, and the authority of his that is corrupted will be improved, and he will delight in messengers and gifts, and something detestable will find some of his children, and he will increase in the power of [his] children, and the father will be respected because of them. **10** Now if the Tail came to be in it, harm will come to him from the children, and he will delight in slaves and be distressed by reports.

11 And if the Head came to be in the sixth from the three positions, then so long as it is in it he will go[111] from a condition of detestable things and distresses to a condition of delight, respect, power, and health, and he will labor much, and move from place to place, and a man having power will become angry with him but then be pleased with him, and he will fall from a raised thing or fall into a place with water in it, and his slaves will submit to him. **12** And if the Tail came to be in it, then an ailment will afflict him in a hidden place, and a blow to one of his limbs, and he will search for obscure things and be distressed because of slaves.

13 Now if the Head was in the seventh from the three positions, then so long as it is in it he will delight because of some women, and be distressed because of some of them, or he will separate from them, and he will be devoted to the nobles and the powerful, and assets having value will come to him, and some of his assets will leave his hands, and his mother will have something detestable, and he will slander and undermine the people. **14** And if the Tail came to be in it, then he will have sex with a despicable, base, or poor woman, and distresses and quarreling will afflict him because of her or with her.

15 And if the Head came to be in the eighth from the three positions, then so long as it is in it he will travel or move from place to place, or he will have much labor, and he will have many expenses, and

---

[111] Tentatively reading for "he will be devoted to" (**B, E**) and "he will speak / be spoken of."

an ailment will afflict him, and he will quarrel with the people repeatedly (and the victory will belong to him), and his enemies will find something detestable, and he will be in charge of work having value. **16** And if the Tail came to be there, misfortune will afflict him due to which he will be on the brink of death, and he will be accused of something he did not do.

17 And if the Head came to be in the ninth from the three positions, then so long as it is in it he will benefit from travels, and he will imitate kings and the nobles, and will engage in open quarrels because of old matters, and his word will be accepted, being victorious, strong in what he judges for the people, and he will benefit for that reason, and assets will come to him from a foreign place, and he will increase in his slaves, servant girls, and entourage, and will desire women, and perhaps he will commit adultery with a woman. **18** And if the Tail was in it, then he will have something detestable from travels and because of them, and generally from what we have mentioned.

19 And if the Head was in the tenth from the three positions, then so long as it is in it he will get assets and respect, and will be spoken of well, and become related to kings and nobles through marriage, and rule over lands, waters, and trees, and command and forbid [things], and be in charge of work relating to villages and cities in deserts and wastelands, and he will benefit in all works he devotes himself to, and be victorious over his enemies, and be entrusted with the assets of people for safekeeping, and an ailment will afflict him in his face. **20** And if the Tail came to be in it, he will have something detestable and evil from the Sultan and generally from what we have mentioned.

21 Now if the Head came to be in the eleventh from the three positions, then so long as it is in it he will be delighted, and will acquire real estate and goods, and build a prominent, famous building, and quarrel and be victorious over everyone who contends with him, and he will befriend the nobles, and connect with people having power, and benefit by them, and he will be in the houses of his parents, and be distressed because of children, and will see the good and what is suitable in all of his works, and his speech will be accepted, being of a suitable condition, and he will travel or move from place to place, and fleeting anxieties will afflict him. **22** And if the Tail came to be in it, he will generally have something detestable from these things.

23 And if the Head was in the twelfth from the three positions, then so long as it is in it various lawsuits will happen to him, and he will be victorious over his enemies, and will associate with kings and the nobles, and assets will come to him from abroad,[112] and he will be freed from detestable things. **24** And if the Tail was in it, something detestable will afflict him from enemies, and he will generally be distressed from these things.

[When the Ascendants do not coincide]

25 And the strongest indication there is for each of them is when these three places agree in one, just as we said, and [a planet] is in one [and the same] houses relative to them.[113]

26 But as for when they differ, the indication of each one of them is in accordance with its place relative to each position: and that is like if a planet is in the second from the Ascendant from the root, and in the fourth from the terminal point, and in the seventh from the Ascendant of the revolution. **27** For if it was like that, its indication would be in accordance with each position and house relative to them, except that its indication for [each of] those things would be weaker than the first [scenario].[114]

28 And if the planet was in one of the signs so that it transited the bodies and rays of the rooted and revolutionary planets, and their rooted and revolutionary Lots and twelfth-parts, and it connected with one of the planets (or one of them connected with it) or they looked at each other, then it produces the indication of each one of them individually.

---

[112] Or, "foreigners."
[113] See Ch. VII.1, **26-27**.
[114] That is, weaker than if all of the Ascendants coincided. Unfortunately, all three will almost never coincide.

29 And for every planet, if it was in one of the positions it will indeed have indications over many things apart from what we have mentioned, but we have left off from mentioning them because we have [already] taught that one should make inferences about the world from the natures of the planets and their indications both in isolation and by mixing [them].

BOOK VIII: ON THE PRESENCE OF THE PLANETS IN THEIR OWN SHARES AND THOSE OF OTHERS

And it is in fifteen chapters

1 In this Book we want to state the indication of each planet when it comes to be in its own house or bound, or in the house or bound of the rest of the planets, as well as when it comes to be in the wells[1] (whether that was at the beginning of the year or in another of its times), because in every position they have a characteristic indication for specific things, according to what we will state. **2** And the planets do have other shares in the signs, some of which we stated in what preceded, though we have left out some of it because it resembles statements about it in other books. **3** But as for the positions of the planet in their houses or the positions of their houses relative to them, we will mention their indications in Book IX, because a discussion of it is more appropriate there.

Chapter VIII.1: On the indication of Saturn by his presence in the shares of the planets[2]

1 If Saturn was in his own house and the revolution was by day, then its owner will befriend the nobles, and will do works because of which he will get something detestable as well as illness. **2** And if the revolution was nocturnal, then he will slander people, and his toil will increase, and an ailment from moisture or hemorrhoids will afflict him.

3 And if Saturn was in a house of Jupiter, he will befriend nobles and be devoted to the mansions of kings, the houses of worship, buying and selling, and household management.

---

[1] That is, the "wells" or welled degrees: see Ch. VIII.15 below.
[2] For this chapter, cf. *Carmen* II.32 and II.37, and *JN* Ch. 39.

4 And if Saturn was in a house of Mars, he will have difficulty, being slow in his works, cowardly, with much worry[3] and sorrow for no reason.

5 And if Saturn was in the house of the Sun and the revolution was by day, then it will increase in the assets of the native's father[4] and in his own good fortune; and if the revolution was by night, his father will become ill from moisture.

6 And if Saturn was in a house of Venus, he will have sex with the poor, servant-girls, the elderly, harlots, and the sterile, and he will be distressed because of children, and his woman will become ill or die.

7 And if Saturn was in a house of Mercury, he will seek obscure sciences, and hidden secrets, and for that reason he will have harm, and an ailment will afflict him in his ear[5] or his tongue, and he will envy people, and he will be criticized.

8 And if Saturn was in the house of the Moon, then he will become ill from cold, or from black bile, and he will corrupt the assets of his mother.[6]

Chapter VIII.2: On the indication of Jupiter by his presence in the houses of the planets[7]

1 If Jupiter was in a house of Saturn, then he will acquire benefits with suitable value even though poverty will [be what] appears,[8] and he will have many thoughts about evil and something detestable, be a

---

[3] Lit. "thought" (الفكرة), but meant in a negative sense.
[4] So reads **B**. But **P** reads, "of the father and of the native." This could reflect *JN* Ch. 39, in which it increases the native's fortune and the father's status: so I have read "his *own*" good fortune in the next clause so both are included.
[5] **B** adds "his hands," which is also a signification of Mercury.
[6] Reading for "father," with *Carmen* and *JN* (and normal astrological symbolism).
[7] For this chapter, cf. *Carmen* II.33 and II.37, and *JN* Ch. 40.
[8] Reading with the sense of Leopold Ch. VII.17, **9**, which says he will profit but will "present himself" as being poor (i.e. he will only appear or seem to be poor), otherwise the text would read "poverty will appear," or "poverty will be apparent," which would imply that the poverty is real—and contradict the previous clause.

coward, and he will do hidden acts, and harm will afflict him from different directions.

2 And if Jupiter was in his own house and the revolution was by day, then assets will come to him from a direction considered good, and he will be well commended, and he will associate with the nobles. **3** And if the revolution was nocturnal, then he will have benefits with suitable value,[9] and he will associate with the religious, and will attend the houses of worship.

4 If Jupiter was in a house of Mars, then he will be praised generally for what works he does, and he will increase in his good fortune, and associate with commanders, the leaders of soldiers, and great men.

5 If Jupiter was in the house of the Sun, he will befriend the nobles and his provisions will be multiplied.

6 If Jupiter was in a house of Venus, he will take over responsibility for household management, or buying and selling, and he will befriend those having importance (among men as well as women), and he will have sex with women (in which there is [already] familiarity between him and them), and he will quarrel with some of them, and he will benefit because of his having sex with them and his quarreling with them.

7 And if Jupiter was in a house of Mercury, then he will be devoted to selling and buying, calculation, and being entrusted with [something], and for that reason he will have what is good, and he will be well praised.

8 If Jupiter was in the house of the Moon, then he will acquire benefits having value, and he will befriend the nobles and be devoted to the religious.

---

[9] *JN* Ch. 40 says there will be some falseness in his statements, and the assets will have to be worked for, which makes more sense for a contrary-to-sect Jupiter.

Chapter VIII.3: On the indication of Mars by his presence in the houses of the planets[10]

1 If Mars was in a house of Saturn, then he will hasten along in matters, and will persist in managing many works, and the father will have harm in his assets, and his brother will become ill or be ruined.

2 If Mars was in a house of Jupiter, then he will inspire awe,[11] and befriend the nobles and soldiers.

3 If Mars was in his own house and the revolution was by night, then state that he will do something <bad>,[12] except that he will gain assets from it; and if the revolution was by day, then an ailment will afflict him in a hidden place of his body, and perhaps the ailment will be from bile.

4 If Mars was in the house of the Sun, then an ailment will afflict him in his eyes, or in his stomach from indigestion, or cutting by iron will afflict him, or a misfortune from fire or from things having four feet, or he will fall from an exalted, elevated place, and he will scatter the wealth of his father, or an ailment will afflict the father on a journey or in another's home.

5 If Mars was in a house of Venus, then he will marry a widow, or he will have sex with a woman he has already known or committed adultery with before that, and a fine or harm will afflict him by reason of women, and he will treat his father's women badly. **6** And it is more confirmed for that if he was in Taurus; but as for if he was in Libra, then along with what we have mentioned, misfortune will find him from iron or fire, or an ailment will afflict him in the hip or in a hidden place of his body.

7 If Mars was in a house of Mercury, then he will have a bad attitude, while increasing in his mind and cleverness, and assets will come to him from a loathsome direction, and it will turn out successfully for him in that area as well, and he will concern himself with robbers and

---

[10] For this chapter, cf. *Carmen* II.34 and II.37, and *JN* Ch. 41.

[11] مهيبًا; but **P** reads فيهمَا, "discerning."

[12] *JN* Ch. 41 says he will be honored and wealthy—which I can understand, but it does not make sense of the "except" which follows.

folks who kill people, and sorcery, books, and scholars, and he will be criticized.

8 If Mars was in the house of the Moon, then he will discuss obscure things, and will seek the sciences and preserve them, and will go along with bad actions, and a powerful catastrophe will afflict him, or an ailment in his belly, or in a hidden place of his body, and his mother will become ill or die, especially if the revolution was diurnal.

Chapter VIII.4: On the indication of the Sun by his presence in the houses of the planets[13]

1 If the Sun was in a house of Saturn and the revolution is diurnal, then he will increase in the strength of his own soul and his risk-taking; and if the revolution was nocturnal, it is the contrary of that.

2 And if the Sun was in a house of Jupiter and the revolution was diurnal, then he will be of a suitable condition in benefits and assets, and he will leave the house of his fathers; and if the revolution was nocturnal, it is the contrary of that.

3 And if the Sun was in a house of Mars, then he will devote himself to eloquence and the sciences,[14] and a bad illness will afflict him or his father. **4** And[15] that is worse if the revolution was diurnal and[16] he was

---

[13] For this chapter, cf. *Carmen* II.37, and *JN* Ch. 42.

[14] This seems like an odd signification, and is not reflected in al-Khayyāt, *Carmen*, or the Latin Māshā'allāh.

[15] Without sentence numbering, the rest of the sentence reads this way: "And that is worse if the revolution was diurnal or he was in Scorpio; but as for if he was in Aries, then he will have manifest good fortune; and if the revolution was by night, it is below that." But this is ambiguous because we have two planets of opposite sects, in signs of opposite sects, in charts of opposite sects—but only two or three options are listed. Only *JN* is very close to this, saying that (1) if it is in Scorpio in diurnal nativities it is good, but in nocturnal nativities less good. In my slightly altered version, a diurnal chart in Scorpio is worse because the Sun would be in a nocturnal sign, without dignity, in the sign of the contrary-to-sect infortune (**4**). However, if he was in Aries by day, then it would not matter that Mars is a nocturnal planet because the Sun is already exalted in Aries, and would also be of the sect, in a diurnal

in Scorpio. **5** But as for if he was in Aries [by day], then he will have manifest good fortune; and if the revolution was by night, it is below that.

6 And if the Sun was in his own house and the revolution diurnal, and he is in a stake, then he will increase in his power and rank; and if the Sun was not in a stake, then assets will come to him or he will be entrusted with the assets of people who have power. **7** And if the revolution was by night, then he will decrease[17] in the power of the father, and assets will come to him from people who have power, and his toil will increase, or he will travel.

8 And if the Sun was in a house of Venus, then he will associate with astrologers and soothsayers, or interpreters of dreams, and in his own dreams he will see things true in [their] interpretation, and he will be devoted to entertainment and pleasures, and his soul will resolve to travel, and his confusion in his actions will multiply, and an ailment from moisture will afflict him.

9 And if the Sun was in a house of Mercury and the revolution diurnal, then he will have little stability in a single matter, and he will discuss lofty matters and hidden secrets, and he will devote himself to calculation. **10** And if the revolution was nocturnal, then he will have an ailment, and will have a nasty tongue.

11 And if the Sun was in the house of the Moon, then an ailment will afflict him in his stomach or in a hidden place of his body, and he will associate with people who handle the situations of *jinn*s and devils.[18]

---

sign (**5**); and it would only be made somewhat less good if it was nocturnal in Aries, because he is still exalted and would also not have a contrary-to-sect infortune ruling him.

[16] Reading for "or." See footnote above.

[17] Reading for "increase," with the sense of *JN* Ch. 42 and the Latin Māshā'allāh (and astrological principles).

[18] This last signification is because Cancer is the twelfth from Leo.

Chapter VIII.5: On the indication of Venus by her presence in the houses of the planets[19]

1 If Venus was in a house of Saturn, then he will have sex with elderly or corrupted women, and evil gossip will be said about him because of them; and that is more confirmed if she was in Capricorn.

2 If Venus was in a house of Jupiter and the revolution was nocturnal, then he will increase in his power, assets, garments, and dishes, and that will be from sons-in-law and brothers-in-law, or from women of the nobles (and because of them), and from a work he takes over for them such as household management or what is like that, and people who have power will support him. **3** And if the revolution was by day, it reduces that.

4 If Venus was in a house of Mars, then he will become ill with a fleeting ailment, and he will have sex with servant girls and corrupted women, and will toil and quarrel with them or because of them, and his thoughts about them will be bad.

5 If Venus was in the house of the Sun, then he will be eager for women and have sex with more than one of them, and perhaps that will not be in a [proper] place for intercourse;[20] and he will be criticized because of them.

6 And if Venus was in her own house and the revolution was by night, then he will delight in women and befriend a corrupt woman, and his amusement and joy will multiply, and he will be criticized, and he will see what he loves in everything he does. **7** And if the revolution was diurnal, then his condition with women will be like that except that detestable things will afflict him from them and because of them, and an ailment will afflict them.

8 If Venus was in a house of Mercury, then he will associate with the leaders of the religious, and will take over responsibility for one of the

---

[19] For this chapter, cf. *Carmen* II.35 and II.37, and *JN* Ch. 43.
[20] Because it is the Sun, Abū Ma'shar probably means a public place.

works of some women, and he will be eager for sexual intercourse, and will concern himself with dyes, images, and decoration.[21]

9 If Venus was in the house of the Moon, he will be eager for sex, and perhaps something detestable will afflict him because of women, and he will be criticized.

Chapter VIII.6: On the indication of Mercury by his presence in the houses of the planets[22]

1 If Mercury was in a house of Saturn, he will have conflicting thoughts, bad thoughts, and he will be entrusted with something for safekeeping, and will be devoted to the houses of worship and the religious, and scholars, astrologers, and the interpreters of dreams.

2 If Mercury was in a house of Jupiter, he will be devoted to judgment, scholars, authorities, and will manage their affairs, and the affairs of groups from among the people.

3 If Mercury was in a house of Mars and the revolution was by day, he will be devoted to false books and speaking about them, and lying, and stratagems, and for that reason something detestable will find him, and evil gossip will be said about him; now if the revolution was by night, it will be below that.

4 If Mercury was in the house of the Sun and the revolution diurnal, he will increase in his reason, and preserve the sciences, and discuss obscure things; and if the revolution was nocturnal, it will be below that.

5 If Mercury was in a house of Venus, he will see affection in all of his affairs, and will increase in his friends and assets, and will be devoted to types of entertainment, building and repairs, and calculation, and obscure books.

---

[21] **P** reads, "the decoration of wood, and what is like that." This phrase is also in al-Khayyāt and Māshā'allāh, and so should probably be assumed.

[22] For this chapter, cf. *Carmen* II.36 and II.37, and *JN* Ch. 44.

6 If Mercury was in his own house, he will be devoted to the sciences, calculation, obscure books, management, buying and selling, and he will befriend the nobles and those having importance.

7 If Mercury was in the house of the Moon and the revolution was nocturnal, he will associate with people having knowledge and an acquaintance with things,²³ and culture, and he will see what he loves from them, and will travel, toil, and often be angry.

Chapter VIII.7: On the indication of the Moon by her presence in the houses of the planets²⁴

1 If the Moon was in a house of Saturn and she is increasing in light, then he will be criticized, and an ailment from wind²⁵ will afflict him; but if she was decreasing in [light], he will become ill from coughing or cold, or a pain of the kidneys or spleen, and perhaps blood will be let from him. **2** And that is harsher if the revolution was nocturnal, while if it was by day it is less.

3 If the Moon was in a house of Jupiter, then he will be well commended, and he will be put in charge in the house of his fathers, and perhaps he will have sex with those women who have a taboo [relation to him].

4 If the Moon was in a house of Mars and she is increasing in light, his anger will multiply, and his sharpness,²⁶ and his quarreling in useless matters, and he will associate with robbers, soldiers, the cavalry, and bad people and dogs; but if she was decreasing in it, it will be below that.

5 If the Moon was in the house of the Sun, his joy will multiply, and an ailment will afflict him in a hidden place of his body, and perhaps

---

²³ Or more strongly, "people having science and the knowledge of things" (قوم لهم علم ومعرفة الأشياء).
²⁴ For this chapter, cf. *Carmen* II.37, and *JN* Ch. 45.
²⁵ That is, gas.
²⁶ Or, "violence" (حدّته).

that will be in his lung or his stomach; and that is harsher if the Moon was at the beginning of the sign or its end.

6 If the Moon was in a house of Venus, he will be loved, delighted, eager for women, and he will be criticized.

7 If the Moon was in a house of Mercury, then he will increase in his understanding and [power of] discrimination, and will desire women, and they will desire him.

8 If the Moon was in her own house and the revolution is nocturnal, he will increase in his power, and will acquire assets from his own labor and from [other] work he does, or in relation to the Sultan; but if it was diurnal, it will be below that.

Chapter VIII.8: On the indication of Saturn by this presence in the bounds of the planets

1 If Saturn was in his own bound, then he will take over work for the Sultan, and will associate with people who have power, and they will need him because of assets, and a fleeting illness will afflict him, and a place in his residence will be corrupted, and he will hate entertainment and singing, and contention will occur between him and his women, and he will hate his children and they will hate him.

2 If Saturn was in a bound of Jupiter, then assets which have value will come to him from theft or something else, and an ailment will afflict him in his eye or in one of the places of his body, and he will increase in his power, and he will gain good from his children and the people of his house, and they will be agreeable to him, and he will discuss obscure things, and will deceive the people and be a ruler over them, and there will be estrangement between him and his women, and people will seek to [see him] stumble and will slander him, and he will acquire assets from where he did not anticipate it, and it will prepare conflict for his parents, and his older brothers will have something detestable.

BOOK VIII: PLANETS IN SIGNS, BOUNDS, & WELLS

3 If Saturn was in a bound of Mars, then he will toil or often be away from his home (or he will travel),[27] and he will be devoted to the houses of worship,[28] and will be distressed because of women, and will corrupt the assets of his father or his own assets, and distress or toil will afflict some of his relatives who are older than him, or misfortune will afflict his brother from the cutting of iron or by some doctors, and something detestable will find him because of people who envy him, and he will handle lies and falseness, and he will be hostile to his friends, and he will say things which are harmful for him, and he will be distressed because of confinement and the imprisoned, and he will love elderly men and women, and the people of his house will have contentions and something detestable.

4 If Saturn was in a bound of Venus, then a pain of the belly or an ailment in his penis will afflict him, and his benefits will decrease, and perhaps a child will be born to him and he will delight in the children of strangers, and he will loathe women, and some of his women will have misfortune, and he will often be away from his home, and his father will become ill, and his parents will benefit from him, and the people of his house will be in agreement with him, and women will loathe him while he will be turned cold by them (though he will love the elderly and widows).

5 If Saturn was in a bound of Mercury, he will be distressed and sad because of women and children, and perhaps some of his children will marry, and he will contend with people who have power, and he will be distressed because of them, and they will slander him and lie about him, and he will be blamed for the betrayal of another man or because of a bounty guaranteed by some of the people, and something will be stolen from him, and he will befriend bad people, and he will be devoted to the desert, and valleys, and inaccessible mountains and elevated places, and he will be distressed because of confinement and

---

[27] Traditionally Mars was a travel planet, and in general the infortunes can show travel because of their destabilizing qualities. See Sahl, *Nativities* Ch. 9.1, **61-62**.

[28] To me the signification of worship does not make sense for this combination of planets.

the imprisoned, and he will contend with the people of his house, even though they will benefit from him.

Chapter VIII.9: On the indication of Jupiter by his presence in the bounds of the planets

1 If Jupiter was in a bound of Saturn, then fetters and punishment will afflict him, and for that reason he will benefit, and he will be victorious over his enemies, and be of a varying condition with women, and some of them will unveil his delighting in the people,[29] and he will be put in charge of his father's assets and the assets of women, and he will acquire assets because of waters and lands, and his costs and lawsuits will multiplied, and he will toil much, and be distressed because of children, and be absent from his home, and an ailment will afflict him in a hidden place of his body, and the results of his works (which he begins in that time) will be suitable.

2 If Jupiter was in his own bound, he will increase in his assets and slaves, and a child will be born to him or to his own children, and the people will need his rank, and he will assist them, and he will be devoted to business.

3 If Jupiter was in a bound of Mars, illnesses and trouble and harm will afflict him because of old things as well as resentment, and his body will be cut by iron, and some of his relatives or his children will be ruined, or something detestable will reach them, and he will increase in the love of his father towards him.

4 If Jupiter was in a bound of Venus, then he will do works of piety, and will increase in the suitability of his women and their integrity, and he will be sad about some of them, and he will be devoted to business and household management for the nobles, and will increase in his siblings, rank, assets, and slaves, and he will be fearful about the slaves, and his body will be healthy, and he will love women and provide for them, and will be eager for them and have sex with them, and

---

[29] ويكشف بعضهنّ سرّه للنّاس. Meaning unclear.

a child will be born to him, and he will enjoy himself, and treat people well, and pay for them out of his own assets, and will build a famous building, and he will be sheltered by it,[30] and the results of his works (which he will begin in those days) will be praised.

5 If Jupiter was in a bound of Mercury, he will devote himself to the sciences, books, calculation and accounting, and [various] types of crafts, and the people will respect him, and he will be present at the doors of kings, and delight in women and children, and ailments will afflict him from things like the fracturing of bones and partial paralysis, and wind, and he will apply treatments, and the assets of his father will be ruined (while he will increase in his own assets), and assets will come to him from theft, and he will be out of view,[31] and he will slander people, [and] the results of his works (which he will begin in those days) will be praised.

Chapter VIII.10: On the indication of Mars by his presence in the bounds of the planets

1 If Mars was in a bound of Saturn, then something detestable will afflict his children, siblings, and relatives, or one of them will die, and he will corrupt the assets of his father, and his toil will multiply, as well as his traveling about to various places, and he will associate with foreign people, and it will corrupt the place of his home,[32] and it will multiply his spending, and he will slander people, and bloodshed will happen at his hands, and he will spread corruption among the people (as well as deception and tricks), and he will harm and despise them, and he will befriend robbers, and his works will be delayed, and he will take assets belonging to someone else, and be entrusted with some things, and associate with the nobles, and if he litigates with a man his

---

[30] Reading somewhat uncertainly for ويكون مستورًا عليه.
[31] ويختفي. But this could mean "and [the assets] will be hidden," but the reason for that is not clear, either.
[32] E reads rather plausibly: "it will corrupt part of his assets."

lawsuit will quickly be cut short, and he will have sex with a foreign woman.

2 If Mars was in a bound of Jupiter, he will increase in his assets and collect them, and some of it will be bribes or gifts, [but] then he will throw it out and corrupt it, and a lawsuit will afflict him as well as a bad illness, and he will toil much or travel, and he will befriend the nobles, and will love singing and entertainment, and will prepare food for the people, and will be devoted to buying and selling, and his enemies will multiply, and women will love him, and he will marry a bad[33] woman and she will become pregnant from him (or a child will be born to him), and some of his children will be ruined or become ill, and what is detestable will find them.

3 If Mars was in his own bound, then he will be devoted to riding animals and beasts, and those who are confined as well as prisons, and blood, heat, and fires, and he will be keen,[34] fighting the people and contending with and beating them, and stealing, and he will lie and be forgiven, and will be successful in the things he wants, and he will free himself quickly from detestable things, and he will see what he loves from kings, and will manage the assets of foreigners and their slaves, and will contend with his elder brothers, his enemies will multiply, and he will feed the people and give to them to drink (and not be praised for that), and fornicate with some women, and his child will suddenly become ill.

4 If Mars was in a bound of Venus, then he will be criticized, and he will be accused of fornication, and desire corrupt women, and have sex with them, and he will take their assets and contend with them, and be distressed because of some of them, while supporting them as well as others besides them, and he will acquire assets from the women of the nobles or from eunuchs, and he will be credited with lies, and he will eat and drink and have fun, and rejoice, and something detestable will

---

[33] **E** reads "beautiful," which could be Jupiterian but I read Jupiter here as the marriage and fertility, while Mars indicates badness.

[34] Or perhaps, "sharp" (حديد).

find him while away from his home and on a journey, and the condition of his children will be good.

5 If Mars was in a bound of Mercury, then he will be nice to none of the people, and because of that they will not praise him, and his enemies will multiply, and he will be distressed because of the Sultan, women, and children, and groups of the people, and he will litigate against them, and an ailment will afflict him from wind or heat, and if he traveled he will find something detestable, and useless things will be said about him, and he will swear false oaths, and be used to lying and speaking falsehoods, and he will envy the people and loathe them, and deceive them, and some of his brothers will be hostile to him, and he will loathe entertainment, singing, and delights, and something detestable will afflict him from riding animals or women, and his parents will have something detestable.

Chapter VIII.11: On the indication of the Sun by his presence in the bounds of the planets

1 If the Sun was in a bound of Saturn, then he will increase in his assets and good fortune, delight in children, and associate with nobles, kings, the powerful, and scholars, and will be devoted to secrets and hidden things, and will be elevated above his siblings and companions, but his body will be beaten,[35] and his labor will multiply, and he will refrain from building and collecting assets, and his joy will be little, and he will withdraw from his people and relatives, or move away from his home, and his life will collapse around him as well as his delight, and he will slander people, and an ailment will afflict him from hemorrhoids, wind, or the fracturing of bones.

2 If the Sun was in a bound of Jupiter, he will be devoted to ornaments of gold and silver, and business, and profit in it, and the houses of worship, and he will increase in his friends, and people will envy

---

[35] يضطرب عليه بدنه. Perhaps this should be better read with the standard Form VIII, "agitated, disturbed"; but I do not understand the use of the preposition على.

him, and his enemies will multiply, and he will build a building, and plant, and be sincere in his conversation, and his speech will be received, and he will treat the people of his house well, and do much spending, and will invite his brothers to his meals, and he will transfer from place to place or be absent [from his home], and the condition of his children will be suitable.

3 If the Sun was in a bound of Mars, then his wrath and anger will multiply, as well as his joking around and his banter, and cutting by iron will afflict him, and it will corrupt <what is> between him and some of the people of his house, and he will associate with some robbers, and will be absent from his home, and will do hard labor.

4 If the Sun was in a bound of Venus, he will increase in his love for women, and have sex with some of his relatives, and will spend money on entertainments and delights, and will speak on the matter of religion and prophecy, and will be devoted to the houses of worship, and scholars, and he will know the secrets of kings, and will do a good deed, and benefit from the people of his house, and his delight will multiply.

5 If the Sun was in a bound of Mercury, he will be devoted to cleanliness and clean things, and writing and speaking, and those of the people having importance, and he will be a big joker, with diverse thoughts, and he will disparage people and slander them, and will delight in children.

Chapter VIII.12: On the indication of Venus by her presence in the bounds of the planets

1 If Venus was in a bound of Saturn, he will associate with corrupt and elderly women, and be distressed by some of them, and contend with them, and detest them, and treat them badly, and he will hate the people of his own house, and labor or travel (or he will resolve to travel), and he will be irritated in a time of his delight,[36] and he will have a

---

[36] This probably means he will be irritated *when he should have* delight.

stingy soul, and spend money on things which will weigh heavily upon him, and he will associate with eunuchs and the nobles, and fear or an ailment will afflict him from wind.

2 If Venus was in a bound of Jupiter, he will be joyful, delighted, and will befriend people having power, and he will increase in the benefits of his parents as well as his own benefits and good fortune, and his dishes and possessions, and gifts will come to him, and he will benefit from business, and some of the people will entrust him with assets, or he will entrust someone with what is like that, and he will be elevated above his relatives and peers, and he will be present at the doors of the nobles, and associate with women having power, and enjoy himself, and a fleeting ailment will appear, and he will be devoted to works of piety, and building in gardens and promenades, and the people will not praise him for his good deeds towards them.

3 If Venus was in a bound of Mars, a disagreement will occur between his parents, and he will increase in his sexual intercourse, and he will be criticized because of women, and he will be distressed because of them and because of children, assets, fines, the sciences, and scholars, and he will be devoted to entertainment, delight, and games, as well as lying, foolish people, and robbers.

4 And if she was in her own bound, then his father, women, and children (as well as the people of his house) will delight in him, and he will increase in his power and servants,[37] and his assets, his gold and silver, and dishes, and he [himself] will be decorated, and have fun or rejoice, and will drink wines, and will associate with some of the nobles and benefit from [that], and he will be respected, and will devote himself to the houses of worship, and delight in slaves.

5 If Venus was in a bound of Mercury, then he will delight in children and benefit from women and slaves, and associate with some of the noble men or eunuchs, and women in whose hands there is a craft such as hair stylists, singers, and wailing women, and the rest of [such] professions, and he will command, and his speech will be received,

---

[37] Or, his "entourage" (حشم).

and he will acquire assets and rob people of their money, or he will loan dirhams, and he will be distressed because of something from moisture and waters, and he will discuss books and obscure things, and will be devoted to lying, slandering people, stratagems, useless things and joking around, and treatments and doctors, and scholars, astrologers, soothsayers, and interpreters of dreams, and dyers, molders, and decorators, and a bite or sting will afflict him from some animal, or cutting by iron, and his enemies will have something detestable, and he will be victorious over those who contend [with him].

Chapter VIII.13: On the indication of Mercury by his presence in the bounds of the planets

1 If Mercury was in a bound of Saturn, then his brothers and the people of his house will have something detestable from enemies, and he will treat them and his parents badly, and one of his children will become sick, and he will have sex with pregnant women (and not remain constant with them), and he will toil or travel, and assets will come to him, and he will make expenditures which will be burdensome for him, and a fine will afflict him, and the work he does will be little except that there will be quarreling and confusion in it, and no one will praise him for the good deed he does, and he will lie in his speech, and swear false oaths, and will seek stumbling-blocks for his brothers and the people, and he will slander them, and fear of the Sultan will afflict him, and his distresses will multiply, and a fleeting ailment will afflict him in one of his eyes or in his legs, and he will be devoted to the houses of worship as well as cheating, deception, and corruption.

2 If Mercury was in a bound of Jupiter, then he will discuss books and obscure matters, and be elevated above his peers, and associate with the nobles and kings on account of managing their works and the affairs of religion and the religious, and reports of prophets and their situations, and he will be honest in his speech and deeds, and will be eager to do the good and be in command in it, and he will be elevated above his peers, and free people from detestable things, and be rewarded [by] the people for [his] good deeds, and he will be victorious over his enemies, and he will have success with one who quarrels[38] with him, and he will be devoted to business, assets, and things deposited [with him] and entrusted [to him], and slave girls among women, or divorced women, and he will delight in children, and assets will come to him and to his parents, and an ailment from dryness and heat will afflict him, and he will attend to buildings and promenades, and he will invite the people to his meals, and the works which he begins in it will be completed. **3** And Mercury in the bound of Jupiter [means that] the outcomes will be good.

4 If Mercury was in a bound of Mars, then he will have much toil, and will be away from his home, and distresses and confusion will find him because of women and children (and some of them will become ill), and he will acquire assets, and be devoted to robbers and thefts, and the assets of the people of his house will be ruined, and he will treat them badly, and a fine will afflict him, and he will behave hypocritically[39] before the people, and he will become corrupted among people and slander them, and his anger will be multiplied, and he will love what is useless, lying, and quarreling. **5** Now if Mercury was in his own sign, in a bound of Mars, then he will have the good and rejoice in women and children.

6 If Mercury was in a bound of Venus, he will increase in his assets and furniture, and be obstinate in his opinion, and he will be devoted to entertainment, music, and corrupt women, and he will spend money because of them, and he will delight in his parents and family, and children and slaves,[40] and they will delight in him, and he will associate with administrators,[41] the nobles, kings, and the religious, and he will benefit from foreigners, travels, and travelers, and he will enter into

---

[38] Or, "litigates."
[39] Reading Form III for what seems to be برای.
[40] Only **B** includes slaves.
[41] الكتاب, the same word which also means "writers" in **8** below; but its inclusion with nobles and kings here suggests the administrative state.

partnerships with people, and see what he loves from his partners, and he will be envied, blamed, and be distressed by [paying] security [for] a man,[42] and he will move from place to place, or be absent from his home,[43] and be distressed because of women. **7** And if Mercury was in this bound, in his fall, then he will be of little importance to his relatives.

8 If Mercury was in his own bound, then he will be respected, with much joy and delight, and he will associate with writers, calculators, scholars, astrologers and soothsayers, and dyers,[44] and he will devote himself to ornamentation, paintings,[45] and decoration, as well as deception and stratagems, and buying and selling, and he will benefit from[46] eunuchs or the women of kings, and he will increase in his culture and ideas, and assets and slaves, and he will treat people well, and be superior to them, and he will love travel as well as thinking about it, and perhaps he will be absent from his home, and he will be distressed because of women, and the people of his house will have something detestable, and he will have dreams in which there are lofty, heavenly things, or he will see prophets and their situations.

Chapter VIII.14: On the indication of the Moon by her presence in the bounds of the planets

1 If the Moon was in a bound of Saturn, he will be distressed because of women and children, and will be slow in his works and in what things he begins, and something detestable as well as quarreling will afflict his parents and the people of his house, and he will devote himself to hidden works, and will quarrel with [some] people and

---

[42] بكفالة إنسان.

[43] Both **E** and **P** omit the rest of this sentence.

[44] Tentatively reading as ملقّبين, which pertains especially to clothing with a red dye. But this could also be ملهيين, "amusing things." See also Ch. VII.4, **4** and **17**.

[45] Or, "sculptures."

[46] **P** reads, "delight in."

support⁴⁷ others, and loss will afflict him as well as pain in a hidden place, and he will build and make repairs, and will manage the conditions of slaves and servant girls, and he will contemplate obscure things.

2 If the Moon was in a bound of Jupiter, then he will apply himself to business, and assets will come to him, and he will toil or be absent from his home, and some of his children will become ill, and he will associate with the nobles, and he will enter among the people in reconciliation,⁴⁸ and his speech will be received, and his character will become bad,⁴⁹ and from some of the people he will hear ugly speech, and he will be victorious over those who contend with him, and he will hear melodies and joke around with women (and have sex with them), and his passion will increase, and he will treat some of the people well, and will have the good from lands and waters, and will benefit from a woman having power (or a eunuch), and he will build and make repairs.

3 If the Moon was in a bound of Mars, then he will be envious, foolish, and angry, and will give no care to what he perpetrates, and will say useless things, and some of his speech will be bad for him, and he will slander people and contend with them (and they will slander him), and his grief⁵⁰ and remorse will multiply, and he will treat his older children badly, and will be distressed at the time he eats and drinks, and will be occupied with homicides and their places, and he will be devoted to robbers and authorities, and riding animals and instruments [pertaining to] them, and lions and beasts, and iron, and hot things, and it will prepare contention and pain for the people of his house.

---

⁴⁷ Reading يعضد with **B** and **P**. **E** reads يغصب ("rob") or يغضب ("be angry with").

⁴⁸ Or more generally, in "peace" (الصّلح).

⁴⁹ يسوء خلقه. Or perhaps, his character or temper will become troubled or turn bad. But, this does not really match much of the rest of the paragraph, or the usual notions of Moon-Jupiter. Perhaps it reflects a sect difference.

⁵⁰ حسرة. But **B** reads "confusion" (حيرة).

4 If the Moon was in a bound of Venus, then he will delight and rejoice, and have sex with some women in secret (or impregnate them), and his fun and games with them will multiply, as well as his associating with them, and he will drink wines with them, and will apply himself to business, and assets will come to him [but] he will have expenses, and gifts will come to him, and he will be proud of himself[51] in producing assets, and he will be entrusted with [the safekeeping of] something, and he will be good to the poor and foreigners, and he will support some of the people, and trade in clothing and household items, and sit in clean, decorated places, and he will plant, build, and make repairs, and decorate, and devote himself to paintings and adornments, and scholars and sages, and he will increase in his logic, and his speech will be received, and he will see what he loves from leaders and the nobles, and he will be in need of some of them, and will toil or be absent from his home.

5 If the Moon was in a bound of Mercury, then he will apply himself to having a friendly attitude and courteous acts, and proverbs and fairy tales, books, and reports, and obscure things, and different sciences, and he will associate with scholars and sages, and interpreters of dreams for that reason, and he will benefit from them, and his speech will multiply, and he will lie about things, and he will devote himself to deception and stratagems, and useless things, and he will disparage people and slander them, and do bad deeds in secret, and expose himself to lawsuits, and his speech will be received, and he will toil much, and a pain will afflict him or he will be harmed by something hot, and he will be eager to seek assets, and the outcomes of the works which he begins in those days, will be suitable.

6 So if a planet in the revolution of the year or the revolution of the month was in the house of one of the planets (or in its bound), then whenever it [later] comes to be in one of the two houses of that planet (or its bound in one of the signs), at any of the times of the year or in

---

[51] Tentatively reading سبّح نفسه, and translating somewhat loosely.

any of the days of the month, it will produce the indication which it had first indicated, at that time. **7** And the strongest of the planets by indication during its course in the bounds, is the lord of the year: so when it encounters a fortune or was in its bound, it indicates good; and when it encounters an infortune or is in its bound, it indicates evil.

8 And[52] the indication of the planet if it was in [1] the bound of its [own] house,[53] [as opposed to being][54] in [2] the houses of the rest of the planets, is not [just] one [and the same] thing. **9** Nor if it was in [3] the bound of one of the planets in one of the signs, is its indication just like its indication if it was in [4] another sign [and] in the bound of that same planet: but rather, it is converted into an increase or decrease in it, according to the condition of the planet in itself at that time, and according to what testimony it has in that sign, and according to its harmonizing or contrasting with that house or bound, or the lord of either one by nature.

Chapter VIII.15: On the indication of the planets by their presence in the wells of the signs

1 If Saturn was in a well,[55] then he will have good fortune and respect, and will have a high opinion of himself, and foreigners will serve

---

[52] In this paragraph, Abū Ma'shar is distinguishing four types of situations: for example, Mercury in (1) the Mercury bound of Gemini, versus (2) the Mercury bound of Cancer; Mercury in (3) the Venus bound of Cancer, versus (4) the Venus bound of Leo. The whole point is that the nature of each bound is connected to its sign, so when a planet is in the Mercury bound of Gemini, it will mean something subtlely different than the Mercury bound of Cancer. (See also VIII.13, **5** and **7** above.) Unfortunately, almost no author really gives us enough information to understand what the principle of interpretation for bounds is.

[53] Reading with **E** for "one of its [own] two houses."

[54] Reading for "or."

[55] See the table below. My sense is that the wells may have been linked to the degrees of the sphere that lacked fixed stars, or were maybe linked to the "empty" degrees. In *Gr. Intr.* V.21 Abū Ma'shar says the following about their interpretation (translation not finalized): "**1** In the signs there are degrees called "wells," such that if one of

him, and he will increase in his slaves (and they will delight in him, and he will delight in them), and benefits will come to him from some of those having importance, and he will earn money outside of his own country, and he will separate from his parents and transfer or travel to a place he had no idea he would come to, and a pain will afflict him in a hidden place of his body, and he will be skilled in useless things, and he will present the truth from his own soul, and he will have good dreams, and in his dreams there will be kings or lofty things, and his mother will have a pain from poison or from medication, or something detestable due to shackles or confinement, and misfortune will find some of his siblings from a man having power, or from iron, and the place of his parents' home will be corrupted.

2 If Jupiter was in a well, then he will do works which will be bad for him, and he will destroy his assets, and be in need of the people, and some of them will scorn him, and part of his good fortune will be decreased, and he will leave his house and homeland, and quarrel and contend [with people], and he will weep over some of the people of his house, and his grief and remorse will multiply, and a catastrophe will afflict him from some animals who lack reason.

---

the planets occurred in those very degrees of the signs, without being powerful, then the disappearance of its brilliance will not be delayed, and the weakness of its indication. **2** So if the fortunes occurred in them, their condition will be like what we stated about weakness; but as for the infortunes, if they occurred in them their indication will be weakened (and sometimes they will indicate incidental good fortune due to their inability to [create] misfortune, and sometimes the nature of their misfortune will be strengthened). **3** And the ancients have already stated the places in which they indicate suitability or corruption, but we will state that in its own place." Steven Birchfield points out that this makes the interpretations sound like the Tail of the Dragon: diminishing the good, but also taking away some of the bad. But below, with the Moon in the wells (**7-19**), it sounds more like the licentious signs and decans.

	Wells (ordinal)	Wells (cardinal)		Wells (ordinal)	Wells (cardinal)
♈	6th 11th 17th 23rd	5°-5°59' 10°-10°59' 16°-16°59' 22°-22°59'	♎	1st 7th 20th 30th	0°-00°59' 6°-6°59' 19°-19°59' 29°-29°59'
♉	5th 13th 18th 24th 25th 26th	4°-4°59' 12°-12°59' 17°-17°59' 23°-23°59' 24°-24°59' 25°-25°59'	♏	9th 10th 17th 22nd 23rd 27th	8°-8°59' 9°-9°59' 16°-16°59' 21°-21°59' 22°-22°59' 26°-26°59'
♊	2nd 13th 17th 26th 30th	1°-1°59' 12°-12°59' 16°-16°59' 25°-25°59' 29°-29°59'	♐	7th 12th 15th 24th 27th 30th	6°-6°59' 11°-11°59' 14°-14°59' 23°-23°59' 26°-26°59' 29°-29°59'
♋	12th 17th 23rd 26th 30th	11°-11°59' 16°-16°59' 22°-22°59' 25°-25°59' 29°-29°59'	♑	2nd 7th 17th 22nd 24th 28th	1°-1°59' 6°-6°59' 16°-16°59' 21°-21°59' 23°-23°59' 27°-27°59'
♌	6th 13th 15th 22nd 23rd 28th	5°-5°59' 12°-12°59' 14°-14°59' 21°-21°59' 22°-22°59' 27°-27°59'	♒	1st 12th 17th 23rd 29th	0°-0°59' 11°-11°59' 16°-16°59' 22°-22°59' 28°-28°59'
♍	8th 13th 16th 21st 25th	7°-7°59' 12°-12°59' 15°-15°59' 20°-20°59' 24°-24°59'	♓	4th 9th 24th 27th	3°-3°59' 8°-8°59' 23°-23°59' 26°-26°59'

Figure 98: The wells in the signs (*Gr. Intr.* V.21)

3 If Mars was in a well, he will increase in his anger and sharpness, and [then] turn away [from it] quickly, and he will have a high opinion of himself, and increase in his friends, and will have the good from his brothers, and his women will obey him, and they will love him, and he will delight in them and in children, and he will free himself from a lawsuit (if he was in it), and he will be received, successful in what he seeks, assets and goods will come to him, and he will be devoted to iron and weapons.

4 If the Sun was in a well, then he will decrease in his brilliance and power, and his parents and the people of his house will scorn him, and they will separate from him, ugly things will be said about him, he will be blamed for something he does not do, part of his home will be corrupted, his condition will turn bad in what he possesses, and misfortune will afflict him from iron or fire.

5 If Venus was in a well, an ailment will afflict him from wind in the eye or in another place, and he will dislike women, and there will be estrangement between him and them, and loss will afflict him in his possessions.

6 If Mercury was in a well, astonishment and confusion will befall him, and weakness of the intellect, and his idleness will increase while his speech will be little, and his language will be obscene, and he will be made fun of, and he will be absent from his home, and be distressed by women and children, and an ailment will afflict him from wind.

7 Now as for the Moon, if she was in the wells of the signs, he will increase in his enemies, and some of the people will scorn him, and he will do works like the works of slaves, and his wandering will increase, and his transferring from place to place, and there will be estrangement between him and his parents, and he will be distressed because of women and children. **8** And she has a special indication if she was in the wells of each sign: so if the Moon was in the wells of Aries, then his power will be weakened as well as his intellect, and worry[56] will overtake him, and his companions will be of little importance, and an ailment will afflict him in his eye. **9** And if she was in the wells of Tau-

---

[56] Lit. "thought" (فكرة), but this usually has a negative connotation.

BOOK VIII: PLANETS IN SIGNS, BOUNDS, & WELLS

rus, he will be eager for women, and will be done wrong by them,[57] and will crave sex with male youths. **10** And if she was in the wells of Gemini, then he will have many thoughts about things full of lust, and will listen to speech of a similar kind, and he will revile and reject the thought of women, and love to have sex with male youths. **11** And if the Moon was in the wells of Cancer, his eating will increase, and an ailment will afflict him from hemorrhoids and swelling, and something detestable from some servant girls and female singers, and he will increase in his love for free[58] women. **12** And if she was in the wells of Leo, he will have sex with women not his own, in the rear and in places the likes of which one scarcely has sex. **13** And if she was in the wells of Virgo, then he will increase in his sexual intercourse, and he will deceive women, and make himself similar to them, and wear their clothing, and he will be criticized because of them. **14** And if the Moon was in the wells of Libra, then he will be confused in thought, with much distress, and an ailment will afflict him from fire or from something hot, and he will be laughed at, and he will steal some things in secret. **15** And if she was in the wells of Scorpio, he will increase in his sexual intercourse and his joking around with women, and he will devote himself to lying. **16** And if she was in the wells of Sagittarius, he will devote himself to weapons, and cutting by iron will afflict his body, and he will rejoice with his companions, though they will despise him. **17** And if she was in the wells of Capricorn, he will increase in his sexual intercourse, and will have sex with some of his relatives, and fear of the darkness or being alone will afflict him. **18** And if she was in the wells of Aquarius, then narrowed circumstances will afflict him in his possessions, and he will be devoted to the religious and works of piety. **19** And if she was in the wells of Pisces, then he will be devoted to birds, fish, and waters, and the places of them, and he will be distressed because of them.

---

[57] Or, he will be offended or hurt by them (يتأذى بهنّ).
[58] And especially, those of higher social rank (الحرائر).

20 And people have disagreed about the degrees of the wells in the signs,[59] but we stand by those who agree on what we have described in the *Book of Introduction*.

21 And the time of the thing which is pointed out by the indicators which we have mentioned in this Book,[60] are of three types.

22 The first is [1] when that planet is the manager for the year or for one of its times; the second is [2] so long as the planet is [actually] in that house, bound, or well, and the third is [3] when the management of one of the months or days reaches[61] the position in which that planet is—and sometimes that will be in all three of these times [simultaneously].

23 And of course a single planet in a different time may indicate something (by means of one of the conditions and positions), but in that [later] time it will indicate something contrary to that (by a different condition and position): so if the indication of the planet was like that, then the strongest of them will manifest, and there will be [only] a small portion of the other thing. **24** But if the strength of the planet in [its] indication of [each of] the two is equivalent, then each one of them will manifest when it manages one of the times of the year, and it indicates [what is] like that [strong] condition: and that is like when a planet is in its own house, and in the houses of the circle (or the sign in which it is by place)[62] indicating good, or it is in the contrary of its domain and in a bound and well, indicating evil. **25** So when that planet manages one of the times of the year with suitability, it will manifest that good; and when it manages with corruption, it will manifest that evil.

---

[59] See for example al-Qabīsī in his *Introduction* I.51 (see *ITA* VI.9.1).
[60] Book VIII, not the entire work. However, it seems to me that the following contains good general advice anyway.
[61] Or "terminates at," Abū Ma'shar's usual term for profections. But perhaps he would include cases where the Ascendant of the month falls on that natal planet.
[62] Reading with **B**. **E** and **P** read, "by condition and place."

26 And if the planets were in diverse places, and at the same time each one of them indicates something contrary to what another indicates, then the indication of each one of them will manifest at the time it manages one of the times of the year, in the manner we mentioned.

27 And if any of the indicators of the year was in a suitable condition, strong, it indicates through that condition a suitability of condition and stability of rank and status, and the duration of assets; and any of them in a bad condition, weak, indicate corruption and alteration in those very same matters. **28** So those good fortunes will not leave him, but he will be fearful, in dread, with many distresses because of them, and he will enact [only] a small thing of it.[63]

29 And in what we have stated in this book of ours, there are manifest matters whose existence a man will not doubt when they occur, and in it are [also] faint, distant[64] things one does not perceive unless it is a perception [of something] corresponding to its conditions and affairs.[65] **30** And indeed that will be in accordance with the strength of the planet or its weakness: for if the planet was strong in indicating something, that will be manifest, and if it was weak, it will be [only] part of the thing it had indicated, or his involvement in that thing will be for [only] a short time, in the sense of seeing, hearing, and talking (and sometimes that will be a wish, idea, dream, and fleeting things). **31** And God is more knowledgeable.

---

[63] Reading with **E**. **B** and **P**: "he will be diverted in a small thing of it."

[64] بعيدة. That is, remote from obvious actions and perceptions: see below.

[65] By "its" conditions and affairs, I believe that Abū Ma'shar is speaking about the planet's condition, and in the next sentence we see he means "strength" (probably, angularity). So if a planet is suitable and fit, or its opposite, it will indicate good things, or their corruption (**27-28**); but its strength will show how outwardly and powerfully it manifests, as opposed to being merely in the mind (**29-30**).

BOOK IX: ON THE KNOWLEDGE OF THE CONDITIONS OF A MAN IN THE MONTHS, DAYS, AND HOURS, AND THE KNOWLEDGE OF THE CUTTERS AND INDICATORS OF THE YEAR

And it is in nine chapters

Chapter IX.1: On the knowledge of the indicators of the months

1 The indications of the planets in this subject are of five types:

2 The first type is rooted,[1] and it is what the planets indicate in the root of the nativity, of the magnitude of lifespans,[2] occupations, and good fortune, and the number of siblings and children, and the rest of the things which one draws conclusions about and [judges] their conditions and times from the planets of the root, in the manner mentioned in *The Book of Nativities*.[3]

3 The second type is annual,[4] and it is what the planets of the revolutions of years indicate (of good or evil): like the lord of the year, the distributor, and the *fardārs*, and their transits over each other, and the rest of what follows that, of what we have stated in this book of ours. **4** So if the planets of the root or the revolution indicated that something will come to be [later on] in one of the months or days, then their indication for that will be according to what emerges from the distribution of the minutes, and the arrival of one of them to the position of another,[5] and the rest of

---

[1] That is, natal interpretation.
[2] Reading as الأعمار, with **P, T,** and possibly **B. E** (and possibly **B**) reads الأعمال, "works."
[3] Again, this may refer to his *Book of the Judgments of Nativities*, in Oxford, Bodleian, Hunt. 546.
[4] That is, everything we have done in this book so far.
[5] By "distribution," he probably means a very precise calculation of the natal distribution for a particular time of the year (Book III). By "arrival," I believe he means the transit of each planet to some natal place at the solar revolution (Book V).

what is like that—and that is a rooted or annual indication, not monthly or daily, because one draws conclusions about one of the two from the root or at the revolution of the year.

5 The third type is monthly, it is what the Ascendants of the revolution of the months indicate, as well as the turning of the twelve signs, a month for every sign.

6 The fourth type is daily.[6]

7 The fifth type is hourly.[7]

8 We will discuss the indication of these three latter types in this Book, and we will begin with the indicators of the months—and there are seven.

[Seven monthly indicators]

9 So the knowledge of the first indicator is that you see [#1] where the year terminates from the Ascendant of the root, by a calculation of a year for every sign, up to the year which you want: when it terminates at one of the signs, then it is the "sign of the terminal point." **10** And it is among the indicators indicating the year as well as the first month of it.[8]

---

[6] These are discussed in Chapter IX.7.
[7] These are discussed in Chapter IX.7.
[8] This is simply the sign of the profected natal Ascendant; but it is included as a monthly indicator because it also stands for the first month of the year, and is used to generate monthly profections.

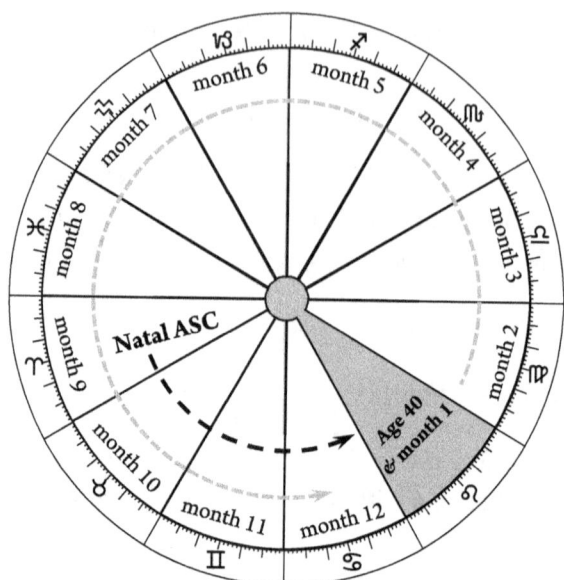

Figure 99: Monthly indicator #1: Basic profection of natal Ascendant (IX.1, 9-10)[9]

11 And the knowledge of the second indicator is that you know [#2] the ninth-part of the sign of the terminal point: and it is that you divide the sign into nine divisions so that every division is 3 1/3 degrees (and it is 200'), and you grant one of these ninth-parts to every planet of the seven: so the planet which is the lord of the first ninth-part belonging to the sign of the terminal point, is among the indicators of the year—and it is also the indicator of the first month of that year (so don't worry about which position in that sign is the terminal point of the year, whether it is 10° of it, or more or less).[10] **12** And the lord of the first ninth-part belonging to the second sign from the sign of the terminal point (which is its house of assets) is the indicator of the condition of the second month of that year. **13** And the lord of the

---

[9] In this hypothetical nativity, the Ascendant is Aries. The native is age 40, so the Ascendant profects to Leo and the 5th (black dotted line). This means that Leo is the profected Ascendant for the whole year as well as its first month, followed by the other signs for the other months (grey dotted line). However, see Abū Ma'shar's special rules for profection below in **26-31**.

[10] See Chs. III.9-III.10: this is the lord of the year according to the Indians.

first ninth-part belonging to the third sign from the terminal point (which is its house of siblings) is the indicator of the third month of that year. 14 And likewise the lord of the first ninth-part of every sign which the turning from the terminal point reaches, is the indicator of a month, until the lord of the first ninth-part belonging to the twelfth [from it] is the indicator of the condition of the twelfth month.

15 And an example of that is [that] the year terminated at Cancer, so the lord of its first ninth-part is the Moon, and she is the lord of the year, as well as the lord of the first month of it. 16 And the lord of the first ninth-part of Leo is Mars, and he is the lord of the second month of it; and the lord of the first ninth-part of Virgo is Saturn, and he is the lord of the third month; and the lord of the first ninth-part of Libra is Venus, and she is the lord of the fourth month—and likewise are the lords of the first ninth-parts belonging to [all] twelve signs, every lord of [the first] ninth-part of the signs being a month.

Rooted	#1	**Profected natal Ascendant** (1st month) and monthly profections from it	*Old, rooted causes Slow to disappear*
	#2	**Ninth-part of sign of year** (1st month) and monthly profections from it	
	#3	**Profected natal Lot of Fortune** (1st month) and monthly profections from it	
	#4	**SR Ascendant** (1st month) and monthly profections from it	*Recent causes Limited to year Not constant*
	#5	**SR Lot of Fortune** (1st month) and monthly profections from it	
Not	#6	**Ascendants** of: monthly revolution charts	*Recent causes Months, days Short duration*
	#7	**Lots of Fortune** in: monthly revolution charts	

Figure 100: Seven annual and monthly indicators (IX.1, 9-25, 35-39; IX.5, 95-98)[11]

---

[11] For comparing the subject-matter of each significator, see IX.5, **99-102**.

17 And the knowledge of the third indicator is that you see [#3] where the Lot of Fortune is in the root of the nativity, and turn from it a sign for every year, up to the year which you want. **18** So when it terminates at one of the signs, then that sign is the sign of the terminal point from the rooted Lot of Fortune: and it is of the indicators indicating the year as well as the first month of it. **19** Then, you turn the twelve signs from it for twelve months, a month for every sign.

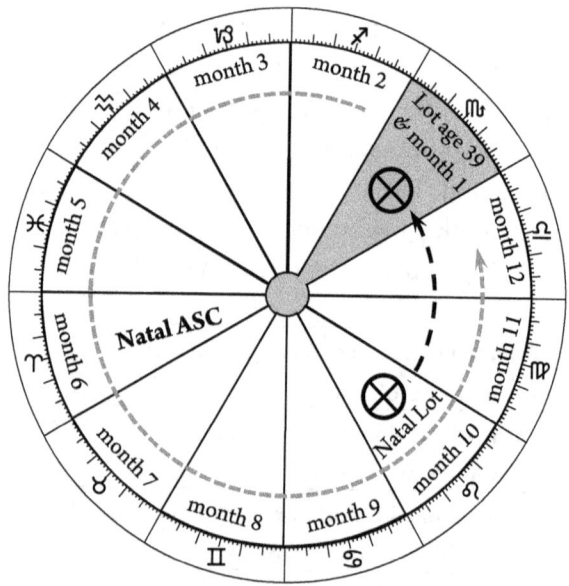

Figure 101: Monthly indicator #3: Basic profection of natal Lot of Fortune (IX.1, 17-19)[12]

20 And the knowledge of the fourth indicator is that you look at [#4] the Ascendant of the revolution of that year, and you assign [it] to the first month, then you turn the twelve signs from it for the twelve months, a month for every sign.

---

[12] In this hypothetical nativity, the Ascendant is Aries and the natal Lot in Leo. The native is age 39, so the Lot profects to Scorpio and the 8th (black dotted line). This means that Scorpio is the profected Lot for the whole year as well as its first month, followed by the other signs for the other months (grey dotted line). *However*, see Abū Ma'shar's special rules for profection below in **26-31**.

BOOK IX: MONTHS, DAYS, HOURS, LONGEVITY, REFLECTIONS 557

21 And the knowledge of the fifth indicator is that you see [#5] where the Lot of Fortune occurred in the revolution of the year, and you assign the sign in which it is to the first month, then turn the twelve signs from it for the twelve months, a month for every sign. **22** And these five indicators are the rooted ones.[13]

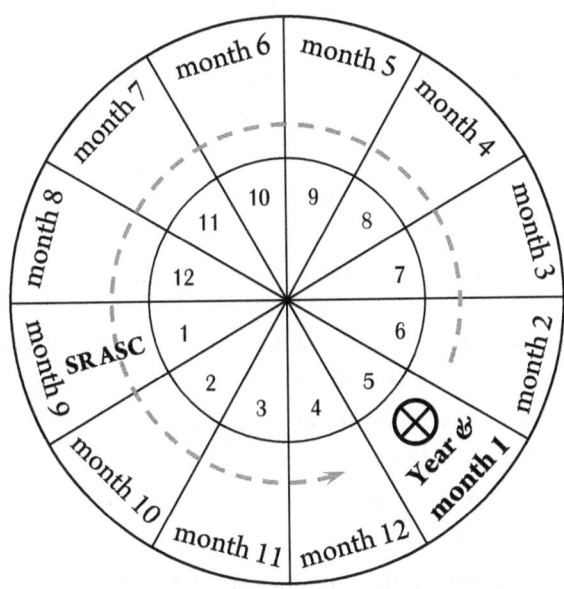

Figure 102: Monthly indicator #5: Basic profection of SR Lot of Fortune (IX.1, 21)[14]

23 And the knowledge of the sixth indicator is that you see [#6] where the Sun is in the root of the nativity: for when he comes to be in the second sign from it, in the like degree and minute to the one he

---

[13] They are "rooted," because the depend directly upon the natal chart and natal Sun: see **37** below. But note that for the most part, he will ignore the ninth-parts. Note also that each of these five indicators is calculated for the beginning of the year, but does double-duty as the first month of the year as well.

[14] In this hypothetical solar revolution, the Lot of Fortune is in the SR 5th: it stands for the year as a whole, as well as its first month. It is then profected forward through the signs for successive months. *However,* see Abū Ma'shar's special rules for profection below in **26-31**.

was in at the root, then see what the Ascendant is at that time, for it is among the indicators of the second month. **24** And when he reaches the third sign from his rooted position and comes to be in it, in the like degree and minute to the root of the nativity, then see what the Ascendant is at that time, for it is among the indicators of the third month—and you will likewise know the Ascendant of the rest of the months of the year.

25 And the knowledge of the seventh indicator is that you [#7] derive the Lot of Fortune for that month from the Sun, Moon, and Ascendant of the revolution of the month, and where it occurs, that is also among the indicators of the month.

[How to profect for successive months]

26 Now as for knowing the turning of the indicators in the signs for the twelve months, you should look at every one of the four [following] rooted indicators (and they are [#1] the sign of the terminal point from the Ascendant of the root, and [#3] the sign of the terminal point from the Lot of Fortune of the root, and [#4] the Ascendant of the revolution of the year, and [#5] the sign of its Lot of Fortune):[15] for if all of these were fixed signs, then one turns from the position of each one of them forwards, a month for every sign, and it is that you assign the position in which [each one] is to the first month, and the second sign from it to the second month, and the third sign from it to the third month, and likewise they are turned equally in succession, sign after sign, until the twelve signs are [assigned] to the twelve months.

27 And if these four indicators were convertible signs, then they are turned from the position of each one of them *backwards*, a month for every sign: and it is that you assign the place in which it is to the first month, and the twelfth sign from it to the second month, and the eleventh sign from it to the third month, and the tenth sign from it to the fourth month, and you do likewise with the rest of the twelve signs until the second sign from its position belongs to the twelfth month.

---

[15] Throughout most of these chapters, Abū Ma'shar will ignore [#2] the ninth-part.

28 And if these four indicators were signs having two bodies, then look: for if all of them[16] were from the beginning of that sign up to 15 complete degrees of it, then it is turned from the position of each one of them equally in succession, sign after sign, just as you did when they are in fixed signs. **29** And if they were <in> signs having two bodies, [but] from the beginning of the sixteenth degree[17] of it up to the end of the sign, then it is turned from the position of each one of them *backwards*, just as one does when they are in the convertible signs. **30** And indeed, they are turned like this because the signs having two bodies, from their beginning to the end of fifteen degrees, are of the nature of the fixed sign which is before it, and after that up to the end of thirty degrees [they] are of the nature of the convertible sign which is after it.

31 Now if some of these four indicators are of the fixed signs, and others of them of the convertible signs, and others of them of the signs having two bodies, then one turns each one of them individually in the manner we mentioned previously.

32 And as for [2] the second indicator which we spoke of before (and it is the lord of the first ninth-part of the sign of the terminal point), it is not turned in the way that these four [other] indicators are turned, but is turned in succession without distinction, whether the sign of the terminal point is convertible, fixed, or having two bodies: because working with the ninth-part and its lord is different from working with these four indicators.

33 But[18] if one of the signs was turned in a revolution of years in order to know the months, and it terminated at one of the signs and it was convertible,[19] then the second one from it in the direct order of signs is its house of assets, and the third is its house of brothers, and

---

[16] Or rather, "any" of them: they are profected independently of one another (**31**).

[17] That is, at precisely 15° (reading more precisely for "the beginning of sixteen degrees of it.")

[18] See the Introduction, §9.

[19] Reading up to here more naturally for "So if one of the signs was turned in one of the years, and it was convertible, for knowing the months, and it terminated at one of the signs."

the fourth its house of real estate—and likewise the rest its houses. **34** And as for the signs which are turned without distinction, there is no doubt that they are like this.

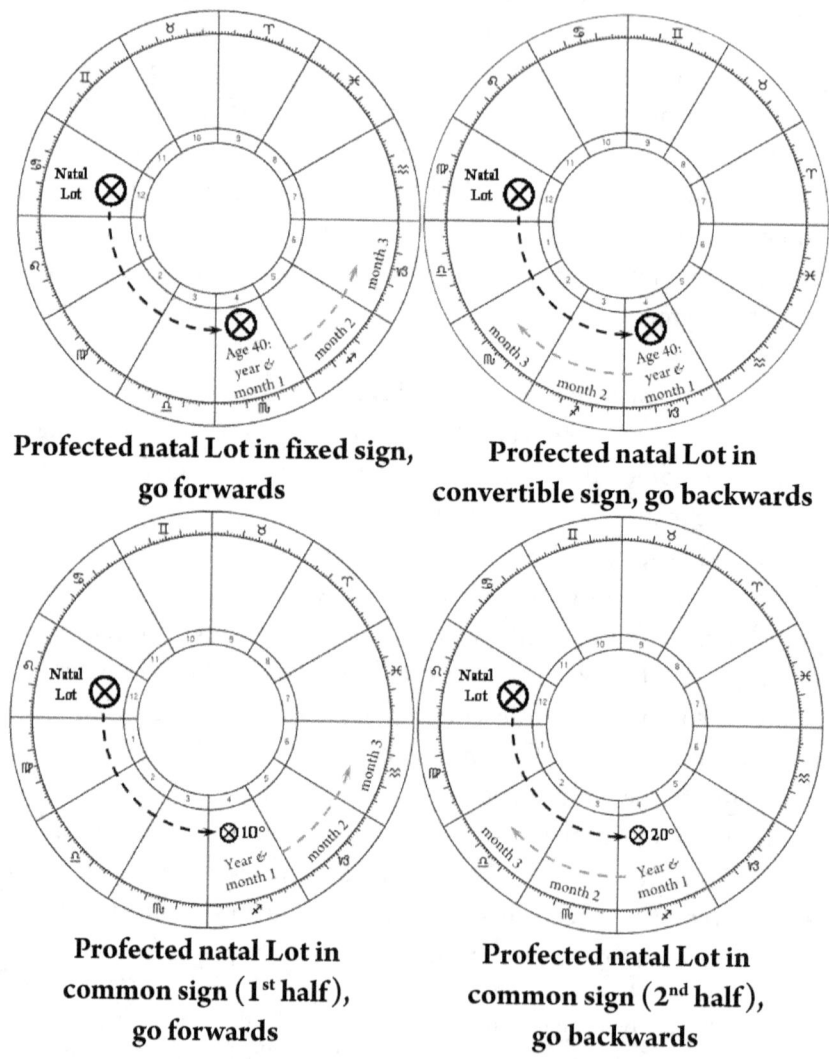

Figure 103: Abu Ma'shar's special rules for quadruplicities in monthly profections (IX.1, 26-34)

[Summary of the seven indicators]

35 And [of] these seven indicators, five of them are rooted, and two are not rooted.

36 As for the five rooted ones, the first of them is [1] the sign of the terminal point, and the second [2] the lord of its first ninth-part, and the third [3] the sign which the rooted Lot of Fortune terminates at, and the fourth is [4] the Ascendant of the revolution of the year, and the fifth is [5] its Lot of Fortune. **37** And we have called these "rooted," because we turn each one of them from their positions which they are in at the revolution of the year, in the twelve signs for the twelve months; and[20] you see where each one of these indicators reaches, relative to three positions: relative to the Ascendant of the root of the nativity, and the sign of the terminal point, and the Ascendant of the revolution of the year.

38 And as for the two last ones (which are [6] the Ascendant of the month and [7] its Lot of Fortune), they are *not* rooted, because each of them indicates the condition of a single month, and [then] changes in the next month.

39 And the first indicator is more universal[21] in indication than the second one, and the second one more universal than the third, and the third more universal than the fourth, and the fourth more universal than the fifth; and as for the sixth and seventh indicators, they are more universal in their indication over the days of the month as well as its hours.

---

[20] Reading for "or."
[21] Or, "general" or "all-embracing" (أعمّ). I have slightly abbreviated what follows, since Abū Ma'shar tediously repeats the same phrasing for each indicator ("and the second indicator is more universal in indication than the third indicator," etc.).

[Three rejected alternatives]

40 And there were certainly some of the ancients who, when they[22] wanted knowledge of the conditions of the months in the revolutions of years, they used to see how many signs, degrees, and minutes were between the Sun in the revolution of that month whose knowledge they wanted, up to the Moon of the root of the nativity, and they preserved that; then they cast it out from the Ascendant of the root, and wherever the counting ran out, they looked at that sign and made it the indicator of that month which they wanted.[23] **41** And this is not correct, because sometimes this indicator will not have an indication in one of the months: and that is because sometimes in some nativities the Moon will be in one of the signs, in the degree and minute corresponding to that of the Sun in *his* sign, so when the Sun in that month reaches[24] that sign and comes to be in that corresponding degree and minute, the month will not have an indicator, because there will be no distance between him and the Moon of the root—so that ruins this method.[25]

---

[22] Arabic is sometimes ambiguous as to whether "some" means only "one" or more than one. I have read it in the plural here, even though it is evident that Abū Ma'shar is thinking of Dorotheus (see below). Abū Ma'shar is apparently being polite in not criticizing Dorotheus by name.

[23] That is, from the monthly Sun to the natal Moon, and projected from the natal Ascendant. This Lot of Fortune-style method for the months is no doubt based on Dorotheus (*Carmen* IV.1, **46-55**), and is similar to Theophilus (*Cosmic Inceptions* Ch. 5, **3**), who might also be based on Dorotheus. (Valens has his own version in *Anth.* V.4.) *Carmen* and Theophilus agree that we should measure from the monthly transiting Sun, but seem to disagree about which Moon to count to, and which Ascendant to project from (natal or revolutionary).

[24] Lit., "terminates at."

[25] That is a poor argument, because the same could be said about the Lots of Fortune and Spirit. If the Sun and Moon occupy the same degree, then this would simply mean that the rising sign is the indicator, but what is wrong with that? The real problem is that if we mix the charts, projecting from a moving Sun to *any* fixed Moon, then the signs indicating the months will always move *backwards*, which is contrary to astrological thinking and is a problem with the special quadruplicity rules in **26-31**. As the Sun moves forward in the zodiac each month, the distance forward to the fixed Moon will shrink, so the amount we project from the Ascendant

42 And there were people[26] who used to look, in deriving the indicator of the month, at the sum of the days of the nativity since the day on which [the native] was born, up to the time in which they wanted knowledge of the condition of that month: then, they cast it out from the Ascendant of the nativity, 28 days for every sign (then after that they made every sign be 2 1/3 days).

43 And among them were [also] those who cast out these days by 30 ½ days (and by this they intended the days of a solar month):[27] and wherever the counting reached, by [either] one of the two amounts,[28] they made that sign the indicator of that month.

44 But we have left [the latter] two behind, because the first one (in which one casts these days out in groups of 28, then calculates from the sign at which it terminates, 2 1/3 days for every sign), intends to approximate the months of the Moon, and the revolutions of months are not appropriate for that.[29] **45** And as for those who cast it out according to the days of the solar months, in our revolutions for the months we dispense with that due to the fact that the days of one "month of the Sun" are different from the days of another, while those people cast out one [and the same] amount for every month.[30]

---

will also shrink, meaning that the signs indicating the months will always get *closer* to the Ascendant by moving backwards, rather than advancing forward.

[26] That is, Ptolemy (*Tet.* IV.10, Robbins p. 453).

[27] That would be a year of 366 days (30.5 * 12 = 366).

[28] That is, by either the 28-day method of Ptolemy or the 30 ½-day method.

[29] See the argument against lunar months in Ch. I.3. The 28 days of the Moon refer to the approximate days of visibility.

[30] Again, see I.3. Because the days allotted to each calendar month differ from each other (such as 30 days to September, and 31 to October), "those people" divided the *calendar* year into 12 equal parts, yielding artificial months of 30.5 days apiece, which do not correspond to calendar months nor the Sun's motion. But since the year is actually based on the *Sun's* motion, Abū Ma'shar prefers to divide the circle into twelve parts using that, so a "month of the Sun" will be however long it actually takes for the Sun to move through each one.

Chapter IX.2: On the knowledge of the condition of the first month

1 Obtaining information about the conditions of the first month is full of uncertainty, because these five rooted indicators are among the indicators of the year as well as having an indication for the first month of it. **2** So if at the beginning of the year they indicate something good or bad, then the condition they are in has indications for both the year and the first month the year, which are difficult to distinguish as being for one of them rather than the other: so with respect to this one should be careful about[31] the indication of the first month, according to the generality of the people of this craft. **3** And indeed the indication of each one of them *for* the first month is if, in the revolution of the year, the lord of every[32] indicator of them is *in* the sign which has the indication of the first month, and it is in[33] the stake of the Ascendant (and the rest of the stakes sometimes indicate that as well, and especially the Midheaven): so if any of them in the revolution of the year indicates that something will come to be in something other than the first month, that indication will pertain to the year, not the month.

---

[31] Reading Form VIII (and translating a little loosely) with **B** and **P**, which strictly means to be obscure or confused. **E** reads, "compare." **T** is illegible.

[32] Abū Ma'shar means "any" indicator. It is a stronger indication if they are all doing it (**4** and **7** below), but we should look at each one. See "any" later in the sentence.

[33] Abū Ma'shar most likely means "and it *should be*." Being in the Ascendant itself (that is, the revolutionary Ascendant) would be best because it would be in that sign; but since the angles show quick manifestation, probably the others would be nearly as good.

To manifest in first month:	
Indicators of topic...	...should ideally be in the five rooted annual indicators:
That *natal* house (and its lord)	1. Profected natal Ascendant
That *profected* house (and its lord)	2. Convertible sign
	3. Profected natal Lot of Fortune
That *SR* house (and its lord)	4. SR Ascendant (especially)
	5. SR Lot of Fortune
The planets should also be in a stake, and fast.[34] For first house matters, the lords of the five rooted indicators themselves should be in those signs.	

Figure 104: General template for the indications of the first month (IX.2)

4 Now as for the knowledge of the condition of the body in the first month, you should look at the five rooted indicators, unless one of them is the "governor" of the indication: and that is if the Lot of Fortune of the root of the nativity is in the Ascendant [of the root], so that[35] the terminal point relative to [#1] the Ascendant of the root and relative to [#3] its Lot of Fortune is one [and the same] sign, and [#4] the Ascendant of the revolution of the year is also that sign, and in it is the [#5] Lot of Fortune of the revolution, and that sign is [#2] convertible.[36] 5 So if one of them combined [all of] these indications,

---

[34] See also IX.2, **36-38** for some extra rules.
[35] Reading for "and." If the natal Lot and natal Ascendant are the same sign, then they will each profect to the same sign every year, which is what Abū Ma'shar says next.
[36] If this sign is convertible, then the lord of the year will also be the lord of the ninth-part, and all five rooted indicators will be the same sign and have the same lord. However, if this sign is convertible then by the normal rules of quadruplicities its effects should only happen once and soon, rather than being repeated (double-bodied) or persistent (fixed).

then it alone is the governor of the first month,[37] while if [only] the generality of the indications belonged to one of them, it will be primary for obtaining information about the year,[38] while the remaining [ones] will have a partnership with it.

Figure 105: Cancer-Moon as governor of 1st house in first month (IX.2, 4-7)[39]

---

[37] Note that such an indicator would also be the governor for the entire year, because the first-month positions are identical to the annual positions.
[38] This should read "month," since that is strictly the context here.
[39] In this chart for Age 39, the natal Lot is on the natal Ascendant (inner circle), so at 39 they both profect to Cancer, the natal 4th. But the Ascendant of the revolution and the Lot of the revolution are also on Cancer as well, and since Cancer is a watery, convertible sign the Moon is the lord of all of them (since the lord of the year in the Indian system is always the lord of the convertible sign). Therefore all five of the rooted indicators from Ch. IX.1 are on the same sign, and Cancer and its lord the Moon fully control the meaning of the first month (and year, since the revolutionary positions stand for both the year and the first month).

Book IX: Months, Days, Hours, Longevity, Reflections

6 And often, two indications coincide with the sign of the terminal point: one of them because it is the sign of the terminal point, and the second if the terminal point is of the convertible signs, so that the lord of the sign of the terminal point is the lord of the first ninth-part for that sign, so it strengthens the indication of the sign of the terminal point—and perhaps it will prepare something like that for the Ascendant of the revolution of the year, so one should examine that.[40] **7** So if the indicator was single, then look at it and at its lord; and if it was many, then look at each one of them individually and at their lords, and at their suitability and their corruption, both in the root of the nativity and in the revolution of the year.

8 Now [the body's] condition in the first month (in terms of health, illness, and the rest of the conditions) will be in accordance with what those indicators point out: so if they were in a suitable condition, they indicate the suitability of the body's condition, and if they were corrupt they indicate its disruption and illness, in relation to their indication—but if there are other indicators of the root or the year indicating illness, the illness will be in relation to that indication.[41]

9 But as for the knowledge of the condition of assets in the first month, look at the indicators of assets, and they are three: the second sign from the Ascendant of the root of the nativity, the second sign from the terminal point, and the second sign from the Ascendant of the revolution of the year. **10** For if these three indicators and their lords mixed with the indicators of the owner of the revolution and their lords (and they are the Ascendant of the root, the four [normal] rooted indicators and their lords, and the lord of the ninth-part of the year), they indicate the suitability of the condition in assets. **11** And if the lords of the indicators [of assets] were quick in course, close to the [exact] aspect of one to the other, or close to the degree of the connec-

---

[40] In **36** below he emphasizes that the Ascendant of the revolution especially indicates the first month, so even if we are hoping that several of them combine, we should favor indicators in it for the first month.

[41] Abū Ma'shar is probably thinking of other predictive techniques, such as distributions.

tion [by body], and they are in the sign of the first month just as we stated before, the indication of what they point out will be in the first month.

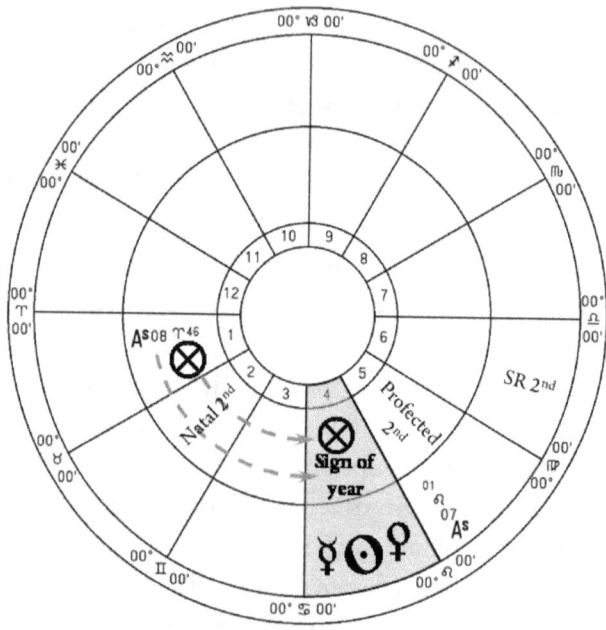

Figure 106: Activation of assets in first month (IX.2, 9-11)[42]

12 And as for the knowledge of the condition of siblings in the first month, you should look at the indicators of siblings, and they are three: the third sign from the Ascendant of the root, and the third sign from the sign of the terminal point, and the third sign from the Ascendant of the revolution of the year. **13** For if these three signs were in a suitable condition, and their lords like that as well, and they are

---

[42] In this chart we again have the natal Lot in the natal Ascendant, so that the profection of each at age 39 reaches Cancer. This allows Cancer greater ability to act as the sign of the first month, even though the Ascendant of the revolution is in Leo. According to **9**, there are three indicators for assets: the natal second (Taurus, and its lord Venus), the second place of the profection (Leo, and its lord the Sun), and the second of the revolution (Virgo, and its lord Mercury). At the revolution all three of these planets are transiting in Cancer, so whatever they indicate for the year should manifest in the first month.

quick in course, in the sign of the first month,[43] they indicate the suitability of the condition of brothers and sisters in it. **14** And if the indicators of the owner of the revolution and their lords were in a good mixture (and they are the Ascendant of the root, the four [normal] rooted indicators and their lords, and the lord of the ninth-part of the year), and they are in the sign of the first month, then it indicates the harmony between them, and their friendly relations, in the first month.

15 And as for the knowledge of the condition of fathers and real estate in the first month, one should look at the three indicators: and they are the fourth sign from the Ascendant of the root, and the fourth sign from the sign of the terminal point, and the fourth sign from the Ascendant of the revolution of the year. **16** For if these three signs were in a suitable condition, and their lords like that as well, and they are quick in course, in the sign of the first month, they indicate the suitability of the condition of fathers and real-estate <in the first month>. **17** And if the indicators of the owner of the revolution and their lords (of the Ascendant of the root, the four [normal] rooted indicators and their lords, and the lord of the ninth-part of the year) were in a good mixture, it indicates their harmony towards him, and the suitability of the condition of possessions among them, and their friendly relations, and the owner of the revolution's benefiting by real estate in the first month.

[Judging the topical indicators and their configuration with the native's]

18 So if the indicators of the house of assets, or the house of siblings, or the house of parents, or whichever house you looked at, were—as well as their lords—made unfortunate in themselves, while the indicators of the owner of the revolution and their lords were in an excellent mixture, then it indicates that something detestable and misfortune will afflict that topic in its own right, but harm will not afflict

---

[43] Again, this is ideally a single sign (and its lord) in which *all* of the rooted indicators coincide (**4-7**), but that will rarely happen.

the owner of the revolution for that reason, but rather he will benefit by what it prepares for him from that.

Relationship of topic to native	
Indicators of topic…	…should be configured to native's indicators:
That *natal* house (and its lord)	1. Natal ASC (and its lord)
That *profected* house (and its lord)	2. Profected natal Ascendant (and its lord)
	3. Ninth-part of year (and its lord)
	4. Profected natal Lot of Fortune (and its lord)
That SR house (and its lord)	5. SR Ascendant (and its lord)
	6. SR Lot of Fortune (and its lord)

Figure 107: Indicators for relationship of topic to native (IX.2)[44]

19 But if the indicators of the owner of the revolution and their lords were the ones made unfortunate, and the indicators of assets, siblings, or other indicators of the rest of the houses (and their lords) were made fortunate, and they were taking part in a mixture with the indicators of the owner of the revolution (and their lords), then the condition of the matter which that house indicates (in terms of assets, siblings or others) will be good, and the owner of the revolution will benefit by it—but he will be distracted in his own right by illness or confinement, or some other detestable thing.

20 If the indicators of that house and their lords, and the indicators of the owner of the revolution and their lords, were [all] made fortunate, then the owner of the revolution will be safe in his body, and in the matter which those indicators point out, he will see what he loves (in terms of suitability and increase in it), and he will rejoice in and benefit by it. **21** So if the examination was about assets, and <the lords

---

[44] For first-house matters, we may only need to take the lord of the natal Ascendant, lord of the year, and lord of the SR Ascendant—not the complete list which includes the ninth-part and the Lots.

of>⁴⁵ the indicators of assets were the ones making the indicators of the owner of the revolution (and their lords) fortunate, then he will benefit because of assets and be fortunate in them, and he will see increase in them without distress[46] and toil. **22** But if the lords of the indicators of the owner of the revolution were the ones making the indicators of assets and their lords fortunate, then he will be earning and seeking out that benefit and good fortune, and toiling and laboring in it.

Topical indicators	Configuration	Native's indicators	Meaning (and sentence)
Bad	Good	Good	(**18**) Bad for topic, good for native.
Good	Good	Bad	(**19**) Good for topic, native benefits but is distracted.
Good	Good	Good	(**20-22**) Good for all, with benefit.
Good	Bad	Bad	(**23-24**) Good topic incompatible with native; distress.
Bad	Bad	Good	(**25**) Bad for topic, incompatible with native; distress.
Bad	Bad	Bad	(**26-28**) Bad for all, with misfortunes.
Mixed	Mixed	Mixed	(**29**) Mixed.

Figure 108: Basic interpretations for configurations (IX.2, 18-31)

23 If the indicators of that house which you are looking at (of assets or something else) and their lords were in a bad mixture with the indicators of the owner of the revolution and their lords, then that matter will not be harmonious for the owner of the revolution, and his worrying[47] will multiply in it, and his distresses because of it. **24** And if,

---

[45] Adding in parallel with the next sentence.
[46] **E** and **P** read "trouble."
[47] Lit., "his thoughts."

along with the badness of the mixture of each of them with its associate, the indicators of the owner of the revolution and their lords are made unfortunate, then something detestable as well as distresses will afflict the owner of the revolution, in the category of what that house indicates, in relation to the nature of the infortune.

25 If the condition of some of the indicators with their associates were like that (in terms of the badness of the mixture), and the lords of the indicators of assets (or other [topic], of the houses of the circle) were the ones made unfortunate, then the owner of the revolution will have his distresses multiply because of the matter which that house indicates, and its harmony with him will be less, and misfortunes will afflict that matter.

26 If the indicators of the owner of the revolution (and their lords), and the indicators of the house which you are looking at (and their lords), were [all] made unfortunate, then [both] the owner of the revolution in himself and that matter will have types of detestable things and misfortunes. **27** And if the ones which make the indicators of the owner of the revolution (and their lords) unfortunate are the lords of the indicators of that house, then something detestable will afflict the owner of the revolution, from the category of the indication of that house (like assets, siblings, or the rest of them), and that will be evident.[48] **28** And if the lords of the indicators of the owner of the revolution are the ones which make the indicators of that house (and their lords) unfortunate, then misfortunes will afflict that matter because of something the owner of the revolution does.

29 Now if some of the indicators of assets (or siblings, or parents) and their lords were in a suitable condition and some of them in a bad condition, and the indicators of the owner of the revolution and their lords were some of them harmonious with those three indicators and their lords (or, made fortunate), and some of them contrary to them

---

[48] عارض. But this could also mean "an obstacle."

BOOK IX: MONTHS, DAYS, HOURS, LONGEVITY, REFLECTIONS 573

(or, made unfortunate), they indicate a confusion[49] of good and evil in that thing.[50]

⁂

30 So the examination of the indication of the rest of the twelve houses with respect to the conditions of the first month, should be in this manner. **31** And everything you examine in it, has a number of [other] indicators (from among the Lots, twelfth-parts, and other things); and likewise you ought to look at their mixture and their resemblance with the indicators of the owner of the revolution and their lords.

32 Now as for an excellent mixture and resemblance, [it is] if the indicators of the owner of the revolution (and their lords), and the indicators of the house which you are looking at (and their lords) are in a connection by sextile or trine, or they look at each other from this direction without a connection, or[51] there is a transfer or collection [of light] between them, or they are in the house, exaltation, bound, triplicity, or face of a single planet. **33** And if they are not looking at each other,[52] [it is also good] if they are in one belt (and that is if they are in the two signs belonging to one planet, like Taurus and Libra, and what is like that), or they are in two signs in which the length of day is one [and the same] (like Gemini and Cancer, for the length of [Gemini's] day is like the length of Cancer), or they are in two signs of matching ascension (like Pisces and Aries, and Virgo and Libra—and that is more firm if the indicators are in two signs, in degrees whose ascension is equivalent, such as the ascension of 20° Pisces being like the ascension of 10° Aries, and the ascension of 10° Pisces being like the ascension of 20° Aries); and you should work like that in the degrees

---

[49] تخليط. But this should probably be understood more mildly as "mixture."
[50] Reading with **B**. **P** and **E** read, "in that meaning."
[51] Abū Ma'shar probably means "and" here, since transfers and collections of light are usually used when planets do look at each other but are not connecting (as he just stated). But perhaps he is simply trying to be complete.
[52] That is, if they are in aversion.

of two signs matching in the length of the day. **34** And the more it is contrary to this, it is a bad mixture.

35 And in all of this, if the indicators were in the sign of the first month, and they are quick in course, in a stake, they indicate the coming-to-be of that matter in the first month; and if they were in the contrary of it[53] or they were slow in course, they indicate its coming-to-be in the rest of the months of the year.

36 And the Ascendant of the revolution of the year, and its houses (such as the house of assets, and siblings, and the rest of them), have a special characteristic in the indication of the months. **37** So if the lords of the indicators which are consulted with respect to assets or the rest of the things, are in the Ascendant of the revolution, they indicate that that will be in the first month; and if they were in its house of assets, it will be in the second month; and if they were in its house of siblings, that will be in the third month, and you look likewise in the rest of the houses for the twelve months.

38 And you should certainly look into it from the perspective of the quadrants as well: so if the lords of the indicators of any of the houses, and the lords of the indicators of the owner of the revolution, were in the second sign or in the third from the Ascendant of the revolution, that will be in the first quarter; and if they were in the fourth,[54] fifth, or sixth, that will be in the second quarter: and the condition in the remaining two quarters will be in this manner (and that is more confirmed if the Ascendant of the revolution was a fixed sign).

---

[53] This probably means being cadent or falling.
[54] **P** adds "sign."

Chapter IX.3: On the image of the revolution of the month

1 As for the first month, one obtains information about the conditions of a man in it from the image of the revolution of the year [itself]. **2** But as for the second month, and the rest of the months which follow it, see when the Sun reaches the second sign from his rooted place, and, within it, comes to be in the like degree and minute which he was in at the root of the nativity: then derive the Ascendant for that time, and it is the Ascendant of the second month. **3** And in this manner we derive the Ascendant of the third month, the fourth, and the rest of the months of the year, until we bring the Sun's motion in the twelve signs to a close, at the completion of twelve months.

4 So once you know the Ascendant of the month you want, then write it down in one of the houses of the image, and in the rest of the houses write down what is in the twelve signs according to what came out for you in the calculation, and in it write down the planets of the revolution of the month, their rays, their twelfth-parts, the twelfth-parts of the twelve houses,[55] the Lots, and the Head and Tail in their positions in the signs, at the time of the revolution of the month.

5 Then after that, write down in it the planets of the revolution of the *year*, as well as their rays, their twelfth-parts, the twelfth parts of the houses, the Lots, and the Head and Tail in the positions they were in at the revolution of the year.

6 Then after that, write down in it the planets of the root of the *nativity*, as well as their rays, their twelfth-parts, the twelfth-parts of the signs,[56] the Lots, and the Head and Tail in the positions they were in at the root of the nativity, [and] each planet according to its condition in terms of direct motion, retrogradation, and other things.

7 And if there occurred, in the degree of the Ascendant of the month (or its tenth),[57] or with one of the luminaries, one of the fixed stars indicating good fortune, then write it down in it.

---

[55] This seems to be the twelfth-parts of the house cusps.
[56] This should be understood as "houses," with the previous sentences.
[57] That is, the degree of the Midheaven.

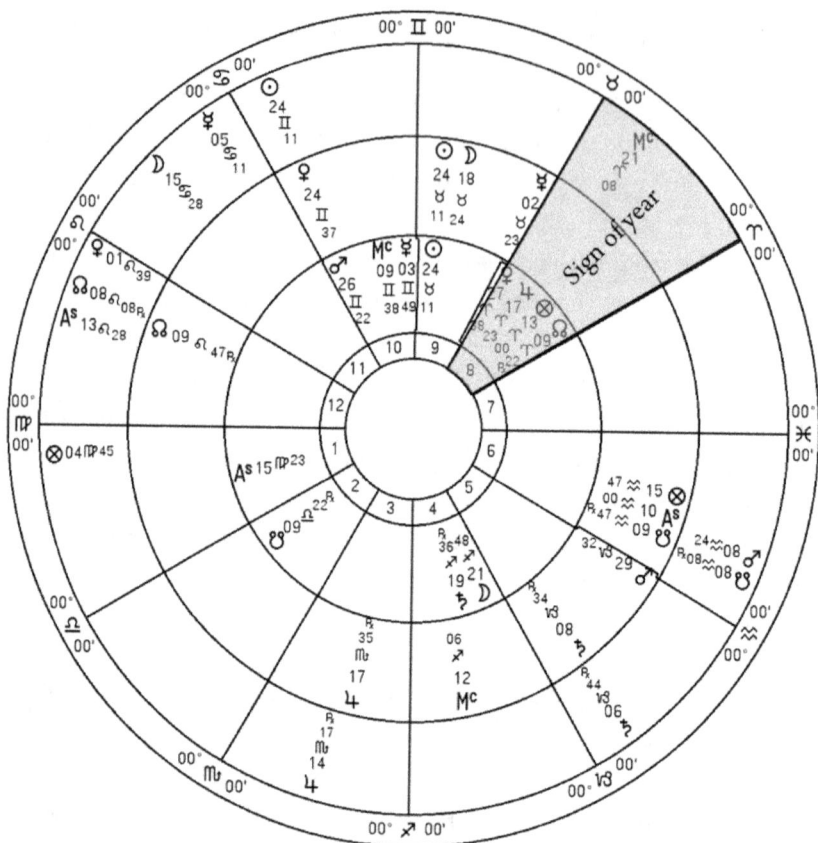

Figure 109: Monthly revolution in a tri-wheel (IX.3)[58]

8 And in the middle of the image, write down the position of the Ascendant of the root, and [1] the sign of the terminal point from the Ascendant of the root, and [3] the terminal sign from the Lot of For-

---

[58] I have greatly simplified this tri-wheel because it cannot include all of Abū Ma'shar's points without making a mess. Here, the nativity is the inner wheel (Ascendant at 15° 23' Virgo), and the native is 31, making the sign of the year Aries, the eighth. Mars is the lord of the year. The middle wheel is the solar revolution for age 31, and you can see that the natal and revolutionary Suns are the same (24° 11' Taurus). The outer wheel is the monthly revolution for the second month of that year, and you can see that the Sun is now 30° later (24° 11' Gemini). Note that the Sun of the MR is exactly on the Venus of the SR, with both falling almost exactly on the natal Mars (who is the lord of the year). The MR Mars is also extremely close to the SR Ascendant. So, Mars should be highly emphasized during this year and month.

tune in the root, and [4] the Ascendant of the revolution of the year, and [5] the Lot of Fortune of the year, and the sign which the month terminated at from each of these four rooted indicators (based on what we stated about it in the first month),[59] and the Lot of Fortune of the revolution of the month, and the terminal point of the distribution (as well as the distributor and the one partnering with it in the management), and the lord of the *fardār*, and the one distributing with it,[60] and the lord of the orb.

9 And once you have done that, then that is the correct image of the revolution of the month. **10** And there are gathered together in it: 21 planets (and the Head and Tail of each of them) in 3 places,[61] and the rays of the planets of the revolution of the month, the revolution of the year, and the root of the nativity, in 147 places,[62] and the twelfth-parts of the signs and planets which are in the revolution of the month, and in the revolution of the year, and in the root of the nativity, in 57 places,[63] and the Lots according to those of them you did, [whether] more or less.

Chapter IX.4: On the combinations of the seven planets

1 Now, of the seven planets, [some] have two houses and [others] one house,[64] and in the revolutions of years and months they have an indication according to the place of their houses relative to them (and their places relative to their houses), and according to their own places and the place of their houses in terms of four positions: [1] from the Ascendant of the root, [2] from the sign of the terminal point, [3]

---

[59] Remember, these numbered items are the four "rooted indicators" (apart from the ninth-part) which rule the year and its first month, in IX.1, **9-10** and **17-22**.
[60] That is the ruler of the sub-period.
[61] That is, according to the three charts: the root, the revolution of the year, and the revolution of the month (7 planets x 3 charts = 21).
[62] Each planet casts 7 rays, in each of the 3 charts: 7 planets x 7 rays x 3 charts = 147.
[63] Twelve signs and seven planets makes 19 twelfth-parts in each chart: 19 twelfth-parts x 3 charts = 57.
[64] Lit., "of them, its asset is two houses, and of them its asset is one house."

from the Ascendant of the revolution of the year, and [4] from the Ascendant of the revolution of the month (and in accordance with the place of these four from them and as well as from their houses).[65] **2** And we call these conditions which belong to them with respect to each other, "combinations," and we have explained those combinations and have assigned a fixed number for them so that it may be evident to us in how many ways there may be a combination of one with another in this subject: for in the knowledge of that are surprising, recondite secrets, profound, and beneficial in all cases of the knowledge of the stars.

[Planets ruling two houses: four divisions]

3 And we begin in that by looking at the planets and their houses, because for a planet which has two houses, its place from its house in the root and in the revolution of the year may be divided into four divisions. **4** The first is if [1] a planet in the root of the nativity *and* in the revolution of the year is in houses other than its own. **5** The second is if [2] a planet in the revolution of the year is in one of its two houses, and in the root of the nativity it is in neither of them. **6** The third is if [3] a planet in the root of the nativity is in one of its two houses, and in the revolution of the year it is in neither of them. **7** The fourth is if [4] a planet in the root of the nativity *and* in the revolution of the year is in one of its two houses.

Combinations for planets with two signs		
Division, sentences	In own sign?	
	In root	In SR
1 (8-12)	N	N
2 (13-16)	N	Y
3 (17-20)	Y	N
4 (21-24)	Y	Y

Figure 110: Combinations for planets with two signs (IX.4, 3-7)

---

[65] The first part of the chapter will deal with the annual Ascendants, and the last part with the monthly Ascendants (see **67**).

BOOK IX: MONTHS, DAYS, HOURS, LONGEVITY, REFLECTIONS   579

[Planets ruling two houses: first division]

8 Now as for the first one (and it is that a planet in the root of the nativity and in the revolution of the year is in houses other than its own),[66] it is combined in the revolution of the year in 32 combinations: and the examination of it is in three ways.

9 The first way is that you look at the place of the planet in the root of the nativity, relative to the Ascendant of the root of the nativity (and the place of the Ascendant of the root of the nativity relative to it), and the place of its two houses from the Ascendant of the root of the nativity (and the place of the Ascendant of the root of the nativity from its two houses), and the place of the planet from its two houses (and the place of its two houses from it), and the place of the planet in the revolution of the year from its two houses (and the places of its two houses from it), <and the place of the planet in the revolution from the Ascendant of the root (and the place of the Ascendant of the root from it)>.[67]

10 The second way is that you look at the place of that planet in the root relative to the sign of the terminal point (and the place of the sign of the terminal point relative to it), and the place of the planet in the revolution of the year from the terminal point (and the place of the terminal point from it), and the place of the planet's two houses from the terminal point (and the place of the terminal point from them both).

11 The third way is that you look at the place of the rooted planet relative to the Ascendant of the revolution of the year (and the place of the Ascendant of the revolution of the year relative to it), and the place of the revolutionary planet from the Ascendant of the revolution of the year (and the place of the Ascendant of the revolution of the year from it), and the place of the planet's two houses from the Ascendant

---

[66] See **4** above.
[67] This must be added, or else the total combinations will not add up to 32. For an example that uses all sixteen combinations from this first way, see **91-106** below.

of the revolution of the year (and the place of the Ascendant of the revolution of the year from its two houses).

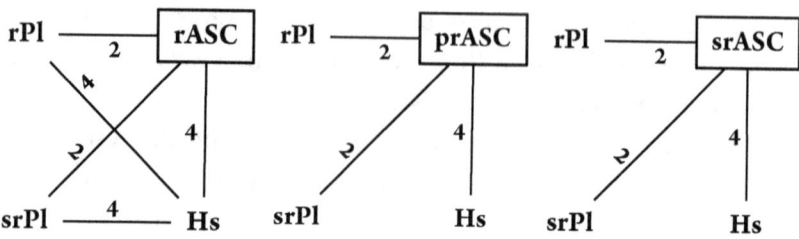

Figure 111: Planets with two houses, 1st division (IX.4, 8-12)[68]

12 And that is 32 combinations, because we have calculated one combination for every [single] sign, and two combinations for two signs.

[Planets ruling two houses: second division]

13 As for the second one (and it is if a planet in the revolution of the year is in one of its two houses, but in the root of the nativity it is in neither of them),[69] it is combined in the revolution of the year in 26 combinations, and the examination of it is in three ways.

14 The first way is that you look at the place of the planet in the root relative to the Ascendant of the root of the nativity (and the place of the Ascendant of the root of the nativity relative to it), and the place of the planet's two houses from the Ascendant of the root of the nativity (and the place of the Ascendant of the root of the nativity from them both), and the place of that planet from its own two houses (and

---

[68] In Figure 111, the three Ascendants are the focal points: the rooted Ascendant (rASC), profected Ascendant (prASC), and solar revolution Ascendant (srASC). They are related to the rooted planet (rPl), solar revolution planet (srPl), and the planet's two houses (Hs), or single house (H) in the case of the Sun and Moon. The numbers list the possible relationships between them. For example, the rPl has a position relative to the rASC, and vice versa, for a total of 2 relationships. But an rPl has 2 relationships to its houses, and vice versa, for a total of 4.

[69] See **5** above.

the place of its two houses from it), and the place of that planet in the revolution of the year from the Ascendant of the root of the nativity (and the place of the Ascendant of the root of the nativity from it in the revolution), and the place of the house of the planet which it is *not* in at the revolution of the year, from the planet (and the place of the planet in the revolution from it).

15 And the second way is that you look at the place of the rooted planet relative to the sign of the terminal point (and the place of the sign of the terminal point relative to it), and the place of the revolutionary planet from the terminal point (and the place of the terminal point from it), and the place of the house of the planet which it is *not* in at the revolution of the year, from the terminal point (and the place of the terminal point from that house).

16 And the third way is that you look at the place of the rooted planet relative to the Ascendant of the revolution of the year (and the place of the Ascendant of the revolution of the year relative to it), and the place of the planet in the revolution of the year from the Ascendant of the revolution (and the place of the Ascendant of the revolution from it), and the place of the house of the planet which it is *not* in at the revolution of the year, from the Ascendant of the revolution of the year (and the place of the Ascendant of the revolution of the year from that house).

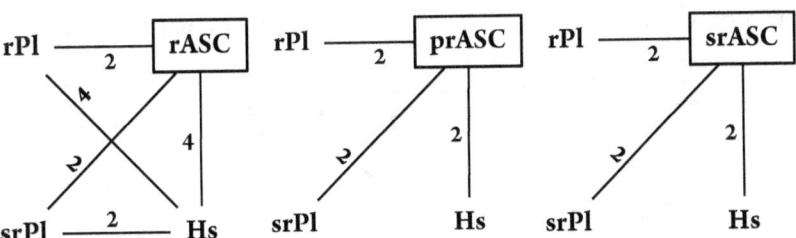

Figure 112: Planets with two houses, 2nd division (IX.4, 13-16)

[Planets ruling two houses: third division]

17 As for the third one (and it is if a planet in the root of the nativity is in one of its two houses, [but] in the revolution of the year it is in neither of them),[70] it is combined in the revolution of the year in 24 combinations, and the examination of it is in three ways.

18 The first way is that you look at its place in the root relative to the Ascendant of the root of the nativity (and the place of the Ascendant of the root of the nativity from it), and the place of its house which it is *not* in at the root, relative to the Ascendant of the root of the nativity (and the place of the Ascendant of the root of the nativity from that house), and the place of the planet from its house which it is *not* in (and the place of that house from it), and its place in the revolution of the year from the Ascendant of the root of the nativity (and the place of the Ascendant of the root of the nativity from it in the revolution), and the place of the planet in the revolution of the year from its two houses (and the place of the planet's two houses in the revolution from it).

19 And the second way is that you look at the place of the rooted planet from the sign of the terminal point (and the place of the sign of the terminal point from it), and the place of the revolutionary planet from the terminal point (and the place of the terminal point from it), and the place of its house which it is *not* in at the root from the terminal point (and the place of the terminal point from that house).

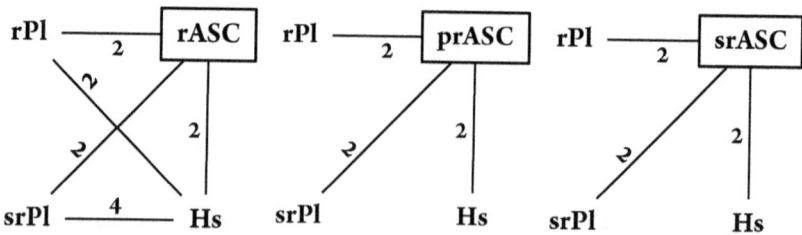

Figure 113: Planets with two houses, 3rd division (IX.4, 17-20)

---

[70] See **6** above.

BOOK IX: MONTHS, DAYS, HOURS, LONGEVITY, REFLECTIONS   583

20 And the third way is that you look at the place of the rooted planet from the Ascendant of the revolution of the year (and the place of the Ascendant of the revolution of the year from it), and the place of the revolutionary planet from the Ascendant of the revolution of the year (and the place of the Ascendant of the revolution of the year from it), and the place of its house which it is *not* in at the root, from the Ascendant of the revolution of the year (and the place of the Ascendant of the revolution of the year from it).

[Planets ruling two houses: fourth division]

21 And as for the fourth (and it is if a planet in the root of the nativity and in the revolution of the year, is in one of its two houses),[71] it is combined in the revolution of the year in 22 combinations, and the examination of it is in three ways.

22 The first way is that you look at the place of the planet in the root relative to the Ascendant of the root of the nativity (and the place of the Ascendant of the root of the nativity relative to it), and the place of the house of the planet which it is *not* in, from the Ascendant of the root (and the place of the Ascendant of the root from that house), and the place of the planet from that one of its two houses which it is *not* in (and the place of that house from it), and its place in the revolution of the year from the Ascendant of the root of the nativity if it was in its other house which it was not in at the root (and the place of the Ascendant of the root of the nativity from the planet), and the place of the planet from its other house (and the place of that house from it).

23 And the second way is that you look at the place of the planet in the root relative to the sign of the terminal point (and the place of the sign of the terminal point relative to it), and the place of the revolutionary planet from the terminal point (and the place of the terminal point from it), and the place of the terminal point from its house which it is *not* in (and the place of that house from it).

---

[71] See **7** above.

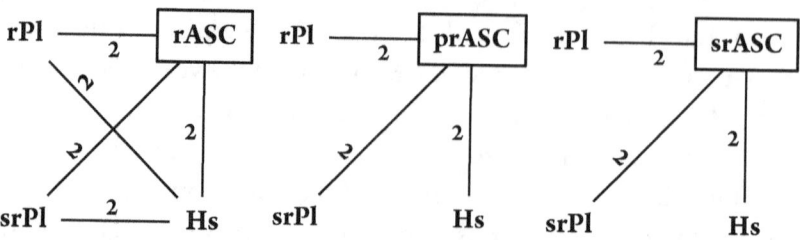

Figure 114: Planets with two houses, 4th division (IX.4, 21-24)

24 And the third way is that you look at the place of the rooted planet relative to the Ascendant of the revolution of the year (and the place of the Ascendant of the revolution relative to it), and the place of the revolutionary planet from the Ascendant of the revolution (and the place of the Ascendant of the revolution from it), and the place of the revolutionary Ascendant from the other house of the planet (and the place of that house from it).

25 These are the combinations of the planets which have two houses.

[Planets ruling one house: four divisions]

26 As for the two planets which each have one house,[72] the place of each of them relative to its own house in the root and in the revolution of the year is also divided into four divisions. **27** As for the first one, it is if [1] one of them is not in its own house in [both] the revolution of the year and the root of the nativity. **28** The second is if [2] one of them is in its house in the revolution of the year, but is not in it in the root of the nativity. **29** The third is if [3] the planet is in its own house in the root of the nativity but is not in it in the revolution of the year. **30** The fourth is if [4] one of them is in its own house in [both] the root of the nativity and in the revolution of the year.

---

[72] Namely, the luminaries.

Combinations for planets with one sign		
Division, sentences	In own sign?	
	In root	In SR
1 (31-36)	N	N
2 (37-42)	N	Y
3 (43-48)	Y	N
4 (49-54)	Y	Y

Figure 115: Combinations for planets with one sign (IX.4, 26-30)

[Planets ruling one house: first division]

31 Now as for the first [division], it is if one of them is not in its own house, in [both] the root of the nativity and the revolution of the year:[73] and if that is the Moon, then she is combined in 22 combinations, and the examination in it is in three ways.

32 The first way is that you look at the place of the [rooted] planet relative to the Ascendant of the root of the nativity (and the place of the Ascendant of the root of the nativity relative to it), and the place of the house of the planet from the Ascendant of the root of the nativity (and the place of the Ascendant of the root of the nativity from it), and the place of the planet from its house (and the place of its house from it), and the place of the planet in the revolution of the year from the Ascendant of the root of the nativity (and the place of the Ascendant of the root of the nativity from it), and the place of the revolutionary planet from its own house (and the place of its house from it).

33 The second way is that you look at its rooted place relative to the sign of the terminal point (and the place of the sign of the terminal point relative to it), and its revolutionary place from the terminal point (and the place of the terminal point from it), and the place of its house from the terminal point (and the place of the terminal point from its house).

---

[73] See **27** above.

34 The third way is that you look at its rooted place relative to the Ascendant of the revolution of the year (and the place of the Ascendant of the revolution of the year relative to it), and its revolutionary place from the Ascendant of the revolution of the year (and the place of the Ascendant of the revolution of the year from it), and the place of its house from the revolutionary Ascendant (and the place of the revolutionary Ascendant from its house).

35 And these 22 [combinations] belong especially to the Moon. **36** But for the Sun, the most combinations he can have in the revolution of the year (of these positions which we have mentioned) is 14, and that is because the Sun returns to his [natal] position, and so there is not a combination of his place in the revolution from his house nor from the Ascendant of the root, nor from the sign of the terminal point, nor the Ascendant of the revolution of the year, because the place of each of them from the other in the revolution is [identical to] his place in the root, so there is no combining between the two.

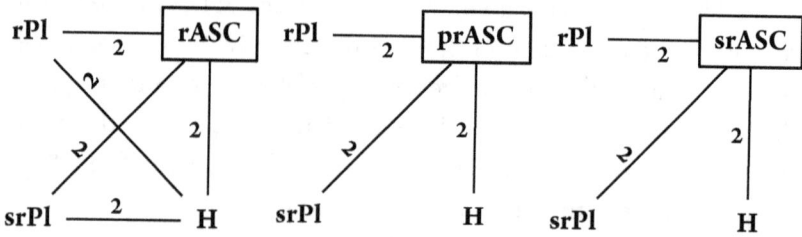

Figure 116: Planets with one house (Moon), 1st division (IX.4, 31-35)

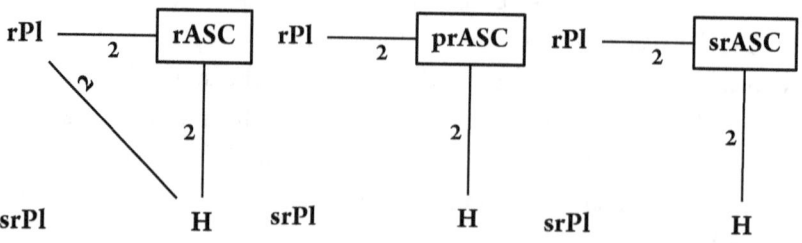

Figure 117: Planets with one house (Sun), 1st division (IX.4, 36)

[Planets ruling one house: second division]

37 As for the second one (and it is if one of them is in its house in the revolution of the year, but in the root of the nativity it is not in its house),[74] it is combined in 14 combinations, and the examination of it is in three ways.

38 The first way is that you look at[75] its place relative to the Ascendant of the root of the nativity (and the place of the Ascendant of the root of the nativity relative to it), and its revolutionary place from the Ascendant of the root of the nativity (and the place of the Ascendant of the root of the nativity from it), and its place in the root of the nativity from its house (and the place of its house from it).

39 And the second way is that you look at its rooted place relative to the sign of the terminal point (and the place of the sign of the terminal point relative to it), and its revolutionary place from the terminal point (and the place of the terminal point from it).

40 And the third way is that you look at its rooted place relative to the Ascendant of the revolution of the year (and the place of the Ascendant of the revolution of the year relative to it), and its revolutionary place from the Ascendant of the revolution of the year (and the place of the Ascendant of the revolution of the year from it).

41 And this situation in the revolution of the year belongs to the Moon especially, because the Sun's variation in his position takes place in the revolutions of months, except that for both of them, even though their situation differs in the revolution of the year just as we mentioned, they do agree in the number, except that there is a difference in the manner of examining it.[76] **42** Because the Sun returns to his [natal] place: so that what there is between him and the terminal

---

[74] See **28** above.

[75] For the first three relationships, reading with **T**; I have written the last one myself, as all three MSS are garbled and incomplete.

[76] Abū Ma'shar means that since the Sun always returns to his natal place, then if (as this division presupposes) he was not in his place at the nativity, he *cannot* be in it at the revolution. Nevertheless, they each have fourteen configurations (see Figures 118-19 below).

point, and what between him and the Ascendant of the revolution of the year in both the root and the revolution is one [and the same] thing (for even if he returns to his [natal] place he is not in his own house), so in the revolution you should look at the place of his house relative to the terminal point and the Ascendant of the revolution of the year, and his place in it.

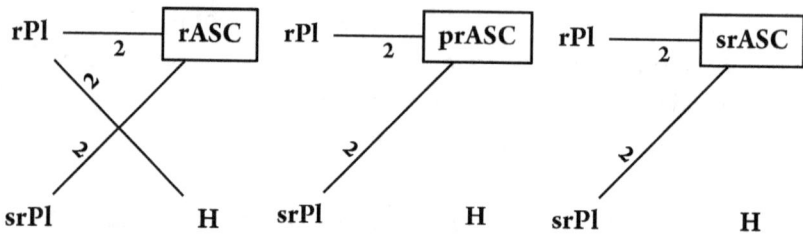

Figure 118: Planets with one house (Moon), 2nd division (IX.4, 37-41)

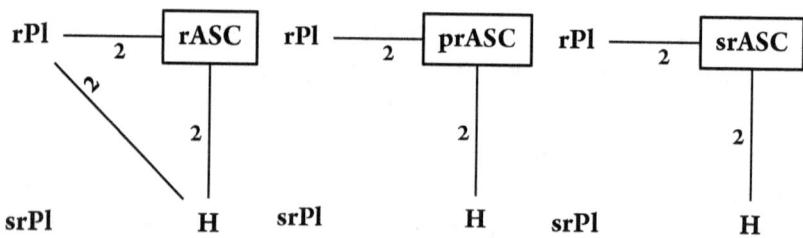

Figure 119: Planets with one house (Sun), 2nd division (IX.4, 41-42)

[Planets ruling one house: third division]

43 And as for the third [division] (and it is if one of them is in its own house in the root of the nativity, but not in its house in the revolution of the year),[77] it is combined in fourteen combinations, and the examination of it is in three ways.

44 The first way is that you look at its [rooted] place relative to the Ascendant of the root of the nativity (and the place of the Ascendant

---

[77] See **29** above.

of the root of the nativity relative to it), and its revolutionary place from the Ascendant of the root of the nativity (and the place of the Ascendant of the root of the nativity from it),[78] and the place of its house from it in the revolution (and its place in the revolution from its house).

45 The second way is that you look at its rooted place relative to the sign of the terminal point (and the place of the sign of the terminal point relative to its rooted place), and its revolutionary place from the terminal point (and the place of the terminal point from it).

46 The third way is that you look at its rooted place relative to the Ascendant of the revolution of the year (and the place of the Ascendant of the revolution of the year relative to it), and its revolutionary place from the Ascendant of the revolution of the year (and the place of the Ascendant of the revolution of the year from it).

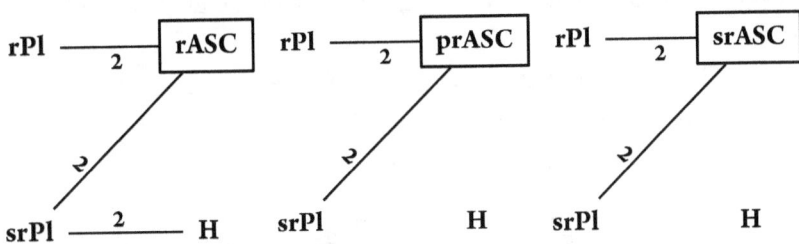

Figure 120: Planets with one house (Moon), 3rd division (IX.4, 43-47)

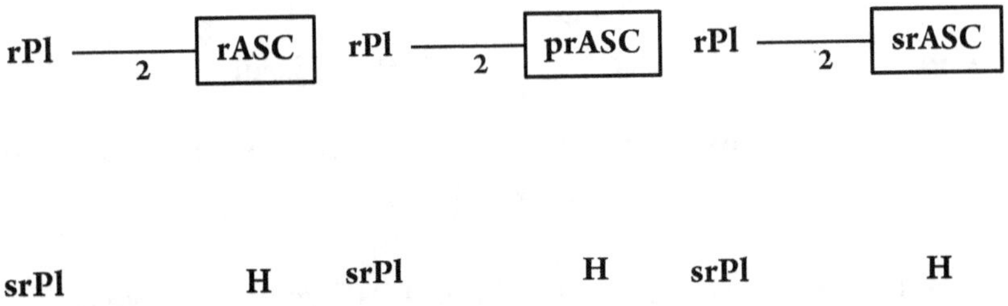

Figure 121: Planets with one house (Sun), 3rd division (IX.4, 48)

---

[78] Omitting "and the place of its house in the revolution from the Ascendant of the root of the nativity (and the place of the Ascendant of the root of the nativity from it)."

47 And this certainly belongs especially to the Moon. **48** But as for the Sun, in this position he has six combinations: because in the revolution of the year he will return to his [natal] house, so his place from those four positions and the place of those four from him in the revolution and the root will be one [and] the same place for the purposes of a combination between the two; but something like that does happen to the Sun in the revolution of months, because if he was in his own house in [both] the root and the revolution of the year, then in the revolution of months he will not be in his own house.

[Planets ruling one house: fourth division]

49 And as for the fourth [division] (and it is if one of them is in its own house in [both] the root of the nativity and the revolution of the year),[79] it is combined in 6 combinations, and the examination of it is in three ways.

50 The first way is that you look at its rooted place relative to the Ascendant of the root of the nativity (and the place of the Ascendant of the root of the nativity relative to it).

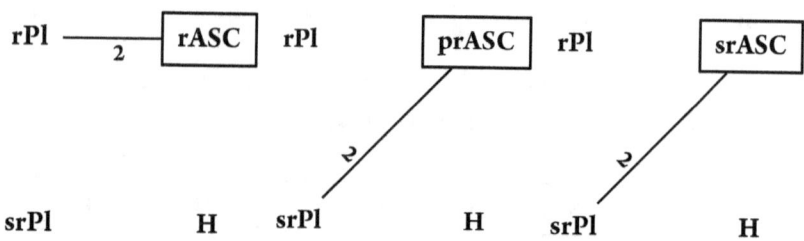

Figure 122: Planets with one house (Sun or Moon), 4th division (IX.4, 49-54)

51 The second way is that you look at its place in the revolution of the year[80] relative to the terminal point (and the place of the terminal point relative to it).

---

[79] See **30** above.

[80] But we could equally use the rooted place, since the planet is in the same sign in both.

52 And the third way is that you look at its revolutionary place[81] relative to the Ascendant of the revolution (and the place of the Ascendant of the revolution relative to it).

53 And this [fourth division] harmonizes with the number which was before,[82] and it certainly belongs to the Sun in the revolution of years,[83] because he will return to his rooted place. **54** And if the Moon was in her house in the root, and happened to be in her house as well in the revolution of any of the years, her situation in the number of these combinations will be like the situation of the Sun.

55 So these are the combinations of the planets in the revolutions of years.

Ranking	Combinations	Which planets
#1	32	Five planets
#2	26	Five planets
#3	24	Five planets
#4	22	Five planets
#5	22	Moon
#6	14	Sun
#7	14	Moon and Sun
#8	14	Moon
#9	6	Sun
#10	6	Moon and Sun

Figure 123: Table comparing planetary combinations (IX.4, 56-61)

56 Now we looked into that, and we found that there has been gathered together for us [in] the composition of these combinations,

---

[81] Again, we could equally use the rooted place.
[82] I.e., the Sun in **48** above.
[83] That is, if in the nativity he was in Leo.

ten [different] numbers, the greatest of them being 32 (and it is the first number), the second one is 26, the third is 24, and the fourth is 22 (and this is the least one which belongs to the five planets in the revolutions of years). **57** But as for the Moon, the greatest number belonging to her 22 (and this is the least which belongs to the five planets), and this is the fifth number. **58** The sixth number is 14, and it is the most that belongs to the Sun. **59** The seventh number is also 14, and it belongs to the Moon and the Sun. **60** The eighth number is 14, and it belongs to the Moon. **61** The ninth and tenth numbers each [belong] to the two [luminaries], and it is six: they both belong to the Sun, but the tenth also belongs to the Moon.

62 And you should know that for each of these combinations, sometimes they will be less than what we have stated due to the coinciding of some of them in one [and the same] position, such as if it happens that the Ascendant of the root, and the sign of the terminal point, and the Ascendant of the revolution of the year are a single sign, or one of the planets in the root is in [the same] place relative to the Ascendant of the root of the nativity as well as from its own house, while in the revolution of the year it is also in that position from it: such as Saturn, since he will be in a sign for 2 ½ years.[84]

63 But when we divided up these combinations we wanted to cover *everything* in the division so that all of it would be clear to us, and we found that the most that a single planet which has two houses would have in the root and in the revolution of the years of nativities, in terms of these three places, is 32 combinations, according to what we have explained.

64 And since we wanted knowledge of the most combinations that they would have in the root and the revolution, we multiplied these 32 (which are the most that a single planet has) by the number of the five planets, it came to 160 combinations: so we knew that [that was] the maximum [number of] combinations in the root and in the revolution

---

[84] Saturn's speed seems to be irrelevant to me here, because the point is simply that he *happens* to occupy the same position relative to several things, not for how many years in a row he may be thus.

BOOK IX: MONTHS, DAYS, HOURS, LONGEVITY, REFLECTIONS

of the year. **65** And as for the Moon, the most combinations she has in the root and the revolution of the year is 22, and as for the Sun the most combinations he has in the root and the revolution of the year is 14. **66** And when we gathered all of these together, it was 196 combinations.

67 But as for the rest of the months of the year, one adds on top of what we stated, and that is because the place of each one of these planets relative to its house in the root, the revolution of the year, and the revolution of the months, is divided into six divisions:[85]

> **68** As for the two planets which each have [only] one house, the first division of each of them relative to its house is if the planet is *not* in its own house in the root of the nativity, the revolution of the year, nor the revolution of the month.
>
> **69** The second is if it is in its own house in the root of the nativity, but not in its own house in the revolution of the year and month.
>
> **70** The third is if it is not in its own house in the root of the nativity, but it is in its own house in the revolution of the year and month.
>
> **71** The fourth is if it is in its own house in the root of the nativity and the revolution of the year, but not in its own house in the revolution of the month.
>
> **72** The fifth is if it is not in its own house in the root of the nativity nor the revolution of the year, but it is in its own house in the revolution of the month.
>
> **73** The sixth is if it is in its own house in the root of the nativity as well as in the revolution of the year and month.

---

[85] These are just the previous variations we have already discussed, but with the months added.

74 And the division of each of the five planets relative to their two houses will [also] be in this manner, but each of these divisions of the year has many combinations (and the most combinations of each planet in the root, the revolution of the year, and the revolution of the month, is if it was in the combination of the first division).[86] **75** So if that was of the planets which each have two houses, then it will be combined in the revolution of that month in 48 combinations (32 of the three positions which we have mentioned, and 16 of the Ascendant of the revolution of the month), and the examination of these combinations will be in four ways (three of them just as we mentioned above, and the fourth the revolution of the month). **76** And that is because once we have combined its place and the place of its two houses with the three positions, after that we see:

[1] Where it is in the revolution of the month relative to the Ascendant of the root of the nativity (and where is the Ascendant of the root of the nativity relative to it),

And [2] where it is in the revolution of the month relative to the sign of the terminal point (and where is the sign of the terminal point relative to it),

And [3] where it is in the revolution of the month relative to the Ascendant of the revolution of the year (and where is the Ascendant of the revolution of the year relative to it),

And [4] where it is in the revolution of the month relative to the Ascendant of the revolution of the month (and where is the Ascendant of the revolution of the month relative to it),

And [5] where are its two houses relative to the Ascendant of the revolution of the month (and where is the Ascendant of the revolution of the month relative to its two houses),

---

[86] The reason for that is because the first division involves the planets *not* being in their houses in any chart: so more house combinations are possible.

And [6] where is the planet in the revolution of the month relative to its two houses (and where are its two houses relative to it).

77 And as for the position of its two houses from the Ascendant of the root of the nativity and from the terminal point, as well as from the [Ascendant] of the revolution of the year, we have already combined them with the revolution of the year, according to our statement which preceded [this].[87]

78 But if that was one of the two planets which each have one house, and it was the Moon, then she is combined in the root, the revolution of the year, and the revolution of the month in 34 combinations (22 relative to the three places which we stated, and 12 from the Ascendant of the revolution of the month). **79** And that is because after we combine [her] with those three places, we see:

[1] Where she is in the revolution of the month relative to the Ascendant of the root of the nativity, and from the terminal point, and from the Ascendant of the revolution of the year, and from the Ascendant of the revolution of the month (and where all of these are from her),

And [2] where is her house relative to the Ascendant of the revolution of the month (and where the Ascendant of the revolution of the month is from her house),

And [3] where is the planet[88] in the revolution of the month from its own house (and where its own house is from it).

80 And if that was the Sun, then he is combined in the revolution of that month in 26 combinations: 14 of them relative to the three positions which we have stated, and 12 from the Ascendant of the revolution of the month, in the manner that we combined the Moon.

---

[87] That is, the long lists from **3-25**.
[88] Abū Ma'shar means the Moon, but uses a more neutral term so that he does not have to repeat everything for the Sun in the next sentence.

81 And the combining of each of these planets in those ways when you combine [them] with the Ascendant of the month, we call "the complete[89] combination."

82 So if we wanted the knowledge of the maximum combinations of planets there is, we would multiply those 48 which belong to each of the five planets in a single month, by 11 months, and it comes to 528, and that is the combinations of one of them. **83** And if we multiplied that by the number of them (and there are five), it comes to 2,640: and that is the maximum [number of] combinations they can have in the root, the revolution of the year, and the revolution of the month. **84** (And of course we multiplied them by 11 because the combination of the first month pertains to the revolution of the year.)

85 Now as for the Moon, the combinations which belong to her are 34, so if we multiplied that by 11 months it would come to 374, and it is the maximum [number of] combinations she has. **86** And as for the Sun, combinations which belong to him are 26, so when we multiply that by 11 months that comes to 286, and it is the maximum [number of] combinations he has.

87 Now if we gather all of it together, it comes to 3,300, and we know that this is the maximum [number of] combinations of the seven planets in the three times, relative to the four positions. **88** (But as for the average and fewest combinations they have, I have left those off because this [way] we have done it [includes] both of them.[90] **89** So if you wanted knowledge of one of those, look at those numbers which we stated, and work with them according to what we have set as an example.)

90 As for what these combinations *indicate*, it will be in accordance with the approach we mentioned in Book V of this book of ours, concerning the transit of the planets to each other's positions: and it is that you make each position be like the Ascendant and the root, then you

---

[89] Reading with **P. B**: "the second," **E**: "the eighth."
[90] Reading a little loosely for what seems to be هو نحويهما.

see where its lord is relative to it according to the number of the signs, so that its indication will be akin to the position of that sign from it, and one proceeds in this subject of all of the planets, by [using] the planetary governor over the year—and the maximum [number of] combinations it can have in the revolution of the year and months is 48 combinations, just as we have mentioned before.

91 And an example of that is a native whose Ascendant was Sagittarius, and his year terminated at Taurus,[91] and the Ascendant of his revolution Scorpio. 92 And Venus was the governor of the year, so we wanted her combination with these three positions: and in the root she was in Gemini, and in the revolution in Cancer.[92]

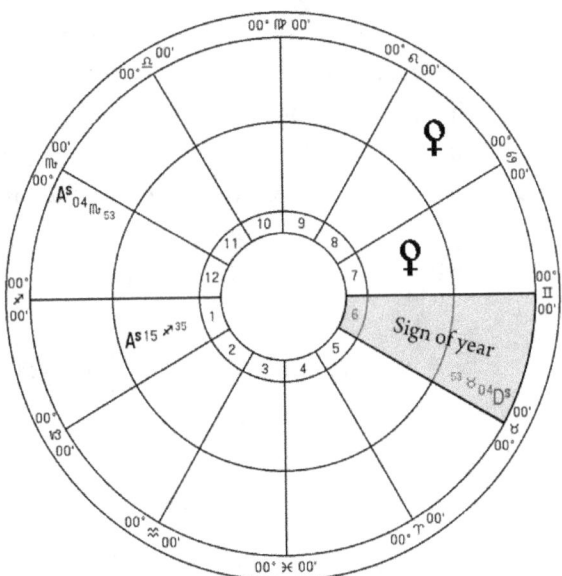

Figure 124: Planet with two houses, 1st division, first way (IX.4, 91-106)

---

[91] Reading with **P** for "Pisces," as this is the only way to have Venus plausibly be the "governor" of the year (which here probably just means "lord of the year," as she does not clearly rule anything else).

[92] In this example, Venus rules two signs and is not in either of them in the root or revolution, so this falls under the first division (**4**). Here, Abū Ma'shar *only* covers the combinations with the natal Ascendant, in accordance with the first way (in **9** above, and Figure 111 there). In **106** he will remind us to do the same with the profected Ascendant and revolutionary Ascendant (as described in **10-11**), and any monthly Ascendants.

93 We[93] began with Sagittarius and treated it as a root, then we looked at [the natal] Venus: and she was [1] in the seventh from Sagittarius, and Sagittarius is her seventh.

94 And [2] one of her houses is the sixth from Sagittarius and the other house its eleventh, and Sagittarius was the third from one of them and the eighth of the other.

95 And [3] Venus is in the second from Taurus and the ninth from Libra, and one of them is her own twelfth and the other her fifth.

96 Then, [4] we looked at her in the revolution, and she was in Cancer, in the eighth from Sagittarius, and Sagittarius is her sixth.

97 And [5] in the revolution she is in the third from one of her own houses and in the tenth from the other, and one of her houses is her own eleventh and the other her fourth.

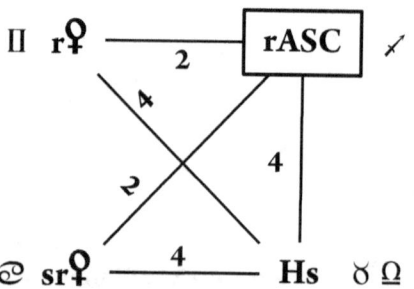

Figure 125: Venus combinations for 1st division, first way (IX.4, 91-106)[94]

98 So, [1] the position of [natal] Venus relative to Sagittarius, and the position of Sagittarius from her, indicates his associating with women, and contrarieties, and their associating with him.

99 And [2] because one of her houses is the sixth from Sagittarius and the other its eleventh, we made Sagittarius be like the root, and we said it indicates mental irritation with female and male servants (and

---

[93] Since there are five fundamental relationships in the first division, first way (see **9** and Figure 111 there), I have numbered them for convenience and added the signs of the example chart in Figure 125.

[94] This is the set of combinations listed above in IX.4, **9**.

perhaps that will be evident to them), and he will be successful in [something] hoped for and assets, and he will delight in women, and they will correspond with him and flatter him, and some of them will become ill, and some of his siblings (of men and women) will be antagonistic towards him because of some servants and slaves, or a man of a bad type, and it will make his enjoyment [of things] be disturbed sometimes due to an ailment he will find in the upper part of the body and in the belly, and various things will be presented to him, [including]⁹⁵ slaves for purchase. **100** And because Sagittarius is the third from one of the houses of Venus and the eighth of the other, we made her houses be like the root and we said it indicates being involved with the siblings, and [his] corresponding with them, and their coming to him, and toil with them, and their conflict because of assets, and he will be devoted to reports about the ancestors and ancient matters, and being present at the funeral of one of those who are burdensome to him, and he will be distressed because of some riding animals.⁹⁶

101 And due to [3] the place of [the natal] Venus from her houses (and she is in the second from one of them and the ninth of the other), we made her houses be like the root, and said he would acquire assets from women, and assets would come to him through his own persistence in seeking them,⁹⁷ and he will toil or travel because of it, and he will get rid of assets or goods which are burdensome for him, and perhaps some of that will be [given] to slaves and servants, and he will hoard clothing and dishes.⁹⁸ **102** And due to the place of her houses from her (and one of them is her twelfth and the other her fifth), we made her place be like the root and said it indicates that he will be irri-

---

⁹⁵ Reading for "and."

⁹⁶ Sagittarius indicates horses, so by its being in the eighth from Taurus, it shows distress (the eighth) from riding animals (Sagittarius).

⁹⁷ Taurus is being treated as an Ascendant, and its lord (Venus) is in its own second (Gemini): so it shows the native seeking assets, in the way that in a horary chart the lord of the Ascendant in the second would show a querent seeking assets (rather than the assets coming to him).

⁹⁸ Or more broadly "receptacles," no doubt Venusian things like fancy vases and such. But I do not understand where this signification of servants comes from.

tated by riding animals, and reports and messengers, and women and children, and he will be distressed by some reports of enemies which will come to him, and he will think about the mistreatment of one of his children, and perhaps he will be blessed with children.

103 And due to [4] the place of Venus in the revolution in the eighth from Sagittarius (and Sagittarius being her sixth), we made Sagittarius be like the root and said it indicates that he and one of his women will fall ill, and his servants and his adversaries, and the illness will return and the funerals publicized, and he will be devoted to cemeteries and ancestors, and female servants and slaves (as well as their purchase) and the market of cattle-dealers, and songs and amusement, and all of it will weigh heavily upon him.

104 And due to [5] her place in the revolution in the third from one of her houses and in the tenth from the other, we made her houses be like the root and said it indicates his being devoted to the conditions of siblings and relatives, and his going to them, and his making an effort in what they need, and some of his relatives will associate with the Sultan or he will increase in the power of [his] kinship. **105** And because one of her houses [in the revolution] is her own eleventh and the other her fourth, and she looks at them both, we made her place be like the root and said it indicates that because of real estate and his being praised for the results of his affairs, it will prepare for him things which he had wished and hoped for.

106 And in this way you would combine her situation and the situation of her houses relative to the terminal point, the Ascendant of the year, and the Ascendant of the month:[99] and you do likewise with every planet which was the governor of the year.

107 And the time in everything we have mentioned, is when the management of the months or days comes to that sign or that planet.

108 And sometimes the combinations of these four positions (or most of them) will come together in a single sign: so if it was like that,

---

[99] This would cover the remaining Ascendant "divisions" that Abū Ma'shar discussed earlier in the chapter, as well as the combinations with the monthly Ascendants.

their combining will be less, while the indication of the indicators will be stronger.[100] **109** And if a planet came to be in any of these positions or looked at it, it will increase in these matters or take away from them, in accordance with its indication.[101]

Chapter IX.5: On looking into the conditions of the eleven months

[Indicators of the body and soul]

1 As for the knowledge of the condition of the body in the second month and in the rest of the months of the year, you look in the revolution of that month at seven indicators (and they are [#2] the lord of the ninth-part of that month, [#1, #3-5] the sign which the month has terminated at from those four rooted indicators,[102] [#6] the Ascendant of the [revolution of the relevant] month, and [#7] its Lot of Fortune)—and their lords. **2** And if the generality of these indicators (or all of them), coincided in one of them, it will be the governor over the indication of that month:[103] so look at it, and at its lord, and at the position of each of them relative to its associate, and at their suitability or corruption in the root of the nativity and at the time of the revolution of the year, *and* in the revolution of the *month*.

---

[100] For example, if Venus's houses were in the eleventh from her in several charts, then there would be fewer distinct combinations, but would reinforce the eleventh-house interpretation.

[101] Here Abū Ma'shar is reminding us that other planets matter, too: so if Saturn was in or squaring one of these positions, we would have to modify the interpretation with Saturnian interpretations. But he probably also means that Venus's own presence in or aspects to these signs will make the matters intensify or slacken.

[102] Note well that all of these act as a kind of Ascendant, so they only indicate that month in general and the native's body and mind in particular, just like a normal Ascendant—they *do not* indicate other things like assets, brothers, and parents. For those, we need to go to their derived houses (see below).

[103] See IX.1, **4-7** for this concept.

Rooted	#1	Profected natal Ascendant *for that month*	Old, rooted causes Slow to disappear
	#2	Ninth-part of sign of year *for that month*	
	#3	Profected natal Lot of Fortune *for that month*	
	#4	SR Ascendant *profected to that month*	Recent causes Limited to year Not constant
	#5	SR Lot of Fortune *profected to that month*	
Not	#6	MR Ascendant	Recent causes Months, days Short duration
	#7	MR Lot of Fortune	

Figure 126: Seven monthly indicators
(IX.1, 9-25, 35-39; IX.5, 1, 95-98)[104]

3 So if the single indicator (or the many indicators) were in an excellent combination in relation to each other,[105] and they are in a suitable condition in themselves, they indicate the safety of the body and his good health in that month. **4** And if they were suitable in their positions in the rotation[106] of the circle, they indicate his power and his hardiness. **5** And if, along with what we stated, the indicators were made fortunate, they indicate the growth of the body and its pleasing quality due to his good health and its repelling [any] affliction[107] from itself.

6 And if the indicators were as we stated, and their *lords* were also in a suitable condition in terms of the signs they are in at the revolution of the month, then in addition to what we stated about the body's suit-

---

[104] For comparing the subject-matter of each significator, see IX.5, **99-103**.

[105] The awkwardness of the singular and plural here is because Abū Ma'shar wants to discuss both the condition of a single governing indicator, and cases where the indicators do not coincide.

[106] دور. This refers either to their being in the good or bad places, or to their dynamic angularity (advancing or withdrawing), here and in **7**, **11**, and **14**.

[107] E: "illnesses."

able condition, they indicate the safety of the soul. **7** And if the lords of the indicators were in a suitable condition in the rotation of the circle (along with the soundness of their condition in their signs), then along with what we stated they indicate thinking about lofty affairs, and the goodness of character as well as happiness. **8** And if, along with what we stated about their condition they were made fortunate, they indicate temperateness, and delight, and joy, and the goodness of the soul. **9** And if the fortunes which make the lords of the indicators fortunate were in the stakes or what follows them, they indicate (along with the rest of what we stated) might, power, rank, reputation, class, and their endurance in that month; while if the fortunes were falling, it subtracts from their indication and they will not be lasting.

10 But if the indicators of the month were in a bad mixture with each other, and they are in a bad condition in themselves, they indicate the disturbance of the body in that month. **11** And if along with that they were in bad positions in the turning of the circle, they indicate the weakness of the body and the quickness of its taking on afflictions. **12** And if they were made unfortunate in addition to what we stated, they indicate powerful adversity and illness in the body.

13 And if their lords were in a bad condition in terms of their positions in the signs, then in addition to what we mentioned they indicate that badness of character will defeat him, as well as bad thoughts and distress. **14** And if (along with the badness of their condition in the signs in which they are) these lords were in a bad condition due to the rotation of the circle, then along with the rest of what we stated they indicate fear, cowardice, and the decline of the soul and its weakness. **15** And if, in addition to what we stated, the lords of these indicators were made unfortunate, they indicate (along with the rest of what we stated) the illness of the soul, and something detestable, mental evil, alarm, cowardice, and depression.

16 But if some of them were in an excellent condition, made fortunate, and others in a bad condition, made unfortunate, it indicates suitability from the indication of the indicator in a suitable condition, and badness from the indication of the indicator in a bad condition. **17**

Then you look at that fortune which indicated the good and good fortune, and at the infortune which indicated evil and misfortune: of what category is it, and from which of the houses does it make these indicators and their lords fortunate or make them unfortunate? **18** For the good and evil will be from the category of the indication of that planet, and its cause will be from the nature of the sign and bound[108] in which the fortune or infortune is, and its greatness or smallness will be in accordance with the power of the planet or its weakness.[109]

[The month in general, as distinct from the native]

19 And[110] as for the knowledge of the things which the houses of the circle indicate in the second month (or in others, of the remaining months of the year), one looks at the seven indicators for each one of the eleven months, each month [taken] separately: and the condition of each one in [its] indication should be understood because from that [is known] what its place and condition indicates about the condition of the month.

20 Then one looks at its mixture with the rest of the indicators, and there are four. **21** The first is [#2] the lord of the ninth-part of the month. **22** The second is [#3] the sign of the terminal point of the month (and its lord), [taken] from the Lot of Fortune of the root (and its lord). **23** The third is [#5] the sign of the terminal point of the

---

[108] **E** omits the bound.

[109] So a square from a planet in the ninth, will indicate problems related to religion or travel; if in a four-footed sign, then from animals; while advancing planets will be stronger, withdrawing ones weaker.

[110] Again, because the Ascendant of any month relates to the month in general as well as the native personally, we must use a special procedure to examine it. Here, Abū Ma'shar divides up the seven indicators into two groups: the Lots (as well as the ninth-part), and the Ascendants. If we ignore the annoying ninth-part, the Lots (**20-25**) refer to general trends and occurrences in the month, while the Ascendants (**26-29**) refer to the native himself. We can look at each separately, but also compare them to see how the native is affected, much like the table found in IX.2, **18-31**. This division of Lots and Ascendants is confirmed in **99-102** below, but the ninth-part is not.

month (and its lord), [taken] from the Lot of Fortune of the revolution of the year. **24** The fourth is [#7] the Lot of Fortune of the revolution of the month, and its lord. **25** And the indication of it is from them, like that.

26 Then after that you erect the Ascendant, then you look for what is sought by the owner of the revolution of the month from its house, and there are three things. **27** The first is [#1] the sign which the month terminates at, from the sign of the terminal point of the Ascendant of the root. **28** The second is [#4] the sign which the month terminates at from the Ascendant of the revolution of the year. **29** The third [#6] is the Ascendant of the revolution of the month.

| General appraisal of months 2-12 ||
Compare these general monthly indicators…	…with the native's monthly indicators
#2: Lord of ninth-part *for that month*	**#1: Profected natal ASC (& lord)** *for that month*
#3: Profected natal Lot (& lord) *for that month*	**#4: SR Ascendant (& lord)** *profected to that month*
#5: SR Lot of Fortune (& lord) *profected to that month*	
#7: MR Lot of Fortune (& lord) *for that month*	**#6: MR Ascendant** *for that month*

Figure 127: Seven monthly indicators, general appraisal of any month (IX.5, 19-29)

[Six indicators and their lords, for topical indicators every month]

30 Then after that you look at the indicators of each of the houses of the circle, like the house of assets, the house of siblings, the house of parents, the house of children, and the rest of them: because each of the houses in the eleven months has six indicators: three of them rooted in the indicators of the beginning of the year, and three in the turning of the sign of the month.[111] **31** Now as for the first of the three rooted ones, it is [1] the Ascendant of the root; as for the second, it is [2] the sign of the terminal point from it; as for the third, it is [3] the Ascendant of the revolution of the year—just as we stated in the first month.[112] **32** But as for the first of the three which are from the turning of the signs, it is [4] the sign which the month terminates at from the sign of the terminal point of the Ascendant of the root; the second is [5] the sign which the month terminates at from the Ascendant of the revolution of the year; and the third is [6] the Ascendant of the revolution of the month.[113]

[A method for assets in the months]

33 So as for the knowledge of the condition of assets in any of the eleven months, at the revolution of the month one looks at the [six] indicators of the year which we mentioned,[114] *and* at their lords, and at the lords of *their* houses of assets: **34** The first of them is [1] the lord of the Ascendant of the root, and the lord of its house of assets. **35** The second is [2] the lord of the sign of the terminal point relative to the Ascendant of the root, and the lord of its house of assets. **36** The third is [3] the lord of the Ascendant of the revolution of the year, and the lord of its house of assets. **37** The fourth is [4] the lord of the sign which the month terminates at from the sign of the terminal point relative to the Ascendant of the root, and the lord of its house of assets. **38** The fifth is [5] the lord of the sign which the month terminates at from the Ascendant of the revolution of the year, and the lord of its house of assets. **39** The sixth is [6] the lord of the Ascendant of the revolution of the month, and the lord of its house of assets.

---

[111] **P**: "the sign of the terminal point." But as we will see in **32**, these are not all by profection because one of them is the Ascendant of the chart of the month.

[112] See the table for IX.1, **17**: these were the three Ascendants listed as items #1, #2, and #5.

[113] Again, the last one [6] is not gotten by profection, but never mind. See the table below for an easy comparison of these in the method of assets.

[114] See **31-32** above, and the table below.

Indicators to judge and combine in any month (Using assets or the 2nd house as an example)		
	Indicators of native and the month	Indicator of topic
Year as a whole	1. Natal ASC (& its lord)	1. 2nd sign from it (& its lord)
	2. Profected natal ASC (& its lord)	2. 2nd sign from it (& its lord)
	3. SR ASC (& its lord)	3. 2nd sign from it (& its lord)
Monthly derivatives from year as a whole	4. Monthly profection from sign of year (& its lord)	4. 2nd sign from it (& its lord)
	5. Monthly profection from SR ASC (& its lord)	5. 2nd sign from it (& its lord)
	6. MR ASC (& its lord)	6. 2nd sign from it (& its lord)
	Evaluate indicators of topic (right) for its suitability, then compare with indicators of native (left) for impact on native.	

Figure 128: Six indicators, general appraisal of any month (IX.5, 30-40, 48-49, 50-53)

40 So if in the revolution of the month there was an excellent, harmonious combination between one of them and its associate—like a combination of the lord of the house of assets of the Ascendant of the root, with the lord of the Ascendant of the root, or the lord of the sign of the terminal point from the Ascendant of the root with the lord of its house of assets (and the rest of what is like this), it indicates the suitability of the condition in assets, benefits, and increase in it. 41 But if it was not like that, and there was a combination of the lord of one of the indicators and the lord of the house of assets of another one (such as the lord of the sign of the terminal point with the lord of the house

of assets of the Ascendant of the month),[115] it weakens the indication of benefit, or there will be something [which is] not huge, [and] from where he does not expect it.

42 (And[116] if the lord of the ninth-part of the month was in an excellent combination with the lord of the house of assets of the indicators of the year, and especially with the lord of the house of assets of the sign which the month terminates at from the sign of the terminal point from the Ascendant of the year, then it indicates the suitability of the condition in assets, and an increase in benefits. **43** And it is likewise if the lord of the sign of the month relative to the Lot of Fortune of the revolution of the year, or the lord of the Lot of Fortune of the revolution of the month, or the lord of the Lot of assets of the root, or the lord of the Lot of assets of the revolution of the year or revolution of the month, or their own Lots,[117] were in an excellent combination with the indicators of the assets of the year and their lords. **44** And that is more confirmed, and stronger and more excellent, if there was [also] an excellent combination between one of those we mentioned with another in the root of the nativity, and in the revolution of the year, and in the revolution of the month: and if it was below that, it will be below that.)

45 So the more that the indicators of rooted benefits are many and strong, the more that the benefit will be greater in power; while if the indicators are few and weak, it will be less, or the benefit will be from

---

[115] That is, combining a significator by *profection* (which is more closely linked to the nativity) with a significator in a *revolution* chart. This kind of weaker combination was discussed in VI.6, **45**.

[116] This paragraph now brings back three indicators from **21-24** above, which generally pertain to the events of the month rather than to the native personally: the ninth part of the month (#2), the monthly profection from the SR Lot (#5), and the lord of the MR Lot (#7). The purpose of this is to bring general events into the picture, rather than simply the relationship between assets narrowly defined, and the native. But Abū Ma'shar is also telling us to bring in the other Lots pertaining to the topic, such as the Lot of assets here, or the Lots of siblings, parents, or others below (**39**, **52**).

[117] This may refer to the Lots of the other house topics, as stated in **39** and **52**).

where he does not expect it (even if perhaps it was be wished for and desired).

46 And the combining of rooted lords of the indicators of assets with the rooted lords of the [native's] indicators,[118] and [those of] the revolutionary ones, with the revolutionary ones, is more powerful for the indication: and that is like the lord of the ninth-part of the sign of the terminal point from the Ascendant of the root, and the lord of the sign of the terminal point from the Lot of Fortune of the root, if [their combination] is with the lord of the second of the Ascendant of the root, or with the lord of the second of the sign of the terminal point, in an excellent combination. **47** And as for the revolutionary ones, it is if the lord of the house of assets of the Ascendant of the revolution of the year, and its Lot of fortune and its lord, were in an excellent, harmonious combination with the Ascendant of the revolution of the year and its lord; and if the lord of the house of assets of the Ascendant of the month, and its Lot of Fortune and its lord, were in an excellent combination with the Ascendant of the revolution of the month and its lord.

[A method for siblings in the months]

48 And as for the knowledge of the condition of siblings, you look in the revolution of the month at the third sign from the indicators of the year, and at their lords:[119] so if each one of them and its lord was in a suitable condition in itself, and their lords are in an excellent combination relative to them,[120] it indicates the goodness of their condition. **49** And if the indicators of siblings and their lords are in an excellent

---

[118] P and T omit "with the rooted lords of the indicators," while T even omits the second instance of "the revolutionary ones." The scribes evidently thought this was a mistake, but as the rest of the sentence makes clear, Abū Ma'shar *is* speaking of the indicators *within* each chart combining with each other (as in **40-41**), rather than across charts. This preference for combinations within each scheme was also discussed in VI.6, **1-5**.

[119] See the table above, but substituting the third sign and its lord for the second.

[120] Or perhaps simply, "with them."

condition with the Ascendant of the root, or the five rooted indicators, and their lords, it indicates the harmony of each with the other, and their friendly relations; and the suitability of their house's essence will also come to be if the rest of the indicators of siblings (of the Lots and their lords, and the rest of the planets) were in an excellent combination with the Ascendant of the root and those five rooted indicators and their lords.

[A method for fathers and real estate in the months]

50 As for knowing the condition of fathers and real estate, you look in the revolution of the month at the fourth from the indicators of the year, and at their lords:[121] so if they were in a suitable condition in themselves, and their lords were in an excellent combination relative to them, it indicates the suitability of the condition of the father and real estate. **51** And if the indicators of both[122] and their lords were in an excellent combination relative to the Ascendant of the root, and the five rooted indicators and their lords, it indicates the harmony of one of them with the other, and benefit in real estate, and an increase in it. **52** And the condition of both will be likewise if the rest of the indicators of the father and real estate (of the Lots and their lords, and the rest of the planets) were in an excellent combination relative to the Ascendant of the root, and the five rooted indicators and their lords. **53** And in all of this, if it was the contrary of what we stated, it will be the contrary of it; and examining the indicators of the house of children, slaves, women, and the rest of the houses of the circle, will [also] be in this manner.

[Timing the indications, combinations across charts]

54 And the revolution of the month has an indicator close <to> the indication [above], and it is that you look at the lord of the sign which the month terminates at, relative to one of the indicators: so if it com-

---

[121] See the table above, substituting the fourth sign and its lord for the second.
[122] This seems to mean fathers and real estate.

bined with the lord of the sought house[123] of the root, or[124] the lord of the sought house of the sign of the terminal point, or the lord of the sought house of the Ascendant of the revolution, it indicates the coming-to-be of that thing.[125] **55** So if there was a combination of the lord of the sign which the month terminates at from one of the indicators, and a combination of the lord of the sought house of the root, or the lord of the sought house relative to the sign of the terminal point, or the lord of the sought house of the revolution, it indicates the coming-to-be of that thing: such as if [1] there was an examination of assets, and the lord of the sign which the month terminates at [from one of the indicators] combines with the lord of the house of assets of the root, or the lord of the house of assets relative to the sign of the terminal point, or the lord of the house of assets of the Ascendant of the revolution of the year; or like if [2] there was an examination of the condition of the siblings, so that the lord of the house which the month terminates at from one of the indicators combines with the lord of the house of siblings of the root, or the lord of the house of siblings of the sign of the terminal point, or the lord of the house of siblings of the Ascendant of the year.

56 And when the *month* relative to one of the indicators terminates at the second sign from the three rooted indicators (and at their

---

[123] That is, the house you are interested in: if fathers, then the fourth; if children, then the fifth, etc.

[124] The MSS differ on whether these should be "or" or "and," but either way the more that are combined, the firmer the indication.

[125] In this paragraph I believe Abū Ma'shar is speaking about events which are *already* shown by the annual and rooted charts (natal, profected, and SR charts). So for example, let the lord of the SR seventh promise marriage: this could happen anytime during the year. But let it also be connecting with Mercury: in that case, the marriage might manifest during the month when the SR Ascendant profects to Gemini or Virgo, activating the connection with the lord of the seventh. But Abū Ma'shar might also want to introduce transits: then we not only want to look at the month when Gemini or Virgo is the sign of the monthly profection, but see if Mercury *in real time* is transiting the lord of the SR seventh.

lords),[126] it will manifest the indication of assets (for good or evil). **57** (And it will be likewise if the month relative to one of them terminates at the rest of the houses and at their lords: such as siblings, parents, children, slaves, women, or the others.)

Four other methods of monthly timing	
If this time lord or point...	*... does this:*
(**54-55**) If the lord of a monthly profection ...	... combines with the lord of the relevant natal, profected, or SR house.
(**56-57**) If the monthly profection from some indicator ...	... reaches some natal, profected, or SR house (or its lord).
(**58**) When a natal or SR indicator of some topic...	... is in the sign of a monthly profection.
(**59**) If the degree of an MR ASC...	... is on a fixed star or nebula.

Figure 129: Four other methods of monthly timing (IX.5, 54-59)

58 And when the rooted or revolutionary indicators of assets (or the indicators of the rest of the things) were in the sign which the *month* terminates at, their indication will be manifested.[127]

59 And if the degree of the Ascendant of the month was the position of one of the fixed stars or nebulas (or any of their rays, or the rest of what is like this), it will produce its indication.

---

[126] In the simplest and weakest sense, this just means that any monthly profection will activate whatever sign it comes to. But maybe Abū Ma'shar means something more: if some MR planet *already* combines with the lord of some natal house, then when the MR profection reaches that natal house or its lord, it will manifest. For example, let the MR Mercury be connecting to the lord of the natal seventh: then when the monthly profection reaches the natal seventh or its lord, it will activate the aspect they had at the monthly revolution.

[127] It is hard to distinguish this from the previous example. Perhaps this is like a transit: if, during some month, a natal planet transits through the sign of a monthly profection, it will activate the natal topic it rules.

[The sign of the month with the fortunes]

60 Now if the month relative to one of the indicators terminated at a sign, and one of the fortunes was looking at it or at its lord in the root of the nativity *and* in the revolution of the year, *and* in the revolution of the month, it indicates great, abundant good, and that will be from a direction he had hoped for, [both] old and recent.

61 But if the month relative to one of the indicators terminated at a sign, and the fortune was looking at it and its lord in the root of the nativity *and* in the revolution of the year, but *not* looking at it in the revolution of the month, then he will attain the good suddenly, from a direction he had hoped for, and perhaps he had always hoped [for it].

62 And if the month relative to one of the indicators terminated at a sign, and the fortune was looking at it or its lord in the root of the nativity, but *not* looking at it in the revolution of the year, *nor* in the revolution of the month, then he will get the good because of something old he had hoped for, [but] then he will be distressed by it after that.

63 And if the fortune was looking at that position or its lord in the revolution of the year but *not* looking at it in the root of the nativity *nor* in the revolution of the month, then he will gain the good because of something new with no foundation to it, and he will hope for it on an occasional basis[128] in that year.

64 And if the fortune was looking at that position or its lord in the revolution of the month, but *not* looking at it in the root of the nativity *nor* in the revolution of the year, then he will gain the good from an unknown direction.

65 So, this is the indication of a fortune if it looked at the sign of the terminal point [of the month] or was in it.

66 Then you look after that: for if one of the infortunes was looking at the fortune indicating the good, but nothing of the infortunes looks at the sign of the terminal point of the month nor its lord, then it is less for the good and weaker for it, but he will [still] delight in and benefit

---

[128] Lit., "in time after time" in that year.

by it. **67** And if the infortune did look at the position of the terminal point of the month or its lord, but nothing of the infortunes looks at that fortune, then it indicates an abundance of the good [thing], but he will not delight in nor benefit by it. **68** And if the infortune looked at the sign of the terminal point of the month or its lord, *and* at the fortune indicating the good, it indicates the scarcity of the good, and its weakness, as well as that he will not delight in nor benefit by it.

\	\	\	Fortunes looking at profected sign of month
Root	*SR*	*Month*	*Meaning*
Y	Y	Y	**60:** Much good from expected direction, in past and present.
Y	Y	N	**61:** Sudden good, from expected direction.
Y	N	N	**62:** Good from something old, but distress afterwards.
N	Y	N	**63:** Sudden new good for no reason, occasional in the year.
N	N	Y	**64:** Good from an unknown direction.

- Infortunes looking at sign: decreases delight.
- Infortunes looking at fortune: decreases benefit.
- Infortunes looking at both: decreases both.

Figure 130: Fortunes looking at profected sign of month (IX.5, 60-71)

69 And if the fortunes looked at the fortune indicating the good, and at the sign of the terminal point of the month or its lord, then it indicates an increase in the good and benefit, and delighting in it.

70 Now as for the scarcity of the good or its abundance, it is known from the condition of that fortune and from its strength or weakness; and its cause will be from the category of its nature and the nature of the sign it is in, and its position in the circle, and from the house which it owns (such as the house of assets, siblings, and the rest of them).

71 And that will affect him when the fortune manages one of the days of the month; and when an infortune reaches the position of that fortune,[129] it will undermine that good fortune.

[The sign of the month with the infortunes]

72 And if the month relative to one of the indicators terminated at a sign and one of the infortunes was in the inspection of that sign or in the inspection of its lord in the root of the nativity, *and* in the revolution of the year, *and* in the revolution of the month, then it indicates powerful evil; and that will be from a direction which he feared, both in the past and recently.

73 And if the month relative to one of the indicators terminated at a sign which an infortune was looking at (or at its lord) in the root *and* in the revolution of the year, but does *not* look at it in the revolution of the month, then the detestable thing will reach him suddenly, from a direction he feared in the past.

74 And if the month relative to one of the indicators terminated at a sign which an infortune was looking at (or at its lord) in the root, but does *not* look at it in the revolution of the year, *nor* in the revolution of the month, then the evil will reach him because of something old which he had feared, but then he will feel safe from it after that.

75 And if that infortune looks at that position (or at its lord) in the revolution of the year, but does *not* look at it in the root of the nativity *nor* in the revolution of the month, then the evil will reach him from something recent, having no foundation, and he will fear it on an occasional basis.[130]

76 And if the month relative to one of the indicators terminated at a sign which an infortune does look at (or at its lord) in the revolution of the month, but does *not* look at it in the revolution of the year *nor* in the root of the nativity, then the detestable thing will reach him from a direction which will be new for him.

---

[129] This must mean "by transit."
[130] Lit., "in time after time."

77 So, these are the indications of an infortune if it looked at the sign of the terminal point of the month, or was in it.

| Infortunes looking at profected sign of month ||||
Root	SR	Month	Meaning
Y	Y	Y	72: Much evil from expected direction in past and present
Y	Y	N	73: Sudden evil, from expected direction in past.
Y	N	N	74: Evil from something old, but relief afterwards
N	Y	N	75: Sudden new evil for no reason, occasional in the year
N	N	Y	76: Evil from an unknown direction
• Fortunes looking at sign: allows assistants. • Fortunes looking at infortune: decreases evil. • Fortunes looking at both: decreases evil, allows assistants.			

Figure 131: Infortunes looking at profected sign of month (IX.5, 72-76)

78 Then, look after that: for if one of the fortunes was looking at the infortune indicating the evil, and nothing of the fortunes looks at the sign of the terminal point (nor at its lord), the evil will be lighter, but it will[131] force the repelling of assistants from him.

79 And if the fortune looked at the sign of the terminal point of the month (or at its lord) and nothing of the fortunes looks at that infortune, the evil will be harsher but it will not[132] force the rejection of assistants from him. 80 (And if an infortune looked at that fortune which is looking at the terminal point of the month, or at its lord, the

---

[131] Omitting a "not" and moving it to the parallel phrase in 79, otherwise we could not make sense of the "not," nor the presence of assistants in 80. The point is that the fortune will relieve the evil impact of the infortune, but because it does not see the sign, it cannot provide assistants. Therefore the infortune will repel them.

[132] Again, because the fortune now looks at the sign, it contributes assistants, even though it cannot relieve the evil impact of the infortune.

evil will be stronger, and his assistants will cheat him and not be loyal towards him.)[133]

81 And if one of the fortunes looked at the infortune indicating evil and[134] at the sign of the terminal point of the month (or its lord), the evil will be lighter, and it will <not>[135] force the rejection of assistants from him.

82 And if one of the infortunes looked at the infortune indicating the evil, and it also looked at the sign of the terminal point of the month (or its lord), he will increase in evil and people will <not> aid him in giving support, so that he is too weak handle it.

83 Now as for the amount of the evil, and its strength or weakness, that is known from the strength of the infortune (or its weakness), and its cause will be from the category of its nature and the nature of the sign which it is in, and from its position in the circle, and from the house which it owns (such as assets, and siblings, and the rest of them).

84 And that will affect him in the time when that infortune manages one of the days of the month, while his release from it and its fading away will be when that infortune withdraws from its place in that month.

85 And if a fortune reached the place of that infortune or the sign of the terminal point of the month, it will shove that evil away from him in his impulses and exploits, and it will make him have assistants in relation to the nature of that fortune.

[Other rules about months: timing and activation]

86 And if the Moon, the Ascendant of the year, and its Lot of Fortune were all corrupted in the revolution of the year, and the Lot was in one of the houses of the infortunes, then when the month termi-

---

[133] In other words, if an infortune looks at the fortune which provides the assistants in **79**, it will spoil their influence.
[134] **E** and **T**: "or."
[135] Adding "not."

nates at the square of those positions, it indicates harm and evil from the category of that sign.

87 Now when the month terminates at the houses of fortunes, and the infortunes in the root of the nativity or in the revolution were in its opposition or square, then due to the nature of the infortunes it indicates something detestable and evil; but because the fortune is the lord of the house, it indicates its scarcity and weakness. **88** And if the month terminated at the houses of the infortunes, and the fortunes in the root or in the revolution were in its square or in its opposition, then due to the nature of the fortunes it indicates the good; but because the infortune is the lord of the house it indicates that something detestable will corrupt it. **89** And if the infortune was in it at the root, while in the revolution it looks at it from a square or opposition, then upon the terminating of the month at it, it indicates intense adversity.

90 And if the month relative to the Lot of Fortune of the year terminated at the sign in which there was a square or opposition of the infortunes at the root of the nativity, and that infortune is not looking at it <at the revolution>,[136] while the fortunes *are* looking at that position in the root and the revolution, then it indicates the dissolving of the evil and the benefit of great good.

91 And the Moon and her movements become a partner with everything we have stated about the indicators, as well as her looking at the planets, connecting with them, and separating from them.

92 And if the planet[137] was in one of the houses of the circle in the revolution of the year or in the revolution of one of the months, its relevance to[138] the thing which that house and its lord indicate in that year, and in that month, is greater than[139] its relevance to the rest of the things.

---

[136] This is probably at the SR, as with the rest of the sentence.
[137] T: "the Moon."
[138] Lit., "pursuit of," "application to" (مزاولة).
[139] Abū Ma'shar should have said "more immediate than," since he means that (a) location is more immediate than rulership, and (b) annual and monthly charts are more immediate and time-sensitive than the natal chart. Because he has emphasized

93 And if in the revolution of the month, the lord of its Ascendant and the lord of the Ascendant of the year, and the lord of the year, and the lord of the distribution, and the one partnering with it, and the lord of the *fardār* and the one distributing with it,[140] and the lord of the orb, were all or mostly in a suitable condition, [then] in that month they indicate the suitability of the condition, relative to the category of their indication (and if they were corrupted, they indicate corruption). **94** And that will be when they manage one of the days of the month, or when the Moon reaches them.

[Comparing the seventh monthly indicators, by time and causation]

95 And of course different things (of illness and health, and the good and the bad) are prepared for a man in the first month of the year, or in the rest of its months, even if the indicators at the beginning of the year or in that month are not indicative of those things: and indeed that comes to be from the rest of the indicators of the year or[141] the root, and everything which [#1] the sign of the terminal point from the Ascendant of the root indicates, as well as [#3] the sign of the terminal point from the position of the Lot of Fortune of the root (and the two signs which the month terminates at from them both, and the lords of these signs), and [#2] the lord of the ninth-part of the month. **96** But most of those will be old, rooted causes, and they are slow to disappear.

97 And the things which [#4] the Ascendant of the revolution of the year and [#5] its Lot of Fortune indicate, as well as the two signs which the month terminates at from them both, and their lords—their causes will be recent, the majority of them being in that year alone, and with little constancy.

---

repeatedly that the nativity is stronger than annual charts, using language like "greater than" is less precise.
[140] That is, the "sub-lord."
[141] E: "and."

98 And the things which [#6] the Ascendant of the revolution of the month and [#7] its Lot of Fortune indicate, as well as their lords, and the indicators of the days and their lords—their causes will be recent, the majority of them being in that month and in those days, and indeed their duration will be for a short time.

[Monthly indicators: personal versus general quality and pursuits]

99 Now as for [#1] the sign of the terminal point relative to the Ascendant of the root, and [#4] the Ascendant of the revolution of the year (and the two signs which the month terminates at from them both), and [#6] the Ascendant of the revolution of the month, the majority of their indication is for the body and its conditions. **100** And as for their lords and [#2] the lord of the ninth-part of the month, the majority of their indication is over the soul and its conditions.

101 And as for [#3] the sign of the terminal point relative to the Lot of Fortune of the root, and [#5] the Lot of Fortune of the revolution of the year (and the two signs which the month terminates at from them both), and [#7] the Lot of Fortune of the revolution of the month, the majority of their indication is for assets, and the social relations[142] of the people and their trade, and good fortune, and elevation and authority, and praise and good reputation,[143] and assistants, and the majority of that will be through action. **102** And as for their lords, and the lords of the indicators of the days, the majority of that indicates *thought* about those matters, and seeking them and pursuing them, and joy and anxiety in them.

103 So, this is the way of examining in detail the indicators of the months, and their indication.

---

[142] معاشرة. But it seems to be a better word would be معايش, "types of livelihood."
[143] Reading somewhat uncertainly with **B** for the rest of this sentence, as **E** and **P** contain an uncertain word and the end of the sentence is somewhat ungrammatical in the Arabic. **T** seems to read, "to the extent that that whole action was with intelligence."

BOOK IX: MONTHS, DAYS, HOURS, LONGEVITY, REFLECTIONS

[Three quick methods for studying the months, using the rooted indicators]

104 And we have not found any of those preceding us in the foregoing situations having mentioned these indicators in the way we have, nor having investigated deeply into them. **105** And it was extremely obscure to the majority of the people of this art, because in this science they looked [only] at what was important and evident, so they took their cue from what was ready-to-hand in it, with respect to the things they wanted knowledge of: so when the indicators grew numerous and their conditions overwhelmed them, they were incapable of distinguishing them due to its difficulty for them. **106** But of course philosophers and scholars are able to distinguish these indicators by means of the natures of the planets, their conditions, and their indications.

107 But *it is* possible for you to know what is manifest in the conditions of the months, and a *summary* of them, from a few of these indicators without [all of] the others, and that is in three ways:

108 The first way is that, of all of them, you look at the lord of the Ascendant of the month: for if it was in a suitable condition just as we mentioned about the suitability of the condition of the planets, it indicates the suitability of the condition and good fortune in that month. **109** And if in addition to that it was in a suitable condition in the revolution of the year and in the root, it indicates an increase in suitability and good fortune.[144] **110** But if it was in a bad condition at the time of the revolution of the month, *and* at the time of the revolution of the year, *and* in the root, it indicates excess in the badness of the condition. **111** And one must consult the condition of the lord of the Ascendant of the month[145] for the [situation of] excellence or badness

---

[144] E adds: "in the revolution of the year."

[145] This seems redundant, because this is the same planet we have been speaking about. But perhaps Abū Ma'shar is just being verbose, and we should focus on what follows: namely, that we use the same criteria for judging this planet, as we do the lord of the year in real time at the revolution. (It is possible that Abū Ma'shar also wants us to look at some profected monthly lord.)

in that month, just as one consults the condition of the lord of the year at the revolution of the year for the condition of the year.

Quick monthly method 1: Monthly revolution only
Rooted indicator #6 - Lord of the MR Ascendant
Evaluate at the monthly revolution, and compare with the condition at the annual SR and in the root.

Figure 132: Quick monthly method 1 (IX.5, 108-11)

112 And the second way is that, of all of them, you look at the sign which the year terminates at from the Ascendant of the root, and from its Lot of Fortune, so that one [then] turns from the position of each one of them, a month for every sign. **113** Then, you see where they land: so in this way the owner of the revolution has three indicators, and his sought matters have two indicators for every house. **114** As for the first of the three indicators, it is the lord of the Ascendant of the root; the second is the sign which the month terminates at from the sign of the terminal point relative to the Ascendant of the root; and the third is the sign which the month terminates at from the sign of the terminal point relative to the Lot of Fortune of the root. **115** And as for the two indicators which each house has, one of them is the house which resembles the nature of that sought matter, from among the houses of the rooted circle; and the second is the house of that sought matter, relative to the sign which the month terminates at from the sign of the terminal point of the Ascendant of the root. **116** So as for the knowledge of the benefit of assets in any of the months, one looks at the combination of the lord of one of the three indicators, with the lord of the house of assets of the root, or the lord of the house of assets of the sign which the month terminates at from the sign of the terminal point relative to the Ascendant of the root.[146] **117** And the examination of the indication of the rest of the houses will be in this manner.

---

[146] That is, the profected second house for that month.

Quick monthly method 2: Monthly profections from nativity	
Rooted indicator #1: Monthly profection from natal Ascendant	
Rooted indicator #3: Monthly profection from natal Lot of Fortune	
Compare these (for native)…	**…with these for topic**
• Lord of natal Ascendant • #1: Monthly profection from natal Ascendant • #3: Monthly profection from natal Lot of Fortune	• Lord of relevant natal house • Lord of monthly profection from that house, in nativity

Figure 133: Quick monthly method 2 (IX.5, 112-17)

118 And the third way is that, of all of them, you look at the Ascendant of the revolution of the year, and its Lot of Fortune, so that one turns from all of them a month for every sign, and you see where they both land: so in this way the owner of the revolution will have three indicators, and his sought matters will have two indicators for every house. 119 As for the first of the three indicators, it is the lord of the Ascendant of the root; the second is the sign which the month terminates at from the Ascendant of the revolution of the year; and the third is the sign which the month terminates at from the Lot of Fortune of the revolution of the year. 120 And as for the two indicators which each house has, the first of them is the house which resembles the nature of that sought matter, from among the houses of the circle in the root; and the second is the house of that sought matter, from the sign which the month terminates at from the Ascendant of the revolution of the year. 121 So as for the knowledge of benefits and assets, one looks at the combination of the lord of one of the three indicators with the lord of the house of assets of the root, or with the lord of the house of assets of the sign which the month terminates at from the Ascendant of the revolution of the year. 122 And the examination of the rest of the matters will be in this manner.

123 And if you did not turn for knowing the months from the sign which the Lot of Fortune of the root terminates at, nor from the Lot of

Fortune of the revolution, but you did indeed turn from each one of those we mentioned separately, that is permitted.[147]

Quick monthly method 3: SR profection only	
Rooted indicator #4: Monthly profection from SR Ascendant	
Rooted indicator #5: Monthly profection from SR Lot of Fortune	
Compare these (for native)...	**...with these for topic**
• Lord of natal Ascendant • #1: Monthly profection from SR Ascendant • #3: Monthly profection from SR Lot of Fortune	• Lord of relevant natal house • Lord of monthly profection of that house, in SR

Figure 134: Quick monthly method 3 (IX.5, 118-23)

124 And in the second and third ways, the turning of the convertible signs among them (and the fixed ones, and those having two bodies), should be according to our preceding statement.[148]

125 And none of these three ways indicates the conditions of the month in their entirety, but the manner of investigating deeply into it is as we stated at the beginning of this chapter; and the Moon and her conditions participate in all of this.

126 And everything we have stated about the indication of the indicators of the months and their lords (in terms of suitability or corruption), and their combining with the indicators of the houses of the months and their lords, and the indication of the sign which the month terminates at, and its lord—the majority of it is to be employed when looking (in the revolution of the year) at its indicators and their combining with the lords of its houses, and upon the year terminating at one of the signs.[149]

---

[147] This seems to mean that the Lot of Fortune is included but less important than the revolutionary and profected Ascendants.

[148] The refers to the special rules for convertible and double-bodied signs, in Ch. IX.1, **26-31**.

[149] I believe this means, "the time of the revolution is more important than ongoing transits."

Chapter IX.6: On the indication of the planets for lasting things [&] change

1 The indication of the circle (and the planets in it) for what there is in this world, is based on different things: some of them are sluggish in occurrence (and that is what will be in one period or another, and in one time or another), and some of them are lasting in occurrence (and that is what will be at every time, in terms of unceasing coming-to-be and corruption, and the rest of what is discovered of the conditions of individuals—various, changing, [and] lasting, due to difference and change).

2 And indeed the unceasing motion of the circle (and what is in it, of planets in various and changing conditions) indicates these things, and it prepares for a single man, on a single day from his beginning,[150] many things lasting in occurrence, which the signs and planets indicate: the management of the condition of assets, and taking and giving, and social relations with siblings and relatives, and increase in them, and focusing on the conditions of fathers and real estate, and delight and anxiety over children and an increase in them, and [whether] he will be a master or servant, and his body healthy or [whether] an ailment is found in it (in all or part of it), and an involvement with women and opponents, and the conditions of the dead, ancestors,[151] and legacies, and [whether] he will travel or labor, or move from place to place, and [whether] authority will come to him or he will associate with people having power, or he will have relations with a brotherhood and people he delights in, or he will associate with people he hates or who hate him.

3 And sometimes his pursuit of these things will be in a single hour, or in the time it takes for a single degree (or less) of the circle to rotate, and indeed it prepares for an individual man praiseworthy or detestable conditions in these matters, and in many matters (of those which

---

[150] That is the nativity.
[151] السلف. But this can also mean "loans."

the signs and planets indicate at every one of these times),[152] all or some of them being below one another in activity. **4** But as for thought, sometimes the man will contemplate all (or much) of what we have stated about their indications (whether the good of them or the evil), to the extent that ten [degrees] of the circle (or less than that) is rotated.[153]

5 So[154] if many of these things which they indicate were already prepared for an individual man in action or thought in any of the times which we have mentioned, then everything which is of their indication after that will be an example of those things. **6** And indeed, they will be in the style of the original indication in resemblance, so that the exploits of a man (or his thought) in the rest of the hours, days, and months, as well as [any] recurring unpleasantness, will resemble the first situation—but of course they will not come to resemble it in the *same* way, because the essence of each one of those things is changed in itself in individual after individual, and time after time, due to the reason which we stated at the beginning of this chapter: and that is the alteration by [1] difference, or by [2] increase or decrease in it.[155]

---

[152] Because of how Abū Ma'shar arranges his clauses, it's a little difficult to say where "at every one of these times" fits. An alternative reading could be that it prepares praiseworthy or detestable *conditions* at every time, based on what the signs and planets indicate.

[153] I think the point is that even actions can be fast, or thoughts last a long time, depending on what is indicated by the charts.

[154] This paragraph is a more abstract way of making the astrological point Abū Ma'shar has constantly emphasized. At the nativity many future things are prefigured in the chart, but in later charts and times these things will only "resemble" the nativity when they manifest: because of the constantly changing circle, each manifestation will be modified by the real-time conditions of the planets and signs indicating them.

[155] See **1**. These alterations are qualitative ("by difference," or rather by being and not being, or being one thing now, and a different thing later), and quantitative ("by increase or decrease").

BOOK IX: MONTHS, DAYS, HOURS, LONGEVITY, REFLECTIONS 627

7 Now[156] as for that which comes to be [1] by difference, like a man who gains assets from a direction he had not gotten from them [before] and will not get them from it after that, that benefit of his will be from a direction different from the directions in which he had gotten it before—or he will travel to a region he had not traveled to [before] and he will not travel to [again], so that journey of his will be in a direction different from the directions which he had traveled to; or a limb of his body will have an ailment which that limb had not ailed from before that, and it will not ail from it after that, so that ailment will be in a limb different from the limbs which had had an ailment [before].

8 But for what comes to be [2] by increase or decrease, it is in accordance with what there is of the scarcity of benefit or its abundance, or according to the nearness of the travel or its distance, or according to the harshness of the pain or its mildness.

[Types of indications, based on potential and duration]

9 And of the known indications belonging to the twelve houses is [1] what belongs to a man since the beginning of his coming-to-be in the belly of his mother, and [2] what he has since the beginning of being born until he dies, and [3] what is prepared for him on an occasional basis[157] in his life, and [4] what is in him as a potential until the time comes in his life when he is able to bring it forth into action, and [5] what afflicts him by compulsion.

10 Now as for [1] the first type, which he has since the beginning of his coming-to-be in the belly of his mother, it is like the indication of the house of the father and mother, because they are both the cause of his coming-to-be, and his kinship to them always stands. **11** And it is like the indication of the house of assets (the meaning of which in this

---

[156] I believe this refers to situations where an annual or monthly chart will indicate something only for that time, so they are unique experiences that are "different" from what is expected in the nativity: for example, IX.5, **63-64** and **75-76**.

[157] Lit., "in time after time."

place is what nourishes his body and supports him), and this is what he has since the beginning of his coming-to-be, so long as he is alive—but as for what is apart from that, of the types of assets which will come to him after childbirth and in the rest of his lifespan (of what his path will be apart from food), they are "provisions."

Type of event	House indicating these:
1: Since beginning to be in mother's belly	4, 2
2: From birth until death	1, 3, 6, 9, 10, 11, 12
3: Occasional	6
4: Potential to activate later	5, 7
5: By compulsion	8

Figure 135: Events indicated by houses (IX.6, 9-20)

12 And as for [2] the second one, which one has since the beginning of being born until he dies, it is like the indication of the Ascendant and its lord, indicating the combination of soul and body, and their remaining [that way] until he dies; and it is like the indication of the house of siblings and relatives, for this belongs to the man from the beginning of when he is born, since all people have siblings and relatives attributed to them even though the closer some are in kind than others are (that is, by [being] the father and mother), the closer they are in attribution, and indeed it comes to be like that because the relationship of the two parents is the closest relationship.[158] **13** And it is like the indication of the house of slaves and servants, because from the first day he is born he will be served and protected and raised up, and for his whole life he will be a servant or master. **14** And it is like the indication of the house of travel, for the meaning of it is "transferring": and it is however he moves and wherever he heads or travels to (for he will transfer from place to place), and indeed [how] one varies from the other by nearness or distance or difference. **15**

---

[158] The reason for comparing other relatives to parents here seems to be because he mentioned parents as belonging to a different category in **10**.

And it is like the house of authority, the house of friends, and the house of enemies: for one is not free to live one's whole life without being governed or being an authority, or having a man love or befriend him, or another hating him or being hostile to him, or he would be the one doing that when he comes to the point of [exercising] preferences.

16 As for [3] the third, which is prepared for him on an occasional basis[159] in his life, it is like the indication of the house of illness: and indeed, the sense of that is that one of the humors inclines towards one of his limbs so that that limb is too weak to do its action completely, and the man suffers pain in his animal soul which he has in that limb, due to its weakness. **17** And this afflicts the whole animal [nature] on an occasional basis in his life, both in the belly of his mother and after he is born, because some of the four humors are sometimes strong or weak, so that in their strength or weakness they incline to one of the limbs and an illness afflicts that limb.

18 And as for [4] the fourth, which he has as a potential until the time comes in his life when he is able to bring it forth into action, that is like sexual intercourse and generating children, because those are both a potential at the beginning of his birth until the time when he does have sexual intercourse and has children, and then each one is brought forth into action.

19 And as for [5] the fifth, which afflicts him by compulsion, that is like the indication of the house of death, because every living thing definitely dies (except for the One God, the Conquering, praise be unto Him).

20 And the planets have indications for other things in accordance with approaches we have not mentioned here, because there is enough in what we have said.

---

[159] Lit., "in time after time," here and in **17**.

Chapter IX.7: On the indicators of the days & hours, & their indications

1 The[160] days and hours have nine indicators which are derived differently, but we will begin in that with the indicators of the "weeks of days," due to the harmonizing of their number with the number of the seven planets.[161]

[Method 1: Planetary "weeks" from the lord of the Ascendant][162]

2 So, the first indicator of them is that you take the days since the day the native was born, up to the year which has just been completed for him, and divide by seven: what arises is the cycles of weeks, and what remains (which does not complete seven) is the remainder of the days of the week. **3** Now each planet grants one of those cycles, and one begins with the lord of the Ascendant of the root, then with the one below it in the circle, then the one below it, until [one gets to] the remainder of those cycles, and the counting reaches the remainder of the days of the week: the year will be introduced in the week of the planet which has those days, and that planet will manage from the beginning of the year in accordance with what remains to it, of the total days of that week.[163] **4** Then, the week which is after it will belong to

---

[160] For **1-6**, cf. Da. 189.

[161] Al-Dāmaghānī also says there were nine methods (Burnett and al-Hamdi p. 337), attributing them to several people, including al-Andarzaghar and Dorotheus. So Abū Ma'shar is probably getting this from his own version of Dorotheus, or from al-Andarzaghar. *Carmen* IV.1, **56-57** also includes another method. One ongoing problem in some of these methods is that we do not know exactly what Abū Ma'shar means by a "day." If it is a 24-hour period that begins at the moment of the nativity, then the calculations are easy because we can start counting by Julian days (and their fractions), and the exact length of the year as measured from the birth time. But if the "day" begins at dawn, then it becomes more complicated because dawn changes from day to day, and latitude to latitude.

[162] For other accounts of this method, see *Carmen* IV.1, **58-62**, and al-Andarzaghar in Burnett and al-Hamdi, p. 337.

[163] See the table below. So, let a native be born with Scorpio rising: Mars rules the first week (and the first day of it), and after seven weeks of the seven planets (or 49

BOOK IX: MONTHS, DAYS, HOURS, LONGEVITY, REFLECTIONS   631

the planet which is below it in the circle, then after it to the planet which is below that planet, until it returns to the planet which introduced the year in its week, then the one below it in the circle, just as in the beginning of the year, [and so on] for the whole lifespan of the man. **5** And when any of the planets manages one of the weeks, it will manage the first day of it as well, and the planet which is below it in the circle will manage the second day from it, and the planet which is below that will manage the third day from it, and the management of the planets will be like that, one after another, for the rest of the days and weeks.

Remainder							Week belongs to:
0	1	2	3	4	5	6	Lord of ASC
7	8	9	10	11	12	13	1st planet below lord ASC
14	15	16	17	18	19	20	2nd planet below lord ASC
21	22	23	24	25	26	27	3rd planet below lord ASC
28	29	30	31	32	33	34	4th planet below lord ASC
35	36	37	38	39	40	41	5th planet below lord ASC
42	43	44	45	46	47	48	6th planet below lord ASC
♄		♃		♂		☉	♀	☿	☽
Multiply age at SR by 365.2422, divide by 49, subtract the whole number, and multiply the remainder by 49. Find the new whole number in the "remainder" cells above.							

Figure 136: Lord of weeks and days, Method 1 (IX.6, 2-6)

days) Mars will do so again. This means we can divide the number of days between birth and the year we want, by 49, cast off the whole number, and the remainder will tell us where in the planetary "weeks" the year begins. Suppose we want to know the lord of the day for the beginning of age 37. We multiply 37 by 365.2422, to yield 13,513.9614 days elapsed. Divide by 49 to yield 275.7951, and cast off the whole number to get .7951. Multiply by 49 to get 38.9614. This means that we are on day 38 in the cycle of days, and the week belongs to the 5th planet after (or "below") Mars. This is Saturn, who at the revolution is halfway through his week. After a few days Jupiter will begin a new planetary week and also rule the day. You can do the same thing for any other possible day by knowing the Julian day of both the nativity and the other day, and dividing the difference between them by 49, as above.

6 And as for their hours, the planet which has the day will manage 3 3/7 hours of its day, and the planet which is below it in the circle will manage like that as well, and the management of each planet over the hours will be like that up to the completion of 24 hours.[164]

[Method 2: Planetary "weeks" from the lord of the orb]

7 And the second indicator is that you look at the lord of the orb which has that year (in the manner which we stated in Chapter VI.1 of this book of ours), for it grants 7 days. **8** And one begins in it from the first day of the revolution of the year, then the planet which is below the lord of the orb in the circle grants another 7 days, and you work like that with the rest of the planets; and whenever the weeks of the seven planets end, you return to the lord of the orb [and so on], until the completion of the year. **9** Now as for the management of the planets over the days of each week,[165] and their hours, it is in the manner of the management of [the first indicator].[166]

[Method 3: The year divided into sevenths]

10 And the third indicator is that you look at the sum of the days of the year (and they are 365 ¼ minus 1/300 of a day),[167] and divide into sevenths, and they are called the "greater sevenths": and a seventh is granted to the lord of the Ascendant of the revolution from the first day of the revolution, and it is one of the "weeks" of the days of the year, its amount being 52 days, 4 hours, and a quarter of an hour (approximately).[168] **11** Then another seventh is granted to the planet

---

[164] A day has 24 hours. Divided by 7, each planet will rule 3.43 hours (or 3 3/7, or 3h 25m).

[165] Reading for "one-seventh."

[166] See **6**.

[167] Again, this is 365.2467 days, Hipparchus's value for the length of the tropical year (and slightly longer than the more accurate 365.2422).

[168] A Hipparchan tropical year of 365.2467 days / 7 = 52d 4h 16m. The period is only about 30 seconds longer than the accurate tropical year, because the 6-minute difference between the two years is spread across the seven divisions.

which is below it in the circle, until the management of the seven planets is completed due to the completion of the year. **12** And each of these sevenths will be divided among the seven planets as well, so that each seventh will be 7 days, 10 hours, and approximately 6/7 of an hour, and each one of them is called a "lesser seventh": so the first of these sevenths (and it is a lesser seventh) is granted to the planet which manages the greater seventh, [but] then the second seventh of it is granted to the planets which are below it in the circle, until the seven planets manage each seventh of those greater sevenths among them. **13** And as for the management of the days of each seventh of the lesser weeks and their hours, that is derived in the manner which we gave an example of [before].[169]

[Method 4: Weeks assigned to the rising sign]

14 And the fourth indicator is that you look at the cycles of the weeks which you knew from the sum of the days of the native (and the remainder of the days of the week) which we mentioned at the beginning:[170] so each of the *signs* grants one of those cycles,[171] and one begins with the Ascendant of the root, then its house of assets, then its house of siblings, up to the twelfth sign. **15** Then, you return to the Ascendant of the root until those cycles run out, and the counting reaches the remainder of the days of the week, and the sign which has those days: for the year will be introduced in its week, and that sign will manage from the beginning of that year for the amount of what remains to it (of the complete amount of days of that seventh). **16** Then the week which is after it will belong to the sign which follows it, then after that to the sign which follows that sign, and the cycle of the weeks will be like that for the days in accordance with the signs of the whole year for the rest of the man's lifespan. **17** And when any of the signs manages one of the weeks, it will manage from the beginning of

---

[169] See **6**.
[170] See **2**.
[171] That is, not the *lord* of the sign as before.

that week[172] for 14 hours,[173] then the sign which follows it will manage for a like number of those hours, then the rest of the signs will manage like that as well, in succession, sign after sign, until the days of the week of that sign are completed.

[Method 5: One day per sign]

18 And the fifth indicator is that you cast out the sum of the days of the native which we mentioned at the beginning, twelve days by twelve [days] (according to the number of the signs), then you cast out what remains of the days below twelve from the Ascendant of the root, a sign for each day: and the sign which the counting terminates at is the manager for that day, and it is the sign which introduces the year in its management. **19** Then after that, each sign grants a day of every year for the whole lifespan of the man. **20** But as for the management of the hours in this method, the sign which manages that day grants two hours, and the sign which follows it [grants] two hours as well, until twenty-four hours is completed over the twelve signs.

21 And look into these five ways which deal with the weeks and the day of a sign of the year. **22** So if the lord of a week of the year, and a day of its sign, are two fortunes in a sound condition, they indicate good in that year;[174] and if they are two infortunes of a bad condition, they indicate evil: and they indicate like that when they manage one of the weeks and the days.

[Method 6: A profection-distribution hybrid]

23 And the sixth indicator is that you look in the revolution of the year at the degree of the sign which the year terminated at, from the Ascendant of the root of the nativity:[175] for if the body of a planet or its

---

[172] Reading for "seventh."

[173] Seven days of 24 hour hours apiece, divided among 12 signs, is 14 hours: $(7*24)/12 = 14$.

[174] But perhaps Abū Ma'shar means "in that 'week' or day"?

[175] Nowadays this is called a "continuous" profection. Normally Abū Ma'shar simply jumps sign-by-sign to find the sign of the year, even though he also wants to know

rays was in the bounds of that degree, then the management of the days will belong to it until another [planet] encounters it by body or ray.[176] **24** And if not, the management will belong to the lord of the bound of that degree, then to the lord of the bound which follows it, until it reaches a planet with its body or ray. **25** Now as for knowing the days of the management, you should see how many degrees and minutes are between the degree of the terminal point and the body of some planet or its rays, and multiply by 12 days, <4 hours>, 10 minutes, and 30 seconds (and that is 1/6 of a day and half a sixth of a tenth of a day):[177] and what it comes to is where the management terminates at after those days, from the first day of the revolution. **26** Now if the planet which the management reached (after those days, from the first day of the revolution) was a fortune, it indicates good in that time, and so long as it is a manager; but if it was an infortune it indicates evil. **27** And you will [also] direct (in this way of knowing the days of the management of good or evil) the degrees of the signs

---

where the 30° increments from the Ascendant occur, so he can locate fixed stars on them (III.8, **9**). We have also seen him profect in 30° increments when doing monthly profections, so that he knows whether to profect forwards or backwards from double-bodied signs (recall this controversial method from IX.1, **26-30**). Now he is doing something advocated by al-Tabarī (in *PN2*): after profecting in the 30° increment, treat that span of degrees as being like a whole year, as though the Ascendant is slowly moving forward through it over the year. As we will see, he then treats this like a distribution, so that as the Ascendant profects "continuously" through the degrees, it will have bound lords and partners just like when we distribute. Steven Birchfield points out it would make more sense to do this using ascensions, as a primary direction or distribution.

[176] This is awkwardly stated and should be put the other way around: until *the degree* encounters another planet, since it is the degree which is being profected. But since this method is a hybrid of profections and distributions, he seems to be blending the vocabulary. But Abū Ma'shar's vocabulary *does* make sense if we are treating this as a distribution only.

[177] Both the time units listed and the fractions are wrong, but it doesn't matter anyway because Abū Ma'shar's year is inaccurate. He wants to divide the year (365.2422 days) into profectional increment of 30°: this would be 12.17474 days per degree, or 12d 4h 11m 38s. Even if he wanted to use the approximate year of 365.25 days as he mentions in **28**, this would be 12d 4h 12m.

which the year terminates at from the Lot of the father, and the Lot of the mother, and all of the houses and Lots, and the rooted things, a year for each sign. **28** And indeed you multiply every degree of the sign of the terminal point by the number of these days (and fractions), because this is the number which, if you multiply it by 30°, comes to 365 ¼ days, approximately the number of days of the year: and this is called the management of the "mighty days."

[Method 7: Distributing the Ascendant of the revolution]

29 And the seventh indicator is that you look at the degree of the Ascendant of the revolution of the year, so that you direct from it (for the knowledge of the conditions of the days), a day for every 59' 08",[178] until it returns to the degree of the Ascendant at the end of the year. **30** Now if in the bounds of the degree of the Ascendant of the revolution there was the body of a planet or its rays, the management of the degree of the Ascendant will belong to it until another besides it encounters it by body or rays; but if not, the management will belong to the lords of the bounds in the way we have stated,[179] until it reaches one of the planets or the rays. **31** And you work like that with everything of the planets, Lots, and houses, of whatever you want the direction of in the twelve signs, for all of the days of the year: and this is called the management of the "small days." **32** And there is an approximation in it, but the correct [approach] is that this way of directing is like the direction of the Sun every day, even though his course [in longitude] in a single day is sometimes 1°, and sometimes less than that or more—except that directing in this work is complicated, and between this sense which is by approximation and the exact

---

[178] Abū Ma'shar should be emphasizing that this is by ascensions (as with all directions), *not* by zodiacal degrees, although in **32** he admits that doing it zodiacally is only an "approximation." But due to the differences in ascensions as the birth latitude increases, it quickly becomes distorted and inaccurate as an approximation.
[179] See **24**.

one, the second one is easy,[180] [with] no harm in the work. **33** And when the management arrives from one of them to a fortune, or it is the manager for that sign, it indicates the good; and when it reaches an infortune or it was the manager for it, it indicates evil.

[Method 8: Other continuous profections]

34 And the eighth indicator is the management of the days of the months (and their hours) based on the signs, and it is in two ways. **35** One of them is that [1] you look at the degree of the sign at which the month terminates from the four rooted indicators,[181] and at the degree of the Ascendant of the month, and the degree of its Lot of Fortune, and the degree of its Moon, and one directs from the position of each one of them, a day for every degree, up to the completion of 30° for the thirty days. **36** And if we wanted to direct the houses of the Ascendant of the month in this manner, then we would do likewise with every house: so if they reached the fortunes they would indicate good, and if they reached the infortunes they would indicate evil.

37 And the second way is that [2] you look at these indicators which we mentioned, and from the position of each one of them you appoint a day for every 12°, and 2 ½ days for every sign, so that there are 12 signs for the 30 days. **38** And [for the hours], when the management of one of these days belongs to any of the signs, then the management will belong that sign itself for 5 hours, then the management will belong to the sign which follows it for the [same] number of those hours as well, up to the completion of 60 hours for the twelve signs.[182] **39** And if the days of any of the months was greater than 30

---

[180] Again, this is not really true because ascensions and zodiacal degrees diverge especially as the birth latitude increases.

[181] See IX.1, **26**: these are the months profected from the natal Ascendant, the month profected from the natal Lot, the month as profected from the SR Ascendant, and the month as profected from the SR Lot.

[182] Each sign is worth 2 ½ days, a total of 60 hours. But when we break the signs into the hours, each sign is also 1/12 of those 60 hours: 60 hours / 12 signs = 5 hours.

days, [then] in the management of the days and hours it will return to the position which it began from.

❧ ❧ ❧

40 And for each indication of these eight indicators, if we wanted to make it more precise to [whatever] fractions of hours we wanted, we would work in it just as we gave an example of in each one of them. **41** And if the manager of the days or hours was a fortune, it indicates the good; and if it was an infortune, it indicates the bad. **42** And everything we initiate from the position of any of the signs for the purpose of managing the days of the months and their hours, is found in succession, sign after sign, whether the sign which we begin with was convertible or something else.

[Method 9: Ninth-parts]

43 And the ninth indicator in the management of the days and hours is from the method of the ninth-parts: and we begin in it at the beginning of the year from three positions: the first of them is [1] the sign of the terminal point, the second is [2] the Ascendant of the revolution of the year,[183] and the third is [3] the Moon.[184]

44 Now as for [1] the first of them, one looks at the lord of the year: and it is the lord of the first ninth-part of the sign of the terminal point, according to what the people of India claim, just as we mentioned in Book III of this book of ours.[185] **45** So it will have the management of the first ninth of the sign of the terminal point (but do not focus on which position in [the sign] the year terminates at); and the management of the second ninth of the sign of the terminal point will belong to the lord of the second ninth-part; and the management of the third ninth of it will belong to the lord of the third ninth-part,

---

[183] See **69** below.
[184] See **70** below.
[185] See III.10, **1**.

until the nine ninths are completed for the sign of the terminal point, and the first month is done.[186]

46 Then, the management for the beginning of the second month shifts over to the beginning of the sign which follows that of the terminal point, so that the management of its first ninth will belong to the lord of the ninth-part itself, and the management of its second ninth will belong to the lord of the second ninth-part, and the management of the third ninth-part will belong to the lord of the third ninth, until the nine ninths belonging to that sign run out, and the second month is completed.

47 Then, the management for the beginning of the third month shifts over to the beginning of the third sign from that of the terminal point, and the management of its first ninth will belong to the lord of the ninth-part itself, and the management of the second ninth will belong to the lord of the second ninth-part. **48** And the management of the 108[187] ninth-parts in the twelve signs will be like that for the twelve months, a month for every sign, and the lord of the first ninth-part belonging to each sign will be the lord of that month, just as we mentioned in what preceded.

49 And if the management of days belonged to one of the ninth-parts, [and] then we wanted a more precise management for that, we would divide the number of degrees of the one ninth-part into thirds, an even division among three planets, so that the lord of the ninth-part itself would manage the first division for one-third of those days, and the lord of the fifth sign from the sign of the lord of the ninth-part would manage the second division for one-third of those days as well, and the lord of the ninth sign from the sign of the lord of the ninth-part would manage the third division for one-third of those days. **50** So, you would divide[188] the management of the degrees of the ninth among three planets in the manner of the lords of the *darījān*, just as

---

[186] I.e., each sign represents a month, and is divided into ninths rather than the normal weeks and days we saw in the previous methods.
[187] Reading for "180," since there are only 108 ninth-parts.
[188] Reading فتقسم for "come to an end" (فتتمّ).

we mentioned in Book III of this book of ours: and this division is called the "management of the thirds of the ninth-part."[189]

51 And if we wanted the management of what is more precise than that, we would divide each of these thirds into ninths (according to the number of ninth-parts), so that one of the planets will rule each ninth, in one-ninth of those hours, and one begins with the lord of the ninth which <manages> this division in its ninth-part, then after that the lord of the ninth-part which follows it according to the first operation: and this is called "the management of the ninths of the thirds of the ninth-part."

52 And if we wanted the management of what is more precise than that, we would divide each of these ninths into thirds among three planets, so that the lord of the first ninth will manage the first division of that third, for one-third of the hours which that ninth gets; and the lord of the fifth sign from the sign of the lord of the [first] ninth will manage the second division of it, for one-third of the hours which that ninth gets as well; and the lord of the ninth sign from the sign of the lord of the [first] ninth manages the third division, for a like time as well: and this is called "the management of the thirds of the ninths of the thirds of the ninth-part."

53 (And if we wanted the management of what is more precise than that, the work in it would be in this manner, and we would divide each division of it by nine, then the division which is after that by three, then the division which is after that by nine, then the division which is after that by three, until it is what we wanted.)

54 And the beginning of the management of each division should be with the lord of the ninth-part which [rules] this whole division in its ninth, and in all of this it will be in charge of equal degrees, every 3° 20' belonging to a single ninth-part, and the management of each ninth will belong to its ninth-part for 3 days, 9 hours, and 1/6 of an hour (and this is the number which, if we multiply it by the number of the ninth-parts of a single sign—and it is nine), will come to 30 days, 10 hours, and ½ an hour—and among the Indians this is the amount

---

[189] See the table of subdivisions in III.9, **14**, and the example in **57-69** below.

of every month, because they make the days of the months of the years of the native in this subject be equal, each month being of a like number of days, hours, and fractions as belongs to the next one. **55** And if we multiplied the days of a single month and its fractions by the number of 12 months, it comes to 365 ¼ days, and that is the days of a solar year, approximately.[190]

56 (And everything in these nine things, and in this book of ours, of the discussion of the management of the planets over hours, is in equal hours,[191] because the amount of each hour is like the amount of the next hour, none of them being increased over another nor being less than it; and the amount of each of the equal hours is like that.)

57 And example of that is: a year terminated at 20° Taurus, so the lord of its first ninth-part became Saturn, the lord of Capricorn, and he is the lord of the year; and [in terms of months and days], he manages 3 days, 9 hours, and 1/6 of an hour from the beginning of the year.[192]

58 So we wanted the management of what is more accurate than that, and divided that ninth-part into thirds with an equal division among three planets, so each division became 1° 06' 40" [in longitude].[193] **59** Saturn, the lord of Capricorn and the lord of the first ninth-part, manages the first division of it for 27 hours, and one-half of a ninth of an hour.[194] **60** And Venus, the lord of Taurus, manages the second division of it, for the amount of those hours and their fraction as well. **61** Then Mercury, the lord of Virgo, manages the third division of it, for the amount of those hours and their fraction as well.

62 But we wanted the management of what is more precise than that, so we divided each of the thirds into ninths, and each division of

---

[190] So in this scheme, the year is 365.25 days long. Each month is 30.4375 days long (or 30d 10h 30m), and one-ninth of each month is 3.381944 days (or 3d 9h 10m).
[191] That is, in our normal civil hours of 60 minutes apiece, rather than the unequal "planetary" hours which differ based on latitude and date.
[192] See the footnote for **55**: Saturn will manage 3d 9h 10m.
[193] A single ninth-part of 3° 20' divided into thirds = 1° 06' 40" (1d 3h 3.333m).
[194] The 1d 3h 3.333m just mentioned, is equivalent to 27h 3.333m (27.0555).

it came to 7' 25" 33'" [in longitude].[195] **63** So, Saturn, the lord of Capricorn and the lord of the first ninth-part, manages the first of the divisions, for three hours and one-third of a sixth of a ninth of an hour.[196] **64** And Saturn, the lord of Aquarius and the lord of the second ninth-part, will manage the second division of them, in a like [amount] of those hours and their fractions, as well. **65** And Jupiter, the lord of Pisces and the lord of the third ninth-part, will manage the third division of them, in a like [amount] of those hours and their fractions, as well.

66 But we wanted the management of what is more precise than that, so we divided each of these ninths into thirds, and each third of them was 2' 28" 31'" [in longitude].[197] **67** So Saturn, the lord of Capricorn and lord of the first ninth-part, will manage the first portion of this third, for 1 hour and one-third of one-ninth of one-third of one-sixth[198] of an hour. **68** Then Venus, the lord of Taurus, manages the second division of this third for a like time as well. **69** Then Mercury, the lord of Virgo rules the third division of this third for a like time as well; and in this manner we work with every ninth-part and make it be more precise to the [level] we want.

70 Now as for [2] the Ascendant of the revolution of the year,[199] the management of the lords of its ninth-parts over [the year], and its days, and the rest of what follows that, will be like what we stated about the sign of the terminal point: and we begin the management of the ninth-part from the beginning of that sign.

---

[195] Abū Ma'shar is incorrect, this should be 7' 24" 26'". For if the one-third just mentioned (1° 06' 40") is divided by 9, we get .123456789 (7' 24" 26.4'"). Abū Ma'shar is probably working from a table with fractional equivalents to degrees, and reading the wrong value.

[196] That is, 3 and 1/162 of an hour, or 3.00617284.

[197] The correct value is 2' 28" 09'": the previous one-ninth (.123456789°) divided into thirds is .041151851° (00° 02' 28" 8.8'").

[198] That is, 1 and 1/486 of an hour, which is highly accurate: the previous one-ninth (3.00617284h) divided into thirds, is 1.0020576h (or 1h 00m 7.4s).

[199] Mentioned in **43** above.

71 And as for [3] the Moon,[200] one sees at the revolution of the year which ninth-part she is in, of the sign she is in, so that the beginning of the management of the days will be from that ninth-part[201] and from that degree she is in: and she herself operates with every ninth-part by means of the ninths and thirds, just as we stated about the sign of the terminal point.

72 And for everything whose direction one wants (of the signs and the planets) for the management of the days of the ninth-parts in the year in which the native was born, and in the rest of the future years, we begin the direction of the *signs* from the beginning of them, and the *planets* from their positions and degrees which they are in at the revolution.

[Some timing methods, and the manifestation of the effect]

73 And in everything we have mentioned in these nine kinds of management of the planets over the week, days, and hours, the indication of the planetary manager will be in one of two ways: as for <the first, it is> if the thing which it had indicated in the root or in the revolution of the year or in the month, would manifest at that time; and as for the second, it is whether it would produce [only] a portion of the indication of its nature and condition: of deeds which are quick to disappear[202] and change, or discussions, the inner heart and thought, ideas, and dreams.

74 So if the Moon reached the indicator of the week, or the indicator of the day, or the indicator of the hour, it will produce the indication of one of the two, whether it was good or bad.

75 And if the indicator of the week, or the indicator of the day, or the indicator of the hour, or the Moon, transited one of the fixed stars

---

[200] Mentioned in **43** above.
[201] That is, *not* from the beginning of the sign as in the previous examples: this is confirmed in **72**.
[202] Or, "to become active" (الزوال). The point is that they are fleeting.

in any of the times, or it corresponded to one of the 36 images in the north or south,[203] it will manifest part of the indication of that thing.

76 And if one of them came to be in the degrees indicating good fortune, or in the bright degrees, or in a face or in the *darījān*,[204] or in a ninth-part or in a twelfth-part, or in the rays, or in the management of one of the Lots indicating good, it indicates a small increase in good fortune at that time. **77** And if it was in the gloomy[205] degrees, or the empty or dark ones, or in the rest of the rays and Lots and bad, unfortunate positions, it indicates corruption.

[Revolutions of days and hours]

78 Now as for the revolution of days and hours, when the Sun moves one full degree from the position he was in in the root, that is a revolution of that day; and when he moves 2' 30", that is the revolution of that hour.[206] **79** So if we wanted the revolution of the days and hours, and we do derive their Ascendants and plants, we would work with them both in the way we described in what has preceded; but there is no need for us [to do] that, because these nine indicators which we have described for the management of the days and hours (and their fractions) are complete for everything needed in the examination of this matter.[207]

---

[203] That is, the 36 non-zodiacal constellations identified by Ptolemy.
[204] See *ITA* VII.6-VII.7, and VII.9.
[205] Also known in English as the "smoky" degrees. Again, see *ITA* VII.9.
[206] One degree of 60' / 24 hours = 2' 30" in longitude. See I.3, **10-11**, where he defines this.
[207] This is pretty disappointing. I should have liked Abū Ma'shar to devise 9 more variations for each of the hours of the day, with their 1,440 minutes and 86,400 seconds, in every permutation of planets and their aspects.

BOOK IX: MONTHS, DAYS, HOURS, LONGEVITY, REFLECTIONS   645

Chapter IX.8: On the cutters, which of them is true, friendly,[208] superior, loved for wisdom[209]

1 Since you have asked me for the characteristic marks of a cutting year in order to know your lifespan from the years of one of the killing bounds (when having doubts about it), it is necessary for you and everyone in our time who is called to the knowledge of this craft, to deny having possession of that, due[210] to the excess of distress which is caused by [even] a little thing affecting you. **2** And how are you permitted to look into the time of a cutting, conclusive disaster involving the soul and body, which has no purpose beyond [seeing] something detestable?

3 But[211] even though I have refrained from that, still my nature has been spurred on to [this] work and the nuisance of it, by thinking [about it] until I collected together for you things to investigate from my book in this chapter,[212] concerning the planetary indicators of that—not doing it out of jealousy of those scholars in this science who have come before, [but] hoping that you will contemplate it when you look for yourself at the lifespan, after a year which has already resulted in[213] [only] a small fear for yourself, so that you are gladdened.[214]

---

[208] الوال. This makes it seem like Abū Ma'shar is making an ironic joke, since the chapter is about disasters and death, and he is chiding his students in **1-2**. But, in **119** he does reaffirm that he is trying to give us the best methods.
[209] See my Introduction for a discussion of this chapter.
[210] The MSS have little differences in their reading of the rest of the sentence, but this is the gist of it.
[211] This paragraph was apparently very confusing for the scribes, as approximately one-third of the words have variations in them, with some apparently ungrammatical structures.
[212] Abū Ma'shar may be thinking of another book as well, but he certainly reuses many statements from this book below, especially from **71-111**.
[213] Reading somewhat loosely for سبق إلى.
[214] Omitting the last few words, which contain two more instances of "gladness" or "delight" but do not make grammatical sense to me. But the point is that you should look back and analyze past years when there was only trouble, so you do not rush in to predict death.

4 And the operative foundation in that is that you look at the indicator of the lifespan[215] in the root of the nativity, [to see] how many years it grants. **5** So if it has increasers and decreasers there,[216] you will make an increase to it due to the increasers, and make a decrease from it due to the decreasers; and you make what happens to the indicator of the lifespan after that (in terms of years, months, days, and hours), be like the foundation of the man's lifespan: and one makes inferences about their soundness[217] from some of the indicators which we will mention.

6 And while you certainly do make those years be *like* the foundation of his lifespan, do not make his [actual] lifespan be like them in the same way:[218] because that indication of his over the lifespan is not complete at every time, [and] one should not use the planets to make inferences about something due to a single indicator, or a single condition—but let it be from two indicators or two conditions, or from more than that (just as we stated in Chapter I.4 of this book of ours).[219] **7** And for this reason, the years of a man's life will not be like the years which are assigned to the indicator of the lifespan from the manner of its indication alone, unless other indicators testify to that, so that the man's life is [understood] by the agreement of several indications similar to those years; and if not, his life will differ from those years by an increase in it or a subtraction from it.[220]

---

[215] That is, the house-master.

[216] That is, other factors (especially planets) which add to or decrease the expected years of the house-master based on their aspects to it. See for example Sahl, *Nativities* Chs. 1.20-1.21.

[217] I believe "their" refers to the units of time: years, months, days. "Soundness" also has connotations of "health" (صحّة).

[218] What Abū Ma'shar means is that the years attributed to the house-master at the nativity are something like the "expected lifespan—unless something cuts it short." This chapter is about precisely that: situations which cut the lifespan short, or present great dangers.

[219] See I.4, **6**.

[220] Since Abū Ma'shar has already spoken about the method of adding and subtracting years, I don't think that's what he means here. I believe he simply means that if the native does not die at the expected time, it's because something is prolonging it;

8 And the indicator which one should be guided by (along with the indicator of the lifespan) for the health of those years, is one of the releasers or the revolution of one of the years: and it is that you direct the positions of the releasers[221] in the root, a year for each degree, and they are turned in the signs, a year for each sign, and along with that you look into the revolutions of the years.[222] **9** For if any of them reaches the cutters by direction or turning in any of the years, months, or days, and that time of years of the native's lifespan was an instance of the completion of those years which are like the foundation [of the lifespan][223] (or it was close to them by a few years, adding to or subtracting from them), or, close to the completion of those years the infortunes governed over[224] the revolution of the year with corruption, the native will have a cutting disaster in it.

10 So[225] if in the root the indicator of the lifespan as well as the increasers were in a suitable condition, strong, the cutting disaster will be the greatest upon [his] completing those years which are similar to the foundation [of the lifespan] (whether in terms of getting close to them or after they are passed by), in accordance with one of[226] the

---

and if he dies early, it's because something cuts it short. In both cases that would be seen astrologically in the charts for the appointed time. See **9**, where he seems to simply mean that the expected longevity is "close" to the actual amount, give or take some years.

[221] **E** reads, "that you direct *one of* the releasers."

[222] **P** adds, "and months." In other words, you look at the releasers in distributions, profections, and revolutions (the very topic of the whole book). But note that he is using the methods with *all* of the releasers, because each one makes a major statement about life even if it is not the *longevity* releaser.

[223] That is, the years attributed to the house-master.

[224] يستولي. This is the word that Abū Ma'shar tends to use for a "governor," a planet which has responsibility for *all* of the main rulerships in a revolution. But more generally it can mean "overpower" or "overwhelm."

[225] See another, shorter version in **120-22** below, and Māshā'allāh's simple version in Sahl, *Nativities* Ch. 1.23, **61-63**.

[226] Or, "any" (بعض), reading with **B**. **P** reads, "in accordance with the powerful releasers," implying multiple ones. **E** reads, "in accordance with the powerful releaser." It seems to me that the direction of the longevity releaser is the most important.

powerful releasers reaching one of the cutters, or the year being corrupted by powerful, corrupting infortunes. **11** And if they[227] were weak, the cutting disaster will be the greatest *before* his reaching the completion of those years, unless—during those years which are close to their completion—his indicators and the indicator of the lifespan are in a suitable condition in them, strong, made fortunate, and none of the releasers reaches any of the cutters in them, and no year is corrupted by any of its indicators.[228] **12** For if it was like that,[229] the cutting disaster *would* be upon the completion of those years (by getting close to them or after them, by a few years), in accordance with damage [and] corruption harming some of the indicators of the year. **13** And sometimes in the root the indicator of the lifespan and the increasers are weak or in a bad condition, so that by their weakness or the badness of their condition they indicate such-and-such about the years of the lifespan, but the direction from the particular[230] releaser terminates at one of the powerful killers in a year which is many years less than the years of the foundation, and powerful, corrupting infortunes *also* govern over[231] the indicators of that year and the indicator of the lifespan, and the number of the man's years from the beginning of his lifespan up to that year matches the years of the indicator of the lifespan (be they the greater, middle, or lesser), or that year matches the amount of one-third, one-half, or two-thirds of one of them or one of the years which are like the foundation: for if it was like that, that will be a cutting year.

---

[227] That is, the house-master and the increasers (but perhaps even the releasers).

[228] In other words, if the natal indicators are weak or weaker, then the native is more likely to have a disaster or death early—*unless* in those years leading up to it, the indicators are in a good condition in real time (in the revolutions), and no clearly bad direction occurs.

[229] That is, if the natal indicators were weak, but an early disaster was prevented by everything looking good.

[230] I believe Abū Ma'shar means, "*whichever* one reached the killer." I don't think he has a specific one in mind, like the longevity releaser (but that would be bad enough).

[231] See above; again, this can mean "overwhelm, overpower."

BOOK IX: MONTHS, DAYS, HOURS, LONGEVITY, REFLECTIONS

[Four types of cutting]

14 And the inability of the indicator of the lifespan to reach the years it had indicated, as well as the cutters of the five releasers, comes to be in four ways:

15 The first way is the stars.[232]
16 The second way is one of the positions.[233]
17 The third way is one of the positions by the management of one of the planets over it.[234]
18 The fourth way is the corruption of the years.[235]

[Cutting type #1: the planets and stars]

19 Now as for the cutters of the first way, it is from the stars, and there are nineteen: five of them are fast in course, seven from among the fixed stars, and seven from among the nebulous ones and what resembles them.

20 Now as for the five which are fast in course, two of them cut by nature (and they are [1] Saturn and [2] Mars), and two of them cut by a differing contingency (and they are [3] the Sun and [5] Moon), and one of them cuts by mixture[236] (and it is Mercury).

21 Now as for Saturn and Mars, they cut off the releasers upon the direction from one of [the releasers] reaching the body of one of [the infortunes], or their opposition, square, trine, or sextile, [whether] the right one or left.

22 And as for the two which cut by a differing contingency, one of them is the Sun, and he cuts off the releasers upon the direction reaching his body, opposition, or square; but if he was in an alien sign and

---

[232] See **19-55** below.
[233] See **56-70** below.
[234] That is, by distributions: see **71-78** below.
[235] See **79-118** below.
[236] Lit., "by a blending mixture," or perhaps even "by a blending humor" (بالخلط الممازج).

was opposing, assembling with, squaring, trining, or sextiling Mars, and [Mars] is corrupting him without the fortunes looking at [the Sun], or [the Sun] was like that with Saturn in terms of the aspect and corruption, then from the trine and sextile he indicates [only] a powerful disaster. **23** And the second is the Moon, and it is if one of the releasers in its direction connects with her body, opposition, or square; but <if> in the root she is made fortunate, in a suitable condition, perhaps she will not kill and the disaster will be powerful [but] passing over him. **24** Now if the Moon in the root of the nativity was not made fortunate, or[237] she was squaring the Sun or opposing him, or in the root she was increasing in glow and corrupted by Mars (or she was decreasing in glow and corrupted by Saturn), from whatever direction her corruption from them was, then she will kill upon the releasers' reaching her body, opposition, or square. **25** And if the Ascendant was the releaser, then the Moon will cut it off with her body no matter what the condition of the Moon is; but if the condition of the Moon in relation to the Sun, Mars, or Saturn was as we stated, then she will cut off in all ways. **26** And the luminaries certainly cut themselves off from the square.[238]

27 And as for the single one which cuts by mixture, it is Mercury: and it is if he was made unfortunate from an assembly, opposition, square, trine, or sextile, and the infortunes were enclosing[239] him without the improving fortunes looking at him: for if he mixes his nature with the nature of the infortunes, he becomes like them. **28** So whichever releaser reached his body by direction, or his rays (from whatever direction[240] the rays were), he will kill; and if he was not like that in terms of the infortunes enclosing him, he will not kill.

---

[237] E reads that she is "made unfortunate, *and*" squaring the Sun, etc. Obviously being made unfortunate is worse than simply not being fortunate, and it also makes a difference whether this must be combined with the relationship to the Sun. But I'm not sure which way Abū Ma'shar means it.
[238] That is, if they are directed to the square of themselves (which will generally happen only in very old age).
[239] That is, "besieging."
[240] That is, from whatever aspect on either side.

BOOK IX: MONTHS, DAYS, HOURS, LONGEVITY, REFLECTIONS

29 So these are the five planets which kill upon the releasers' reaching them by direction, in the ways which we have mentioned.

30 And if the turning of the years from any of the five releasers (or from the indicator of the lifespan) reached their bodies, oppositions, or squares, then they also kill. **31** But as for if the turning from them reached the rest of the rays' direction,[241] that is a weak testimony not having power in it for killing, unless there is testimony in addition to them apart from that.

32 And as for [6-19] the rest of the remaining cutters which we mentioned in this first way, they cut off the [other] releasers upon [the releasers'] reaching them by direction only; and the indicator of the lifespan alone is turned in the signs, sign-by-sign, and is not directed degree-by-degree.

33 So as for the seven cutting fixed stars, four of them are the Hearts of a hot complexion, and they are of the first and second magnitudes:

34 The first of them is [6] Aldebaran,[242] and it is in Taurus 23° 28',[243] and its latitude in the south, 5° 10'.

35 The second is [7] the Heart of Leo,[244] and it is in Leo in 13° 18', and its latitude in the north, 10°.

36 And the third is [8] the Heart of Scorpio,[245] and it is in Scorpio 23° 28', and its latitude in the south, 4°.

37 And the fourth is [9] the Shoulder of the Horse,[246] and it is in Pisces 12° 58', and its latitude in the north, 31°.

---

[241] Again, from other aspects (the sextile and trine).
[242] See *Almagest* p. 362, star #14.
[243] This is not true even by Ptolemy's too-slow precession, but it doesn't matter because many of these longitudes have probably been written badly by scribes anyway. Note that this degree is the same as Antares in **36**, which supports the "scribal error" explanation.
[244] That is, *Cor Leonis* or Regulus (*Almagest* p. 367, star #8).
[245] That is, *Cor Scorpionis* or Antares (*Almagest* p. 372, star #8).

Cutter	Name / Description	Modern Designation
1-5	(Malefics, luminaries, Mercury)	(n/a)
6	Aldebaran (*Oculus Tauri*)	α Tauri
7	Regulus / *Cor Leonis*	α Leonis
8	Antares / *Cor Scorpii*	α Scorpii
9	Scheat	β Pegasi
10	Cluster near Algol	16 Persei
11	In eyebrows of Leo (Rasalas)	μ Leonis
12	In eyebrows of Leo (Ras Elased)	ε Leonis
13	Nebula in r. hand of Perseus	Clusters 884, 869
14	Meissa *et al.*	λ + φ Orionis
15	Praesepe	Nebula (M44/ MCG 2632)
16	Cluster at sting of Scorpio	G Scorpii, Cluster 6441
17	Nebula in eye of Sagittarius	ν¹ and ν² Sagittarii
18	Tip of arrow of Sagittarius (Alnasl)	(γ² Sagittarii)
19	Nebula, right knee of Cygnus	ω Cygni

Figure 137: Nineteen cutters, planets, and fixed stars (IX.8, 19-50)

38 And there are three stars below them in magnitude:

39 One of them is [10] the Giant[247] which precedes the star of Algol, and it is in Taurus 5° 28', and its latitude in the north, 20° 40'.

---

[246] This is the Arabic term for Scheat (see Kunitzsch and Smart p. 47). Its being grouped with the other three ought to make us think of the four Persian royal stars, which should make this Fomalhaut instead (α Piscis Austrinus). But Fomalhaut is not really at the "heart" of a constellation like Scheat is. See *Almagest* p. 358, star #3.

[247] الجبّار, *al-Jabbār*. This is the usual name for Orion, and Abū Ma'shar not only says it *is* the Giant (not "in" the Giant), but that it precedes Algol—but Perseus and Algol precede Orion. Instead, it seems to be 16 Persei, a small cluster next to Algol slightly earlier in longitude, which Ptolemy describes as being "in advance of those

Book IX: Months, Days, Hours, Longevity, Reflections 653

40 The second is [11] in the head of Leo,[248] and it is in Leo 5° 08', and its latitude in the north, 12°.

41 The third is [12] a star also in the head of Leo, and it is in Leo 4° 58', and its latitude in the north, 9° 30'.

42 And as for the seven others, five of them are dark, corrupting nebulae cutting off life:

43 The first of them is [13] one which is at the tip of the right hand of Perseus,[249] and it is in Taurus, 9° 28',[250] and its latitude in the north, 40° 30'.

44 The second is [14] the nebulous one which is at the head of Orion, and it is in Gemini, 7° 48',[251] and its latitude in the south, 13° 50'.[252]

45 The third is [15] the nebulous one which is in the chest of the Crab, and it is in Cancer 21° 08', and its latitude in the north, 40'.

46 The fourth is [16] the nebulous one which follows the Sting [of Scorpio], and it is in Sagittarius 11° 58', and its latitude in the south, 13° 15'.[253]

---

in the Gorgon-head" (*Almagest* p. 353, star #29). Nevertheless it seems obvious to me that we ought to include Algol itself.

[248] This star and the next seems to be two stars in the eyebrows of Leo, μ and ε. I would have expected al-Jabbah and Aldhafer, but they are further back and do not have the right relationship of latitude and longitude. See Allen pp. 260 and 263, and *Almagest* p. 367 (stars #3-4), which gives these a longitude that would make sense.

[249] This nebulous mass is described in *Almagest*, p. 352 (and listed today as Galactic Clusters 884 and 869).

[250] E reads 7° 28'.

[251] P has 9° 48'.

[252] This is the cluster of stars around and including Meissa (*Almagest* p. 382, star #1).

[253] This is G Scorpii and Galactic Cluster 6441 (*Almagest* p. 373, star #21).

47 The fifth is [17] the nebulous one which is in the eye of the Archer, and it is in Sagittarius 25° 58', and its latitude in the north, 5° 40'.[254]

48 And two are comparable to them:

49 One of them is [18] in the tip of the arrows of the Archer, and it is in 16° 28' Sagittarius, and its latitude northern, 2° 50'.[255]

50 The other is [19] in the right knee of the Hen, in Aquarius 28° 58',[256] and its latitude northern, 63° 45'.[257]

51 And these degrees and minutes which these fixed and nebulous stars are in by latitude, are their positions in the year 1150 of Alexander the Two-Horned:[258] and every 100 years on top of what we mentioned, adds 1° on top of these positions [so that] you correct their positions in that time, as opposed to [using] rings or other instruments. **52** But as for their latitudes and directions towards the north or south, they always [remain] in one state. **53** (And as for the six planets Saturn, Jupiter, Mars, Venus, Mercury, and the Moon, their latitudes change in distance, while the Sun has no latitude.)

54 So you ought to know the latitude of each one of them[259] and their direction,[260] at every time, so that you may know the amounts of which degree of those signs you should rotate[261] at that time, because these 14 [fixed] stars are killers: if one of them connected with one of

---

[254] This is a nebulous double star, ν¹ and ν² Sagittarii (*Almagest* p. 373, star #8). However, the longitude and latitude are pretty far off, no doubt due to scribal errors.
[255] Again, this must be Alnasl (γ Sagittarii), but the degrees are way off (*Almagest* p. 373, star #1).
[256] Abū Ma'shar most likely meant 18° 58'.
[257] This is the nebula or "multiple star system" ω Cygni (*Almagest* p. 351, star #17).
[258] This means that Abū Ma'shar has calculated his star positions for about 820 AD.
[259] Omitting "and the inclination of the Sun."
[260] جهاتها. This probably means being northern or southern in latitude: see the rest of the paragraph.
[261] That is, "direct."

the releasers by direction, and it is running in the direction of the releaser's course (in terms of inclination or latitude), it kills. **55** And that is [even] more confirmed if, when they met, they were matching in inclination and²⁶² latitude—but if the direction of their inclination differed, or their latitude, and one of them is northern and the other southern, there will be a disaster but it will not kill (and especially if the time was far from the years which are like the root).

[Cutting type #2: by positions]

56 As for the second way of cutting, which is by means of the places, there are ten [of them]:

57 The first is the Head.

58 The second is the Tail.

59 The third is the degree which the meeting before the birth of the native was in.

60 The fourth is the degree which the opposition before the birth of the native was in.

61 The fifth is the degree of the west in the root.

62 So, these are five positions [such that] whichever releaser connects with them by direction, they kill. **63** And if the turning from one of the releasers reached them in any of the years, then it indicates a disaster resembling cutting; and if one of the indicators testifies to that along with them, they kill.

64 The sixth is the Ascendant of the root. **65** Now if the Moon was the releaser, and especially by direction she connected with the degree of the Ascendant of the nativity, she kills, because the Ascendant is of the nature of the day and heat, while the Moon is of the nature of the night and cold: so due to the contrariety of each to the other by na-

---

²⁶² Reading for "or."

ture, one of them will cut the other off.²⁶³ **66** And if one of them was the releaser so that the turning from it terminated at the other, then perhaps it will kill, or [only] indicate a powerful disaster.

67 The seventh is if the direction of the releaser ran out due to the completion of the sign, so upon the direction's switching over to the next sign, it kills.

68 The eighth is the two places in which the Moon and Sun were in a square²⁶⁴ before the birth of the native (whether she was increasing in glow or decreasing in it), for they both indicate a powerful disaster upon the direction reaching them, and sometimes they will kill.

69 The ninth is if the direction of one of the releasers shifts from the bound of a fortune to the bound of an infortune.

70 The tenth is if the direction of one of them shifts from the bound of an infortune to the bound of an infortune, for then in that year it will cut—or so long as the distribution is in the bound which it has switched over to (and it will be like that if the management shifted from an infortune to an infortune, by body or ray).²⁶⁵

[Cutting type #3: by distributions]

71 And as for the third way of cutting, which is due to one of the positions by the management of the planets over it, there are five [types]:

72 The first is if the direction of one of the releasers shifts from the bound of a fortune to the bound of an infortune, in the *management* of an infortune, or the management shifts from a fortune to an infortune, in the *bound* of an infortune: for then it indicates cutting in that year.²⁶⁶

---

²⁶³ See also **25** above. Abū Ma'shar is perhaps being clumsy here, because the Ascendant cannot be moved as a promittor—unless he really means to direct its zodiacal degree (a tendency that we see later in the tradition).

²⁶⁴ يربعان. This is probably whichever one was more recent. Earlier, Abū Ma'shar mentioned the conjunction or opposition (**59-60**).

²⁶⁵ That is, it can kill if the distribution either (1) goes from an infortune to infortune, *or* (2) from a partnering infortune to partnering infortune, *if* it is still in the bound of an infortune. See below.

²⁶⁶ See III.2, **98**.

73 The second is if the direction of one of the releasers shifts from the bound of an infortune to the bound of an infortune, in the *management* of a fortune, or the management shifts from an infortune to an infortune, in the *bound* of a fortune: for then it indicates cutting in that year.[267]

74 The third is if the direction of one of the releasers shifts from the bound of an infortune to the bound of an infortune, in the *management* of an infortune, or the *management* shifts from an infortune to an infortune in the *bound* of an infortune: for it indicates cutting in that year.[268]

75 The fourth is if the direction of one of the releasers shifts from the bound of an infortune to the bound of an infortune, *and the management* of the manager over it shifts from an infortune to an infortune, by body or rays: for this is an indicator of cutting in that year, and it is the harshest and most powerful.[269] **76** And this power which belongs to the shifting will be like that if the four came together.[270] **77** (Now as for if one of the releasers is directed so that the direction from it shifts from the *bound* of an infortune to the bound of an infortune, and with regards to the direction of *another* releaser the *management* shifts from a planetary infortune to another infortune,[271] that is below the first one in power; and the strongest shift is if three of them or four of them coincide in a single releaser).

78 And the fifth is if the direction from one of the releasers reached the beginning of the bound in which Mars is: for that kills.

---

[267] See III.2, **99**.
[268] See III.2, **100**.
[269] See III.2, **101**.
[270] That is, if *both* the distributor *and* the releaser were changing from an infortune to an infortune.
[271] That is, if two different releasers each change distributions from one infortune to the other, around the same time: for example, if around the same time the Moon went from an infortune to an infortune in the bounds, and the Sun did the same with the partners.

[Cutting type #4: by the corruption of years]

79 And as for the fourth way of cutting, which comes to be through the corruption of one of the years, one looks at the revolution of the year: for[272] if the distributor was one of the infortunes, and in that bound in the root there was the body of a fortune (or its rays), and in the root that distributor was made unfortunate by one of the infortunes, and the position in which that infortune was in the root was the sign of the terminal point or the Ascendant of the year, or the lords of both were made unfortunate by that infortune in the root, and the infortune returned to its place in the revolution, and the Moon and the bound in which the distribution was in that year were in a bad place (of the houses of the circle), or made unfortunate without the fortunes assisting them, then it indicates cutting in that year.

80 If[273] the distribution belonged to one of the planets (be it a fortune or infortune), and in that bound is the body of a rooted fortune (or its rays) from a weak place, and in it was the rooted body of an infortune (or its rays) from a stake,[274] and the lord of the year and Ascendant of the year and its lord, and the lord of the distribution, and the Moon, all of them (or most of them) were made unfortunate or in a bad condition, then it indicates cutting in that year.

81 If[275] the distribution belonged to an infortune, in the management of the body of a rooted infortune (or its rays), and the distributor, the lord of the year, the Ascendant of the year and its lord, and the Moon are in a bad condition or made unfortunate, it indicates cutting in that year. **82** And if all of these were just as we stated, and at the revolution there was the ray of an infortune in the distribution,[276] then it will not free him from death.

---

[272] For this scenario, cf. III.2, **40**.

[273] Cf. III.2, **41-42**. This is the more severe version alluded to in **42**, where there are influences from two partners, but the infortune is stronger.

[274] This could also be read as "in it was the body of an infortune (or its rooted rays from a stake)." In that case, there could be an infortune in the bound by transit at the revolution.

[275] See III.2, **44-45**.

[276] Probably, into the bound of the distribution.

BOOK IX: MONTHS, DAYS, HOURS, LONGEVITY, REFLECTIONS

83 If[277] the distributor was a fortune or infortune, and in the root and the revolution it was falling away from the view of the fortunes, and in the year the distributor and the Moon are both made unfortunate, and the lord of the year corrupted, in a bad place, it indicates cutting in that year.

84 If[278] Saturn was the distributor, and at the revolution both he and Mars are making that bound unfortunate (in which the distribution is), without the fortunes looking at the position of the distribution, and the lord of the year and the Moon are corrupted, then it indicates cutting in that year.

85 If the direction of the releaser in one of the years reached an infortune without a fortune casting its rays upon that degree, and the lord of the year and the lord of the Ascendant of the year were both made unfortunate by that infortune, then it indicates death[279] in that year.

86 If[280] the distribution belonged to an infortune and that infortune was in a bad condition in both the root and the revolution of the year, and a fortune is not looking at that bound in the root nor in the revolution, and the Moon in the revolution is corrupted, and[281] the Ascendant of the revolution and its lord are in the square of the infortunes (or their opposition), it indicates cutting in that year.

87 If[282] the year terminated at the Ascendant of the root, or the Ascendant of the revolution and the Ascendant of the root were a single sign, and the distributor and the lord of the year were both infortunes, and they were both in the bad positions (in the houses of the circle), and the planets in that year were in a condition relative to the Ascendant of the revolution such that if it was like that relative to the

---

[277] See III.8, **45**.
[278] See III.8, **46**.
[279] **E** reads, "fear."
[280] See III.2, **28**.
[281] Reading with **E** for "or."
[282] See III.8, **47**.

Ascendant of the root of the nativity, it would not indicate upbringing,[283] it indicates despairing of life in that year.

88 If an infortune of the root of the nativity was in [some] degree, and the year was revolved so that that degree is the Ascendant of the year or the degree of the west, and that infortune in that year was corrupting the Ascendant as well as the Moon and the lord of the year, then it indicates cutting in that year.

89 (And along with everything we have said, one should seek information from the lord of the orb of the year—I mean, the planet which the cycle reaches from the lord of the hour of the root—in terms of the suitability of its condition or its corruption in that year, just as one seeks information from the lord of the Ascendant of the revolution.)[284]

90 If[285] the sign of the terminal point and the Ascendant of the year, and the lords of both, and the Moon, were in a bad condition, made unfortunate, then he will come to the brink of death in that year, or he will die.

91 If[286] the lord of the year was in a bad condition in the two times, and it was in a stake of the Ascendant of the year, and a planet not receiving it made it unfortunate from the square or opposition, it indicates powerful misfortunes; now if that infortune was retrograde or going toward burning, it indicates that the detestable thing will reach him from no [particular] direction; and if along with that it was made unfortunate in the root, also in a stake, death will be feared for him in that year.

92 If[287] Jupiter was the lord of the year and assembled with the Sun in the two times (or he was under [the Sun's] rays), and the Sun is stronger than him, and [the Sun] is made unfortunate, death will be feared for him in that year.

---

[283] See Sahl, *Nativities* Ch. 1.8, 1.29-1.30, and *Carmen* I.12.
[284] See Ch. VI.1.
[285] See III.2, **35**.
[286] See II.3, **12-14**.
[287] Cf. II.7, **13-14**.

93 If[288] Mars was the lord of the year and both he and the Moon are in a bad condition in the two times, and they looked at each other from the square in both [times], and Mars is looking down upon her,[289] then death will be feared for him in that year.

94 If[290] the lord of the year was a fortune, and in the revolution there was an infortune in the Ascendant of the revolution, and the other infortune in the setting, [opposite] it, and the Moon in the year is corrupted by one of them (or by another apart from them), death will be feared for him in that year.

95 If[291] the year reached the rooted stake of the earth or stake of the west, and Saturn is in it or looking at it by an aspect of hostility, then death will be feared for him in that year.

96 And[292] if the *fardār* belonged to Mercury, and Saturn distributed with him for 1 year, 10 months, 8 days, then death will be feared for him in that year, as well as [those] months and days.

97 And[293] if the *fardār* belonged to Mercury and the Moon distributed with him for the like [amount] that Saturn did, then death will be feared for him in that time as well.

98 If[294] the *fardār* belonged to Mars, and the Sun distributed in the *fardār* for 1 year, then death will be feared for him in that year; and if Saturn distributed in the *fardār* of Mars for 1 year, death will be feared for him in that year <as well>.

99 If[295] the Moon in the root of the nativity was in the Ascendant of the nativity, and then in the revolution of one of the years Saturn reached the place of the Moon,[296] then death will be feared for him in that year.

---

[288] Cf. II.11, **36**.
[289] That is, overcoming her from the superior square.
[290] See II.23, **49** and Da. 9.
[291] See II.23, **64**.
[292] See IV.3, **6-7**.
[293] See IV.3, **4-5**.
[294] Cf. IV.7, **4-5** and **12-13**.
[295] Cf. V.2, **13** and **16**.
[296] This is by transit, here and below.

100 If[297] the Sun in the root was in some position, and Jupiter reached his place and assembled with him, and he is burned by him, and Jupiter had testimony in the Ascendant of the root or in the Ascendant of the revolution, or in the sign of the terminal point, then death will be feared for him until Jupiter goes past burning, or the Sun goes past the degree of the terminal point or the Ascendant of the revolution.

101 If[298] in the revolution Jupiter reached the place of Venus in the root, and Venus had testimony in the root or in the revolution, and one of the infortunes made her unfortunate in the revolution, then death will be feared for him in that year.

102 If[299] Mars was the lord of the year and assembled with the Sun in the revolution of the year, and the revolution in that year was by day, then death will be feared for him in that year.

103 If[300] Mars in the revolution of the year reached the place of Venus in the root, and Venus had testimony in the root or in the revolution, and she is made unfortunate, then death will be feared for him in that year.

104 If[301] Mars in the revolution of the year reached the place of Mercury in the root, and Mercury had testimony in the year, and he was made unfortunate by Mars, then death will be feared for him in that year.

105 If[302] the Sun had testimony in the revolution and was in Pisces,[303] made unfortunate, then death will be feared for him in the year.

106 If[304] the Moon in the revolution of the year reached the place of [the natal] Saturn, and the Moon had testimony in that year, and was made unfortunate, then death will be feared for him in that year.

---

[297] See V.3, **4**.
[298] See V.3, **7-8**.
[299] Cf. II.11, **15** and **19**.
[300] See V.4, **16**.
[301] See V.4, **17-18**.
[302] Cf. V.5, **15-16**.
[303] Pisces is in the eighth sign from Leo (the domicile of the Sun), so this is an example of Abū Ma'shar's derived-house theory of transits.

107 If[305] Mercury in the revolution of the year reached the place of [the natal] Mars, and Mercury had testimony in the year, and he is corrupted by Mars in the revolution, then death will be feared for him in that year.

108 If[306] the year reached the sign in which Saturn was in the root, and that sign was the Ascendant of the year, and Saturn and[307] Mars looked at that place in the revolution with an aspect of hostility without the aspect of the fortunes to that position, then death will be feared for him in that year.

109 If[308] in the revolution of the year, [1] the lord of the Ascendant of the root, and [2] the lord of the sign of the terminal point, and [3] the lord of the revolution of the year, were connecting—one of them—with the lord of the fourth from its own place, and the lord of the fourth was making it unfortunate, then death will be feared for him in that year. **110** If the lord of one of these three positions was connecting in the revolution of the year with the lord of its own eighth and it was corrupted, made unfortunate by the lord of its eighth, death will be feared for him in that year. **111** And if the lord of its own eighth connected with one of them and the lord of its eighth was making it unfortunate, the indication is more firm.

112 And in what we have stated about the fourth way of cutting which comes to be by the corruption of the indicators of the year, when we have found some of its indicators indicating cutting, and some of them indicating [only] the fear of death, then as for the indication of the cutters among them, they are clear [and] not in doubt; but as for the indication of a year to be feared, the indication of each one of them is individually weak. **113** So if two or more of them occurred in the revolution of years, there will be cutting in it; and the lord of the *fardār* is powerful in indication in this topic.

---

[304] Cf. V.8, **1-2**.
[305] See V.7, 7.
[306] Cf. VI.4, **3** and **8**.
[307] **B** reads "or."
[308] For this paragraph, see VI.6, **25-26**.

114 And in this book of ours, mention is made in many places of the conditions of the planets one seeks information from in the revolution, concerning what is detestable and powerful corruption in that year, [and] those are explained in their own place.[309] **115** But we have omitted mention of them in this chapter, because in their conditions they do not have a power indicating death as do the indication of these indicators which we have mentioned—but if there was agreement in the indication of several of them for detestable things in the revolution of one of the years, there will be cutting.

116 And sometimes the generality of the planets in the revolution of one of the years will evidently be of a suitable condition, except that one of the 14 cutters[310] in that year will mix with the degree of one of the two Ascendants (I mean, the Ascendant of the root and the Ascendant of the revolution), or with the degree of the sign of the terminal point, or it will be with their lords or with the Moon—so if it was like that at the completion of the years which are like the root (or close to it by a little increase or decrease), there will be cutting in that year.

117 Now if the cutter was one of the bounds or the completion of the sign and its shifting to the next sign,[311] and the condition of the lord of that bound or the lord of the sign into which the management shifts in that year was like what we stated, then it indicates cutting in that year.

118 Now as for the month and day of that year in which the cutting will happen, that is known from the indicators of the months and days, in the manner that we stated in what preceded.[312]

---

[309] See for example Chs. II.3 and III.8.
[310] This must be the 14 fixed stars and nebulae above (**32-55**).
[311] See **67, 69-70**, and **71-78**.
[312] See the many references in IX.2 and IX.5, and in my discussion in the Introduction.

[Abū Ma'shar's reflections on the methods]

119 And due to my desire to explain to you which of them is truthful [and] preferred for wisdom, I believe I will repeat for you some of what preceded of my statement, because there will be [some] assurance in that.

120 So[313] I say that if the indicators of the lifespan are strong, and then the year or the turning from one of the releasers reaches one of the cutters in one of the years, or the harming infortunes govern over [the year], and that time is *not* among the years of the native's lifespan which are close to the completion of the years which are like the foundation [of the lifespan], the year will be a disaster that can be gotten over. **121** But if that was upon their completion or after he had passed [those years], then [even] a small corruption of the year will cut off life for him. **122** And if the indicators of the lifespan were weak, but then the corrupting infortunes governed over one of the years which was less than the completion of the years which are like the foundation [of the lifespan], and their condition was like what we stated in the preceding, there will be cutting in that year.

123 And there is great difficulty and much confusion in deriving the years of the indicator of the lifespan which is like the root: and generally for those who are called to this knowledge, those who look into it are wandering around in the dark;[314] but a statement of the truth of that, and its correctness, is found in the book which we worked on concerning nativities.[315]

124 Now as for knowing the year in which there will be cutting for the father, mother, women, children, or those who are like them, one looks at the indicator of each one of them in the root, based on how

---

[313] See the longer version in **10-13** above, and Māshā'allāh's version in Sahl, *Nativities* Ch. 1.23, **61-63**.

[314] Omitting here a confusing clause that reads somewhat differently in all MSS, that simply emphasizes how wrong other astrologers are.

[315] This may refer to Book V of his *On the Judgments of Nativities* (Oxford Bodleian, Hunt. 546).

many years of a lifespan are indicated for them,³¹⁶ and you assign those years to that man just like a root; then, you do it for each one of those indicators, by directing to the cutters, degree by degree, and by turning in the signs, sign by sign, just as we stated for the three ways.³¹⁷ **125** And if the indicator corresponded to one of them in corruption in one of the years (in the manner which we described of the corruption of the indicator of the owner of the revolution in the fourth way),³¹⁸ the man whose indicator had that corrupting condition will have a cutting disaster in that year.

126 And in this book of ours we have already stated in many places (concerning the indication of the conditions of the planets), things which one should consult for information on the year in which there was death, [for] each one of them.

127 But as for the Indians, they derive the years which are like the root for the lifespan of a man in a different way than what the people of other regions do: for they direct the ninth-parts from the degree³¹⁹ of the Ascendant of the root of the nativity in the way we stated in what preceded,³²⁰ and they grant the distribution to the ninth-part which the directing from the Ascendant reaches, and they make its lord be the distributor, and they make the lord of the first ninth-part belonging to the sign of the terminal point be the lord of the year, and they derive the Ascendant of the revolution of the year. **128** Then they look: for if the distribution, the distributor, the lord of the year (and the first lord of the ninth-part), and the Ascendant of the year, and the Moon, are [all] corrupted, and that time is close to the years whose amount is like the root, they say there is cutting in it; and God is more knowledgeable.

---

³¹⁶ There are methods for doing this for parents (such as Sahl, *Nativities* Ch. 4.12). Sahl's Ch. 4.13 mentions methods for other people.
³¹⁷ That is, the first three ways of cutting earlier in this chapter.
³¹⁸ The fourth way of cutting above, from **79-118**.
³¹⁹ **E** reads, "face."
³²⁰ Perhaps referring to III.8-III.9.

Chapter IX.9: On the special indicators in the indication of the conditions of the year

1 There are eight special indicators to look at in the revolution of the years of nativities:[321]

2 The first is the lord of the year.

3 The second is the distributor from the Ascendant.

4 The third is the distributor from the [longevity] releaser.

5 The fourth is the partner to them both,[322] by body and rays.

6 The fifth is the lord of the *fardār*.

7 The sixth is the lord of the orb.

8 The seventh is the one accepting the connection of the Moon, or the lord of her house.[323]

9 The eighth is the first lord of the Ascendant of the revolution,[324] for the first one is stronger in indication.

10 Now if these eight indicators would combine together in a single planet, then it alone would be the governor of the indication for the condition of the year; and if one of them had [only] some of the testimonies, it will be more primary than the others, and the rest of them will have a partnership with it in the indication.

11 So if the indicators indicated his survival, and in the root and the revolution the governor over the year was in a suitable condition in its essence (and that is if the three superior ones were easternizing from

---

[321] Note that this is the same list which was said to indicate the soul, in Ch. II.2, **10-18**.
[322] That is, of the two distributors in **3** and **4**.
[323] That is, if she is empty in course, use the lord of her sign.
[324] That is, the lord of the Ascendant of the *annual* revolution, not the monthly revolutions.

the Sun, in their *halb*, not retrograde, and not made unfortunate,[325] and the inferior ones westernizing from him, in the same condition as well, and they are in their *halb*), then it indicates strength in the soul, thought, cleverness, and excellence in judgment, and the goodness of [his] character. **12** And if it was in a suitable condition in terms of its sign (and that is if the sign harmonized with it by nature, or it had testimony in it), then it indicates the strength of the body, and a suitable condition in it. **13** And if it was in a suitable condition in terms of the rotation of the circle (and that is if it was in a stake or in what follows a stake) as well as in its sign, then it indicates a suitability of condition in rank, power, and class.

14 And when a planet has rulership of the year, the distribution, the *fardār*, or the rest of what we have mentioned in terms of an indication, and in the revolution of the year it returns to its rooted position, it increases in its strength.

15 And after that, you should look into the condition of each planet according to the combinations which we have mentioned in this book of ours, in Book after Book, and Chapter after Chapter.

16 And let their positions in the houses be examined, because sometimes that planet, in its transit and position in the houses of the circle in the root and in the revolution, will indicate something similar to what other planets indicate by nature. **17** Because the one which indicates assets by nature, is the second sign, its lord, and the rest of its indicators; and the one which indicates siblings by nature is the third sign, its lord, and the rest of its indicators, and likewise the rest of the signs. **18** But as for the one which is indicative by its position and by its transit *in* the houses of the circle, that is if a planet in the root of the nativity is *in* the second from the Ascendant, but in the revolution it came to be *in* [1] the fifth from the Ascendant of the root, [2] the tenth from the terminal point, and [3] the ninth from the Ascendant of the revolution of the year. **19** So, one needs to mix its place with these positions, one to the other: and it is that you look at that planet, and if it was a fortune or made fortunate, assets will go *from* him *to* the

---

[325] **P** reads that they are not made unfortunate *by the Sun*.

children and the Sultan, and he will spend assets for reasons of travel, and travelers, and invisible things, and men of godliness, and he will delight in that.

20 But if that planet was an infortune or made unfortunate, it indicates that the children will steal money from him, and he will spend money because of the Sultan, travel, and travelers, and he will be distressed by that.

21 And if the planet in the root of the nativity was in the ninth, and in the revolution it

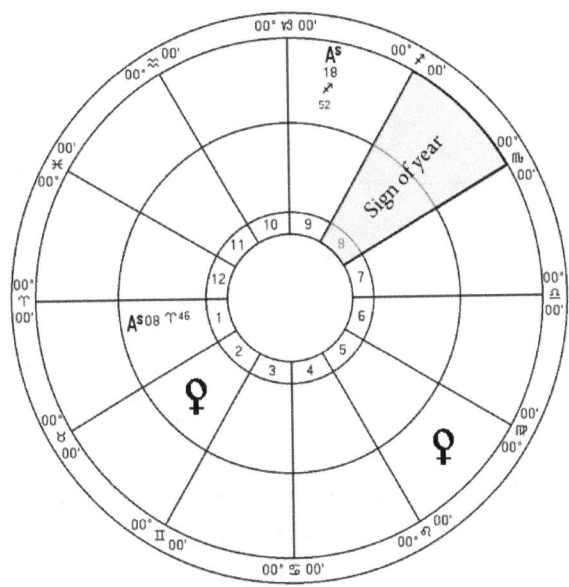

Figure 138: Combining house meanings (IX.9, 16-20)

came to be in [1] the fifth from the Ascendant of the root, and [2] the tenth from the terminal point, and [3] the second from the Ascendant of the revolution of the year <and if it is a fortune or made fortunate>,[326] it indicates that the child will travel, and will gain authority or benefits in his travel, and assets or gifts will pass to the owner of the revolution from his children because of the travel, or from an absent person, and he and his children will delight in that. **22** But if the planet was an infortune or made unfortunate, it indicates distress and something detestable in relation to these. **23** (And if some of them were fortunes and some infortunes, it indicates good from the fortunes, and evil from the infortunes.)[327]

---

[326] Adding on the model of **19**.
[327] Abū Ma'shar is probably thinking of cases where there are multiple planets in the same house.

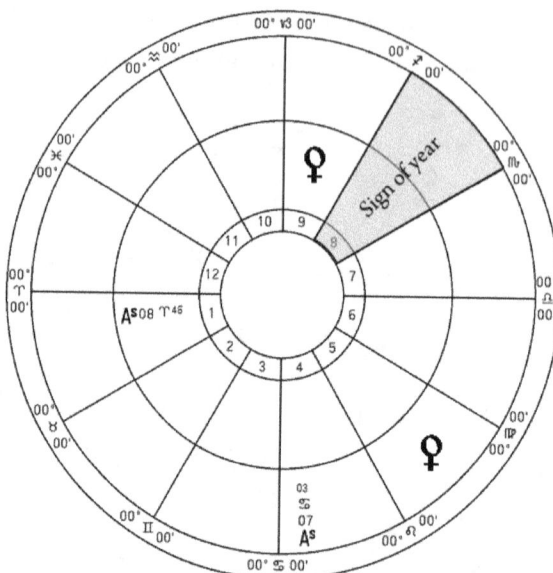

Figure 139: Combining house meanings (IX.9, 21-23)

24 And you should look likewise into the condition of each one of the indicators individually; and in this book of ours we have already stated many different things about the indication of every planet in each time and each condition. **25** And indeed, [if you do this] you will know which of those things will come to the man, from the nature of the planet, and its condition in itself, and its position in its sign, and in the houses of the circle, and the positions of those looking at it,[328] and their conditions.

The book is ended.

---

[328] Lit. "them."

Appendix A: Calculating Distributions

In this Appendix I will show you how to calculate distributions of the Ascendant and Midheaven quickly, using the animation function of your astrology computer program. You can also use a table of ascensional times or the free software from Morinus.com. I'll also mention the settings to use in Janus.

Important: the simple animation function here *only* works if you are distributing the Ascendant or Midheaven. If you are distributing anything else—a Lot, planet, or something else—you can use animation but the procedure is more complicated. I have an audio download lecture on this topic at bendykes.com, and it's fully covered in my traditional natal astrology course.

The celestial sphere rotates 1° for every 4 minutes of clock time.[1] Since 1° on the celestial equator is also normally equivalent to 1 year, there is a regular relationship between how much time passes and how old the native will be at any distribution or direction. We only need to multiply an age by 4, or divide minutes by 4, and animate the chart. But how fast or slow the Ascendant moves in the zodiac, depends on the birth latitude: that's why we need the computer to do those calculations. We can ask two questions:

Question	Answer
What age will I be at distribution X?	• Animate to that distribution. • Divide the number of *minutes* elapsed, by 4.
What distribution will I be in at age X?	• Multiply age by 4. • Add that many minutes to the birth time. • Animate to that time.

---

[1] It is actually 3m 59.34s, which makes no difference to our purposes here.

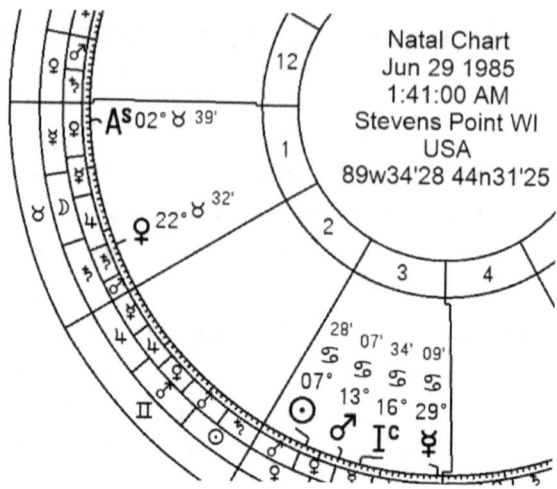

Let's take this nativity as an example:

What age will the native be at the distribution of Mars-Mercury, at 29° 09' Taurus?

- Animate the chart until the Ascendant is on 29° 09' Taurus. This happens at 2:52:54 AM, which means 1h 11m 54s have elapsed, or 71.9 minutes.
- Divide 71.9 by 4: **Age 17.97**.

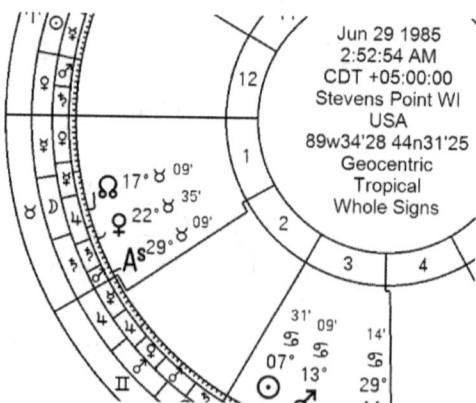

Figure 140: Distribution of Mars-Mercury, Age 17.97

What distribution will the native be in, at age 42?
- Multiply 42 x 4: 168.
- Add 168m (or 2h 48m) to the birth time: 4:29 AM.
- Animate the chart to 4:29 AM.
- The Ascendant is in the bounds of Saturn in Gemini. In this nativity Jupiter (at 16° 02' Aquarius, not visible here) was the latest partner by trine at 16° 02' Gemini: so the full distribution is Saturn-Jupiter.

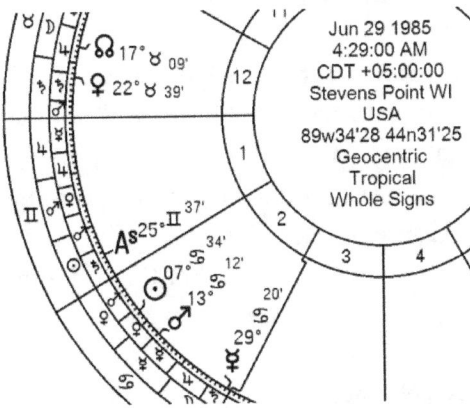

Figure 141: Distribution of Saturn-Jupiter, Age 42

You can do the same thing with the degree of the Midheaven for actions, profession, and life projects: animate the MC to the distribution you want and divide the elapsed minutes by 4 to get the age; and multiply the age by 4 and add those minutes to the birth time, to see where the MC lands at that age. This must be done separately from the Ascendant, because they move at different rates through the signs.

To get distributions in the **Janus astrology program**, open the chart and go to: **Predictive > Distributions**. Do the following:

- Settings > Calculation Options: choose Egyptian bounds or terms, and Zero Latitude.

- Arc to Time Conversion menu: for natal distributions, click "Deg for a year"; for SR distributions, click "59° 08' for a day."
- Choose your age range.
- Timing should be "One Degree."
- Choose the point to distribute. This will almost always be the Ascendant, Midheaven, a luminary, or the Lot of Fortune. You can also define custom points.
- The Calculate button will give you a full set of distributions, ascensional times, and other things.

If you use the **free Morinus.com software**, make these changes:
- Options > Appearance I. Click "Terms" and decide whether you want color or black and white.
- Options > Minor Dignities > Terms. Choose "Egyptian."
- Options > Housesystems > Whole Sign
- Options > Primary Directions. Starting from the top left and working downwards, choose:
  - Placidus (semiarc).
  - Zodiacal, Neither.
  - Aspects of promissors to significators.
  - Promissors: choose the 7 traditional planets and the terms. You could choose fixed stars and then select from the list, but remember that these are not proper partners.
  - Middle: choose the conjunction and classical aspects.
  - Significators: choose the Ascendant ("Asc") or some other releaser/significator, but but only do one at a time.
- Options > Primary Keys. Choose "Static" and "Ptolemy."
- To calculate the distributions, go to Tables > Primary Directions. Choose the age range, "Direct," and the resulting table will give you both the bounds (identifying the sign and distributor) and the partners in the Promissor ("Prom") column, the natives age in the Arc column, and the date when the distribution begins. (Note that Morinus only allows degrees and minutes for birthplace calculation, so the dates might differ from Janus by a few days, especially over the course of life.)

Appendix B: Table of Ascensional Times

This updated table was calculated by Microsoft Excel based on equations in Peter Duffett-Smith's *Practical Astronomy with Your Calculator* (Cambridge University Press, 3rd edition 1988). It uses an obliquity of the ecliptic value of 23° 26' (mid-late 20th Cent.).

Ascensional times (AT) are given by sign and degrees, in the northern (N) and southern (S) hemispheres. They can be used for the maturation of planets in the signs, or for calculating distributions of the Ascendant (both natally and in the SR). For example:

- Let a native be born in the northern hemisphere, at 37° N. The AT of both Cancer and Sagittarius is 35.19568. Dividing this by 30° shows that each degree is worth 1.17319 AT. If the Ascendant was in Cancer, one could direct it at the rate of 1.17319 years or days per degree, until one reaches Leo and discovers the new rate.

- Let a native be born in the southern hemisphere, at 42° S. The AT of both Aries and Pisces is 38.43781. Dividing this by 30° shows that each degree is worth 1.28126 AT. If the Ascendant was in Aries, one could direct it at the rate of 1.28126 years or days per degree, until one reaches Taurus and discovers the new rate.

The AT for individual degrees is approximate, because the heavens are curved: in reality the degrees at one end of a sign will be slightly different from those at the other end. There will be some distortion especially around the end of Sagittarius and the end of Gemini, where the signs change ascension.

N:	♈ – ♓ ♍ – ♎		♉ – ♒ ♌ – ♏		♊ – ♑ ♋ – ♐		♋ – ♐ ♊ – ♑		♌ – ♏ ♉ – ♒		♍ – ♎ ♈ – ♓	
S:		Yrs/1°		Yrs/1°		Yrs/1°		Yrs/1°		Yrs/1°		Yrs/1°
0°	27.91162	0.93039	29.90829	0.99694	32.18009	1.07267	32.18009	1.07267	29.90829	0.99694	27.91162	0.93039
5°	26.89452	0.89648	29.08617	0.96954	31.84612	1.06154	32.51407	1.08380	30.73040	1.02435	28.92872	0.96429
10°	25.86140	0.86205	28.24975	0.94166	31.50572	1.05019	32.85447	1.09515	31.56682	1.05223	29.96183	0.99873
15°	24.79521	0.82651	27.38365	0.91279	31.15193	1.03840	33.20826	1.10694	32.43293	1.08110	31.02803	1.03427
20°	23.67666	0.78922	26.47016	0.88234	30.77655	1.02588	33.58364	1.11945	33.34642	1.11155	32.14658	1.07155
21°	23.44473	0.78149	26.27996	0.87600	30.69802	1.02327	33.66216	1.12207	33.53662	1.11789	32.37851	1.07928
22°	23.20959	0.77365	26.08681	0.86956	30.61814	1.02060	33.74205	1.12473	33.72976	1.12433	32.61365	1.08712
23°	22.97103	0.76570	25.89051	0.86302	30.53679	1.01789	33.82340	1.12745	33.92606	1.13087	32.85220	1.09507
24°	22.72883	0.75763	25.69084	0.85636	30.45386	1.01513	33.90632	1.13021	34.12573	1.13752	33.09441	1.10315
25°	22.48273	0.74942	25.48756	0.84959	30.36925	1.01231	33.99094	1.13303	34.32902	1.14430	33.34050	1.11135
26°	22.23250	0.74108	25.28041	0.84268	30.28282	1.00943	34.07737	1.13591	34.53616	1.15121	33.59074	1.11969
27°	21.97785	0.73260	25.06914	0.83564	30.19444	1.00648	34.16575	1.13886	34.74744	1.15825	33.84539	1.12818
28°	21.71851	0.72395	24.85345	0.82845	30.10397	1.00347	34.25622	1.14187	34.96312	1.16544	34.10472	1.13682
29°	21.45419	0.71514	24.63305	0.82110	30.01124	1.00037	34.34895	1.14496	35.18353	1.17278	34.36905	1.14564
30°	21.18455	0.70615	24.40760	0.81359	29.91610	0.99720	34.44409	1.14814	35.40897	1.18030	34.63868	1.15462
31°	20.90927	0.69698	24.17676	0.80589	29.81835	0.99394	34.54184	1.15139	35.63981	1.18799	34.91396	1.16380
32°	20.62799	0.68760	23.94015	0.79800	29.71779	0.99059	34.64240	1.15475	35.87643	1.19588	35.19524	1.17317
33°	20.34032	0.67801	23.69736	0.78991	29.61421	0.98714	34.74597	1.15820	36.11921	1.20397	35.48291	1.18276
34°	20.04586	0.66820	23.44795	0.78160	29.50737	0.98358	34.85281	1.16176	36.36862	1.21229	35.77738	1.19258
35°	19.74416	0.65814	23.19145	0.77305	29.39701	0.97990	34.96318	1.16544	36.62512	1.22084	36.07907	1.20264
36°	19.43477	0.64783	22.92733	0.76424	29.28283	0.97609	35.07736	1.16925	36.88924	1.22964	36.38847	1.21295
37°	19.11716	0.63724	22.65503	0.75517	29.16451	0.97215	35.19568	1.17319	37.16154	1.23872	36.70608	1.22354
38°	18.79080	0.62636	22.37394	0.74580	29.04170	0.96806	35.31849	1.17728	37.44264	1.24809	37.03243	1.23441

APPENDIX B: TABLE OF ASCENSIONAL TIMES

39°	18.45511	0.61517	22.08336	0.73611	28.91400	0.96380	35.44619	1.18154	37.73321	1.25777	37.36813	1.24560
40°	18.10945	0.60365	21.78257	0.72609	28.78096	0.95937	35.57922	1.18597	38.03400	1.26780	37.71379	1.25713
41°	17.75314	0.59177	21.47073	0.71569	28.64210	0.95474	35.71809	1.19060	38.34584	1.27819	38.07010	1.26900
42°	17.38543	0.57951	21.14695	0.70490	28.49684	0.94989	35.86335	1.19544	38.66962	1.28899	38.43781	1.28126
43°	17.00551	0.56685	20.81021	0.69367	28.34456	0.94482	36.01563	1.20052	39.00636	1.30021	38.81772	1.29392
44°	16.61252	0.55375	20.45939	0.68198	28.18451	0.93948	36.17568	1.20586	39.35718	1.31191	39.21072	1.30702
45°	16.20548	0.54018	20.09324	0.66977	28.01588	0.93386	36.34431	1.21148	39.72333	1.32411	39.61776	1.32059
46°	15.78334	0.52611	19.71035	0.65701	27.83771	0.92792	36.52248	1.21742	40.10622	1.33687	40.03989	1.33466
47°	15.34496	0.51150	19.30913	0.64364	27.64887	0.92163	36.71132	1.22371	40.50744	1.35025	40.47828	1.34928
48°	14.88906	0.49630	18.88779	0.62959	27.44809	0.91494	36.91210	1.23040	40.92878	1.36429	40.93418	1.36447
49°	14.41424	0.48047	18.44429	0.61481	27.23381	0.90779	37.12637	1.23755	41.37229	1.37908	41.40899	1.38030
50°	13.91896	0.46397	17.97627	0.59921	27.00425	0.90014	37.35594	1.24520	41.84031	1.39468	41.90428	1.39681
51°	13.40150	0.44672	17.48105	0.58270	26.75721	0.89191	37.60297	1.25343	42.33553	1.41118	42.42174	1.41406
52°	12.85994	0.42866	16.95549	0.56518	26.49008	0.88300	37.87011	1.26234	42.86108	1.42870	42.96330	1.43211
53°	12.29215	0.40974	16.39597	0.54653	26.19962	0.87332	38.16057	1.27202	43.42061	1.44735	43.53109	1.45104
54°	11.69574	0.38986	15.79818	0.52661	25.88184	0.86273	38.47835	1.28261	44.01840	1.46728	44.12750	1.47092
55°	11.06802	0.36893	15.15703	0.50523	25.53169	0.85106	38.82849	1.29428	44.65954	1.48865	44.75522	1.49184
56°	10.40595	0.34687	14.46644	0.48221	25.14271	0.83809	39.21748	1.30725	45.35013	1.51167	45.41729	1.51391
57°	9.70609	0.32354	13.71902	0.45730	24.70643	0.82355	39.65376	1.32179	46.09756	1.53659	46.11715	1.53724
58°	8.96449	0.29882	12.90569	0.43019	24.21150	0.80705	40.14869	1.33829	46.91089	1.56370	46.85874	1.56196
59°	8.17667	0.27256	12.01517	0.40051	23.64228	0.78808	40.71790	1.35726	47.80140	1.59338	47.64656	1.58822
60°	7.33745	0.24458	11.03320	0.36777	22.97641	0.76588	41.38378	1.37946	48.78377	1.62611	48.48579	1.61619
61°	6.44080	0.21469	9.94132	0.33138	22.18049	0.73935	42.17970	1.40599	49.87525	1.66251	49.38244	1.64608
62°	5.47973	0.18266	8.71516	0.29051	21.20170	0.70672	43.15849	1.43862	51.10142	1.70338	50.34350	1.67812
63°	4.44602	0.14820	7.32152	0.24405	19.94967	0.66499	44.41052	1.48035	52.49505	1.74983	51.37722	1.71257
64°	3.32989	0.11100	5.71355	0.19045	18.25095	0.60837	46.10924	1.53697	54.10303	1.80343	52.49334	1.74978
65°	2.11972	0.07066	3.82180	0.12739	15.70264	0.52342	48.65755	1.62192	55.99478	1.86649	53.70352	1.79012
66°	0.80141	0.02671	1.53651	0.05122	10.88222	0.36274	53.47797	1.78260	58.28006	1.94267	55.02182	1.83406

Glossary

This Glossary contains terms from all branches of traditional astrology, from all of my translations. Most entries also provide the Greek, Latin, and Arabic source words. Boldface terms in the definitions and descriptions indicate that the Glossary also contains that word.

- **Absent from** (Ar. عن غائب). See **Aversion**.
- **Accident** (Lat. *accidens*, Ar. حادث, عرض). An event which "befalls" or "happens" to someone, though not necessarily something bad.
- **Adding in course.** See **Course**.
- **Advancement, advancing** (إقبال \ مقبل; Lat. *accedens*). Refers to being (1) dynamically **angular** or **succeedent**, i.e. moving by **primary motion** toward an **axial** degree. (But occasionally might refer to angular or succeedent **whole signs**). Its two antonyms are **retreat/retreating**, and **withdrawal/withdrawing**. It can also refer to (2) the **eastern quadrants**.
- **Advantageous places.** One of two schemes of **houses** which indicate affairs/planets which are more busy or good in the context of the chart. The seven-place scheme according to Timaeus and reported in *Carmen* includes only certain signs which **look at** the **Ascendant** by **whole-sign**, and suggests that these places are advantageous for the *native* because they look at the Ascendant. The eight-place scheme according to Nechepso lists all of the **angular** and **succeedent** places, suggesting places which are stimulating and advantageous for a planet *in itself*.
- **Ages of Man** (Ar. أسنان الإنسان). Ptolemy's division of a typical human life span into periods ruled by planets as **time lords**.
- **Agreeing signs.** Groups of signs which share some kind of harmonious quality. Sometimes planets are said to agree with one another, although this meaning must be taken in context.
- **Alcochoden.** Latin transliteration for *kadkhudhāh*, the **House-master**.
- **Alien** (Lat. *alienus*, Ar. غريب). Lit., "a stranger, foreigner." When a planet is not in one of its five **dignities**. In later astrology in English this is often called "peregrine," from Lat. *peregrinus* ("foreigner, pilgrim").
- **Almuten.** A Latin transliteration for Ar. *mubtazz*: see **Victor**.
- **Angles, succeedents, cadents.** A division of houses into three groups which show how powerfully and directly a planet acts. The angles are the 1st, 10th, 7th and 4th; the succeedents are the 2nd, 11th, 8th and 5th; the cadents

are the 12th, 9th, 6th and 3rd. But the exact regions in question will depend upon whether and how one uses **whole-sign** and **quadrant houses**, especially since traditional texts refer to an angle or pivot (Gr. *kentron*, Ar. وتد) as either (1) equivalent to the **whole-sign** angles from the **Ascendant**, or (2) the **axial degrees** of the **Ascendant-Midheaven** themselves, or (3) **quadrant houses** (and their associated strengths) as measured from the degrees of the axes.

- **Antiscia** (sing. *antiscion*), Greek for "throwing shadows." Refers to a degree mirrored across an axis drawn from 0° Capricorn to 0° Cancer. For example, 10° Cancer has 20° Gemini as its antiscion.
- **Apogee of eccentric/deferent** (Ar. أوج). The point on a planet's **deferent circle** that is farthest away from the earth; as seen from earth, it points to some degree of the zodiac.
- **Applying, application** (Lat. *applicatio*). When a planet is in a state of **connection**, moving so as to make the connection exact. Planets **assembled** together or **looked at** by sign, but not yet connecting by the relevant degrees, are only "wanting" to be connected.
- **Apsides, apsidal line.** In geocentric astronomy, the line passing through the center of the earth, which points at one end to the **apogee** of a planet's **deferent**, and at the other end to its **perigee**.
- **Arisings** (Lat. *orientia*). See **Ascensions**.
- **Ascendant.** Usually the entire rising sign, but often specified as the exact degree on the horizon (the **axial degree**). In **quadrant houses**, a space following the exact rising degree up to the cusp of the 2nd house.
- **Ascensions** (Ar. مطالع, Lat. *ascensiones*). Degrees on the celestial **equator**, measured in terms of how many degrees pass the **meridian** as an entire sign or **bound** (or other spans of zodiacal degrees) passes across the horizon. They are often used in the predictive technique of ascensional times, sometimes as an approximation of primary **directions**.
- **Aspect** (Lat. *aspectus*, Ar. نظر). For the verb, see **look at**. As a noun, a **configuration** between two things (such as two planets or a planet and a sign): see **sextile**, **trine**, **square**, and **opposition**. See also **Connection** and **Assembly**
- **Assembly** (Lat. *conventus*, Ar. مقارنة). When two or more planets are in the same sign, and more intensely if within 15°. (It is occasionally used in Arabic to indicate the conjunction of the Sun and Moon at the New Moon, but the more common word for that is **meeting**).

- **Aversion.** Being in the second, sixth, eighth, or twelfth sign from a place, as a planet in Gemini is in the twelfth from, and therefore in aversion to, Cancer. Such places are not **configured** and so cannot **look at** or see each other by the classical scheme of **aspects**.
- **Axial degree, axis.** The degree of the **zodiac** which the horizon or **meridian**: the **Ascendant, Midheaven, Descendant,** and *Imum Caeli/IC.*
- **Ayanamsha.** In sidereal astrology, a point or degree which acts as the beginning of the zodiac. The **equinoctial point** acts as the ayanamsha in the tropical **zodiac**.
- *Azamene.* Equivalent to **Chronic illness.**
- **Bad ones.** See Fortune/Infortune.
- **Barring.** See **Blocking.**
- **Bearing** (Lat. *habitudo*). Hugo's term for any of the many possible planetary conditions and relationships.
- **Benefic:** see **Fortune/Infortune.**
- **Benevolent.** See **Fortune/Infortune.**
- **Besieging** (Lat. *obsido*). Equivalent to **Enclosure.**
- **Bicorporeal signs.** Equivalent to "common" signs. See **Quadruplicity.**
- **Blocking** (Lat. *prohibitio*, Ar. منع), sometimes called "prohibition." When a planet blocks another planet from completing a **connection,** either through its own body or **ray.** This may happen in several ways: see Sahl's *Introduction* Ch. 3, **31-48.**
- **Body** (Lat. *corpus*, Ar. جرم). Normally, a planet considered by itself, in the degree where it is located. But in **aspect** theory, also equivalent to an **orb.**
- **Bodyguarding.** See **Spear-bearing.**
- **Bound, bounds** (Gr. *horion*, Lat. *terminus*, Ar. حدّ). Unequal divisions of the zodiac in each sign, each bound being ruled by one of the five non-**luminaries.** Sometimes called "terms," they are one of the five classical **dignities.**
- **Bright, smoky, empty, dark degrees.** Certain degrees of the zodiac said to affect how conspicuous or obscure the significations of planets or the Ascendant are.
- **Burned up, burning** (Lat. *combustus, combustio*; Ar. محترق, احتراق). Normally, when a planet is between about 1° and 7.5° away from the Sun. See also **In the heart.**
- **Burnt path** (Lat. *via combusta*). A span of degrees in Libra and Scorpio in which a planet (especially the Moon) is considered to be harmed or less

able to effect its significations. Some astrologers identify it as between 15° Libra and 15° Scorpio; others between the exact degree of the **fall** of the Sun in 19° Libra and the exact degree of the fall of the Moon in 3° Scorpio.
- *Bust*. Certain hours measured from the New Moon, in which it is considered favorable or unfavorable to undertake an action or perform an **election**.
- **Busy places**. Equivalent to the **Advantageous places**.
- **Cadent** (Lat. *cadens*, "falling"; Ar. ساقط). Typically, when a planet is one of the following **whole sign** or **quadrant houses** (called "cadent/falling" from the **angles**): 3rd, 6th, 9th, 12th. But see also **falling away from**, which is equivalent to **Aversion**.
- **Cardinal**. Equivalent to "movable" or "convertible" signs. See **Quadruplicity**.
- **Cardine**. Equivalent to **Angle**.
- **Cazimi**: see **In the heart**.
- **Centers of the Moon**. Also called the "posts" or "foundations" of the Moon. Angular distances between the Sun and Moon throughout the lunar month, indicating possible times of weather changes and rain.
- **Choice**. See **Election**.
- **Choleric**. See **Humor**.
- **Chronic illness (degrees of)**. Sometimes called the "azamene" degrees, which are especially said to indicate chronic illness, due to their association with certain fixed stars.
- **Claim** (Ar. مزاعمة). See **Dignity**.
- **Cleansed** (Ar. نقيّ, Lat. *mundus*). Ideally, when a planet is in **aversion** to the **infortunes** (but certainly not in an **assembly**, **square**, or **opposition** to them.
- **Clothed**. Equivalent to one planet being in an **assembly** or **aspect** with another, and therefore partaking in (being "clothed in") the other planet's characteristics.
- **Collection** (Lat. *collectio*, Ar. جمع). When two planets **aspecting** each other but not in an applying **connection**, each **apply to** a third planet.
- **Combust** (Lat. *combustus*). See **Burned up**.
- **Commanding/obeying**. A division of the signs into those which command or obey each other (used sometimes in **synastry**).
- **Common signs**. See **Quadruplicity**.

- **Complexion.** Primarily, a mixture of elements and their qualities so as to indicate or produce some effect. Secondarily it refers to planetary combinations, following the naturalistic theory that planets have elemental qualities with causal power, which can interact with each other.
- **Confer.** See **Handing over.**
- **Configuration.** A geometrical relationship, figure, or **aspect** between signs, which allows things to **look at** each other or **connect.**
- **Configured.** To be in an **aspect** by **whole-sign** (though not necessarily **connecting** by degree).
- **Conjunction** (Lat. *conjunctio*, Ar. قران). As a relationship of planets, normally equivalent to **assembly** and **connecting** by body. In mundane astrology it refers to the **mean** conjunction (normally, of Saturn and Jupiter).
- **Conjunction/prevention.** The position of the New (conjunction) or Full (prevention) Moon most immediately prior to a **nativity** or other chart. For the prevention, some astrologers use the degree of the Moon, others the degree of the luminary which was above the earth at the time of the prevention.
- **Connection** (Lat. *continuatio*, Ar. اتّصال). When a planet **applies** to another planet (by body in the same sign, or by **ray** in **configured** signs), within a particular number of degrees up to exactness.
- **Conquer** (Lat. *vinco*). Normally, the equivalent of being a **victor**, which comes from the same Latin verb.
- **Convertible** (Lat. *conversivus*, Ar. منقلب). See **Quadruplicity.** But sometimes planets (especially Mercury) are called convertible because their **gender** is affected by their placement in the chart.
- **Convey.** See **Handing over.**
- **Corruption.** Normally, the harming of a planet, such as being in a **square** with an **infortune.** But sometimes, equivalent to **Detriment.**
- **Counsel** (Lat. *consilium*). See **Management.**
- **Counting** (Ar. عدد). In the context of **house** theory, it refers to **whole-sign** houses (namely, assigning the house numbers by counting each sign); it is opposed to **quadrant houses** (by **division** or **equation**).
- **Course, increasing/decreasing in.** For practical purposes, this means a planet is quicker than average in motion. But in geometric astronomy, it refers to what **sector** of the **deferent** the center of a planet's **epicycle** is. (The planet's position within the four sectors of the epicycle itself will also

affect its apparent speed.) In the two sectors that are closest to the planet's **perigee**, the planet will apparently be moving faster; in the two sectors closest to the **apogee**, it will apparently be moving slower.

- **Crooked/straight.** A division of the signs into those which rise quickly and are more parallel to the horizon (crooked), and those which arise more slowly and closer to a right angle from the horizon (straight or direct). In the northern hemisphere, the signs from Capricorn to Gemini are crooked (but in the southern one, straight); those from Cancer to Sagittarius are straight (but in the southern one, crooked).
- **Crossing over** (Gr. *parallagē*). When a planet begins to **separate** from an exact **connection**. See also **Right/left**.
- **Cusp** (Lat. *cuspis*). In **quadrant houses**, the degree which marks the division between one house and another.
- **Cutter, killer, destroyer** (Ar. قاطِع, قاتِل). A planet or point which ends the life when the **releaser** meets it by distribution.
- **Cutting of light** (Ar. قطع النّور). Any of several ways in which a **connection** is prevented, such as by **blocking**.
- *Darījān*. An alternative **face** system attributed to the Indians.
- **Dastūriyyah** (دستوريّة). See **Spear-bearing**.
- **Decan** (Lat. *decanus*). A division of the **zodiac** into 36 divisions or **faces** of 10° each.
- **Decimation.** A form of **overcoming**, specifically from the superior **square** (i.e., the tenth sign from something else).
- **Declination.** The equivalent on the celestial **equator**, of geographical latitude. The signs of northern declination (Aries through Virgo) stretch northward of the **ecliptic**, while those of southern declination (Libra through Pisces) stretch southward.
- **Decline, declining** (Gr. *apoklima*, Ar. حدر, سقط). Equivalent to **cadence** or **falling** by whole sign, but perhaps in some Arabic texts referring rather to cadence by **quadrant house** divisions.
- **Decreasing in number.** See **Increasing/decreasing in number**.
- **Deferent.** The large circle which is off-center or **eccentric** to the earth, on which a planet's system rotates.
- **Degrees of equality** (سواء), **equal degrees**. Degrees of the zodiac, as opposed to degrees of **ascensions** or measured on the celestial **equator**.
- **Descension** (Lat. *descensio*). Equivalent to **fall**.

- **Detriment** (Lat. *detrimentum*, Ar. ضدّ, وبال). The sign opposite a planet's **domicile**. For example, Libra is the detriment of Mars.
- **Dexter.** "Right": see **Right/left**.
- **Diameter.** Equivalent to **Opposition**.
- **Dignity** (Lat. *dignitas*, Ar. مزاعمة, نصيب, حظّ). Any of (typically) five ways of assigning rulership or responsibility to a planet (or sometimes, to a **Node**) over some portion of the zodiac. They are often listed in the following order: **domicile, exaltation, triplicity, bound, face/decan**. The opposite of domicile is **detriment**, the opposite of exaltation is **fall**.
- **Directions, directing** (Ar. تسيير, Lat. *directio*). A predictive technique in which a point in the chart (the significator) is considered as stationary, and other planets and their **connections** by degree (or even the **bounds**) are sent forth (**promittors**) as though by **primary motion** until they come to the significator. The degrees between the significator and promittor are converted into years of life. This is the method used in **distributions**. An astronomically less accurate version is done by **ascensions**. Some astrologers also allow "converse" directions, in which points may be directed contrary to primary motion.
- **Disregard.** Equivalent to **Separation**.
- **Distribution** (Lat. *partitio, divisio*; Ar. قسمة). The primary **direction** of a **releaser** (often the degree of the **Ascendant**) through the **bounds**. The bound **lord** of the distribution is the **distributor**, and any body or **ray** which the **releaser** encounters is the **partner**.
- **Distributor** (Lat. *divisor*, Ar. قاسم). The **bound lord** of a **directed releaser**. See **Distribution**.
- **Diurnal.** See **Sect**.
- **Division** (Ar. تسويّة, قسمة). In the context of **house** theory, it refers to any **quadrant house** system, as these are derived by dividing each of the the **quarters** by three. Synonymous with houses by **equation**, and opposed to **whole-sign** houses by **counting**.
- **Domain** (حيّز). Sometimes, a synonym for **sect**. But also used for a specific sect and **gender**-based planetary condition, in which a planet is in a sign of its own gender and also in its preferred hemisphere relative to the Sun (for example, Jupiter being in a male sign and above or below the horizon, wherever the Sun is).

- **Domicile.** One of the five **dignities**. A sign of the **zodiac**, insofar as it is owned or managed by one of the planets. For example, Aries is the domicile of Mars, and so Mars is its domicile **lord**.
- **Doryphory** (Gr. *doruphoria*). Equivalent to **Spear-bearing.**
- **Double-bodied.** Equivalent to the common signs. See **Quadruplicity.**
- **Dragon:** see **Node.**
- **Drawn back** (Lat. *reductus*). Equivalent to being **cadent** from an **angle**.
- **Dodecametorion.** Equivalent to **Twelfth-part.**
- *Duodecima*. Equivalent to **Twelfth-part.**
- **Dustoria** (Lat. transliteration of Ar. *dastūriyyah*). See **Spear-bearing.**
- **East** (Lat. *oriens*). The **Ascendant.**
- **Eastern** (Lat. *orientalis*, Ar. شرقيّ) and **western** (Lat. *occidentalis*, Ar. غربيّ). Four primary meanings: (1) when a planet rises before the Sun or Moon in an earlier zodiacal degree (eastern), or setting after it in a later degree (western); (2) to be outside the **Sun's rays** and visible (eastern) or under them and invisible (western). See also **Easternize, easternization**. (3) When a planet is in an eastern/diurnal or western/nocturnal **quadrant** of the chart: the eastern quadrants are from the horizon/Ascendant to the **meridian**/Midheaven, and from the Descendant to the IC; the western quadrants are the opposite. (4) In an eastern or western quadrant relative to the Sun: eastern is to be in the 90° span of the zodiac which precede the Sun, and the opposite 90°; the other two are western.
- **Easternize, easternization** (شرّق \ تشريق), and **westernize, westernization** (غرّب \ تغريب). Two meanings: (1) when a planet is coming out of or going under the **Sun's rays**, with different distances for different planets (normally around 15° from the Sun); (2) when a planet is close enough to the Sun that *within 7 or 9 days* it will come out of our go under the rays. **Superior planets** easternize and westernize when rising before or setting after the Sun, respectively. The **inferior planets** Venus and Mercury are ambiguous, since each can come out of or go under the rays on either side. See **Eastern and western.**
- **Eccentric.** As an adjective, it describes circles that are "off-center" to the earth; it is also a synonym for the **deferent circle**, the larger circle in a planetary model (which is likewise eccentric or off-center).
- **Ecliptic.** The path defined by the Sun's motion through the **zodiac**, defined as having 0° ecliptical latitude. In tropical astrology, the ecliptic (and

therefore the zodiacal signs) begins at the intersection of the ecliptic and the celestial **equator** (the **equinoctial point**).

- **Election** (Lat. *electio*, Ar. اختيار). Literally, "choice": the deliberate choosing of an appropriate time to undertake an action (called an **inception**), or avoid something unwanted.
- **Element** (Lat. *elementum*, Ar. طبيعة, أصل). One of the four basic bodies or qualities (fire, air, water, earth) describing how matter and energy operate, and used to describe the significations and operations of planets and signs. They are usually described by pairs of four other basic qualities (hot, cold, wet, dry). For example, Aries is a fiery sign, and hot and dry; Mercury is typically treated as cold and dry (earthy).
- **Emptiness in course** (Lat. *vacuum cursu*, Ar. خلاء السّير, Gr. *kenodromia*). Medievally, when a planet does not complete a **connection** for as long as it is in its current sign. In Hellenistic astrology, when a planet does not complete a connection within the next 30°.
- **Enclosure** (Gr. *perischesis, emperischesis*; Lat. *obsido*; Ar. احتوى, حصر, ضغط). When a planet has the rays or bodies of the **infortunes** (or alternatively, the **fortunes**) on either side of it, by degree or sign.
- **Epicycle**. A circle on the **deferent**, on which a planet turns.
- **Equant**. In Ptolemaic astronomy, a mathematical point in outer space from which measurements are made. At the equant, planetary motion is seen as virtually constant and unchanging in speed.
- **Equation, Equate**. (1) In astronomical theory, a correction that is made to the **mean motion/position** of a planet, in order to convert its idealized or **mean** position to its **true motion/position**. Equations are found in a table of equations calculated individually for each planet. (2) In **house** theory, it refers to any **quadrant house** system, where house divisions are derived by exact calculation or equation (Ar. التّسوية); synonymous with house division by **division**, and **whole-sign** houses by **counting**.
- **Equation of the center (planetary theory)**. The angular difference between where the center of a planet's **epicycle** is, as seen from the **equant** (also known as its **mean position**), and its **true position** as seen from earth.
- **Equation of the center (solar theory)**. The angular difference between the **mean Sun** (where we expect it to be) and the **true Sun** (where we observe it to be).

- **Equator (celestial).** The projection of the earth's equator into space, forming a great circle. Its equivalent of latitude is called **declination**, while its equivalent of longitude is called **right ascension** (and is measured from the beginning of Aries, from the intersection of it and the **ecliptic**).
- **Equinoctial point, equinox.** The point where the circles of the **ecliptic** and celestial **equator** cross, which defines the beginning of spring (and 0° Aries, in the tropical **zodiac**) or beginning of autumn (and 0° Libra).
- **Escape** (Ar. فوت, Lat. *frustratio, evasio*). When a planet wants to **connect** with a second one, but the second one moves into the next sign before it is completed, and the first planet makes a **connection** with a different, unrelated one instead.
- **Essence** (Lat. *substantia*, Ar. جوهر). Deriving ultimately from Aristotelian philosophy, the fundamental nature or character of a planet or sign, which allows it to indicate or cause certain phenomena (such as the essence of Mars being responsible for indicating fire, iron, war, *etc.*). This word has often been translated as "substance," which is a less accurate term.
- **Essential/accidental.** A common way of distinguishing a planet's conditions, usually according to **dignity** (essential) and some other condition such as its **configurations** or **connections** or rulership (accidental).
- **Exaltation** (Lat. *exaltatio*, Ar. شرف). One of the five **dignities**. A sign in which a planet (or sometimes, a **Node**) signifies its matter in a particularly authoritative and refined way. The exaltation is sometimes identified with a particular degree in that sign.
- **Excellent place** (Ar. مكان جيّد). Includes several of the **advantageous places**, among which the Ascendant, Midheaven, and eleventh are consistently mentioned. (These may be the only excellent places.)
- **Exile** (Ar. غربة) In Arabic astrology, an **alien** (or "peregrine") planet. But in some later Latin astrology (Lat. *exilium*), it denotes being in **detriment**.
- **Face** (Lat. *facies*, Ar. وجه). One of the five **dignities**. The **zodiac** is divided into 36 faces of 10° each, starting with the beginning of Aries. Each division is equivalent to a **decan**.
- **Facing** (Ar. مواجهه). See **Proper face**.
- **Fall** (Gr. *hupsōma*, Ar. هبوط, Lat. *casus, descensio*). The sign opposite a planet's **exaltation**; sometimes called "descension."
- **Falling** (Lat. *cadens*, Ar. ساقط). Several uses. (1) Refers to being **cadent**, but sometimes ambiguous as to whether dynamically by **quadrant division** or by **whole sign** (which is also called **declining**). When understood

dynamically, it is equivalent to **retreating** and **withdrawing**. (2) A planet coming down from its **apogee** (sometimes with Ar. هبط).
- **Fall away from** (Ar. سقط عن). See **Aversion**.
- **Familiar** (Lat. *familiaris*). A hard-to-define term which suggests a sense of belonging and close relationship. (1) Sometimes it is contrasted with being **alien**, suggesting that a familiar planet is one which is a **lord** over a degree or **place** (that is, it has a **dignity** in it): for a dignity suggests belonging. (2) At other times, it refers to a familiar **configuration** or **connection** (and probably the **sextile** or **trine** in particular): all of the family houses in a chart have a **whole-sign** aspect to the **Ascendant**.
- *Firdāriyyah*. See *fardār*.
- **Feminine**. See **Gender**.
- **Feral** (Ar. وحشيّ, Lat. *feralis*). Equivalent to **Wildness**.
- **Figure** (Lat. *figura*). One of several polygons implied by a **configuration**. For example, a planet in Aries and one in Capricorn do not actually form a **square**, but they imply one because Aries and Capricorn, together with Libra and Cancer, form a square amongst themselves.
- *Fardār, firdāriyyah* (Ar. فردار, فرداريّة). A **time lord** method in which planets rule different periods of life, with each period broken down into sub-periods (there are also mundane versions).
- **Firm**. In terms of signs, the **fixed** signs: see **Quadruplicity**. For houses, equivalent to the **Angles**.
- **Fixed**. See **Quadruplicity**.
- **Fixing** (Gr. *pēxis*). See **Root**.
- **Flow away** (Lat. *defluo*, Ar. انصبّ). See **Separation**.
- **Foreign** (Lat. *extraneus*, Ar. غريب). Usually equivalent to **Peregrine**.
- **Fortunate, made fortunate** (Lat. *fortunatus*, Ar. مسعود). A planet whose condition is made better, often by a **trine** or **sextile** from a **fortune**.
- **Fortune/Infortune** (Ar. سعد \ نحس, Lat. *fortuna / infortuna*). A division of the planets into groups that cause or signify typically "good" things (Jupiter, Venus, usually the Sun and Moon) or "bad" things (Mars, Saturn). Mercury is considered variable.
- **Foundation of the lifespan** (Ar. أصل العمر). The expected longevity shown by the **house-master**.
- **Foundations of the Moon**. See **Centers of the Moon**.
- **Free** (Ar. بري, Lat. *liber*). Sometimes, being **cleansed** of the **infortunes**; at other times, being out of the **Sun's rays**.

- **Gender.** The division of signs, degrees, planets and hours into masculine and feminine groups.
- **Glow** (Ar. ضوء). This has three primary meanings: (1) a planet in "its own glow" is of the **sect** of the chart, or in some sect-related rejoicing condition; (2) the Moon increases and decreases in her light or glow by waxing and waning; (3) a planet can be "in its own glow" when it is out of the **Sun's rays** so as to be visible.
- **Good ones.** See **Fortune/Infortune**.
- **Good places.** Equivalent to **Advantageous places**.
- **Governor** (Ar. المستولي \ الوالي). Normally a generic term referring to a **victor** over a place, such as the Ptolemaic victor (by rulership and **aspect**). Sometimes used to denote the **house-master** or a **time lord**.
- **Greater, middle, lesser years.** See **Planetary years**.
- **Halb** (Ar. حلب). Probably Pahlavi for **sect**, but normally describes a special sect-related rejoicing condition. For **diurnal** planets, when they are in the same hemisphere as the Sun (upper or lower); for **nocturnal** planets, when they are in the hemisphere opposite the Sun. For example, if Saturn during the day is above the earth (where the Sun by definition also is).
- **Handing over** (دفع إلى) When a planet applies by **connection** to another, it hands over its **management**.
- **Harm.** A broad category of conditions by which a planet may be made **unfortunate**.
- **Hayyiz.** (Ar. حيّز). Arabic for **domain**, technically equivalent to **halb**, except that the planet is also in a sign of its own **gender**. But sometimes this term simply means **sect**.
- **Head (of the Dragon).** See **Node**.
- **Hexagon.** See **Sextile**.
- **Hīlāj** (Ar. هيلاج, from the Pahlavi for "releaser"). Equivalent to **releaser**.
- **Hold onto.** Hugo's synonym for a planet being in or **transiting** a **sign**.
- **Honor guard, paying honor** (تكرمة). A synonym for **Spear-bearing**.
- **Horary astrology.** A late historical designation for **questions**.
- **Hours (planetary).** The assigning of rulership over hours of the day and night to planets. The hours of daylight (and night, respectively) are divided by 12, and each period is ruled first by the planet ruling that day, then the rest in descending planetary order. For example, on Sunday the Sun rules the first planetary "hour" from daybreak, then Venus, then Mercury, the Moon, Saturn, and so on.

- **House** (Gr. *oikos*, Lat. *domus*, Ar. بيت). A twelve-fold spatial division of a chart, in which each house signifies one or more areas of life. Two basic schemes are (1) **whole-sign** houses, in which the **signs** are equivalent to the houses, and (2) **quadrant houses**. But in the context of dignities and rulerships, "house" is the equivalent of **domicile**: so, Aries is the house of Mars.
- **House-master** (Gr. *oikodespotēs*, Ar. كدخذاه). Often called the *alcochoden* in Latin, from the Arabic transliteration of a Persian word (*kadkhudhāh*). One of the **lords** of the longevity **releaser**, preferably the **bound lord**. But the Greek word is also used in a general way to mean simply any **lord**, or even a **victor**.
- **Humor** (Lat. *humor*, Ar. خلط). Any one of four mixtures or substances in the body (according to traditional medicine), the balance between which determines one's health and **temperament** (outlook and energy level). Choler or yellow bile is associated with fire and the choleric temperament; blood is associated with air and the sanguine temperament; phlegm is associated with water and the phlegmatic temperament; black bile is associated with earth and the melancholic temperament.
- **Hundred, Hundreds** (الألف). A Persian mundane **time lord**, which rules the world for a period of 100 years.
- *Hyleg.* See *Hīlāj* and **Releaser**.
- *IC.* See *Imum Caeli*.
- *Imum Caeli* (Lat. "lowest part of heaven"). The **axial degree** or degree of the zodiac on which the lower half of the **meridian** circle falls; in **quadrant house** systems, it marks the beginning of the fourth **house**.
- **In the heart**. Often called *cazimi* in English texts, from the Ar. كصميمي. A planet is in the heart of the Sun when it is either in the same degree as the Sun (according to Sahl b. Bishr and Rhetorius), or within 16' of longitude from him.
- **Inception** (Lat. *inceptio*, Ar. ابتداء). See **Election**.
- **Increaser, decreaser** (Ar. زائد, ناقص). A planet which natally connects by body or ray to the **house-master**, and increases or decreases the **foundation of the lifespan**.
- **Increasing/decreasing in calculation**. A planet is increasing in calculation when its **equation** is added to the **mean motion/position**, because the **true motion/position** is farther ahead in the zodiac than the mean one. It is decreasing in calculation when the equation is subtracted.

- **Increasing/decreasing in number**. When the daily speed of a planet (or at least the speed of the center of its **epicycle**) is seen to speed up (or slow down). When moving from its **perigee** to its **apogee**, it slows down or decreases in number, because it is moving farther away from the earth; when moving from the apogee to the perigee, it speeds up or increases in number because it is coming closer to the earth.
- **Indicator**. A generic term synonymous with **significator**. See also *namūdār*.
- **Indicator of the lifespan** (Ar. دليل العمر). The **house-master**.
- **Inferior** (Lat. *inferior*, Ar. سفليّ). The planets lower than the Sun: Venus, Mercury, and sometimes the Moon.
- **Infortunes**. See **Fortune/Infortune**.
- **Inspection** (مناظرة). Equivalent to an **aspect**, but might specifically refer to a degree-based **connection** from another sign.
- **Intercepted** signs. In **quadrant houses**, a sign which does not have a **cusp** on it, but is wholly contained by two cusps: one in the sign before it, and one in the sign after it.
- **'Ittisāl** (Ar. اتّصال). Equivalent to **Connection**.
- **Jārbakhtār** (Ar. جاربختار, from the Pahlavi for "distributor of time"). Equivalent to **Distributor**; see **Distribution**.
- **Joy** (Lat. *gaudium*, Ar. فرح). Signs or houses in which the planets are said to "rejoice" in acting or signifying their natures.
- **Kadkhudhāh** (كدخذاه). An Arabic transliteration from Pahlavi or Middle Persian for the **House-master**, often called the *alcochoden* in Latin transliteration.
- **Kardaja** (Ar. كردجة, from Sansk. *kramajyā*). The numerical interval used in rows of an astronomical table, when entering an **argument** and then finding the result in the relevant column (and therefore sometimes seems to refer to portions of the astronomical circles themselves). Ptolemy's tables often used intervals of 6°, while Indian tables often used 3° 45', which is 1/24 of 90°.
- **Kasmīmī** (Ar. كصميمي). See **In the heart**.
- **Kingdom**. See **Exaltation**.
- **Largesse and recompense** (Ar. نعمة والمكافة). A reciprocal relation in which one planet is rescued from being in its own **fall** or a **well**, and then returns the favor when the other planet is in its fall or well.

- **Leader** (Lat. *dux*). Equivalent to a **significator** for some topic. The Arabic word for "significator" means to indicate something by pointing the way toward something: thus the significator for a topic or matter "leads" the astrologer to some answer. Used by some less popular Latin translators (such as Hugo of Santalla and Hermann of Carinthia).
- **Linger in** (Lat. *commoror*). Hugo's synonym for a planet being in or **transiting** through a **sign**.
- **Lodging-place** (Lat. *hospitium*). Hugo's synonym for a **house**, particularly the **sign** which occupies a house.
- **Look at** (Lat. *aspicio*, Ar. نظر). Two things may look at each other if they are in signs which are **configured** or in **aspect** to each other by a **sextile**, **square**, **trine**, or **opposition**. See also **Whole signs**. Places and planets which cannot see or look at each other, are in **aversion**.
- **Look down upon** (Ar. أشرف). A synonym for **overcoming**, and in particular **decimation**.
- **Lord of the year.** Usually, the **domicile lord** of a **profection**, namely where the profection **terminates**. But in mundane astrology it can also refer to a kind of **victor**, the planet in the chart which is the most powerful and sums up the meaning of the year.
- **Lord.** A designation for the planet which has a particular **dignity**, but when used alone it usually means the **domicile** lord. For example, Mars is the lord of Aries.
- **Lord of the orb.** See **Orb**.
- **Lord of the question.** See **Owner**.
- **Lord of the year.** In mundane ingress charts, the planet that is the **victor** over the chart, indicating the general meanings of the year. But in **profections**, the lord of the sign of the **terminal point**.
- **Lot** (Gr. *klēros*, Lat. *pars, sors*, Ar. قرعة, سهم). Sometimes called "Parts" (and falsely called "Arabic Parts"). A place (often treated as equivalent to an entire sign) expressing a ratio derived from the position of three other parts of a chart. Normally, the distance between two places is measured in zodiacal order from one to the other, and this distance is projected forward from some other place (usually the Ascendant): where the counting stops, is the Lot. The Lot of Fortune is the most famous Lot.
- **Lucky/unlucky.** See **Fortune/Infortune**.
- **Luminary** (Lat. *luminarium*, Ar. نيّر). The Sun or Moon.
- **Lunation.** See **Conjunction/prevention**.

- **Malefic.** See **Fortune/Infortune**.
- **Malevolent.** See **Fortune/Infortune**.
- **Management** (Ar. تدبير). A generic term referring to how a planet "manages" a topic by signifying it. Typically, planets **hand over** and "accept" management to and from each other, simply by **applying** to one another.
- **Manager** (Ar. المدبّر). Sometimes, the planetary **partner** in **distributions**; sometimes a term for the longevity **releaser**. But also a generic name for planets which have any kind of **management**.
- **Masculine.** See **Gender**.
- **Maximum equation.** In solar theory, the greatest angular amount of the **equation of the center**, which occurs when the **mean Sun** is perpendicular to the **apsidal line**.
- **Mean motion/position.** The motion or position of a planet as measured from the **equant**, namely assuming a constant rate of speed. To be contrasted with **True motion/position**.
- **Mean Sun.** A fictitious point which revolves around the earth in exactly one year, in a line parallel with the **true Sun**. The mean Sun represents where we would expect the Sun to be, if it traveled in a perfect circle around the earth. It coincides with the true Sun at the Sun's **apogee** and **perigee**.
- **Meeting** (Ar. اجتماع). The **conjunction** of the Sun and Moon at the New Moon, which makes it a **connection** by body. See **Conjunction/prevention**.
- **Melancholic.** See **Humor**.
- **Meridian.** The great circle which has its center at the middle of the earth, and points north-south relative to the horizon. The degree which intersects the **ecliptic** (or **axial degree**) is called the degree of the **Midheaven** or *Imum Caeli/IC*.
- **Midheaven.** Either the tenth sign from the **Ascendant**, or the **axial degree** on which the celestial **meridian** falls.
- **Minister.** A synonym for **Governor**.
- **Movable signs.** See **Quadruplicity**.
- *Mubtazz* (Ar. مبتزّ). See **Victor**.
- **Mutable signs.** Equivalent to "common" signs. See **Quadruplicity**.
- *Namūdār.* (Ar. نمودار) Persian for "indicator," a special way of determining the moment of conception or the nativity (if they are known only approximately).

- **Native** (Lat. *natus*, Ar. مولود, مولد). The person whose birth chart it is.
- **Nativity.** Technically, a birth itself, but used by astrologers to describe the chart cast for the moment of a birth.
- **Ninth-part** (Ar. نهبر, Lat. *novenarium*). Divisions of each sign into 9 equal parts of 3° 20' apiece, each ruled by a planet. Used predictively by some astrologers as part of the suite of **revolution** techniques.
- **Nobility.** Equivalent to **Exaltation**.
- **Nocturnal.** See **Sect**.
- **Node** (Lat. *nodus*, Ar. عقدة), lit. "knot." The point on the ecliptic where a planet passes into northward latitude (its North Node or Head of the Dragon) or into southern latitude (its South Node or Tail of the Dragon). Normally only the Moon's Nodes are considered.
- **Northern/southern.** Either planets in northern or southern latitude in the **zodiac** relative to the ecliptic, or in northern or southern **declination** relative to the celestial **equator**.
- **Not-reception** (Ar. غير مقبول). When an **applying** planet is in the **fall** of the planet being applied to, or applies from a place in which the other planet has no **dignity**.
- **Number** (Ar. عدد). For house theory, see **counting**. For its use in calculating planetary positions, see **Increasing/decreasing in number**.
- **Oblique ascensions.** The **ascensions** used in making predictions by ascensional times or primary **directions**.
- **Obstruction.** See **Resistance**.
- **Occidental, occidentality.** See **Eastern and western**.
- **Opening of the portals/doors.** Times of likely weather changes and rain, determined by certain **transits**.
- **Opposition** (Lat. *oppositio, oppositum*; Ar. استقبال, مقابلة). A **configuration** or **aspect** either by **whole sign** or degree, in which the signs have a 180° relation to each other: for example, a planet in Aries is opposed to one in Libra.
- **Optimal place** (Lat. *optimus*). See **Excellent place**.
- **Orb** (Ar. دور, Lat. *orbis*), **lord of the orb**. Denotes a natal **time lord** technique; this same word is the basis of **Turn** (a mundane technique), and sometimes **Turning** (see **Profections**).
- **Orbs/bodies** (Lat. *orbis*, Ar. جرم). A space of power or influence on each side of a planet's **body** or position, used to determine the intensity of interaction between different planets.

- **Oriental, orientality.** See **Eastern and western**.
- **Overcoming**. When a planet is in the eleventh, tenth, or ninth sign from another planet (i.e., in a superior **sextile**, **square**, or **trine**); being in the tenth sign is considered **decimation**, a more domineering or even harmful position.
- **Overlord** (Ar. المسلّط). Refers to a **victor** over a place, but often used to designate the primary **triplicity lord**.
- **Own light** (Ar. ضوء, Lat. *lumen suum*). See **Glow**.
- **Owner** (صاحب). The person who "owns" or is the subject of a chart: the **native** is the owner of a nativity, the **querent** is the owner of the question chart, etc.
- **Part.** See **Lot**.
- **Partner** (Ar. شريك, Lat. *particeps*). The body or **ray** of any planet which a **directed releaser** encounters while being **distributed** through the **bounds**.
- **Peregrine** (Lat. *peregrinus*, Ar. غريب), lit. "a stranger, foreigner." See **Alien**.
- **Perigee (of eccentric/deferent)**. The point on a planet's **deferent circle** that is closest to the earth; as seen from earth, it points to some degree of the zodiac. It is opposite the **apogee**.
- **Perverse** (Lat. *perversus*). Hugo's occasional term for (1) the **infortunes**, and (2) **places** in **aversion** to the **Ascendant** by **whole-sign**: definitely the twelfth and sixth, probably the eighth, and possibly the second.
- **Phlegmatic.** See **Humor**.
- **Pitted degrees.** Equivalent to **Welled degrees**.
- **Pivot** (Lat. *cardo*). Equivalent to **Angle**.
- **Place** (Gr. *topos*, Lat. *locus*, Ar. مكان). Equivalent to a **house**, and more often (and more anciently) a **whole-sign** house, namely a **sign**.
- **Planetary years.** Periods of years (or, other units of time) which the planets signify according to various conditions.
- **Portion** (Ar. جزء, Lat. *pars, portio*). Normally, refers to either (1) a specific zodiacal degree, especially the degree of the Ascendant or the degree where a **ray** falls, or (2) the degrees within a particular **bound**: especially, the bound in which the Ascendant falls.
- **Possess.** Hugo's synonym for a planet being in or **transiting** a **sign**.
- **Post** (Ar. مركز). A **stake** or **angle**. (The Arabic verb is virtually equivalent to Ar. *watada*, used for a stake.) Sometimes translated as **center**, as in the centers of the Moon.

- **Posts of the Moon.** See **Centers of the Moon**.
- **Prevention.** See **Conjunction/prevention**.
- **Predominator** (Gr. *epikratētōr*). See **Victor**.
- **Primary directions.** See **Directions**.
- **Primary motion.** The clockwise or east-to-west motion of the heavens. See **secondary motion**.
- **Profection** (Lat. *profectio*, "advancement, setting out"). A predictive technique in which some part of a chart (usually the **Ascendant**) is advanced by an entire sign or in 30° increments for each year of life.
- **Prohibition.** Equivalent to **Blocking**.
- **Promittor** (lit., something "sent forward"). A point which is **directed** by **primary motion** to a **significator**, or to which a significator is **released** or directed (depending on how one views the mechanics of directions).
- **Proper face** (Gr. *idioprosōpos*). A relationship between a planet and a **luminary**, so that the **signs** the occupy have the same relationship as the **domiciles** they rule. For example, Leo (ruled by the Sun) is two signs to the **right** of Libra (ruled by Venus): so whenever Venus is **western** and two signs away from the Sun, she will be in the proper face of the Sun.
- **Pushing.** See **Handing over**.
- **Qāsim/qismah** (Ar. قاسم, قسمة) See **distributor** and **distribution**.
- **Quadrant.** A division of the heavens into four parts, defined by the circles of the horizon and **meridian**, marked out by the **axial degrees** of the **Ascendant-Descendant**, and **Midheaven-IC**.
- **Quadrant houses.** A division of the heavens or local space into twelve spaces which overlap the **whole signs**, and are assigned topics of life and ways of measuring strength (such as Porphyry, Alchabitius Semi-Arc, or Regiomontanus houses). For example, if the degree of the **Midheaven** fell into the eleventh sign, the space between the Midheaven and the Ascendant would be divided into sections that overlap with, and are not coincident with the signs.
- **Quadruplicity.** A "fourfold" group of signs indicating certain shared patterns of behavior. The movable (or cardinal or convertible) signs are those through which new states of being are quickly formed (including the seasons): Aries, Cancer, Libra, Capricorn. The fixed (sometimes "firm") signs are those through which matters are fixed and lasting in their character: Taurus, Leo, Scorpio, Aquarius. The common (or mutable or bicorporeal)

signs are those which make a transition and partake both of quick change and fixed qualities: Gemini, Virgo, Sagittarius, Pisces.
- **Quaesited/quesited.** In **horary** astrology, the matter asked about.
- **Querent.** In **horary** astrology, the person asking the question (or the person on behalf of whom one asks).
- **Questions.** The branch of astrology dealing with inquiries about individual matters, for which a chart is cast.
- **Radical** (Lat. *radicalis*). See **Root**.
- **Radix** (Lat. *radix*). See **Root**.
- **Ray, raying** (Lat. *radius, radiatio*; Ar. شعاع). An imaginary line which represents an exact **aspect** cast from a planet to the corresponding degree in another sign, such as if a planet is in 15° Gemini and casts a **square** ray to 15° Virgo. See also **Sun's rays**.
- **Receive, reception** (Lat. *recipio*, Ar. قبل). What one planet does when another planet **hands over** or **applies** to it, and especially when they are related by **dignity**, or by a **trine** or **sextile** from an **agreeing** sign of various types. For example, if the Moon applies to Mars, Mars will accept her application; and if he rules the sign in which she is, he will receive her (an intensified condition).
- **Reflection** (Ar. رد, Lat. *redditus*). When two planets are in **aversion** to each other, but a third planet either **collects** or **transfers** their light. If it collects, it reflects the light elsewhere.
- **Refrenation.** See **Revoking**.
- **Regard** (Lat. *respectus*). Equivalent to **looking at** or an **aspect**.
- **Releaser** (Ar. هيلاج). The point which is the focus of a **direction**, often one of a standard set of five (the luminaries, **Ascendant**, **Lot** of Fortune, and the prenatal **lunation**. In determining longevity, it is the **victor** among a set of possible points, which often includes the five just mentioned.
- **Remote** (Lat. *remotus*, prob. a translation of Ar. زائل). Equivalent to **cadent**: see **Angle**. But see also *Judges* §7.73, where al-Tabarī (or Hugo) distinguishes being **cadent** from being **remote**, probably translating the Ar. زائل and ساقط (**withdrawing** and **falling**).
- **Render.** When a planet **hands over** to another planet or place.
- **Resistance** (Ar. اعتراض). When one planet is moving towards a second (wanting to be **connected** to it), but a third one in a later degrees goes **retrograde**, connects with the second one, and then with the first one.

- **Retreat, retreating** (إدبار \ مدبر). Refers to being (2) dynamically **cadent**, i.e. moving by **primary motion** away from an **axial** degree. (But occasionally might refer to being cadent by **whole signs**.) A near synonym to **withdrawal**. Its antonym is **Advancement**. It may also refer to (2) the **western** quadrants.
- **Retrograde, retrogradation** (Lat. *retrogradus*, Ar. راجع). When a planet seems to move backwards in its **secondary motion**.
- **Return, Solar/Lunar.** Equivalent to **Revolution**.
- **Returning** (Ar. رذ, Lat. *redditus, reditio*). What a **burned** or **retrograde** planet does when another planet **hands over** to it.
- **Revoking** (Ar. انتكاث, Lat. *refrenatio*). When a planet making an applying **connection** stations and turns **retrograde**, not completing the connection.
- **Revolution** (Lat. *revolutio*, Ar. تحويل). Sometimes called the "cycle" or "transfer" or "change-over" of a year. Technically, the **transiting** position of planets and the **Ascendant** at the moment the Sun returns to a particular place in the zodiac: in the case of nativities, when he returns to his exact natal position; in mundane astrology, usually when he makes his ingress into 0° Aries. But the revolution is also understood to involve an entire suite of predictive techniques, including **distribution**, **profections**, and *fardārs*.
- **Right ascensions.** Degrees on the celestial **equator** (its equivalent of geographical longitude), particularly those which move across the **meridian** when calculating arcs for **ascensions** and **directions**.
- **Right/left.** Right (or "dexter") degrees and **configurations** or aspects are those earlier in the zodiac relative to a planet or sign, up to the **opposition**; left (or "sinister") degrees and configurations are those later in the zodiac. For example, if a planet is in Capricorn, its right aspects will be towards Scorpio, Libra, and Virgo; its left aspects will be towards Pisces, Aries, and Taurus.
- **Right-siding, being on the right, right-sidedness** (تنامن \ ميمنة). A synonym for **Spear-bearing**.
- **Root** (Gr. *pēxis*, Lat. *radix*, Ar. أصل). A chart used as a basis for another chart; a root particularly describes something considered to have concrete being of its own. For example, a **nativity** acts as a root for an **election**, so that when planning an election one must make it harmonize with the na-

tivity. A horary or **question** chart is considered "radical" or "rooted" if it fits certain criteria, such as harmonizing with the **querent's nativity**.

- **Safe** (Ar. سليم). When a planet is not being harmed, particularly by an **assembly** or **square** or **opposition** with the **infortunes**. See **Cleansed**.
- **Sālkhuday / sālkhudāh** (Ar. سالخداه \ سالخدى, from Pahlavi, "lord of the year"). Equivalent to the **lord of the year** in a **profection**.
- **Sanguine**. See **Humor**.
- **Scorched** (Lat. *adustus*). See **Burned up**.
- **Secondary motion**. The motion of planets forward in the zodiac, rather than the **primary motion** of the heavens around the earth.
- **Sect** (Gr. *hairēsis*). A division of charts, planets, and signs into "diurnal/day" and "nocturnal/night." For similar terms, see **Glow, Share**, and **Domain**.
- **Sector** (Ar. نطاق). A division of the **deferent** circle or **epicycle** into four parts, used to determine the position, speed, visibility, and other features of a planet.
- **See**. See **Look at**.
- **Seeing, hearing, listening signs**. A way of associating signs similar to **commanding/obeying**.
- **Separation** (Lat. *separatio*, Ar. انصراف). When planets have completed a **connection** by **assembly** or **aspect**, and move away from one another.
- **Sextile** (Lat. *sextilis*, Ar. تسديس). A **configuration** or **aspect** either by **whole sign** or degree, in which the signs have a 60° relation to each other: for example, Aries and Gemini.
- **Share** (Ar. حظّ, but sometimes نصيب, or حصّة, "allotment, share"). Often equivalent to **dignity**, but sometimes used to mean **sect** (where it is synonymous with and perhaps confused with **domain** (Ar. حيّز).
- **Shift**. (1) Equivalent to **sect** (Ar. نوبة), referring not only to the alternation between day and night, but also to the period of night or day itself. The Sun is the lord of the diurnal shift or sect, and the Moon is the lord of the nocturnal shift or sect. (2) In mundane astrology, it refers to the shift (Ar. انتقال, Lat. *mutatio*) of the Saturn-Jupiter conjunctions from one **triplicity** to another about every 200 (tropical zodiac) or 220 (sidereal zodiac) years.
- **Sign**. One of the twelve 30° divisions of the **ecliptic** or **zodiac**, named after the constellations which they used to be roughly congruent to.

- **Significator** (Lat. *significator*, Ar. دليل). Either (1) a planet or point in a chart which indicates or signifies something for a topic (either through its own character, or house position, or rulerships, *etc.*), or (2) the stationary point in primary **directions**.
- **Significator of the king.** In mundane ingress charts, the **victor** planet which indicates the king or government.
- **Sinister.** "Left": see **Right/left**.
- **Slavery.** In Hugo of Santalla's Latin, equivalent to **Fall**.
- **Sought matter, sought thing** (Ar. حاجة). See **Quaesited**.
- **Sovereignty** (Lat. *regnum*). In Hugo of Santalla's Latin, equivalent to **Exaltation**.
- **Spear-bearing** (Ar. دستوريّة, Lat. *dustoria*, Gr. *doruphoria*). A special configuration in a chart showing eminence and prosperity, of which there were several types and definitions. Spear-bearing requires that there be a royal planet (usually, a **luminary**), which is accompanied by a spear-bearing planet.
- **Square.** A **configuration** or **aspect** either by **whole sign** or degree, in which the signs have a 90° relation to each other: for example, Aries and Cancer.
- **Stake** (Ar. وتد). Equivalent to **Angle**.
- **Sublunar world.** The world of the four **elements** below the sphere of the Moon, in classical cosmology.
- **Substance** (Lat. *substantia*). Sometimes, indicating the real **essence** of a planet or sign. But often it refers to financial assets (perhaps because coins are physical objects indicating real value).
- **Succeedent.** See **Angle**.
- **Suitable, suitability** (Ar. صالح \ صلاح). For **places** of the chart, equivalent to the schemes of **advantageous places**. Otherwise, a general term for the good or bad condition of a planet.
- **Sun's rays** (or Sun's beams). In earlier astrology, equivalent to a regularized distance of 15° away from the Sun, so that a planet under the rays is not visible at dawn or dusk. But a later distinction was made between being **burned up** (about 1° - 7.5° away from the Sun) and merely being under the rays (about 7.5° - 15° away).
- **Superior** (Lat. *superior*, Ar. علوي). The planets higher than the Sun: Saturn, Jupiter, Mars.

- **Supremacy** (Lat. *regnum*). Hugo's word for **exaltation**, sometimes used in translations by Dykes instead of the slightly more accurate Latin **sovereignty**.
- **Synastry**. The comparison of two or more charts to determine compatibility, usually in romantic relationships or friendships.
- **Tail (of the Dragon)**. See **Node**.
- *Tasyir* (Ar. تسيير, "dispatching, sending out"). Equivalent to primary **directions**.
- **Temperament** (Lat. *temperamentum*, Ar. مزاج). The particular mixture (sometimes, "complexion") of **elements** or **humors** which determines a person's or planet's typical behavior, outlook, energy level, and health.
- **Terminal point, termination, terminate** (Ar. انتهاء). The sign or degree which a **profection** comes to, at a particular day or time.
- **Testimony** (Lat. *testimonium*, Ar. شهادة). From Arabic astrology onwards, a little-defined term which can mean (1) the planets which have **dignity** in a place or degree, or (2) the number of dignities a planet has in its own place (or as compared with other planets), or (3) a planet's **assembly** or **aspect** to a place of interest, or (4) generally *any* way in which planets may make themselves relevant to the inquiry at hand. For example, a planet which is the **exalted** lord of the **Ascendant** but also **looks at** it, maby be said to present two testimonies supporting its relevance to an inquiry about the Ascendant.
- **Tetragon.** See **Square**.
- **Thought-interpretation**. The practice of identifying a theme or topic in a **querent's** mind, often using a **victor**, before answering the specific **question**. Called the "extraction of the heart" in Arabic (استخراج الضمير), it was sometimes used to identify an object in the hand prior to a consultation.
- **Thousand, Thousands** (المائة). A Persian mundane **time lord**, which rules the world for a period of 1000 years.
- **Time lord.** A planet or sign ruling over some period of time according to one of the classical predictive techniques. For example, the **lord of the year** in nativities is the time lord over a **profection**.
- **Transfer** (Lat. *translatio*, Ar. نقل) When one planet **separates** from one planet, and **connects** to another. Not to be confused with a **shift** of triplicities in Saturn-Jupiter conjunctions, or annual **revolutions**, either mundane or natal.

- **Transit** (Lat. *transio*, Ar. مرّ). The passing of one planet across a planet or point (by body or **aspect** by exact degree), or even through a particular sign.
- **Translation** (Lat. *translatio*). Equivalent to **Transfer**.
- **Traverse** (Lat. *discurro*). Hugo's synonym for a planet being in or **transiting** through a **sign**.
- **Triangle**. Normally, equivalent to **trine**, but sometimes **triplicity**.
- **Trigon**. Normally, equivalent to **trine**, but sometimes **triplicity**.
- **Trine** (Lat. *trinus*, Ar. تثليث). A **configuration** or **aspect** either by **whole sign** or degree, in which the signs have a 120° relation to each other: for example, Aries and Leo.
- **Triplicity** (Ar. مثلّثة, Lat. *triplicitas*). A set of three signs which form a triangle, such as Aries-Leo-Sagittarius. (Arabic texts sometimes use the plural "triplicities" when they mean the singular.)
- **Triplicity lords**. A set of three planets which jointly rule a **triplicity** as a whole. One planet is primary by day, another by night, and the third lord always acts as their partner. For example, the Sun, Jupiter, and Saturn are the triplicity lords of Aries-Leo-Sagittarius: the Sun is primary by day, Jupiter by night, and Saturn is always the last, partnering lord.
- **True motion/position**. The motion or position of a planet as measured from the earth, once its **mean motion/position** has been adjusted or corrected by various types of **equations**.
- **True Sun**. The zodiacal position of the Sun, as seen from the earth, after its **mean** position has been **equated** or corrected.
- **Turn** (Ar. دور). A predictive technique in which responsibilities for being a **time lord** rotates among different planets. It may also refer to other methods in which cycles through the planets, assigning them roles as **time lords**. See **Lord of the orb**.
- **Turned away from** (Gr. *apostrophē*). See **Aversion**.
- **Turning** (Ar. دور \ إدوار, Gr. *kuklōmenon*). See **Profection**.
- **Turning signs** (Lat. *tropicus*). Normally, equivalent to **movable** or **convertible** signs. See **Quadruplicity**. But sometimes refers to the tropical signs Cancer and Capricorn, in which the Sun turns back from his most extreme **declinations**.
- **Twelfth-part** (Lat. *duodecatemorion, duodecima*; Ar. اثنى عشرية). Signs of the zodiac defined by 2.5° divisions of other signs. For example, the twelfth-part corresponding to 4° Gemini is Cancer.

- **Two-parted signs.** Equivalent to the double-bodied or common signs: see **Quadruplicity.**
- **Under the rays.** See **Sun's rays.**
- **Underground.** Equivalent to *Imum caeli/IC.*
- **Unfortunate** (Lat. *infortunatus*, Ar. منحوس). When a planet's condition is made more difficult, usually by **assembly**, **square**, or **opposition** with the **infortunes**.
- **Unhealthiness** (Ar. وبال). Equivalent to **Detriment.**
- **Union** (Ar. اقتران). Usually, any **conjunction** of planets by body; but sometimes, a **mean** conjunction or even the New Moon (see **Conjunction/prevention**).
- **Unlucky.** See **Fortune/Infortune.**
- **Upright** (Ar. قائم). Describes the axis of the MC-IC, when it falls into the tenth and fourth signs, rather than the eleventh-fifth, or ninth-third.
- *Via combusta.* See **Burnt path.**
- **Victor** (Ar. مبتزّ). A planet or point identified as the most authoritative over a particular topic, **place** or **house**, or for a chart as a whole. Dykes distinguishes procedures that find victor "over" several places at once, and a victor "among" several candidate victors, usually on a ranked list.
- **Void in course.** See **Emptiness in course.**
- **Well, welled degrees** (Lat. *puteum*, Ar. بئر). A degree in which a planet is said to be more obscure in its operation. In later, English-speaking astrology, sometimes called the "pitted" degrees.
- **Western.** See **Eastern and western.**
- **Westernize, westernization** (غرّب \ تغريب). See **Easternize, easternization.**
- **Whole signs.** The oldest system of assigning house topics and **aspects**. The entire sign on the horizon (the **Ascendant**) is the first house, the entire second sign is the second house, and so on. Likewise, aspects are considered first of all according to signs: planets in Aries **look at** planets in Gemini, even if aspects which **connect** by degree are more intense.
- **Wildness** (Ar. وحشيّة, Lat. *feralitas*). When a planet is not **looked at** by any other planet.
- **Withdrawal, withdrawing** (زوال \ زائل; in some Latin translations, *recedens*). Refers to being (1) dynamically **cadent**, i.e. moving by **primary motion** away from an **axial** degree. (But occasionally might refer to being

cadent by **whole signs**.) A near synonym to **retreat**. Its antonym is **Advancement**. It may also refer to (2) the **western** quadrants.

- **Zīj** (Ar. زيج). The Arabic for a Persian word meaning a set of astronomical tables for calculating planetary positions and other things. Ptolemy's *Almagest* can be considered a *zīj*.
- **Zodiac**. Three ways of dividing the **ecliptic** into signs. The "constellational" zodiac uses the actual constellations, which are of different sizes. The "sidereal" zodiac divides the ecliptic into twelve equal divisions, starting from some fixed star which acts as the **ayanamsha**. The "tropical" zodiac also uses equal divisions, but starts from the **equinoctial point**.

Bibliography

Abū Ma'shar, *De Revolutionibus Nativitatum*, ed. David Pingree (Leipzig: B.G. Teubner, 1968)

Allen, Richard Hinckley, *Star Names: Their Lore and Meaning* (New York: Dover Publications Inc., 1963)

ibn Bishr, Sahl, trans. and ed. Benjamin N. Dykes, *The Astrology of Sahl b. Bishr Volume I: Principles, Elections, Questions, Nativities* (Minneapolis, MN: The Cazimi Press, 2019)

Burnett, Charles and Ahmed al-Hamdi, "Zādānfarrūkh al-Andarzaghar on Anniversary Horoscopes," *Zeitschrift für Geschichte der Arabisch-Islamischen Wissenschaften*, Vol. 7, 1991/1992, pp. 294-400.

Burnett, Charles, and David Pingree eds., *The Liber Aristotilis of Hugo of Santalla* (London: The Warburg Institute, 1997)

Cumont, Franz ed., *Catalogus Codicum Astrologorum Graecorum* vol. VIII.1 (Brussels: Maurich Lambertin, 1929)

Dorotheus of Sidon, *Carmen Astrologicum*, trans. and ed. Benjamin N. Dykes (Minneapolis, MN: The Cazimi Press, 2017)

Dykes, Benjamin trans. and ed., *Works of Sahl & Māshā'allāh* (Golden Valley, MN: The Cazimi Press, 2008)

Dykes, Benjamin, trans. and ed., *Persian Nativities I: Māshā'allāh & Abū 'Alī* (Minneapolis, MN: The Cazimi Press, 2009)

Dykes, Benjamin trans. and ed., *Introductions to Traditional Astrology: Abū Ma'shar & al-Qabīsī* (Minneapolis, MN: The Cazimi Press, 2010)

Dykes, Benjamin, trans. and ed., *Persian Nativities II: 'Umar al-Tabarī & Abū Bakr* (Minneapolis, MN: The Cazimi Press, 2010)

Dykes, Benjamin, trans. and ed., *Persian Nativities III: On Solar Revolutions* (Minneapolis, MN: The Cazimi Press, 2010)

Dykes, Benjamin, trans. and ed., *Astrology of the World II: Revolutions & History* (Minneapolis, MN: The Cazimi Press, 2014)

Firmicus Maternus, *Mathesis*, ed. P. Monat (Paris: Les Belles Lettres, 1992-1997)

Firmicus Maternus, *Mathesis*, trans. and ed. Benjamin N. Dykes (forthcoming)

Gansten, Martin, *Primary Directions: Astrology's Old Master Technique* (England: The Wessex Astrologer, 2009)

Kennedy, E.S., "A Survey of Islamic Astronomical Tables," *Transactions of the American Philosophical Society*, New Ser., Vol. 46, No. 2 (1956), pp. 123-77.

Kunitzsch, Paul and Tim Smart, *A Dictionary of Modern Star Names* (Cambridge, MA: New Track Media, 2006)

Leopold of Austria, *A Compilation on the Science of the Stars*, trans. and ed. Benjamin N. Dykes (Minneapolis, MN: The Cazimi Press, 2015)

Morin, Jean-Baptiste, trans. and ed. James Herschel Holden, *Astrologia Gallica Book Twenty-Three: Revolutions* (Tempe, AZ: American Federation of Astrologers, Inc., 2003)

Al-Nadīm, Muhammad b. Ishāq b., ed. and trans. Bayard Dodge, *The Fihrist of al-Nadīm*, 2 vols. (New York & London, Columbia University Press, 1970)

Pingree, David, "Historical Horoscopes," in *Journal of the American Oriental Society* v. 82 (1962), pp. 487-502.

Ptolemy, Claudius, *Tetrabiblos*, trans. F.E. Robbins (Cambridge and London: Harvard University Press, 1940)

Ptolemy, Claudius, *Ptolemy's Almagest*, trans. and ed. G.J. Toomer (Princeton, NJ: Princeton University Press, 1998)

Al-Qabīsī, *The Introduction to Astrology*, eds. Charles Burnett, Keiji Yamamoto, Michio Yano (London and Turin: The Warburg Institute, 2004)

Rhetorius of Egypt, *Astrological Compendium*, trans. and ed. James H. Holden (Tempe, AZ: American Federation of Astrologers, Inc., 2009)

Schmidt, Robert, *The Astrological Record of the Early Sages in Greek* (Berkeley Springs, WV: The Golden Hind Press, 1995)

Schmidt, Robert trans. and Robert Hand ed., *Dorotheus, Orpheus, Anubio, & Pseudo-Valens: Teachings on Transits* (Berkeley Springs, WV: The Golden Hind Press, 1995)

Sezgin, Fuat, *Geschichte des Arabischen Schrifttums* vol. 7 (Leiden: E.J. Brill, 1979)

Theophilus of Edessa, trans. Eduardo Gramaglia and ed. Benjamin Dykes, *Astrological Works of Theophilus of Edessa* (Minneapolis, MN: The Cazimi Press, 2017)

Valens, Vettius, *The Anthology*, vols. I-VII, ed. Robert Hand, trans. Robert Schmidt (Berkeley Springs, WV: The Golden Hind Press, 1993-2001)

Vescovini, Graziella Federici, "La Versio Latina Degli *Excerpta de Secretis Albumasar di Sadan*," in *Archives d'Histoire Doctrinale et Litteraire du Moyen Age*, Vol. 65 (1998), pp. 273-330.

INDEX

Above/under the earth....196-97, 208, 234, 242, 277, 344, 346, 415, 417

Advancing...29, 31-32, 43, 79-81, 138, 171, 216, 298, 563, 602, 604

Ages of Man...13, 20, 22, 116, 121, 146, 165, 169, 171

al-'Amīn ('Abbāsid Caliph)...3, 75

al-Andarzaghar, Zādānfarrūkh...4-5, 44, 60, 115, 119-21, 241, 264, 279-80, 299, 318, 320, 365, 369, 374, 380, 388-91, 393, 630

al-Dāmaghānī...4, 44, 115, 119

al-Fadl b. Sahl (Persian vizier)...3, 75

Alien (peregrine) planets....28-29, 115, 192, 196-97, 210-12, 216, 219, 228, 230-31, 253, 274, 282, 458, 464, 469-70, 481, 483, 486, 493, 649

al-Khayyāt, Abū 'Alī...34, 527, 530

al-Ma'mūn ('Abbāsid Caliph)....3, 75

al-Musta'īn ('Abbāsid Caliph)......3

al-Nadīm (historian)................2-3

al-Qabīṣī (Alchabitius) 5, 116-17, 286, 550

al-Ṭabarī, 'Umar........697

Ascensions, ascensional times...9, 24, 64, 101, 159, 186, 287-88, 291, 334-36, 346, 353-55, 358, 403, 635-37

Aversion...27, 45, 48, 80, 133, 163, 186, 189, 197, 212, 227, 265, 278, 282, 323, 334, 340-41, 345, 413, 459, 461-62, 469, 473, 573, 615, 659

Babylon, Babylonians...61, 121, 129, 158, 291, 347, 426

Besieging................650

Bonatti, Guido................50

Bounds (apart from distributions)............147, 532-45

Brahmagupta................157

Burning (combustion)...48, 165, 187, 189, 196, 231, 244-45, 279, 282, 284, 411, 422, 459, 481, 660, 662

Collection of light................573

Comets................142-43, 338-39

Cumont Franz................453

Cusps...1, 38, 41, 49-60, 159, 433-35, 476-77, 575

Cutters/cutting (longevity)..137, 139, 552, 645, 647-49, 651-53, 655-60, 663-66

Daily and hourly revolutions and profections...151, 630, 632-34, 636-38, 643-44

Darījān................353, 360-61, 639

Degrees
  bright................186, 644
  dark................186, 644
  empty................545, 644
  gloomy/smoky................186, 644
  glowing................186

Detriment................29, 416

Distributions... 2, 4, 12-13, 20-21, 24, 51-52, 60-61, 64-71, 73-74, 76, 85, 112, 119-20, 129-32, 134-39, 142, 146-47, 161, 179, 183, 241, 245, 265, 268, 283, 286-88, 289-09, 312-30, 332-39, 341-42, 345, 347, 355-56, 359-60, 364-71, 374-94, 424, 552, 567, 577, 634-35, 647, 649, 656-59, 666, 668, 671-74

   distributor...... 9, 44, 60, 62, 64-72, 78, 132, 134, 136, 138, 141, 146-47, 161, 179, 184, 241, 245, 264, 268, 283, 286-91, 293-307, 309, 315-17, 319, 322, 325, 327, 330-35, 337, 338, 340-46, 424, 552, 577, 619, 657-59, 666-67, 674

   partner ..60, 62, 64-72, 74, 119, 136-38, 146-47, 161, 179-80, 184, 286, 291, 293-95, 298, 300-01, 303-07, 309, 311-12, 315-30, 332, 334-35, 359-61, 635, 656-58, 667, 673-74

Domain (*hayyiz*)...164, 187, 191, 198, 228, 233, 236, 277, 550

Dorotheus of Sidon... 4, 33-34, 51, 109, 135, 141, 562, 630

Eastern/western planets..........165, 191, 193, 213, 231, 243, 274, 282, 411, 412, 456, 486

Easternization, westernization 165, 187, 215, 294, 366, 417, 420, 496, 667

Eclipses... 118, 142, 276, 338, 339

Egypt, Egyptians..36, 61, 129, 158, 347

Emptiness in course...44, 46, 106-07, 180, 184, 265-67, 438, 667

Exaltation... 29, 38, 82, 107, 171, 185, 191, 242, 250, 275, 282, 294, 332, 339, 361, 366, 387, 527, 573

Exile (peregrination)... 163, 187, 219, 250, 253, 361

Faces... 186, 294, 332, 353, 573, 644

Fall (contrary of exaltation) 19, 29, 38, 45, 48, 84, 360, 542

Fardārs... 4, 20, 24, 112, 115-21, 129, 147, 161, 171, 180, 184, 286, 337, 364-71, 374-94, 552, 577, 619, 661, 663, 667-68

Firmicus Maternus..............34, 431

Fixed stars... 5, 60, 135, 142, 161, 315, 338-39, 545, 575, 612, 635, 643, 649, 651-52, 654, 664, 674

Glow
   out of rays.. 165, 187, 191, 227, 269

Good/suitable places 26-29, 138, 184, 187, 227, 242, 270, 273, 280, 282, 301, 319, 337, 361, 412

Governor
   as victor......... 77, 80, 89, 95, 99, 565-66, 597, 600-01, 647, 667

Halb (a sect condition) 668

Handing over.............. 44, 241, 292

Head/Tail of the Dragon 116, 147, 160-61, 181, 276, 279-80, 289, 329, 364-65, 367, 374, 380, 392-93, 438, 440, 442-43, 445, 447, 449-50, 452, 454, 456-57, 463, 478, 517-21, 546, 575, 577, 655

Hermes ... 121, 370, 426, 432, 436

Hipparchus 5-6, 158, 632

House-master..135-36, 138-39, 646-49, 651, 665

Hugo of Santalla 5, 390, 391

In the heart (*cazimi*) 165, 244

India, Indians ... 5, 60, 89, 115, 129-31, 147, 158, 179, 347, 352-53, 361-63, 554, 566, 638, 640, 666

Intercepted signs ... 1, 49, 51, 54-58, 476-77

Joys/rejoicing 332, 514

Lilly, William 35, 50, 135

Lord of the orb ... 1, 20, 24, 115, 121-22, 124-29, 147, 161, 180, 184, 286, 426-27, 429, 577, 619, 632, 660, 667

Lots
  assets 50, 430, 608
  authority 432
  brothers/siblings 140, 346, 409
  children 195, 203, 219, 260, 412
  courage 73, 290-92
  father . 201, 219, 275, 344, 431, 636
  Fortune ... 12, 22-23, 39, 40, 80, 91-92, 96, 100, 136, 140, 161, 286, 316, 331, 337-38, 344, 408-09, 430, 433, 555-58, 561-62, 565-66, 570, 577, 601-02, 604-05, 608-09, 617-20, 622-24, 637, 674
  illness 432
  marriage . 13, 80, 141, 164, 194, 202, 253, 325, 397
  mother 219, 431, 636
  prosperity 290, 291, 292
  real estate 433
  reason 290, 292
  slaves 195, 203, 432
  Spirit 562
  wedding 202, 230
  work 195, 203, 260, 341, 432

Lunation (esp. pre-natal) 136, 286, 316, 655-56

Māshā'allāh b. Atharī..2, 5, 34, 50, 51, 68, 102, 137, 270, 432, 527-28, 530, 647, 665

Metonic cycle 117, 118

Monthly revolutions and profections ... 1, 15, 24, 39, 51-52, 60, 80, 85, 88-97, 100, 102-04, 131, 133, 156, 172, 179, 183, 209, 339, 362, 396, 400, 544, 553-58, 563, 574-78, 593-96, 601-13, 615, 618-24, 627, 635, 667

Moon
  waning . 25, 120, 205, 231, 265-66, 650
  waxing ..25, 120, 196, 218, 265, 650, 656

Morin, Jean-Baptiste ... 50, 81, 152

Nawbakht the Persian............. 317
Ninth-parts... 5, 97, 100, 129-31, 186, 347-53, 355-62, 554-55, 558-59, 561, 565, 567, 569-70, 577, 601, 604-05, 608-09, 619-20, 638-44, 666
Overcoming... 199-201, 203-05, 219-24, 233-37, 251-52, 254-55, 259, 261, 268, 278, 283, 661
Persia. Persians... 3, 5, 14, 36, 61, 75, 115, 129, 157-58, 288, 347, 397, 430, 444, 652
Planetary hours... 20, 121-22, 124-28, 428-29
Planetary years... 22, 71, 117-18, 136, 166-69, 335-37, 403, 648
Planets
  diurnal/nocturnal .25, 33, 116-18, 121, 164, 236, 267, 455, 457, 526-29, 655
  orbs or bodies....... 31, 112, 395, 397, 403-04
Primary directions... 45, 51-52, 61, 64, 74, 85, 102, 133, 135-36, 138, 147, 152, 155-56, 177, 286-88, 290, 293, 295, 302, 305, 315-16, 346-47, 352, 358, 360, 362, 430, 434, 635-36, 643, 647-51, 655-57, 659, 671
  longevity releaser...... 44, 49, 65, 136-37, 139-40, 142, 183-84, 241, 245, 264-65, 286, 316-17, 341, 647-48, 667
  releasers.. 44, 62, 64-65, 69, 73, 135-40, 245, 286-87, 315-17, 647-51, 655-57, 659, 665
Profections... 4, 9-10, 12, 17-18, 20-22, 24, 37, 38, 40-41, 43, 51-62, 71, 75-76, 88, 90, 95, 97-98, 102, 106, 110-11, 118, 120-21, 124-25, 127, 129-31, 140-41, 147, 156, 161, 177, 180, 183, 270, 300-01, 338, 346, 361-62, 405, 423, 428, 430-35, 550, 553, 555-60, 603, 606, 608, 624, 635, 637, 647, 651, 655-56, 665-66
  in increments...59-60, 338, 635
  lord of the year... 10, 18, 21-22, 27, 37-40, 42-47, 59, 71, 75-78, 81, 84-85, 91, 93, 106, 109-13, 120-21, 124-126, 128, 130, 132, 135, 140-41, 146-47, 180, 184-96, 198-200, 202-03, 205-28, 231, 233, 235, 237-43, 245-46, 248-51, 253-54, 256-62, 264, 267-70, 275-83, 294, 296, 297, 300, 303-04, 323, 325, 328, 336-46, 361-62, 375, 399, 413, 423, 428-29, 435, 545, 552, 554-55, 565-66, 570, 576, 597, 619, 621-22, 638, 641, 658-62, 666-67
  sign of the year...... 9, 38-45, 60, 75-76, 79-80, 83, 88-89, 94, 103-04, 109-10, 124, 127-28, 133, 135, 146-47, 156, 179-81, 183, 185-87, 209, 213, 241, 249, 258, 264,

268, 271, 274, 281, 294, 299-302, 304, 339-44, 346, 361-62, 402, 411, 413, 429, 435-37, 439-40, 442-43, 445, 447, 449-50, 453, 455-56, 458, 462-63, 465-69, 472-74, 479-80, 489, 494, 500, 503, 508, 514, 517, 553-54, 556, 558-59, 561, 567-69, 576-77, 579, 581-83, 585-87, 589, 592, 594, 604-09, 611, 613-14, 616-17, 619-20, 622, 634, 636, 638-39, 642-43, 658, 660, 662-64, 666

Ptolemy, Claudius... 5, 24, 49, 51, 136, 142, 157-58, 168-70, 287-88, 563, 644, 651-52

Quadrant house divisions........29, 31, 41, 49-59, 159, 433-34, 476

Quadrants 345, 574

Reception... 28, 107, 164, 188-89, 193-95, 207, 210-13, 225-28, 231-32, 237-40, 248-50, 256-58, 262-64, 266, 269, 285, 359, 409, 416, 421-22, 458, 469-70, 471, 660

Retrogradation...29, 159, 163, 187, 189, 193-94, 196, 210-13, 215, 219, 226, 231, 239, 253, 256, 262-63, 274-75, 279-80, 284, 289, 294, 342, 396, 420, 459, 471, 483, 575, 660, 668

Returns (planets)...276, 280, 395-97, 400-02, 408, 410, 413, 418, 420, 423

Rhetorius of Egypt...4, 35, 437, 439-40, 442-43, 445, 447, 449-50, 453, 455-56

Schmidt, Robert 24, 707

Sect of chart...25, 116-17, 120-22, 125, 193, 196-98, 201-02, 208, 218, 224, 231, 233-34, 236, 239, 243, 267, 279, 364-71, 374-75, 378-86, 393, 408, 413, 423, 430-33, 437, 451-57, 523-32, 662

Shadhān b. Bahr..........................73

Shahriyār (*Zīj al-Shāh*) 5, 157

Signs

airy 129, 130, 351, 353

convertible (movable).. ....89, 102, 104, 129-30, 331, 333-35, 345-46, 351-53, 403-05, 558-60, 565-67, 624, 638

diurnal/nocturnal................ 527

double-bodied.......60, 102, 197, 333-35, 403, 559, 565, 624, 635

earthy........... 130, 229, 353, 482

equal ascensions 573

female/feminine...... ... 197, 429, 481, 483, 490

fiery........ 129-30, 192, 229, 348, 351-53

fixed........102-03, 331, 333-335, 403, 558-60, 574, 624

four-footed..200, 206, 486, 604

human/of people........ 199, 206, 228, 232, 253, 266, 281, 338

in same belt.................. 186, 573

lecherous/licentious......35, 546

male/masculine 197, 429, 481, 483, 485, 490, 492
of same ascensions 573
riding animals 410
royal 192, 229
same length of day 186, 573
social classes 229
watery 200, 228, 267, 353, 482, 566
wild animals 206, 240, 410
Sindhind 5, 157
Slow planets ... 197, 208, 232, 343, 412, 471, 477, 574
Solar revolutions ... 5, 7, 14-15, 23-24, 54, 68, 77, 112, 145-47, 149, 152-56, 158-62, 164-65, 172-77, 179-84, 186-89, 191-92, 197-99, 205, 207-08, 212-13, 227, 241, 243, 249, 258, 264, 267, 269-85, 294-304, 315, 329, 336-45, 359, 382, 395-98, 400-03, 405-25, 428-31, 435-37, 439, 441-42, 444, 446-47, 449, 451, 453, 455, 457-73, 476-78, 484, 544, 552-53, 557-58, 561-62, 564-65, 567-69, 574-98, 600-02, 605-11, 613, 615, 617-24, 631-32, 634, 636, 638, 642, 643, 647, 658-59, 661-64, 666-69
Stations, stationary planet 197, 232, 274
Theophilus of Edessa 562
Time lords ... 12-15, 18-22, 25, 37, 44, 61-62, 64-65, 67, 70-71, 73, 75-79, 101, 110-11, 115-16, 120-21, 124, 132-33, 135, 140-41, 152, 171-72, 293, 330-31, 333-34, 336-37, 362, 365, 612
Transfer of light 573
Transits ... 4, 13-16, 19, 27, 43, 45, 54-58, 60, 68, 75, 77-78, 80, 83-86, 95, 107-14, 118-19, 133-35, 141, 147, 151-52, 155, 159, 164, 179-81, 208, 241, 258, 275, 277, 279, 282-84, 286, 300, 329, 331, 334, 342, 344, 395-97, 399-401, 403-04, 406-08, 410, 412, 414, 417, 419, 421, 423-24, 435, 476-77, 478-80, 489, 494, 500, 503, 508, 514, 517, 521, 552, 562, 568, 596, 611-12, 615, 624, 643, 658, 661-62, 668
Triplicity lords
of Mars 431
of sect light 430
of the Moon 431
of Venus 431
Twelfth-parts ... 159-62, 164, 181-82, 185-87, 189, 192, 198, 219, 228, 233, 245, 250, 253, 259, 261, 266, 286, 288-90, 293, 424, 430, 465, 479, 521, 573, 575, 577, 644
Under the rays ... 165, 187, 196, 198, 201, 215, 219, 231-32, 237, 243-47, 253, 277, 282, 343, 420, 438
Valens, Vettius ... 4, 24-25, 35, 37, 43, 49, 337, 562, 706
Victors 77, 80, 89, 163

Wells of the signs...35-37, 147, 523, 545-48

Whole signs...8, 43, 49-50, 53-54, 58, 254

Withdrawing...29, 31, 273, 275, 277, 284, 331, 346, 413, 415, 418, 420, 451, 602, 604

Zīj al-Shāh...See Shahriyār (Zīj al-Shāh)